WELL-BEING

Positive Development Across the Life Course

CROSSCURRENTS IN CONTEMPORARY PSYCHOLOGY
A series of volumes edited by Marc H. Bornstein

WELL-BEING

Positive Development
Across the Life Course

Edited by

Marc H. Bornstein
Lucy Davidson
Corey L. M. Keyes
Kristin A. Moore
The Center for Child Well-being

LEA

LAWRENCE ERLBAUM ASSOCIATES, PUBLISHERS
2003   Mahwah, New Jersey   London

Lawrence Erlbaum Associates, Inc., Publishers
10 Industrial Avenue
Mahwah, NJ 07430

Cover design by Kathryn Houghtaling Lacey

Library of Congress Cataloging-in-Publication Data

Well-being : positive development across the life course / edited by Marc H.
Bornstein … [et al.].
p. cm. — (Crosscurrents in contemporary psychology)
Proceedings of a conference held June 20–22, 2000 in Atlanta, GA.
Includes bibliographical references and index.
ISBN 0-8058-4035-4 (cloth : alk. paper)
1. Developmental psychology. 2. Health.   I. Bornstein, Marc H.   II. Series.
BF713.5 .W45   2002
155—dc21   2002029756
                                                                          CIP

Books published by Lawrence Erlbaum Associates are printed on acid-free paper, and their bindings are chosen for strength and durability.

Printed in the United States of America
10   9   8   7   6   5   4   3   2   1

Contents

PART IV: ADULT DEVELOPMENT DOMAIN

PART V: OVERARCHING ISSUES AND THEMES

Series Prologue

CROSSCURRENTS IN CONTEMPORARY PSYCHOLOGY

Contemporary psychological science is increasingly diversified, pluralistic, and specialized, and most psychologists venture beyond the confines of their substantive specialty only rarely. Yet psychologists with different specialties encounter similar problems, ask similar questions, and share similar concerns. Unfortunately, there are today too few arenas available for the expression or exploration of what is common across psychological subdisciplines. The *Crosscurrents in Contemporary Psychology* series is intended to serve as such a forum.

The chief aim of this series is to provide integrated perspectives on supradisciplinary themes in psychology. The first volume in the series was devoted to a consideration of *Psychological Development from Infancy*; the second volume to *Comparative Methods in Psychology*; volumes three, four, and five examined relations between *Psychology and Its Allied Disciplines* in the humanities, the social sciences, and the natural sciences; volume six concerned itself with *Sensitive Periods in Development*; volume seven focused on *Interaction in Human Development*; volume eight addressed *Cultural Approaches to Parenting*; and volume nine examined the intersection of *Child Development and Behavioral Pediatrics.*

The Center for Child Well-being appreciates this approach and, under it aegis, pursued an in-depth interdisciplinary assessment of life course well-being. The Center focuses on the next frontier of developing strengths from birth through adolescence and explores how to nurture children's thriving in all aspects of life—the physical, socioemotional, and cognitive. Toward that end, the Center gathered scholars, practitioners, public health professionals, and principals in the child development community to examine, from their respective disciplinary perspectives and expertise, the common question, "What are the central elements of child well-being—the fundamental strengths that support children's early health and development and sustain positive development throughout the life course?" In response, this group prepared analytic reviews of key positive capacities for well-being. The

Center then used an experts' work group meeting and supplemental discussion groups at a larger conference to refine these written reviews. Revisions of that process became chapters for this tenth book in the *Crosscurrents in Contemporary Psychology* series, *Well-Being: Positive Development Across the Life Course*.

Well-Being presents a science-based framework for elements of well-being and how those elements can be fostered across the life course. Several features about the nature and structure of this collection will orient the reader. To aid in exposition, chapters on child well-being are grouped into three sections corresponding to the physical, socioemotional, and cognitive domains of well-being, but the editors and contributors alike are fully cognizant of the thoroughly integrated nature of the elements within and across these domains. The review of elements of well-being is perforce selective, rather than exhaustive; some known elements could not be covered, others will emerge in the future. A section examining adult well-being extends those on childhood and rounds out the life course perspective. Concluding chapters examine overarching issues in well-being and invite the reader to consider implications for science, practice, and policy. Finally, this collection has an admittedly European American perspective, reflective of the state of the contemporary scientific literature in well-being.

Each volume in the *Crosscurrents in Contemporary Psychology* series treats a different issue and is self-contained, yet the series as a whole endeavors to interrelate psychological subdisciplines by bringing shared perspectives to bear on a variety of concerns common to psychological theory and research. As a consequence of this structure and the flexibility and scope it affords, volumes in the *Crosscurrents in Contemporary Psychology* series will appeal, individually or as a group, to scientists with diverse interests. Reflecting the nature and intent of this series, contributing authors are drawn from a broad spectrum of humanities and sciences—anthropology to zoology—but representational emphasis is placed on active contributing authorities to the contemporary psychological literature.

Crosscurrents in Contemporary Psychology is a series whose explicit intent is to explore a broad range of cross disciplinary concerns. In its focus on such issues, the series is devoted to promoting interest in the interconnectedness of research and theory in psychological study.

—*Marc H. Bornstein*
Series Editor

ACKNOWLEDGMENTS

The editors express special gratitude to Maureen Marshall for continuing efficiency and good cheer during the production of this volume; Patrice Lee and Susan Toal for continuing support of child well-being; and the production staff at LEA for continuing editorial excellence.

Foreword
Well-Being: Positive Development Across the Life Course

Our children are here to stay, but our babies and toddlers and preschoolers are gone as fast as they can grow up—and we have only a short moment with each.
—St. Clair Adams Sullivan

We articulate our dreams in order to make them real. The Center for Child Well-being shares a vision of all children having the supports, strengths, and opportunities they need to grow and experience full lives, right from the start. These foundations of well-being would help children develop satisfying relationships, optimal health, lifelong learning abilities, social responsibility, and purposefulness. Well-being across the life course is a vision to be brought to reality through the efforts of all those who have contributed to this book and the families we serve.

Part of articulating this dream comes in identifying the foundational strengths that children should have in order to thrive, the interrelatedness of these strengths, and the contexts in which they are fostered. Such articulation helps move knowledge into action and provides a framework to galvanize community investment in the policies and works that support child well-being. Like child health and development, well-being doesn't automatically unfold and flourish as the child gets older. I am profoundly grateful to all those who have captured knowledge for action in this book and in so doing, moved our ability to actively promote well-being forward.

This book, *Well-Being: Positive Development Across the Life Course*, is the first scientific book to consider well-being holistically, integrating physical, cognitive, and social-emotional dimensions and the first taking a developmental perspective across the life course. It is also a first in describing foundational strengths for well-being—the capacities that can be actively developed, supported, or learned. These foundational strengths—such as problem solving, emotional regulation, and physical safety—are the positive underpinnings of early child health and development and of ongoing well-being across the life course. More than fifty experts in psychology, sociology, child development, and medicine have contributed to the book, working together and blending their respective disciplinary perspectives and expertise.

Well-Being focuses on a set of core strengths or elements grouped within three areas or domains: the physical, social-emotional, and cognitive. Integrating the concepts of well-being at different points in the life course, the book also includes a fourth section on developmental strengths throughout adulthood—which broadly examines a continuum of health and development as well as transitions in well-being.

The sponsoring organization for this book, the Center for Child Well-being (Center), was formed in 1999 with support from The Robert Wood Johnson Foundation to explore ways to improve the lives of children. The Center began an in-depth assessment of the science and practice of what we believed to be the next frontier of children's health: a focus on developing strengths from birth throughout childhood and adolescence, which would nurture a child's ability to thrive in all aspects of life—physically, cognitively, and socioemotionally.

Our efforts over the past three years have focused on four key questions:

1. What are the central elements of child well-being, that is, the fundamental strengths that support children's early health and development and sustain well-being throughout the life course?
2. What characteristics of child-serving environments support improvements in children's daily lives?
3. Which individuals and organizations could partner for collective leadership and action to improve child well-being?
4. How can information about child well-being best be used to support decision making and action by the adults entrusted with children's care and development?

Well-Being: Positive Development Across the Life Course, in content and through the process of developing the book, represents part of our answers to each key question.

We look forward as a Center to continuing to address these questions with readers and partners across the nation and around the world. Six principles provide the framework for all activities of the Center. As we plan and carry forward the articulation of a dream for all children, we strive to be:

- **Collaborative:** No one group or discipline can accomplish this vision alone. This work requires the participation and collective knowledge of children and parents, national and local groups, both public and private, in many areas, such as education, early childhood development, health, psychology, social services, faith communities, civic groups, and many others.
- **Positive:** The Center embraces a strength-based model for child health and development. Many organizations that are working in risk areas incorporate strengths into their prevention models, such as the development of

self-worth, trust, attachment to positive role models, creativity, or habits to promote physical health among children. The work of the Center is designed to help increase the momentum toward developing positive capabilities, thereby promoting the health and well-being that buffers risks and may prevent problems.

- **Evidence-based:** Using science and the evidence resulting from practice to support the needs of program and policy development is key in the Center's work. Knowledge about what works to foster the well-being of children comes from many disciplines. Integrating this information will support families and others who support children in making sound decisions.

- **Developmental:** Different positive characteristics are more or less influential throughout different stages across the life course. At various points in human development, one's sense of self and connectedness to others are more closely attuned to particular sets of skills, competencies, and activities. The Center recognizes the different expressions of well-being and contributions to it across development and seeks to work with multiple partners whose combined interests can encompass all stages of human development.

- **Ecological:** The Center's work recognizes the interactions among parents, children, caregivers, community, and the environment that shape children's well-being. One task of the Center is to integrate what is known about children's unique, inherent capabilities and these interactions.

- **Universal:** The Center is committed to ensuring that all people have equal access to opportunities and supports for their children's development. We seek to eliminate disparities that may be attributable to such differences as race or ethnicity, gender, education or income, disability, age, sexual orientation, or geographic location. This principle recognizes and accepts the value of cultural diversity and the call to social justice. Our work must help those who are in greatest need while being broadly inclusive.

Thank you for the opportunity that this book affords to extend our shared commitment to children in knowledge and action.

—William H. Foege
Founding Executive Director
The Center for Child Well-being

1

A Brief History of the Study of Well-Being in Children and Adults

Kristin A. Moore
Child Trends, Washington, DC

Corey L. M. Keyes
Emory University, Atlanta, GA

INTRODUCTION

Social commentators and politicians running for election often lay out a vision for what they see as the good or desired society and its vision of human functioning. Only recently, however, have researchers systematically joined in this endeavor. At present, and at last, a number of scientific disciplines are contributing to the current work on positive social and human development, and they have arrived at that place from quite different starting points. In addition to the treatment and prevention of problems and disease, there appears to be an interest in, and a desire to identify and promote, positive outcomes in children, in adults, and in their social environments.

The past century has seen remarkable progress in the eradication, treatment, and prevention of infectious diseases. Equally important, however, have been the public health advances that have helped to prevent the occurrence of disease, illness, and accidents (McGinnis & Foege, 1993; Foege, 1996). For example, the developments of vaccines and sanitation have prevented much sickness and early death. This concern with prevention has long moved public health researchers to work with community practitioners. Similarly, this concern has led public health researchers to consider ways to influence people's environments, health habits, and decision making in order to reduce the risk of injury, chronic illness, and contagious diseases.

However, the focus of public health efforts remained more on the prevention of negative outcomes than on the promotion of positive development. Moreover, as one would expect, the goals of public health prevention efforts have traditionally focused on improving health outcomes. Despite those efforts, many social indicators suggest that problems, for example, of suicide, substance use, precocious sexual activity, and violence, have worsened rather than improved over the past three to five decades (U.S. Department of Health and Human Services, 2000). Moreover, even when rates plateau or decline, rates of problem behavior remain very high. For example, since the teen birth rate peaked in 1991 at 61 births per 1,000 females aged 15–19, the rate has fallen to 49, but remains higher than any other developed nation except Armenia. (Moore, Manlove, Terry-Human, Papillo, & Williams, 2001). Persistently high levels of risk taking and problem behaviors suggest that new approaches are needed. As Sir Francis Bacon said many years ago, "He that will not apply new remedies must expect new evils, for time is the greatest innovator." We believe the investigation and application of positive human development is a new perspective that is needed now more than ever. We now turn to a brief history of the nature and origins of the study of well-being in children and adults.

THE NATURE AND ORIGIN OF WELL-BEING IN CHILDREN

Well-being in children is usually equated with the absence of problem behavior and the presence of positive behaviors that reflect academic, interpersonal, athletic, and artistic success (see e.g., Moore, 1997; Scales, Benson, Leffert, & Blyth, 2000). However, in recent decades, the focus has been on the prevention of problem behaviors. For example, school counselors, psychologists, the police, religious leaders, and other youth workers more generally have sought to prevent problem behaviors, such as the use of illicit drugs, delinquency and violence, alcohol use, smoking, and adolescent pregnancy. Concern about these behaviors has stimulated numerous programs and policies designed to prevent these problems (Catalano, Berglund, Ryan, Lonczak, & Hawkins, 1999). Programs, however, have tended to focus singly on one problem at a time.

Funders have also tended to concentrate their focus on specific problem behaviors. For example, government agencies have been formed and funded to focus solely on adolescent pregnancy (The Office of Adolescent Pregnancy Programs), mental health (The National Institute of Mental Health), substance abuse (The National Institute on Drug Abuse), and juvenile delinquency (The Office of Juvenile Justice and Delinquency Prevention). Many foundations also funded prevention and demonstration programs directed at specific social problems.

Perhaps reflecting these narrow funding mandates, researchers, particularly researchers studying adolescent behavior, have also tended to focus on specific problem behaviors (Hawkins, Catalano, & Miller, 1992; Moore, Miller, Morrison, & Glei, 1995; Kirby, 1997). However, through the 1980s, researchers increasingly documented that risk-taking behaviors tend to cluster and that adolescents who engage in one risky behavior have a higher probability of engaging in additional risky behaviors (Mott & Haurin, 1988; Elliott, Huizinga, & Mendard, 1989).

Catalano and colleagues (1999) suggested that a key turning point came when longitudinal studies began to generate information about the predictors of problem behavior, and this information was then incorporated into prevention programs. Inevitably, researchers came to look across problem areas, and they noted that different problem behaviors have common antecedents. In addition, researchers began to look across the separate or "silo" literatures that were accumulating. Again, they noted that the predictors of different problem behaviors are very similar (Moore & Sugland, 1996). For example, the four broad categories of predictors of adolescent childbearing identified by Moore and Sugland (1996)—early school failure, early behavior problems, family dysfunction, and poverty—are echoed in other reviews of quite different problem behavior literatures (e.g., Mendel, 1995). The discovery of common predictors led many researchers to suggest that more comprehensive intervention strategies might reduce multiple negative outcomes (Dryfoos, 1998). The empirical studies that have informed this paradigm shift have moved beyond simple correlational research and now encompass numerous longitudinal studies that employ multivariate statistical techniques and rich sets of control variables (e.g., Moore, Manlove, Glei, & Morrison, 1998; Paley, Conger, & Harold, 2000).

However, there have been too few experimental, intervention, or genetic studies as yet to distinguish between mere predictors and actual causes, and the causes are likely to be complex. Thus, only rarely do we have evidence of a causal nature. Nevertheless, identification of common predictors has led researchers to suggest that program providers focus on these predictors as "best bets" for improving children's outcomes (Moore & Sugland, 1996).

Meanwhile, in response to this expanding knowledge base and their own insights from work in the field, service providers were also developing increasingly comprehensive programs and/or positive, strength-focused, asset-building programs. One insight from the service provider community was that adolescents are more responsive to programs that meet their needs and address their goals than they are to programs that attempt to simply eliminate problem behaviors. Another insight is succinctly summarized by youth advocate Karen Pittman, who stated, "Problem-free does not mean fully prepared" (Pittman & Fleming, 1991, p. 3). Others noted that programs provided by religious groups and organizations such as the Scouts have for many years provided positive experiences and challenges to children and youth. Local programs with a prevention focus began to evolve positive goals to augment their prevention goals (United Way, 2000).

Several social commentators also stepped forward with their own definitions of positive development. For example, William Bennett (1993) in his widely reviewed *The Book of Virtues: A Treasury of Great Moral Stories*, highlights a set of desired outcomes for children and youth. These virtues include perseverance, faith, friendship, courage, responsibility, and compassion. The Council on Civil Society calls for a stronger focus on civility, emphasizing the role of the family, local neighborhoods, the faith community, and voluntary civic organizations in restoring a civil society (Institute for American Values, 1998).

Despite this major change in orientation in the program, policy, and service fields, the research field as a whole was slow to shift. In particular, the major national databases continued to focus on problem behaviors, such as substance abuse, adolescent pregnancy, and delinquency. This limited the ability of researchers to address positive development. Analysts examined outcome variables such as drug use and teen parenthood; consideration of positive outcomes was therefore limited to the avoidance of these negative outcomes (i.e., not using drugs and not becoming a teen parent). Positive outcomes such as civility, sibling closeness, exercise, parent–child relationships, religiosity, character, and volunteering (Moore & Halle, forthcoming) were only occasionally included in national databases (the National Survey of Children being the early exception). Therefore, empirical studies using nationally representative samples only occasionally examined the presence and development of positive characteristics and behaviors. In addition, the system of child well-being indicators that developed in the 1980s and expanded dramatically in the early 1990s retained a negative cast. Calls for new measures of positive development started to be heard, for example, at the 1994 conference on indicators of child well-being organized by the National Institute of Child Health and Human Development, the Office of the Assistant Secretary for Planning and Evaluation, the Annie E. Casey Foundation, the Poverty Institute, and Child Trends (Moore, 1997; Takanishi, Mortimer, & McGourthy, 1997; Aber & Jones, 1997). However, the child well-being indicators field then and now was unable to provide more than a handful of positive indicators because the indicators had not been conceptualized, measured, and included in nationally representative surveys.

However, outside the Federal statistical system, individual researchers and groups had begun to conduct relevant research studies and to develop new constructs and measures. Several researchers have focused specifically on conceptualizing and measuring positive development. Key among these initial efforts is the assets framework developed by the Search Institute (Benson, 1993; Leffert, Benson, Scales, Sharma, Drake, & Blyth, 1998; Scales & Leffert, 1999). Internal assets within youth were identified as a commitment to learning, positive values, social competencies, and positive identity. External assets that support children's development were also identified in families, schools, and communities.

Karen Pittman has consistently argued for a positive approach (International Youth Foundation, 1998) and has developed a definition of youth development that incorporates four desirable youth outcomes: confidence (a sense of self-worth, mastery, and future), character (a sense of accountability, control, self-awareness, and a relation to a deity, the family, and the larger culture), connection (a sense of safety, structure, membership, and belonging), and competence (the ability and motivation to be effective in terms of physical and emotional health, intellectual development civic action, and employment). She noted that the phrase "youth development" is often used to include "the range of informal education programs and organizations that operate in the out-of-school hours and focus on 'non-academic' outcomes such as recreation, wellness, service, the arts, leadership development, and life skills training." (International Youth Foundation, 2001).

The report, *Turning Points*, prepared by the Carnegie Council on Adolescent Development (1989), defined desirable outcomes for youth, including being intellectually reflective; being en route to a lifetime of meaningful work; being a good citizen; being a caring and ethical individual; and being healthy. Lerner, Fisher, and Weinberg (2000) posited the five C's of positive development: competence, confidence or positive identity, connections, character or positive values, and caring. Roth, Brooks-Gunn, and Galen (1997) identified positive youth development programs as those that counter risk factors and enhance protective factors, that use an asset-based approach instead of a remedial approach, and that focus on the development of skills and competencies rather than the prevention of specific problem behaviors.

In a series of papers, Moore and her colleagues outlined a set of positive outcomes ranging from positive parent–child relationships to character and social capacity and began to explore the antecedents and consequences of these positive characteristics (Moore & Glei, 1995; Moore & Halle, forthcoming; Moore, Evans, Brooks-Gunn, & Roth, forthcoming; Zaff, Moore, Papillo, & Williams, 2001). However, they noted that the definition of positive outcomes is controversial, that the research evidence for positive constructs is thin and methodologically weak, that few longitudinal studies have examined positive development, and that substantial measurement and psychometric work is needed.

WELL-BEING IN ADULTHOOD

Well-being in adulthood, like childhood, needs to be defined broadly and includes the domains of cognitive functioning, behavioral functioning, physical health, and mental health. These domains, which are reviewed in this volume's section on aging include positive thought processes, social engagement with one's community, positive health behaviors including restorative sleep and resistance training.

From inception, social science has focused on the investigation of well-being. However, until about forty years ago, most research equated health and well-being with the absence of physical disease or mental disorder. At least three major developments have marked the rise of the study of positive aspects of adulthood. First, the period of humanism following World War II provided both methodological and conceptual tools for the study of how individuals view the quality of their lives. Second, the rise of gerontology and the study of successful aging provided conceptions of positive human development. Third, the study of stress and health matured to include models of the individual's perception of stress and their coping strategies.

Humanism and Subjective Well-Being

Well-being in human life has been a paramount concern of philosophers and thinkers since ancient times. It began to be a topic of systematic research only at the end of the 1950s and the 1960s. The interest in fostering the good life was probably facilitated by the Zeitgeist following World War II. The recovery from the physical and moral devastation of the war appeared to stimulate appreciation of the individual as a cherished entity together with commitment to social welfare. This historical climate manifested itself in philosophical, sociological, and psychological movements that focused on the centrality of the individual's perceptions and viewpoints (phenomenology), and the importance of personal meaning and concerns (existentialism and symbolic interactionism).

Humanistic writings emphasized several concerns (see Severin, 1965) and constructs that set the stage for the study of well-being in adulthood. In reaction to orthodox psychoanalysis, humanistic scholars catalogued the capacity for positive adjustment and for the development of positive characteristics such as maturity, ego-strength, and generativity. In reaction to the hegemony of behaviorism, humanistic writers lauded introspection and subjective appraisal as meaningful data. Humanists sought to understand whole lives by asking people how their lives looked to them and how they felt about their own lives. As stated by Allport (1961, cited in Severin, 1965), "It is not enough to know how man reacts: we must know how he feels, how he sees his world, … why he lives, what he fears, for what he would be willing to die. Such questions of *existence* must be put to man directly" (p. 42).

Since Jahoda's (1958) seminal review of elements of positive psychological health, scholars have spent the past forty years operationalizing various facets of subjective well-being. Defined as an individual's perception and evaluation of the quality of their own lives, subjective well-being consists of a variety of criteria against which individuals judge their own lives. Keyes and Waterman (this volume) review this literature and conclude that subjective well-being consists of three domains: emotional well-being, psychological well-being, and social well-being. In other words, individuals evaluate their lives in terms of whether they feel good about it, function well personally, and function well socially. Aspects of emotional well-being that contribute to subjective well-being include feeling satisfied and happy about one's life and experiencing more positive than negative emotion over time. However, being well is more than feeling good; it means that adults report that they are functioning well in their personal and social lives. Personally, individuals may view their lives in terms of psychological well-being, which consists of dimensions such as a sense of personal growth, a purpose in life, and self-acceptance. Socially, individuals may view their lives in terms of social well-being, which consists of dimensions such as a sense of social integration and social contributions.

Adult Development and Successful Aging

Erik Erikson (1950, 1959) provided the first comprehensive theory of development throughout the entire life span. In it, Erikson proposed several stages of development each characterized by distinctive life challenges. Unlike prior theorists, Erikson believed that such life challenges were necessary for human growth, and he also portrayed each stage of development in terms of a negative and a positive outcome.

Despite Erikson's positive and comprehensive conception of adult development, the social reality of aging during the 20th century until about the 1980s was that many older adults lived in poverty. As late as 1967, 29.5% of adults aged 65 or older lived at or below the government's standard of poverty (Kutzka, 1981; see also Miringoff & Mirongoff, 1999). During the same time, adults aged 65 or older reported on average between 30 and 40 days a year in which they experienced restricted activity due to their health (Kutzka, 1981). Not surprisingly, the early theories and models of aging portrayed it as a process of disengagement (e.g., Cumming & Henry, 1961). Contrary to the theories of aging as decline, studies have repeatedly shown that aging is associated with either the maintenance of well-being or an increase in well-being (Diener & Suh, 1997; Keyes & Ryff, 1998; Mroczek & Kolarz, 1998).

A host of theories that build on the paradigm of successful aging (Rowe & Kahn, 1998) have emerged to explain how individuals adapt or compensate for loss at the same time they resolve new challenges and optimize extant skills (e.g., Baltes & Baltes, 1990). Moreover, the study of life transitions now reveals that many individuals actively shape the meaning of stressful experience, resolve those stressors to their satisfaction, and thereby learn new coping skills and information about their own strengths and abilities (Aldwin, Sutton, & Lachman, 1996; Thoits, 1994; Turner & Avison, 1992).

Stress Perception and Coping

Since Holmes and Rahe (1967), objective life events have been the centerpiece of the social science of health and well-being. Life events such as marriage, relocating to a new residence, or childbirth, because they demand readjustment from an organism that seeks or desires equilibrium, are precursors to stress. Repeated and extensive exposure to myriad life events has been repeatedly shown to increase individuals' risk for mood disorders such as depression (Turner, Wheaton, & Lloyd, 1995; Pearlin, 1989, Thoits, 1995). However, the association of life event exposure with mental health outcomes remains modest.

Whether life events create stress appears to depend on how individuals perceive those events, the ways that individuals cope with demands and stress, as well as the availability of social supports. Stress process models suggest that a critical linkage between life and health outcomes is the perception of demands and events (Lazarus & Folkman, 1984; Pearlin, Lieberman, Menaghan, & Mullan, 1981). Events perceived as threatening, uncontrollable, or unpredictable are more predictive of health outcomes. Events that are perceived as unresolved are stronger predictors of mental illness than demands and events that are perceived as resolved (i.e., successfully handled, personally enlightening; Thoits, 1994; Turner & Avison, 1992). Moreover, studies of the stress process reveal that individuals often successfully cope with life events and the stress reactions (Thoits, 1995). In particular, research has shown that individuals who actively cope via seeking social support and by managing the source of the stress often show better physical and mental health outcomes than individuals who have little social support and who cope by using techniques to sedate the emotional sequelae of stress.

WHERE ARE WE NOW? WHAT NEXT?

One scientific discipline that has developed an explicit focus on positive development is the "positive psychology" group. Reacting to a field that focuses "almost exclusive attention to pathology" and "concentrates on repairing damage within a disease model of human functioning," Martin Seligman (Seligman & Csikszentmihalyi, 2000) and colleagues have turned their focus to understanding "what makes life worth living" and "how normal people flourish under more benign conditions." Similar to other disciplines, many psychologists have come to focus not only on remediation but also on prevention. In so doing, they have recognized that preventing problems, such as mental illness, requires a focus on building competency rather than simply healing deficiencies (Keyes & Lopez, in press). However, prevention and promotion are not synonymous, though they may be more distinctive as health objectives than as procedures or interventions. In other words, the objective of prevention is avoidance of pathology, whereas promotion is the objective of elevating health. As procedures, prevention and promotion may share common features in that each technique seeks to reduce risk factors (i.e., reducing weaknesses) and increase protective factors (i.e., increasing strengths and competencies).

Another recent effort was completed at the National Academies of Science, where a panel on positive development was convened with a focus toward informing programs for youth. Chaired by Jacquelynne Eccles, members took an interdisciplinary perspective and focused on indicator measurement as well as programs. Interestingly, this panel was funded by the Office of the Assistant Secretary for Planning and Evaluation in the Department of Health and Human Services, reflecting the emerging policy interest in taking a positive and developmental approach to adolescent issues. The office of the former Surgeon General (Satcher, 2000) has also urged a focus on a healthy start for children, with good mental health being emphasized along with good physical health.

In sum, despite a slow start for child well-being, a logical progression has occurred from an emphasis on treating problems, to preventing problems, to promoting positive development. This "positive" approach has recently begun to gain considerable momentum. Despite this upsurge in interest, critical conceptual, measurement, methodological, and empirical work remains to be done. Thus, the current book takes its place in a field that has begun to acquire critical mass, but which has much work left to do.

REFERENCES

Aber, J. L., & Jones, S. M. (1997). Indicators of positive development in early childhood: Improving concepts and measures (pp. 395–408). In R. M. Hauser, B. V. Brown, & W. R. Prosser (Eds.), *Indicators of children's well-being*. New York: Russell Sage Foundation.

Aldwin, C. M., Sutton, K. J., & Lachman, M. (1996). The development of coping resources in adulthood. *Journal of Personality, 64*(4), 837–869.

Allport, G. W. (1961). *Pattern and growth in personality*. New York: Holt, Rinehart & Winston.

Baltes P. B., & Baltes, M. M. (1990). *Successful aging: Perspectives from the behavioral sciences*. New York: Cambridge University Press.

Bennett, W. J. (Ed.). (1993). *The book of virtues: A treasury of great moral stories*. New York: Simon & Schuster.

Benson, P. L. (1993). *The troubled journey: A portrait of 6th–12th-grade youth*. Minneapolis, MN: Search Institute.

Carnegie Council on Adolescent Development. (1989). *Turning points: Preparing American youth for the 21st century*. New York: Carnegie Corporation of New York.

Catalano, R. F., Berglund, M. L., Ryan, J. A. M., Lonczak, H. S., & Hawkins, J. D. (1999). *Positive youth development in the United States: Research findings on evaluations of positive youth development programs*. Washington, DC: Government Printing Office.

Cumming, E., & Henry, W. H. (1961). *Growing old: The process of disengagement*. New York: Basic Books.

Diener, E., & Suh, E. (1997). Subjective well-being and age: An international analysis. In K. W. Schaie & M. P. Lawton (Eds.), *Annual review of gerontology and geriatrics* (pp. 304–324). New York: Springer.

Dryfoos, J. G. (1998). *Safe passage: Making it through adolescence in a risky society*. New York: Oxford University Press.

Elliott, D. S., Huizinga, D., & Menard, S. (1989). *Multiple problem youths: Delinquency, substance use, and mental health problems*. New York: Springer-Verlag.

Erikson, E. H. (1950). *Childhood and society*. New York: Norton.

Erikson, E. (1959). Identity and the life cycle. *Psychological Issues, 1*, 18–164.

Foege, W. H. (1996). Preventive medicine and public health. *Journal of the American Medical Association, 275*(23), 1846–1847.

Hawkins, J. D., Catalano, R. F., & Miller, J. Y. (1992). Risk and protective factors for alcohol and other drug problems in adolescence and early adulthood: Implications for substance abuse prevention. *Psychological Bulletin, 112*, 64–105.

Holmes, T. H., & Rahe, R. H. (1967). The social readjustment scale. *Journal of Psychosomatic Research, 11*, 213–218.

Institute for American Values. (1998). *A call to civil society: Why democracy needs moral truths*. New York: Institute for American Values.

International Youth Foundation. (1998). What is youth development? In *Programs that work* [On-line]. Available: www.iyfnet.org/programs/dyo.html

International Youth Foundation. (2001). *Aligning youth agendas: A rationale for the Forum for Youth Investment*. Takoma Park, MD: Author.

Jahoda, M. (1958). *Current concepts of positive mental health*. New York: Basic Books.

Keyes, C. L. M., & Lopez, S. J. (2002). Toward a science of mental health: Positive directions in diagnosis and intervention. In C. R. Snyder & S. J. Lopez (Eds.), *Handbook of positive psychology* (pp. 45–59). New York: Oxford.

Keyes, C. L. M., & Ryff, C. D. (1998). Generativity in adult lives: Social structural contours and quality of life consequences. In D. McAdams & E. de St. Aubin (Eds.), *Generativity and adult development:*

Perspectives on caring for and contributing to the next generation (pp. 227–263). Washington, DC: American Psychological Association.

Kirby, D. (1997). *No easy answers: Research findings on programs to reduce teen pregnancy.* Washington, DC: National Campaign to Prevent Teen Pregnancy.

Kutzka, E. A. (1981). *The benefits of old age. Social-welfare policy for the elderly.* Chicago: University of Chicago Press.

Lazarus, R. S., & Folkman, S. (1984). *Stress, appraisal, and coping.* New York: Springer.

Leffert, N., Benson, P. L., Scales, P. C., Sharma, A., Drake, D., & Blyth, D. A. (1998). Developmental assets: Measurement and prediction of risk behaviors among adolescents. *Applied Developmental Science*, *2*(4), 209–230.

Lerner, R. M., Fisher, C. B., & Weinberg, R. A. (2000). Toward a science for and of the people: Promoting civil society through the application of development science. *Child Development*, *71*, 11–20.

McGinnis, J. M., & Foege, W. H. (1993). Actual cases of death in the United States. *Journal of the American Medical Association*, *270*(18), 2207–2212.

Mendel, R. A. (1995). *Prevention or pork? A hard-headed look at youth-oriented anti-crime programs.* Washington, DC: American Youth Policy Forum.

Miringoff, M., & Miringoff, M. (1999). *The social health of the nation: How America is really doing.* New York: Oxford University Press.

Moore, K. A. (1997). Criteria for indicators of child well-being. In R. M. Hauser, B. V. Brown, & W. R. Prosser (Eds.), *Indicators of children's well-being* (pp. 36–44). New York: Russell Sage Foundation.

Moore, K. A., Evans, V. J., Brooks-Gunn, J., & Roth, J. (2001). What are good child outcomes? In A. Thornton (Ed.), *The well-being of children and families: Research and data needs* (pp. 59–84). Ann Arbor, MI: University of Michigan Press.

Moore, K. A., & Glei, D. A. (1995). Taking the plunge: New measures of youth development that cross outcome domains and assess positive outcomes. *Journal of Adolescent Research*, *10*(1), 15–40.

Moore, K. A., & Halle, T. G. (forthcoming). Preventing problems vs. promoting the positive: What do we want for our children? In S. Hofferth & T. Owens (Eds.), *Children at the millennium: Where have we come from, where are we going?* Stamford, CT: JAI Press.

Moore, K. A., Manlove, J., Glei, D. A., & Morrision, D. R. (1998). Nonmarital school-age motherhood: Family, individual, and school characteristic. *Journal of Adolescent Research*, *13*(4), 433–457.

Moore, K. A., Manlove, J., Terry-Humen, E., Papillo, A. R., & Williams, S. (2001). *Facts at a glance.* Washington, DC: Child Trends.

Moore, K. A., Miller, B. C., Morrison, D. R., & Glei, D. A. (1995). *Adolescent sex, contraception and childbearing: A review of recent research.* Washington, DC: Child Trends.

Moore, K. A., & Sugland, B. W. (1996). *Next steps and best bets: Approaches to preventing adolescent childbearing.* Washington, DC: Child Trends.

Mott, F. L., & Haurin, R. J. (1988). Linkages between sexual activity and drug use among American adolescents. *Family Planning Perspectives*, *20*, 129–136.

Mroczek, D. K., & Kolarz, C. M. (1998). The effect of age on positive and negative affect: A developmental perspective on happiness. *Journal of Personality and Social Psychology*, *75*(5), 1333–1349.

Paley, B., Conger, R. D., & Harold, G. T. (2000). Parents' affect, adolescent cognitive representations, and adolescent social development. *Journal of Marriage and Family*, *62*, 761–776.

Pearlin, L. I. (1989). The sociological study of stress. *Journal of Health and Social Behavior*, *30*(3), 241–256.

Pearlin, L. I., Lieberman, M. A., Menaghan, E. G., & Mullan, J. T. (1981). The stress process. *Journal of Health and Social Behavior*, *22*, 337–356.

Pittman, K. J., & Fleming, W. E. (1991). *A new vision: Promoting youth development.* Testimony by Karen J. Pittman before the House Select Committee on Children, Youth and Families. Washington, DC: Center for Youth Development and Policy Research.

Roth, J., Brooks-Gunn, J., & Galen, B. (1997). *Promoting health adolescence: Youth development frameworks and programs.* New York: Center for Children and Families, Teachers College, Columbia University.

Rowe, J. W., & Kahn, R. L. (1998). *Successful aging.* New York: Pantheon.

Satcher, D. (2000). *Welcome.* Surgeon General's Conference on Children's Mental Health: Developing a National Action Agenda, September 18–19, 2000. Washington, DC.

Scales, P. C., Benson, P. L., Leffert, N., & Blyth, D. A. (2000). Contribution of developmental assets to the prediction of thriving among adolescents. *Applied Developmental Science, Vol. 4*(1), 27–46.

Scales, P. C., & Leffert, N. (1999). *Developing assets: A synthesis of the scientific research on adolescent development*. Minneapolis, MN: Search Institute.

Seligman, M. E. P., & Csikszentmihalyi, M. (2000). Positive psychology: An introduction. *American Psychologist, 55*(1), 5–14.

Severin, F. T. (1965). *Humanistic viewpoints in psychology*. New York: McGraw-Hill.

Takanishi, R., Mortimer, A. M., & McGourthy, T. J. (1997). Positive indicators of adolescent development: Redressing the negative image of American adolescents. In R. M. Hauser, B. V. Brown, & W. R. Prosser (Eds.), *Indicators of children's well-being* (pp. 428–441). New York: Russell Sage Foundation.

Thoits, P. A. (1994). Stressors and problem solving: The individuals as psychological activist. *Journal of Health and Social Behavior, 35*, 143–159.

Thoits, P. A. (1995). Stress, coping, and social support processes: Where are we? What next? *Journal of Health and Social Behavior* (Extra Issue), 53–79.

Turner, R. J., & Avison, W. R. (1992). Innovations in the measurement of life stress: Crisis theory and the significance of event resolution. *Journal of Health and Social Behavior, 33*, 36–50.

Turner, R. J., Wheaton, B., & Lloyd, D. A. (1995). The epidemiology of social stress. *American Sociological Review, 60*, 104–125.

U.S. Department of Health and Human Services, Office of the Assistant Secretary for Planning and Evaluation. (2000). *Trends in the well-being of America's children and youth*. Washington, DC: Government Printing Office.

United Way. (2000). *Agency experiences with outcome measurement: Survey results*. Alexandria, VA: United Way.

Zaff, J. F., Moore, K. A., Papillo, A. R., & Williams, S. W. (April, 2001). *The longitudinal effects of extracurricular activities on academic achievement and civic involvement*. Paper presented at the biennial conference of the Society for Research in Child Development, Minneapolis, Minnesota.

2

The Strengths-Based Approach to Child Well-Being: Let's Begin With the End in Mind

Elizabeth L. Pollard
Mark L. Rosenberg
The Center for Child Well-being, Decatur, GA

INTRODUCTION

If you were given the charge to dramatically improve the lives of children, what would you do? When we were confronted with this question, we began by thinking about what those "dramatically improved" lives would be like and what the children who led those "dramatically improved" lives would be like. This lays the foundation for improving the lives of children and the adults they will become by identifying the strengths that they should have.

We took some lessons from the way we have already improved the physical health of children. Just 100 years ago, at the beginning of the last century, the life expectancy in this country was only 45 years; by 1999 the life expectancy had increased by 30 years to 75. That was the equivalent of adding on 8 hours a day, every day for close to a century. This did not come about because of better treatment of heart disease, cancer, and stroke; rather it was health promotion and better preventive care for mothers, infants, and children. It was the public health focus on immunizations, better nutrition, clean drinking water, better housing, better nutrition, and more exercise. It was this focus on promotion of physical strengths and the prevention of problems—rather than the treatment of problems once they occurred—that was so important in extending the life expectancy.

However, there is more to well-being than good physical health. The idea behind the current effort is to apply the same focus on promotion of strengths and prevention of problems not just to children's physical health, but to their psychological development as well. The term we use to encompass both their physical health and psychological development is *well-being*.

To focus on promoting strengths in children, we need a clear idea of what those strengths are. We need to know what we are aiming for. In photography we have something that helps us know what we are aiming for. It is called the viewfinder, and the person who invented this deserves more credit that she ever gets. The viewfinder on the camera lets us see what we are going to get in our picture before we ever take it. It lets us see ahead in time to what we are going to have in our picture, whether we get it weeks later as an old-fashioned glossy print, or seconds later as a digitized image. We need the equivalent of a viewfinder for picturing how we would like our children to turn out. Another way to put it would be to say that we need to begin with the end in mind. We don't usually do this when it comes to rearing children. We pretty much rear them by the seat of our pants. We develop strategic plans for so many relatively unimportant things in our life, and we spend so much time working on these plans that never get used, that in the end strategic planning has given strategic planning a bad name. But we don't take the time to make strategic plans for the most important things in our lives, our children. Part of the reason we do this is that we don't know what we want our children to be in the end. We may say we want them to be healthy, to be happy, to be content. But what does that really mean? This book is meant to be a viewfinder to help to focus our attention on the end that we have in mind, and it constructs that end with the elements of well-being.

Well-Being: Positive Development Across the Life Course presents the reader with an integrative summary of the evidence base for elements that contribute to an individual's well-being. The term *element* is used to represent the foundational strengths contributing to an individual's well-being in the physical, social and emotional, and cognitive domains. The aim of this book is to consolidate what is known about a strengths-based approach to well-being by identifying these strengths within the physical, social and emotional, and cognitive domains. This book also suggests new directions for well-being research, practice, and policy.

The book editors and authors adopted the following formal definition of well-being: Well-being is a state of successful performance throughout the life course integrating physical, cognitive, and social-emotional function that results in productive activities deemed significant by one's cultural community, fulfilling social relationships, and the ability to transcend moderate psychosocial and environmental problems. Well-being also has a subjective dimension in the sense of satisfaction associated with fulfilling one's potential.[1] This definition takes a positive, ecological approach and encompasses developmental stages across the life course. We further acknowledge that the expression of well-being, its subjective experience, and the elements that undergird well-being, all exist in a particular cultural context. Fur-

---

[1]The Surgeon General's (1999) definition of mental health and Thomas Weisner's (1998) definition of well-being both contributed aspects to our definition.

thermore, the knowledge base we are drawing on for the majority of the book is written to refer to Western populations.

This work has been a collaborative effort, and we wish to thank the many contributors and section editors. We are also deeply grateful to the Robert Wood Johnson Foundation for their support in this endeavor.

STRENGTHS-BASED APPROACH

"Health," according to the World Health Organization, "is a state of complete physical, mental, and social well-being and not merely the absence of disease or infirmity" (World Health Organization, 1983). However, most people when they think about health think about illness. Most efforts have focused on children's disorders, disabilities, and deficits. (Pollard & Lee, in press) This book is an effort to begin to integrate and consolidate what we know about children's strengths, assets, and competencies. A strengths-based approach focuses on cultivating children's assets, positive relationships, morals, and capacities that give them the resources they need to grow successfully across the life course.

The knowledge base for child development is largely segmented into separate disciplines; most of it reflects a deficit or dysfunction orientation and addresses the biological and environmental influences separately. This book integrates expert knowledge and guidance on child well-being. The book is divided into four sections; three of these address domains of well-being: physical, social and emotional, and cognitive. The fourth integrates notions of well-being at different points in the life course.

A Simplified Model That Goes Beyond Prevention

We would like to avoid the presumption that the best model is either focused on treating problems, preventing problems, or promoting strengths. Rather, we would like to develop an integrative model that combines the best of all of these approaches. Neal Halfon has described a model called the "The Health Development Trajectory" which shows the impact of risk factors and risk reduction measures as well as protective factors and health promotion interventions over the life trajectory (Halfon & Inkelas, 2000). Here we present a simpler model that will help us discuss several assumptions about these models and the thinking that goes into them.

The *problem-treatment* approach has traditionally been the dominant approach to health. The United States currently spends about one trillion dollars a year on health and health care. Of that amount, more than 95% is spent on treating problems that have already occurred. Probably only about 1% is spent on preventing health problems. Although every bit as important, the corresponding figures for spending on the cognitive and socioemotional domains are not yet available. However, we would guess that the balance here is also steeply in the direction of fixing up problems that have already occurred. This balance probably reflects the fact that people

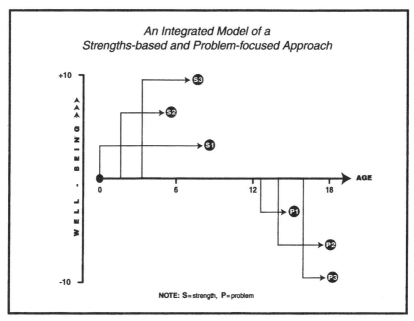

FIG. 2.1. An integrated model of a strengths-based and problem-focused approach.

with problems are much stronger advocates for attention to their problem than are people who do not yet have problems. Physical realities make for much stronger voices than statistical possibilities.

With the prevention-focused approach, people typically begin to pay attention to specific problems close to the time when these problems actually occur or begin to emerge. This approach has the advantage of being able to address problems with a prevention program delivered close in time to when children are at greatest risk for developing these problems. Programs for older children and adolescents can have measurable outcome data available relatively soon after the program is initiated. For example, if you want to start a program to prevent violence in teens, you might start the program with children aged 12 and be able to measure the results at age 17. Thus, you might have measurable outcomes within 5 years. These specific outcomes of interest might also be easier to measure than the outcomes of strength-promoting programs. Similarly, prevention programs are easier to evaluate because measures and data sets containing indicators of problems are abundant. In addition, by identifying risk factors and selecting a group of children who demonstrate these risk factors, children who are at greatest risk can be selected for intervention and thus program resources are concentrated on the children most likely to demonstrate the problems. It has also been demonstrated that early targeting of risk factors can lead to success in prevention. Some problems, such as smoking, alcohol abuse, and violence, share common risk factors, so prevention programs can sometimes target the same high-risk population and be able to impact multiple outcomes simultaneously. Finally, political support and popular attention tend to gravitate towards problem-focused approaches.

When a *strengths-based approach* is used, strengths can be described across the life course and precursors to those strengths defined in age-specific terms. These precursors can be identified and used to measure outcomes beginning at birth, outcomes that occur much earlier than most prevention programs begin. In fact, parents can begin to think about strengths, and perhaps even influence some of them, beginning at conception. Strengths can be promoted at any age. Neuroscience suggests that early developmental influences are critical to the development of strengths.

In addition, strengths can and do appear, even when they are not explicitly named or cultivated. Strengths also provide some measure of protection against problems, although much work remains to be done to measure this effect on specific problems of childhood.

Strengths-based programs usually take longer to carry out because they begin at or before birth, and to attain their optimal impact, usually need to be maintained through adolescence. Thus, a strengths-based approach requires a longer period of time from program initiation to the measurement of results. This is part of the explanation for why it is usually harder to get popular and political attention for strengths than it is to get attention to problems. Finally, it is difficult to evaluate strengths-based programs because there are, as of yet, few indicators and data sets that measure strengths.

A model that permits one to view the benefits of a strengths-based approach together with the potential benefits of a problem-prevention approach can be quite useful. Many prevention programs also utilize strengths-based developmental components. Prevention programs have a longer history than strengths-based approaches; thus we have more experience with them. An important route for promoting strengths-based approaches then might be to add strength-promotion components to prevention programs. Measuring the benefits of both components requires a comprehensive model that can assess the promotional benefits of strengths in terms of improved levels of well-being (i.e., ranking above the line) and the benefits of strengths in terms of preventing the undesirable outcomes of problems (i.e., which could make a person rank below the line).

The Foundational Strengths of Well-Being

As a first step in building the foundation for a knowledge base, a systematic review of the literature was conducted to assess the current state of child well-being research (Pollard & Lee, 2001). This review updated and expanded an earlier systematic literature review spanning 1974 to 1992 (Toles et al., 1993). The review extended our understanding of child well-being to include current definitions of well-being, indicators of well-being, and instruments used to measure these indicators, thus contributing to a more integrated understanding of the state of the well-being research base. This initial effort showed that the definitions, indicators, and measures of well-being are highly variable and often do not use a strengths-based perspective.

The well-being literature base spanned the following domains: physical, social and emotional, cognitive, and economic. Indicators for each domain were grouped into deficit and positive clusters. The review revealed that well-being has been defined by positive individual characteristics, such as happiness, and on a continuum from positive to negative, such as how one might measure self-esteem. Well-being has also been defined in terms of an individual's context, such as standard of living. It is frequently defined by the absence of well-being, such as the absence of depression, and also defined in a collective manner (e.g., shared understanding). There is a clear need for a consistent vocabulary and framework that spans a wide range of disciplines, age groups, cultures, communities, and environments in which well-being has been studied. Child well-being is more than the absence of problems; however, a core set of positive indicators has not yet been determined.

Examples of the Strengths-Based Approach: Research and Practice

There are a number of organizations that incorporate a strengths-based approach to their work, and we would like to mention two of them: The Values in Action Institute and Prevent Child Abuse America.

The Values in Action Institute (VIA), funded by the Mayerson Foundation, is creating a list of human strengths and virtues and a reliable and valid strategy for measuring them. The project is linking the positive psychology with youth development groups to encourage program evaluation in terms of their catalog and measurement system. The program's long-term goal is to identify active ingredients in youth development programs, and ultimately design exemplary way of promoting the components of character among our society's youth (C. Peterson, personal communication, February 22, 2001).

Prevent Child Abuse America is an organization that has adopted a strengths-based approach to the prevention of child abuse. After years of focusing on prevention of child abuse, they came to the conclusion that they could prevent child abuse most effectively by focusing on the family and individual strengths. Their Healthy Families America (HFA) program helps prepare first-time parents to promote positive childhood outcomes and prevent child abuse and neglect. Home visitors to new parents provide support, parenting education and referral to services, along with training and employment opportunities for up to 5 years after the child is born.

Indicators and Measurement

The necessary prerequisite for developing indicators and measures of child well-being is developing operational definitions of the foundational strengths. This book is a first step towards achieving this goal. Expanding measurement of well-being is critical to evaluate programs, guide policy decisions, and identify areas of strengths as well as areas that need improvement.

However, presently there are no standardized metrics or indicators for measuring well-being, especially those related to children. Individual studies and programs tend to derive their own measures of well-being and, consequently, measures and indicators of well-being tend to vary greatly. Standardization of indicators and measures of well-being is necessary to advance research and practice in this arena. We could measure overall well-being or we could measure strengths. Ideally, we would like to know how particular strengths relate to outcomes in the future.

At the beginning of a movement, qualitative concepts often suffice. It is important now, for example, to increase the nation's attention to developing strengths and focusing on positive measures from the child's earliest years. We will soon need to be able to measure the difference between two distinct approaches to developing strengths in children. Until we have quantitative indicators of these strengths, we will not be able to determine which approach is more effective or cost-effective. To measure these outcomes we might employ measures such as Disability-Adjusted Life Years (DALYs), a measure that incorporates both morbidity and mortality. DALYs lets us measure not only deaths, but the impact of the problem in terms of disability and disease as well. (Anand & Hansen, 1998). Unfortunately, there is no set of obvious indicators of well-being to adopt. There are significant obstacles to identifying and reaching consensus on indicators of well-being. One might assume that *America's Children: Key National Indicators of Well-Being*, prepared by the Federal Interagency Forum on Child and Family Statistics (the Forum), would be a prime source; however, it contains primarily negative indicators. Although the Forum would like to include more positive indicators, they have had problems in the past coming up with positive indicators the Forum members agree are important and valid. (K. Heck, personal communication, December 5, 2000). In a commentary on the America's Children report, Karen Pittman (1998) wrote, "Hiding behind concerns about the quality of data sources is unacceptable. The educational value of presenting data which tell the whole story should not only outweigh our concern about data quality, it should drive it" (p. 55).

Despite the challenges of measuring strengths, the Search Institute provides us with an example of a widely adopted system for measuring strengths in youth. The Search Institute's conceptual model of youth development is based on the young people's strengths and the resources of their communities and families that can foster these strengths to transform them into components of positive development across the life span. Based on this model, the Search Institute developed a list of 40 internal and external developmental assets for youth (Benson, 1990). The developmental assets are positive experiences, relationships, opportunities, and personal qualities that young people need to grow into healthy, caring, and responsible adults. Since 1989, Search Institute has measured developmental assets in more than 1 million 6th to 12th graders in communities across the United States (Scales & Leffert, 1999). Their approach would be further strengthened by identifying developmentally comparable types of measures linked to an evidence base, and then finding ways to promote these strengths.

Clearly, there is a compelling need to measure more than children's and youth's problems. We hope that the chapters that follow will help meet this need by identifying core strengths in the physical, social and emotional, and cognitive domains, on which future work on measurement and indicators can be based.

DEVELOPMENT OF THIS WORK

Creating a book aimed at depicting the core strengths of well-being presents a formidable challenge. To begin our task, section editors developed a list of core strengths in their domains (physical, social and emotional, cognitive, and well-being in adulthood). We asked the following questions for each of the proposed strengths: (a) Is the strength generalizable to all children? (b) Is there an evidence base that supports the strength? (c) Does the strength promote health and child well- being and mitigate illness and dysfunction? (d) Can the strength be cultivated? (e) Can the strength be measured?

Next, the section editors assembled a team of scientists, representing expertise from diverse disciplines, to write chapters on each of the proposed strengths. Chapters in the book introduce and review the evidence base for a foundational strength. Chapter authors integrated existing knowledge from developmental theory, empirical data, expertise, and professional experience. Each chapter follows a three-part outline consisting of (a) theoretical and empirical review of the literature, (b) developmental stability of the strength, and (c) factors affecting the development and promotion of the strength. In addition, chapter authors commented on how the strength contributes to one's sense of well-being and how we promote it in a general sense.

Section editors and selected authors met for a two-day meeting in May of 2000 to review the preliminary work that had been done on the chapters of the proposed strengths, and reach consensus on which strengths would be included in this book. At this meeting, some of the proposed strengths were eliminated as a result of our deliberations. For example, the group omitted resiliency as a strength in favor of a chapter on coping. The consensus among participants at the meeting was that resiliency is more of an outcome than an actual strength. After much discussion, the group converged on a set of strengths that met our criteria and now form the foundation of the book. In selecting the core strengths of well-being that would be represented in the book, we could not be exhaustive. The list of core strengths does not represent everything needed for healthy development. We acknowledge that many variables, including genetics, biology, the environment, and individual experience, contribute to the development of well-being.

Although the chapters follow a similar format, the reader will note some differences. For example, chapters in the physical domain tend to make recommendations for application of the knowledge base based on what is known, whereas the socioemotional and cognitive sections tend to make recommendations for future research initiatives.

A unique contribution of the book is that it is comprehensive and incorporates the physical, social and emotional, and cognitive domains, each of which is essential for well-being. The concluding section addresses overarching issues, implications for policy and practice, and defines a vision for what is next in the study and practice of well-being.

This book aims to advance children's health and development by identifying, describing, and organizing strengths of well-being. We hope that this work will direct attention to the importance of fostering developmental well-being in children and ensuring continuity across the life course.

REFERENCES

Anand, S., & Hanson, K. (1998). DALYs: Efficiency versus equity. *World Development*, *26*, 307–310.

Benson, P. L. (1990). *The troubled journey: A portrait of 6th–12th-grade youth.* Minneapolis, MN: Search Institute.

Halfon, N., & Inkelas, M. (2000). *Motivating investment in "Health Development" in children's health care.* Unpublished manuscript.

Pittman, K. (1998). Move over, Greenspan. *Youth Today*, *7*, 55.

Pollard, E. L., & Lee, P. (in press). *Child well-being: A systematic review of the literature.* Social Indicators Research.

Scales, P., & Leffert, N. (1999). *Developmental assets: A synthesis of the scientific research on adolescent development.* Minneapolis, MN: Search Institute.

Toles, M., Marks, S., Fallon, B., & Offord, D. (1993). *A literature review of child well-being: Concepts, measurements and determinants.* Unpublished manuscript.

U.S. Department of Health and Human Services. *Mental health: A report of the Surgeon General.* Rockville, MD: U.S. Department of Health and Human Services, Substance Abuse and Mental Health Services Administration, Center for Mental Health Services, National Institutes of Health, National Institute of Mental Health, 1999.

World Health Organization. *A WHO report on social and biological effects on perinatal mortality*, *1.* Statistical Publishing House, Budapest, 1978. Re-issued by Saudi Med. J. 1983; 4: Suppl 1.

Weisner, T. S. (1998, Fall). Human development, child well-being, and the cultural project of development [Review]. *New Directions for Child Development*, *81*, 69–85.

3

Holistic Well-Being and the Developing Child

Jonathan F. Zaff
Child Trends, Washington, DC

D. Camille Smith
Centers for Disease Control and Prevention, Atlanta, GA

Martha F. Rogers
Caroline H. Leavitt
The Center for Child Well-being, Decatur, GA

Tamara G. Halle
Child Trends, Washington, DC

Marc H. Bornstein
National Institute of Child Health and Human Development Bethesda, MD

INTRODUCTION

Research and scholarship present a picture of child well-being that is detailed in the same way as a mosaic or pointillist painting. The whole is articulated more clearly with the distinct contributions of each piece. In this book, life-course well-being is detailed through examination of three domains or dimensions—the physical, socioemotional, and cognitive—and the contributions of specific foundational elements of well-being within each domain. Nonetheless, well-being must be appreciated as a holistic and integrated state. We distinguish between manner of presentation and conceptual state.

This chapter examines interrelations among dimensions and elements of well-being during child development and ways that overall well-being is fostered. The actions and environments that promote child well-being operate across the whole and also by impacting specific factors that then have reciprocal effects on the whole. We begin with a description of dimensions of well-being as seen through the lens of child development and maturation.

CHILD DEVELOPMENT AND DIMENSIONS OF WELL-BEING

Physical Well-Being

Physical health and safety is a primary dimension grounding children's overall well-being. Vital elements of physical well-being include good nutrition, preventive healthcare, physical activity, safety and security, substance abuse prevention, and reproductive health. Although the behaviors and components that are needed to foster each element may change as the individual matures, the elements or strengths themselves provide a coherent core around which physical health and safety guidelines and standards can be structured for each stage of childhood and adulthood. Adults not only need to ensure children's physical well-being during their early years, but also teach and demonstrate the importance of children continuing healthy habits into adolescence and adulthood.

Responsibility for accomplishing these complementary health and safety goals shifts as children develop, for as they mature, children progress from dependence to autonomy in their ability to make decisions about their own physical well-being. In early childhood, parents or caregivers are primarily responsible for ensuring physical health and safety. Early attention to this dimension is critical for several reasons. First, young children experience rapid growth and development during infancy and during the first five years of life. This stage of most rapid growth can have a lasting impact on subsequent development. Sustaining a good physical, social-emotional, and cognitive environment for this period undergirds the whole developmental trajectory. Second, young infants and children may be more vulnerable to harm than older children. The immaturity of young children's immune systems makes them more susceptible to infection and disease. Promoting health and safety in early childhood can help protect young children when they most need external safeguards to sustain their holistic development.

This early period is an ideal time for parents and caregivers to begin teaching children the importance of maintaining healthy behaviors throughout their lives as a primary way in which they can promote their own health and safety. Throughout middle childhood, while parental opportunities and responsibilities continue, parents and caregivers relinquish more and more duties and decision-making to the child. This transition continues during adolescence when parents accelerate their trust of responsibility and children assume a greater role in ensuring their own health and safety. In addition, adolescence gives children the opportunity to test and experiment with the lessons they have learned from their caregivers about healthy lifestyles and decisions, while still having the benefit of adult supervision.

In sum, when parents and caregivers are actively attentive to their children's physical health and safety, demonstrate the relations between physical health, safety, and well-being, and allow children increasing opportunities to test these lessons and make their own choices under adult supervision, children typically develop into healthy individuals and achieve good developmental outcomes. Without the provision of an adequate foundation in the physical domain and encouragement of physical health and safety elements, positive development would almost certainly be compromised. Fortunately, over the past century, advances in technology, the growth of the health and medical knowledge base, improvements in accessibility to information and services, and increased efforts to educate policymakers and individuals about the benefits of physical health and safety have contributed to vast improvements in this dimension of well-being.

Social and Emotional Well-Being

Having a balanced, internal emotional "center," being able to adapt to different circumstances and manage stress, knowing how to interact effectively in social situations, and feeling good about oneself are all characteristics of a healthy and productive individual. Developing these social and emotional competencies is a vital task for children and youth. Collectively, these competencies are markers of social and emotional well-being. Social and emotional well-being encompasses the development of emotion understanding and regulation; the ability to cope with stressors; the development of autonomy and trust; the maturation of the self-system, including identity, self-concept, and self-esteem; the development of empathy and sympathy; and the formation of positive social relationships with parents, siblings, and peers. These elements of social and emotional well-being influence each other across the life course. In other words, they are both outcomes of and contributors to positive overall social and emotional development.

The social and emotional elements of well-being develop from birth and, like the physical attributes of the child, become more refined as the child ages. Social relationships, for instance, typically begin within a parent-child dyad in which a warm and responsive relationship predicts positive social-emotional and cognitive outcomes. Siblings, and subsequently peers, broaden the child's social world. Under the guidance of warm and responsive adults (such as parents or teachers), children learn how to use conflict resolution skills and how to act prosocially. Through interactions with siblings and peers, children learn how to coordinate play behavior, and how to respond appropriately to others. Highly important to the development of social relationships are empathy and sympathy (i.e., the ability to feel what another person is feeling and the ability to react out of concern for that person's distress or sorrow). Not only are empathy and sympathy integral components of healthy relationships, but they are also correlated with prosocial behaviors. In fact, associations among empathy, sympathy, and prosocial behaviors strengthen as the child ages.

Empathy and sympathy would be impossible, however, without the ability to feel and regulate emotions. Although emotions have a biological basis, biology interacts with the environment, resulting in the interpretation of specific feelings corresponding with specific situations. Understanding when an emotion is appropriate for a situation is a necessary ability for social competence (e.g., laughing, an indicator of joy, when a friend is hurt would be considered inappropriate).

The environment-child fit can also be seen with coping strategies. Through experience, children develop the knowledge that certain coping strategies work better in certain situations. The complex dynamic of the child-environment interaction is also present in the development of the child's sense of self. How children perceive themselves to be and how they feel about that perception are determined, predominantly, through social interactions and through living in a given community or society. Overall, the development of any single social or emotional element of well-being is dependent on the development of one or several other elements.

Cognitive Well-Being

From earliest infancy, children develop the cognitive structures that allow them to assimilate information more and more efficiently from the environment. At the same time, they acquire a broad set of communication skills, including understanding and speaking words in sentences, pragmatics, reasoning with and thinking about language, and literacy, that allow them to use their cognitions effectively. Thinking, communicating thought, and using the products of thought in everyday life—cognitive skills broadly construed—are essential to individual well-being. Cognition encompasses the processes of perceiving, remembering, conceiving, judging, and reasoning in order to obtain and use knowledge. Communication refers to skills that permit the exchange of thoughts, wishes, and feelings so necessary to developing and maintaining social relationships with others. Cognition is basic to adapting and making one's way in the world, to maintaining health, to engaging in productive activity, and to taking profitable advantage of the social world and object environment.

These various cognitive and language abilities underlie success in school, positive social interactions, and future employability. Although educators are prepared to teach basic literacy skills, children must come to school with the cognitive and communicative foundations that are prerequisites for learning to read, write, and perform quantitative operations. Thereafter, academic achievement in many subjects and success in various walks of life depend on understanding what is heard and what is read. Children use their conceptual grounding to provide the context for comprehending information acquired by ear and eye. Cognitive and language competencies influence not only academic success, but success in communicating with others and finding ways to problem-solve. Just as early interactions between caregivers and infants promote the child's first cognitive and communication skills, cognition and language, in turn, support personal and interpersonal social-emotional development across the life course.

Cognitive abilities include mental capacities often vernacularly referred to as intelligence. Although definitions of intelligence are diverse, surveys of professionals indicate that three attributes—abstract thinking or reasoning, the capacity to acquire knowledge, and problem solving—are key. In addition, a majority of respondents also rate adaptation, creativity, general knowledge, linguistic and mathematical competence, memory, and mental speed as fundamental elements of a strengths-based approach to cognition and intelligence.

INTERRELATEDNESS OF DIMENSIONS AND ELEMENTS OF CHILD WELL-BEING

These dimensions and elements of well-being closely interrelate, and two aspects of their interrelatedness warrant elaboration. First, elements of each domain impact and influence one another. Second, there are interrelated effects among the elements of each domain and elements of other domains.

First, each element in a domain is independently important to the well-being of children and adults. However, elements also articulate with one another as, for example, individuals' overall level of physical health depends on their ability to attain and sustain high levels of all elements of well-being in the physical domain. Cognitive and communicative abilities develop in tandem, and competence in one promotes competence in the other. Some cognitive abilities are prerequisites for language acquisition; for example, mental categorization (grouping based on shared similarity) is believed to be a necessary, although not sufficient, skill for vocabulary acquisition. At the same time, linguistic development facilitates the refinement of cognitive concepts. As the child's communication skills develop, language becomes one of the major vehicles for thinking and for acquiring further knowledge. Children learn to abstract concepts through comprehension of the oral and written word, and verbalization skills are useful for reasoning and solving problems. In addition, of course, lapses in one element can impede the promotion and maintenance of one or more other elements in domain.

Elements in a domain are also interrelated because of a propensity for particular elements to be present as groupings of either strengths or deficits in individuals. For example, an individual's quality of diet and amount of physical activity are frequently correlated. In addition, adolescents who either use or refrain from using tobacco often make similar decisions with regard to drugs, alcohol, precocious sexual behavior, and other high-risk activities. These relations among the physical elements produce either positive or negative outcomes and also can be advantageous in trying to establish how best to promote positive development. For example, preventing the use of tobacco and alcohol, often considered gateway substances to more serious drug use, may allow concerned parties to stave off the use of illegal drugs and promiscuous sexual behavior. The recognition and study of behavioral clusters such as these therefore helps scientists, practitioners, and policymakers to achieve more informed, efficient, and successful efforts in the areas of promotion, prevention, and treatment.

Likewise, social and emotional domain elements influence and promote one another. For example, children's ability to regulate their internal emotional reactions is a key contributor to the quality of relationships with parents, siblings, and peers. At the same time, warm and supportive relationships with parents, siblings, and peers help to increase feelings of happiness and contentment, and reduce the prevalence of depression and anxiety. Thus, the child's emotional state both affects and is affected by social interactions with others. It is clear that the core elements of social and emotional well-being included in this book are related to each other and influence each other in a dynamic and recursive manner.

The elements of cognition discussed in this book link in a nomological network with one another as well as with other domains of well-being. Certainly memory depends on information processing; for example, if information is not processed, it cannot enter into memory. It is possible, then, that if one element of cognitive well-being is neglected, other elements of cognitive well-being will suffer. However, the full ramifications of a local nomological net that involves all of the elements of well-being are not well understood, nor is the nature and structure of the mind with respect to how these elements are organized and mutually dependent.

Second, just as elements within a domain influence one another, they also exercise a substantial impact on the development of elements in other domains. For example, within the physical domain, good nutrition, particularly during the critical early years of rapid brain development, can encourage and improve social-emotional and cognitive development and performance. Alternatively, deficits in nutritional intake, even for only a short period of time, can have severe and harmful effects on development in other domains of well-being not only in childhood, but lasting into adulthood.

Physical domain elements influence those of the social-emotional and cognitive domains, just as the physical domain is also affected by social-emotional and cognitive elements. For example, healthy social-emotional development is grounded in caregiver relationships that are warm, consistent, and nurturing. These relationships are also essential for physical well-being and safety. Secure attachment to a caregiver is likely to enable children to better resist the temptation of drugs and alcohol and early, promiscuous, unsafe sexual behavior. Parental involvement in their children's lives and parental responsibility for their children's care will better ensure that children receive the preventive medical attention, physical activity, and proper nutrition they require. Finally, positive cognitive development will prepare many children to make better choices and understanding the consequences of their behavior and decisions about their physical health, development, and safety, particularly as they begin to assume more responsibility over their own physical well-being.

So, too, elements of social and emotional well-being promote and are promoted by core elements in the physical and cognitive domains. For example, the warmth and responsiveness of the parent-child relationship promotes the development of trust and autonomy, which in turn leads to increases in child exploration of the physical environment, thus stimulating both motor and cognitive development. Ongoing acquisition of information and development of well-being in the cognitive realm hinges on social-emotional well-being. Positive interpersonal relationships are associated with the development of cognitive abilities, such as social cognition and perspective taking—the ability to understand other people's thoughts, emotions, and intentions. Other cognitive gains associated with positive interpersonal relationships are the development of moral reasoning and school engagement.

Reciprocally, the development of cognitive abilities, such as information processing and perspective taking, are also essential for the development of many social and emotional elements of well-being, including emotion understanding, empathy, and the development of positive interpersonal relationships. Coping and the sense of self have strong cognitive undercurrents. Good cognitive functioning is vital to processing health and safety information. That is, children need a solid cognitive appreciation of why nutrition, exercise, and good decision making with regard to risk are important as well as how to conduct themselves.

Because there are reciprocal influences on the development of the elements of well-being both within and across domains, physical, social and emotional, and cognitive aspects of well-being cannot be segregated from one another. Relations among domains of well-being are so intertwined that which way causal arrows of association and influence point cannot be determined. Presumably it takes a certain level of cognitive maturity to be able to take another person's perspective and so gain empathy into a situation; however, one may share feelings at an emotional level and only later come to understand why and analyze the situation cognitively.

Early in school, children's educational achievement and their self-perceptions or motivations are independent of one another: Virtually all young children hold high perceptions of their competencies, and they persist in academic endeavors even in the face of failure. Later, however, children use grades to judge their ability. Moral development is associated with and fostered by influences that are consistent with healthy development in other areas. In sum, there are reciprocal influences on the development of the elements of well-being both within and across domains. Physical, social and emotional, and cognitive aspects of well-being are not separate entities. Indeed, physical strengths, social strengths, and cognitive strengths reverberate in synergy.

PROMOTING HOLISTIC WELL-BEING

The environmental context influences the development and expression of all elements of well-being. For example, emotional competence depends in part on the expression of emotions appropriate for a particular situation. Children who do not laugh at another person's expense are judged as more socially competent than children who do. Similarly, there are different coping strategies that are optimal for different circumstances, but no one type of strategy is optimal for all situations. Even self-esteem is thought to be specific to a particular context (e.g., academic, interpersonal, athletic, and so forth).

Biological factors, too, have acknowledged importance in how elements of well-being manifest themselves. However, even elements of well-being with a significant biological basis require social contexts to trigger their full and appropriate expression.

An important feature of well-being is that its elements can be targeted for promotion and may be responsive to intervention activities. The many facets of the child's environment, including the individual's personal practices, family and societal systems and values, neighborhood security, quality and affordability of the public health system, institutional practices, provision of basic needs, and economic considerations, largely determine well-being and promotion of the discrete elements within any domain. A child's ability to develop positively can only be fully appreciated by taking each of these environmental contexts into account.

For instance, the factors that promote positive development within the social and emotional domains reside at different levels within the ecological system: individual, interpersonal, and environmental. The most intimate of these systemic environments encompasses everyday facets of a child's life such as parents and siblings, peers, teachers, and classmates. Promotional factors at the individual level include temperament (i.e., a set of personal and constitutional characteristics such as activity and arousal level, and a capacity to be soothed, express pleasure, and adapt to change), personality traits, and cognitive abilities. Some of these individual characteristics, in particular temperament, personality traits, and other biologically based processes, are at present difficult to alter. However, others, particularly cognitive characteristics, are amenable to intervention. Mastery of cognitive and linguistic skills is particularly important for the development of empathy, conflict resolution skills, and social support.

Looking to another domain, parents are primarily responsible for ensuring a child's health and safety and can do so through, for example, attending to a child's preventive healthcare needs such as immunizations, teaching the child how to maintain a healthy diet, modeling and participating with the child in physical activity, and ensuring the provision of a safe and secure environment. Teachers also educate students about many physical domain issues and help provide for physical development while students are in their care. In addition, classmates and peers can promote or impede physical well-being by contributing to the classroom environment, influencing decisions individual children make about safety, drugs, alcohol, and sexuality, and providing the social context in which children make decisions about health and safety.

At the interpersonal level, a range of factors promotes positive social and emotional development. They include qualities of the interaction itself, such as the level of reciprocity and synchronicity of behaviors, and interactions among individual characteristics of people involved in the relationship, such as the dynamics between individuals' cognitive abilities. Factors at this level also include sentiments directed from one person to another. Most specifically, we see that mutual respect and responsiveness are important factors in producing positive, nurturing, and supportive relationships, which in turn lead to the development of trust, autonomy, sympathy, and empathy.

It is important to reinforce the idea that each of the elements of well-being depends on and is amenable to improvement by external influences. Human interchange is necessary for language acquisition: Children must speak to others and be spoken to in order to learn language, and exposure to spoken language on television does not substitute for human interactive conversation. Many questions remain however because we lack experimental evidence of malleability of many elements of well-being. Finally, few effect sizes have been reported in studying interventions that promote well-being, so we cannot tell how much of an effect each individual element has on an individual's overall well-being.

ADDITIONAL CONSIDERATIONS

Several important features of all these elements of well-being merit additional comment. Each element is marked by individual variation; that is, some people have more or do better in an element than others. Language growth, for example, is marked by notable individual differences among children in terms both of developmental status and rates of change. It is also the case that people improve in most of these elements as they mature (particularly in childhood). Some come "on line" early; others do so later. Whereas abilities such as problem solving, acquiring knowledge, and memory are evident in young children, abstract reasoning, general knowledge, and numeracy begin as elements of cognitive well-being in the preschool years. Moreover, most elements of well-being show good stability. That is, people whose foundational capacities would be rated highly in childhood would also tend to be rated highly in adolescence, barring non-normative developmental events. Even moral ability measured in middle childhood predicts the developmental sophistication of moral judgment in late childhood and adolescence.

Regardless of the characteristics included in the multidimensional construct of well-being, research supports both top-down and bottom-up theories of well-being development. From the top-down perspective, overall life satisfaction or global quality of life is assumed to permeate the positive valence accorded any particular dimensional assessment within the whole of well-being. Conversely, the bottom-up view assumes that overall quality of life represents a formulaic calculus from all the separate dimensions of well-being (Headey, Veenhoven, & Wearing, 1991).

In addition to factors that promote positive outcomes, there are many factors that can undermine positive development, such as poverty, discrimination, and abuse and neglect. Other factors may not necessarily promote or hinder positive outcomes but will cause variance in positive outcomes among individuals. These factors include family configuration, social class, cultural background, status differences between individuals, and age. For example, first born children experience different parent-child relationships than later born children, and the meaning of a supportive and nurturing parent-child, sibling, or peer relationship will change with the birth order of the child.

Many of the contributors to this book discuss the importance of nurturing and supportive environments in promotion of the elements of well-being. For young children, the most important environments are home and school, but other important settings include childcare, the extended family, neighborhoods, and media influences. Supporting children so that they can succeed in school, form resilient personalities, engage in fulfilling interpersonal relationships, and acquire meaningful work will contribute holistically to successful development across the life course.

REFERENCE

Headey, B., Veenhoven, R., & Wearing, A. (1991). Top-down versus bottom-up theories of subjective well-being: a systematic evaluation. *Social Indicators Research*, *24*, 81–100.

PART I

PHYSICAL DOMAIN

Edited by

Martha F. Rogers

Caroline H. Leavitt
The Center for Child Well-being, Decatur, GA

Anita Chawla

4

Good Nutrition—The Imperative for Positive Development

Caroline H. Leavitt
The Center for Child Well-being, Decatur, GA

Thomas F. Tonniges
University of Nebraska Medical Center, Omaha, NE

Martha F. Rogers
The Center for Child Well-being, Decatur, GA

INTRODUCTION

Children develop more rapidly during the first few years—socioemotionally, cognitively, and physically—than any other time of life and good nutrition is imperative to this rapid development. Nutritional habits that are developed during early childhood will have long-term consequences because these habits are among the most difficult to change in adulthood (Centers for Disease Control and Prevention [CDC], 2000). In this chapter the operational definition of *nutrition* addresses issues related to two topics: (1) providing good nutrition to young children so as to foster the best possible developmental outcomes and (2) establishing the practice of healthy eating in early childhood so as to optimize well-being throughout the life span.

NUTRITION AS A CORE ELEMENT OF WELL-BEING

A wealth of evidence supports nutrition as crucial to well-being throughout the life span by preventing morbidity and mortality and promoting positive attributes.

35

Typically, poor nutrition stems from either excess (diets composed primarily of too much food and/or foods high in fat, salt, cholesterol, and sugar), or deficiency (diets lacking energy and essential vitamins and minerals). These problems can occur in isolation or concurrently, and effects can be either immediate and/or long-term.

Short-Term Impact of Nutrition

Fat is essential for development in infants and children under the age of 2. Once children reach the age of 2 however, their dependency on fat for development lessons and therefore, their intake of fat and cholesterol should be decreased (Story, Holt, & Sofka, 2000). For children older than 2, the immediate effects of high fat diets can impair young children's well-being by contributing to high cholesterol levels and obesity (CDC, 2000). However, the effects of high fat diets are cumulative and often become more apparent and severe later in life, once consumption of this type of diet has been habitual for many years. The immediate effects of under nutrition often manifest in physical, behavioral, cognitive, or emotional problems during early childhood. For example, deficient diets often contribute to anemia (typically caused by iron deficiencies in the diet), failure to thrive, short stature (low height for age), underweight (low weight for height), poor academic performance, and poor social and emotional skills such as increased aggression, anxiety, and irritability (Briefel, Murphy, Kung, & Devaney, 1999).

The Effects of Micronutrient Deficiency on Young Children.   Micronutrients, such as vitamin A, zinc, iodine, and iron, are the foundations on which good health and development are built. The lack of these nutrients in the diets of young children can lead to profound developmental delays, illness, and death (Alnwick, 1999; Young & Berti, 2000). In addition, dietary deficiencies can also lead to substantial impairment and delay in cognitive development and performance. The effect of nutritional deficits on cognitive development will be discussed more thoroughly in the next section.

Nutritional Deficiencies and Cognitive Development.   Scientists have found that specific nutrients in food consumed affect biochemical and hormonal processes in the body and brain and are intricately involved in early development. Therefore, researchers have proposed that individuals who do not receive proper nutrition during early childhood, which is the primary period for rapid brain development, may be developmentally disadvantaged and this developmental delay could affect future cognitive outcomes (Briefel et al., 1999).

Briefel, et al. (1999) discuss another, related theory by Levitsky, which suggests that poor nutrition during early childhood strongly affects cognition due to "functional isolationism." According to this theory, undernourished children have poor motor development and lower levels of responsiveness and activity. Due to their lack of physical activity, these children are less likely to explore and receive stimulation from their environment. Therefore, this theory posits that poor nutrition leads to physical delay, which in turn, contributes to cognitive impairment (Briefel et al., 1999).

Experimental studies have, to a large extent, borne out these theories of cognitive delay. As discussed later in this chapter, future cognitive impairment can be affected by maternal nutrition while the child is in utero. Morley and Lucas (1997) demonstrated that children whose nutritional needs are not being met perform less well on a variety of types of cognitive performance tests than their well-nourished peers. Poor performance on attention and visual tasks, and especially short-term memory assessments, has been shown to be significant for undernourished children. Other, recent studies by the Center on Hunger, Poverty, and Nutrition Policy (1998) have shown that even short-term nutritional deficits can have a profound impact on young children's cognitive development. Alternatively, Brown and Pollitt (1996) demonstrated that short-term consumption of nutrient rich diets can have a moderate impact on the cognitive performance of habitually undernourished children. However, Brown and Pollitt's study also indicated that adults who had insufficient nutrition during childhood were still performing at a lower level on certain cognitive tasks than adults who had received adequate nutrition as children. This finding suggests that poor nutrition may have a short- and long-term impact on cognition thereby adding additional evidence that good nutrition is imperative to lifelong well-being (Briefel et al., 1999).

Long-Term Impact of Nutrition

Obesity.   The scientific evidence showing the link between lifelong excesses in the diet and life-threatening disease is well documented (National Institute of Health [NIH] and National Heart, Lung and Blood Institute, 1998; American Heart Association, 1998). Various combinations of genetic, dietary, and physical activity factors typically cause overweight, which is defined as a body mass index (BMI) of 25 to 29.9 kg/m^2 and obesity, which is defined as a body mass index of greater than or equal to 30 kg/m^2 (it should be noted that obese individuals are also considered to be overweight; NIH and National Heart, Lung, and Blood Institute, 1998). Obesity has been shown to be responsible for a significant increase of morbidity and mortality from numerous diseases including: hypertension, type 2 diabetes, stroke, osteoarthritis, gallbladder disease, respiratory problems, sleep apnea, coronary heart disease, and certain types of cancer (NIH and National Heart, Lung, and Blood Institute, 1998; American Heart Association, 1998). However despite the wealth of information about the dangers of unhealthy eating, a large percentage of the population of developed countries continues to consume excessive amounts of sugar, fat, sodium, and cholesterol in their diets (American Heart Association, 1998). Estimates show that almost one third of U.S. adults are categorized as obese (American Heart Association, 1998). This combined with findings from longitudinal studies such as the Framingham Longitudinal Heart Study (National Heart,

Lung, and Blood Institute, 1998b) and the Clinical Guidelines on the Identification, Evaluation, and Treatment of Overweight and Obesity in Adults study (NIH and National Heart, Lung, and Blood Institute, 1998) provide good evidence that particular excesses in the diet (and often, a lack of physical activity) are a significant cause of illness and mortality in the United States.

Additionally, research has shown that the greatest challenge toward effective treatment of obesity is determining how adults can successfully maintain the necessary behavioral changes in diet over time (National Heart, Lung, and Blood Institute, 1998a). When treating overweight children however, researchers have found dietary changes established early in life are often permanent, especially when the entire family is involved in the intervention (National Heart, Lung, and Blood Institute, 1998a). Research has also found that overweight children, if left untreated, will most likely become obese adults (National Heart, Lung, and Blood Institute, 1998b). This lends support to the theory that dietary habits established early in life can greatly affect lifelong health and development and are extremely difficult to change in adulthood (National Heart, Lung, and Blood Institute, 1998a). Therefore, establishing a healthy diet during early childhood is vital to ensuring well-being throughout life.

Nutritional Deficits.   The long-term impact of nutritional deficits in adulthood is also now receiving attention. Women of childbearing age and pregnant women are particularly at risk for micronutrient deficiencies such as iron and iodine (Alnwick, 1999; Unicef and WHO, 1999). These dietary deficiencies in adulthood often impair the immune system increasing the incidence and severity of infections, cause a loss of energy, and in the case of pregnant women, can negatively impact the developing fetus (Alnwick, 1999; Unicef and WHO, 1999).

One example of a typically adult condition that results from a lack of calcium and vitamin D in the diet during childhood and adult years is osteoporosis. Calcium contributes to proper functioning of the heart, muscles, nerves, and blood clotting processes while the body uses vitamin D to facilitate the intestinal absorption of calcium from food and supplements. When an individual receives less than 1000 to 1300 mg of calcium a day and/or does not receive an adequate supply of vitamin D, the body removes calcium from the bones. This causes bones to become brittle and have an increased risk of breakage (National Osteoporosis Foundation, 2000a).

Osteoporosis affects over half of the population 65 years of age and older. Often thought of as a women's disease, osteoporosis also affects a smaller percentage of men. A fracture of the hip, spine, or wrist typically raises suspicion of osteoporosis and a bone density scan can confirm diagnosis. Osteoporosis-related bone fractures could lead to loss of height, severe back pain, permanent disability, and deformity (U.S. Department of Health and Human Services [HHS], 1999; CDC, 1994).

Fortunately, in most cases, osteoporosis is preventable. The National Osteoporosis Foundation recommends that all individuals consume a diet rich in calcium and vitamin D, participate regularly in weight bearing exercise such as walking or weight training, avoid smoking and excessive alcohol consumption, and receive bone density scans when appropriate. The dietary and exercise recommendations are particularly effective if followed regularly before the age of 30 and then continued throughout the life span. There are treatments for osteoporosis but, there is no cure and often diagnosis is not made until after the individual has had complications. Therefore, prevention, particularly through the promotion of adequate calcium and vitamin D intake and physical exercise in early childhood is particularly important (National Osteoporosis Foundation, 2000b, 2000c).

NUTRITIONAL MEASUREMENT AND POLICY IN THE UNITED STATES

Measuring various indicators of nutritional well-being enables nutritionists, clinicians, policymakers, and the general public to evaluate the improvements made in the area of nutrition and the work that still must be done to encourage healthy diets. Also, materials distributed to the general population indicate which nutritional policies are being promoted. The following are examples of both public policy and measurement tools used to influence and assess nutritional status and dietary intake in the United States.

Food Guide Pyramid for Young Children

In an effort to promote policies about good nutrition and dietary habits among the U.S. public, the U.S. Department of Agriculture (USDA) developed a food guide pyramid to provide information about healthy eating and to improve the quality of the average diet in an illustrative, easy to understand format. The traditional food guide pyramid is based on USDA research about both the types of food that contribute to healthy nutrition and that individuals in the U.S. actually consume (United States Department of Agriculture [USDA] and Center for Nutrition Policy and Promotion [CNPP], 1996). The food guide is a general guide to eating a variety of foods to obtain the nutrients and energy needed to maintain a healthy weight. The pyramid encourages individuals to eat a particular number of servings from each of the five major food groups (breads, cereals, rice, and pasta; fruit; vegetables; milk, yogurt, and cheese; and meat, poultry, fish, dry beans, eggs, and nuts) and to consume fats, oils, and sweets only in limited quantities.

Recently, the USDA has distributed a food guide pyramid specifically designed for young children over the age of two (see diagram 1). Like the original food guide pyramid, the food pyramid for young children is based on USDA research and data about what foods constitute a healthy diet and about what types of food children already eat. The same food categories are represented on the young children's pyramid. However, the category names have been simplified; a specific number of servings, rather than a range, is suggested; and the pyramid pictures foods that are popular with children ages 2 to 6. In addition, the amount of food constituting one

FOOD Guide PYRAMID

for Young Children

A Daily Guide for 2- to 6-Year-Olds

Fats & Sweets — Eat Less

MILK Group 2 servings

MEAT Group 2 servings

VEGETABLE Group 3 servings

FRUIT Group 2 servings

GRAIN Group 6 servings

U.S. Department of Agriculture
Center for Nutrition Policy and Promotion

January 2000
Program Aid 1651

USDA is an equal opportunity provider and employer.

FOOD IS FUN and learning about food is fun, too. Eating foods from the Food Guide Pyramid and being physically active will help you grow healthy and strong.

WHAT COUNTS AS ONE SERVING?

GRAIN GROUP
1 slice of bread
½ cup of cooked rice or pasta
½ cup of cooked cereal
1 ounce of ready-to-eat cereal

VEGETABLE GROUP
½ cup of chopped raw or cooked vegetables
1 cup of raw leafy vegetables

FRUIT GROUP
1 piece of fruit or melon wedge
¾ cup of juice
½ cup of canned fruit
¼ cup of dried fruit

MILK GROUP
1 cup of milk or yogurt
2 ounces of cheese

MEAT GROUP
2 to 3 ounces of cooked lean meat, poultry, or fish.
½ cup of cooked dry beans, or 1 egg counts as 1 ounce of lean meat. 2 tablespoons of peanut butter count as 1 ounce of meat.

FATS AND SWEETS
Limit calories from these.

Four- to 6-year-olds can eat these serving sizes. Offer 2- to 3-year-olds less, except for milk. Two- to 6-year-old children need a total of 2 servings from the milk group each day.

EAT a variety of FOODS AND ENJOY!

serving has been decreased to approximately two thirds (2/3) of an adult portion (USDA and CNNP, 1999a).

The USDA has also published a booklet to assist parents in using the food guide pyramid for young children. In addition to explaining the importance of good nutrition and providing detail about the pyramid itself, the booklet provides recommendations for meals and snacks, encourages physical activity, teaches parents ways to reduce the risk of choking on food, and offers a meal planning chart. This booklet is available by contacting the USDA and also through the Internet (USDA and CNNP, 1999b).

The Healthy Eating Index

The USDA also publishes the Healthy Food Index (HFI), which is a summary of the dietary quality of U.S. population. The index's data is accumulated from the USDA's Continuing Survey of Food Intake by Individuals, a national survey that contains information on food and nutrient intake and consumption (Bowman, Lino, Gerrior, & Basiotis, 1998).

The HFI is made up of 10 sections. The first five measure the extent to which individuals' diets conform to the USDA's food guide pyramid recommendations for the five major food groups. The sixth section measures total fat consumption as a percentage of the person's total caloric intake. Section 7 more specifically measures saturated fat ingestion. Sections 8 and 9 measure cholesterol and sodium intake respectively. Finally, section 10 measures the level of variety of a person's diet (Bowman et al., 1998).

Based on the results, nutrition researchers determined that although the average diet in the United States is healthier, there is still much room for improvement. Overall, the average score on the HFI for the U.S. population over the age of 2 was 64 out of 100%. A score of 80 is necessary for an individual's diet to fall into the "good" range, while a score of 51 or less is indicative of a "poor" diet. Therefore, the score of 64 falls within the "needs improvement" range (Bowman et al., 1998).

Factors such as education level, socioeconomic status, geographic region, gender, race and culture are believed to contribute to quality of dietary intake of individuals. Researchers have hypothesized that these factors impacted the results because there are discrepancies in the amount of nutritional knowledge possessed by members of the various groups (Bowman et al., 1998). Therefore, increasing the nutritional knowledge of the general population is an important component to achieving healthier nutrition.

Growth Monitoring

Growth monitoring is another method that can be used to make sure that children are receiving proper nutrition. Growth monitoring usually takes place during well child visits to health professionals and can involve the use of the recently revised growth charts and/or the Body Mass Index (BMI; National Center for Health Statistics, 2000 [NCHS]). Growth charts are used to track the physical growth of infants and children by plotting the child's age, weight, and height and then comparing the individual's growth with that of the larger population (NCHS, 2000). This allows health and nutrition experts to determine if growth is adequate and to indicate the presence of diseases such as growth hormone deficiency (NCHS, 2000). Growth charts can also be used to educate parents about their children's growth patterns, to identify goals for change, and to evaluate and reinforce changes in growth over time. Growth patterns are usually more accurate indicators of proper growth and nutrition than any single measurement (NCHS, 2000).

The BMI (which is defined as wt/ht^2) is used to determine whether an individual's weight is appropriate for their height, and the BMI is strongly related to assessment of an individual's percentage of body fat. This measure is not appropriate for infants, who typically need to have a higher proportion of body fat than older individuals, but can be used beginning at age 2. As in the case of other growth charts, the BMI can be a helpful tool for assessing whether a young child's nutritional needs are being met (NCHS, 2000). Growth monitoring should be a standard element of well child care, particularly if the health care professional suspects deficiencies in growth and nutrition.

PROMOTING GOOD NUTRITION

The effects of poor nutrition are preventable if good nutritional habits are established early in life. There are three entities that are central to the promotion of good nutrition in early childhood—parents, educational settings (including schools and child care settings), and the government. Parents typically establish nutritional habits in their children. Therefore, they are primarily responsible for providing their children with developmentally appropriate education about the habits that contribute to good nutrition and why it is important to maintain these habits. Schools and child-care settings are also responsible for the nutritional well-being and the development of dietary habits in young children who eat many meals and snacks while in their care. In addition, for those families and schools without the resources to provide adequate nutrition for their children, governmental programs play an important role. Methods for ensuring good nutritional outcomes for children and a number of governmental programs, such as The Special Supplemental Nutrition Program for Women, Infants, and Children (WIC), which provide nutritional assistance are discussed in this section.

Maternal Nutrition During Pregnancy

Even before conception, women can take steps to help promote good nutrition for their newborns. The B vitamin, folic acid, has been shown to be an important addition to the diets of all women who are of childbearing age. The U.S. Department of Health and Human Services (HHS), the American Academy of Pediatrics (AAP), and the Centers for Disease Control and Prevention (CDC) recommend that 0.4 milligrams of folic acid be taken daily both before conception and during pregnancy. If this regimen is followed, folic acid can decrease the risk of neuronal tube defects by up to 70% (HHS, 1996; AAP, 1999; Acuna, Yoon, & Erickson, 1999). Because neuronal tube defects typically occur during the earliest weeks of gestation, they may form before a woman is even aware that she is pregnant (AAP, 1999;

American College of Obstetricians and Gynecologists, 1996; Acuna, et al., 1999). This explains why preconception ingestion of folic acid is especially important. Folate, the nonsynthetic version of folic acid is found naturally in some foods while folic acid is typically found in pill form such as a multivitamin. Therefore, adding folic acid to one's diet is an easily accessible preventive measure for women of childbearing age. In addition, the United States has taken positive steps toward increasing the consumption of folic acid by fortifying breakfast cereals and some grain products with the vitamin (HHS, 1996).

Prepregnancy weight at the time of conception and maternal weight gain during pregnancy also may affect the well-being of the developing infant. Women who are either significantly underweight at the time of conception or who do not gain enough gestational weight (the Health Resources and Services Administration's Office of Maternal and Child Health recommends that on average, women should gain between 25 and 35 pounds during pregnancy; Maternal and Child Health Department of Public Health City of Philadelphia, 1998), risk their infant's well-being. In both cases, these women have an increased likelihood of having low birth weight babies. In addition, inadequate weight gain may contribute to premature delivery (Perry, Zykowski, Clark, & Yu, 1994).

Mothers who are significantly overweight at conception are at a greater risk of having babies with macrosomia (high birth weight). Macrosomia is a risk factor for perinatal morbidity and mortality. In addition, women whose gestational weight gain is excessive also put their babies at an increased risk of macrosomia and increase the chances of complications during delivery (Perry et al., 1994).

Another nutritional issue that affects many pregnant women and their babies is maternal anemia. Maternal anemia is most often caused by iron deficiency in the mother's diet (Perry et al., 1994; Scholl, Hediger, Fischer, & Shearer, 1992). Maternal anemia is so common that a significant percentage of all pregnant women become anemic during their third trimester. As in the cases of unsuitable prepregnancy weight and gestational weight gain, maternal anemia can have serious consequences for infants, especially if the anemia is severe and occurs during the first and/or second trimesters. For example, maternal anemia is thought to contribute to low birth weight and premature delivery (Perry et al., 1994; Scholl et al., 1992).

The use of drugs during pregnancy, including all legal and illegal substances, can have harmful effects on the developing fetus (AAP, 1995; Skolnick, 1994). Therefore, legal medications should only be taken under the advice and supervision of a doctor. Illegal drugs may impair the development and well-being of children who are prenatally exposed. Effects of in utero illegal drug exposure include withdrawal symptoms after birth; premature labor; intrauterine growth retardation; neonatal seizures; perinatal cerebral infarctions; long-term physical, socioemotional, and cognitive developmental delays; and death (AAP, 1995; Skolnick, 1994). In addition, maternal alcohol and drug consumption during pregnancy can cause severe developmental delays, such as fetal alcohol syndrome (Perry et al., 1994). Therefore, pregnant women should never consume illegal drugs or alcohol.

Breastfeeding

The majority of doctors and children's health organizations (e.g., the AAP, the CDC, WHO, and Unicef), have long advocated that breastfeeding is the preferred method for feeding young babies. Research has demonstrated that, in most situations, human milk is considered superior to formula particularly for babies less than 6 months of age. In fact, the AAP recommends that babies should be exclusively breastfed until twelve months of age with moderate complementary feeding introduced slowly between 4 and 6 months of age (AAP, 1997, 2000).

Human milk is specially designed for infants' digestive systems. It is highly absorbable and differs in its protein structure, fats, and micronutrients than formula or cow's milk. Therefore, infants have an easier time digesting and absorbing the nutrients they need for rapid development from human milk than from any other alternative (Story et al., 2000).

In addition, human milk often provides infants with added protection from a variety of illnesses such as food allergies and gastrointestinal and respiratory illnesses both during infancy and early childhood (Story et al., 2000; Williams, 1995). Human milk also provides additional immunity from diseases in the baby's immediate environment. The mother's mature immune system, if not impaired, produces antibodies to fight infections that are present in her environment. These antibodies are passed to the baby through the mother's human milk, which bolsters the infant's developing immune system and protects him from disease (Story et al., 2000; Williams, 1995). There is also tentative evidence suggesting that breastfeeding may help prevent chronic immune system related diseases that typically develop in late childhood such as Crohn's disease, type I diabetes, and lymphoma (AAP, 1997; CDC, 1999).

Aside from the preventive health benefits, breastfeeding may contribute to the emotional quality of the relationship between mother and infant. Through breastfeeding, the mother and child typically develop an intense emotional and psychological bond. This bonding process allows the baby to develop feelings of security and trust and strengthens the mother's parental competence though the reinforcement and encouragement she receives when her baby signals that she is satisfying his needs (Story et al., 2000; Unicef, 1999; Williams, 1995). Formula feeding does not prevent the establishment of bonding, nor does it necessarily impair the emotional quality of the mother—child relationship. However, bottle-feeding does not provide the same degree of close physical contact and essential sensory stimulation for the infant through skin and eye contact (Story et al., 2000). Therefore, breastfeeding is typically a more ideal method through which infants and mothers can learn to communicate with one another.

There are two additional reasons why the use of infant formula should be discouraged. First, for many families in the United States and internationally, buying infant formula puts additional strain on the already limited financial resources of most families. For example, in Uganda, the average annual income of a village family is less than the average cost of providing infant formula for one year (Unicef, 1999). Second, developing countries often do not have clean water or easily accessible sterilization and refrigeration resources necessary to make infant formula a safe alternative to human milk. The lack of clean water can put infants at risk of developing severe gastrointestinal illness and may even cause death, and sterilization creates extra work that keeps family members from being able to spend more time caring for their children (Unicef, 1999).

Of course, some mothers are unable to breastfeed and in these circumstances, iron fortified infant formula does provide a suitable alternative. Mothers in the United States, who have tested positive for Human Immunodeficiency Virus (HIV), should formula feed their infants. HIV can be transmitted through human milk and there is, as yet, an unclear risk to infants from breastfeeding (AAP, 1997; Fowler, Bertolli, & Nieburg, 1999). In less developed countries however, the risk of HIV transmission through human milk must be weighed against the risk of infant morbidity and mortality from artificial feeding.

In addition, women who are infected with herpes, hepatitis, untreated active tuberculosis, or beta streptococcus infections should consult with their physician before breastfeeding (AAP, 1997; Williams, 1995). Also, while the majority of maternal medications pose no risk for the breastfed infant, particular medications (e.g., those used to treat Parkinson's disease, cancer, bipolar disorder, migraine headaches, and arthritis) may harm infants if passed through human milk (Williams, 1995). Mothers taking medication should therefore consult their physician before breastfeeding. Finally, breastfeeding mothers should not use illegal drugs or smoke as these substances produce harmful effects, such as illness and addiction in the infant and mother (Williams, 1995).

The Special Supplemental Nutrition Program for Women, Infants, and Children

WIC, run by the USDA, is one example of a successful governmental effort to improve the nutritional health and general well-being of young children. Started in 1972, the program now exists in all 50 states (although the amount of funding differs depending on the state) and serves over 7 million people each month (USDA, 2000). Four requirements—categorical, residential, income, and nutrition risk—must be fulfilled in order for an individual to be eligible for WIC. Individuals who are categorically eligible for WIC include pregnant women until 6 weeks after pregnancy, breastfeeding women until their infant's first birthday, nonbreastfeeding postpartum women for up to 6 months after pregnancy, infants until their first birthday, and children until the age of 5. The residential requirement necessitates all potential participants meet residency requirements for the state in which they wish to receive benefits. With regard to income, WIC participants must fall at or below 185% of the U.S. Poverty Income Guidelines. For example, a family of four cannot earn more than $31,543 a year in pretax income to remain eligible for WIC. Finally, the nutritional risk requirement requires that individuals seeking WIC assistance have either a medical- or diet-based risk for undernutrition (USDA, 2000).

Individuals who qualify for WIC receive supplemental food, nutrition education and counseling, and screening and referral for other health-related services. The food that WIC participants receive is designed to bolster their intake of calcium, iron, vitamins A and C, and protein. In many areas, WIC participants also receive coupons to use at local farmers markets to purchase additional fruit and vegetables. Although new mothers participating in WIC are encouraged to breastfeed, they are provided with coupons for iron-enriched infant formula if they choose not to breast-feed (USDA, 2000).

The WIC program has positively impacted the lives of millions of women, infants, and young children. Participation in WIC can help prevent developmental delays, illness, and permanent physical and mental impairment (USDA and CNPP, 1999c). Although participants in WIC are nutritionally better off than non-WIC participants who meet the WIC qualification requirements, a 1999 study by the USDA reports that on average, WIC participants, and especially women, are still deficient in many of the key nutritional areas that WIC targets (USDA and CNPP, 1999c). These results indicate that research is needed to address why these nutritional deficits still exist and to attempt to establish new methods of eliminating dietary shortcomings in nutritionally at-risk women and children.

School Breakfast Program

Eating breakfast has been associated with improved cognitive and academic performance, emotional and social well-being, and improved nutritional intake throughout the day (Briefel et al., 1999). Unfortunately, a large number of children have been found to not eat breakfast on a regular basis or at all. Children who do not eat breakfast were found to be lacking calcium, magnesium, phosphorus, riboflavin, folate, and vitamins A and B_{12}. Children who live in impoverished conditions, come from single-parent homes, or come from homes in which the mother is employed have been found to be more likely to not consume breakfast than other children (Briefel et al., 1999).

In order to correct this preventable problem, the federal government authorized The School Breakfast Program (SBP) under the Child Nutrition Act of 1966. This program offers either free or reduced cost breakfasts for children in an effort to improve nutrition and school performance. When breakfast is defined as intake of dietary energy greater than 10% of the Recommended Daily Allowance (RDA) of total food energy intake, the SBP has been shown to substantially increase the number of children consuming breakfast. In fact, one large study predicted that the SBP is providing nutritional breakfasts to over 3 million children who otherwise would not have an adequate meal. In addition, recently, the quality of the food served during SBP meals has improved with the "Eat Smart" program. This program has attempted to lower the amount of total fat, saturated fat, and sodium while increasing the amount of essential nutrients in school breakfasts. Nutritionally speaking, therefore, the SBP has successfully supplemented the diets of many young children (Briefel et al., 1999).

In terms of improving academic and cognitive performance, the results from the SBP are still unclear. It is widely agreed that providing school breakfasts increases school attendance and reduces tardiness. However, results from studies that specifically measure cognitive performance have been mixed (Briefel et al., 1999). While some researchers have demonstrated significant improvements in math and verbal fluency, other studies have shown positive, but nonsignificant results. Therefore, breakfast programs may improve cognitive performance on certain tasks; however, questions of which cognitive processes are affected and the magnitude of improvement still exist (Briefel et al., 1999).

Finally, there is a similar program, known as The Child and Adult Care Food Program (CACFP) that provides or supplements the provision of meals and snacks for young children in out-of-home day-care settings including the federally funded Head Start Program (USDA, 1997). This program provides additional opportunities for researchers to attempt to improve the research that has been performed on the SBP.

CONCLUSIONS

In most areas, the evidence supporting the theory that good nutrition leads to child well-being is very strong. Research has shown that young children's rapid growth is highly affected by the nutrition they receive from their diets—both excesses and deficiencies pose serious problems for development and short- and long-term well-being. This knowledge has affected policy decisions in the past, such as the introduction of the very successful WIC program, and continues to do so now as demonstrated by the examples of governmental programs and policies discussed in this chapter.

Despite this strong evidence, research is needed in the areas of education, prevention, promotion and behavioral change. Although nutrition scientists are knowledgeable with regard to the effects of nutrition on well-being, there is a lack of knowledge about best-practices—How can healthy nutrition most effectively be promoted in and provided for children? In addition, if children have poor nutritional habits, what is the best way to educate and permanently alter their behavior? These are questions that must be investigated if good nutrition is to be the norm for all children.

REFERENCES

Acuna, J., Yoon, P., & Erickson, J. D. (1999) *The prevention of neural tube defects with folic acid [La prevención del los defectos del tubo neural con ácido folico]*. Atlanta, GA: Centers for Disease Control and Prevention.

Alnwick, D. (1999). *Candidate noninfectious disease conditions*. (CDC MMWR Supplements 48 (SU01); 67–75). Atlanta, GA: Centers for Disease Control and Prevention.

American Academy of Pediatrics. (1995, August). Drug-exposed infants (re9533). *Pediatrics, 96*, 364–367.

American Academy of Pediatrics. (1997, December). Breastfeeding and the use of human milk (re9729). *Pediatrics, 100*, 1035–1039.

American Academy of Pediatrics. (1999, August). Folic acid for the prevention of neural tube defects (re9834). *Pediatrics, 104*, 325–327.

American Academy of Pediatrics. (2000, November). Research Priorities in Complementary Feeding: International Paediatric Association (IPA) and European Society of Paediatric Gastroenterology, Hepatology, and Nutrition (ESPGHAN) Workshop. *Pediatrics, 106*(Suppl. 2), 1271–1272.

American College of Obstetricians and Gynecologists. (1996, October). Nutrition and women. *ACOG Education Bulletin, 229*, 1–12.

American Heart Association. (1998). *Questions and answers about obesity* [On-line]. Available: www.americanheart.org

Bowman, S. A., Lino, M., Gerrior, S. A., & Basiotis, P. P. (1998). *The healthy eating index 1994–1996* (CNPP-5). Washington, DC: U.S. Department of Agriculture, Center for Nutrition Policy and Promotion.

Briefel, R., Murphy, J. M., Kung, S., & Devaney, B. (1999). *Universal-free school breakfast program evaluation design project: Review of literature on breakfast and learning.* Unpublished manuscript.

Brown, J. L., & Pollitt, E. (1996). Malnutrition, poverty, and intellectual development. *Scientific American, 274*, 38–43.

Center on Hunger, Poverty and Nutrition Policy. (1998). *The link between nutrition and cognitive development in children.* Tufts University.

CDC. (1994). *Vital and health statistics: Plan and operation of the third national health and nutrition examination survey, 1988–94.* Atlanta, GA: Author.

CDC. (1999). *Breastfeeding* (Nutrition and Physical Activity). Atlanta, GA: Author.

CDC. (2000). *CDC's Guidelines for school and community health programs: Promoting lifelong healthy eating.* Atlanta, GA: Author.

Fowler, M. G., Bertolli, J., & Nieburg, P. (1999). When is breastfeeding not best? The dilemma facing HIV-infected women in resource-poor settings. *Journal of the American Medical Association, 282*, 781–783.

Maternal and Child Health Department of Public Health City of Philadelphia. (1998). *Healthy foods, healthy baby.* Philadelphia, PA: Department of Health and Human Services.

Morley, R., & Lucas (1997). Nutrition and cognitive development. *British Medical Bulletin, 53*, 123–134.

National Center for Health Statistics. (2000). *CDC Growth Charts: United States.* Atlanta, GA: Centers for Disease Control and Prevention.

National Heart, Lung, and Blood Institute (1998a). *National Heart, Lung, and Blood Institute report on the task force on behavioral research in cardiovascular, lung, and blood health and disease.* Washington, DC: Author.

National Heart, Lung and Blood Institute. (1998b). *You changed America's heart.* Washington, DC: Author.

National Heart, Lung, and Blood Institute. (1998). *NIH Clinical guidelines of the identification, evaluation, and treatment of overweight and obesity in adults* (NIH Publication No. 98-4083). Washington, DC: Authors.

National Osteoporosis Foundation. (2000a). *Osteoporosis* [On-line]. Available: www.nof.org

National Osteoporosis Foundation. (2000b). *Patient info* [On-line]. Available: www.nof.org

National Osteoporosis Foundation. (2000c). *Prevention* [On-line]. Available: www.nof.org

Perry, G. S., Zykowski, C. L., Clark, L. D., & Yu, S. (1994). Pregnancy-Related Nutrition. In L. S. Wilcox & J. S. Marks (Eds.), *From data to action: CDC's public health surveillance for women, infants, and children* (pp. 119–128). Washington, DC: U.S. Department of Health & Human Services.

Scholl, T. O., Hediger, M. L., Fischer, R. L., & Shearer, J. W. (1992). Anemia vs. iron deficiency: Increased risk of preterm delivery in a prospective study. *American Journal of Clinical Nutrition, 55*, 985–988.

Skolnick, A. A. (1994). Collateral casualties climb in the drug war. *Journal of the American Medical Association* [On-line]. Available: www.tfy.drugsense.org

Story, M., Holt, K., Sofka, D. (Eds.). (2000). *Bright futures in practice: Nutrition.* Washington, DC: National Center for Education in Maternal and Child Health.

Unicef. (1999, August). *Breastfeeding: Foundation for a healthy future.* New York: Author.

Unicef. (1999, February). *WHO Prevention and control of iron deficiency anemia in women and children*. Geneva, Switzerland: Authors.

U.S. Department of Agriculture. (1997). *Early childhood and child care study: Summary of findings.* Washington, DC: Author.

U.S. Department of Agriculture. (2000). Women, infants, and children [On-line]. Available: www.fns.usda.gov/wic/

U.S. Department of Agriculture & Center for Nutrition Policy and Promotion. (1996, October). *The food guide pyramid* (Home and garden bulletin number 252). Washington, DC: Authors.

U.S. Department of Agriculture & Center for Nutrition Policy and Promotion. (1999a, March). *Tips for using the food guide pyramid for young children 2 to 6 years old* (program aid 1647). Washington, DC: Authors.

U.S. Department of Agriculture & Center for Nutrition Policy and Promotion. (1999b, March). *Food guide pyramid for young children: A daily guide for 2- to 6-year-olds* (program aid 1647). Washington, DC: Authors.

U.S. Department of Agriculture & Center for Nutrition Policy and Promotion. (1999c). *Review of the nutritional status of WIC participants: Final report.* Washington DC: Authors.

U.S. Department of Health and Human Services. (1996). *Folic acid to fortify U.S. food products to prevent birth defects.* Washington, DC: Author.

U.S. Department of Health and Human Services. (1999). *Health, United States, 1999: Health and aging chartbook.* Washington, DC: Author.

Williams, R. D. (1995, October). Breastfeeding best bet for babies. *Food and Drug Administration Consumer Magazine, 29*, 19–23.

Young, M., & Berti, P. (2000). *Insecticide treated nets and vitamin A supplementation: An integrated approach to control malaria and micronutrient deficiency.* Ottawa, Canada: The Micronutrient Initiative.

5

Preventive Health Care in Early Childhood and Through the Life Span

Thomas F. Tonniges
University of Nebraska Medical Center, Omaha, NE

Caroline H. Leavitt
The Center for Child Well-being, Decatur, GA

INTRODUCTION

Preventive health care is an essential element of well-being. Receiving preventive health care during the first years of life has been shown to provide children with both immediate and long-term benefits. For example, children who receive regular care and preventive services are likely to have better health and developmental outcomes. Recent brain research that has been conducted on young infants and children demonstrates that the early period of life is one in which there is a tremendous potential for rapid neurological development and learning (Illig, 1998; Shore, 1997; National Research Council and Institute of Medicine, 2000). Ensuring young children's health and well-being through preventive health care supports and fosters this rapid growth, whereas neglecting early health care can impede brain development. In addition, by receiving regular health care, children are taught the importance of practicing preventive care throughout their lives. Immunizations for children are as important to well-being as cholesterol screening, PAP smears, and mammograms are for adults. Parents, health professionals, and other caregivers need to make certain that children are taught the importance of not only seeking health care when they are sick, but also using health services to prevent illness and disease.

It is important to keep in mind that at the core of preventive health care services is the interface of public health (those health and well-being issues that have an impact on the larger community) and individual health. Therefore, in terms of prevention, the intersection of public and private health care leads to the improved health and well-being of not only the individual, but also the community.

Sporadic well-child care, although preferable to a complete absence of preventive measures, is not nearly as effective as well-child care that is continuous. Gaps in care lead children and adults to experience poorer health and developmental outcomes. These gaps lead to a decline in community health. For example, *herd immunity*, which is a term often associated with immunization issues, can result from continuous well-child care. When an individual child receives her immunizations, she is not only protecting herself from disease but also doing her part to protect the rest of the community (Berger, 1999; Begg & Gay, 1997).

This chapter focuses on children ages 0 to 5 and describes several aspects of well-child care that have been proven to make a difference. Each of these preventive health care measures is discussed in turn, followed by a review of the literature discussing the impact these measures have had on early child health and well-being. Finally, a life span perspective is addressed, followed by an evaluation of the factors that influence the promotion of preventive health care for young children.

IMPORTANT ELEMENTS OF WELL-CHILD CARE FOR CHILDREN AGES 0 TO 5

Well-child care is a means through which parents and primary health care professionals can collaborate to help ensure that young children receive a healthy start to life as well as promote preventive health care throughout the life span. Well-child care visits for children ages 0 to 5 typically comprise a number of services such as complete medical and social history, physical examination, nutrition and physical safety counseling, hearing and vision screening, review of developmental progress, laboratory screening, immunizations, and preventive dental practices, such as regular teeth brushing and use of fluoride and dental referral (Centers for Disease Control and Prevention [CDC], 2001; American Academy of Pediatrics [AAP], 2000). In addition, parents often ask their child's primary health care professional for information about topics pertaining to the care of their child, such as sleep and feeding difficulties and appropriate behavioral and emotional development. Because the scope of this paper does not allow for complete discussion of all topics, the focus is primarily on newborn screening, sleep, immunizations, and hearing and vision screening. The purpose of and benefits afforded by attention to these areas are discussed in this section. Individuals interested in any of the other aforementioned topics may find them discussed in other chapters of this book, other pediatric text-books, or may refer to AAP policy statements. All AAP policy statements are located on the AAP web site at www.aap.org.

Newborn Screening

Since 1962, newborn screening for metabolic and genetic diseases has allowed physicians to prevent the serious complications of these diseases through early detection and treatment. Phenylketonuria, or PKU, was the first disease for which screening was performed and was the precursor of the current screening programs (Guthrie & Susi, 1963). Typically, newborn screening occurs soon after birth and constitutes testing infants' blood for metabolic and genetic diseases (e.g., PKU, sickle cell disease, hypothyroidism, and galactosemia). Some states have begun screening for up to 12 disorders (Newborn Screening Task Force, 2000). With the Human Genome Project underway, it is likely that the number of diseases that can be screened and treated will exponentially increase. Newborn screening has been paramount in preventing mental retardation, illness, and in some cases, premature death.

Newborn screening has been shown to be cost-effective and is generally supported by policymakers. The 1988 U.S. Congress Office of Technology Assessment study showed that for every 100,000 infants screened there was a savings of 3.2 million (1986) dollars. All states participate in newborn screening and, given the fact that the screening is regulated by state statute, there are currently 51 different programs in the United States. This lack of uniformity has led many to be interested in developing national standards that would ensure that all children in every state have access to the same standard of care. These national standards could potentially guarantee that all children would obtain the benefit of receiving appropriate tests and would help clarify and standardize which tests and services are necessary to satisfy the basic needs of the child. For an additional review of newborn screening, the Task Force on Newborn Screening's report, "Serving the Family From Birth to the Medical Home," can be found in the Supplement to the August 2000 issue of *Pediatrics*.

Sleep and Infant Positioning

Sleep plays an important role in the growth and development of young children. Sleep scientists have determined that there are five stages to sleep for the average, healthy person. Eye movement, speed of brain waves, and the presence or absence of muscle contractions differentiate these stages. During stage one, sleep is very light. Sleep becomes deeper as the individual progresses to stage four—the deepest stage of sleep. The fifth stage, known as rapid eye movement (REM) sleep is when dreaming typically occurs (National Institute of Neurological Disorders and Stroke [NINDS], 2000).

Contrary to popular belief, research has shown that sleep is an active, not a passive, state for the brain. Some experts believe that sleep allows for two functions to occur. First, active daytime neuronal connections have the opportunity to make needed repairs and rid themselves of the by-products that result from normal use. Second, it is hypothesized that during sleep, those neurons and neuronal pathways that are inactive during daytime receive the exercise needed to prevent decay. Sleep has also been found to be imperative for proper immune and nervous system functioning (NINDS, 2000).

Sleep plays additional, important roles for children. During deep sleep, scientists have found that important growth hormones are released in children and young adults. Studies have also shown that daytime neuronal patterns are often repeated during deep sleep. Researchers hypothesize that this repetition aids in memory encoding processes and contributes to learning (NINDS, 2000). Finally, REM sleep is believed to make important contributions to the learning process (NINDS, 2000). This may explain why infants under 3 months of age typically spend up to half of their sleep time in REM, unlike older children and adults where REM constitutes approximately 20% of sleep (NINDS, 2000; Anders, Goodlin-Jones, & Zelenko, 1998).

The sleep patterns of young infants differ substantially from adults. Parents often seek advice from primary health care professionals as to the best way to encourage appropriate sleeping habits in their young children. Difficulties arise because young infants' sleep patterns are erratic, thereby disrupting typical adult sleep patterns. Newborns usually sleep for 16 hours a day. However, they wake every 3 to 4 hours for feeding (AAP Task Force on Infant Sleep Position and Sudden Infant Death Syndrome, 2000). Typically, by the fourth month, the infant's brain matures allowing her to regulate her sleep patterns. This allows for longer periods of sleep during the night with typically two naps during the day. By 1 to 2 years of age, the sleeping habits of young children who do not have sleeping problems more closely resemble those of adults and daytime sleeping decreases (Cohen, 1999; AMA, 1997).

Young children often can experience a number of sleep-related difficulties including nightmares, night terrors, separation anxiety, and irregular sleep patterns (Cohen, 1999). One of the most dangerous sleep problems for infants is Sudden Infant Death Syndrome (SIDS). Until the mid-1990s, SIDS was one of the most common causes of death for children under the age of 1 year. Recent preventive health measures and a sleep positioning campaign have drastically reduced SIDS cases in the United States (AAP Task Force on Infant Sleep Position and Sudden Infant Death Syndrome, 2000). An infant death is classified as being caused by SIDS when an otherwise healthy infant dies and the cause of death cannot be determined after autopsy. Despite recent reductions in frequency, SIDS still poses a significant risk for infants, especially those whose caretakers do not abide by risk reduction recommendations.

Much uncertainty exists about the actual cause of SIDS. One recent theory states that abnormalities in the portion of the brain responsible for controlling breathing and sleep/wake cycles may cause SIDS. Another similar theory hypothesizes that the combination of a brain abnormality and environmental conditions, such as excessive inhalation of carbon dioxide or exposure to cigarette smoke, cause oxygen deprivation which leads to SIDS (AAP Task Force on Infant Sleep Position and Sudden Infant Death Syndrome, 2000).

Due to the fact that previously 1 infant out of every 600 died from SIDS, new scientifically supported guidelines were introduced that recommended positioning infants on their back, rather than on their stomach when sleeping. Since the recommendation was made, there has been a 40% decrease in infant deaths due to SIDS (AAP Task Force on Infant Sleep Position and Sudden Infant Death Syndrome, 2000). In addition, concerns that supine sleeping babies were at an increased risk of choking have been unfounded. Due to the success of this policy, it is recommended that all babies, unless medically contraindicated, be placed on their back for sleep. Side sleeping, although safer than prone sleeping, still poses a slightly increased risk for SIDS over supine sleeping.

Despite the benefits of supine sleeping, approximately 20% of infants 1 to 3 months of age are still placed on their stomachs during sleep (Gibson, 2000). Primary health care professionals, other health care providers, and educators have a responsibility to educate all new parents about the benefits of supine sleeping and to follow up with parents during well-child visits. Research has shown that a doctor's endorsement of back sleeping is the single most important factor for influencing mothers to place their babies in the supine position for sleep. In addition, one study has shown that mothers who receive instruction about the benefits of back sleeping and who observe nurses placing their new babies on their backs for sleeping are much more likely to do the same (Willinger, Ko, Hoffman, Kessler, & Corwin, 2000). Medical personnel also should continue to encourage mothers not to smoke during pregnancy and to create a "smoke-free zone" around their young children. Even though decreases in smoking have not directly correlated with decreases in SIDS, maternal smoking during pregnancy emerged as a risk factor in many epidemiologic studies of SIDS (AAP Task Force on Infant Sleep Position and Sudden Infant Death Syndrome, 2000).

Immunizations

One of the most significant advances in modern history is the development of disease-preventing vaccines. From the advent of the diphtheria vaccine in 1921 to the recent licensure of the pneumococcal vaccine, there are now vaccines to prevent 11 life-threatening diseases. Since the first vaccine was introduced, the United States has seen a reduction in infection rates of over 99% in 8 of these 11 preventable diseases (CDC, 1999).

Despite the extremely low incidence of many of these diseases in the United States due to high rates of vaccination, the modern capacity for travel makes it highly possible that a disease in one country can easily cause an outbreak in another country (e.g., an outbreak in the United States). Therefore, it remains imperative that all individuals receive their childhood vaccines and continue to receive immunizations through adulthood.

Immunizations successfully allow for disease eradication because they create artificially induced immunity from infection without causing disease. Vaccines mimic the disease pathogen without causing the serious symptoms and complications of the natural infection. These vaccines are delivered into the body through injection into the skin or muscle, inhalation through the nose, or ingestion into the mouth. When given, the vaccine stimulates the immune system to produce antibodies. In general, these antibodies remain in the body and provide lifelong protection against the disease (CDC, 1994).

Immunizations are particularly important for children ages 0 to 5. Although infants are born with natural immunity that they acquire from antibodies passed from their mother through their mother's placenta, this immunity quickly wears off leaving the young children susceptible to infection. In some diseases, the complications in younger children are often more serious than they would be for an older child or an adult. As an example, the bacterium Haemophilus influenzae type b (Hib) typically targets children ages 0 to 5 and is most serious for children 6 months to 1 year of age. Hib can cause very serious infections, such as meningitis and pneumonia. Since the Hib vaccine has been administered regularly, there has been a 99% reduction in these infections. Also, as deafness is a major complication of Hib, there has been a substantial reduction in the cases of deafness in young children (CDC, 1999).

Due to the success of vaccine administration programs, immunizations are now considered the most cost-effective preventive health measure. The ease and effectiveness of vaccine administration has led many organizations, including the AAP, the American Academy of Family Physicians (AAFP), and the CDC, to endorse immunization schedules that recommend children be fully immunized by the age of 2. Due to the fact that most states require that children receive at least some vaccines before they attend school, more than 95% of all children are immunized for DTP, polio, measles, mumps, and rubella by school age (CDC, 1999).

There is no question that immunizations have dramatically improved child health and particularly the health of children under the age of 5. As immunizations continue to prevent disease, society will move to a time when most parents will not have seen the consequences of epidemic diseases. As a result, parents may become lackadaisical about their children's immunization status. Some advocate the use of immunization tracking systems or registries and using the Internet as a means to ensure that all children continue to receive age-appropriate immunizations. These methods of tracking will be particularly useful for those populations of children who receive their medical care from a variety of different sources, in that every health care professional will be able to easily access the child's immunization history. The use of combination vaccines will also improve immunization rates, as children would receive multiple vaccines with fewer administrations. Most importantly, however, health care professionals must continue to work vigilantly toward ensuring vaccine safety and increasing public and parental knowledge about the benefits and necessity of immunization for individuals throughout the life span.

Finally, vaccines are especially important for the health of children internationally. The importance of vaccines as a basic need for all children is demonstrated by the eradication of many diseases in countries with high immunization rates such as the United States. Groups such as the World Health Organization, Rotary International, and the Bill and Melinda Gates Foundation are supporting efforts to eradicate diseases, such as polio, in countries around the world.

Hearing and Vision Screening

Incorporating hearing and vision screening into the well-child care protocol is important for diagnosing and treating hearing and vision conditions common to early childhood. Even mild hearing loss is a condition that, if left undetected and untreated, will likely impede speech, language, cognitive, and psychosocial development (Yoshinaga-Itano, Sedey, Coulter, & Mehl, 1998). Since the first three years of life are known to be extremely important for early brain development, preventing, detecting, and/or treating hearing problems at an early age is critical.

At present, the average age of diagnosis for hearing impairment is 30 months (Harrison & Roush, 1996). By this age, precious time has been lost and treatment efficacy is impaired. To encourage early testing, the AAP and the Joint Committee on Infant Hearing recommend that all newborns be tested for hearing loss before leaving the hospital (Joint Committee on Infant Hearing, 2000). Timely and effective screening can lead to appropriate monitoring and follow-up and, ultimately, will result in more age-appropriate developmental outcomes for the child.

The technology is currently available to objectively measure hearing loss in newborns and very young infants. Otoacoustic emissions (OAEs) and auditory brainstem response (ABR) are both methods that have been successfully implemented in hospital-based newborn hearing screening programs (Finitzo, Albright, & O'Neal, 1998; Mason & Hermann, 1998; Vohr, Carty, Moore, & Letourneau, 1998). The cost-effectiveness of implementing these programs is difficult to ascertain. While the actual cost of identifying children with hearing loss through universal screening may be substantial, early treatment has demonstrated that these children will be capable of being appropriately educated in a less restrictive and less expensive environment (White, 1997).

As in the case of hearing, vision impairment affects the child's emotional, neurological, and physical development and therefore, prevention and early detection and treatment of vision difficulty is extremely important. Early brain research has determined that children without vision impairment are able to see at birth. For children who do have early vision impairment, better outcomes can be achieved if they receive timely vision screening. In order for the vision system to develop normally, both eyes must see clearly and send and receive neurological information to and from the brain. Because during the first five years the vision system continues this maturation process, treatments that would not be effective in later years can prevent serious impairment if initiated at an early age (Campos, 1995). In particular, detection and treatment of conditions such as amblyopia (reduction of vision in an otherwise healthy eye secondary to disuse, more commonly known as *lazy eye*) and strabismus (misalignment of the eyes, commonly known as *cross-eye*) prior to 6 years of age can prevent loss of vision.

The eyes should be carefully examined in infancy, and children should receive regular vision screening starting at the age of 3. Many children are not tested early enough, frequently enough, or at all. Current obstacles to universal screening include difficulty in screening at an early age due to lack of screening modalities for the very young, a lack of uniform guidelines, barriers to health professionals' implementation, difficulties with appropriate follow-up, the absence of regular well-child care, and lack of insurance. For example, with regard to implementation, it is unfortunately the case that a 3- or 4-year-old who fails a vision screening is often not asked to return for a follow-up screening until a year later. This common practice often results in the loss of important time and, once again, can negatively impact the treatment and ultimate outcome.

Due to the time-sensitive nature of diagnosis and treatment, early hearing and vision screening is imperative. In addition, these early screening procedures, if administered regularly and correctly, provide health care professionals with an important preventive tool for promoting child well-being.

MEASUREMENT AND IMPLEMENTATION
OF PREVENTIVE HEALTH CARE

A continuing challenge has been to determine the best method of evaluating and measuring the effectiveness of preventive care. Until recently, pediatric practice has been guided largely by expert opinion rather than empirical evidence. In addition, the evolution of the medical field has resulted in a haphazard system of unlinked, often redundant, programs, therapies, and screening measures that are difficult to evaluate and measure. In an attempt to consolidate and organize the procedures, screening measures, and concepts, the AAP published what is known as the "Periodicity Schedule," which provides primary health care professionals with expert knowledge, guidelines, and timelines for administering the best care for children (AAP Committee on Practice and Ambulatory Medicine, 2000).

With the development of the concept of evidence-based medicine, the expert opinion approach has been challenged. In addition, in 1992, the AAP publicly recognized the negative impact that the nonunified health care approach was having on children and families. Therefore, the pediatric community has undertaken two efforts to change the implementation and measurement of preventive health care for children. First, pediatricians are attempting to measure the impact preventive health care has on child health and well-being. Second, the pediatric community now supports and advocates for the concept of the "medical home" (AAP, 1992). This concept embodies the classical primary health care model. However, it also recognizes the very significant role and responsibility of the family and the primary health care professional in providing comprehensive, community-based, coordinated care that is compassionate and culturally effective. This kind of care recognizes that the family and the child are central. In addition, a child who has a medical home has a primary health care professional who is working in partnership with the child's family to ensure that all medical, nonmedical, psychosocial, and educational needs of the child and the family are met.

It is believed that the medical home model addresses the categorical basic needs of children, adults, and families. This system of care, in combination with new technologies, will allow a linkage of services, will assist in identifying children who have missed out on preventive health care measures, and will partner the primary health care professional with the family to better address the child's basic needs.

States have been asked by the federal government to measure and evaluate the delivery of health care services for children in a medical home. A special effort has been made in the area of children with special health care needs. An example of this is the various performance measures being developed by the Maternal and Child Health Bureau. In addition, the federal government has enlisted assistance from the states to help ensure the provision of medical homes for children by specifying as a primary objective that children will receive regular, ongoing, comprehensive care within the medical home. Having a firm commitment from the federal government in this effort not only secures the support of various state agencies, but also encourages health care practitioners in the community to provide care through a medical home.

Early results from classic evaluation and measurement procedures have been mixed. On the one hand, studies have shown that individual aspects of health care maintenance, well-child care, and preventive care are beneficial to child well-being and are cost-effective (examples include immunizations and metabolic screening). However, when viewed in the aggregate, it has been difficult to demonstrate which particular combination of health care services makes a significant difference. Clinical experience suggests, however, that when infants and children receive their care within the context of a medical home, child health and family satisfaction improves (Family Voices, 2000).

The AAP has developed a tool to assess the number of pediatricians who are providing medical homes for children. The AAP Periodic Survey of Fellows #44: Health Services for Children With and Without Special Needs—The Medical Home Concept, (2000) a national survey of pediatricians, was designed to explore pediatricians' attitudes and practice of various elements of the medical home, as well as to identify barriers to providing this level of care. The Health Resources and Services Administration's Maternal and Child Health Bureau has funded several model projects that aim to assess the capacity of pediatric practices to provide care through a medical home. Tools developed by these demonstration projects will allow for further investigation into the impact that medical homes and the preventive health care movement is having on child development and well-being.

FACTORS AFFECTING ACCESSIBILITY AND PROMOTION
OF PREVENTIVE HEALTH CARE

A number of factors, including family awareness and attitude, professional responsibility and effort, community involvement, and systemic issues, all can impact favorably or unfavorably on the availability and utilization of preventive health measures.

Awareness of the necessity of preventive health care and a positive attitude toward health care accessibility and services by families is essential to ensuring that children receive well-child care. If family members either do not know about the benefits of preventive care or have had negative experiences with the health care system, they may be less likely to access these services for their children. Another hindrance is that the procedures and tests that are recommended as part of a child's basic needs have become more complex, and the task of learning about and providing all of the aspects of care can be daunting for many families. This complexity has been magnified during a time when the public must cope with a health care system that has become increasingly impersonal. Many families do not fully realize the implications of devastating infectious disease because, fortunately, most children in the United States are typically not exposed to life-threatening epidemics. Combined with the many stresses of everyday life with which most families must cope, parents may not make learning about and providing their children with preventive health care a priority.

In addition, the attitude of the health care professional has a profound effect on whether the community accepts preventive health measures. If pediatricians, family physicians, and nurses promote prevention, it will be incorporated into everyday practice. If they do not, preventive medicine will likely remain foreign to standard medical practice. Today, in an ever-changing health care environment, each community and health system is different. For example, if immunization is valued while managed care refuses to pay for it, health care professionals will be conflicted with regard to making this preventive health option available to their patients. With the training of most health professionals still dominated by a biomedical model, where little formal education is dedicated to preventive measures, it is difficult for the primary care professional to make preventive practices a major focus. However, with tools such as the "Bright Futures" (National Center for Education in Maternal and Child Health, 2000), the *Every Child Deserves a Medical Home* training program (AAP, 2000) and "Healthy Steps Program" (Guyer, Hughart, Strobino, Jones, & Scharfstein, 2000), there is a call for a continued and persistent focus on prevention.

The attitude of the community is also very important. If the community equates a "healthy community" with a "good community in which to live," individuals will see how preventive measures, implemented on a population- or community-wide basis, can have a profound impact. One program working toward achieving community-based preventive health is the Healthy Communities Program. This initiative brings together diverse community members to discuss issues and solve problems related to community preventive health practices. This program also attempts to promote preventive practices that will benefit the entire population in a systematic way. It may encourage the fluoridation of water, address housing conditions, or tackle land-use issues. The program brings institutions like businesses, hospitals, and school systems together to form partnerships and work toward a common goal (The Coalition for Healthier Cities and Communities, 2001).

As the United States has moved from a time when health care was provided by individual health care professionals to a time when many people are cared for by large systems, including managed care organizations (MCOs), implementation of preventive care has become very difficult. As support for the development of health maintenance organizations in the 1960s and 1970s, proponents offered the concept of prevention as being a key component of comprehensive care. However, as "high tech/high cost" health care has developed and now dominates medical care, MCOs have felt pressured to cut other types of care—especially "low tech/low cost" health care measures. Unfortunately, preventive health care procedures are one of the primary low tech/low cost methods that are frequently not reimbursed. For example, enrollees' patterns of frequently changing from one plan to another could make it possible for MCOs to not be concerned about the immunization levels of their enrollees. Fortunately, HEDIS (Health Plan Employer Data and Information Set) measures now require managed care plans to be evaluated by the same criteria. Since the development of these measures, MCOs use HEDIS measures to evaluate the adequacy of their care (Mainous & Talbert, 1998). The use of these measures has compelled MCOs to make sure that children receive timely and appropriate immunizations. As can be seen from this example, the present state of the health care industry forces patients' needs to give way to such issues as cost, regulation, and the desire of the employer when considering whether a preventive service will be covered.

In addition, with the movement toward the concept of evidence-based medicine, there is increasing pressure on health care professionals to provide an evidence base for these practices. Professional medical societies place painstaking efforts into making recommendations for care based on physician expertise, literature review, and case studies. However, provision of an evidence base for their recommendations is not always possible. Physicians can argue that the child who is diagnosed with a hearing impairment or vision deficit through early screening programs will benefit tremendously in prognosis, treatment options, and quality of life as opposed to the child who is diagnosed later in life. This argument frequently, however, is not fully supported by payors when conclusive evidence does not exist and/or is not proven to be cost-effective. The medical community must evaluate how they can do a better job measuring the effectiveness of their recommendations. With the current health care system, the lack of consistency and lack of evaluation of recommendations only add to the confusion and uncertainty as to which practices are important for the individual and the community.

Our ever-changing health care environment requires that the public voice their opinion as to what they feel is important. One example of how powerful public opinion can be occurred in the 1960s when parents' groups brought about legislation that lead to the practice of screening newborns for metabolic disorders in the United States (Paul, 1997). The combination of expert opinion, evidence-based research, and community and family opinion all need to be considered as the United States moves forward in developing preventive programs for children.

CONCLUSIONS

The key to the future impact of preventive health care is the use of new technology to develop a system of care that is seamless, coordinated, comprehensive, and family-centered. Our current system of categorical procedures or tests has many shortcomings. A "system" of care should promote health for the individual and the community at large. As noted earlier, a system that allows children to not be immunized puts the child and others at risk. Not using the technology available to detect treatable conditions early not only costs the child and family but also costs the community. Children who do not have the benefit of a comprehensive preventive health care system may be negatively impacted as adults. For example, it is well known that breastfeeding has a positive impact on development and health throughout the life span, yet only 68.4% of children are breastfed at birth and only 31.4% at six months of age (Ross Products Division, 2000). Yet with the evidence being overwhelmingly in favor of breastfeeding, 45% of pediatricians in a recent, periodic survey did not think that there was any difference between breastfeeding and formula feeding (AAP, 1996). This example shows how our current system fails to provide adequate preventive services, recommendations, and information—prevention that could drastically improve the health and well-being of individuals and communities.

In order to make meaningful recommendations, health care professionals first must evaluate which existing systems and services work. As a society that says that it values children, we need to make sure that all children receive the benefits of preventive care. Every child in the United States should have access to basic health care, immunizations, screening procedures such as hearing, metabolic, and vision, and other beneficial practices such as breastfeeding.

Second, the preventive systems will only be successful if they support families, health care professionals, communities, and states in providing and accessing these services. Stand-alone, uncoordinated programs are very expensive, fail to be comprehensive, and are time intensive. America's children must have routine care provided within the context of a medical home.

Third, we need better research to prove the effectiveness of preventive measures. Research methods need to be developed that answer the public's desire to know if a specific preventive measure improves child health and at what cost. For families, private payors, and the government to value these services, preventive health care benefits need to be proven.

Finally, in order to continue the advancement of preventive measures, pediatricians and other health care professionals who care for children must determine how to better serve the needs of families and communities. The Human Genome Project and new research on child and family development provide enormous opportunities to improve child health. By the end of the second decade of the 21st century, what is unheard of today may be considered routine preventive practice. As families, professional organizations, government, and industry continue to work in collaboration, preventive health care will continue to advance and to improve child health.

REFERENCES

American Academy of Pediatrics, Ad Hoc Task Force on Definition of the Medical Home. (1992). The medical home (RE9262). *Pediatrics*, *90*, 774.

American Academy of Pediatrics, Division of Child Health Research. (1996, February). *Periodic survey of fellows: Number 30: Executive summary*. Elk Grove Village, IL. Available at: www.aap.org/research/surv2.htm   Accessed February 25, 2002.

American Academy of Pediatrics, Work Group on Breastfeeding. (1997, December). Breastfeeding and the use of human milk (RE9729). *Pediatrics*, *100*, 1035–1039.

American Academy of Pediatrics, Task Force on Newborn and Infant Hearing. (1999, February). Newborn and infant hearing loss: Detection and intervention. (RE9846). *Pediatrics*, *103*, 527–530.

American Academy of Pediatrics, Committee on Practice and Ambulatory Medicine. (2000, March). Recommendations for preventative pediatric health care (RE9535). *Pediatrics*, *105*, 645–646.

American Academy of Pediatrics, Task Force on Infant Sleep Position and Sudden Infant Death Syndrome. (2000, March). Changing concepts of sudden infant death syndrome: Implications for infant sleeping environment and sleep position (RE9946). *Pediatrics*, *105*, 650–656.

Anders, T. F., Goodlin-Jones, B. L., & Zelenko, M. (1998, October/November). Infant regulation and sleep-wake state development. *Zero to Three*, *19*, 5–8.

Berger, A. (1999, December). How does herd immunity work? *British Medical Journal*, *319*, 1466–1467.

Campos, E. (1995). Amblyopia. *Survey of Ophthalmology*, *40*, 23–39.

Centers for Disease Control and Prevention. (1994, January). *General Recommendations on Immunizations: Recommendations of the Advisory Committee on Immunization Practice*. Morbidity and Mortality Weekly Report, 43 (RR–1).

Centers for Disease Control and Prevention. (1999, April). *Impact of vaccines universally recommended for children: United States, 1990–1998*. Morbidity and Mortality Weekly Report, 48, 243–248.

Centers for Disease Control and Prevention. (2001). *Dietary fluoride supplement schedule* [On-line]. Available: www.cdc.gov/nccdphp/Oh/child-flsupp.htm

The Coalition for Healthier Cities and Communities. (2001). The communities movement. Available at: http://www.healthycommunities.org/usa/portal2.cfm   Accessed February 27, 2002.

Cohen, G. J. (Ed.). (1999). *Guide to your child's sleep*. Elk Grove Village, IL: American Academy of Pediatrics.

Family Voices. (2000). *The health care experiences of families of children with special health care needs: Summary report of findings from a national survey, and summary of California Family Survey Results*. Algodones, NM. Available at: http://www.familyvoices.org/publist.html   Accessed February 27, 2002.

Finitzo, T., Albright, K., & O'Neal, J. (1998). The newborn with hearing loss: Detection in the nursery. *Pediatrics*, *102*, 1452–1460.

Gibson, E., Dembofsky, C. A., Rubin, S., & Greenspan, J. S. (2000, May). Infant sleep position practices 2 years into the "back to sleep" campaign. *Clinical Pediatrics*, *39*, 285–289.

Gill, J. M., Mainous, A. G., III, & Nsereko, M. (2000, April). The effect of continuity of care on emergency department use. *Archives of Family Medicine*, *9*, 333–338.

Guthrie, R., & Susi, A. (1963). A simple phenylalanine method for detecting phenylketonuria in large populations of newborn infants. *Pediatrics, 32*, 338–343.

Guyer, B., Hughart, N., Strobino, D., Jones, A., & Scharfstein, D. (2000, March). Assessing the impact of pediatric-based developmental services on Infants, Families, and Clinicians: Challenges to evaluating the Healthy Steps program. *Pediatrics, 105*, e33.

Harrison, M., & Roush, J. (1966). Age of suspicion, identification and intervention for infants and young children with hearing loss: A national study. *Ear and Hearing, 17*, 55–62.

Illig, D. C. (1998). *Birth to kindergarten: The importance of the early years.* Sacramento, CA: California Research Bureau.

Joint Committee on Infant Hearing (2000, October). Year 2000 position statement: Principles and guidelines for early hearing detection and intervention programs. *Pediatrics, 106*, 798–816.

Mainous, A. G., III, & Talbert, J. (1998, September/October). Assessing quality of care via HEDIS 3.0: Is there a better way? *Archives of Family Medicine*, 410–413.

Mason, J., & Hermann, K. R. (1998). Universal infant hearing screening by automated auditory brainstem response measurement. *Pediatrics, 101*, 221–228.

National Research Council and Institute of Medicine. (2000). *From neurons to neighborhoods: The science of early childhood development.* Committee on Integrating the Science of Early Childhood Development. J. P. Shonkoff & D. A. Phillips (Eds.), Board on Children, Youth, and Families, Commission on Behavioral and Social Sciences and Education. Washington, DC: National Academy Press.

National Institute of Neurological Disorders and Stroke. (2000). *Brain basics: Understanding sleep* (NIH Publication No. 98–3440–c). Washington, DC: National Institutes of Health, National Institute of Neurological Disorders and Stroke.

Newborn Screening Task Force. (2000, August). Serving the family from birth to the medical home: A report from the Newborn Screening Task Force convened in Washington, DC, May 10–11, 1999. *Pediatrics, 106*, 386–422.

Paul, D. B. (1997). The history of newborn phenylketonuria screening in the U.S. In N. A. Holtzman & M. S. Watson, (Eds.), *Promoting safe and effective genetic testing in the United States: Final report of the Task Force on Genetic Testing.* Bethesda, MD: National Institutes of Health. Available at http://www.nhgri.nih.gov/ELSI/TFGT%5Ffinal Accessed February 25, 2002.

Ross Products Division, Abbott Laboratories. (2000). *Ross mothers survey.* Columbus, OH.

Shore, R. (1997). *Rethinking the brain: New insights into early development.* New York: Families & Work Institute, 27.

Vohr, B. R., Carty, L., Moore, P., & Letourneau, K. (1998). The Rhode Island Hearing Assessment Program: Experience with statewide hearing screening (1993–1996). *Journal of Pediatrics, 133*, 353–357.

White, K. R. (1997). *Universal newborn hearing screening: Issues and evidence.* Presented at the Centers for Disease Control and Prevention workshop on early hearing detection and intervention, Atlanta, GA.

Willinger, M., Ko, C. W., Hoffman, H. J., Kessler, R. C., & Corwin, M. J. (2000, April). Factors associated with caregivers' choice of infant sleep position, 1994–1998: The national infant sleep position study. *Journal of the American Medical Association, 283*, 2135–2142.

Yoshinaga-Itano, C., Sedey, A., Coulter, D., & Mehl, A. (1998). Language of early and later identified children with hearing loss. *Pediatrics, 102*, 1161–1171.

6

Physical Activity and Well-Being

Jeanette M. Conner
Vermont Oxford Network, Burlington, VT

INTRODUCTION

The physical health and well-being of children in the United States today is a leading national public health concern. Trends indicate that children are leading increasingly sedentary lifestyles and an alarming rise in childhood obesity is evident. National efforts are underway to define, measure, and promote the physical well-being of the nation's children. The purpose of this paper is to identify the core components of physical activity and well-being in children and outline the supporting literature, to describe the effects of physical activity in children across the life span, and to identify biological, psychological, social, and environmental determinants of physical activity and well-being.

OPERATIONAL DEFINITION

Physical well-being has been defined by measuring health status, functional outcome, or quality of life (American Academy of Pediatrics [AAP], 2000b). Physical activity level, which is predominantly measured as either energy expended (Gavarry et al., 1998; Kimiecik, Horn, & Shurin, 1996; Kimiecik & Horn, 1998; Trost et al., 1997; Trost, Pate, Ward, Saunders, & Riner, 1999a; Trost, Pate, Freedson, Sallis, & Taylor, 2000; Ward et al., 1997) or by self-report, (Anonymous, 1997; Booth, Macakill, Phongsavan, McLellan, & Okely, 1998; Boreham, Twisk, Savage, Cran, & Strain, 1997; Crocker, Bailey, Faulkner, Kowalski, & McGrath, 1997) is a primary indicator of a healthy physical state for children in the majority of the literature.

Physical activity or functioning is defined as the ability to be physically active, to play, and to participate in activities or sports without limitation or restriction. Physical activity can be thought of as a continuum and is defined as the degree or extent of activity or energy expended. The lowest end of the activity continuum would be a child who is sedentary with no activity, in contrast to the highest end of the activity continuum which would be the child with vigorous physical activity, endurance, and stamina. A child with optimal physical stamina has the ability to be involved in extended periods of vigorous play or strenuous physical activity without limitation. When determining physical activity level and functioning, however, one must consider what is developmentally appropriate for the child.

For the purposes of this paper, physical activity is operationally defined as a positive state of physical health, encompassing normal growth and development and physical activity or functioning level. This paper addresses only the physical activity of the child without physical or cognitive disability, or chronic illness. Children with disability or chronic illness are certainly capable of physical activity, but it is beyond the scope of this manuscript to address these special groups.

During the first six years of life, remarkable growth and development occur. In infancy, the child learns to use muscles voluntarily such as raising the head and then develops complex tasks, such as manipulation of objects with both hands. During the second year, there is notable development in the expansion of vocabulary, gross motor development, such as walking alone, and fine motor development, such as turning book pages. During the third to fifth year, children learn to speak fluently, develop complex motor movements, such as skipping and hopping, and learn to bathe, eat, and dress independently. For more specific information, see the Denver Developmental Screening Test II (Frankenburg, 1969, 1984; Frankenburg & Dodds, 1967; Frankenburg, Camp, Van Natta, & Demersseman, 1971; Frankenburg, Goldstein, & Camp, 1971; Frankenburg, Fandal, Sciarillo, & Burgess, 1981) which defines expected milestones for gross motor, language, fine motor, and personal-social aspects of development from birth through 6 years of age (Table 6.1).

Beyond six years of age, motor and cognitive development of the child has been well defined (Erickson, 1976). Development during these years is individualized, and there is a wide spectrum of normal growth. Development of large and small muscle movements becomes increasingly coordinated as the child begins to participate in more rigorous physical activities. Notable changes in development during these years are the prepubescent growth spurt, in which children have disproportional development in growth of arms, legs, and trunk; and puberty, in which the body composition begins to change and sexual development commences.

THEORETICAL AND EMPIRICAL REVIEW OF THE LITERATURE

Physical activity level is measured in a number of ways. Physiologic measures of physical activity include measuring basal energy expenditure in kilocalorie per day

TABLE 6.1
Developmental Milestones: Birth Through Age 5

Age	Gross Motor	Fine Motor
1 month	Raises head slightly, crawling movements	Tight grasp, follows to midline
2 months	Holds head midline, lifts chest	No longer tight clench, follow object past midline
3 months	Supports on forearm while prone, holds head up steadily	Holds hands open, follows in circular fashion
4–5 months	Rolls, sits well if propped, supports on wrists, shifts weight	Arm movements in unison to grasp, touches placed object
6 months	Sits well unsupported, puts feet in mouth while supine	Reaches with hands, transfers, grasps
9 months	Creeps, crawls, pushes to stand, pivots when sitting	Pincer grasp, probes, holds bottle, fingerfeeds
12 months	Walks alone	Throws objects, lets go of toys, hand release, mature pincer grasp
15 months	Creeps upstairs, walks backwards	Imitates building block tower (2 blocks), scribbles in imitation
18 months	Throws toys while standing, runs	Turns pages a few at a time, holds spoon, feeds self
21 months	Squats, goes up steps	Builds tower of 5 blocks, drinks from cup
24 months	Walks up and down steps without assistance	Turns pages one at a time, begins to undress-remove shoes, pants
30 months	Jumps, throws ball overhand	Unbuttons, holds pencil
3 years	Pedals tricycle, alternate feet going up steps	Dresses and undresses partially, draws a circle
4 years	Hops, skips, alternates feet going down steps	Buttons clothing fully, catches ball
5 years	Skips, alternating feet, jumps over low objects	Ties shoes, spread using knife

Note. Adapted from *Pediatric Clinics of North America, 20*(1), 8–14, by A. J. Capute & R. F. Biehl, 1973.

(energy at rest; Wong et al., 1999), total daily energy expenditure (Spurr & Reina, 1987; Wong et al., 1999), or energy expended during an activity (Spurr & Reina, 1987). Other physiologic indicators of activity include estimating energy expenditure and measuring median metabolic equivalents of energy expenditure above resting metabolic rate (Eisenmann et al., 2000). Physical activity level has also been measured by the number or duration of regular activity episodes per week. A child with no or low levels of physical activity (NLPA) expends little to no time engaging in physical activities in a week. A child with moderate levels of physical activity (MPA) expends approximately three episodes of moderate to vigorous physical activity per week. A child with vigorous physical activity (VPA) expends greater than three episodes of vigorous physical activity per week (Gavarry et al., 1998; Keays & Allison, 1995; Kimiecik et al., 1996, 1998; Trost et al., 1997, 1999a, 2000; Ward et al., 1997). Some investigators report percentage of time of children engage in sedentary, moderate, or vigorous physical activity (Simons-Morton, Pate, & Simons-Morton, 1988; Simons-Morton, Parcel, Baranowski, Forthofer, & O'Hara, 1991; Simons-Morton, Taylor, Snider, & Huang, 1993).

Appropriate activity levels during infancy and the preschool years are difficult to define. Programs have been developed that promote infant swimming, reportedly to improve the psychomotor development of the infant (Kliorin & Aleksandrovich, 1989; Weidle & Aagaard; 1990). These programs have been met with unfavorable review (Kropp & Schwartz, 1982; Phillips, 1987) and were determined to be unjustified programs (AAP, 1985). The American Academy of Pediatrics (AAP) states that "infant exercise programs are unnecessary and they do nothing to improve a baby's physical fitness" (AAP, 2000c). In addition, the AAP discourages team sports for children under the age of 6 (AAP, 2000c). Surveys, such as the National Children and Youth Fitness Study, have identified norms for physical fitness in school-aged children. An accepted standard for appropriate physical activity levels for school aged children and adolescents is 30 minutes of activity, 3 days a week (Ross & Gilbert, 1985; Ross, 1987).

Benefits and Risks of Rigorous Physical Activity

There are many health benefits to regular physical activity. Perhaps one of the most commonly known benefits of physical activity in adults is an improved psychological state. In children, physical activity has been found to improve self-esteem and to decrease anxiety and stress (Calfas, Sallis, & Nader, 1991). Rigorous physical activity, especially sports with increased bone loading, such as gymnastics, are known to have a positive effect on bone tissue and can produce increased bone mineral density (BMD). This effect is especially true for prepubescent girls (Anderson & Metz; 1993; Barr & McKay, 1998; Courteix et al., 1998). To evaluate the effect of intensive physical training on BMD, researchers studied a group of elite prepubertal girls (Courteix et al., 1998). Girls participated either in sports requiring significant bone loading impact (either swimming or gymnastics), or in sports without impact loading. Forty-one healthy prepubertal girls took part in this study. There was no significant difference found between swimmers and controls in BMD measurements. The mean BMD in gymnasts was statistically higher than in the control group. The authors concluded that physical activity in childhood might be an important factor in bone mineral acquisition in prepubertal girls, only if the sport can induce bone strains, such as gymnastics. Similar results have been found in other studies evaluating bone mineral density in high impact bone loading sports (Cassell, Benedict, & Specker, 1996; Daly, Rich, Klein, & Bass, 1999).

High levels of physical activity have also been found to enhance cardiorespiratory endurance. In a study that investigated the relationship between the habitual level of physical activity (HLPA) and cardiorespiratory endurance capacity, 257 healthy children ages 5 to 19 years underwent graded exercise tests on a treadmill. It was determined that more active prepubescent boys demonstrated higher cardiorespiratory endurance capacity, compared to those who were less active. In girls, the level of habitual physical activity was low, and no effect of exercise performance was found on cardiorespiratory endurance (Weymans & Reybrouck, 1989).

While there are many benefits to physical activity, physical exercise during childhood that is too rigorous and intense may have harmful effects. The child athlete who engages in rigorous physical activity may suffer alterations in bone maturation and be at greater risk for fractures, have diminished immune system response, suffer menstrual dysfunction, and be at greater risk for eating disorders. The female athlete is particularly at risk for these harmful effects (Malina, 1994; Lindholm, Hagenfeldt, & Ringertz, 1995; Shepard & Shek, 1996).

One study has shown that although some differences between female athletes and female nonathletes may exist, these differences are not necessarily harmful to development. In this study, 19 young women who had been elite gymnasts during their prepubertal and pubertal years were evaluated with regard to their health, menstrual data, and bone mineral mass and then compared to 21 similar young women (Lindholm et al., 1995). The age of menarche of the gymnasts was 14.8 compared to 12.1 years for the control group. Although the gymnasts had delayed puberty, no difference was found in total body bone mineral mass compared to controls. In addition, other investigators have not found delayed puberty in girls with vigorous activity levels (Malina, 1994).

There is some concern among investigators that excessive physical activity may play a role in eating disorders. Adolescents with anorexia nervosa and bulimia nervosa were given a detailed examination about their physical activity during and prior to the onset of the disorder (Davis et al., 1997). Excessive overexercising was found more in adolescents with anorexia nervosa, particularly during an acute phase of the disorder. These researchers believe that physical activity level is central to the development and maintenance of some eating disorders.

Vigorous physical activity in adults may lead to suppression of the immune system. Whether this alteration is true for children is unknown. During vigorous physical activity, the athlete's muscles suffer injury and undergo an inflammatory response, with suppressed natural killer (NK) cell function, impaired lymphocytes, and decreased immunoglobulin production (Shepard & Shek, 1996). Similar findings were found in a randomized controlled trial of athletes involved in a regular intensive exercise program (Garagiola et al., 1995). These findings should be interpreted cautiously, as NK activity and lymphocyte proliferative assays are sensitive to stimulation and depression, and these findings most likely represent a normal anti-inflammatory response to vigorous exercise.

Organized Sports versus Non-Organized Sports

It has not been clearly delineated whether organized, structured sports compared to nonorganized sports enhance long-term physical well-being. Readiness of the preschool child to participate in structured sports depends on multiple factors including the child's eagerness to participate, enjoyment of the activity, development of motor skills, social development, and cognitive level (AAP, 1992). For preadolescent children, the goal of organized sports should be to enhance the child's self image and mastery of the sport (AAP, 1989). Recent literature suggests that nonorganized sports, which can become "life sports," such as swimming, jogging, and golfing, are more likely to lead to sustained levels of physical activity and be continued throughout life (AAP, 2000a).

CONTINUITY OVER THE LIFE SPAN

Physical well-being of the child is a good predictor of overall long-term health and well-being, and has many proven benefits. Physical activity has been shown to prevent hypertension and reduce the risk of cardiovascular disease, to prevent osteoporosis, to reduce the risk of breast cancer and diabetes, to enhance self-esteem, and to promote learning and lifelong healthy habits.

The influence of physical activity in reducing coronary artery disease in adults is well known (Francis, 1996). Also, the relationship between cholesterol and lipids to coronary artery disease is equally well understood (Katzmarzyk, Malina, & Bouchard, 1999). What is less well known, however, is that the build up of atherosclerosis begins in childhood, and children with elevated levels of cholesterol and blood pressure are at risk for coronary artery disease (Cresanta, Burke, Downey, Freedman, & Dietz, 1986). For children, low- and high-density lipoprotein and cholesterol levels can be improved with physical activity. In a study of girls 8 to 11 years of age, low-density lipoprotein cholesterol (LDL-C), high-density lipoprotein (HDL-C), total cholesterol, and other lipoproteins were measured along with energy expenditure (Craig, Bandini, Lichenstein, Schaefer, & Dietz, 1996). Moderate to high levels of energy expenditure predicted LDL-C, when adjusted for body fat and dietary saturated fat. Similar results in improved lipoproteins were found in gymnasts with high levels of physical activity (Lopez Benedicto, Muviala Mateo, Gomez Diaz-Bravo, Sarria Chueca, & Giner Soria, 1988; Zonderland, Erich, Peltenburg, Bernink, & Saris, 1985; Zonderland et al., 1986).

Peak bone mass is an important determinant in the prevention of osteoporosis. A longitudinal study of peak bone mass was evaluated by identifying the relationships between childhood growth, lifestyle, and peak bone mass in women (Cooper et al., 1995). One hundred and fifty women were traced and evaluated over approximately 22 years. Strong relationships were found between infant weight at 1 year and adult bone mass, and childhood height and adult bone mass. The major determinant of bone mineral density in adulthood was physical activity level during childhood (Burrows Argote et al., 1996; Cassell et al., 1996; Courteix et al., 1998; Daly et al., 1999; Lindholm et al., 1995; Nickols-Richardson, O'Connor, Shapses, & Lewis, 1999; Nickols-Richardson, Modlesky, O'Connor, & Lewis, 2000).

Studies have suggested that adolescent physical activity may reduce the risk of breast cancer (Marcus et al., 1999; Verloop, Rookus, Vanderkooy, & Van Leeuwen, 2000). One group of researchers analyzed data on physical activity at age 12 that had been collected from the Carolina Breast Cancer Study (CBCS; Marcus et al., 1999). The CBCS was a case-control study of 527 European-American and 337 African-American cases and 790 controls, matched on age and race. Women were asked whether, and to what extent, they participated in walking to school, biking to school, competitive training, and performing vigorous household chores at age 12. Women who reported participation in any of the activities had a statistically significant lower risk (OR 0.8) of breast cancer than those women who did not engage in these activities (Marcus et al., 1999).

In another study, the risk of breast cancer in relation to lifetime physical activity was assessed using data from a population-based case-control study of 918 case subjects (aged 20–54 years) and 918 matched (by age) control subjects (Verloop et al., 2000). Associations between breast cancer risks and physical activity at ages 10 to 12 years and 13 to 15 years, and lifetime recreational activity. Women who were more active at ages 10 to 12 years had a statistically significant lower risk of breast cancer (OR 0.68). Women who had ever participated in recreational physical activity also had a reduced risk of breast cancer (OR 0.70) compared to inactive women. In addition, women who started physical activity earlier and continued their activities throughout adult life experienced a similar risk reduction.

Few studies have investigated childhood determinants of adult physical activity patterns. Those that have, have shown that regular physical activity in childhood has long-term effects on physical activity in adulthood (Dennison, Straus, Mellits, & Charney, 1988). For example, in a prospective study of 453 young men 23 to 25 years of age, childhood determinants of adult physical activity patterns were evaluated. The men's physical fitness test scores as children (10–11 years of age and 15–18 years of age) were compared to their physical activity levels as adults. The physically active adults had significantly better childhood physical fitness test scores compared to inactive adults. Specifically, the risk of physical inactivity in young adulthood was linearly related to the number of low scores on the 600-yard run and sit-ups tests as children. The childhood 600-yard run score was the best discriminator between currently physically active and inactive adults. Reported parental encouragement of exercise, level of education, participation in organized sports after high school, and reported spousal encouragement of exercise also contributed significantly to the discriminant function. These results demonstrate that physical fitness testing in boys facilitates the identification of those at increased risk of becoming physically inactive young adults (Dennison et al.).

FACTORS AFFECTING PHYSICAL WELL-BEING

A number of factors influence the development of sustained physical activity and well being, and these include biological, environmental, psychological, and social determinants.

Biological Influences

Numerous studies have identified differences in physical activity levels between male and female children (Allison, 1996; Allison, Dwyer, & Makin, 1999; Brustad, 1996; DiLorenzo, Stucky-Ropp, Vander Wal, & Gotham, 1998). Males tend to spend greater amounts of time in moderate to vigorous physical activities compared to females (Manios, Kafatos, & Codrington, 1999; Michaud, Narring, Cauderay, & Cavadini, 1999; Pate, Dowda, & Ross, 1990; Pate et al., 1997). Differences in physical activity level have also been found to be related to ethnicity. One particular study evaluated children ages 8 through 16 years as part of the National Health and Nutrition Examination Survey III (Andersen, Crespo, Bartlett, Cheskin, & Pratt, 1998). The surveys recorded weekly episodes of vigorous activity and daily hours of television viewing and were related to body mass index (BMI) and fatness. Of the entire sample ($N = 4,063$), 80% of children reported three or more episodes of vigorous activity per week. Rates of physical activity were lower in Hispanic black (69%) and Mexican American girls (73%). TV viewing was highest in non-Hispanic black children (42% watch 4 hours per day), and BMI and body fat were greater in those who watched 4 hours per day of TV. Another important study evaluated the extent to which physical activity patterns varied by ethnicity among subpopulations of U.S. adolescents (Gordon-Larsen, McMurray, & Popkin, 1999). A nationally representative sample of data was obtained from the 1996 National Longitudinal Study of Adolescent Health US adolescents. The population included 3,135 non-Hispanic blacks, 2,446 Hispanics, and 976 Asians. Hours per week of TV viewing, playing video or computer games, and times per week of moderate to vigorous physical activity were collected. After adjusting for sociodemographic factors, significant ethnic differences were seen for inactivity, particularly for hours of TV or video viewing per week. Results showed that non-Hispanic blacks, viewed 20.4 hours of TV compared to non-Hispanic whites (13.1 hours). Moderate to vigorous levels of physical activity (greater than five episodes per week) were found to be lowest in female and minority adolescents. Female levels of physical activity were the lowest in non-Hispanic black and Asian females, in contrast to males, who had higher levels of physical activity.

A longitudinal study conducted on children in Alabama explored the influence of ethnicity and gender, as predictors of TV viewing and physical activity level (Lindquist, Reynolds, & Goran, 1999). In this study, few ethnic differences in childhood physical activity were found when researchers accounted for social class and family type (single parent vs. dual parent). However, girls were more likely to have lower habitual physical activity levels, and African American children were noted to have less school based physical education.

Environmental Influences

The environment has a strong influence on the physical activity well-being of the child. Environmental influences can come from within the home, the school system, or the community of residence.

Nutrition.   Nutrition plays an important role in physical health and well-being. In particular, calcium intake during childhood and adolescence is crucial to the development of bone mass, yet most children and adolescents receive less than the recommended daily calcium intake (Ilich, Skugor, Hangartner, Baoshe, & Matkovic, 1998; Stallings, 1997). Studies have documented that dietary calcium can enhance bone mass density (BMD), especially for peripubertal girls (Anderson et al., 1993; Ilich et al., 1998; Rubin et al., 1993). A randomized, double-blind, controlled trial of calcium supplementation was conducted to determine calcium's effects on bone acquisition in 8-year-old Chinese children. Bone mineral content (BMC), bone density, and height were evaluated every 6 months. The treatment group received 300 mg calcium per day and control subjects received placebo tablets for 18 months. After 18 months, the treatment group had greater bone mineral content and density than the control subjects, but no changes in height (Lee et al., 1994). For more information on nutrition's impact on children's development and activity refer to the Nutrition chapter in the physical domain section of this book.

Home Environment.   In the home, parental role modeling is strongly associated with the child's development and persistence in physical activities and healthy behaviors. Mothers who are physically active typically have children who are more likely to physically active (Aarnio, Winter, Kujala, & Kaprio, 1997; DiLorenzo et al., 1998). In a cross-sectional study of 129 obese children and 142 normal weight children parental inactivity was a strong and positive predictor of child inactivity (Fogelholm, Nuutinen, Pasanen, Myohanen, & Saatela, 1999). In addition, parent obesity was a strong predictor of child obesity.

TV viewing or playing computer games is another determinant of physical activity level. TV viewing and computerized games tend to enhance physical inactivity, and alter a child's eating habits to less nutritional foods that often leads to obesity. A number of studies have documented the strong association between TV viewing, reduced activity levels, altered eating habits, and increased body fat (Bernard,

Lavalle, Gray-Donald, & Delisle, 1995; Dietz, 1991; Gortmaker, Dietz, & Cheung, 1990; Gupta, Saini, Acharya, & Miglani, 1994; Hernandez et al., 1999; Jason & Brackshaw, 1999; Katzmarzyk, Malina, Song, & Bouchard, 1998; Robinson, 1999; Wong et al., 1992).

School Environment.   The school environment also strongly influences the physical activity and well-being of children. The Child and Adolescent Trial for Cardiovascular Health (CATCH) evaluated the outcomes of health behavior interventions in the elementary school system on 5,106 third-grade students (Luepker et al., 1996). A randomized controlled trial was conducted in 96 elementary schools in California, Louisiana, Minnesota, and Texas. Schools randomized to intervention participated in a 3-year program (third through fifth grade) including school food service modifications, enhanced physical education, and classroom curricula. The children in the intervention program had increased levels and intensity of physical activity and reduced dietary fat intake as compared to the control schools.

Psychological and Social Influences

A child's enjoyment and perceived ability of physical activity has been found to be a consistent predictor of physical activity levels (DiLorenzo et al., 1998). In this particular study, self-efficacy for physical activity and interest in sports media were found to be important determinants for physical activity in boys between the fifth and ninth grades. For girls in the same grades, enjoyment of physical activity and self-efficacy were also important determinants of physical activity (DiLorenzo et al., 1998). In another study, fifth and eighth graders in Cambridge, Massachusetts, were surveyed about their perceived behavioral control (how easy or difficult it was to engage in physical activity (Craig et al., 1996; see also, Trost, Pate, Ward, Saunders, & Riner, 1999b). The children's attitude and perceived control predicted their intent to participate in physical activities. Activities in which the children feel competency and enjoyment are more likely to sustain vigorous physical activity (Allison et al., 1999; Craig, Goldberg, & Dietz, 1996).

CONCLUSIONS

Physical well-being of the child is a positive health state encompassing normal growth and development, and the ability to be physically active to play, and to participate in activities or sports without limitation or restriction. Regular physical activity has been found to have many benefits. Moderate physical activity for 30 minutes, 3 days a week can lead to enhanced overall health, improved self esteem and self image, increased bone density and muscle strength, and prevent chronic disease in children. Physical well-being is a multidimensional concept, and many biological, environmental, psychological, and social factors influence physical activity and well-being.

Children need to be encouraged and supported in their home and school environments to be physically active and to develop healthy lifelong physical activity patterns. Until age appropriate levels of physical activity are established for children, children should be encouraged to sustain moderate levels of physical activity of 30 minutes, 3 days a week. Children should also be encouraged to develop interests in physical activities that can be sustained throughout the life span such as walking, jogging, bicycling, swimming, and golfing.

The home and school environment can play important roles in modeling and influencing the establishment of proper diet and regular physical activity for all children. Parents and schools can teach children the health benefits of eating a well balanced diet, and can use a variety of techniques to promote lifelong physical activity.

REFERENCES

Aarnio, M., Winter, T., Kujala, U. M., & Kaprio, J. (1997). Familial aggregation of leisure-time physical activity—A three-generation study. *International Journal of Sports Medicine, 18*, 549–556.

Allison, K. R. (1996). Predictors of inactivity: An analysis of the Ontario Health Survey. *Canadian Journal of Public Health. Revue Canadienne de Sante Publique, 87*, 354–358.

Allison, K. R., Dwyer, J. J., & Makin, S. (1999). Self-efficacy and participation in vigorous physical activity by high school students. *Health Education & Behavior, 26*, 12–24.

American Academy of Pediatrics. (1985). Policy Statement: Infant Swimming Programs (RE5045). *Pediatrics, 75*.

American Academy of Pediatrics. (1989). Policy Statement: Organized athletics for preadolescent children (RE9165). *Pediatrics, 84*.

American Academy of Pediatrics. (1992). Policy Statement: Fitness, Activity, and Sports Participation in the Preschool Child (RE9265). *Pediatrics, 90*, 1002–1004.

American Academy of Pediatrics. (2000a). *Better health and fitness through physical activity* [On-line]. Available: www.aap.org

American Academy of Pediatrics. (2000b). *Functional outcomes project: Spring 2000* [On-line]. Available: www.aap.org

American Academy of Pediatrics. (2000c). *Sports and your child* [On-line]. Available: www.aap.org

Andersen, R. E., Crespo, C. J., Bartlett, S. J., Cheskin, L. J., & Pratt, M. (1998). Relationship of physical activity and television watching with body weight and level of fatness among children: Results from the Third National Health and Nutrition Examination Survey [see comments]. *Journal of the American Medical Association, 279*, 938–942.

Anderson, J. J., & Metz, J. A. (1993). Contributions of dietary calcium and physical activity to primary prevention of osteoporosis in females. *Journal of the American College of Nutrition, 12*, 378–383.

Anonymous. (1997). Youth Risk Behavior Surveillance: National College Health Risk Behavior Survey—United States, 1995. *Morbidity & Mortality Weekly Report. CDC Surveillance Summaries, 46*, 1–56.

Barr, S. I., & McKay, H. A. (1998). Nutrition, exercise, and bone status in youth. *International Journal of Sport Nutrition, 8*, 124–142.

Bernard, L., Lavalle, C., Gray-Donald, K., & Delisle, H. (1995). Overweight in Cree schoolchildren and adolescents associated with diet, low physical activity, and high television viewing. *Journal of the American Dietetic Association, 95*, 800–802.

Booth, M. L., Macakill, P., Phongsavan, P., McLellan, L., & Okely, T. (1998). Methods of the NSW Schools Fitness and Physical Activity Survey, 1997. *Journal of Science & Medicine in Sport, 1*, 111–124.

Boreham, C. A., Twisk, J., Savage, M. J., Cran, G. W., & Strain, J. J. (1997). Physical activity, sports participation, and risk factors in adolescents. *Medicine & Science in Sports & Exercise, 29*, 788–793.

Brustad, R. J. (1996). Attraction to physical activity in urban schoolchildren: Parental socialization and gender influences. *Research Quarterly for Exercise & Sport, 67*, 316–323.

Burrows Argote, R., Leiva Balich, L., Lillo Ganter, R., Pumarino Carte, H., Maya Castillo, L., & Muzzo Benavides, S. (1996). [*Influence of physical activity upon bone mineralization of school age children of both sexes*]. *Archivos Latinoamericanos de Nutrición, 46,* 11–15.

Calfas, K. J., Sallis, J. F., & Nader, P. R. (1991). The development of scales to measure knowledge and preference for diet and physical activity behavior in 4- to 8-year-old children. *Journal of Developmental & Behavioral Pediatrics, 12,* 185–190.

Capute, A. J., & Biehl, R. F. (1973). Developmental milestones: Birth through age 5. *Pediatric Clinics of North America, 20,* 3.

Cassell, C., Benedict, M., & Specker, B. (1996). Bone mineral density in elite 7- to 9-year-old female gymnasts and swimmers. *Medicine & Science in Sports & Exercise, 28,* 1243–1246.

Cooper, C., Cawley, M., Bhalla, A., Egger, P., Ring, F., & Morton, L. (1995). Childhood growth, physical activity, and peak bone mass in women. *Journal of Bone & Mineral Research, 10,* 940–947.

Courteix, D., Le Spessailles, E., Peres, S. L., Obert, P., Germain, P., & Benhamou, C. L. (1998). Effect of physical training on bone mineral density in prepubertal girls: A comparative study between impact-loading and non-impact-loading sports. *Osteoporosis International, 8,* 152–158.

Craig, S. B., Bandini., L. G., Lichenstein, A. H., Schaefer, E. J., & Dietz, W. H. (1996). The impact of physical activity on lipids, lipoproteins, and blood pressure in preadolescent girls. *Pediatrics, 98,* 389–395.

Craig, S., Goldberg, J., & Dietz, W. H. (1996). Psychosocial correlates of physical activity among fifth and eighth graders. *Preventive Medicine, 25,* 506–513.

Cresanta, J. L., Burke, G. L., Downey, A. M., Freedman, D. S., & Dietz, W. H. (1986). Prevention of atherosclerosis in childhood. *Pediatric Clinics of North America, 33,* 835–858.

Crocker, P. R., Bailey, D. A., Faulkner, R. A., Kowalski, K. C., & McGrath, R. (1997). Measuring general levels of physical activity: preliminary evidence for the Physical Activity Questionnaire for Older Children. *Medicine & Science in Sports & Exercise, 29,* 1344–1349.

Daly, R. M., Rich, P. A., Klein, R., & Bass, S. (1999). Effects of high-impact exercise on ultrasonic and biochemical indices of skeletal status: A prospective study in young male gymnasts. *Journal of Bone & Mineral Research, 14,* 1222–1230.

Davis, C., Katzman, D. K., Kaptein, S., Kirsh, C., Brewer, H., & Kalmbach, K. (1997). The prevalence of high-level exercise in the eating disorders: Etiological implications. *Comprehensive Psychiatry, 38,* 321–326.

Dennison, B. A., Straus, J. H., Mellits, E. D., & Charney, E. (1988). Childhood physical fitness tests: Predictor of adult physical activity levels? *Pediatrics, 82,* 324–330.

Dietz, W. (1991). Physical activity and childhood obesity. *Nutrition, 7,* 295–296.

DiLorenzo, T. M., Stucky-Ropp, R. C., Vander Wal, J. S., & Gotham, H. J. (1998). Determinants of exercise among children. II. A longitudinal analysis. *Preventive Medicine, 27,* 470–477.

Eisenmann, J. C., Katzmarzyk, P. T., Theriault, G., Song, T. M., Malina, R. M., & Bouchard, C. (2000). Cardiac dimensions, physical activity, and submaximal working capacity in youth of the Quebec Family Study. *European Journal of Applied Physiology & Occupational Physiology, 81,* 40–46.

Erickson, M. (1976). *Assessment and Management of Developmental Changes in Children.* St. Louis. MO: Mosby.

Fogelholm, M., Nuutinen, O., Pasanen, M., Myohanen, E., & Saatela, T. (1999). Parent-child relationship of physical activity patterns and obesity. *International Journal of Obesity & Related Metabolic Disorders, 23,* 1262–1268.

Francis, K. (1996). Physical activity in the prevention of cardiovascular disease. *Physical Therapy, 76,* 456–468.

Frankenburg, W. K. (1969). The Denver developmental screening test. *Developmental Medicine & Child Neurology, 11,* 260–2.

Frankenburg, W. K. (1984). Developmental screening. *Primary Care; Clinics in Office Practice, 11,* 535–47.

Frankenburg, W. K., Camp, B. W., Van Natta, P. A., & Demersseman, J. A. (1971). Reliability and stability of the Denver developmental screening test. *Child Development, 42,* 1315–25.

Frankenburg, W. K., & Dodds, J. B. (1967). The Denver developmental screening test. *Journal of Pediatrics, 71,* 181–91.

Frankenburg, W. K., Fandal, A. W., Sciarillo, W., & Burgess, D. (1981). The newly abbreviated and revised Denver Developmental Screening Test. *Journal of Pediatrics, 99,* 995–999.

Frankenburg, W. K., Goldstein, A. D., & Camp, B. W. (1971). The revised Denver developmental screening test: Its accuracy as a screening instrument. *Journal of Pediatrics, 1971, 79,* 988–95.

Garagiola, U., Buzzetti, M., Cardella, E., Confalonieri, F., Giani, E., & Polini, V. (1995). Immunological patterns during regular intensive training in athletes: Quantification and evaluation of a preventive pharmacological approach. *Journal of International Medical Research, 23,* 85–95.

Gavarry, O., Bernard, T., Giacomoni, M., Seymat, M., Euzet, J. P., & Falgairette, G. (1998). Continuous heart rate monitoring over 1 week in teenagers aged 11–16 years. *European Journal of Applied Physiology & Occupational Physiology,* 125–132.

Gordon-Larsen, P., McMurray, R. G., & Popkin, B. M. (1999). Adolescent physical activity and inactivity vary by ethnicity: The National Longitudinal Study of Adolescent Health. *Journal of Pediatrics, 135,* 301–306.

Gortmaker, S. L., Dietz, H. W., Jr., & Cheung, L. W. (1990). Inactivity, diet, and the fattening of America. *Journal of the American Dietetic Association, 90,* 1247–1255.

Gupta, R. K., Saini, D. P., Acharya, U., & Miglani, N. (1994). Impact of television on children. *Indian Journal of Pediatrics, 61,* 153–159.

Hernandez, B., Gortmaker, S. L., Colditz, G. A., Peterson, K. E., Laird, N. M., & Parra-Cabrera, S. (1999). Association of obesity with physical activity, television programs and other forms of video viewing among children in Mexico City. *International Journal of Obesity & Related Metabolic Disorders, 23,* 845–854.

Ilich, J. Z., Skugor, M., Hangartner, T., Baoshe, A., & Matkovic, V. (1998). Relation of nutrition, body composition and physical activity to skeletal development: A cross-sectional study in preadolescent females. *Journal of the American College of Nutrition, 17,* 136–147.

Jason, L. A., & Brackshaw, E. (1999). Access to TV contingent on physical activity: Effects on reducing TV-viewing and body-weight. *Journal of Behavior Therapy & Experimental Psychiatry, 30,* 145–151.

Katzmarzyk, P. T., Malina, R. M., & Bouchard, C. (1999). Physical activity, physical fitness, and coronary heart disease risk factors in youth: The Quebec family study. *Preventive Medicine, 29,* 555–562.

Katzmarzyk, P. T., Malina, R. M., Song, T. M., & Bouchard, C. (1998). Television viewing, physical activity, and health-related fitness of youth in the Quebec Family Study. *Journal of Adolescent Health, 23,* 318–325.

Keays, J. J., & Allison, K. R. (1995). The effects of regular moderate to vigorous physical activity on student outcomes: A review. *Canadian Journal of Public Health. Revue Canadienne de Sante Publique, 86,* 62–65.

Kimiecik, J. C., & Horn, T. S. (1998). Parental beliefs and children's moderate-to-vigorous physical activity. *Research Quarterly for Exercise & Sport, 69,* 163–175.

Kimiecik, J. C., Horn, T. S., & Shurin, C. S. (1996). Relationships among children's beliefs, perceptions of their parents' beliefs, and their moderate-to-vigorous physical activity. *Research Quarterly for Exercise & Sport, 67,* 324–336.

Kliorin, A. I., & Aleksandrovich, N. (1989). [Characteristics of the neuropsychological development of infants during the first year of life, engaged in swimming.] *Pediatriia, 2,* 16–18.

Kropp, R., & Schwartz, J. F. (1982). Water intoxication from swimming. *Journal of Pediatrics, 101,* 947.

Lee, W. T., Leuign, S. S., Wang, S. H., Xu, Y. C., Zeng, W. P., & Lau, J. (1994). Double-blind, controlled calcium supplementation and bone mineral accretion in children accustomed to a low-calcium diet [see comments]. *American Journal of Clinical Nutrition, 60,* 744–750.

Lindholm, C., Hagenfeldt, K., & Ringertz, H. (1995). Bone mineral content of young female former gymnasts. *Acta Paediatrica, 84,* 1109–1112.

Lindquist, C. H., Reynolds, K. D., & Goran, M. I. (1999). Sociocultural determinants of physical activity among children. *Preventive Medicine, 29,* 305–312.

Lopez Benedicto, M. A., Muviala Mateo, R. J., Gomez Diaz-Bravo, E., Sarria Chueca, A., & Giner Soria, A. (1988). Lipids, lipoproteins, apoproteins and physical exercise in young female athletes. *Anales Espanoles de Pediatria, 28,* 395–400.

Luepker, R. V., Perry, C. L., McKinlay, S. M., Nader, P. R., Parcel, G. S., & Stone, E. J. (1996). Outcomes of a field trial to improve children's dietary patterns and physical activity. The Child and Adolescent Trial for Cardiovascular Health. CATCH collaborative group. *Journal of the American Medical Association, 275,* 768–776.

Malina, R. M. (1994). Physical activity and training: Effects on stature and the adolescent growth spurt. *Medicine & Science in Sports & Exercise, 26*, 759–766.

Manios, Y., Kafatos, A., & Codrington, C. (1999). Gender differences in physical activity and physical fitness in young children in Crete. *Journal of Sports Medicine & Physical Fitness, 39*, 24–30.

Marcus, P. M., Newman, B., Moorman, P. G., Millikan, R. C., Baird, D. D., & Qaqish, B. (1999). Physical activity at age 12 and adult breast cancer risk (United States). *Cancer Causes & Control, 10*, 293–302.

Michaud, P. A., Narring, F., Cauderay, M., & Cavadini, C. (1999). Sports activity, physical activity and fitness of 9- to 19-year-old teenagers in the canton of Vaud (Switzerland). *Schweizerische Medizinische Wochenschrift. Journal Suisse de Medecine, 129*, 691–699.

Nickols-Richardson, S. M., Modlesky, C. M., O'Connor, P. J., & Lewis, R. D. (2000). Premenarcheal gymnasts possess higher bone mineral density than controls. *Medicine & Science in Sports & Exercise, 32*, 63–69.

Nickols-Richardson, S. M., O'Connor, P. J., Shapses, S. A., & Lewis, R. D. (1999). Longitudinal bone mineral density changes in female child artistic gymnasts. *Journal of Bone & Mineral Research, 14*, 994–1002.

Pate, R. R., Dowda, M., & Ross, J. G. (1990). Associations between physical activity and physical fitness in American children. *American Journal of Diseases of Children, 144*, 1123–1129.

Pate, R. R., Trost, S. G., Felton, G. M., Ward, D. S., Dowda, M., Saunders, R. (1997). Correlates of physical activity behavior in rural youth. *Research Quarterly for Exercise & Sport, 68*, 241–248.

Phillips, K. G. (1987). Swimming and water intoxication in infants [letter]. *Canadian Medical Association Journal, 136*, 1147.

Robinson, T. N. (1999). Reducing children's television viewing to prevent obesity: A randomized controlled trial. *Journal of the American Medical Association, 282*, 1561–1567.

Ross, J. (1987). The national children and youth fitness study II: A summary of findings. *Journal of Physical Education, Recreation and Dance, 58*, 51–56.

Ross, J., & Gilbert, G. (1985). The national children and youth fitness study: A summary of findings. *Journal of Physical Education, Recreation and Dance, 56*, 45–50.

Rubin, K., Schirduan, V., Gendreau, P., Sarfarazi, M., Mendola, R., & Dalsky, G. (1993). Predictors of axial and peripheral bone mineral density in healthy children and adolescents, with special attention to the role of puberty [see comments]. *Journal of Pediatrics, 123*, 863–870.

Shepard, R. J., & Shek, P. N. (1996). Impact of physical activity and sport on the immune system. *Reviews on Environmental Health, 11*, 133–147.

Simons-Morton, B. G., Parcel, G. S., Baranowski, T., Forthofer, R., & O'Hara, N. M. (1991). Promoting physical activity and a healthful diet among children: Results of a school-based intervention study. *American Journal of Public Health, 81*, 986–991.

Simons-Morton, B. G., Pate, R. R., & Simons-Morton, D. G. (1988). Prescribing physical activity to prevent disease. *Postgraduate Medicine, 83*, 165–166, 169–172, 175–176.

Simons-Morton, B. G., Taylor, W. C., Snider, S. A., & Huang, I. W. (1993). The physical activity of fifth-grade students during physical education classes. *American Journal of Public Health, 83*, 262–264.

Spurr, G. B., & Reina, J. C. (1987). Marginal malnutrition in school-aged Colombian girls: Dietary intervention and daily energy expenditure. *Human Nutrition–Clinical Nutrition, 41*, 93–104.

Stallings, V. A. (1997). Calcium and bone health in children: A review. *American Journal of Therapeutics, 4*, 259–273.

Trost, S. G., Pate, R. R., Freedson, P. S., Sallis, J. F., & Taylor, W. C. (2000). Using objective physical activity measures with youth: How many days of monitoring are needed? *Medicine & Science in Sports & Exercise, 32*, 426–431.

Trost, S. G., Pate, R. R., Saunders, R., Ward, D. S., Dowda, M., & Felton, G. (1997). A prospective study of the determinants of physical activity in rural fifth-grade children. *Preventive Medicine, 26*, 257–263.

Trost, S. G., Pate, R. R., Ward, D. S., Saunders, R., & Riner, W. (1999a). Correlates of objectively measured physical activity in adolescent youth. *American Journal of Preventive Medicine, 17*, 120–126.

Trost, S. G., Pate, R. R., Ward, D. S., Saunders, R., & Riner, W. (1999b). Determinants of physical activity in active and low-active sixth grade African-American youth. *Journal of School Health, 69*, 29–34.

Verloop, J., Rookus, M. A., Vanderkooy, K., & Van Leeuwen, F. E. (2000). Physical activity and breast cancer risk in women aged 20–54 years. *Journal of the National Cancer Institute, 92*, 128–135.

Ward, D. S., Trost, S. G., Felton, G., Saunders, R., Parson, M. A., & Dowda, M. (1997). Physical activity and physical fitness in African-American girls with and without obesity. *Obesity Research*, *5*, 572–7.

Weidle, B., & Aagaard, P. (1990). Infant swimming programs in Norway during the last 10 years. *Tidsskrift for Den Norske Laegeforening*, *110*, 3847–3850.

Weymans, M., & Reybrouck, T. (1989). Habitual level of physical activity and cardiorespiratory endurance capacity in children. *European Journal of Applied Physiology & Occupational Physiology*, *58*, 803–807.

Wong, N. D., Hei, T. K., Qaqundash, P. Y., Davidson, D. M., Bassin, S. L., & Gold, K. V. (1992). Television viewing and pediatric hypercholesterolemia. *Pediatrics*, *90*, 75–79.

Wong, W. W., Butte, N. F., Ellis, K. J., Hergenroeder, A. C., Hill, R. B., & Stuff, J. E. (1999). Pubertal African-American girls expend less energy at rest and during physical activity than Caucasian girls. *Journal of Clinical Endocrinology & Metabolism*, *84*, 906–911.

Zonderland, M. L., Erich, W. B., Peltenburg, A. L., Bernink, M. J., & Saris, W. H. (1985). Nutrition of premenarcheal athletes: Relation with the lipid and apolipoprotein profiles. *International Journal of Sports Medicine*, *6*, 329–335.

Zonderland, M. L., Erich, W. B., Peltenburg, A. L., Bernink, M. J., Havekes, L., & Thijssen, J. H. (1986). Plasma lipoprotein profile in relation to sex hormones in premenarcheal athletes. *International Journal of Sports Medicine*, *7*, 241–245.

7

Promotion of Safety, Security, and Well-Being

David A. Sleet
Division of Unintentional Injury Prevention,
National Center for Injury Prevention and Control,
Centers for Disease Control and Prevention, Atlanta, GA

James A. Mercy
Division of Violence Prevention,
National Center for Injury Prevention and Control,
Centers for Disease Control and Prevention, Atlanta, GA

INTRODUCTION

Safety and security are basic human needs (Maslow, 1943) and are prerequisites to health and well-being (Dane, Sleet, Lam, & Roppel, 1987; Maurice, 1998; Sleet & Dane, 1985). The United Nations in their 1994 report on human development stated that safety is a fundamental right and an essential condition for the sustainable development of societies (United Nations, 1994). Injury and physical trauma threaten safety and security and are barriers to healthy development (American Academy of Pediatrics, 1997; World Health Organization [WHO], 1989, 1996). As a positive characteristic, safety and security imply not only the absence of injury but also the presence of safety-promoting behaviors and environments. Specifically, safety suggests immediate freedom from harm and security implies freedom from anxiety or apprehension of harm.

Unfortunately, the safety and security required to ensure well-being is often compromised by intentional or unintentional injury. In every single industrialized country, injury is the leading killer of children, accounting for almost 40% of all deaths among children ages 1 to 14 (United Nations Foundation, 2001). In the United States, about 20 children die everyday from an injury, more than from all other diseases combined (Sleet, Schieber, & Dellinger, 2002).

Injury is the leading cause of death in each 5-year age group from ages 1 to 44 years and the eighth leading cause of death overall (Centers for Disease Control and Prevention [CDC], 2002). Table 7.1 describes the 10 leading causes of death by age group in 1998.

Injury also accounts for nearly three quarters of the deaths to 15- to 24-year-olds (CDC, 2002). Motor vehicle crashes account for the largest proportion (30%), followed by homicide (16%), other unintentional injuries (13%), and suicide (12%). The first three causes of death for young people are unintentional injuries resulting from motor vehicle crashes, violence due to homicide, and self-inflicted suicide. More than 5.5 million children ages 5 to 14 years and 7.4 million adolescents and young adults ages 15 to 24 years also suffer nonfatal injuries requiring emergency department care (Burt & Fingerhut, 1998). For each death due to injury, there are approximately 19 hospitalizations, 233 emergency department visits, and 450 physician visits (CDC, 2000b). Injuries requiring medical attention or resulting in restricted activity affect more than 20 million children and adolescents and cost $17 billion annually for medical care (Danseco, Miller, & Spicer, 2000).

These are startling statistics about the well-being of young people. Even more startling is that most of these injuries are preventable. Former U.S. Surgeon General C. Everett Koop reminds us optimistically that "we can make our world a safer place for future generations to grow up unharmed by the dangers that surround us" (O'Donnell & Mickalide, 1998).

Variables that affect safety and security and contribute to injury include sociocultural variables (e.g., crime, crowding, social norms), economic variables (e.g., income), caregiver behaviors (e.g., supervision), alcohol and drug use, risk-taking behavior (e.g., drinking and driving), behavioral disorders (e.g., conduct disorders, impulsivity); environmental variables (e.g., neighborhoods, streets, housing), and unsafe products (Brown & Peterson, 1997; Lowry, Sleet, Duncan, Powell, & Kolbe, 1995). Because of the variety of injury threats related to environments, sociocultural variables, and behavioral risks, injuries present a tremendous threat to children's physical, cognitive, and social-emotional development (Tolan, 1988). Young people are at greatest risk for this type of harm.

Despite the threats to safety and security, today there is a better understanding of how to promote safety and define and prevent injury. Injuries are defined as "unintentional or intentional damage to the body resulting from acute exposure to thermal, mechanical, electrical, or chemical energy or from the absence of such essentials as heat or oxygen" (National Committee for Injury Prevention and Control, 1989). In addition, the term injury includes bodily harm that results from either violence or un-

TABLE 7.1
10 Leading Causes of Deaths by Age Group—1998

Rank					Age Groups						
	<1	1–4	5–9	10–14	15–24	25–34	35–44	45–54	55–64	65+	Total
1	Congenital Anomalies 6,212	Unintentional Injuries 1,935	Unintentional Injuries 1,544	Unintentional Injuries 1,710	Unintentional Injuries 13,349	Unintentional Injuries 12,045	Malignant Neoplasms 17,022	Malignant Neoplasms 45,747	Malignant Neoplasms 87,024	Heart Disease 605,673	Heart Disease 724,859
2	Short Gestation 4,101	Congenital Anomalies 564	Malignant Neoplasms 487	Malignant Neoplasms 526	Homicide 5,560	Suicide 5,365	Unintentional Injuries 15,127	Heart Disease 35,056	Heart Disease 65,068	Malignant Neoplasms 384,186	Malignant Neoplasms 541,532
3	SIDS 2,822	Homicide 399	Congenital Anomalies 198	Suicide 317	Suicide 4,135	Homicide 4,565	Heart Disease 13,593	Unintentional Injuries 10,946	Bronchitis Emphysema Asthma 10,162	Cerebro-vascular 139,144	Cerebro-vascular 158,448
4	Maternal Complications 1,343	Malignant Neoplasms 365	Homicide 170	Homicide 290	Malignant Neoplasms 1,699	Malignant Neoplasms 4,385	Suicide 6,837	Liver Disease 5,744	Cerebro-vascular 9,653	Bronchitis Emphysema Asthma 97,896	Bronchitis Emphysema Asthma 112,584
5	Respiratory Distress Synd. 1,295	Heart Disease 214	Heart Disease 156	Congenital Anomalies 173	Heart Disease 1,057	Heart Disease 3,207	HIV 5,746	Cerebro-vascular 5,709	Diabetes 8,705	Pneumonia & Influenza 82,989	Unintentional Injuries 97,835
6	Placenta Cord Membranes 961	Pneumonia & Influenza 146	Pneumonia & Influenza 70	Heart Disease 170	Congenital Anomalies 450	HIV 2,912	Homicide 3,567	Suicide 5,131	Unintentional Injuries 7,340	Diabetes 48,974	Pneumonia & Influenza 91,871

(continued on next page)

TABLE 7.1 (continued)

Rank	<1	1–4	5–9	10–14	15–24	25–34	35–44	45–54	55–64	65+	Total
7	Perinatal Infections 815	Septicemia 89	Bronchitis Emphysema Asthma 54	Bronchitis Emphysema Asthma 98	Bronchitis Emphysema Asthma 239	Cerebro-vascular 670	Liver Disease 3,370	Diabetes 4,386	Liver Disease 5,279	Unintentional Injuries 32,975	Diabetes 64,751
8	Unintentional Injuries 754	Perinatal Period 75	Benign Neoplasms 52	Pneumonia & Influenza 51	Pneumonia & Influenza 215	Diabetes 636	Cerebro-vascular 2,650	HIV 3,120	Pneumonia & Influenza 3,856	Nephritis 22,640	Suicide 30,575
9	Intrauterine Hypoxia 461	Cerebro-vascular 57	Cerebro-vascular 35	Cerebro-vascular 47	HIV 194	Pneumonia & Influenza 531	Diabetes 1,885	Bronchitis Emphysema Asthma 2,828	Suicide 2,963	Alzheimer's Disease 22,416	Nephritis 26,182
10	Pneumonia & Influenza 441	Benign Neoplasms 53	HIV 29	Benign Neoplasms 32	Cerebro-vascular 178	Liver Disease 506	Pneumonia & Influenza 1,400	Pneumonia & Influenza 2,167	Septicemia 2,093	Septicemi 19,012	Liver Disease 25,192

Source: National Center for Health Statistics, 2000. Chart developed by the National Center for Injury Prevention and Control, CDC.

intentional causes. Prior to 1960, there was a perception that injuries were caused by accidents—random events that occurred suddenly and unpredictably. However, scientists in the injury prevention field have demonstrated that public health can use the same epidemiological techniques for injury control that are used to control infectious disease (Bonnie, Fulco, & Liverman, 1999). It has also been recognized that injury patterns change over the course of life and are closely related to developmental stage (Dahlberg & Potter, 2001; Williams, Guerra, & Elliott, 1997; Zuckerman & Duby, 1985). This knowledge, combined with the understanding that the prevention of injuries and the promotion of safety are integral to improving safety, security, and well-being, has also enabled experts to determine the behaviors and activities necessary to promote safety and security at various points across the lifespan.

The purpose of this chapter is to describe the major threats to safety and security in childhood and adolescence, recognize the individual, social, and environmental determinants of injury, and identify the elements of safety and security that can be promoted to prevent injury and increase well-being for infants, children, and adolescents.

ENVIRONMENTAL AND DEVELOPMENTAL INFLUENCES ON SAFETY AND SECURITY

The likely causes of injury, the appropriate safety promotion activities, and the individual characteristics that improve children's safety and security change as an individual matures. Figure 7.1 shows the major causes of injury as they relate to developmental changes in injury death rates by single year of ages from birth to age 17. Death rates are higher for unintentional injuries than violence at every age, and the U-shaped death rate curves by manner of death parallel one another. They show quite dramatically the high rates of injury in young children, followed by a drop in middle childhood, then a sharp rise in late childhood and early adolescence that continues through late adolescence and early adulthood.

With regard to safety promotion, the influences of the social environment (families, peers, schools, communities), the physical environment (streets, neighborhoods, playgrounds, pools), and products (cribs, toys, weapons) also change as the individual develops. These changes profoundly affect the potential safety and health outcomes during a child's or adolescent's growth and development. Specific ecological contexts may also influence risk and protection as displayed in Figure 7.2. This ecological model of life course development (adapted from Williams et al., 1997) reinforces the fluidity of levels of influence on safety and security as the life course progresses.

According to this model, during infancy through early adolescence, the family and home are primary influences on safety. Also influential in early and late childhood is the acquisition and adoption of individual skills and safety behaviors, school and peer influences, and the community's actions. Moving into and through adolescence, schools and peers have even greater influence. In addition, attributes related to social bonds and personal protective practices assume greater importance, although characteristics of the family and home environment remain essen-

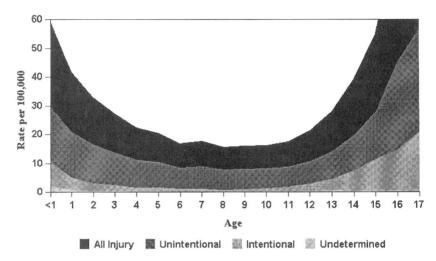

FIG. 7.1.   Injury fatality rates by single year of age and manner of death, United States, 1998.

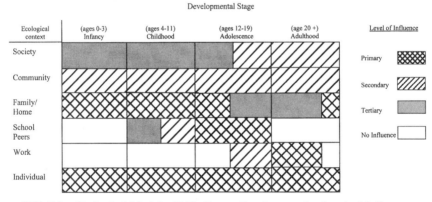

FIG. 7.2.   Ecological Model of Life Course Development by Level of Influence. Adopted from Williams, Guerra, and Elliott, 1997.

tial to ensure safety. In late adolescence and early adulthood, the work setting and social norms emerge as important influences on safety.

With this ecological model in mind, safety promotion strategies should be matched to the developmental stage of children and adolescents and be linked across stages, beginning in infancy. Programs that address developmental needs, remove barriers to meeting developmental milestones, and foster support for healthy development across a variety of ecological contexts are crucial to promoting safety and security (Williams et al., 1997). Table 7.2 provides some examples of attributes of safety and security across developmental stages and ecological contexts.

TABLE 7.2

Attributes of Safety and Security by Developmental Stage and Ecological Context

Infancy

Family/Home: Strong emotional bond between infant and caregiver
                  Use of positive reinforcement by caregiver to promote pro-social behavior
                  High caregiver awareness and knowledge of home safety measures
                  Active supervisory style by parent
                  Absence of home hazards

Community: Presence of parental support networks
                  High population awareness of indicators of child abuse and neglect
                  Home visitation programs
                  Environmental protections (e.g. reduced lead exposure)

Childhood

Individual: Development of social skills and ability to regulate emotions
                  Involvement in activities that promote positive attachments and pro-social norms
                  Acquisition of early academic skills and knowledge
                  Impulse control (e.g. crossing a street after a ball)
                  Frequent use of personal protection (e.g. bike helmets, safety seats)

Family/Home: High awareness and knowledge child management and parenting skills
                  Caregiver participation in child's education and social activities
                  Frequent parent protective behaviors (e.g. use of child safety seats)
                  Presence of home safety equipment (e.g. smoke alarms, cabinet locks)

School/Peers: Promotion of home-school partnerships
                  Availability of enrichment and tutoring programs
                  Social norm development for protective behaviors (e.g. wearing helmets)
                  Absence of playground hazards
                  Management support for safety and injury prevention
                  Injury reduction and safety promotion policies and programs

Community: Availability of pro-social activities for children and their parents
                  Active surveillance of environmental hazards
                  Effective prevention policies in place (e.g. pool fencing)
                  Commitment to emergency medicals services for children and trauma care
                  Adoption of safety culture

Adolescence

Individual: Involvement with pro-social peers
                  Building friendships
                  Developing a sense of self identity
                  Using personal protective equipment often (e.g., seat belts)
                  Refusal skills training for alcohol and drug use

Family/Home: High awareness and knowledge of adolescent management and parenting skills
                  Monitor access to lethal weapons
                  Caregiver participation in adolescent's education and social activities
                  Active involvement in teen driving contracts and monitoring
                  Installation and frequent testing of smoke alarms

(continued on next page)

TABLE 7.2   (*continued*)

Schools/Peers:	Availability of programs to facilitate entry into the workforce
	Availability of instruction in problem-solving, refusal skills and anger management
	School safety policies and programs (e.g. bike helmet use, firearms)
	Frequent contact with positive peer modeling
Community:	Low availability of lethal weapons and alcohol
	Availability of safe places for adolescents to socialize
	Policies that support enforcement of safety laws
	Effective emergency medical services and trauma care
	A commitment to environmental safety

INTERVENTIONS TO PROMOTE SAFETY AND SECURITY

Interventions to promote safety and security include social and environmental change, individual behavioral change, family and parental change, and changes in exposure to hazardous products. These interventions vary in their application and implementation across developmental stages. Effective interventions for promoting safety and security, by developmental stage, are presented next.

Infancy

An infant's safety is primarily dependent on three factors: an appropriately safe home and community environment, adequate and responsible parenting, and access to regular and affordable health care. Safety in the home can be achieved through a variety of means including close monitoring of the child's environment. For example, monitoring lead levels and removing environmental toxins will help prevent brain damage and subsequent learning disabilities in young infants (U.S. General Accounting Office [USGAO], 1999; Williams et al., 1997). In addition, efforts to reduce exposure of children to domestic violence will help reduce potential for aggression, phobias, and poor academic performance and reduce effects such as depression, low self-esteem, violence, and criminal behavior later in life (Packard Foundation, 1999). Other environmental interventions, such as installing stair gates and window guards above the first floor, avoiding the use of infant walkers, storing medications in child resistant containers, installing four-sided fencing in residential pools, and using approved child safety seats, are effective means of reducing unintentional injury among very young children (Grossman, 2000).

There are many programs that help promote parenting skills and provider behaviors that are necessary to ensure the safety of very young children. Interventions such as home visitation, parent training, and clinical preventive services have been found to help parents improve the safety and well-being of infants and children (DiGuiseppi & Roberts, 2000; Green, 1994; Krugman, 1993; Tertinger, Greene, & Lutzker, 1984). For example, home visitation involves weekly to monthly visits by a trained professional to provide parenting and health information, emotional support, counseling, and referrals to outside agencies for high-risk families (Kellermann, Fuqua-Whitley, Rivara, & Mercy, 1998). Although findings are mixed, some studies have found evidence that, over the long-term, visited children have lower rates of antisocial behavior, drug use and abuse, and injuries than those who did not receive home visits (Olds, 1998).

Parenting programs are also helpful. Parenting programs are designed to improve the emotional bond between parents and their children, to encourage parents to use consistent and contingent child-rearing methods, and to help develop parental problem-solving skills and self-control in raising children. Several programs have found this type of training to be successful and there is some evidence of a long-term impact in reducing antisocial behavior in children (Hawkins, Von Cleve, & Catalano, 1991; Patterson, Capaldi, & Bank, 1991).

In addition, clinical preventive services offer another option for helping parents ensure infant safety. Counseling and brief inventions delivered by pediatricians and clinical counselors to parents of infants and young children have been found to modify some parent practices related to preventing unintentional injury by encouraging parents to follow basic safety guidelines with their babies. (DiGuiseppi et al., 2000).

Finally, among the most fundamental of safety promotion activities for very young children is regular health screenings. These screenings can alert medical providers and parents to possible safety risks that can be caused by genetic predispositions, temperament, environmental causes, or a combination of these factors. For example, neurological impairments and brain damage can affect risk patterns and expressions of behavior that influence safety and security especially related to violent behavior (Loeber & Hay, 1994; Mirsky & Siegel, 1994; National Research Council, 1993; Reiss & Roth, 1993; Tolan, 1988). Screening may help identify these risks early in life.

Childhood

Access to child injury prevention resources and opportunities, the quality of the environments where children spend their time, the involvement of caring, responsible adults, as well as the expression of individual risk behaviors are important determinants of safety and security in childhood. For example, safety as well as health is related to access to quality educational opportunities. Early childhood education resources such as Head Start can be helpful by giving young children the skills and self-esteem necessary to be successful in school and to increase school bonding (Kellermann et al., 1998). Long-term, follow-up studies have found that participation in early enrichment activities have positive benefits for children, including less involvement in violent and other delinquent behaviors (Berrueta-Clement, Schweinhart, Barnett, Epstein, & Weikart, 1984; Lally, Mangione, & Honig, 1988; Schweinhart, Barnes, & Weikart, 1993).

Similarly, social development programs seek to improve children's social skills with peers and others and to promote behavior that is positive, friendly, and cooperative (Guerra & Williams, 1996; Richards & Dodge, 1982). These programs typically focus on one or more of the following dimensions: anger management, perspective taking, moral development, social skills, social problem solving, or conflict resolution (Hawkins, Catalano, Kosterman, Abbott, & Hill, 1999). These programs can be effective in reducing problem behaviors and improving social skills (Hawkins et al., 1999; Howell & Bilchick, 1995). Such programs have been shown to have short- and long-term positive impacts for children's safety.

In addition to formal program efforts, involvement by parents, teachers, and other involved community members are needed to promote children's safety. Increased supervision of children at home and in the community is necessary to reduce many childhood injuries (Peterson, Ewigman, & Kivlahan, 1993). Increased involvement of parents in rule setting and enforcement can affect child injury risk behaviors at an early age (Peterson & Roberts, 1992; Roberts & Peterson, 1984). Also, social and environmental change such as speed enforcement and traffic calming—a method to slow speeds of vehicles on residential streets—are methods to reduce child pedestrian injuries (CDC, in press; Stevenson & Sleet, 1996). Using childproof medication containers to reduce poisoning, using cabinet locks, keeping guns unloaded, locked, and out of reach, installing window guards and smoke alarms, and reducing home hazards to prevent falls are also effective injury prevention measures. In the community, providing access to 911 telephone service and making streets pedestrian- and bike-friendly are other system-level strategies.

Physicians and other health care professionals can also continue their role in ensuring the safety of individuals as they move developmentally from infants to children through the provision of anticipatory guidance (Smith, 1990). Guidance by physicians to parents of small children in the clinical setting has been found effective in reducing injury risk exposure through modifications in parent practices and home environments (Bass, Christoffel, Widome, 1993).

Finally, older children can do their part in taking responsibility for their own safety. Adults can encourage and model particular safety behaviors but, in certain circumstances, it is up to the child to carry out safety guidelines and behaviors that parents and other adults have taught, provided they possess the developmentally appropriate ability (Schieber & Thompson, 1996).

Actions that prevent or reduce unintentional injury that are often under the child's direct control include wearing bicycle helmets, using safety belts, and using personal protective equipment like shin guards and face masks while playing sports. Child training programs directed to modify some individual child safety behaviors have been found to be effective (Jones, Kazdin, & Haney, 1981; Peterson, 1984; Peterson & Roberts, 1992).

Adolescence

Achieving safety for adolescents includes many of the same features, such as parental involvement and individual behavior change, as in earlier stages of life. At the same time, however, as adolescents mature, more intensive personalized interventions may be necessary to reduce the chances of injury (CDC, 2000a). For example, in many cases, mentoring can give adolescents the outside help they need to stay safe. Mentoring programs that match youth (particularly youth growing up in a single parent family or in adverse situations) with a nonfamilial caring adult is one example (Mihalic & Grotpeter, 1997). The goals of mentoring are to assist youth in developing skills and to provide a sustained relationship with a more experienced person who serves as a positive role model and guide (Guerra & Williams 1996). An evaluation of the Big Brothers/Big Sisters Program found that a positive mentoring relationship led to reductions in self-reported antisocial behaviors, such as hitting and drug use (Grossman & Garry, 1997).

Family therapy also has been proven effective in reducing the likelihood of adolescent involvement in high-risk activities. Family therapy has the goal of improving communication, interaction, and problem solving between parents and their children (Guerra & Williams, 1996). These programs are most appropriate for families experiencing a high level of conflict and behavioral problems (Guerra & Williams, 1996). There is substantial evidence that family therapy can be effective in improving family functioning and reducing child behavior problems (Hazelrigg, Cooper, & Borduin, 1987; Shadish, 1992).

Parental involvement remains essential for safety promotion in adolescence. Authoritative yet warm parenting styles have been shown to help reduce the risks of adolescent risk-taking behavior (Hartos, Eitel, Haynie, & Simons-Morton, 2000; Simons-Morton & Hartos, 2002). Parents can be influential in helping teenagers limit their risks, as in driving, and reinforce laws designed to protect teens, such as graduated licensing (Rosenberg & Martinez, 1996).

Modifying individual behavior of adolescents is also essential to safety. Behavior change strategies that encourage the use of personal protection such as safety belts, motorcycle helmets, personal flotation devices, and protective sports gear, and the reduction of drinking and driving can help reduce adolescent injuries. Reducing bullying and gang involvement can help prevent violence-related injury among youth. Injury risk behavior change can also be changed through laws, policies, and environmental modifications (Schieber, Gilchrist, & Sleet, 2000). Examples of such policies that can reduce the risk for the leading cause of death to adolescents (vehicle occupant injuries) include zero tolerance alcohol laws, minimum drinking age laws, lowering legal limits on blood alcohol levels to 0.08g/dL, and primary safety belt use laws (CDC, 2001; Zaza, Carande-Kulis, & Sleet, 2001).

CONCLUSIONS

Promoting safety and security should include efforts to: (a) eliminate or reduce hazards and risks in the physical environment, social, and family life of children; (b) eliminate or reduce the occurrence of injury by modifying behaviors, environments, and hazardous products, or by reducing exposure to injury; (c) implement programs to reduce both violence and unintentional injuries; (d) enhance emergency services and urgent care to minimize trauma when an injury occurs; and (e) increase access to appropriate treatment and adequate rehabilitation services to reduce re-injury.

It is important to keep in mind that taking risks is an important part of growing up. Risk taking can enhance learning by providing children an opportunity to test their limits and increase the adaptation to their environment. Life would be boring without some risks. The goal of promoting safety and security is not to eliminate all risk but to minimize, manage, and control risk exposures and outcomes.

Individuals, families, communities, workplaces, schools, and other social institutions are important partners in creating a "culture of safety" for children. Promoting safety and security in all of these settings will increase the chances for child well-being. Therefore, an approach that can be tailored within the context of multiple environments according to developmental stage is what is needed to prevent injury and violence and promote safety and security through the life span.

Table 7.3 presents a matrix of injury prevention strategies. This model allows for strategies to be considered together, by developmental stage (infancy, childhood, adolescence), and in ecological context (family/home, community, schools/peers, societal). Some interventions within an ecological context influence several developmental periods (e.g., lead monitoring in the community or parent training in the family). The framework in Table 7.3 reinforces the common theme of this chapter: What is ultimately needed to promote safety and security of children is a continuum of effective programs and services across the developmental spectrum that addresses salient ecological contexts. Continuity in promoting safety and in safety practices is important through the life course because, typically, those who exhibit safety early in life are more likely to continue to be safe later in life. Safety promotion has the strong potential for increasing well-being related to many elements in the physical, cognitive, and social-emotional domains, and throughout the life cycle. Programs that promote safety and security by implementing science-based interventions at each developmental stage will decrease the likelihood of injury and increase the likelihood that optimal well-being will be achieved.

TABLE 7.3

Prevention Strategies by Developmental Stage (Infancy Through Adolescence) and Ecological Context

| | *Developmental Stage* | | |
Ecological Context	*Infancy (ages 0–3)*	*Childhood (ages 3–11)*	*Adolescence (ages 12–19)*
Family/Home	• Home visitation services to strengthen families • Parenting training for new parents • Respite day care centers or drop–in programs • Increase access to prenatal and postnatal service • Install 4–sided fencing on pools • Avoid infant walkers • Use stair gates • Use approved child safety seats	• Parenting training • Remove home hazards • Avoid dog breed likely to bite • Provide screens or grills on upstairs windows • Use bicycle helmets • Use child safety seats, booster seats and seat belts • Reduce access to poisons • Install working smoke alarms • Monitor pedestrian crossing • Keep guns unloaded and locked	• Home–school partnership programs to promote parental involvement • Family therapy • Install and test smoke alarms on all floors • Wear safety belts • Enforce zero tolerance alcohol policies • Support graduated licensing programs
School/Peers		• Social development training • Preschool enrichment programs including Head Start • Bullying prevention programs • School policies to prevent injuries • Use protective equipment in sports	• Mentoring • Academic enrichment programs • Provide education to promote healthy relations with the opposite sex and decrease dating violence • Social development training in anger management, social skills, and problem–solving • Develop and enforce school safety policies • Insist on using protective gear in sports

(continued on next page)

93

TABLE 7.3 (continued)

Developmental Stage

Ecological Context	Infancy (ages 0–3)	Childhood (ages 3–11)	Adolescence (ages 12–19)
Community	• Lead monitoring and toxin removal • Foster care programs • Inspect and modify playground hazards • Institute traffic calming • Reduce hot water heater temperatures	• Lead monitoring and toxin removal • Foster care programs • Provide safe pedestrian and bike paths • Dial 911 access and child training	• Create safe havens for children on high–risk routes to and from school • Provide after–school programs to extend adult supervision • Recreational programs • Multi–component gang prevention programs • Train health care professionals in identification and referral of high–risk youth • Separate bicyclists from motorists
Social/Cultural Level	• Deconcentrate lower–income housing • Reduce income inequality	• Public information campaigns to promote pro–social norms • Reduce levels of media violence • Develop a "culture of safety" • Educate drivers to share the road	• Reduce levels of media violence • Public information campaigns to promote pro–social norms • Educational incentives for at–risk, disadvantaged high school students • Enforce laws prohibiting illegal transfers of guns to youth • Support bicycle and motorcycle helmet laws • Support restrictions on access to alcohol

REFERENCES

American Academy of Pediatrics. (1997). *Injury control.* Oak Brook, IL: Author.

Bass, J. L., Christoffel, K. K., & Widome, M. (1993). Childhood Injury prevention counseling in primary care settings: A critical review of the literature. *Pediatrics, 9,* 544–550.

Berrueta-Clement, J. R., Schweinhart, L. J., Barnett, W. S., Epstein, A. S., & Weikart, D. P. (1984). *Changed lives: The effects of the Perry Preschool Program on youth through age 19.* Ypsilanti, MI: High/Scope Press.

Bonnie, R. J., Fulco, C. E., & Liverman, C. T. (Eds.). (1999). *Reducing the burden of injury: Advancing prevention and treatment.* Committee on Injury Prevention and Control, Division of Health Promotion and Disease Prevention, Institute of Medicine. Washington, DC: National Academy Press.

Brown, D., & Peterson, L. (1997). Unintentional injury and child abuse and neglect. In R. T. Ammerman & M. Hersen (Eds.), *Handbook of prevention and treatment with children and adolescents* (pp. 332–356). New York: Wiley.

Burt, C. W., & Fingerhut, L. A. (1998). Injury visits to hospital emergency departments: United States, 1992–1995. *Vital Health Statistics, 13,* 1–76.

Centers for Disease Control and Prevention. (2000a). *Best practices for violence prevention.* Atlanta, GA: Author.

Centers for Disease Control and Prevention. (2000b). *President's task force on environmental health risks and safety risks to children: Briefing document.* Unpublished manuscript.

Centers for Disease Control and Prevention. (2002). *Web-based injury statistics query and reporting system (WISQARS).* National Center for Injury Prevention and Control. Available: http://www.cdc.gov/ncipc/wisqars

Centers for Disease Control and Prevention. (in press). Proceedings of the Panel to Prevent Pedestrian Injuries. National Center for Injury Prevention and Control, Atlanta, GA: Author.

Centers for Disease Control and Prevention. (2001). Motor-vehicle occupant injury: strategies for increasing use of child safety seats, increasing use of safety belts, and reducing alcohol-impaired driving. A report on recommendations of the Task Force on Community Preventive Services. *MMWR*; *50* (RR-7): 1–13.

Dahlberg, L. L., & Potter, L. B. (2001). Youth violence. Developmental pathways and prevention challenges. *American Journal of Preventive Medicine, 20,* 3–14.

Dane, J. K., Sleet, D. A., Lam, D. J., & Roppel, C. E. (1987). Determinants of wellness in children: An exploratory study. *Health Values, 11,* 13–19.

Danseco, E. R., Miller, T. R., & Spicer, R. S. (2000). Incidence and costs of 1987–1994 childhood injuries: Demographic breakdowns. *Pediatrics, 105.* [On-line] Available: www.pediatrics.org/cgi/content/full/105/2/e27

DiGuiseppi, C., & Roberts, I. (2000). Individual level injury prevention strategies in the clinical setting. *The Future of Children, 10,* 53–82.

Green, M. (Eds.). (1994). *Bright futures: Guidelines for health supervision of infants, children and adolescents.* Arlington, VA: Center for Education in Maternal and Child Health.

Grossman, D. C. (2000). The history of injury control and the epidemiology of child and adolescent injuries. *The Future of Children, 10,* 23–52.

Grossman, J. B., & Garry, E. M. (1997). Mentoring—A proven delinquency prevention strategy. *Juvenile Justice Bulletin.* Washington, DC: U.S. Department of Justice.

Guerra, N. G., & Williams, K. R. (1996). *A program planning guide for youth violence prevention: A risk focused approach.* Boulder, CO: Center for the Study and Prevention of Violence.

Hartos, J. L., Eitel, P., Haynie, D. L., & Simons-Morton, B. G. (2000). Can I take the car? Relations among parenting practices and adolescent problem-driving practices. *Journal of Adolescent Research, 15,* 352–367.

Hawkins, J. D., Catalano, R. F., Kosterman, R., Abbott, R., & Hill, K. G. (1999). Preventing adolescent health-risk behaviors by strengthening protection during childhood. *Archives of Pediatrics & Adolescent Medicine, 153,* 226–34.

Hawkins, J. D., Von Cleve, E., & Catalano, R. F. (1991). Reducing early childhood aggression: Results of a primary prevention program. *Journal of the American Academy of Child and Adolescent Psychiatry, 30*, 208–217.

Hazelrigg, M. D., Cooper, H. M., & Borduin, C. M. (1987). Evaluating the effectiveness of family therapies: An integrative review and analysis. *Psychological Bulletin, 101*, 428–442.

Howell, J. C., & Bilchick, S. (Eds.). (1995). *Guide for implementing the comprehensive strategy for serious violent and chronic juvenile offenders* (NCJ-153681). Washington, DC: Office of Juvenile Justice and Delinquency Prevention.

Jones, R. T., Kazdin, A. E., & Haney J. I. (1981). Social validation and training of emergency fire safety skills for potential injury prevention and life saving. *Journal of Applied Behavior Analysis, 14*, 245–260.

Kellermann, A. L., Fuqua-Whitley, D. S., Rivara, F. P., & Mercy, J. A. (1998). Preventing youth violence: What works? *Annual Review of Public Health, 19*, 271–292.

Krugman, R. D. (1993). Universal home visiting: A recommendation from the U.S. Advisory Board on child abuse and neglect. *The Future of Children, 3*, 184–191.

Lally, J. R., Mangione, P. L., & Honig, A. S. (1988). The Syracuse University Family Development Research Project: Long-range impact of an early intervention with low-income children and their families. In D. R. Powell (Ed.), *Annual advances in applied developmental psychology: Parent education as an early childhood intervention* (p. 59). Norwood, NJ: Ablex.

Loeber, R., & Hay, D. F. (1994). Developmental approaches to aggression and conduct problems. In M. Rutter & D. F. Hay (Eds.), *Development through life: A handbook for clinicians* (pp. 488–516). Malden, MA: Blackwell Scientific.

Lowry, R., Sleet, D., Duncan, C., Powell, K., & Kolbe, L. (1995). Adolescents at risk for violence. *Educational Psychology Review, 7*, 7–39.

Maslow, A. (1943). A theory of human motivation. *Psychological Review, 50*, 370–396.

Maurice, P. (1998). *Safety and safety promotion: Conceptual and operational aspects.* Quebec City; (Unpublished report).

Mihalic, S. F., & Grotpeter, J. K. (1997). *Blueprints for violence prevention: Big brothers/Big sisters of America, book two.* Boulder, CO: Center for the Study and Prevention of Violence.

Mirsky, A. F., & Siegel, A. (1994). The neurobiology of violence and aggression. In A. J. Reiss, K. A. Miczek, & J. A. Roth (Eds.), *Understanding and preventing violence: Vol. 2. Biobehavioral influences* (pp. 59–172). Washington, DC: National Academy Press.

National Committee for Injury Prevention and Control. (1989). Injury prevention: Meeting the challenge. [suppl.] *American Journal of Preventive Medicine, 5*, 1–303. New York: Oxford University Press.

National Research Council. (1993). *Losing generations: Adolescents in high-risk settings.* Washington, DC: National Academy Press.

Olds, D. L. (1998). Long-term effects of nurse home visitation on children's criminal and antisocial behavior: 15-year follow-up of a randomized controlled trial. *Journal of the American Medical Association, 280*, 1238–1244.

O'Donnell, G. W., & Mickalide, A. D. (1998). *SafeKids at home, at play, and on the way. A report to the Nation on unintentional childhood injury.* Washington, DC: National SafeKids Campaign, May.

Packard Foundation. (1999). Domestic violence and children. *The Future of Children, 9*(3), 4–144.

Patterson, G. R., Capaldi, D., & Bank, L. (1991). An early starter model for predicting delinquency. In D. J. Pepler & K. H. Rubin (Eds.), *The development and treatment of childhood aggression.* Hillsdale, NJ: Lawrence Erlbaum Associates.

Peterson, L. (1984). The "safe at home" game. Training comprehensive safety skills to latchkey children. *Behavior Modification, 8*, 474–494.

Peterson, L., & Roberts, M. C. (1992). Compliance, misdirection and effective prevention of children's injuries. *American Psychologist, 23*, 375–387.

Peterson, L., Ewigman, B., & Kivlahan, C. (1993). Judgments regarding appropriate child supervision to prevent injury: The role of environmental risk and child age. *Child Development, 64*, 934–950.

Reiss, A. J., & Roth, J. A. (Eds.). (1993). *Understanding and preventing violence: Vol. 1.* Washington, DC: National Academy Press.

Richards, B. A., & Dodge, K. A. (1982). Social maladjustment and problem solving in school-aged children. *Journal of Consultative Clinical Psychology, 50*, 226–233.

Roberts, M. C., & Peterson, L. (1984). *Prevention of Problems in Childhood.* New York: Wiley.

Rosenberg, M. L., & Martinez, R. (1996). Graduated licensure: A win-win proposition for teen drivers and parents. *Pediatrics, 98,* 959–960.

Schieber, R. S., & Thompson, N. (1996). Developmental risk factors for childhood pedestrian injuries. *Injury Prevention, 2,* 228–236.

Schieber, R. S., Gilchrist, J., & Sleet, D. A. (2000). Legislative and regulatory strategies to reduce childhood unintentional injuries. *The Future of Children, 10*(1), 111–136.

Schweinhart, L. J., Barnes, H. V., & Weikart, D. P. (1993). *Significant benefits: The High/Scope Perry Preschool Project Study through age 27.* Ypsilanti, MI: High/Scope Press.

Shadish, W. R. (1992). Do family and marital psychotherapies change what people do? A meta-analysis of behavior outcomes. In T. D. Cook, H. Cooper, D. S. Cordray, H. Hartmann, L. V. Hedges, & R. J. Light (Eds.), *Meta-analysis for explanation: A casebook* (pp. 129–208). New York: Russell Sage Foundation.

Simons-Morton, B. G., & Hartos, J. (2002). Application of authoritative parenting to adolescent health behavior. In R. DiClemente, R. Crosby, & M. Kegler (Eds.), *Emerging theories and models in health promotion research and practice.* San Francisco: Jossey-Bass.

Sleet, D. A., Schieber, R. A., & Dellinger, A. (2002). Childhood injuries. In *The Encyclopedia of Public Health* (pp. 184–187). (L. Breslow, Ed.) New York: Macmillan.

Sleet, D. A., & Dane, J. K. (1985). Wellness factors among adolescents. *Adolescence, 20,* 910–920.

Smith, G. S. (1990). The physician's role in injury prevention: Beyond the United States preventive services task force report. *Journal of General Internal Medicine, 5* (Suppl. 5), 67–73.

Stevenson, M., & Sleet, D. A. (1996). Which Prevention Strategies for Child Pedestrians? A Review of the Literature. *International Quarterly of Community Health Education, 16*(3), 207–217.

Tertinger, D. A., Green, B. F., & Lutzker, J. R. (1984). Home Safety: Development and validation of one component of an ecobehavioral treatment program for abused and neglected children. *Journal of Applied Behavior Analysis, 17,* 154–174.

Tolan, P. H. (1988). Socioeconomic, family, and social stress correlates of adolescent antisocial and delinquent behavior *Journal of Abnormal Child Psychology, 16,* 317–331.

United Nations Foundation. (2001). *Injuries: OECD could prevent 12,000 child deaths per year—report.* UNICEF Innocenti Research Center, United Nations Foundation UNWire, 6 February.

United Nations. (1994). *United Nations Development Program.* Human Development Report 1994. New York: Oxford University Press.

U.S. General Accounting Office. (1999). *Lead poisoning: Federal health care programs are not effectively reaching at-risk children.* (GAO/HEHS No. 99–18). Washington, DC: Author.

Williams, K. R., Guerra, N. G., & Elliott, D. S. (1997). *Human development and violence prevention: A focus on youth.* Boulder, CO: University of Colorado, Center for the Study and Prevention of Violence, Institute of Behavioral Science.

World Health Organization. (1989). *Manifesto for safe communities. Safety–A universal concern and responsibility for all.* Joint Policy Document. First World Conference on Accident and Injury Prevention. Lund, Sweden: Karolinska Institute.

World Health Organization. (1996). *Violence: A Public Health Priority.* Working Group Report. Document EHA/SPI/POA.2. Geneva, Switzerland: Author.

Zaza, S., Carande-Kulis, V. G., Sleet, D. A., Sosin, D. M., Elder, R. W., Shults, R. A., Dinh-Zarr, T. B., Nichols, J. L., Thompson, R. S., Task force on community preventive services. (2001). Methods for conducting systematic reviews of the evidence of effectiveness and economic efficiency of interventions to reduce injuries to motor vehicle occupants. *American Journal of Preventive Medicine, 21*(45), 23–30.

Zuckerman, B. S., & Duby, J. C. (1985). Developmental approach to injury prevention. *Pediatric Clinics of North America, 32,* 17–29.

8

Reproductive Health

Jeanette M. Conner
Vermont Oxford Network, Burlington, VT

James E. Dewey
Quality Metric, Inc., Lincoln, RI

INTRODUCTION

At the International Conference on Population and Development in Cairo in 1994, the World Health Organization (WHO) defined reproductive health as:

> a state of physical, mental, and social well-being in all matters relating to the reproductive system at all stages of life. Reproductive health implies that people are able to have a satisfying and safe sex life and that they have the capability to reproduce and the freedom to decide if, when, and how often to do so. Implicit in this are the rights of men and women to be informed and to have access to safe, effective, affordable, and acceptable methods of family planning of their choice, and the right to appropriate health-care services that enable women to safely go through pregnancy and childbirth. (World Health Organization [WHO], 1994)

This is an excellent starting point for the discussion of reproductive health as a core element of well-being. Sexuality, pregnancy, and childbirth are a necessary part of the human life cycle. Reproductive health is an integral part of basic human development. It affects health through all aspects of life, from childhood through adolescence and adulthood. It is a key aspect of general health and life expectancy even after the reproductive years are over (Mbizvo, 1996).

Reproductive health is of major importance in the adolescent years. On average, in the U.S. sexual maturation is occurring earlier, and marriage is occurring later. Therefore, the at-risk period is extended for nonmarital pregnancy, sexually transmitted diseases (STDs), and the likelihood of multiple sexual partners. Single parenthood, dual working parents, same-sex parents, and other changes in the family and societal patterns and values have also resulted in further relaxation of some social taboos on sexual activity. Television, movies, advertising and other forms of mass media emblazon sexuality as an integral part of even casual relationships. It is no wonder that children of childbearing age are confused as to what behaviors are expected of them (McCauley & Salter, 1995).

While much of the literature on reproductive health focuses on international and third world applications, this review places its emphasis on those issues of reproductive health most relevant to citizens of the United States. This review focuses on major content areas: family planning; reproductive health in women throughout the lifecycle; men and reproductive health; and finally, and most appropriately, reproductive health and adolescents.

OPERATIONAL DEFINITION

There is strong evidence that effective family planning has a positive effect on the well-being and quality of life of men, women, and children. However, despite the availability of effective methods of birth control, approximately 75% of teen pregnancies each year in the United States are unplanned (National Center for Health Statistics, 2000). The percentage of intended pregnancies drops below 40% for the poor and to under 25% for teenage mothers (Henshaw, 1998). Family planning improves health and well-being by preventing unplanned and high-risk pregnancies, assuring adequate spacing of children, and reducing the need for unsafe abortions. The consequences of unintended pregnancy are not limited to the young, the poor, or the unmarried. The negative effect on well-being of an unplanned pregnancy affects females of all ages and life stages (Brown & Eisenberg, 1995).

When pregnancy is unplanned, the mother is less likely to seek or receive effective prenatal care and more likely to expose the fetus to substances such as tobacco, alcohol, or drugs (Brown & Eisenberg, 1995; Kost, Landry, & Darroch, 1998b). When the pregnancy is unintended, there is a 30% greater likelihood that the infant's health will be compromised (Kost et al., 1998a). Kost and colleagues (1998a, 1998b) found that with unplanned pregnancy there was a lower proportion of babies that received well-baby care by age 3 months, as well as a lower proportion of babies who were breastfed. The child of an unplanned pregnancy is also at greater risk for low birth weight, death within the first year of life, and abuse (Kost et al., 1998b). In addition, a larger proportion of women who have an unplanned pregnancy are at either end of the reproductive age span, creating an increase in medical cost and social burden to children, adults, and society in general (Kost et al., 1998b).

When used correctly, contraceptives prevent unwanted pregnancy and enable both couples and individuals to plan the number and spacing of their children or to avoid conception altogether. Use of condoms in at-risk sexual relationships prevents the transmission of STDs, including human immunodeficiency virus (HIV). When properly used, currently available contraceptive methods are both safe and effective for the majority of users (Santelli et al., 1997).

REPRODUCTIVE HEALTH ISSUES FOR WOMEN AND MEN

Sexuality affects individuals' health needs throughout their lifecycles. Biological differences between men and women such as childbearing, breast cancer, and menopause create unique health issues for women. There are differences between the sexes in heart disease, osteoporosis, depression, and other health problems that are related to reproductive health practices as well (Paykel, 1991).

Women and Reproductive Health

The health needs of women in the childbearing age revolve around their fertility. Family planning can help women chose if, when, and how many children to have. As women complete their families, their family planning needs change from spacing to preventing births. Older women need to consider the increased risk of negative side effects from certain methods of contraception. This population should also take into account their declining fertility and impact of contraceptives on the symptoms and health risks associated with menopause (Blaney, 1997).

Once reaching menopause, women's health needs no longer center on childbearing. The first challenge is to help women through the menopausal transition, a period of hormonal and clinical changes that culminates with the end of menstruation (Dennerstein, 1996). Postmenopause hormonal changes greatly increase the risk of cardiovascular disease and osteoporosis, which affects over 22 million American women (Levinson & Altkorn, 1998). Older women experience other reproductive health disorders as well, such as cervical and breast cancer, genital prolapse, and increased urinary tract infections (Dennerstein, 1996).

Men and Reproductive Health

In the past, most reproductive health programs focused on family planning and, therefore, specifically targeted women. Little attention was paid to the roles that men take in reproductive health decision making and the effect of their behaviors. The few programs that were developed focused mainly on encouraging men to use condoms or undergo vasectomy and to be an active participant in reproductive responsibility (Helzner, 1996).

In the 1990s, many women's health programs started focusing on the role of men in reproductive health services (Berer, 1996). The International Conference on Population Development in Cairo in 1994 devoted an entire segment of its summary action plan to male responsibilities and participation, when it recommended that:

> Special efforts should be made to emphasize men's shared responsibility and promote their active involvement in responsible parenthood; sexual and reproductive behavior, including family planning; prenatal, maternal and child health; prevention of STDs, including HIV; prevention of unwanted and high-risk pregnancies; shared control and contribution to family income, children's education, health and nutrition; and recognition and promotion of the equal value of children of both sexes. (WHO, 1994)

ADOLESCENT REPRODUCTIVE HEALTH

Puberty, defined as the biological change of adolescence (Steinberg, 1999), is a state of transition to biological-sexual maturation. Puberty, beginning as early as 8 years of age, is characterized by a growth spurt, change in body composition, and the development of primary and secondary sex characteristics. The growth spurt is distinguished by increased bone length and density, and increased proportion of muscle and fat. Body composition changes include the development of breast tissue, pubic hair, and underarm hair for girls, and growth of the testes, scrotal sac, penis, underarm hair, and larynx for boys. Additional physical changes include the production of oil and sweat glands for both sexes, and the onset of menarche for girls between the ages of 10 to 16 years. Hormonal changes include the release of estrogen by female ovaries causing the breasts, uterus, and vagina to mature and contribute to the regulation of menarche. In addition, androgens in girls are secreted contributing to growth and development of pubic and underarm hair. Hormonal changes in boys include the release of testosterone contributing to growth and development of body and facial hair and sex characteristics (Steinberg, 1999).

The health and well-being of adolescents is closely linked with their physical, psychological, and social development. Adolescent reproductive health is put in jeopardy by the increasing sexual and reproductive health risks within the environment (Friedman, 1994). As individuals enter puberty, they face not only powerful hormonal and physical growth changes but also increased social pressures to become sexually active. In order to make healthy decisions, all adolescents need information about human sexuality and access to reproductive health services. Individuals also must learn how to refuse unwanted sexual relations and insist on condom use in order to protect themselves against pregnancy and STDs.

Adolescents are a large and growing segment of the population. During adolescence, young people develop their adult identity, move toward physical and psychological maturity, and become economically independent. However, many adolescents are often less informed, less experienced, and less comfortable accessing family planning and reproductive health services than adults. They are at an increased risk of STDs, HIV, unintended pregnancy, and other health consequences that can affect their futures (McCauley & Salter, 1995; Program for Appropriate Technology in Health, 1998).

As stated previously, adolescents in the United States are reaching sexual maturity at an earlier age, yet are marrying later. As a result, a significant number of adolescents are engaging in premarital sex. Surveys show that 68% of adolescents in the United States have had premarital sex by age 20. Along with increased risk of STDs and unintended pregnancy, adolescents who engage in nonmarital sexual activity face family conflicts, educational difficulties, and the potential stress and anxiety associated with abortion, adoption, or single parenthood. Married adolescents who become pregnant may not encounter the same social risks as their unmarried counterparts, but they may face the emotional and relationship difficulties of early-age marriage and childbirth (Alan Guttmacher Institute [AGI], 1998).

In the United States, about 19% of adolescent women give birth by age 20 (Noble, Cover, & Yanagaishita, 1996). In 1997, over 400,000 adolescent girls had abortions (National Campaign to Prevent Teen Pregnancy, 1998). Complications of pregnancy, childbirth, and unsafe abortion are major causes of death for women age 15 to 19 years (AGI, 1994, 1998).

STDs also pose significant risk for adolescents. The highest rates of infection for STDs, including HIV, are found among young people age 20 to 24; and the second highest rate occurs among adolescents 15 to 19 years of age (Noble et al., 1996). Each year, one out of every 20 adolescents contracts an STD, some of which can cause lifelong health problems, such as infertility, if left untreated.

These are the challenges confronting reproductive health professionals in this country and around the world. The question is, what programs can be designed and implemented to meet the information and service needs of adolescents? Many believe that targeting young people for health information and services can be an important gateway to promoting healthy behaviors as adults. If parents, community leaders, and health professionals work together, programs can be offered that address young people's needs and help them grow into healthy and responsible adults (PATH, 1998). Examples of effective adolescent reproductive health programs will be discussed in the following section.

ADOLESCENT REPRODUCTIVE HEALTH PROGRAMS

School-Based Programs

Sex education and reproductive health programs in schools often face stiff opposition from those who fear that these programs will encourage earlier and/or more frequent sexual experimentation, yet research shows otherwise (Adams, Adams-Taylor, & Pittman, 1989; AGI, 1994). To win public support, however, programs should work with parents and within community norms (McCauley & Salter, 1995).

Schools with trained educators represent perhaps the most efficient way to reach young people and their families about reproductive health. There is evidence in the literature to suggest that general education has a positive effect on the reproductive health of young people. Young women who remain in school generally delay marriage and childbearing. It can also provide valuable time to help them develop decision making skills and self-esteem. Reproductive programs administered in school can help prevent early pregnancy, HIV/AIDS, and STDs. Reproductive education at the earliest possible age can help the formation of healthy sexual attitudes and practices before the child is sexually active. Prevention is easier and more effective than trying to change unhealthy habits later in life (Kirby, 1994; Birdthistle & Vince-Whitman, 1997).

Elements of an Effective School-based Program: Values Clarification

Students should not only receive sexuality/reproductive health information in the classroom but also explore their own values and attitudes to acquire the personal skills they need to maintain healthy behavior. By exploring and clarifying their values through debates and discussions, students are able to reflect on the implications of their sexual decisions and the attitudes and values that influence them. This clarification can help equip them with the knowledge and skills necessary to negotiate safer sex.

Skill Building

Many existing education curricula are primarily information based and focus on anatomy, the biology of reproduction, and symptoms of STDs. Information alone rarely teaches young people the skills necessary to lead healthy sexual lives. A better strategy is to include learning activities that focus on acquiring the skills necessary for responsible behavior in the context of specific reproductive health issues and to build confidence in using the behaviors (Birdthistle & Vince-Whitman, 1997).

School-based programs that have curricula designed as a sequence from the primary through the secondary grade levels are most effective at staging learning through an adolescent's evolving life experience. Content and teaching methods that are age appropriate are recommended (Birdthistle & Vince-Whitman, 1997).

Health-Facility Programs

Reproductive health services are much needed by young men and women and are often not available or accessible. Adolescents may be reluctant to seek care from their family medical providers because of the lack of anonymity or fear of parental exposure. In addition, typically, a full array of contraceptive methods is not provided by local drugstores or other outreach projects. Therefore, STD diagnosis and treatment, reproductive health information, and contraceptives are commonly available only at a community clinic. Community health clinics are established in many communities and are designed to handle the special needs of young people. Many young people already go to community health clinics for other reasons and could be served with needed reproductive health services at the same time and location (Senderowitz, 1997).

Outreach Programs

Outreach has emerged as an innovative way to connect with young people. Increasingly, educational programs about reproductive health are offered at special youth sites or through the efforts of roving health educators who bring information directly to adolescents. Outreach efforts include special programs conducted by trained professionals in community youth centers. These can include programs that seek to both prevent early and unplanned pregnancy and other risky behaviors while, at the same time, focus on the enhancement of life skills and assisting pregnant and parenting teens to pursue educational and vocational objectives. Peer counseling programs are also used to deliver information and services in the community and workplace through individuals similar in age and background. These programs are intended to appeal to difficult-to-reach populations such as school dropouts. Programs provided by youth-oriented organizations are frequently characterized by a high degree of youth involvement in their operations (Senderowitz, 1997).

Social Marketing and Mass Media

In recent years, modern marketing and mass communications have been used with increasing success to promote the reproductive health of young adults. These efforts take advantage of marketing's ability to analyze target audience behavior and use the media's persuasive power to support health-enhancing objectives. Social marketing refers to a process for designing health promotion interventions that utilize techniques drawn from commercial advertising, market research, and the social sciences. These strategies have been used to achieve a variety of health promotion objectives, including increased condom use, increased access to health services, and changes in health behavior and practices such as abstinence or monogamy. Mass media can also be used as a major channel of communication in social marketing intervention strategies. Mass media refers here to self-contained audio, visual, or printed material distribution systems that can reach large numbers of people with similar messages. Examples include radio, television, computers (and the Internet), newspapers, magazines, billboards, direct mail, and telemarketing (Israel & Nagano, 1997).

CONCLUSIONS

Reproductive health is an integral element in human development from childhood though adulthood. Sexuality, pregnancy, and childbirth are natural phases in the human lifecycle. Sexuality and reproductive health are particularly crucial during adolescence when this developmental period is fraught with sexual and reproductive risks including increased sexual activity, STDs, and unintended pregnancy. Challenges in promoting reproductive health arise from lack of social clarity regarding sex education, the role of mass media in the perception of sexuality, and age and gender expectations regarding responsibility for reproductive health.

Promotion of reproductive health must be endorsed at all levels: the individual, the family, the school, the community, and society. Both men and women have a responsibility in reproductive health, and efforts should be made to further promote men's involvement in responsible sexual and reproductive behavior. Families should promote reproductive health through family planning, and early teaching and discussions with children regarding healthy sexual behaviors. Schools contribute an important role in promoting reproductive health by offering educational programs. School-based reproductive health programs led by trained educators that target children at an early age are effective in preventing unintended pregnancy and STDs. Schools should also develop programs that help children explore their values and attitudes about sexuality while teaching skills for responsible sexual behavior.

Communities can also contribute to reproductive health by providing programs targeted for adolescents, offering reproductive health information while providing access to health services. Services that should be offered by a community health clinic include contraceptive methods, diagnosis and treatment of STDs, and educational support and guidance. Communities can also contribute by sponsoring outreach programs as an effective method of relating to young people.

Finally, marketing and mass media can play an important role in supporting and endorsing healthy sexuality and sexual behaviors. Mass media can use their broad scope of communication, often targeted at children, to establish social consciousness by promoting healthy sexual practices.

REFERENCES

Adams, G., Adams-Taylor, S., & Pittman, K. (1989). Adolescent pregnancy and parenthood: Review of the problem, solutions, and resources. *Family Relations, 38*, 223–229.

Alan Guttmacher Institute. (1994). *Sex and America's teenagers*. New York: Author.

Alan Guttmacher Institute. (1998). *Into a new world: Young women's sexual and reproductive lives*. New York: Author.

Berer, M. (1996, May). Men. *Reproductive health matters, 7*, 7–10.

Birdthistle, I., & Vince-Whitman, C. (1997, May). Reproductive health outreach programs for young adults: School-based programs. *FOCUS on Young Adults Research Series*.

Blaney, C. (1997). Contraceptive needs after age 40. *Network, 18*, 4–7.

Brown, S. S., & Eisenberg, L., (Eds.). (1995). *The best intentions: Unintended pregnancy and the well-being of children and families*. Washington, DC: National Academy Press.

Dennerstein, L. (1996). Well-being, symptoms and the menopausal transition. *Maturitas, 23*, 147–157.

Friedman, H. L. (1994). Reproductive health in adolescence. *World Health Statistics Questionnaire, 47*, 31–35.

Helzner, J. F. (1996). Men's involvement in family planning. *Reproductive Health Matters, 7*, 146–154.

Henshaw, S. K. (1998). Unintended pregnancy in the United States. *Family Planning Perspectives, 30*, 24–29, 46.

Israel, R. C., & Nagano, R. (1997). Promoting reproductive health for young adults through social marketing and mass media: a review of trends and practices. *FOCUS on Young Adults Research Series*.

Kirby, D. (1994). *A proposed adolescent reproductive health initiative.* (POPTECH Report No. 94–004–012). Arlington, VA: Population Technical Assistance Project.

Kost, K., Landry, D. J., & Darroch, J., (1998a). The effects of pregnancy planning status on birth outcomes and infant care. *Family Planning Perspectives, 30,* 223–230.

Kost, K., Landry, D. J., & Darroch, J., (1998b). Predicting maternal behaviors during pregnancy: Does intention status matter? *Family Planning Perspectives, 30,* 79–88.

Levinson, W., & Altkorn, D. (1998). Primary prevention of postmenopausal osteoporosis. *Journal of the American Medical Association, 280,* 1821–1822.

Mbizvo, M. T. (1996). Reproductive and sexual health: A research and developmental challenge. *Central African Journal of Medicine, 42,* 80–85.

McCauley, A. P., & Salter, C. (1995). *Meeting the needs of young adults.* (Population Rep. Series J, No. 41). Baltimore, MD: Johns Hopkins School of Public Health, Population Information Program.

National Campaign to Prevent Teen Pregnancy. (1998). *A statistical portrait of adolescent sex, contraception, and childbearing.* Washington, DC: Author.

National Center for Health Statistics. (2000). *Health, United States 2000 with adolescent health chartbook.* Hyattsville, MD: U.S. Department of Health and Human Services.

Noble, J., Cover, J., & Yanagaishita, M. (1996). *The world's youth 1996.* Washington, DC: Population Reference Bureau, Inc.

Paykel, E. (1991). Depression in women. *British Journal of Psychiatry, 158* (Suppl. 10), 22–29.

Program for Appropriate Technology in Health. (1998). Adolescent reproductive health: Making a difference. *Outlook, 16*(3).

Santelli, J., Warren, C., Lowry, R., Sogolow, E., Collins, J., Kann, L., Kaufman, R., & Senderowitz, J. (1997). Reproductive health outreach programs for young adults: Health facility programs. *FOCUS on Young Adults Research Series.*

Senderowitz, J. (1997). Reproductive health outreach programs for young adults: Outreach programs. *FOCUS on Young Adults Research Series.*

Steinberg, L. (1999). *Adolescence* (5th ed.). Boston, MA: McGraw-Hill College.

World Health Organization. (1994, September). *Report of the International Conference on Population and Development.* Paper presented at the International Conference on Population and Development, Cairo.

9

Growing Up Drug Free: A Developmental Challenge

Bruce G. Simons-Morton

Denise L. Haynie

Prevention Research Branch
Division of Epidemiology, Statistics, and Prevention Research
National Institute of Child Health and Human Development,
Bethesda, MD

INTRODUCTION

Healthful child and adolescent development can be threatened by any number of challenges, including family dissolution, delinquency, violence, and substance abuse. Each of these threats could precipitate or accentuate a departure from a normal and positive developmental trajectory, sometimes referred to as the "good path." The good path is a metaphor for the type of developmental experiences that facilitate achievement motivation, competence, prosocial values, positive social relations, and psychological adjustment. Of course, there are many possible good paths up the proverbial developmental mountain, and some of the most interesting may include minor deviations from the usual. However, there is a great difference between a brief experimentation with unconventional behavior and an irreversible detour that can seriously threaten normal development. Irresponsible substance use that leads to abuse, addiction, and injury/disease is one such detour (Felner & Felner, 1989). Consequently, avoiding adolescent substance abuse is one of the fundamental challenges faced by adolescents in modern society.

109

Substance use increases dramatically during early adolescence (Johnston, O'Malley, & Bachman, 2000; Kann et al., 2000). Early experimentation with drug use is a particularly powerful risk factor for subsequent abuse and long-term behavioral, social, and health problems (Gruber, Di Clemente, Anderson, & Lodico, 1996). Therefore, the primary goals of prevention are delaying the age of initiation and reducing the extent of experimentation (Coie et al., 1993). Fortunately, a growing body of research is helping to identify risk and protective factors and the types of social actions that can help protect youth from drug abuse. This chapter defines the nature and prevalence of adolescent substance use, examines the evidence that avoiding precocious substance use is an important developmental challenge, reviews theoretical perspectives on adolescent substance use, and identifies a range of protective and risk factors. Finally, the social options that can be adopted to protect adolescents from substance use and keep them on a good developmental path are examined.

TECHNICAL ISSUES

Definition of the Challenge

Adolescent substance use is a complicated problem, given that both illegal and restricted drugs are widely available. Illicit drugs, such as marijuana, cocaine, and heroin, are illegal for persons of any age to use, possess, or sell, except for limited medical and research purposes. Tobacco and alcohol, by far the most popular recreational drugs, are regulated but widely marketed.

Illicit Drugs.   Due to their medical uses and intoxication effects, drugs have been a part of human culture for centuries (Schivelbusch, 1992). Opium and its derivatives, morphine and heroin, as well as cocaine, amphetamines, barbiturates, and other drugs have potential medical benefits, for which they can be obtained and used by prescription. Due to their intoxication properties, recreational use of these drugs has long been a feature of modern society.

Illicit drugs are the focus of substantial interdiction and law enforcement efforts in what has come to be known as the "war on drugs." Whereas the merits of interdiction and legal containment can be debated on many levels, there is general agreement that these policies and practices have lead to innovations in drugs and their increased potency, without appreciable reductions in supply (Cahalan, 1991; Falco, 1992). Moreover, as a side effect of the war on drugs, U.S. prisons are full beyond capacity with individuals incarcerated for drug-related crimes. Critics note that the potential benefits of the interdiction and criminalization of drugs must be balanced by an appreciation of the substantial social costs of these approaches (Cahalan, 1991; Falco, 1992). Although about one third of the current federal drug control budget of nearly $15 billion is devoted to prevention and treatment (Office of National Drug Control Policy, 2001), little of this is devoted to tobacco and alcohol, which are the most heavily promoted, readily available, and frequently abused drugs.

Tobacco and Alcohol.   If they were newly introduced today, alcohol and to-bacco might well be categorized as illicit, based on their addictive properties and health effects. But because they have been a part of society for centuries and legitimate industries have developed around their production and sale, they are legal for adults to purchase, possess, and consume. Sadly, these drugs are heavily promoted to youth (DuRant et al., 1997; Grube, 2000), readily obtainable (Kann et al., 2000), and invariably the first drugs used by teens (Kandel, 1989).

Definitions of Use

Most of our understanding about the prevalence of substance use is based on self-reports, the primary means by which type, recency, age of initiation, frequency, amount, and population prevalence of the substance used can be determined. Biochemical verification indicates that self-report is reasonably accurate (Dolcini, Adler, & Ginsberg, 1996), with both overreporting and underreporting limited to a small percentage of respondents. Self-reports of drug use, with minor variations, have been found to be stable from year to year and from one region of the country to another (Johnston et al., 2000).

Substance use is commonly assessed during the past 30 days (recent use) and past 12 months. Frequency of use refers to how many times or on how many days a substance was used (e.g., "How many times/how many days in the past 30 days have you smoked/had alcohol beverages/used marijuana?"). Frequency assessments have the advantage of providing a continuous measure of use, for example, from 0 to 30 days. Amount used daily is the preferred measure of habitual use (e.g., "How many cigarettes have you smoked in the past 30 days?"). Sometimes amount and frequency are combined in the same question (e.g., "How many times in the past 30 days have you had five or more alcoholic drinks within a few hours?").

Prevalence

National probability surveys of substance use have been administered for several decades. The Monitoring the Future Study (Johnston et al., 2000) has provided national survey results on high school students and young adults since 1975. Additional information is provided by the National Household Survey of Drug Use (SAMHSA, 2000). In the past decade, data on substance use have also been available by state for high school students from the Youth Risk Behavior Survey (Kann et al., 2000). Data on early adolescents/middle school students is available only from regional surveys.

In general, the prevalence of illicit substances among teens and adults has declined from its peak in the 1980s and has remained more or less steady in recent years (Johnston, et al., 2000). Use rates, however, vary by substance, sex, age, and race, as shown in Table 9.1. Generally, use has varied little year to year, despite occasional spikes in the use of one drug or decline in use of another. Just under 11% of

TABLE 9.1

Percentages of Current (30-day) Cigarette Smoking, Alcohol, Marijuana,
and Illicit Drug* Use by Grade, Gender, and Race

	Cigarette	Alcohol	Marijuana	Cocaine	Inhalants
Total	34.8	50.0	26.7	4.0	4.2
Sex					
Males	34.7	52.3	30.8	5.2	4.4
Females	34.9	47.7	22.6	2.9	3.9
Grade					
9	27.6	40.6	21.7	3.4	6.4
10	34.7	49.7	27.8	3.7	3.7
11	36.0	50.9	26.7	4.5	3.3
12	42.8	61.7	31.5	4.8	2.2
Race					
White	38.6	52.5	26.4	4.1	4.4
Black	19.7	39.9	26.4	1.1	2.3
Hispanic	32.7	52.8	28.2	6.7	4.9

*Source: Youth Risk Behavior Survey, 1999 (Kann et al., 2000).

12- to 17-year-old youth report the recent use of any illicit drug, 4.4% excluding marijuana (SAMHSA, 2000).

In contrast, recent smoking increases from about 10% among sixth graders to 18% among eighth graders (Simons-Morton, Crump, Haynie et al., 1999), 35% among tenth graders, and 43% among twelfth graders (Kann et al., 2000). The prevalence of current drinking increases from less than 7% among sixth graders to nearly 20% among eighth graders (Simons-Morton, Crump, Haynie, et al., 1999), 50% among tenth graders, and 62% among twelfth graders (Kann et al., 2000). Less than 2% of sixth graders report drinking five or more drinks at one time, contrasted with 8% of eighth graders (Simons-Morton, Haynie, Crump et al., 1999), 32% of tenth graders, and 42% of twelfth graders (Kann et al., 2000).

Male and female youth tend to report similar rates of cigarettes and alcohol use, as shown in Table 9.1 (Kann et al., 2000), but males report higher rates of marijuana and other illicit drug use (Johnston et al., 2000). The prevalence of recent smoking and drinking is highest among European Americans and lowest among African Americans (Johnston et al., 2000; Kann et al., 2000). Recent smoking is reported by 39% of European Americans, 33% of Hispanic Americans, and 20% of African Americans (Kann et al., 2000). Similarly, the prevalence of recent use of alcohol is 53% among European

Americans, 53% among Hispanic Americans, and 40% among African Americans. This pattern is less clear for other substance use; for example, 26–28% of European Americans, Hispanic Americans, and African Americans report recent use of marijuana. Current cocaine use is about 7% among Hispanic Americans, 4% among European Americans, and 1% among African Americans. Substance use among other racial or ethnic groups is less well known (Wallace et al., 1999). Hence, it is clear that alcohol and tobacco are the primary substances used by adolescents, that prevalence increases sharply from sixth to twelfth grade, and use varies modestly by sex and race.

AVOIDING SUBSTANCE USE: AN IMPORTANT DEVELOPMENTAL CHALLENGE

Avoiding precocious substance use is an important challenge for two major reasons. First, substance nonuse co-varies with prosocial behavior, while precocious substance use co-varies with other problem behaviors. Second, nonusers avoid the substantial long-term health and social consequences experienced by many early substance users. Hence, even a delay in the age of initial use may reduce the likelihood that experimentation may lead to long-term negative consequences.

Covariance of Substance Use With Other Problem Behaviors

Tobacco and alcohol tend to be the drugs first used by experimenting youth (Kandel, 1989), used by the largest proportion of youth, and used concurrently with other drugs. Cigarettes and alcohol are the first drugs used because they are most readily available, but the process of procuring these restricted substances brings the user into contact with other users and opportunities for other antisocial behavior. So nonusers are not only spared the actual effects of the substances themselves, but also the antisocial contacts with substance users (Fisher & Bauman, 1988; Petraitis, Flay, Miller, Torpy, & Greiner, 1998).

Compared with adolescent substance users, nonusers have higher academic achievement motivation (Ellickson, Saner, & McGuigan, 1997) and are less likely than users to engage in delinquent and violent behavior (Dawkins, 1997; Ellickson et al., 1997) and unprotected sex (Alan Guttmacher Institute, 1994). To some extent, substance use can be seen as a cause of these other problem behaviors. Adolescent substance use is an act of rebellion that may drive youth toward the social periphery and undermine social bonding, enhance their sense of non-conformity and social disengagement, and introduce them to social contexts and pressures that mediate future behavior. Moreover, adolescent substance use is a covert behavior that often occurs in groups of unsupervised youths, who, in the process of engaging in one antisocial behavior, may be prone to engage in other dangerous, risk-taking, or antisocial behavior.

Consequences of Substance Use

The consequences of psychoactive drugs can be particularly devastating for teens in the early stages of identity formation and intense psychological, social, and physical development. Due to their relative immaturity and inexperience with drugs, adolescents may be particularly vulnerable to intoxication (Thombs, Beck, & Pleace, 1993). Adolescents who avoid early initiation of illicit substance use are less likely than precocious users to abuse these substances as adults (Grant & Dawson, 1998; Gruber et al., 1996), avoiding the long-term negative health and social effects of a lifetime of abuse, including lower educational attainment, greater involvement in the criminal justice system, and more mental health problems (Leukefeld et al., 1998).

WHY DO YOUTH EXPERIMENT WITH DRUGS?

Why do some youth develop substance use problems, whereas others do not? Youth may be attracted to drugs for social and psychological reasons, for example, because they associate them with maturity, social popularity, and independence (Chassin, Presson, & Sherman, 1990; Petraitis et al., 1998). Given the insidious physiological properties of drugs, even casual experimentation can lead to habituation and addiction. There is surprisingly little evidence that precocious substance use is associated with depression, home stress, family conflict, disrupted families, or socioeconomic status. However, there is substantial evidence that substance use is associated with modifiable perceptions and attitudes. Youthful substance use can best be understood within a social context. Here we examine the utility of several theories or categories of theories in explaining adolescent resistance to substance use and identify variables that have been identified as risk or protective factors for substance use. A comprehensive review of the literature is beyond the scope of this paper; however, several excellent reviews are available (see Hawkins, Catalano, & Miller, 1992; Petraitis et al., 1998).

Societal Context

Drugs are easily available and widely promoted. Tobacco and alcohol account for much of the advertising revenue in teen-oriented magazines and the popular media (Grube, 2000; Pierce, Choi, Gilpin, Farkas, & Berry, 1998); movies and rock videos (DuRant et al., 1997) treat drug use as a common and attractive aspect of youth culture. Marketing to youth is a particular problem because most adult smokers start as adolescents and relatively few nonsmoking teenagers start smoking later as adults (Centers for Disease Control and Prevention, 1994; Chassin, Presson, Sherman, & Edwards, 1990). Sadly, most high school students report that they would have little difficulty obtaining drugs if they wanted (Forster, Hourigan, & McGovern, 1992; Johnston et al., 2000; Kann et al., 2000). The general availability to youth of tobacco and alcohol may confer a sense that their use is common and normal.

Personality

Drug use may be particularly attractive and habituating for youth with certain personality traits. Youth who score high on measures of sensation seeking (Pedersen, 1991), and those who are both extroverted and disinhibited (Brook, Brook, Gordon,

Whiteman, & Cohen, 1990; Shedler & Block, 1990; Teichman, Barnea, & Ravav, 1989) may be more likely to experiment with drugs than others. Moreover, aggressive and hostile youth (Block, Block, & Keyes, 1988; Pandina & Johnson, 1990; Schulenberg, Bachman, O'Malley, & Johnston, 1994) and those who lack self-restraint (Kazdin, 1989; Simons-Morton, Haynie et al., 1999) are susceptible to drugs' appeal of immediate gratification.

Perceptions and Attitudes

Most preteens have negative attitudes toward drugs, but over time they are exposed to new information, situations, and people that reshape their views (Ellickson & Hays, 1991). Perceptions and attitudes are strongly related to behavior (Weiner, 1992), but which perceptions and attitudes predispose or protect youth from substance use? According to the Theory of Reasoned Action (Fishbein & Ajzen, 1975), adolescents' perceptions about the expected outcomes of substance use (e.g., how much they would enjoy it; how likely they would be to get into trouble) and what others would think of them if they used a substance (e.g. their friends' approval; their parents' disapproval) influence initiation and continuation of substance use. In addition, efficacy expectations may influence the likelihood an adolescent will or will not engage in substance use (Bandura, 1986). Efficacy expectations refer to one's confidence in one's ability to obtain and use a substance, or to resist social pressure to use the substance. Numerous studies have reported relationships between drug use and perceived expectations (Bailey, Flewelling, & Rachal, 1992; Johnson, 1988). Those who expect negative consequences are less likely to initiate and continue to use drugs (Bailey, et al., 1992; Bauman, & Chenoweth, 1984; Johnson, 1988; Simons-Morton, Crump, Haynie et al., 1999; Simons-Morton, Haynie et al., 1999). Adolescents with more positive expectations may be more likely to initiate substance use and, if they perceive the experience favorably, are likely to continue use (Christiansen, Roehling, Smith, & Goldman, 1989). Relatedly, adolescents' substance-specific perceptions are thought to mediate the influence on substance use behavior of other important variables, such as personality traits, developmental status, or social influences. Perceptions predispose or motivate behavior, and the best measure of this motivation is intent (Fishbein & Ajzen, 1975). Accordingly, intent not to use drugs is higher among those with negative perceptions about drug use than among those with positive perceptions (Newcomb & Bentler, 1986). Actual use, however, may depend on the frequency and circumstances of opportunities to use drugs.

Social Influences

Substantial evidence links social influences to substance use. Peer influences have consistently been found to be associated with substance use (Petraitis et al., 1998). Social cognitive theory (Bandura, 1986) emphasizes the influence of substance-specific beliefs and behavior of role models such as peers, parents, and media figures on expectations. Accordingly, adolescents' outcome and efficacy expectations about substance use are shaped directly through experience and vicariously through observation.

Substance use by close friends is the most consistent predictor of adolescent substance use (Flay, et al., 1994; Jessor, Donovan, & Costa, 1991; Johnson, 1988; Simons-Morton, Crump, Haynie et al., 1999; Simons-Morton, Haynie et al., 1999; Simons-Morton, et al., 2001). In a recent paper, Patterson and colleagues (2000) reported that most of the variance in the growth in deviant behavior, including substance use, could be explained by early and concurrent association with deviant peers. There are several explanations for these findings. One is the tendency for youth to experiment with drugs with their friends due to a desire to maintain the friendship, social pressure, or increased availability. Alternatively, youth who are inclined toward risk taking behaviors may tend to select as friends others who engage in those same behaviors.

There is also evidence that parenting behavior protects youth against substance use and other problem behavior (Baumrind, 1991; Maccoby & Martin, 1994; Resnick, Bearman, Blum, & Bauman, 1998; Simons-Morton, et al., 2001), but the evidence is not as consistent or as strong as that of peer influences. Several studies have reported that youth whose parents were firm and demanding when they were young were less likely than youth whose parents had treated them permissively to experiment with marijuana at an early age (Baumrind, 1985; Kandel & Logan, 1984). One important function of parenting is to teach impulse control and delayed gratification. The failure of children to develop impulse control may make them susceptible to behaviors such as substance use that promise immediate gratification, despite negative consequences. The ability to control one's emotions appears to protect against smoking (Simons-Morton, Crump, Haynie et al., 1999), drinking (Simons-Morton, Haynie et al., 1999), and marijuana use (Baumrind, 1985).

A growing literature documents the importance of parental behavior during early adolescence. Youth who report that their parents are responsive and supportive of their interests and aspirations were less likely to engage in precocious substance use than youth who felt that their parents were unresponsive and granted them little autonomy (Baumrind, 1985; Brook et al, 1990). Parental expectations and behaviors such as monitoring and involvement also appear to protect against drug use (Bailey & Hubbard, 1990; Biglan, Duncan, Ary, & Smolkowski, 1995; Chilcoat, Dishion, & Anthony, 1995; Cohen, Richardson, & LaBree, 1994; Simons-Morton, Haynie, Crump, Eitel, & Saylor, 2001; Steinberg, Fletcher, & Darling, 1994), although there appears to be some variation in what parental behaviors are protective for boys and girls (Simons-Morton, Crump, Haynie et al., 1999; Simons-Morton, Haynie et al., 1999).

Notably, the children of alcoholics are at increased risk of becoming alcoholics themselves (Cuda, Rupp, & Dillon, 1993; Johnson & Leff, 1999; Leiberman, 2000; Sher, 1997), probably stemming from a confluence of biological, psychological, and environmental factors. Less well understood are the associations between other forms of parental substance abuse and adolescent outcomes (Johnson & Leff, 1999), factors that relate to resilience in youth from families with a substance-abusing parent (Lieberman, 2000), and the long-term effects of parental substance use on their children (Barber & Gilbertson, 1999).

Social Control

The values and institutions of conventional society, including family, school, and religious institutions, are generally hostile toward drug use. Therefore, youth who develop commitments to conventional values and institutions may be less likely to use drugs than youth who develop weak or ineffectual bonds (Elliott, Huizinga, & Ageton, 1985; Gottfredson & Hirschi, 1994; Hawkins & Weis, 1985). Relatedly, those who develop and maintain attachments with prosocial, antisubstance using people are less likely to take up drug use than those who develop attachments to antisocial, substance-using people (Oetting & Donnermeyer, 1998). But why do some youth fail to develop conventional commitment and attachments? Presumably, most youth are socialized by their parents to adopt conventional standards, accept the rules of social institutions, and develop attachments to others who are similarly socialized. However, this process of socialization is not uniform and can be further undermined by weak family attachments and social disorganization caused by neighborhood crime, unemployment, and transience. Weak attachment to family may also undermine the development of self-restraint (Gottfredson & Hirschi, 1994).

Some empirical evidence indicates that social bonding may protect youth from problem behavior. Adolescents are less likely to experiment with drugs when they feel that their parents have been nurturing, responsive, and encouraging at an early age (Shedler & Block, 1990) and during adolescence (Hansell & Mechanic, 1990; Baumrind, 1991; Simons-Morton, Crump, Haynie et al., 1999; Simons-Morton, Haynie et al., 1999; Simons-Morton et al., 2001). When teens are closely attached to parents, they may be more responsive to parental management and, presumably, more responsive to the mission and requirements of social institutions such as school. Participation in prosocial activities might be protective against problem behavior by providing opportunities to become involved with other prosocial youth under the leadership of positive adult role models (Eccles & Barber, 1999). There is some evidence that teens that develop positive affiliation with their school are less likely to use drugs or engage in other problem behavior (McBride et al., 1995; Simons-Morton, Crump, Saylor, & Haynie, 1999).

WHITHER PREVENTION?

Given the prominence of tobacco and alcohol in society, prevention is a daunting task. How should limited resources be spent to prevent adolescent substance use? Clearly, it would seem to be important to reduce availability and opportunities for use in ways that would minimize substantial negative social consequences, as well as strengthen the resilience of youth. Although there is clear evidence that education, treatment, and policy approaches can be effective, not every type of prevention works. For example, comprehensive policy approaches, which include increased price, restricted advertising, and enforcement of the regulations on sales, are thought to be more effective than isolated measures (Willemsen & DeZwart, 1999). Moreover, research on the effectiveness of school-based substance abuse prevention programs indicates that theory-based programs that alter perceptions and attitudes of youth about norms and expectations and improve social skills are more effective (Hansen, 1992; Schinke, Botvin, & Orlandi, 1991) than information-oriented programs (Hansen, 1992). However, the effects of these programs are transitory, so intervention must be applied continually. Therefore, one challenge is to increase the adoption and maintenance of quality prevention programs.

CONCLUSIONS

Based on the available literature and relevant theory, the following conclusions about adolescent substance use are warranted. First, avoiding early initiation of substance use is an important aspect of staying on the good path of adolescent development. Tobacco and alcohol should be given primary attention because their use by youth (a) is great compared with other drugs and increases substantially during adolescence; (b) co-varies with other problem behaviors; (c) is associated with a host of acute and long-term health problems; and (d) increases involvement with antisocial peers and behavior. Non-users are protected from these untoward effects. Second, perceptions and attitudes are important precursors of use and are amenable to intervention. Finally, associating with non-using peers, having involved and supportive parents, and developing positive attachments with family, school, and other social institutions appear to protect against substance use.

In light of the current information on substance use and abuse, it is recommended that prevention policy and program initiatives take the causes of substance abuse into account when designing interventions. Programs that stress tobacco and alcohol control, the development of protective attitudes and social skills, the quality of youth attachment to parents and conventional social institutions, and increased parental involvement and support will most likely be effective in keeping youth free from substance use and promoting the good path of youth development.

REFERENCES

Alan Guttmacher Institute. (1994). *Sex and America's Teenagers*. New York: Author.

Bailey, S., Flewelling, R. L., & Rachal, J. V. (1992). Predicting continued use of marijuana among adolescents: The relative influence of drug-specific and social context factors. *Journal of Health and Social Behavior, 33*, 51–66.

Bailey, S., & Hubbard, R. L. (1990). Developmental variation in the context of marijuana initiation among adolescents. *Journal of Health and Social Behavior, 31*, 58–70.

Bandura, A. (1986). *Social Foundations of thought and action: A social cognitive theory.* Englewood Cliffs, NJ: Prentice Hall.

Barber, J. G., & Gilbertson, R. (1999). The drinker's children. *Substance Use and Misuse*, *34*(3), 383–402.

Bauman, K. E., & Chenoweth, R. L. (1984). The relationship between the consequences adolescents expect from smoking and their behavior: A factor analysis with panel data. *Journal of Applied Social Psychology*, *14*, 28–41.

Baumrind, D. (1985). Familial antecedents of adolescent drug use: A developmental perspective. In C. L. Jones & R. J. Battjes (Eds.), *Etiology of drug abuse: Implications for prevention* (pp. 13–44). Rockville, MD: NIDA Research Monograph 56.

Baumrind, D. (1991). Effective parenting during the early adolescent transition. In P. A. Cowan & E. M. Hetherington (Eds.), *Family transitions. Advances in family research series* (pp. 111–123). Hillsdale, NJ: Lawrence Erlbaum Associates.

Biglan, A., Duncan, T. E., Ary, D. V., & Smolkowski, K. (1995). Peer and parental influences on adolescent tobacco use. *Journal of Behavioral Medicine*, *8*(4), 315–330.

Block, J., Block, J. H., & Keyes, S. (1988). Longitudinally foretelling drug usage in adolescence: Early childhood personality and environmental precursors. *Child Development*, *52*, 336–355.

Brook, J. S., Brook, D. W., Gordon, A. S., Whiteman, M., & Cohen, P. (1990). The psychosocial etiology of adolescent drug-use: A family interactional approach. *Genetic, Social, and General Psychology Monographs*, *116*(2), 111–267.

Centers for Disease Control and Prevention. (1994). *Preventing tobacco use among young people: Report of the Surgeon General*. Atlanta, GA: USDHHS (PHS), CDC, National Center for Chronic Disease Prevention and Health Promotion, Office on Smoking and Health.

Cahalan, D. (1991). *An ounce of prevention: Strategies for solving tobacco, alcohol, and drug problems*. San Francisco: Jossey-Bass.

Chassin, L., Presson, C. C., & Sherman, S. J. (1990). Social psychological contributions to the understanding and prevention of adolescent cigarette smoking. *Personality and Social Psychology Bulletin*, *16*(1), 133–151.

Chassin, L., Presson, C. C., Sherman, S. J., & Edwards, D. A. (1990). The natural history of cigarette smoking: Predicting young-adult smoking outcomes from adolescent smoking patterns. *Health Psychology*, *9*(6), 701–716.

Chilcoat, H. D., Dishion, T. J., & Anthony, J. C. (1995). Parent monitoring and the incidence of drug sampling in urban elementary school children. *American Journal of Epidemiology*, *141*(1), 25–31.

Christiansen, B. A., Roehling, P. V., Smith, G. T., & Goldman, M. S. (1989). Using alcohol expectancies to predict adolescent drinking behavior after one year. *Journal of Consulting and Clinical Psychology*, *57*(1), 93–99.

Cohen, D. A., Richardson, J., & LaBree, L. (1994). Parenting behaviors and the onset of smoking and alcohol use: A longitudinal study. *Pediatrics*, *94*(3), 365–375.

Coie, J. D., Watt, N. F., West, S. G., Hawkins, J. D., Asarnow, J. R., Markman, H. J., Shure, M. B., Ramey, S. L., & Long, B. (1993). The science of prevention: A conceptual framework and some directions for a national research program. *American Psychologist*, *48*, 1013–1022.

Cuda, S., Rupp, R., & Dillon, C. (1993). Adolescent children of alcoholics. *Adolescent Medicine*, *4*(2), 439–452.

Dawkins, M. P. (1997). Drug use and violent crime among adolescents. *Adolescence*, *32*(126), 396–405.

Dolcini, M. M., Adler, N. E., & Ginsberg, D. (1996). Factors influencing agreement between self-reports and biological measures of smoking among adolescents. *Journal of Research on Adolescents*, *6*(4), 515–542.

DuRant, R. H., Rome, E. S., Rich, M., Allred, E., Emans, S. J., & Woods, E. R. (1997). Tobacco and alcohol use behaviors portrayed in music videos: A content analysis. *American Journal of Public Health*, *87*(7), 1131–1135.

Eccles, J. S., & Barber, B. (1999). Student council, volunteering, basketball, or marching band: What kind of extracurricular involvement matters? *Journal of Adolescent Research*, *14*(1), 10–43.

Ellickson, P. L., & Hays, R. D. (1991). Antecedents of drinking among young adolescents with different alcohol use histories. *Journal of Studies on Alcohol*, *52*(5), 398–408.

Ellickson, P. L., Saner, H., & McGuigan, K. A. (1997). Profiles of violent youth: Substance use and other concurrent problems. *American Journal of Public Health*, *87*, 985–991.

Elliott, D. S., Huizinga D., & Ageton, S. S. (1985). *Explaining Delinquency and Drug Use*. Beverly Hills, CA: Sage.

Falco, M. (1992). *The making of a drug-free America: Programs that work*. New York: Times Books.

Felner, R. D., & Felner, T. Y. (1989). Primary prevention programs in the educational context: A transactional-ecological framework and analysis. In L. A. Bond & B. E. Compas (Eds.), *Primary Prevention and Promotion in the Schools* (pp. 13–49). Newbury Park, CA: Sage.

Fishbein, M., & Ajzen, I. (1975). *Beliefs, attitude, intention, and behavior: An introduction to theory and research*. Reading, MA: Addison-Wesley.

Fisher, L. A., & Bauman, K. E. (1988). Influence and selection in the friend-adolescent relationship: Findings from studies of adolescent smoking and drinking. *Journal of Applied Social Psychology, 18*, 289–314.

Flay, B. R., Hu, F. B., Siddiqui, O., Day, L. E., Hedeker, D., Petraitis, J. et al. (1994). Differential influence of parental smoking and friends' smoking on adolescent initiation and escalation of smoking. *Journal of Health and Social Behavior, 35*, 248–265.

Forster, J. L., Hourigan, M., & McGovern, P. (1992). Availability of cigarettes to youth in three communities. *Preventive Medicine, 21*, 320–328.

Gottfredson, M. R., & Hirschi, T. (1994). A general theory of adolescent problem behavior: Problems and prospects. In R. D. Ketterlinus & M. E. Lamb (Eds.), *Adolescent Problem Behavior: Issues and Research* (pp. 41–56). Hillsdale, NJ: Lawrence Erlbaum Associates.

Grant, B. F., & Dawson, D. A. (1998). Age at onset of alcohol use and its association with DSM-IV alcohol abuse and dependence: Results from the National Longitudinal Alcohol Epidemiological Survey. *Journal of Substance Abuse, 9*, 103–110.

Grube, J. W. (2000). Alcohol advertising and alcohol consumption: A review of recent research. In NIAA *Tenth Special Report to Congress on Alcohol and Health*. Bethesda, MD: National Institute on Alcohol Abuse and Alcoholism.

Gruber, E., DiClemente, R. J., Anderson, M. M., & Lodico, M. (1996). Early drinking onset and its association with alcohol use and problem behavior in late adolescence. *Preventive Medicine, 25*, 293–300.

Hansell, S., & Mechanic, D. (1990). Parent and peer effects on adolescent health behavior. In K. Hurrelmann & F. Losel (Eds.), *Health Hazards in Adolescence: Prevention and Intervention in Childhood and Adolescence, Vol. 8* (pp. 43–65). New York: deGruyter.

Hansen, W. B. (1992). School-based substance abuse prevention: A review of the state of the art in curriculum, 1980–1990. *Health Education Research, 7*, 403–430.

Hawkins, J. D., Catalano, R. F., & Miller, J. Y. (1992). Risk and protective factors for alcohol and other drug problems in adolescence and early adulthood: Implications for substance abuse prevention. *Psychological Bulletin, 112*(1), 64–105.

Hawkins, J. D., & Weis, J. G. (1985). The social development model: An integrated approach to delinquency prevention. *Journal of Primary Prevention, 6*, 73–97.

Jessor, R., Donovan, J. E., & Costa, F. M. (1991). *Beyond Adolescence: Problem Behavior and Young Adult Development*. New York: Cambridge University Press.

Johnson, J. L., & Leff, M. (1999). Children of substance abusers: Overview of research findings. *Pediatrics, 103*, 1085–1099.

Johnson, V. (1988). Adolescent alcohol and marijuana use: A longitudinal assessment of a social learning perspective. *American Journal of Drug and Alcohol Abuse, 14*, 419–439.

Johnston, L. D., O'Malley, P. M., & Bachman, J. G. (2000). *Monitoring the future study, National survey results on drug use, 1975–1999. Vol. 1: Secondary school students*. (NIH Pub. No. 00-4802). Rockville, MD: U.S. Department of Health and Human Services, National Institute on Drug Abuse.

Kandel, D. B. (1989). Issues of sequencing of adolescent drug use and other problem behaviors. *Drugs and Society, 3*, 55–76.

Kandel, D. B., & Logan, J. A. (1984). Patterns of drug use from adolescence to young adulthood: I. Periods of risk for initiation, continued use, and discontinuation. *American Journal of Public Health, 74*(7), 660–666.

Kann, L., Kinchen, S. A., Williams, B. I., Ross, J. G., Lowry, R., Hill, C. V., Grunbaum, J. A., & Kolbe, L. J. (2000). Youth risk behavior surveillance—United States, 1999. *MMWR, 49*(5), 1–96.

Kazdin, A. E. (1989). *Behavior modification in applied settings* (4th ed.). Pacific Grove, CA: Brooks/Cole.

Leukefeld, C. G., Logan, T. K., Clayton, R. R., Martin, C., Zimmerman, R., Cattarello, A., Milich, R., & Lynam, D. (1998). Adolescent drug use, delinquency, and other behaviors. In T. P. Gullatta, G. R. Adams, & R. Montemayor (Eds.), *Delinquent violent youth: Theory and interventions* (pp. 98–128). Thousand Oaks, CA: Sage.

Lieberman, D. Z. (2000). Children of alcoholics: An update. *Current Opinion in Pediatrics*, *12*(4), 336–340.

Maccoby, E. E., & Martin, J. A. (1994). Socialization in the context of the family: Parent–child interaction. In J. Wiley (Ed.), *Socialization, Personality, and Social Development* (pp. 2–101) New York: Wiley.

McBride, C. M., Curry, S. J., Cheadle, A., Anderman, C., Wagner, E. H., Diehr, P., & Psaty, B. (1995). School-level application of a social bonding model to adolescent risk-taking behavior. *Journal of School Health*, *65*(2), 63–68.

Newcomb, M. D., & Bentler, P. M. (1986). Frequency and sequence of drug use: A longitudinal study from early adolescence to young adulthood. *Journal of Drug Education*, *16*, 101–120.

Office of National Drug Control Policy. (2001). *Summary: FY2002 National Drug Control Budget*. Washington, DC: The White House.

Oetting, E. R., & Donnermeyer, J. F. (1998). Primary socialization theory: The etiology of drug use and deviance. *Substance Use and Misuse*, *33*(4), 995–1026.

Pandina, R. J., & Johnson, V. (1990). Serious alcohol and drug problems among adolescents with a family history of alcoholism. *Journal of Studies on Alcohol*, *51*, 278–282.

Patterson, G. R., Dishion, T. J., & Yoerger, K. (2000). Adolescent growth in new forms of problem behavior: Macro- and micro-peer dynamics. *Prevention Science*, *1*(1), 3–13.

Pedersen, W. (1991). Mental health, sensation seeking and drug use patterns: A longitudinal study. *British Journal of Addiction*, *86*, 195–204.

Petraitis, J., Flay, B. R., Miller, T. Q., Torpy, E. J., & Greiner, B. (1998). Illicit substance use among adolescents: A matrix of prospective predictors. *Substance Use and Misuse*, *33*(13), 2561–2604.

Pierce, J. P., Choi, W. S., Gilpin, E. A., Farkas, A. J., & Berry, C. C. (1998). Tobacco industry promotion of cigarettes and adolescent smoking. *Journal of the American Medical Association*, *279*, 511–515.

Resnick, M. D., Bearman, B. S., Blum, R. W., & Bauman, K. E. (1998). Protecting adolescents from harm: Findings from the National Longitudinal Study on Adolescent Health. *American Journal of Public Health*, *86*, 956–965.

SAMHSA. (2000). *Summary of findings from the 1999 National Household Survey on Drug Abuse*. National Clearing House for Alcohol and Drug Information [on-line] http://www.samhsa.gov/oas/oasftp.htm   Accessed 10/6/00.

Schinke, S. P., Botvin, G. J., & Orlandi, M. A. (1991). *Substance abuse in children and adolescents: Evaluation and intervention*. Newbury Park, NJ: Sage.

Schivelbusch, W. (1992). *Tastes of paradise: A social history of spices, stimulants, and intoxicants*. New York: Vintage.

Schulenberg, J., Bachman, J. G., O'Malley, P. M., & Johnston, L. D. (1994). High school educational success and subsequent substance use: A panel analysis following adolescents into young adulthood. *Journal of Health and Social Behavior*, *35*, 45–62.

Shedler, J., & Block, J. (1990). Adolescent drug use and psychological health. *American Psychologist*, *45*, 612–630.

Sher, K. J. (1997). Psychological characteristics of children of alcoholics. *Alcohol Health and Research World*, *21*(3), 247–254.

Simons-Morton, B. G., Crump, A. D., Haynie, D. L., Eitel, P., Saylor, K., & Yu, K. (1999). Psychosocial, school, and parent factors associated with smoking among early adolescent boys and girls. *Preventive Medicine*, *28*, 138–148.

Simons-Morton, B. G., Crump, A. D., Saylor, K., & Haynie, D. L. (1999). Student-school bonding and adolescent problem behavior. *Health Education Research*, *14*(1), 99–107.

Simons-Morton, B. G., Haynie, D. L., Crump, A. D., Eitel, P., & Saylor, K. (2001). Peer and parent influences on smoking and drinking among early adolescents. *Health Education and Behavior*, *28*(1), 95–107.

Simons-Morton, B. G., Haynie, D. L., Crump, A. D., Eitel, P., Saylor, K., & Yu, K. (1999b). Expectancies and other psychosocial factors associated with alcohol use among early adolescent boys and girls. *Addictive Behaviors*, *24*(2), 229–238.

Steinberg, L., Fletcher, A., & Darling, N. (1994). Parental monitoring and peer influences on adolescent substance use. *Pediatrics*, *93*(6), 1060–1064.

Teichman, M., Barnea, Z., & Ravav, G. (1989). Personality and substance use among adolescents: A longitudinal study. *British Journal of Addiction*, *84*, 181–190.

Thombs, D. L., Beck, K. H., & Pleace, D. J. (1993). The relationship of social context and expectancy factors to alcohol use intensity among 18- to 22-year-olds. *Addiction Research*, *1*(1), 59–68.

Wallace, J. M., Forman, T. A., Guthrie, B. J., Bachman, J. G., O'Malley, P. M., & Johnston, L. D. (1999). The epidemiology of alcohol, tobacco and other drug use among black youth. *Journal of Studies on Alcohol*, *60*(6) 800–809, 1999.

Weiner, B. (1992). *Human motivation: Metaphors, theories, and research*. Newbury Park, NJ: Sage.

Willemsen, M. C., & DeZwart, W. M. (1999). The effectiveness of policy and health education strategies for reducing adolescent smoking: A review of the evidence. *Journal of Adolescence*, *22*(5), 587–599.

PART II

SOCIAL-EMOTIONAL DOMAIN

Edited by

Tamara G. Halle
Child Trends, Washington, DC

Jonathan F. Zaff

10

Emotional Development and Well-Being

Tamara G. Halle
Child Trends, Washington, DC

INTRODUCTION

Psychologists identify emotions as the essential "building blocks" of well-being (Kahneman, Diener, & Schwarz, 1999). This chapter examines the theoretical and empirical basis for this claim. First, it discusses the operational definitions of emotions and the theoretical perspectives that underlie these definitions, along with the measurement techniques that are associated with these perspectives. Second, it traces the processes associated with emotional development from infancy through adolescence. Next, it reviews the evidence for emotions being essential elements of positive development, both as contributors to and measures of well-being. The chapter also addresses the factors that may affect the promotion of positive emotions, emotion understanding, and emotion regulation during childhood and adolescence. Finally, it suggests directions for future research.

OPERATIONAL DEFINITIONS OF EMOTION

Emotion researchers do not agree on a single definition of emotions (Kleinginna & Kleinginna, 1981). Indeed, a scan of the research indicates that operational definitions of emotion span biological, physiological, cognitive, motivational, and behavioral dimensions. For example, emotions have been defined as (a) states of autonomic arousal (Schachter & Singer, 1962); (b) attitudes (Bull, 1951); (c) mechanisms that control shifts in goal states or motivations to act (Frijda, 1986; Lang, 1995); (d) affective reactions preceding and/or lacking perceptual and cognitive encoding (Zajonc, 1980); and (e) cognitive appraisals of social events (Lazarus, 1991).

Despite the multitude of operational definitions, most emotion researchers agree that emotions consist of several components within the domains of physiological responses, subjective experience, and observable behaviors that interact in complex ways (Frijda, 1999). The extent to which each of these components contributes to emotions, the ways in which the components are linked across domains, and the primacy of one component over others comprise the issues that distinguish one operational definition from another.

The various operational definitions of emotion also differ from each other because they stem from different theoretical perspectives on emotions and emotional development. The literature on emotional development identifies two major theoretical frameworks used to understand emotions: the structural approach and the functional approach.

Structural Approaches to Emotional Development

The structural view of emotions has its roots in human evolutionary biology. Emotions are characterized as "discrete, coherent constellations of physiological, subjective, and expressive activity" (Thompson, 1993, p. 374). "Basic" emotions such as sadness, happiness, and fear are considered distinct entities and are thought to be biologically based and constrained. Furthermore, each distinct emotion is claimed to be associated uniquely with particular patterns of behavioral expression and cognitive and subjective experience; these unique patterns of association develop over time.

Emotion researchers from a structuralist perspective tend to use measurement techniques that focus on specific, discrete physiological and behavioral elements that signify emotions. Elaborate and detailed coding schemes and apparatus have been developed for capturing physiological expressions of emotional arousal (e.g., measures that index brain electrical activity, electrodermal activity, respiratory activity, or cardiovascular activity) and facial expressions of emotion (e.g., the Facial Action Coding System [FACS]; Ekman & Friesen, 1975, 1978, and the Maximally Discriminative Facial Movement Coding System [MAX]; Izard, 1979).

These types of measurement systems have been found to be valid indices of emotional arousal (e.g., Cacioppio, Petty, Losch, & Kim, 1986) and have been used widely by developmental and emotion researchers to identify and monitor emotional responses among infants, children, and adults. However, these measurement techniques can be problematic. For example, although validity of facial expression measures have been established, some researchers question the reliability of these measures as indices of emotion, especially during infancy and early childhood (Camras, 1992). Furthermore, some measures of autonomic nervous system activity can be invasive (e.g., electrodes placed on the face or chest) and could potentially elicit emotional responses in and of themselves, thereby compromising the measures' validity (Larsen & Frederickson, 1999).

Recently, there have been challenges to the structuralist approach on theoretical grounds. Some theorists have questioned whether emotions are truly biologically based or physiologically and expressively distinct (Ortony & Turner, 1990). Emotion researchers who voice these concerns are more likely to hold a functionalist view of emotions.

Functional Approaches to Emotional Development

The functionalist view of emotions derives from ecological and dynamic systems approaches to development. Rather than being biologically based, emotions are seen as emerging from ongoing transactions between an organism and its environment (Campos, Campos, & Barrett, 1989; Camras, 1992). Though acknowledging that emotions may be biologically adaptive, functionalists emphasize the flexibility of emotional responses; that is, physiological or behavioral components of emotion are not thought to be mapped onto distinct emotional states, but rather are believed to serve different functions depending on context or social circumstance. Functionalists define emotions as "processes of establishing, maintaining, or disrupting the relations between the person and the internal or external environment, when such relations are significant to the individual" (Campos, Campos, & Barrett, 1989, p. 395; see also Saarni, Mumme, & Campos, 1998, p. 238). Although this definition of emotion has been criticized for being too broad (e.g., capturing processes which some emotion researchers would question as expressions of emotion—such as hunger or boredom), it has become the dominant view of emotion in the past decade (Thompson, 1993).

The functionalist view of emotional development suggests that changes in person–environment relations will bring about changes in emotional development. Evidence that is often cited to support this claim is the finding that infants develop a sense of wariness only after they master the ability to crawl (Campos, Bertenthal, & Kermoian, 1992). Social events, such as school entry or childbirth, also change the person–environment relationship and are therefore expected to reorganize emotion as well, according to this theory (Saarni, Mumme, & Campos, 1998). The functionalist view of emotion also emphasizes the importance of the socialization process in the development of emotional experience, as well as the importance of context.

Emotion researchers from a functionalist perspective tend to use measurements that emphasize subjective perceptions of emotion (gathered either through self-reports of emotions, observer ratings, or reports from third-party informants), although they also sometimes gather objective, physiological indexes of emotion (e.g., heart rate). Self- or other-reports that are in survey form (e.g., multi-item rating scales, checklists, or single-item questions) are popular among researchers, but they also pose some serious methodological concerns (see Bracken, Keith, & Walker,

1998; Larsen & Frederickson, 1999). In a recent review of the psychometric properties of 13 preschool measures of social-emotional functioning (all third-party informant measures), Bracken et al. (1998) found that most of the measures had inadequacies, such as problems with internal consistency, stability, inter-rater reliability, and evidence of validity. Furthermore, self-report measures may be subject to response biases and only capture the cognitive aspects of emotion (Diener, 1994). In sum, no measurement of emotions is without shortcomings, but researchers can increase the odds of capturing the construct by using multiple methods of measurement concurrently (Larsen & Frederickson, 1999).

CONTINUITY AND CHANGE IN EMOTIONS FROM INFANCY THROUGH ADOLESCENCE

Emotions develop very early and are therefore believed to have a biological basis. Some of the earliest developing regions of the brain are associated with emotional expression (National Research Council & National Institute of Medicine, 2000); indeed, newborns have the capacity to display distress. However, emotions are also relational by nature and are believed both to emerge from and provide the basis for human interactions and attachments (Emde, 1987, 1998).

Emotional states in infancy are extreme and not well-regulated. Infants learn, through social interactions with caregivers, to associate meanings and expectations with different behavioral and physical manifestations of emotion. Over time, children learn both to moderate and regulate their emotions. Over the second and third years of life, child-initiated behaviors and affective expressions increase and parent-initiated affect correspondingly decreases, signaling an increased ability on the part of the child to self-regulate her emotion states (Grolnick, Cosgrove, & Bridges, 1996). Emotions get "labeled" through conversations with caregivers and children learn social rules accompanying the expression of emotion (Denham & Auerbach, 1995). By the end of the preschool years, children are able to generate and regulate their emotional expressions to fit the social context appropriately—even to the point of hiding their emotions from others (Harris, 1993). A child's emotional repertoire also expands during the preschool years to include socially influenced emotions such as shame and guilt. By the age of 2, children also express genuine empathy for others (Zahn-Waxler & Radke-Yarrow, 1990). Both of these latter accomplishments reflect further growth in cognitive and social capabilities, as well as signal a burgeoning self-system.

Across the preschool and school-age years, children hone their understanding of emotions in themselves and others through experience with a broader set of social agents, including friends, classmates, teachers, coaches, and other adults. An expanded set of social circumstances also provides opportunities to experience the consequences of restrained and unrestrained emotional expressions. With increased experience, young children's emotional expressions start to conform to the social norms of the culture in which they live (Saarni, Mumme, & Campos, 1998).

It is popularly believed that adolescents are "more emotional" than are younger children and older adults, and that adolescents experience more pronounced mood swings (Sharp, 1980). Although it is true that adolescence is a time of rapid physiological, psychological, and social change, recent research indicates that adolescents are not necessarily more emotionally variable than younger children (Kochanska, Coy, Tjebkes, & Husarek, 1998; Larson & Lampman-Petraitis, 1989), nor do they differ from adults in mean levels of emotion (Larson & Ham, 1993). Some studies have suggested that adolescents experience more negative daily events than do younger children (Larson & Ham, 1993), and report more occasions of both negative and positive emotional extremes than adults (Larson, Csikszentmihalyi, & Graef, 1980). These studies seem to suggest that adolescents may not be "more emotional" than younger or older individuals, but may have more experiences that elicit extreme emotional responses at this point in development.

The only aspect of emotions that shows strong continuity is the physiological expression of emotions. Changes in heart rate, for example, are remarkably consistent across individual development, across individuals, and across cultures. Facial and vocal behaviors (e.g., smiling, crying) also show stability across development and have a universal quality (Van Bezooijen, Otto, & Heenan, 1983), although cross-cultural differences in expressiveness and intensity of emotion have been found among infants (Camras et al., 1998).

The theoretical constructs of emotional states, traits, and moods are crucial to any discussion of continuity and change in emotions. Emotions that are fleeting but intense, and that are associated with a particular event or action are called *states* (Ortony, Clore, & Collins, 1988). Emotions that are less intense, more diffuse, and more enduring are called *moods* (Forgas, 1991). Affective styles that are even more consistent over time are considered *traits*. The consistency of emotional traits across the life course suggests a biological component that is linked to temperament and personality development (Rothbart & Posner, 1985).

The more stable, consistent, trait-like aspects of emotions are thought to be more strongly linked to overall well-being than are more transient and context-specific emotional states (Lazarus, 1991). However, research indicates that both our general outlook on life and the hassles and joys we experience on a day-by-day basis can promote or diminish our perceived sense of well-being (Feist, Bodner, Jacobs, Miles, & Tan, 1995; Saarni, 1999).

HOW ARE EMOTIONS RELATED TO POSITIVE DEVELOPMENT?

Emotions as Contributors to Positive Development

Emotions, both positive and negative,[1] are understood to play a pivotal role in a host of positive life outcomes, including the establishment of secure attachment relation-

---

[1]There is an ongoing debate in the literature about whether positive and negative affect are separate entities or are at opposite poles of a single affective dimension (Diener, Smith, & Fujita, 1995). Due to space limitations, as well as the intended focus of this chapter, I will not address this theoretical debate.

ships (Saarni, 1990), good sibling and peer relations (Denham, McKinley, Couchoud, & Holt, 1990; Dunn, Slomkowski, & Beardsall, 1994), the development of empathy (Hoffman, 1984), adherence to social rules (Banerjee, 1997; Lay, Waters, & Park, 1989), attention and concentration (Rose, Futterweit, & Jankowski, 1999), motivation (Patrick, Skinner, & Connell, 1993), memory (Fagen, Ohr, Fleckstein, & Ribner, 1985; Nasby & Yando, 1982), creativity (Greene & Noice, 1988; Larson, 1990), school achievement (Chen & Dornbusch, 1998; Yasutake & Bryan, 1995), physical health (Salovey, Rothman, Detweiler, & Steward, 2000), job satisfaction (Fisher, 2000), and life satisfaction (Pilcher, 1998).[2]

Some research suggests that positive emotions are associated with the promotion of positive developmental outcomes, whereas negative emotions are associated with nonoptimal and/or problematic outcomes, especially in the area of health. For example, there appears to be a direct connection between emotions and the functioning of the human immune system: Positive mood states decrease susceptibility to illness and negative mood states increase susceptibility (Cohen et al., 1995; Salovey et al., 2000). However, most researchers agree that positive emotions are not universally associated with positive outcomes, nor are negative emotions always linked to negative outcomes. For example, experiencing anger when one's moral code has been violated may be an appropriate expression of righteous indignation (Saarni, 1999). Likewise, feeling extreme sadness or melancholy after suffering a major loss is an entirely appropriate reaction. Indeed, not expressing appropriate sadness in such a situation may signal abnormal social and emotional adjustment. Thus, so-called negative emotions such as deep sadness or anger may actually be adaptive for mental health and overall well-being (Saarni, 1999).

Just as negative emotions do not always lead to bad outcomes, positive emotions do not always lead to positive outcomes (Bloom & Capatides, 1987; Diener, Colvin, Pavot, & Allman, 1991; Mackie & Worth, 1989; Rose et al., 1999). For example, infants who display more positive affect, compared to infants who display more neutral or negative affect, are found to lag behind in their language development (Bloom & Capatides, 1987) and learning (Rose et al., 1999). The fact that positive affect interferes with learning among adults (e.g., Mackie & Worth, 1989; Sinclair & Mark, 1995) lends support for the validity of these findings and for the continuity of the phenomenon across development. The explanation offered for these counter-intuitive findings is that positive mood states prime positive emotional memories that take up room in short-term memory, leaving less room for processing other information (Mackie & Worth, 1989). This research suggests that neutral expressions of emotion may be more conducive to efficient information processing than are positive emotional states (Rose et al., 1999; Ruff, 1982).

---

[2]While emotions are critical contributors to cognitive, social and physical functioning, they are also mediated by mechanisms in these very domains (Lewis, 1993; National Research Council & Institute of Medicine, 2000). Thus, positive emotional development is also dependent upon positive development in each of these other domains.

Emotion regulation researchers suggest that moderation in emotional expression may be more optimal than intense emotions of either positive or negative valence. Thus, it is not positive or negative emotions per se that lead to positive outcomes, but rather the ability to regulate the overt expression of one's emotional responses (in terms of intensity, duration, and social appropriateness) that leads to optimal outcomes (Salovey, Hsee, & Mayer, 1993).[3] For example, a child who resists laughing at another person's expense (even if the situation is funny) would be judged as more socially competent than a child who did express laughter in this context. Similarly, a child who mitigates her disappointment for not getting what she wanted as a birthday gift would be judged as more mature than a child who has a temper tantrum.

Emotion understanding (i.e., the ability to recognize and label emotions in oneself and others, and the ability to distinguish internal emotional experiences from external emotional expression) is related to the development of emotion regulation and to the development of social competence (Banerjee, 1997; D'Andrade, 1987; Dunn & Brown, 1994; Saarni, 1999; Wellman, Harris, Banerjee, & Sinclair, 1995). As such, emotion understanding is another important contributor to positive development. However, because emotion understanding is believed to develop as part of a child's "theory of mind" (i.e., the psychological understanding of self and others) during the preschool years (Banerjee, 1997; D'Andrade, 1987; Wellman, Harris, Banerjee, & Sinclair, 1995), this aspect of emotional competence is also part of the system of positive cognitive developmental processes, and therefore is not exclusively within the socioemotional domain. Similarly, emotion regulation can also be cross-referenced within the physical domain of positive development, because it in part concerns the intentional regulation of physiological arousal. In fact, as noted throughout this volume, it is difficult to consider well-being without acknowledging the mutually interactive roles played by cognition, emotion, physiology, and the self-system (Harter, 1986; Lewis, 1993; National Research Council & Institute of Medicine, 2000).

Emotions as Measures of Positive Development

Emotions are not only used as predictors of positive development, but also as outcome measures. Due to the historical prominence of a deficit model of well-being, there are many more studies that use the reduction of negative emotions (e.g., depression) as their measure of well-being than there are studies that use the promotion of positive emotions (e.g., happiness). Although this trend has begun to change (Diener, 2000; Halle & Moore, 1998; Moore & Halle, 2001), the use of positive emotions (e.g., joy, happiness, and contentment) as outcome measures in extant research is rare, especially in the child development literature. Indeed, most of the recent work on happiness as a dependent variable, as well as psychometric work on

---

[3]Suppressing or inhibiting emotions may lead to poor outcomes in some cases (Frijda, 1999; Gross, 1998).

measures of positive affect, are based on research with adults (e.g., Pilcher, 1998; Roesch, 1998; Seligman & Csikszentmihalyi, 2000).

In contrast, the developmental literature has many examples of studies focused on emotion understanding and emotion regulation as outcomes among children and youth. For instance, Judy Dunn and her colleagues (Dunn & Brown, 1994; Dunn, Brown, & Beardsall, 1991) conducted several naturalistic, longitudinal studies that demonstrated that talk about emotions within the family during the third year of life is related to children's social cognitive understanding of emotions at age 6. Another study showed a link between emotion language used at 33 months and the child's emotion understanding at 40 months (Dunn, Brown, Slomkowski, Tesla, & Youngblade, 1991). In these studies, the associations between emotion language and emotion understanding were not mediated by the child's verbal fluency or general linguistic experience, emphasizing the importance of social interactions in the promotion of socioemotional competencies. We explore factors that promote emotional development next.

FACTORS AFFECTING THE PROMOTION OF POSITIVE EMOTION DEVELOPMENT

Factors that are found to promote positive emotional development may have implications for interventions designed to promote overall well-being.

Promoting Positive Affect

As mentioned earlier, positive emotions do not always produce optimal outcomes and are therefore not a prerequisite for positive development (Bloom & Capatides, 1987; Larson, 1990; Rose et al., 1999; Ruff, 1982). Nevertheless, there are several studies that indicate promoting positive affect can lead to positive outcomes. The technique most often used to promote positive affect is mood induction. The typical mood induction technique often used with children is a visualization task, where children are asked to think of an event that makes them feel happy or sad (Yasutake & Bryan, 1995). Studies of school-age children show that inducing a positive mood state improves performance on creative problem-solving and mathematics tasks (Bryan & Bryan, 1991; Greene & Noice, 1988; Yasutake & Bryan, 1995). Impressive results have also been achieved in the physical health of AIDS and cancer patients by inducing positive mood states (Salovey et al., 2000). Despite the noted successes of mood induction interventions, there are some concerns with this research. First, much of this research has been conducted on small samples within specialized populations (e.g., Yasutake & Bryan, 1995) and therefore the generalizability of the findings is unclear. Second, the mood induction techniques used in these studies have questionable ecological validity. It is also important to know how effective such techniques would be if used repeatedly in the same context. Finally, it is not clear that changes in transient mood states can have long-term effects on outcomes. Additional long-term, follow-up studies need to be conducted on the duration of mood-inducement effects on positive development.

Promoting Emotion Understanding

Parent socialization practices are considered the primary factor that influences emotion understanding (Denham, Zoller, & Couchoud, 1994; Eisenberg, Fabes, Carlo, & Karbon, 1992; Harris, 1994; Laible & Thompson, 1998). Parents promote emotion understanding by responding to infants' early behavioral expressions of emotion (e.g., crying, smiling), by modeling emotional expressiveness (Denham & Grout, 1992; Wilson & Gottman, 1995), and by talking about emotions (Denham & Auerbach, 1995; Dunn & Brown, 1994). The quality of the parent–child relationship is also considered to be an important factor in the development of emotion understanding (Laible & Thompson, 1998). Researchers have theorized that children who have a warm and secure relationship with their parent(s) would have more advanced understanding of emotions than children who have a relationship marked by ambivalence or lack of trust. The emotional state of the parent may have a significant effect on the quality of the parent–child relationship. For instance, a parent who is severely depressed may have a harder time responding effectively to his/her child's emotional (and physical) needs, thus encouraging the development of an insecure attachment relationship between parent and child.

Because the parent–child relationship is so critical to the development of emotion understanding, interventions that target parents may be useful in promoting children's emotional development. In particular, programs that educate parents on their important role in fostering their children's emotional development may be quite effective, especially if an awareness campaign is coupled with parenting skills classes. In addition, efforts to screen parents for emotional disorders, and provide treatment when needed, may be effective in bringing about gains in children's emotional well-being as well as that of the parents.

Parent–child interactions are not the only factor that promotes emotion understanding. Engagement in pretend play also has been found to be associated with more advanced understanding of mental states, including emotional states (Harris, 1994). Early interventions and preschool programs that encourage pretend play may serve to promote emotion understanding among young children. For older children, interventions that focus on understanding emotions within peer interactions become important.

Promoting Emotion Regulation

The factors that influence the promotion of emotion regulation are primarily elements of cognitive development, specifically attention, memory, and information processing (Rothbart & Posner, 1985). During the second and third years of life, these cognitive abilities emerge and influence the development of intentional, autonomous control (Grolnick et al., 1996; Rothbart & Posner, 1985). As mentioned earlier in this chapter, emotion regulation is based, in part, on the ability to recognize internal emotional states, label them, and simultaneously assess the social context and the appropriate behavior required in that context. Therefore, promoting emotion understanding may also serve to promote emotion regulation in children and adolescents.

The parent–child relationship also plays a critical role in the development of emotion regulation. In particular, researchers note the importance of the attachment relationship (Cassidy, 1994) and parental coaching in appropriate emotional expression (Miller & Sperry, 1987) in promoting emotion regulation. Thus, interventions that include parent education may help promote emotion regulation among young children.

CONCLUSIONS

Emotions may have a biological basis, but they are made manifest and acquire meaning within social contexts. Emotions affect the successful development of individuals in a number of ways: directly through the experience of emotions and also through the processes of emotion understanding and emotion regulation. It is important to note that positive emotions are not always associated with optimal outcomes, nor are negative emotions always associated with nonoptimal outcomes. In some situations, particularly those requiring attention, concentration, or complex information processing, neutral emotional states may be superior to positive emotional states for achieving positive outcomes. However, both transient mood states and more enduring emotional dispositions are important components of emotional well-being. The ability to regulate the intensity, duration, and appropriateness of emotional states—both positive and negative—is key to maintaining a sense of well-being. The ability to label and understand the emotions that we and others are feeling is also key to our own emotional health and to our ability to relate effectively to others (Howes, 1987; Sroufe, Schork, Motti, Lawrowski, & LaFreniere, 1984; Walter & LaFreniere, 2000). From the cumulative evidence, it is clear that emotions and emotional processes are essential building blocks of well-being.

Despite the vast amount we already know about emotional development, more longitudinal studies are needed to understand more fully the continuity and change in emotion development across the life course. The current knowledge base relies mainly on separate studies of infants, toddlers, preschoolers, and school-age children. Likewise, there are very few studies that follow the same individuals from adolescence into adulthood (but see Offer, Kaiz, Howard, & Bennett, 1998). Longitudinal research is also needed to understand the underlying mechanisms by which emotions and emotional processes affect positive outcomes across multiple domains (Salovey et al., 2000).

Another limitation of the current knowledge base is the relative lack of diversity in the samples collected within the United States. Most of what is known about emotional development in the U.S. population is based on studies of middle-class white children (National Research Council & Institute of Medicine, 2000). There is suggestive evidence that socioeconomic and cultural contexts are responsible for significant variability in how children learn to interpret and express emotions. Consequently, it is important for future research to address cultural and economic variability within the United States and to strive for more nationally representative samples. With a growing immigrant population in the United States, a closer examination of cross-cultural studies of emotional development may also provide important insights.

Finally, it is believed that emotional development both advances and is advanced by other developmental systems—in particular, the physiological system, cognitive structures, and the self-system (National Research Council & National Institute of Medicine, 2000). Future research on emotional development and its influence on well-being should begin to integrate the best knowledge and methodologies across these multiple domains.

ACKNOWLEDGMENT

I thank Carolyn Saarni for her review of an earlier draft of this chapter.

REFERENCES

Banerjee, M. (1997). Hidden emotions: Preschoolers' knowledge of appearance-reality and emotion display rules. *Social Cognition*, *15*, 107–132.

Bloom, L., & Capatides, J. (1987). Expression of affect and the emergence of language. *Child Development*, *58*, 1513–1522.

Bracken, B. A., Keith, L. K., & Walker, K. C. (1998). Assessment of preschool behavior and social-emotional functioning: A review of thirteen third-party instruments. *Journal of Psychoeducational Assessment*, *16*, 153–169.

Bryan, T., & Bryan, J. (1991). Positive mood and math performance. *Journal of Learning Disabilities*, *24*, 490–494.

Bull, N. (1951). The attitude theory of emotion. *Nervous and Mental Disease Monographs*, No. 81.

Cacioppo, J. T., Petty, R. E., Losch, M. E., & Kim, H. S. (1986). Electromyographic activity over facial muscle regions can differentiate the valence and intensity of affective reactions. *Journal of Personality and Social Psychology*, *50*, 260–268.

Campos, J., Bertenthal, B., & Kermoian, R. (1992). Early experience and emotional development: The emergence of wariness of heights. *Psychological Science*, *3*, 61–64.

Campos, J. J., Campos, R. G., & Barrett, K. C. (1989). Emergent themes in the study of emotional development and emotion regulation. *Developmental Psychology*, *25*, 394–402.

Camras, L. A. (1992). Expressive development and basic emotions. *Cognition and Emotion*, *6*, 269–283.

Cassidy, J. (1994). Emotion regulation: Influences of attachment relationships. *Monographs of the Society for Research in Child Development* (2/3, serial No. 240), *59*, 228–249.

Chen, Z., & Dornsbusch, S. M. (1998). Relating aspects of adolescent emotional autonomy to academic achievement and deviant behavior. *Journal of Adolescent Research*, *13*, 293–319.

Cohen, S., Doyle, W. J., Skoner, D. P., Fireman, P., Gwaltney, J. M., & Newsom, J. T. (1995). State and trait negative affect as predictors of objective and subjective symptoms of respiratory viral infections. *Journal of Personality and Social Psychology*, *68*, 159–169.

D'Andrade, R. (1987). A folk model of the mind. In D. Holland & N. Quinn (Eds.), *Cultural models in language and thought* (pp. 112–148). New York: Cambridge University Press.

Denham, S. A., & Auerbach, S. (1995). Mother-child dialogue about emotions and preschoolers' emotional competence. *Genetic, Social, and General Psychology Monographs*, *121*, 311–337.

Denham, S. A., & Grout, L. (1992). Mothers' emotional expressiveness and coping: Relations with preschoolers' social-emotional competence. *Genetic, Social, and General Psychology Monographs, 118*, 73–101.

Denham, S. A., McKinley, M., Couchoud, E. A., & Holt, R. (1990). Emotional and behavioral predictors
of preschool peer ratings. *Child Development, 61*, 1145–1152.

Denham, S. A., Zoller, D., & Couchoud, E. A. (1994). Socialization of preschoolers' emotion understanding. *Developmental Psychology, 30*, 928–936.

Diener, E. (1994). Assessing subjective well-being: Progress and opportunities. *Social Indicators Research, 31*, 103–157.

Diener, E. (2000). Subjective well-being: The science of happiness and a proposal for a national index.
American Psychologist, 55, 34–43.

Diener, E., Colvin, C. R., Pavot, W. G., & Allman, A. (1991). The psychic costs of intense positive affect.
Journal of Personality & Social Psychology, 61, 492–503.

Diener, E., Smith, H., & Fujita, F. (1995). The personality structure of affect. *Journal of Personality and
Social Psychology, 69*, 130–141.

Dunn, J., & Brown, J. (1994). Affect expression in the family, children's understanding of emotions, and
their interactions with others. *Merrill-Palmer Quarterly, 40*, 120–137.

Dunn, J., Brown, J., & Beardsall, L. (1991). Family talk about feeling states and children's later understanding of others' emotions. *Developmental Psychology, 27*, 448–455.

Dunn, J., Brown, J., Slomkowski, C., Tesla, C., & Youngblade, L. (1991). Young children's understanding of other people's feelings and beliefs: Individual differences and their antecedents. *Child Development, 62*, 1352–1366.

Dunn, J., Slomkowski, C., & Beardsall, L. (1994). Sibling relationships from the preschool period
through middle childhood and early adolescence. *Developmental Psychology, 30*, 315–324.

Eisenberg, N., Fabes, R., Carlo, G., & Karbon, M. (1992). Emotional responsivity to others: Behavioral correlates and socialization antecedents. In N. Eisenberg & R. Fabes (Eds.), *New directions in child development: Emotion and its regulation in early development* (Vol. 5, pp. 57–73). San Francisco: Jossey-Bass.

Ekman, P., & Friesen, W. (1975). *Unmasking the face.* Englewood Cliffs, NJ: Prentice-Hall.

Ekman, P., & Friesen, W. (1978). *Facial action coding system.* Palo Alto, CA: Consulting Psychologists Press.

Emde, R. N. (1987). The infant's relationship experience: Developmental and affective aspects. In A. J. Sameroff
& R. N. Emde (Eds.), *Relationship disturbances in early childhood* (pp. 33–51). New York: Basic.

Emde, R. N. (1998). Early emotional development: New modes of thinking for research and intervention. In J. G. Warhol (Ed.), *New perspectives in early emotional development* (pp. 29–45). New
Brunswick, NJ: Johnson & Johnson Pediatric Institute.

Fagen, J. W., Ohr, P. S., Fleckstein, L. K., & Ribner, D. (1985). The effect of crying on long-term memory in infancy. *Child Development, 56*, 1584–1592.

Feist, G., Bodner, T., Jacobs, J., Miles, M., & Tan, V. (1995). Integrating top-down and bottom-up structural models of subjective well-being: A longitudinal investigation. *Journal of Personality and Social Psychology, 68*, 138–150.

Fisher, C. D. (2000). Mood and emotions while working: Missing pieces of job satisfaction? *Journal of
Organizational Behavior, 21*, 185–202.

Forgas, J. P. (1991). Affect and social judgments: An introductory review. In J. P. Forgas (Ed.), *Emotion
and social judgments* (pp. 3–30). Tarrytown, NY: Pergamon.

Fridja, N. H. (1986). *The emotions.* Cambridge: Cambridge University Press.

Fridja, N. H. (1999). Emotions and hedonic experience. In D. Kahneman, E. Diener, & N. Schwarz
(Eds.), *Well-being: The foundations of hedonic psychology* (pp. 190–210). New York: Russell Sage.

Greene, T. R., & Noice, H. (1988). Influence of positive affect upon creative thinking and problem solving in children. *Psychological Reports, 63*, 894–898.

Grolnick, W. S., Cosgrove, T. J., & Bridges, L. J. (1996). Age-graded change in the initiation of positive
affect. *Infant Behavior and Development, 19*, 153–157.

Gross, J. J. (1998). The emerging field of emotion regulation: An integrative review. *Review of General
Psychology, 2*, 271–299.

Halle, T., & Moore, K. (1998). Creating indicators of positive development. In *A Report of the Four-
teenth Annual Rosalynn Carter Symposium on Mental Health Policy: Promoting Positive and
Healthy Behaviors in Children* (pp. 59–65). Atlanta, GA: The Carter Center.

Harris, P. L. (1993). Understanding emotion. In M. Lewis & J. M. Haviland (Eds.), *Handbook of emotions* (pp. 237–246). New York: Guilford.

Harris, P. (1994). The child's understanding of emotion: Developmental change and the family environment. *Journal of Child Psychology and Psychiatry, 35*, 3–28.

Harter, S. (1986). Cognitive-developmental processes in the integration of concepts about emotions and the self. *Social Cognition, 4*, 119–151.

Hoffman, M. (1984). Empathy, its limitations, and its role in a comprehensive moral theory. In W. Kurtines & J. Gewirtz (Eds.), *Morality, moral behavior, and moral development* (pp. 283–302). New York: Wiley.

Howes, C. (1987). Social competence with peers in young children: Developmental sequences. *Developmental Review, 7*, 252–272.

Izard, C. E. (1979). *Emotions in personality and psychopathology*. New York: Plenum.

Kahneman, D., Diener, E., & Schwarz, N. (1999). *Well-being: The foundations of hedonic psychology*. New York: Russell Sage.

Kleinginna, P. R., & Kleinginna, A. M. (1981). A categorized list of emotion definitions, with suggestions for a consensual definition. *Motivation and Emotion, 5*, 345–379.

Kochanska, G., Coy, K. C., Tjebkes, T. L., & Husarek, S. J. (1998). Individual difference in emotionality in infancy. *Child Development, 64*, 375–390.

Laible, D. J., & Thompson, R. A. (1998). Attachment and emotional understanding in preschool children. *Developmental Psychology, 34*, 1038–1045.

Lang, P. J. (1995). The emotion people. *American Psychologist, 50*, 372–385.

Larsen, R. J., & Frederickson, B. L. (1999). Measurement issues in emotion research. In D. Kahneman, E. Diener, & N. Schwarz (Eds.), *Well-being: The foundations of hedonic psychology* (pp. 40–60). New York: Russell Sage.

Larson, R., Csikszentmihalyi, M., & Graef, R. (1980). Mood variability and the psychosocial adjustment of adolescents. *Journal of Youth and Adolescence, 9*, 469–490.

Larson, R., & Ham, M. (1993). Stress and "storm and stress" in early adolescence: The relationship of negative events with dysphoric affect. *Developmental Psychology, 29*, 130–140.

Larson, R., & Lampman-Petraitis, C. (1989). Daily emotional states as reported by children and adolescents. *Child Development, 60*, 1250–1260.

Larson, R. W., & Almeida, D. M. (1999). Emotional transmission in the daily lives of families: A new paradigm for studying family process. *Journal of Marriage and the Family, 61*, 5–20.

Larson, R. W. (1990). Emotions and the creative process: Anxiety, boredom, and enjoyment as predictors of creative writing. *Imagination, Cognition & Personality, 9*, 275–292.

Lay, K., Waters, E., & Park, K. A. (1989). Maternal responsiveness and child compliance: The role of mood as a mediator. *Child Development, 60*, 1405–1411.

Lazarus, R. S. (1991). *Emotion and adaptation*. New York: Oxford University Press.

Lewis, M. (1993). The emergence of human emotion. In M. Lewis & J. Haviland (Eds.), *Handbook of emotions* (pp. 223–235). New York: Guilford Press.

Mackie, D. M., & Worth, L. T. (1989). Processing deficits and the mediation of positive affect in persuasion. *Journal of Personality and Social Psychology, 57*, 27–40.

Miller, P. J., & Sperry, L. L. (1987). The socialization of anger and aggression. *Merrill-Palmer Quarterly, 33*, 1–31.

Moore, K. A., & Halle, T. G. (2001). Preventing problems vs. promoting the positive: What do we want for our children? In S. L. Hofferth & T. Owens (Eds.), *Children at the Millennium: Where have we come from, where are we going?* (pp. 141–170). Greenwich, CT: JAI Press.

Nasby, W., & Yando, R. (1982). Selective encoding and retrieval of affectively valent information: Two cognitive consequences of children's mood states. *Journal of Personality and Social Psychology, 43*, 1244–1253.

National Research Council & Institute of Medicine (2000). *From neurons to neighborhoods: The science of early childhood development*. J. P. Schonkoff & D. A. Phillips (Eds.). Washington, DC: National Academy Press.

Offer, D., Kaiz, M., Howard, K. I., & Bennett, E. S. (1998). Emotional variables in adolescence, and their stability and contribution to the mental health of adult men: Implications for early intervention strategies. *Journal of Youth & Adolescence, 27*, 675–690.

Ortony, A., Clore, G., & Collins, A. (1988). *The cognitive structure of emotions*. Cambridge: Cambridge University Press.

Ortony, A., & Turner, T. J. (1990). What's basic about basic emotions? *Psychological Review, 97*, 315–331.

Patrick, B. C., Skinner, E. A., & Connell, J. P. (1993). What motivates children's behavior and emotion? Joint effects of perceived control and autonomy in the academic domain. *Journal of Personality and Social Psychology, 65*, 781–791.

Pilcher, J. J. (1998). Affective and daily event predictors of life satisfaction in college students. *Social Indicators Research, 43*, 291–306.

Roesch, S. C. (1998). The factorial validity of trait positive affect scores: Confirmatory factor analyses of unidimensional and multidimensional models. *Educational and Psychological Measurement, 58*, 451–466.

Rose, S. A., Futterweit, L. R., & Jankowski, J. J. (1999). The relation of affect to attention and learning in infancy. *Child Development, 70*, 549–559.

Rothbart, M. K., & Posner, M. I. (1985). Temperament and the development of self-regulation. In L. C. Hartlage & C. F. Telzrow (Eds.), *The neuropsychology of individual differences* (pp. 93–123). New York: Plenum.

Ruff, H. A., (1982). Role of manipulation of infants' responses to invariant properties of objects. *Developmental Psychology, 18*, 682–691.

Saarni, C. (1999). *The development of emotional competence*. New York: Guilford Press.

Saarni, C., Mumme, D. L., & Campos, J. J. (1998). Emotional development: Action, communication, and understanding. In W. Damon (Series Ed.) & N. Eisenberg (Vol. Ed.), *Handbook of child psychology: Vol. 3. Social, emotional, and personality development* (5th ed., pp. 237–309). New York: Wiley.

Salovey, P., Hsee, C. K., & Mayer, J. D. (1993). Emotional intelligence and the self-regulation of affect. In D. M. Wegner & J. W. Pennebaker (Eds.), *Handbook of mental control* (pp. 258–277). Englewood, NJ: Prentice-Hall.

Salovey, P., Rothman, A. J., Detweiler, J. B., & Steward, W. T. (2000). Emotional states and physical health. *American Psychologist, 55*, 110–121.

Schachter, S., & Singer, J. (1962). Cognitive, social and physiological determinants of emotional state. *Psychological Review, 63*, 379–399.

Seligman, M. E. P., & Czikszentmihalyi, M. (2000). (Guest Eds.), Special issue on happiness, excellence, and optimal human functioning. *American Psychologist, 55*.

Sharp, V. (1980). Adolescence. In J. Bemorad (Ed.), *Child development in normality and psychopathology* (pp. 174–218). New York: Brunner/Mazel.

Sinclair, R. C., & Mark, M. M. (1995). The effects of mood state on judgmental accuracy: Processing strategy as a mechanism. *Cognition and Emotion, 9*, 417–438.

Sroufe, L. A., Schork, E., Motti, F., Lawrowski, N., & LaFreniere, P. J. (1984). The role of affect in social competence. In C. E. Izard, J. Kagan, & R. Zajonc (Eds.), *Emotions, cognition and behavior* (pp. 289–319). New York: Plenum.

Thompson, R. A. (1993). Socioemotional development: Enduring issues and new challenges. *Developmental Review, 13*, 372–402.

Van Bezooijen, R., Otto, S. A., & Heenan, T. A. (1983). Recognition of vocal expressions of emotion: A three-nation study to identify universal characteristics. *Journal of Cross-cultural Studies, 14*, 387–406.

Walter, J. L., & LaFreniere, P. J. (2000). A naturalistic study of affective expression, social competence, and sociometric status in preschoolers. *Early Education & Development, 11*, 109–122.

Wellman, H., Harris, P. L., Banerjee, M., & Sinclair, A. (1995). Early understanding of emotion: Evidence from natural language. *Cognition and Emotion, 9*, 117–149.

Wilson, B. J., & Gottman, J. M. (1995). Marital interaction and parenting. In M. H. Bornstein (Ed.), *Handbook of parenting* (Vol. 4, pp. 33–55). Mahwah, NJ: Lawrence Erlbaum Associates.

Yasutake, D., & Bryan, T. (1995). The influence of affect on the achievement and behavior of students with learning disabilities. *Journal of Learning Disabilities, 28*(6), 329–334.

Zahn-Waxler, C., & Radke-Yarrow, M. (1990). The origins of empathic concern. *Motivation and Emotion, 14*, 107–130.

Zajonc, R. B. (1980). Thinking and feeling: Preferences need no inferences. *American Psychologist, 35*, 151–175.

11

Emotion Regulation From Infancy Through Adolescence

William G. Graziano

Renée M. Tobin
Department of Psychology
Texas A&M University, College Station, TX

INTRODUCTION

In its common usage, *regulation* refers to a process in which a system is brought into compliance with a standard. These processes may be external to the system, as in legal regulation of property transfers. The law prescribes the standard and when deviations are identified, they are challenged by the legal system. When systems are *self-regulating*, the system is assumed to contain two additional components beyond the standard: (a) a mechanism for detecting deviation from the standard, and (b) a mechanism for bringing a system back from deviation toward the standard. It is important to differentiate systems that are regulated externally from systems that are self-regulating, especially for biological and psychological systems. A self-regulated child with a strong conscience (internal standard) will not steal or cheat even when authority figures are absent, whereas an externally regulated child will refrain from deviation only when authority figures are present to sanction the deviation. Both children are regulated, but the former is self-regulated.

139

A wide range of psychological systems are assumed to be regulated, and a subset of these are assumed to become self-regulating as part of normal development, including control of emotions, reactions to failure and disappointment, and most forms of achievement activities. Subsequent self-regulation is necessary for healthy social and emotional development. Indeed, when certain systems fail to show self-regulation, we assume that normal development has been disrupted, as in the case of the school-age child who steals or cheats when adults are not watching (Graziano, Jensen-Campbell, & Finch, 1997; Graziano & Waschull, 1995).

TECHNICAL ISSUES

Operational Definitions of Regulation

A little more than 10 years ago, in their edited volume entitled *The development of emotional regulation and dysregulation*, Dodge and Garber (1991) offered a comprehensive conceptual analysis and summary of empirical work available at that time. They noted that as a semantic term, *emotion regulation* is ambiguous, with at least three meanings. First, the term may refer to processes external to the emotion that influence emotion. In this sense, emotional regulation processes are inherently relational and involve at least two components, one of which is outside of emotion, per se. A second meaning reverses the flow of relational influence, suggesting that emotions regulate some component external to emotion, such as cognition. A third meaning implies that some forms of regulation are internal to emotion, and other forms are external.

To reduce ambiguity, Dodge and Garber (1991) proposed a general conceptual scheme of emotional regulation system that involved three types of regulation. In *intradomain* regulation, modulation of one aspect of responding occurs as a result of processes in another aspect of the same domain. An example is the regulation of vagal tone by means of respiratory activity. In *interdomain* regulation, modulation of one aspect of responding occurs as a result of processes in another domain. An example is the inhibition of impulsive behavior by means of distraction from the goal. The process of emotional regulation through *interpersonal* processes involves the modulation of emotion in one person through the activity of another. An example is an infant's use of his or her mother to regulate the infant's emotional responses to strange, ambiguous objects. Given this state of affairs, it is not surprising that operational definitions of regulation include such diverse items as spontaneous heart rate fluctuations, adrenal secretions in blood, gaze aversion, proximity seeking to mother, and even look-backs during reading.

Conceptual Base for Regulation

The Dodge-Garber scheme is useful conceptually, but it has some potential shortcomings. For example, the intrapersonal domains cover a wide variety of processes, and it is not clear how to define boundaries among them. Intuitively, vagal tone and respiration patterns seem to be within the same domain as physiological processes, but are electromyogram (EMG)-assessed motor behaviors within the same domain with them as a physiological process or in a different domain as a perceptual/cognitive process? Furthermore, because emotional regulation processes may be qualitatively different in infants than in older persons (Kagan, 1994), it is also useful to segregate studies by the general age groups of the research participants in the studies (infants, toddlers, preschoolers, school-age children, adolescents).

It is possible to expand the Dodge-Garber scheme to generate a more precise classification in terms of content area and developmental level of research participants. The *content area* refers to the main process or substantive focus of the research and consists of (a) physiological processes, (b) perceptual/cognitive processes, (c) individual-centered social/personality processes, (d) interpersonal processes, and (e) applied issues. *Developmental level* refers to age of the research participants, and consists of (a) infants, (b) toddlers, (c) preschoolers, (d) school-age children, and (e) adolescents. Specifically, for purposes of this review we searched for all empirical studies dealing with regulation in infants, children, and adolescents from 1986 to March 2000. (Outcomes are reported on Table 11.1.)

Instruments and Measures of Regulation

Physiological Measures of Regulation.   Regulation has been assessed based on physiological measures such as vagal tone (Porges, 1991) and electroencephalography (EEG) activity (Fox, Schmidt, Calkins, Rubin, & Coplan, 1996). Vagal tone is an index of the influence of the parasympathetic nervous system on the heart, as measured by the magnitude of respiratory sinus arrhythmia (RSA). It has been used as an indicator of regulation in infants (Field, Pickens, Fox, Nawrocki, & Gonzalez, 1995; Portales et al., 1997) and toddlers (Calkins, 1997).

Other Ratings.   Regulation often is assessed based on the reports of individuals who know the child well. One of the most common methods is to obtain parental reports of a child's regulatory abilities. Carter, Little, Briggs-Gowan, and Kogan (1999) conducted a multimethod examination of emotional regulation in infants. In this study, parents completed the Infant–Toddler Social and Emotional Assessment (ITSEA; Carter & Briggs-Gowan, 1993) and the Infant Behavior Questionnaire (IBQ; Rothbart & Derryberry, 1981). The ITSEA provides ratings for seven competence scales and three problem domains: Externalizing, Internalizing, and Dysregulation. The IBQ is a 94-item instrument completed by parents using a 7-point Likert-type scale.

Rothbart and colleagues (Ahadi, Rothbart, & Ye, 1993; Derryberry & Rothbart, 1988) have generated several other temperamental measures of regulation in older children (e.g., preschoolers, school-aged children) including an Effortful Control factor on the Children's Behavior Questionnaire. This measure is a 195-item ques-

TABLE 11.1

Numbers of Empirical Publications on Regulation by Age Group and Content Area for 1986 - March 2000

Content	Infants			Toddlers			Preschool			School			Adolescents			Totals		
	A	B	Total	A	B	Total	A	B	Total	A	B	Total	A	B	Total	A	B	Total
Physiological	12	7	19	0	1	1	0	3	3	1	5	6	0	0	1	13	16	29
Perception/Cognition	3	2	5	0	0	0	7	2	9	8	5	13	0	1	1	18	10	28
Social/Personality	1	2	3	2	2	4	7	4	11	9	8	17	2	1	3	21	17	38
Interpersonal	12	8	20	3	4	7	12	8	20	2	14	16	1	2	3	30	36	66
Applied	0	0	0	1	0	1	1	0	1	11	5	16	0	3	3	13	8	21
Longitudinal	1	12	13	2	1	3	1	6	7	2	5	7	0	3	3	6	27	33
Totals	29	31	60	8	8	16	28	23	51	33	42	75	3	10	13	101	114	215

Note. The A Column represents the time period between 1986 and 1994. The B column represents the time period between 1995 and March, 2000.

tionnaire yielding 15 scale scores. Parents complete the instrument based on the child's behavior over the last 6 months using a 7-point Likert-type scale. Derryberry and Rothbart (1988) present another parent-report measure of temperamental differences in regulation that Eisenberg and Fabes (1995) adapted in their study examining social competence, regulation, and emotionality. In addition, Eisenberg and Fabes presented parents with vignettes to which parents reported their expectations for their children's behavior. These responses to the vignettes then were used as indicators of emotional regulation.

Block and Block (1980) generated another type of parent-report instrument that has been used as a measure of regulation. The Block and Block measure assesses Ego Control and Ego Resiliency using a Q-sort method.

Another measure of regulation, Lack of Control, has been used to assess regulation in preschool children (Caspi, Henry, McGee, Moffitt, & Silva, 1995).

Behavioral/Observational Ratings.   Behavioral observations also have been used as measures of emotional regulation in children of all ages including infants. Along with two parent-report measures, Carter et al. (1999) present measures of infant reactivity, regulation, and coping behaviors. Using this method, measures of reactivity and regulation are coded in real-time using a computer-videotape-linked system. Ratings of swaddling, regulation, and maternal reunion episodes were coded on a 6-point Likert-type scale.

One of the earliest and best known measures of regulation is delay of gratification tasks (Mischel & Ebbesen, 1970; Mischel & Baker, 1995; Shoda, Mischel, & Peake, 1990). During these tasks, children's ability to wait for a desirable object (e.g., candy) is recorded and coded. Regulation methods (e.g., looking away, distraction) are also examined. According to Metcalfe and Mischel (1999), the ability to shift attention from the tempting object and delay gratification is a measure of emotional regulation.

Kochanska and colleagues (Kochanska, Murray, & Harlan, 2000; Kochanska, Tjebkes, & Forman, 1998) examined regulation among children between the ages of 12 and 52 months. The Kochanska measures of effortful control involve a series of activities the child is asked to perform, such as moving an animal at various speeds across a game board, whispering, walking a straight line, and resisting the temptation of a candy. Children's behaviors are recorded and coded as indicators of effortful control, a type of regulation reflecting the ability to shift and focus attention voluntarily.

Van der Meere and Stemerdink (1999) present another behavioral measure of state regulation. They examine the impulse control of 7- to 12-year-old boys using a go-no-go task used in previous research (van der Meere, Stemerdink, & Gunning, 1995). It involves presenting children with letters and symbols on a video monitor. Children are instructed to press a response button when a certain letter (e.g., P) appears on the screen. The experimenters record the total number of omissions (Correct stimulus is presented, but child does not press button) and commissions (Incorrect stimulus is presented and child presses button).

Although it may not be intuitively obvious, attachment measures also may be considered interpersonal measures of emotional regulation. Attachment initially was assessed in childhood, but it now is measured across the life span. Numerous methods have been established to assess attachment. The widely used methodology is the Ainsworth Strange Situation procedure (Ainsworth, Blehar, Waters, & Wall, 1978). Attachment also has been assessed using parental Q-sort methodology (Waters & Deane, 1985) and various other methods. In 1985, the *Monographs of the Society for Research in Child Development* dedicated an entire issue to the topic of attachment theory and measurement (Bretherton & Waters, 1985).

A final way to examine regulation is to observe the interpersonal processes and code them. Feldman, Greenbaum, Yirmiya, and Mayes (1996) assessed mother–child regulation during videotaped play sessions. Their ratings of maternal regulation reflected the parent's adjustment in amount of stimulation to the infant.

ASSESSMENT OF THE QUALITY OF THE EVIDENCE BY DOMAIN

One way to conceptualize emotional regulation is in terms of a sequence of sets of processes. That is, emotion regulation can be seen as a critical "middle" Process Y, located between a set of antecedent Processes X, and consequent set of Processes Z. In this approach, Y may be seen as a promoter of Z, but also as a consequence or outcome of X. Within the framework of this conceptualization, we divided this section into two parts. First, we consider factors that contribute to emotion regulation (i.e., the X-Y link). In general, physiological processes and cognitive/perceptual processes are regarded as antecedents or promoters of emotion regulation. Second, we consider emotion regulation as a promoter of other processes and outcomes (i.e., the Y-Z link). In general, social/personality differences and interpersonal processes are seen as outcomes of emotion regulation processes. This system is not perfect, in part because most of the available research is correlational or quasi-experimental. In some cases apparent antecedent processes couid be regarded as outcomes, or vice versa.

Factors that Contribute to Emotion Regulation

Physiological Processes.   Physiological studies described in this section examine vagal tone, blood composition, and psychophysiological measures (e.g., EEG, EKG, EMG). Typically, physiological studies involve small numbers of participants.

Vagal tone may be related to individual differences in capabilities for physiological reactivity and self-regulation (Porges, 1991). Respiratory sinus arrhythmia (RSA) decreases during bottle-feeding for 33-42 week old infants (Portales et al., 1997), suggesting that the gustatory-vagal response system can be systematically elicited during feeding. Porges et al. (1996) measured vagal activity in 7- to 9-month-old infants ($N = 24$) during various attention-demanding tasks. Subsequently, the mothers rated their infants for behavioral/emotional problems at 3 years of age. The data support a psychobiological model of social behavior hypothesizing that infants with difficulties in regulating the "vagal brake" (decreasing cardiac vagal tone) during attention tasks have later difficulties in social interactions that require reciprocal engagement. In other words, a lack of emotion regulation results in reduced social competency. Calkins (1997) measured vagal tone in toddlers ($N = 41$), and exposed them to emotion-eliciting episodes. She found that baseline vagal tone was related to reactivity to positive and negative tasks (but not to delay tasks), and that children who consistently suppressed vagal tone began with higher vagal baselines. Field et al. (1995) found that infants of depressed mothers showed lower vagal tone than their peers, and did not show the developmental increase in vagal tone occurring from 3 to 6 months for infants of nondepressed mothers.

Blood chemistry also may provide information about regulation. Gunnar, Mangelsdorf, Larson, and Hertsgaard (1989) found that 9- and 13-month-old infants who were more prone to distress than their peers during laboratory tests showed greater adrenocortical activity (an indicator of stress). Adrenocortical activity was not associated with the strength of attachment between child and caregiver. Gunnar, Isensee, and Fust (1987) compared normal newborns (Group 1) of 32 to 222 hours with neonates with perinatal complications (Group 2) and found few correlations between behavioral responding and levels of plasma cortisol. However, Group 1 neonates who were more competent in behavioral control and state regulation had higher levels of plasma cortisol. In Group 2, neonates who showed the greater adrenocortisol response to the examination also showed more behavior indicative of behavioral arousal and distress. Spangler and Scheubeck (1993) found inconsistent correlations with infant adrenocortical response and newborn irritability, but Spangler, Schieche, Ilg, Maier, and Ackermann (1994) observed mothers and infants during play, and collected measures of behavioral and adrenocortical activity. Elevated cortisol was more frequently observed among children of highly insensitive mothers, suggesting a role for maternal behavior in infant behavioral regulation.

Physiological processes associated with regulation in preschool children have been examined by Cole, Zahn-Waxler, Fox, Usher, and Welsh (1996). Emotion regulation was assessed during a negative mood induction, and used to categorize preschoolers ($N = 79$) into three groups: Inexpressive, modulated expressive, and highly expressive. Inexpressive preschoolers had the highest heart rate, lowest vagal tone, and smallest ANS change during induction. Inexpressive preschoolers appeared to have more depressive and anxious symptoms at follow-up in first grade.

Perceptual and Cognitive Processes.   Perceptual and cognitive studies discussed in this section examine sensory stimulation, private speech, memory, and impulse control. This category varies greatly in terms of participant numbers, although larger participant numbers appear in the older children categories.

Perceptual and cognitive researchers working with infants have focused on basic processes like attention, sensory stimulation, distraction from distress, motor control, and crying. Feldman and Mayes (1999) examined cyclic oscillations of attention and nonattention in 3- and 6-month-olds ($N = 40$). Patterns of oscillations were related to recognition memory, suggesting that regulation of attention in recurrent patterns is a correlate of efficient processing in the early stages of perceptual development. Ashmead and McCarty (1991) examined the self-regulation of posture in the light and dark for 12- to 24-month-old infants, in comparison with adults. Infants did not sway more in the dark than in the light, whereas adults did. Outcomes suggest that infants' regulation of early standing posture is adequate in the absence of visual surroundings (cf., Nougier, Bard, Fleury, & Teasdale, 1998, with school age children). Buss and Goldsmith (1998) examined the regulation of emotional distress in 6-, 12- and 18-month-olds ($N = 148$). Outcomes suggest that certain putative self-regulatory behaviors like distraction are effective for reducing the observed intensity of some emotions (e.g., anger) but not others (e.g., fear). The results suggest caution in assuming that postulated regulatory behavior actually has general distress-reducing effects and that "distress" is too general a construct for research on emotional regulation.

Private speech refers to speech that is produced for one's self, not for another listener. In one sense, this is the ability to regulate one's inner monologue. In general, private speech appears to be more common, or at least more obvious, in younger children than in adults (John-Steiner, 1992). Private speech, which has been linked to self-regulation in theory, has continued to be examined in the play of toddlers and preschoolers over the last fifteen years. Krafft and Berk (1998) found that children in a Montessori preschool program showed lower incidence private speech than children in a traditional preschool. Structural aspects of instruction and contextual factors also contribute to the drop in private speech for children at age 5.

Regulation research on school-age children focuses on school-related tasks like reading and memory for written material. Bossert and Schwantes (1995) examined "looking back" at previously read material as a form of regulatory behavior in fourth graders. Children trained to look back produced more correct responses than children in a control group. Alexander and Schwanenflugel (1994) examined metacognitive attributions for a sort-recall task in first and second graders. Knowledge base was a powerful predictor of strategic looking behavior whereas metacognitive attributions were influential in the low knowledge base condition.

Miller and Byrnes (1997) examined self-regulation during risk-taking decisions in third, fourth, fifth, sixth, seventh and eighth graders. Inappropriate risk taking was associated with overconfidence, falling prey to potential deregulatory influences (e.g., impulsivity, peer presence), and insensitivity to outcomes. In addition, risk taking was correlated with ability beliefs, preferences for thrill seeking, peer status, and competitiveness.

Interpersonal Processes.   These studies examine the domains of attachment, referencing, and parent–infant affect synchrony. Studies show that infants' interpersonal processes and emotional regulation are influenced reliably by both temperament and attachment-related presence of others (e.g., Manglesdorf, Shapiro, & Marzolf, 1995). The need for qualifications of these general patterns also is reported (see Gottman, Guralnick, Wilson, Swanson, & Murray, 1997). Walden and Baxter (1989) examined infant social referencing during parental expressions. They showed that younger infants (6–40 months) looked more often when parents expressed positive reactions, whereas older infants (24–40 months) looked equally at fearful and positive expressions. Only older infants showed regulation. Braungart and Stifter (1991) found that infants ($N = 80$) who were overtly upset in the Strange Situation oriented less toward people, more toward objects, and engaged in less toy exploration than their peers. Infants' attachment classification was related to self-regulation, but the pattern was complex and not consistent with attachment theory. Zach and Keller (1999) examined the connection between infant attachment patterns and emotional regulation in the United States and Germany. In novel situations, infants regulated emotional reactions but referred to their mothers more, and explored less, than they did in familiar situations. U.S. infants conformed more closely to attachment theory prediction than did German infants, whose age-appropriate exploration was not related to physical contact, but significantly and negatively to visual referencing. Blackford and Walden (1998) showed that temperament is more closely associated with regulation and responsiveness to differences in parent messages, but not to child looking at parents, per se.

Calkins, Smith, Gill, and Johnson (1998) examined the link between physiological processes and maternal interactive style on the behavior of toddlers. Negative maternal behavior was related to less adaptive emotional regulation and noncompliant behavior.

Emotion Regulation as a Promoter of Outcomes

Perceptual/Sensory Outcomes.   Lewis, Koroshegyi, Douglas, and Kampe (1997) examined emotional responses to infant separation at 2, 6, and 10 months, and related them to sensorimotor coordination at 4, 8, and 13 months. Separation distress at 2 months predicted lower sensorimotor scores. Emotional responses and cognitive performance may be linked by individual differences in self-regulation and attention management.

Social and Personality Differences.   Studies of social and personality differences in self-regulation examine the following domains: Temperament, socioeconomic status (SES), socialization, attachment, conscience, social-cognitive expectancies, social support, and parenting stress. This category centers on outcomes of regulatory activity in individual children.

Regulation research examining social and personality differences in infants often focus on temperament and emotional reactivity. Stifter and Braungart (1995) examined differences in the regulation of negative arousal in 5- and 10-month-olds. Self-comforting behaviors were exhibited most often during periods of decreasing negative arousal. Avoidance and communicative behavior were exhibited most often during increasing distress.

Cournoyer and Trudel (1991) classified 33-month-olds ($N = 48$) on patterns of self-control behavior in two delay-of-gratification tasks. Low delay children looked at and touched the forbidden toy often, medium delay children engaged in more social referencing, and high delay children were more likely to reference non-forbidden objects and use self-distracting tactics. The observed delay tactics were stable from task to task. Kochanska, DeVet, Goldman, Murray, and Putnam (1994) studied the emergence of conscience and its link to temperament in two studies. For most aspects of conscience, major developmental shifts occurred around 3 years. Two components of early conscience were *affective discomfort* (guilt, apology, concern for good feelings following wrongdoing, and empathy) and *active moral regulation/vigilance* (confession, reparation for wrongdoing, internalization of rules of conduct). Low impulsivity and high inhibitory control were associated with active moral regulation for both sexes.

Grolnick, Bridges, and Connell (1996) examined the expression of negative emotion and strategies to reduce or change them in 2-year-olds ($N = 37$). Active engagement was most commonly used and was negatively associated with child distress. Strategies varied with task context. Eisenberg et al. (1996) found that for second graders, vagal tone was related positively to boys' self-reported sympathy, whereas the pattern was reversed for females. In general high levels of self-regulation, teacher-reported positive emotionality, and physiological reactivity to stress were related to sympathy.

Grolnick and Ryan (1989) used a structural interview to assess parental style, the amount of support parents give for the child gaining autonomy, involvement, and provision of structure on self-regulatory behavior of third to sixth graders. Parental autonomy support was related to children's self-report of autonomous self-regulation, teacher-rated competence, school grades, and achievement. The structure dimension was primarily related to children's understanding of control.

Interpersonal Processes.   These studies examine the domains of attachment, referencing, and parent-infant affect synchrony. This category differs from the social/personality category in that it reports data for at least two persons who are interacting.

Stifter, Spinrad, and Braungart-Rieker (1999) investigated early emotional regulation, as indexed by vagal tone, and later compliance. Heart rate measures were assessed at 5, 10, and 18 months of age during a frustration task. At 30 months of age, children were given several compliance tasks. Infants who showed low levels of regulatory behavior were less compliant as toddlers.

Fabes et al. (1999) found that preschoolers high in the temperamental dimension of effortful control were unlikely to experience high levels of negative emotional arousal in response to peer interactions. When interactions were of high intensity, highly regulated preschoolers were likely to show socially competent responses.

Rubin, Coplan, Fox, and Calkins (1995) reported similar links between tempera-ment and peer relations.

Building on Kochanska's (1991) earlier work on temperament and regulation, Kochanska et al. (1998) examined children's restraint and attention in multiple set-tings at 8–10 months, and children's compliance to mother and internalization of pro-hibitions at 13–15 months of age. Committed compliance had different developmental antecedents than did situational compliance, with girls surpassing boys in committed compliance. The internalization of maternal prohibition was re-lated to committed compliance, but not to situational compliance (cf., Gralinski & Kopp, 1993).

Research on regulation among school-age children and adolescents echoes themes found in research with younger children. Regulation is not a single process or set of processes. The data suggest that regulation processes in which children en-gage are probably moderated by the relationship with the interaction partners and by the types of emotion (Collins, Laursen, Mortensen, Luebker, & Ferreira, 1997; Eisenberg et al., 1996; Zeman & Shipman, 1996, 1997).

Eisenberg et al. (1997) followed children from early to middle childhood, collect-ing data on parents' and teachers' reports on children's social behavior, emotionality, and regulation. In addition, children engaged in puppet-based analog "peer con-flicts." High-quality social functioning was predicted by earlier high regulation, neg-ative emotionality, and general emotional intensity. Eisenberg et al. (1999) explored the relations between self-reported parental reactions to children's early (4 years of age) negative emotions and children's later (12 years of age) appropriate/problem be-havior. Evidence suggests that parent's reported reactions to children's negative emo-tions, especially punitive reactions, affect children's regulations and externalizing negative emotions. The evidence also suggests bi-directional influence (i.e., child to parent, as well as parent to child). In a related study, Eisenberg et al. (1998) found that earlier regulatory abilities and emotionality predicted later teacher-rated disposi-tional sympathetic tendencies in school-age children.

Nelson, Martin, Hodge, Havill, and Kamphaus (1999) used parental ratings of temperament at age 5 to predict school performance problems, behavior problems, and positive social behavior as rated by teachers at 8 years of age. Early parental rat-ing of negative emotionality predicted later externalizing behavioral problems, and was a modest (inverse) predictor of positive social behavior. Katz and Gottman (1995) examined the hypothesis that a child's ability to regulate emotions (as in-dexed by vagal tone) could buffer children from the effects of marital hostility. They measured vagal tone in children when they were 5 years old, and teachers com-pleted Child Adaptive Behavior Inventory 3 years later. Outcomes suggest that high vagal tone can buffer children from the negative effects of parental hostility.

Applied Studies.   All but six of the applied studies are based on school-age children and generally examine school-related activities. For example, Wentzel, Weinberg, Ford, and Feldman (1990) examined the concurrent effects of motivational, affective, and self-regulatory processes on sixth graders' GPA and school motivation. Student self-report and teacher's ratings both suggest that self-restraint is an important contributor to success in school. Jensen-Campbell and Graziano (2001) collected daily diary records of interpersonal conflicts from sixth-, seventh-, and eighth-grade adolescents and found that individual differences in agreeableness were closely related to self-regulatory processes during interpersonal conflicts.

DEVELOPMENTAL STABILITY OF REGULATION ACROSS THE LIFE COURSE

Do physiological processes associated with regulation show a developmental pattern? Bornstein and Suess (2000) measured infant vagal tone and heart rate at 2 months and at 5 years in both children ($N = 81$) and their mothers. Assessments were taken at rest and during an environmental task. Children reached the adult baseline for vagal tone by 5 years of age and did not differ from their mothers in baseline-to-task change in vagal tone or heart rate. Baseline-to-task change in vagal tone showed consistent mother–child concordance. These researchers interpret their data to suggest that experiential or environmental influences shape children's developing characteristic physiological response style.

Doussard-Roosevelt, Porges, Scanlon, Alemi, and Scanlon (1997) examined heart rate and RSA, neonatal ECG beginning at 48 hours after birth, and followed 3 years later. RSA measures predicted 3-year outcomes beyond the effects of birth weight, medical risks, and SES. A measure of joint RSA and heart rate was associated with better behavioral regulation at 3, as measured by Child Behavior Check List and Parenting Stress Index scores. Generalizing these outcomes must be done with caution, however, in that the sample consisted of 41 very low birth weight infants.

Attention management is an aspect of regulation and may have antecedents that can be discovered in longitudinal research. Feldman et al. (1996) videotaped infant attentive states at 3 and 9 months during free-play with their mothers. Patterns in the early synchrony between mothers and infants predicted verbal and general IQ at age 2. How these processes map onto regulation is not yet clear.

CONCLUSIONS

In assessing the overall quality of the evidence, we note that firm conclusions about the development of emotion regulation are hampered by several problems. First, most of the studies currently available are short term, cross-sectional studies involving relatively small samples. To the best of our knowledge, there are no longitudinal studies that track individual persons' regulatory activities from infancy through adolescence. It is difficult to find long-term antecedents or consequences of emotion regulation without prospective longitudinal studies. Second, small sample sizes are associated with low statistical power, so it difficult to detect effects even when they are present. Third, most of the available studies focus narrowly on one aspect of emotion regulation, so it difficult to know how different aspects of emotion regulation are related to each other.

Complicating the process further, self-regulation and emotional regulation are complex processes that have been examined in many domains, age groups, and at many levels of abstraction. The evidence is not perfectly clear, but recent research evidence suggests that basic biobehavioral processes associated with cardiovascular function index some basic regulatory processes, and appear to contribute to the development of subsequent regulatory processes in other domains. The biobehavioral processes associated with cardiovascular function (e.g., vagal tone) have been established most clearly in infancy. The presence of strong biological precursors of regulation does not exclude social and interpersonal forces. Even in infancy, social networks and interpersonal relations, especially with caregivers, can influence developing regulatory systems.

During development, basic biobehavioral processes come into contact with cognitive and social forces. One may conceptualize these forces as a three-legged stool. Each of the three legs contributes to the stability of the system, and none is independent of the other, although different processes may be more active than another at certain developmental periods.

REFERENCES

Ahadi, S. A., Rothbart, M. K., & Ye, R. (1993). Children's temperament in the U.S. and China: Similarities and differences. *European Journal of Personality, 7*(5), 359–377.

Ainsworth, M. D. S., Blehar, M. C., Waters, E., & Wall, S. (1978). *Patterns of attachment: A psychological study of the Strange Situation*. Hillsdale, NJ: Lawrence Erlbaum Associates.

Allexander, J. M., & Schwanenflugel, P. J. (1994). Strategy regulation: The role of intelligence, metacognitive attributions, and knowledge base. *Developmental Psychology, 30*(5), 709–723.

Ashmead, D. H., & McCarty, M. E. (1991). Postural sway of human infants while standing in light and dark. *Child Development, 62*(6), 1276–1287.

Blackford, J. U., & Walden, T. A. (1998). Individual differences in social referencing. *Infant Behavior & Development, 21*(1), 89–102.

Block, J. H., & Block, J. (1980). The role of ego-control and ego-resiliency in the organization of behavior. In W. A. Collins (Eds.), *Development of cognition, affect, and social relations. The Minnesota symposium on child psychology* (Vol. 13, pp. 39–101). Hillsdale, NJ: Lawrence Erlbaum Associates.

Bornstein, M. H., & Seuss, P. E. (2000). Child and mother cardiac vagal tone: Continuity, stability, and concordance across the first 5 years. *Developmental Psychology, 36*(1), 54–65.

Bossert, T. S., & Schwantes, F. M. (1995). Children's comprehension monitoring: Training children to use rereading to aid comprehension. *Reading Research & Instruction, 35*(2), 109–121.

Braungart, J. M., & Stifter, C. A. (1991). Regulation of negative reactivity during the strange situation: Temperament and attachment in 12-month-old infants. *Infant Behavior & Development, 14*(3), 349–364.

Bretherton, I., & Waters, E. (1985). Growing points of attachment theory and research. *Monographs of the Society for Research in Child Development, 50*(1–2, Serial No. 209).

Buss, K. A., & Goldsmith, H. H. (1998). Fear and anger regulation in infancy: Effects on the temporal dynamics of affective expression. *Child Development, 69*(2), 359–374.

Calkins, S. D. (1997). Cardiac vagal tone indices of temperamental reactivity and behavioral regulation in young children. *Developmental Psychobiology, 31*(2), 125–135.

Calkins, S. D., Smith, C. L., Gill, K. L., & Johnson, M. C. (1998). Maternal interactive style across contexts: Relations to emotional, behavioral, and physiological regulation during toddlerhood. *Social Development, 7*(3), 350–369.

Carter, A. S., & Briggs-Gowan, M. (1993). The Infant-Toddler Social and Emotional Assessment (ITSEA). Unpublished measure.

Carter, A. S., Little, C., Briggs-Gowan, M. J., & Kogan, N. (1999). The infant-toddler social and emotional assessment (ITSEA): Comparing parent ratings to laboratory observations of task mastery, emotion regulation, coping behaviors, and attachment status. *Infant Mental Health Journal, 20*(4), 375–392.

Caspi, A., Henry, B., McGee, R., Moffitt, T. E., & Silva, P. A. (1995). Temperamental origins of child and adolescent behavior problems: From age three to age fifteen. *Child Development, 66*, 55–68.

Cole, P. M., Zahn-Waxler, C., Fox, N. A., Usher, B. A., Welsh, J. D. (1996). Individual differences in emotion regulation and behavior problems in preschool children. *Journal of Abnormal Psychology, 105*(4), 518–529.

Collins, W. A., Laursen, B., Mortensen, N., Luebker, C., & Ferreira, M. (1997). Conflict processes and transitions in parent and peer relationships: Implications for autonomy and regulation. *Journal of Adolescent Research, 12*(2), 178–198.

Cournoyer, M., & Trudel, M. (1991). Behavioral correlates of self-control at 33 months. *Infant Behavior & Development, 14*(4), 497–503.

Derryberry, D., & Rothbart, M. K. (1988). Arousal, affect, and attention as components of temperament. *Journal of Personality and Social Psychology, 55*, 958–966.

Dodge, K. A., & Garber, J. (1991). Domains of emotion regulation. In J. Garber & K. A. Dodge (Eds.), *The development of emotion regulation and dysregulation* (pp. 3–14). New York: Cambridge University Press.

Doussard-Roosevelt, J. A., Porges, S. W., Scanlon, J. W., Alemi, B., & Scanlon, K. B. (1997). Vagal regulation of heart rate in the prediction of developmental outcome for very low birth weight preterm infants. *Child Development, 68*(2), 173–186.

Eisenberg, N., & Fabes, R. A. (1995). The relation of young children's vicarious emotional responding to social competence, regulation, and emotionality. *Cognition & Emotion, 9*(2–3), 203–228.

Eisenberg, N., Fabes, R. A., Murphy, B., Karbon, M., Smith, M., & Maszk, P. (1996). The relations of children's dispositional empathy-related responding to their emotionality, regulation, and social functioning. *Developmental Psychology, 32*(2), 195–209.

Eisenberg, N., Fabes, R. A., Shepard, S. A., Guthrie, I., Murphy, B. C., & Reiser, M. (1999). Parental reactions to children's negative emotions: Longitudinal relations to quality of children's social functioning. *Child Development, 70*(2), 513–534.

Eisenberg, N., Fabes, R. A., Shepard, S. A., Murphy, B. C., Guthrie, I. K., Jones, S., Friedman, J., Poulin, R., & Maszk, P. (1997). Contemporaneous and longitudinal prediction of children's social functioning from regulation and emotionality. *Child Development, 68*(4), 642–664.

Eisenberg, N., Fabes, R. A., Shepard, S. A., Murphy, B. C., Jones, S., & Guthrie, I. (1998). Contemporaneous and longitudinal prediction of children's sympathy from dispositional regulation and emotionality. *Developmental Psychology, 34*(5), 910–924.

Fabes, R. A., Eisenberg, N., Jones, S., Smith, M., Guthrie, I., Poulin, R., Shepard, S., & Friedman, J. (1999). Regulation, emotionality, and preschoolers' socially competent peer interactions. *Child Development, 70*(2), 432–442.

Feldman, R., Greenbaum, C. W., Yirmiya, N., & Mayes, L. C. (1996). Relations between cyclicity and regulation in mother-infant interaction at 3 and 9 months and cognition at 2 years. *Journal of Applied Developmental Psychology, 17*(3), 347–365.

Feldman, R., & Mayes, L. C. (1999). The cyclic organization of attention during habituation is related to infants' information processing. *Infant Behavior & Development, 22*(1), 37–49.

Field, T., Pickens, J., Fox, N. A., Nawrocki, T., & Gonzalez, J. (1995). Vagal tone in infants of depressed mothers. *Development & Psychopathology, 7*(2), 227–231.

Fox, N. A., Schmidt, L. A., Calkins, S. D., Rubin, K. H., & Coplan, R. J. (1996). The role of frontal activation in the regulation and dysregulation of social behavior during the preschool years. *Development & Psychopathology, 8*(1), 89–102.

Gottman, J. M., Guralnick, M. J., Wilson, B., & Swanson, C. C., & Murray, J. D. (1997). What should the focus of emotion regulation in children be? A nonlinear dynamic mathematical model of children's peer interaction in groups. *Development & Psychopathology, 9*(2), 421–452.

Gralinski, J. H., & Kopp, C. B. (1993). Everyday rules for behavior: Mothers' requests to young children. *Developmental Psychology, 29*(3), 573–584.

Graziano, W. G., Jensen-Campbell, L. A., & Finch, J. F. (1997). The self as a mediator between personality and adjustment. *Journal of Personality & Social Psychology, 73*(2), 392–404.

Graziano, W. G., & Waschull, S. (1995). Social development and self-monitoring. *Review of Personality & Social Psychology, 15*, 233–260.

Grolnick, W. S., Bridges, L. J., Connell, J. P. (1996). Emotion regulation in two-year-olds: Strategies and emotional expression in four contexts. *Child Development, 67*(3), 928–941.

Grolnick, W. S., & Ryan, R. M. (1989). Parent styles associated with children's self-regulation and competence in school. *Journal of Educational Psychology, 81*(2), 143–154.

Gunnar, M. R., Isensee, J., & Fust, L. S. (1987). Adrenocortical activity and the Brazelton Neonatal Assessment Scale: Moderating effects of the newborn's biomedical status. *Child Development, 58*(6), 1448–1458.

Gunnar, M. R., Mangelsdorf, S., Larson, M., & Hertsgaard, L. (1989). Attachment, temperament, and adrenocortical activity in infancy: A study of psychoendocrine regulation. *Developmental Psychology, 25*, 355–363.

Jensen-Campbell, L. A., & Graziano, W. G. (2001). Agreeableness as a moderator of interpersonal conflict. *Journal of Personality, 69*(2), 323–361.

John-Steiner, V. (1992). Private speech among adults. In R. M. Diaz & L. L. Berk (Eds.), *Private speech: From social interaction to self-regulation* (pp. 285–296). Hillsdale, NJ: Lawrence Erlbaum Associates.

Kagan, J. (1994). On the nature of emotion. In N. A. Fox (Ed.), *Monographs of the Society for Research in Child Development, 59*(2–3, Serial No. 240), pp. 7–24, 250–283.

Katz, L. F., & Gottman, J. M. (1995). Vagal tone protects children from marital conflict. *Development & Psychopathology, 7*(1), 83–92.

Kochanska, G. (1991). Socialization and temperament in the development of guilt and conscience. *Child Development, 62*(6), 1379–1392.

Kochanska, G., DeVet, K., Goldman, M., Murray, K., & Putnam, S. P. (1994). Maternal reports of conscience development and temperament in young children. *Child Development, 65*(3), 852–868.

Kochanska, G., Murray, K. T., & Harlan, E. T. (2000). Effortful control in early childhood: Continuity and change, antecedents, and implications for social development. *Developmental Psychology, 36*(2), 220–232.

Kochanska, G., Tjebkes, T. L., & Forman, D. R. (1998). Children's emerging regulation of conduct: Restraint, compliance, and internalization from infancy to the second year. *Child Development, 69*(5), 1378–1389.

Krafft, K. C., & Berk, L. E. (1998). Private speech in two preschools: Significance of open-ended activities and make-believe play for verbal self-regulation. *Early Childhood Research Quarterly, 13*(4), 637–658.

Lewis, M. D., Koroshegyi, C., Douglas, L., & Kampe, K. (1997). Age-specific associations between emotional responses to separation and cognitive performance in infancy. *Developmental Psychology, 33*(1), 32–42.

Mangelsdorf, S. C., Shapiro, J. R., & Marzolf, D. (1995). Developmental and temperamental differences in emotional regulation in infancy. *Child Development, 66*(6), 1817–1828.

Metcalfe, J., & Mischel, W. (1999). A hot/cool-system analysis of delay of gratification: Dynamics of willpower. *Psychyological Review, 106*(1), 3–19.

Miller, D. C., & Byrnes, J. P. (1997). The role of contextual and personal factors in children's risk taking. *Developmental Psychology, 33*(5), 814–823.

Mischel, W., & Baker, N. (1995). Cognitive appraisals and transformations in delay behavior. *Journal of Personality and Social Psychology, 31*, 254–261.

Mischel, W., & Ebbesen, E. B. (1970). Attention in delay of gratification. *Journal of Personality and Social Psychology, 16*, 329–337.

Nelson, B., Marin, R. P., Hodge, S., Havill, V., & Kamphaus, R. (1999). Modeling the prediction of elementary school adjustment from preschool temperament. *Personality & Individual Differences, 26*(4), 687–700.

Nougier, V., Bard, C., Fleury, M., & Teasdale, N. (1998). Contribution of central and peripheral vision on the regulation of stance: Developmental aspects. *Journal of Experimental Child Psychology, 68*(3), 202–215.

Porges, S. W. (1991). Vagal tone: An autonomic mediator of affect. In J. Garber & K. A. Dodge (Eds.), *The development of emotion regulation and dysregulation* (pp. 111–128). New York: Cambridge University Press.

Porges, S. W., Doussard-Roosevelt, J. A., Portales, A. L., & Greenspan, S. I. (1996). Infant regulation of the vagal "brake" predicts child behavior problems: A psychobiological model of social behavior. *Developmental Psychobiology, 29*(8), 697–712.

Portales, A. L., Porges, S. W., Doussard-Roosevelt, J. A., Abedin, M., Lopez, R., Young, M. A., Beeram, M. R., & Baker, M. (1997). Vagal regulation during bottle feeding in low-birth weight neonates: Support for the gustatory-vagal hypothesis. *Developmental Psychobiology, 30*(3), 225–233.

Rothbart, M. K., & Derryberry, D. (1981). Development of individual differences in temperament. In M. E. Lamb, A. L. Brown, & B. Rogoff (Eds.), *Advances in developmental psychology* (Vol. 1, pp. 37–86). Hillsdale, NJ: Lawrence Erlbaum Associates.

Rubin, K. H., Coplan, R. J., Fox, N. A., & Calkins, S. D. (1995). Emotionality, emotion regulation, and preschoolers' social adaptation. *Development & Psychopathology, 7*(1), 49–62.

Shoda, Y., Mischel, W., & Peake, P. K. (1990). Predicting adolescent cognitive and self-regulatory competencies from preschool delay of gratification: Identifying diagnostic conditions. *Developmental Psychology, 26*, 978–986.

Spangler, G., & Scheubeck, R. (1993). Behavioral organization in newborns and its relation to adrenocortical and cardiac activity. *Child Development, 64*(2), 622–633.

Spangler, G., Schieche, M., Ilg, U., Maier, U., & Ackermann, C. (1994). Maternal sensitivity as an external organizer for biobehavioral regulation in infancy. *Developmental Psychobiology, 27*(7), 425–437.

Stifter, C. A., & Braungart, J. M. (1995). The regulation of negative reactivity in infancy: Function and development. *Developmental Psychology, 31*(3), 448–455.

Stifter, C. A., Spinrad, T. L., & Braungart-Rieker, J. M. (1999). Toward a developmental model of child compliance: The role of emotion regulation in infancy. *Child Development, 70*(1), 21–32.

Thompson, R. A. (1994). Emotion regulation: A theme in search of definition. In N. A. Fox (Ed.), *Monographs of the Society for Research in Child Development, 59* (2–3, Serial No. 240).

van der Meere, J., & Stemerdink, N. (1999). The development of state regulation in normal children: An indirect comparison with children with ADHD. *Developmental Neuropsychology ,16*(2), 213–225.

van der Meere, J. J., Stemerdink, B. A., & Gunning, W. B. (1995). Effect of presentation rate of stimuli on response inhibition in ADHD children with and without tics. *Journal of Perceptual and Motor Skills, 81*, 259–262.

Walden, T. A., & Baxter, A. (1989). The effect of context and age on social referencing. *Child Development, 60*(6), 1511–1518.

Waters, E., & Deane, K. E. (1985). Defining and assessing individual differences in attachment relationships: Q-methodology and the organization of behavior in infancy and early childhood. In I. Bretherton, & E. Waters (Eds.), *Monographs of the Society for Research in Child Development, 50*(1–2, Serial No. 209), pp. 41–104.

Wentzel, K. R., Weinberber, D. A., Ford, M. E., & Feldman, S. S. (1990). Academic achievement in preadolescence: The role motivational, affective, and self-regulatory processes. *Journal of Applied Developmental Psychology, 11*(2), 179–193.

Zach, U., & Keller, H. (1999). Patterns of the attachment-exploration balance of 1-year-old infants from the United States and Germany. *Journal of Cross-Cultural Psychology, 30*(3), 381–388.

Zeman, J., & Shipman, K. (1996). Children's expression of negative affect: Reasons and methods. *Developmental Psychology, 32*(5), 842–849.

Zeman, J., & Shipman, K. (1997). Social-contextual influences on expectancies for managing anger and sadness: The transition from middle childhood to adolescence. *Developmental Psychology, 33*(6), 917–924.

12

Coping as an Element of Developmental Well-Being

Lisa J. Bridges

Child Trends, Washington, DC

INTRODUCTION

In early research and theory on children's coping, coping strategies were frequently confounded with the outcomes of coping. Coping was essentially synonymous with adaptive functioning (see Sandler, Wolchik, MacKinnon, Ayers, & Roosa, 1997; Skinner & Wellborn, 1994). Recent conceptualizations, however, recognize that individuals often engage in cognitive and behavioral strategies to reduce stress that may or may not be effective. These conceptualizations are the foundation for a growing body of research and theory involving coping processes in children and adolescents. Key issues within this literature include whether different coping strategies are more or less likely to lead to positive outcomes in differing contexts, whether there are consistent individual differences in coping styles, and the developmental antecedents and consequences of such individual differences. In this chapter we discuss these issues, focusing on research relevant to the question of whether coping can be considered an element of developmental well-being.

TECHNICAL ISSUES

Definition

One of the most widely accepted definitions of coping was provided by Lazarus and Folkman (1984): Coping involves "constantly changing cognitive and behavioral efforts to manage specific external and/or internal demands that are appraised as taxing or exceeding the resources of the person" (p. 141). Although there are numerous theoretical and empirical approaches to describing coping styles and strategies, present within most approaches is a common distinction between two fundamentally different styles of coping (see Compas, Banez, Malcarne, & Worsham, 1991). The first style involves efforts to alter or master aspects of the environment or of the individual, thereby altering a stressful situation in order to make it less stress provoking. The second coping style involves regulating negative emotion aroused within stressful contexts. With this type of coping, there may be no objective change in the stressful situation, but the individual uses behavioral or cognitive strategies to reduce perceived distress.

Measurement

Most research on coping utilizes instruments tapping multiple, narrowly defined coping strategies. These strategies are generally derived from the broad distinction described previously and frequently also on the basis of actual coping strategies described by adult and child participants during open-ended interviews (see Skinner & Wellborn, 1994). From these same types of measures, a few studies have also attempted to assess coping styles by including alternative forms of coding or scoring. These include indices of flexibility in the use of a variety of coping strategies, perceived efficacy of coping efforts, reliance on avoidance or aggression as coping strategies, and the extent to which proposed coping strategies are appropriate given the perceived controllability of the situation (e.g., Fournet, Wilson, & Wallander, 1998; Hardy, Power, & Jaedicke, 1993). Fournet and her colleagues (1998) refer to these later measures as indicators of "adaptive competence in coping," with the individual strategy measures as indicators of "technical competence in coping."

In studies of children's coping, children are typically asked to think about a stressful situation, and they are then asked about the ways in which they might respond. In some cases, questions take the form of open-ended interviews, whereas other studies use checklists and questionnaires. Measures also differ in the general or specific nature of the stressful situations probed (e.g., going to the doctor to get a shot vs. bad things that happen at school). There are also differences in the number of situations included and whether situations are standard for all respondents versus real-life examples provided by respondents themselves. Measures are frequently adapted for different studies to be either general or specific, and to use individually selected or standard stressors. Measures such as Kidcope (Spirito, Stark, & Williams, 1988), the Coping Scale for Children and Youth (Brodzinsky, Elias, Steiger, Simon, Gill, & Hitt, 1992), and the Self-Report Coping Scale (Causey & Dubow, 1992) are in common use, demonstrate adequate psychometric properties, and are representative of the measures currently used in studies of children's coping.

THEORETICAL AND EMPIRICAL REVIEW OF THE LITERATURE

Theoretical Overview

One of the most common distinctions between different types of coping was initially articulated by Lazarus and Folkman (1984), who differentiated between *problem-focused coping* and *emotion-focused coping*. Problem-focused coping involves actions designed to alter a situation to make it less stressful. Emotion-focused coping involves the use of cognitive or behavioral strategies to help the individual manage distress produced by a problematic situation.

Similar distinctions have been made by other researchers. Weisz and his colleagues (e.g., Rothman, Weisz, & Snyder, 1982) distinguish between *primary* and *secondary coping*. Primary coping refers to efforts to modify a stressful condition, whereas secondary coping involves efforts to improve one's "goodness of fit" with existing conditions. Ebata and Moos (1991) identify two broad dimensions of coping: *approach* and *avoidance*. Approach coping includes cognitions and behaviors that maintain focus on the stressful situation, whereas avoidance involves cognitions and behaviors designed to minimize focus on the stressful situation. For example, persistence in efforts to solve a difficult problem is an example of approach coping; ignoring a difficult problem is an example of avoidance coping. Miller and Green (1985) refer to similar strategies as *monitoring* (approach) and *blunting* (avoidance).

Most current conceptualizations of coping also make a distinction between coping styles and coping strategies (Sandler et al., 1997). Coping styles are generalized ways of coping that individuals exhibit across a variety of contexts. In other words, coping styles are individuals' preferred methods for coping with stressors in general. The broad dimensions of coping described earlier (i.e., problem-focused vs. emotion-focused coping, primary vs. secondary coping, approach vs. avoidance, monitoring vs. blunting) may reflect general coping styles, to the extent that they remain fairly consistent across different types of stressful conditions.

Coping strategies, in contrast, are behaviors and cognitions exhibited by individuals in response to specific stressors within specific contexts. The distinction is important because no single type of coping strategy can be optimal in every stressful situation, and positive coping must involve flexibility in utilizing different strategies to fit situation-specific exigencies. Problem-focused coping strategies may be optimal when the individual can in fact alter the objective conditions of stress, but may be detrimental to well-being when the individual has little or no control over the situation causing distress. For example, in an academic setting where studying can lead to improved grades, problem-focused responses (i.e., increased studying) to a negative outcome (i.e., a poor test grade) are likely to lead to the most positive outcomes over time. In contrast, however, problem-focused responses to negative events that are primarily out of the control of the children, such as high-intensity verbal or physical conflict between parents, may lead to increased distress and poorer outcomes. In such cases, children's efforts aimed at reducing their own distress (e.g., through self-distraction or distancing themselves from parents during times of conflict) may be more adaptive in the long run.

Coping theorists agree that positive coping involves flexibility in the use of coping strategies according to the types of stressors encountered (see Compas, 1987; Compas et al., 1991; Weisz & Dennig, 1993). Thurber and Weisz (1997) propose that a mixture of primary and secondary coping may be most adaptive. Fournet, Wilson, and Wallander (1998) emphasize the importance of both technical competence in using particular coping strategies in stress-provoking situations and adaptive competence in the deployment of different coping strategies in differing contexts. Skinner and Wellborn (1994) hold that individuals should not be thought of as having "styles" of coping at all, but rather as demonstrating patterns or profiles of coping responses.

Most researchers and theorists further agree that long-term adaptiveness is enhanced when individuals preferentially use problem-focused (i.e., primary or approach) coping strategies when faced with controllable stressors across multiple domains of functioning (Lazarus & Folkman, 1984; Dweck & Wortman, 1982; Skinner & Wellborn, 1997; Weisz & Dennig, 1993). Continued engagement with stressful elements of the environment can lead to mastery of these elements. Stress is therefore reduced and perceived competence enhanced. For example, students who responds to low test scores with increased studying or the use of improved studying techniques are likely to improve their performance on subsequent tests. In contrast, individuals who develop coping styles involving avoidance (i.e. emotion-focused) or who cope by becoming increasingly passive limit their opportunities for enhanced competence and may experience increased anxiety and helplessness when confronted with challenging tasks in the future.

In summary, the theoretical literature on coping is remarkably consistent, despite variations in terminology and specific foci found within the major theories of coping. Positive coping is considered a flexibility in the deployment of coping strategies that are appropriate to situational demands. Problem-focused coping efforts are seen as optimal under conditions where outcomes are, at least to some extent, under the control of the individual. When stressful events are uncontrollable, however, emotion-focused coping efforts may lead to more positive developmental outcomes. Overall, a predominantly problem-focused coping style is likely to promote positive growth, not only through the minimization of stressful encounters, but through the promotion of mastery and perceived competence as well. The conceptual coherence of coping as an element of developmental well-being is quite strong.

Empirical Overview

Although the body of research on children's coping has been growing over the past two decades, the total amount of research is still relatively small. Few longitudinal studies have been reported, and most work that has been conducted to date has been descriptive, aimed at defining and operationalizing coping processes (see Kliewer, 1991).

The largest area of research on children's coping deals with coping in medical settings. Included in this area is coping with painful and invasive medical procedures, ranging from immunizations to spinal taps and surgery (e.g. Cohen, Blount, Cohen, Schaen, & Zaff, 1999; Manimala, Blount, & Cohen, 2000; Peterson, Oliver, & Saldana, 1997) and on coping processes among children whose parents are suffering from chronic and severe medical conditions (e.g. Steele, Forehand, & Armistead, 1997; Worsham, Compas, & Ey, 1997). Perhaps of most relevance in this area for understanding effects of coping styles and strategies on children's developmental well-being is the research on children's coping with chronic medical problems such as sickle cell anemia and diabetes. Although not entirely consistent, the bulk of this literature suggests that children who use more active, problem-focused coping strategies tend to fare better both physically and emotionally than do children who use more avoidant coping strategies or who tend to use self-directed strategies such as self-blame (e.g., Frank, Blount, & Brown, 1997; Gil et al., 1997; Grey, Cameron, & Thurber, 1991; Kliewer, 1997).

A second major area of research focuses on children's coping with interparental conflict and divorce. Coping styles have been proposed to mediate or moderate the effects of conflict and divorce on child outcomes. Rogers and Holmbeck (1997) found that low scores on a measure of maladaptive coping (a composite including relatively low levels of social support, "change situation" and "change self" coping, and relatively high levels of aggression, self-destruction, and ventilation) were associated with higher perceived self-worth and lower levels of externalizing behavior and depression in middle-school-age children. In looking at individual coping strategies, they found that social support coping was negatively associated with externalizing behavior and depression among children living in high-conflict homes.

Sandler and his colleagues (e.g. Sandler, Tein, Mehta, Wolchik, & Ayers, 2000; Sandler, Tein, & West, 1994) have conducted short-term longitudinal studies of children's adjustment following divorce. Sandler et al. (1994) reported that higher levels of both distraction and approach coping strategies uniquely predicted lower levels of depression and anxiety 5½ months later. These researchers also found that active coping moderated associations between negative life events and later psychological symptoms. Specifically, negative life events were positively associated with later anxiety for children who reported using low levels of active coping, but not for children who were relatively high in their use of active coping strategies.

Sandler et al. (1994) also found an unexpected positive association between support seeking coping and later depression—a finding opposite to that reported by Rogers and Holmbeck (1997). Further, they found that negative life events predicted later conduct problems among children who reported using relatively high levels of support-seeking coping, but not among children who reported less use of support seeking as a coping strategy. The researchers suggested that, in this sample of children experiencing a parental divorce, the apparently negative effects of support seeking may indicate that the children were not able to obtain satisfactory levels of support at a time when parents were dealing with their own problems following divorce. Consistent with the view that flexibility in coping strategy use is necessary for positive functioning, children who persist in the use of support seeking strategies when such support is not forthcoming may be at increased risk for negative outcomes, at least in the short run, relative to children who use alternative forms of coping.

In a more recent study of children experiencing parental divorce, Sandler et al. (2000) highlighted the importance of assessing children's coping efficacy, defined as their perceptions that they can deal effectively with problems that arise, and with the negative emotions aroused by those problems. In analyses involving cross-sectional, short-term longitudinal, and growth curve models, these authors found that approach coping strategies were negatively associated with internalizing behavioral problems (i.e., depression and anxiety), and that avoidant coping was positively associated with these same types of problems. In all analyses, however, coping efficacy partially or fully mediated these relations.

A growing body of research examines children's coping in everyday stressful situations. One focus has been on children's coping within the academic domain. Brodzinsky et al. (1992) and Causey and Dubow (1992) assessed concurrent associations between coping strategies in response to school-related problems and children's perceived competence. Brodzinsky et al. (1992) found that assistance seeking and cognitive-behavioral problem solving coping strategies were positively related to feelings of self-worth, whereas cognitive and behavioral avoidance strategies were negatively associated with self-worth. Behavioral avoidance was also negatively associated with perceived academic, social, and behavioral competence. Causey and Dubow (1992) similarly found that global self-worth was positively associated with self-reported problem-solving coping in response to receiving a poor grade in school, and negatively associated with distancing in the same situation.

Thurber and Weisz (1997) examined associations between self-reports of strategies for coping with homesickness and self-reported homesickness in a sample of 8- to 16-year-old boys and girls attending summer camp. In their sample, the most effective way of coping with homesickness appeared to be the secondary control strategy of engaging in distracting physical activities. Children who primarily reported doing nothing or simply letting their feelings out by crying or yelling rated their experiences at camp lower and their feelings of homesickness higher than did children who predominantly used primary and secondary coping strategies.

Eisenberg and her colleagues (Eisenberg et al., 1997) examined children's coping, problem behavior, and school social competence at three different time points: In preschool or kindergarten and at follow-ups 2 and 4 years later (at ages 6–8 and 8–10). The most consistent results from this study were that destructive forms of coping (high levels of aggression and venting, and low levels of avoidance and cognitive restructuring)—particularly as reported by teachers—showed concurrent and predictive relations with low social competence. Associations between constructive coping styles (high levels of instrumental coping and emotional support seeking, and low levels of doing nothing) and positive outcomes were not as strong and, in some cases, ran counter to expectations. Interestingly, the strongest positive association was between constructive coping as rated by preschool and kindergarten teachers and social competence as rated by elementary school teachers 4 years later.

Fournet et al. (1998) examined concurrent associations between self-reported use of a set of five coping strategies (aggressive-confrontive, escape-denial, problem-solving, acceptance, and social-support), two coping styles (use of primary or problem-focused strategies vs. secondary or emotion-focused strategies), and five measures of adaptive competence in coping (match between primary vs. secondary coping and perceived controllability, efficacy of coping efforts, use of approach strategies, use of nonaggressive strategies, and variety of strategies reported) and parent- and self-reported behavior problems. This study is particularly noteworthy because the sample was quite different from those used in other coping studies—97 15-year-old African American adolescents with learning disabilities from low-income households. In this study, adaptive competence in coping was a better predictor of self-reported behavior problems than were coping strategies. In particular, perceived efficacy of coping efforts and the use of nonaggressive strategies were associated with lower levels of self-reported behavior problems. This same finding is reflected when looking at the individual strategies: The use of aggressive-confrontive coping was positively associated with behavior problems, and the use of problem solving was negatively associated with behavior problems. Finally, only the adaptive competence measures of match and nonaggressive strategy use were associated with parent-reported behavior problems, and these associations appeared only for girls.

To summarize the empirical literature, there is substantial evidence that active forms of coping, at least in situations where outcomes are to some extent under the control of the child, are associated with positive outcomes. In less controllable situations, such as situations of parent conflict, divorce, and dealing with homesickness while away at summer camp, forms of coping involving self-distraction may be adaptive as well. Several studies have also indicated the importance of assessing coping efficacy when examining associations between coping strategy use and outcomes. The research base remains thin, however, and there are numerous gaps in the literature. The measures used are seldom entirely consistent across studies. Most studies have been conducted with white, middle-class samples. Perhaps most problematic is the lack of truly longitudinal research. Concurrent and short-term longitudinal associations are suggestive, but cannot distinguish between true predictive relations and the possibility that coping and other measures are manifestations of the same underlying construct. Therefore, the empirical support for coping as an element of developmental well-being is suggestive, but far from conclusive.

DEVELOPMENTAL STABILITY OF COPING OVER THE LIFE SPAN

Very little research has been conducted to address the issue of developmental stability in coping styles or strategy use across age. There is research that has indicated general age trends in coping, however. One age trend that has been found fairly consistently is an increase in emotion-focused (i.e., avoidance, secondary control) coping (e.g. Altshuler & Ruble, 1989; Band & Weisz, 1988; Compas, Malcarne, & Fondacaro, 1988).

In a widely cited study, Altshuler and Ruble (1989) presented children with scenarios involving children facing uncontrollable stressors. At all ages, avoidance strategies (behavioral or cognitive distraction, escape, and denial) were much more frequently suggested than approach strategies (e.g., information-seeking, cooperating, changing the situation constructively) or emotion manipulation/tension reduction strategies (e.g., doing something to relax, cry, express feelings). Among the avoidance strategies, behavioral distraction (e.g., play, read, watch TV) was the most commonly suggested type of coping strategy. For negatively valenced stories (i.e., waiting to get a shot or to have a cavity filled), there was also an increase with age in the suggested use of cognitive distraction coping (e.g., think about something else, fantasy) and suggestions of trying to completely escape the situation decreased.

Findings of developmental changes in problem-focused coping have not been consistent across studies. Some have found increases in problem-focused coping (e.g., Compas et al., 1991), some have found decreases (Band & Weisz, 1988), and others have found no change (Altshuler & Ruble, 1989; Compas et al., 1988). Studies finding no change involved a wide range of stressors. Compas et al. (1991) utilized an interpersonal stressor; Band & Weisz (1988) used a medical/dental stressor. Given the different types of stressors, these different findings do not appear to be quite so contradictory. With age, children may come to understand that there is little that they can actually do when required to have a cavity filled or to go for a visit to the doctor, while developing an increased sense of control in interpersonal contexts. Theoretically, when perceived control is low, emotion-focused coping should be higher, and problem-focused coping should be higher under conditions of higher perceived control.

FACTORS AFFECTING DEVELOPMENT AND PROMOTION
OF POSITIVE COPING

Characteristics of children and their environments have ben found to be associated with individual differences in coping. Few longitudinal studies have been conducted, however, which precludes conclusions about causality.

Perceived Control

Kliewer (1991) used a very short-term longitudinal design to predict children's self-reported coping behaviors. Children who were rated by teachers as being more socially competent, and children who self-reported higher levels of perceived control, reported using more cognitive avoidance (i.e., efforts to avoid thinking about the problem, or ignoring the problem) and avoidant actions (i.e., behavioral efforts to avoid a stressful situation, such as walking away). Aside from the short time-frame of 10 weeks, the author did not specify what types of stressors were reported by the children. It is therefore impossible to determine whether the finding that social competence and perceived control are positively associated with cognitive and behavioral avoidance is generalizable across situations. It might be expected, for example, that children with high levels of social competence and perceived control would still use avoidant strategies in situations that are perceived to be uncontrollable, while situations that are perceived to be more controllable would be responded to with more approach-oriented strategies.

Similar findings of relations between perceived control and emotion-focused (versus problem-focused) coping have been reported by Compas and his colleagues (e.g., Compas et al., 1988). In contrast, however, high levels of perceived control within an academic setting have been found to be associated with increased mastery efforts in the face of negative events (e.g., doing poorly on an assignment or a test)—efforts that may be conceived of as consistent with problem-focused coping (see Dweck & Leggett, 1988; Dweck & Wortman, 1982; Skinner, 1995; Skinner & Wellborn, 1997). Most of this work, however, has not been longitudinal. Measures of coping and perceived control are generally obtained at the same point in time.

Parents

Few studies have examined associations between parent characteristics and children's coping styles. There are some suggestive findings from research on children's reactions to painful medical procedures indicating that parents and other adults can reduce children's fear and distress by reinforcing distraction techniques (attending to a cartoon, using a party blower) and that such techniques are more effective than providing reassurance to the child (e.g. Cohen et al., 1999; Manimala et al., 2000). Such reports may indicate that parents who model positive coping strategies and who actively instruct their children in the use of these skills can promote positive coping in their children, although there is little research directly examining the intergenerational transmission of coping styles and strategy use.

Hardy et al. (1993) obtained concurrent measures of parenting characteristics and child coping with everyday stressful situations in a sample of 10-year-olds and their mothers. In this study, the stressful situations used were originally identified for each child by his or her mother. Children were then interviewed about their responses within these situations. High levels of maternal support (a composite of family cohesiveness and adaptability, nurturance, and monitoring of the child), and low levels of structure (a composite of family organization and consistency), were positively related to flexible coping (i.e., the number of coping strategies mentioned by the child). High levels of support were also associated with high levels of child avoidant coping, but only in situations involving relatively uncontrollable stressors. High structure was associated with low levels of aggressive coping.

The relation between low levels of structure and flexible coping was unexpected, as structure is proposed to be a positive element of caregiving environments that should promote more adaptive functioning. Hardy et al. (1993) suggest that the positive association in this sample of mostly White, highly educated families was due to a truncation at the lower end of the possible range of structure in the home environments. Few or none of the children came from families in which structure was so low as to result in a chaotic, unpredictable childrearing environment.

CONCLUSIONS

Few studies have been conducted to date that can conclusively point to positive developmental precursors of effective coping styles or strategies. The limited research evidence available suggests that positive coping is facilitated by the availability of supportive, nurturant caregivers (including parents, teachers, and others) who model positive coping styles for their children, and by social and physical environments that allow children to perceive themselves as being in control of outcomes as much as possible.

It should be pointed out here that there is something of a disconnect between the results of the few prospective studies and the results of studies in which coping is used to predict positive outcomes: Whereas positive precursors have been shown to predict relatively high levels of avoidant coping strategy use, active coping strategies have been found to be most associated with positive outcomes. Compas and his colleagues (1991) suggest that the skills required for true emotion-focused coping emerge later in development than do skills required for problem-focused coping. This suggestion is supported by the age-related increases found in emotion-focused coping responses, particularly in response to uncontrollable stressors. It is possible, then, that these prospective studies capture individual differences in coping sophistication that are, in part, a function of characteristics of the caregiving environment. Further longitudinal studies tapping both potential precursors and outcomes of coping that systematically obtaining information on coping responses in both controllable and uncontrollable situations will be necessary to untangle some of the discrepancies within the extant coping literature.

Despite this, however, the existing theoretical and empirical literature provides substantial evidence supporting coping as a meaningful element of developmental well-being. Individual differences in coping can be reliably assessed with brief self-report measures. Using these measures, both approach and avoidant forms of coping have been shown to be associated with positive development. Approach coping strategies, such as continued efforts to solve a difficult problem and information seeking, promote positive outcomes when conditions are objectively controllable (and when they are subjectively perceived to be controllable), whereas avoidant coping strategies, such as distracting oneself from a difficult situation by thinking about or doing something else, are associated with positive outcomes when conditions are less controllable. In sum, positive development is characterized by the ability to flexibly deploy both problem-focused and emotion-focused coping strategies in appropriate circumstances, within an overall coping style of problem-focused responding.

REFERENCES

Altshuler, J. L., & Ruble, D. N. (1989). Developmental changes in children's awareness of strategies for coping with uncontrollable stress. *Child Development, 60*, 1337–1349.

Band, E. B., & Weisz, J. R. (1988). How to feel better when it feels bad: Children's perspectives on coping with everyday stress. *Developmental Psychology, 24*, 247–253.

Brodzinsky, D. M., Elias, M. J., Steiger, C., Simon, J., Gill, M., & Hitt, J. C. (1992). Coping scale for children and youth: Scale development and validation. *Journal of Applied Developmental Psychology, 13*, 195–214.

Causey, D. L., & Dubow, E. F. (1992). Development of a self-report measure for elementary school children. *Journal of Clinical Child Psychology, 21*, 47–59.

Cohen, L. L., Blount, R. L., Cohen, R. J., Schaen, E. R., & Zaff, J. F. (1999). Comparative study of distratction versus topical anesthesia for pediatric pain management during immunizations. *Health Psychology, 18*, 591–598.

Compas, B. E. (1987). Coping with stress during childhood and adolescence. *Psychological Bulletin, 101*, 393–403.

Compas, B. E., Banez, G. A., Malcarne, V., & Worsham, N. (1991). Perceived control and coping with stress: A developmental perspective. *Journal of Social Issues, 47*(4), 23–34.

Compas, B. E., Malcarne, V. L., & Fondacaro, K. M. (1988). Coping with stressful events in older children and young adolescents. *Journal of Consulting and Clinical Psychology, 56*, 405–411.

Dweck, C. S., & Leggett, E. L. (1988). A social-cognitive approach to motivation and personality. *Psychological Review, 95*, 256–273.

Dweck, C. S., & Wortman, C. B. (1982). Learned helplessness, anxiety, and achievement motivation: Neglected parallels in cognitive, affective, and coping responses. In H. W. Krohne & L. Laux (Eds.), *Achievement, stress, and anxiety* (pp. 93–115). New York: Hemisphere.

Ebata, A. T., & Moos, R. (1991). Coping and adjustment in distressed and healthy adolescents. *Journal of Applied Developmental Psychology, 12*, 33–54.

Eisenberg, N., Fabes, R. A., Shepard, S. A., Murphy, B. C., Guthrie, I. K., Jones, S., Friedman, J., Poulin, R., & Maszk, P. (1997). Contemporaneous and longitudinal prediction of children's social functioning from regulation and emotionality. *Child Development, 68*, 642–664.

Fournet, D. L., Wilson, K. L., & Wallander, J. L. (1998). Growing or just getting along? Technical and adaptive competence in coping among adolescents. *Child Development, 69*, 1129–1144.

Frank, N. C., Blount, R. L, & Brown, R. T. (1997). Attributions, coping, and adjustment in children with cancer. *Journal of Pediatric Psychology, 22*, 563–576.

Gil, K. M., Edens, J. L., Wilson, J. J., Raezer, L. B., Kinney, T. R., Schultz, W. H., & Daeschner, C. (1997). Coping strategies and laboratory pain in children with sickle cell disease. *Annals of Behavioral Medicine, 19*, 22–29.

Grey, M., Cameron, M. E., & Thurber, F. W. (1991). Coping and adaptation in children with diabetes. *Nursing Research, 40*, 144–199.

Hardy, D. F., Power, T. G., & Jaedicke, S. (1993). Examining the relation of parenting to children's coping with everyday stress. *Child Development, 64*, 1829–1841.

Kliewer, W. (1991). Coping in middle childhood: Relations to competence, Type A behavior, monitoring, blunting, and locus of control. *Developmental Psychology, 27*, 689–697.

Kliewer, W. (1997). Children's coping with chronic illness. In S. A. Wolchik & I. N. Sandler (Eds.), *Handbook of children's coping. Linking theory and intervention* (pp. 275–300). New York: Plenum.

Lazarus, R. S., & Folkman, S. (1984). *Stress, appraisal and coping*. New York: Springer.

Manimala, M. R., Blount, R. L., & Cohen, L. L. (2000). The effects of parental reassurance versus distraction on child distress and coping during immunizations. *Children's Health Care, 29*, 161–177.

Miller, S. M., & Green, M. L. (1985). Coping with stress and frustration: Origins, nature, and development. In M. Lewis & C. Saarni (Eds.), *The socialization of emotions* (pp. 263–314). New York: Plenum.

Peterson, L., Oliver, K. K., & Saldana, L. (1997). Children's coping with stressful medical procedures. In S. A. Wolchik & I. N. Sandler (Eds.), *Handbook of children's coping. Linking theory and intervention* (pp. 333–360). New York: Plenum.

Rogers, M. J., & Holmbeck, G. N. (1997). Effects of interparental aggression on children's adjustment: The moderating role of cognitive appraisal and coping. *Journal of Family Psychology, 11*, 125–130.

Rothman, F., Weisz, J. R., & Snyder, S. S. (1982). Changing the world and changing the self: A two-process model of perceived control. *Journal of Personality and Social Psychology, 42*, 5–37.

Sandler, I. N., Tein, J.-Y., Mehta, P., Wolchik, S., & Ayers, T. (2000). Coping efficacy and psychological problems of children of divorce. *Child Development, 71*, 1099–1118.

Sandler, I. N., Tein, J.-Y., & West, S. G. (1994). Coping, stress, and the psychological symptoms of children of divorce: A cross-sectional and longitudinal study. *Child Development, 65*, 1744–1763.

Sandler, I. N., Wolchik, S. A., MacKinnon, D., Ayers, T. S., & Roosa, M. W. (1997). Developing linkages between theory and intervention in stress and coping processes. In S. A. Wolchik, & I. N. Sandler (Eds.), *Handbook of children's coping. Linking theory and intervention* (pp. 3–40). New York: Plenum.

Skinner, E. A. (1995). *Perceived control, motivation, and coping*. Thousand Oaks, CA: Sage.

Skinner, E. A., & Wellborn, J. G. (1994). Coping during childhood and adolescence: A motivational perspective. In D. Featherman, R. Lerner, & M. Perlmutter (Eds.), *Life-span development and behavior* (pp. 91–133). Hillsdale, NJ: Lawrence Erlbaum Associates.

Skinner, E. A., & Wellborn, J. G. (1997). Children's coping in the academic domain. In S. A. Wolchik & I. N. Sandler (Eds.), *Handbook of children's coping. Linking theory and intervention* (pp. 387–422). New York: Plenum.

Spirito, A., Stark, L. J., & Williams, C. (1988). Development of a brief coping checklist for use with pediatric populations. *Journal of Pediatric Psychology, 13*, 555–574.

Steele, R. G., Forehand, R., & Armistead, L. (1997). The role of family processes and coping stratregies in the relationship between parental chronic illness and childhood internalizing problems. *Journal of Abnormal Child Psychology, 25*, 83–94.

Thurber, C. A., & Weisz, J. R. (1997). "You can try or you can just give up": The impact of perceived control and coping style on childhood homesickness. *Developmental Psychology, 33*, 508–517.

Weisz, J. J., & Dennig, M. D. (1993). *The search for an understanding of "good" stress and coping in childhood*. Paper presented at the Biennial Meeting of the Society for Research in Child Development. New Orleans, LA, March 29.

Worsham, N. L., Compas, B. E., & Ey, S. (1997). Children's coping with parental illness. In S. A. Wolchik & I. N. Sandler (Eds.), *Handbook of children's coping. Linking theory and intervention* (pp. 195–213). New York: Plenum.

13

Autonomy as an Element of Developmental Well-Being

Lisa J. Bridges
Child Trends, Washington, DC

INTRODUCTION

Autonomy, mastery motivation, and control are highly interrelated constructs. Perceptions of autonomy arise out of experiences of being able to control the environment and effectiveness in producing desired effects. Mastery motivation[1] has been proposed as an innate need that drives interactions with the environment, thus promoting perceived control and autonomy (e.g., Harter, 1978; White, 1959). Motivational and educational theorists and researchers have been particularly active in focusing on these three constructs as elements of developmental well-being. This chapter focuses on the assessment of autonomy throughout childhood and adolescence and the associations among autonomy, mastery motivation, and perceived control.

TECHNICAL ISSUES

Autonomy is an inherently psychological construct: Although different environments may afford greater or lesser opportunities for autonomy, it is the perception of autonomy that is of greatest importance for well-being. Because of this, auton-

---

[1]For a detailed review of mastery motivation as an essential component of cognitive development and well-being, see Jennings' chapter, "Mastery Motivation," pp. 295–310, in this text.

omy is a particularly difficult construct to define or assess in preverbal children. In infancy, the predominant approach to assessing individual differences in autonomy involve examinations of exploration and play. Perhaps the most influential body of work pertaining to autonomy in infancy and toddlerhood is that of Yarrow and his colleagues (e.g., MacTurk & Morgan, 1995). Based on the theoretical writings of White (1959) and others, these researchers have established a body of work examining mastery motivation in infants and young children.

One component of mastery motivation that has been shown to be associated with other indices of well-being is persistence at tasks. More specifically, it is persistence at tasks that provide moderate, developmentally appropriate challenges to the infant or young child that are proposed to be most strongly associated with mastery motivation and the development of autonomy. In support of the hypothesis that moderate challenge is important in understanding mastery motivation, Redding, Morgan, and Harmon (1988) found that persistence was greater for moderately challenging tasks than for easy or very difficult tasks among infants and toddlers at 12, 24, and 36 months of age.

In studies with children and adolescents, persistence at tasks continues to be used to assess mastery motivation or intrinsic motivation (e.g., Deci & Ryan, 1985, Lepper & Greene, 1975). Numerous experimental studies have included persistence at tasks as a dependent measure in studies investigating the effects of rewards and other environmental manipulations on children's and adolescents' intrinsic motivation. In childhood and adolescence, however, elements of autonomous functioning can also be assessed through self-report or other-report questionnaires.

One approach to autonomy in childhood and beyond is the conceptualization of autonomy as self-regulation. This refers to the extent to which activities are perceived by the individual to be self-chosen. Within the literature on motivation in education, in particular, there has been considerable interest in examining children's and adolescents' perceived reasons for engaging in activities, such as doing homework or trying to do well in school. For example, students may do schoolwork because it is intrinsically enjoyable or interesting, because the knowledge gained is perceived to be of value, to avoid feelings of shame or guilt, or out of fear of punishment for failure to do so. The first two of these reasons (intrinsic interest or self-perceived value) are thought to reflect high levels of autonomy because they involve internal forms of self-regulation. The latter two (to avoid shame or punishment), in contrast, reflect low autonomy because in both cases students feel that they are being forced to engage in activities that are in no sense self-chosen. Perceived Autonomy is one of the three components of Beliefs About Self that are described by Connell and Skinner and their colleagues (e.g., Connell & Wellborn, 1991; Skinner & Wellborn, 1997). An assessment of perceived autonomy is included in the Research Assessment Package for Schools—Student Self-Report (RAPS-S), developed by Connell and his colleagues (e.g., Connell & Wellborn, 1991; Institute for Research and Reform in Education, 1998).

THEORETICAL AND EMPIRICAL REVIEW OF THE LITERATURE

Theoretical Review

The importance of autonomy as an element of developmental well-being has a solid theoretical foundation in theories of motivation and motivational development. In a pivotal paper, White (1959) outlined a theory of *effectance*, or mastery, motivation. According to White, from earliest infancy, humans exhibit a need to act on the environment and to receive feedback that tells them that their actions have been effective. Harter (1978) and others have expanded on White's work by emphasizing that, from infancy onward, the environment plays a role in facilitating or undermining effectance motivation. According to Harter, effectance motivation is facilitated by the provision of competence feedback (i.e., by information that tells the individual that his or her actions have been successful) and by the provision of social encouragement for autonomous activity. Such feedback promotes continued activity which, in turn, promotes further competence. In contrast, effectance motivation and competence are undermined when the environment discourages or punishes autonomous activity and when the balance of feedback from attempts to affect the environment are negative.

White (1959) further went on to say that activity that is motivated by effectance motivation is not random but focused and purposive. It is based on this view of mastery motivation as reflected in focused activity, and as being importantly affected by the environment from earliest infancy, Yarrow and his colleagues proposed that persistence at tasks could be used as a measure of individual differences in mastery motivation in infancy (e.g., MacTurk & Morgan, 1995).

How is mastery motivation in infancy theoretically related to autonomy in later childhood and beyond? Infants who demonstrate high levels of mastery motivation, primarily because their environments have provided positive feedback based on their activities, continue to be active explorers of their environments, seeking out new experiences and new challenges. This allows them many opportunities to receive competence feedback, even when they move into new environments, such as classrooms. Infants who are lower in mastery motivation, primarily because their environments have not supported independent exploration and have provided feedback conveying incompetence, may have fewer opportunities to gain competence due to reduced tendencies to explore and to persist at challenging problems. This may promote a negative cycle of increasing passivity and incompetence.

Children who perceive themselves to be relatively competent tend also to perceive themselves as the originators of most of their own activity, even in settings such as schools, where a substantial amount of activity is both required and not inherently fun. In contrast, children who perceive themselves to be relatively incompetent tend not to choose to engage in activities where further failure is a possibility. Because of this, they tend to feel controlled by external forces such as teachers and parents or negative internal forces such as shame or guilt. Thus, individual differences in persistence in infancy may reflect the origins of a cycle of person–environment interaction that is subsequently reflected in individual differences in perceived autonomy.

Since White published his paper, numerous theorists have described the importance of perceived autonomy and competence feedback for human activity and development. While focusing on different age groups and using different terminologies, all of these theorists, and others, promote the view that autonomy in the sense of self-regulation (i.e., feeling in control of one's own activities) is a key element of developmental well-being (e.g., Connell, 1985; Connell & Wellborn, 1991; deCharms, 1976; Deci, 1980; Deci & Ryan, 1985; Dweck, 1991; Dweck & Leggett, 1998; Seligman, 1975; Seligman, Kamen, & Nolen-Hoeksema, 1988; Skinner & Wellborn, 1997). This literature suggests that when individuals perceive themselves to be in control of their own behaviors, and that their behaviors lead to predictable and positive outcomes, they are likely to maintain high levels of engagement with their environments and to develop positive self-feelings and increased competence. In contrast, when individuals feel controlled by external forces they are expected to reduce their levels of engagement with their environments, to develop more negative self-feelings, and to exhibit decreasing levels of competence. Connell, Skinner, and their colleagues (Connell & Wellborn, 1991; Skinner & Wellborn, 1997) proposed perceived autonomy as one of three interrelated sets of beliefs about self (along with perceived competence and perceived relatedness) that promote engagement, and subsequently positive outcomes, within any domain of action.

Finally, it is important to briefly note the theoretical link between the development of autonomy and attachment. Although attachment and autonomy can in some ways be seen as opposites, attachment theorists and motivational theorists alike support the view that secure attachments promote true autonomy (e.g., Bowlby, 1969/1982; Bretherton, 1985; Erikson, 1963; Ryan & Lynch, 1989). Attachment and autonomy may be linked in part because the same sort of contingent, consistently responsive, and affectively positive caregiving that is linked with secure attachment is also linked with the facilitation of mastery motivation. Theoretically, the link may also be causal: Secure attachments allow infants to use their caregivers as bases for independent exploration. Insecure attachments undermine independent exploration because infants are required to expend more energy either in actively maintaining close proximity to the caregiver (in the case of insecure/ambivalent relationships) or in hypervigilance (in the case of insecure/avoidant relationships). This may leave very little opportunity or energy for exploration, and hence for the development of autonomy.

Empirical Review

Infant mastery motivation has been understudied relative to other aspects of infant socioemotional development, such as attachment. Even to date, a large percentage of the research that has been conducted has been aimed at improving conceptualization and measurement of mastery motivation components, rather than at examining short- and long-term predictiveness of mastery motivation indices for other elements of developmental well-being.

Several studies have been conducted examining the relations between mastery motivation in infancy and later intellectual functioning. This has been a particular area of interest for two reasons. First, early measures of infant "developmental functioning" (DQ) have not been found to be highly associated with later measures of intellectual development. Second, the persistent, focused exploration that is the hallmark of mastery motivation is hypothesized to lead to gains in competence, including cognitive competence. Many of the reported studies have found fairly weak associations, however (e.g., Yarrow et al., 1983).

Other studies (e.g., Jennings, Yarrow, & Martin, 1984; Messer, et al., 1986) have reported significant associations between persistence in task- or goal-directed behaviors at 1 year of age and children's developing competence. These positive associations, however, have been confined largely to girls. Messer and colleagues suggested that this gender difference may be partially accounted for in their study by greater difficulty in obtaining compliance with McCarthy testing procedures for boys versus girls.

Finally, a few studies have examined associations between mastery motivation and indicators of socioemotional functioning. Frodi, Bridges, and Grolnick (1985), for example, examined the associations between mastery-related behaviors (persistence, competence, and affect at a series of structured tasks) and infant–mother attachment classifications. They found that both secure and insecure-avoidant infants were more persistent and displayed more positive affect during tasks than did insecure-ambivalent infants. Most findings were not significant, however, due to very small cell sizes for the two insecure attachment groups.

Researchers and theorists continue to work to refine theory and operationalization of infant mastery motivation (see MacTurk & Morgan, 1995), but the research base that would be required to demonstrate meaningful predictive relations between early mastery motivation and later cognitive and affective outcomes has not yet been established.

There is an enormous body of research relevant to the issue of the importance of autonomy to developmental well-being in childhood and adolescence. A small portion of this research has focused specifically on perceived autonomy or self-regulation. Research with the RAPS-S Perceived Autonomy scales (Connell & Wellborn, 1991; Institute for Research and Reform in Education, 1998) indicates that elementary- and middle-school students' self-reports of autonomous forms of self-regulation were positively associated with self-reported engagement with school. At both ages, reasons for doing schoolwork and classwork that reflected intrinsic self-regulation were also positively associated with teacher-reported student engagement. Relations between introjected self- regulation and engagement were lower and inconsistent across grade levels and across gender.

In earlier studies using the same or similar items tapping the four forms of self-regulation—external, introjected, identified, and intrinsic—Ryan and Connell (1989) found significant associations between self-regulation styles and outcomes in both the academic and prosocial behavior domains. Results in the academic domain suggested that, in general, more autonomous, internal forms of self-regulation were associated with positive outcomes, while more external forms of self-regulation tended to be associated with negative outcomes. In the prosocial domain, Ryan and Connell reported that introjected and identified self-regulation in refraining from negative interpersonal behaviors and engaging in positive behaviors were positively associated with empathy in a sample of urban elementary school students. Intrinsic self-regulation was not assessed in the prosocial domain.

In one final study, Miserandino (1996) used a "relative autonomy index" score to examine associations between perceived autonomy and academic outcomes in a sample of high-ability elementary school students. She found that perceived autonomous (i.e., more internally self-regulated) children subsequently received higher grades than did less autonomous (i.e., more externally self-regulated) children. Autonomous children also reported higher levels of a number of positive engagement-related characteristics, such as curiosity, involvement, and persistence, and lower levels of negative engagement-related characteristics, such as anxiety, anger, and boredom. Further, these associations of autonomy with school engagement and grades were significant controlling for achievement test scores.

DEVELOPMENTAL STABILITY OF AUTONOMY

Very few studies have been conducted demonstrating significant consistency in individual differences in mastery motivation across the infant–toddler period. In one study, Frodi et al. (1985) found that three indicators of mastery motivation at 12 months—persistence, competence, and affect—all predicted competence in a parallel mastery task at 20 months. Competence at 12 months also significantly predicted persistence at 20 months. Studies examining consistency in mastery-related behaviors between early infancy (typically 6 months of age) and later infancy (typically 12 months) have not found significant levels of consistency (e.g., Yarrow et al., 1982; Yarrow et al., 1983).

Studies examining perceived autonomy in later childhood and adolescence have seldom been longitudinal. Thus, little is known about the consistency of individual differences across time, and little is known about direct predictions to adult functioning. Connell and his colleagues have found support for their theoretical model, however, that perceived autonomy is part of a set of beliefs about self that predict subsequent engagement with school. Engagement, in turn, is a predictor of positive school outcomes that are important for successful transitions into young adulthood (e.g., Connell & Wellborn, 1991; Connell, Spencer, & Aber, 1994; Connell, Halpern-Felsher, Clifford, Crichlow, & Usinger, 1995; Ensminger & Slusarcick, 1992).

FACTORS AFFECTING DEVELOPMENT AND PROMOTION
OF AUTONOMY

Theoretically, autonomy at any age is promoted by environments that provide opportunities for individuals to act on their environments and to experience competence—to feel that their actions have been effective in producing positive outcomes. In infancy, environments that provide opportunities for visual and physical exploration through the provision of safe environments and stimulating toys, as well as caregivers who are contingently and appropriately responsive to infant signals, will promote autonomy. In contrast, environments that are restrictive, that do not provide opportunities and appropriate materials for play, and caregivers who restrict and react negatively to exploration will undermine autonomy development.

There is some evidence to support these theory-derived hypotheses. For example, Frodi et al. (1985) correlated maternal characteristics exhibited in a structured infant–mother play with infant mastery motivation (persistence, competence, and affect) in an infant–experimenter structured task setting. The focus was on the extent to which mothers attempted to control their infants' activities versus providing support while allowing the infant to manipulate and experiment with the provided toys independently. These researchers found that mothers' autonomy supportive interactive styles were positively associated with persistence at mastery tasks at 12 months and marginally associated with competence as well. At 20 months, correlations were higher: Maternal autonomy-supportive style was positively associated with both persistence and competence and marginally associated with infant positive affect as well. Associations across age were not significant, however.

Yarrow and his colleagues (1982) had home observations at 6 months for a small sample of infants seen in a laboratory-based mastery motivation assessment at 13 months. Positive correlations were found between persistence at tasks at 13 months and measures of the stimulation available to the infant from the inanimate home environment and from the mother. Competence at 13-month mastery tasks was also associated with the same characteristics of maternal stimulation, as well as maternal contingent responsiveness to infant distress.

There is little research available that would demonstrate associations between early experience and outcomes in later childhood or adolescence. There is, however, a substantial body of research that is suggestive of a link between environmental conditions and concurrent perceptions of autonomy (see Deci & Ryan, 1985). Among the most directly relevant to the element of autonomy, Ryan and Connell (1989) examined the associations between children's perceptions of their teachers and classroom environments as being either autonomy-supportive or controlling, and their self-reported reasons for engaging in homework and classwork (i.e., their perceived autonomy) in two separate elementary school samples. They found that children who described their classrooms as having autonomy-supportive characteristics were also higher on identified and intrinsic self-regulation. Finally, Grolnick and Ryan (1989) found that parents who were more autonomy-supportive in their parenting styles had children who gave more autonomous reasons for their school-related behaviors.

CONCLUSIONS

Measurements of autonomy present several difficulties when considered as indicators of developmental well-being. Because infants and young children cannot articulate their feelings and motivations, researchers generally use observational measures that are expensive and time consuming. Measurement obstacles are not insurmountable, however. Brief observational measures of persistence at tasks could be incorporated into developmental assessments that can be carried out by individuals with minimal training. Coding of these measures are fairly direct, generally involving frequency counts or recording durations of activities. Measurement in later childhood and adolescence is generally conducted via self-report. Difficulties here may primarily involve establishing construct validity of the measures.

The primary difficulty for proposing assessments of autonomy as indicators of positive development, therefore, does not involve measurement costs or reliability. More problematic are questions regarding the extent to which early mastery motivation and later perceptions of autonomy and self-regulation may be predictive of positive outcomes. Predicted associations between measures of mastery motivation and other outcomes have frequently been low or nonsignificant. Measures of autonomy and self-regulation (as well as measures of related motivational constructs) have been found to be associated with predicted outcomes, particularly in the academic domain, but the empirical literature is quite thin. Particularly troubling is the relative lack of longitudinal research on autonomy, earlier predictors of autonomy, and later positive outcomes. Considerably more research is required on this aspect of development before a determination can be made as to the importance of autonomy as an element of developmental well-being.

REFERENCES

Bowlby, J. (1969/1982). *Attachment and loss, Vol. 1. Attachment*. New York: Basic.

Bretherton, I. (1985). Attachment theory: Retrospect and prospect. In I. Bretherton & E. Waters (Eds.), Growing points of attachment theory and research. *Monographs of the Society for Research in Child Development*, *50*(1–2, Serial No. 209), pp. 3–35.

Connell, J. P. (1985). A new multidimensional measure of children's perceptions of control. *Child Development*, *56*, 1018–1041.

Connell, J. P., & Wellborn, J. G. (1991). Competence, autonomy, and relatedness: A motivational analysis of self-system processes. In M. R. Gunnar & L. A. Sroufe (Eds.), *Self processes in development: Minnesota Symposium on Child Psychology* (Vol. 23), pp. 43–77. Chicago: University of Chicago Press.

Connell, J. P., Spencer, M. B., & Aber, J. L. (1994). Educational risk and resilience in African-American youth: Context, self, action, and outcomes in school. *Child Development*, *65*, 493–506.

Connell, J. P., Halpern-Felsher, B. L., Clifford, E., Crichlow, W., & Usinger, P. (1995). Hanging in there: Behavioral, psychological, and contextual factors affecting whether African-American adolescents stay in high school. *Journal of Adolescent Research*, *10*, 41–63.

DeCharms, R. (1976). *Personal causation: The internal affective determinants of behavior*. New York: Academic Press.

Deci, E. L. (1980). *The psychology of self-determination*. Lexington, MA: Lexington Books.

Deci, E. L., & Ryan, R. M. (1985). *Intrinsic motivation and self-determination in human behavior.* New York: Plenum.

Dweck, C. S. (1991). Self-theories and goals: Their role in motivation, personality and development. In R. Dienstbier (Ed.), *Nebraska Symposium on Motivation, 1990: Perspectives on motivation* (pp. 199–235). Lincoln, NE: University of Nebraska Press.

Dweck, C. S., & Leggett, E. L. (1988). A social-cognitive approach to personality and motivation. *Psychological Review, 95*, 256–273.

Ensminger, M. E., & Slusarcick, A. L. (1992). Paths to high school graduation or dropout: A longitudinal study of a first-grade cohort. *Sociology of Education, 65*, 95–113.

Erikson, E. H. (1963). *Childhood and society.* New York: Norton.

Erikson, E. H. (1980). *Identity and the life cycle.* New York: Norton.

Frodi, A. M., Bridges, L. J., & Grolnick, W. S. (1985). Correlates of mastery-related behavior: A short-term longitudinal study of infants in their second year. *Child Development, 56*, 1291–1298.

Grolnick, W. S., & Ryan, R. M. (1989). Parent styles associated with children's self-regulation and competence in school. *Journal of Educational Psychology, 81*, 143–154.

Harter, S. (1978). Effectance motivation reconsidered: Toward a developmental model. *Human Development, 21*, 34–64.

Institute for Research and Reform in Education (1998). Research Assessment Package for Schools (RAPS). Student supports and opportunities in school: Engagement, beliefs about self, and experiences of interpersonal support. *Manual for elementary and middle school assessments.* Philadelphia, PA: Author.

Jennings, K., Yarrow, L., & Martin, P. (1984). Mastery motivation and cognitive development: A longitudinal study from infancy to three and one half years. *International Journal of Behavioral Development, 7*, 441–461.

Lepper, M. R., & Greene, D. (1975). Turning play into work: Effects of adult surveillance and extrinsic rewards on children's intrinsic motivation. *Journal of Personality and Social Psychology, 31*, 479–486.

MacTurk, R. H., & Morgan, G. A., (Eds.). (1995). *Mastery motivation: Origins, conceptualizations, and applications.* Norwood, NJ: Ablex.

Messer, D. J., McCarthy, M. E., McQuiston, S., MacTurk, R. H., Yarrow, L. J., & Vietze, P. M. (1986). Relation between mastery behavior in infancy and competence in early childhood. *Developmental Psychology, 22*, 366–372.

Miserandino, M. (1996). Children who do well in school: Individual differences in perceived competence and autonomy in above-average children. *Journal of Educational Psychology, 88*, 203–214.

Redding, R. E., Morgan, G. A., & Harmon, R. J. (1988). Mastery motivation in infants and toddlers: Is it greatest when tasks are moderately challenging? *Infant Behavior and Development, 11*, 419–430.

Ryan, R. M., & Connell, J. P. (1989). Perceived locus of causality and internalization: Examining reasons for acting in two domain. *Journal of Personality and Social Psychology, 57*, 749–761.

Ryan, R. M., & Lynch, J. H. (1989). Emotional autonomy versus detachment: Revisiting the vicissitudes of adolescence and young adulthood. *Child Development, 60*, 340–356.

Seligman, M. E. P. (1975). *Helplessness: on depression, development, and death.* San Francisco: Freeman.

Seligman, M. E. P., Kamen, L. P., & Nolen-Hoeksema, S. (1988). Explanatory style across the life span: achievement and health. In E. M. Hetherington, R. M. Lerner, & M. Perlmutter (Eds.), *Child development in life-span perspective.* Hillsdale, NJ: Lawrence Erlbaum Associates.

Skinner, E. A., & Wellborn, J. G. (1997). Children's coping in the academic domain. In S. A. Wolchik & I. N. Sandler (Eds.), *Handbook of children's coping. Linking theory and intervention.* New York: Plenum.

White, R. W. (1959). Motivation reconsidered: The concept of competence. *Psychological Review, 66*, 297–333.

Yarrow, L. J., McQuiston, S., MacTurk, R. H., McCarthy, M. E., Klein, R. P., & Vietze, P. M. (1983). Assessment of mastery motivation during the first year of life: Contemporaneous and cross-age relationships. *Developmental Psychology, 19*, 159–171.

Yarrow, L. J., Morgan, G. A., Jennings, K. D., Harmon, R. J., & Gaiter, J. L. (1982). Infants' persistence at tasks: Relationships to cognitive and early experience. *Infant Behavior and Development, 5*, 131–141.

14

Trust, Attachment, and Relatedness

Lisa J. Bridges
Child Trends, Washington, DC

INTRODUCTION

Research and theory pertaining to trust as an element of developmental well-being has focused largely on attachment relationships, as defined by the Bowlby/ Ainsworth theory of attachment (e.g., Ainsworth, Blehar, Waters, & Wall, 1978; Bowlby, 1969/1982). Briefly, attachments are affective bonds between individuals. Primary attachments are established in infancy, between infants and one or a very few caregivers, and are expected to persist throughout life, although manifestations of these attachments change dramatically. Beyond infancy, attachment relationships are established with significant others in an individual's life—teachers, best friends, and romantic partners in adolescence and beyond. The quality of these relationships is theorized to be strongly influenced by the primary attachment relationship(s).

There is a large and growing body of literature demonstrating that the security of attachments to caregivers and, at later ages, friends and romantic partners, is of central importance to positive development. This chapter reviews this literature, and discusses the extent to which attachment quality or security, assessed with varying techniques, should be considered a core element of developmental well-being.

TECHNICAL ISSUES

The operational definitions of attachment vary dramatically across development. During the infant and toddler periods, researchers must rely on observations of behavior in order to evaluate infant–caregiver attachment quality. The security of attachment relationships is determined by observing the tendencies of infants and toddlers to seek and obtain comfort from their caregivers when distressed, versus the tendency to avoid or actively resist interaction with their caregivers, and the ability of infants and toddlers to use their caregivers as "secure bases" from which to explore the environment during periods of low stress.

Two observational procedures have become dominant in the assessment of attachment in infancy and early childhood: the Strange Situation (Ainsworth et al., 1978) and the Attachment Q-Set (Waters & Deane, 1985; Waters, Vaughn, Posada, & Kondo-Ikemura, 1995). The Strange Situation is a laboratory playroom procedure designed to place moderate stress on an infant or toddler through a series of separations from, and reunions with, the caregiver, generally used with children under 2 years of age. In recent years, researchers have modified the coding systems for use with older toddlers and preschool children (Cassidy & Marvin, 1991; see Teti & Gelfand, 1997). The Attachment Q-Set was originally designed to be used by researchers who observe the behavior of infants and young children (from approximately 1 to 5 years of age) in naturalistic settings. Modifications have been made that make it possible to have parents use an adapted version of the Q-Set as well to rate their own infants and young children.

As with any observational procedure, these procedures are time- and labor-intensive. Although the use of q-sort methodology reduces the amount of time required for coding of attachment, it is still a very expensive and time-consuming procedure. In part for this reason, the use of parents as informants on young children's attachments using the Attachment Q-Set has been promoted by some researchers (Teti & McGourty, 1996). However, little research has been conducted using this type of methodology with mothers and fathers who are not well educated and who are not of middle- to upper-middle socioeconomic status. It is likely that the time-consuming nature of the task and the complexity of the instructions that need to be provided in how to arrange a q-sort limit the usefulness of this method for large-scale and nationally representative studies.

Beyond the infant-toddler period, dramatic advances in behavioral and cognitive capacities require a very different form of attachment assessment. No longer can the quality of a relationship be evaluated by examining children's specific behaviors directed toward a caregiver. Therefore, the major focus of attachment research and theory has been on individuals' *internal working models* of relationships. The quality of attachments are evaluated by examining the manner in which children talk about important relationships, rather than by their behavior toward their caregivers.

No single form of assessment of internal working models of attachment is dominant at this time, as is the case with behavioral assessments. However, the majority of assessment procedures used with children and adolescents involve projective or semiprojective techniques administered in individual interviews (e.g., Cassidy, 1988; Oppenheim, 1997; Verschueren, Marcoen, & Scoefs, 1998). Typically, children are presented with vignettes including threats to attachment relationships. In most cases, the threat is resolved. For example, a child might be presented a story in which a similar-aged child is left with a babysitter for 2 weeks while his or her parents go on a vacation. The child being interviewed is asked questions about what the child in the story might feel or do during the separation and on reunion with the parent(s).

Once again, on the basis of the style and content of the narratives that they provide, hypotheses are made regarding the nature of children's internal working models of attachment relationships. Children are judged to be secure when they acknowledge that a child experiencing a separation or some other threat to an attachment relationship would experience negative emotions, but would find positive ways of dealing with those emotions. When children's narratives involve denials of negative emotion, or include intense negative reactions and high levels of anxiety and anger toward others in the story, their internal working models of attachment are hypothesized to be insecure.

In studies with older children and adolescents, attachment assessments frequently involve interview techniques in which individuals are asked to discuss their own current and past attachment relationships. Such assessments are highly personal, sometimes quite painful for the interviewee, and require a great deal of clinical skill to conduct. There are, however, several questionnaire measures that have been developed that may be useful for tapping the core element of trust with much shorter formats. Among these measures are the Inventory of Parent and Peer Attachment (Armsden & Greenberg, 1987) and the Relatedness component of the Research Assessment Battery for Students (RAPS-S) developed by Connell and his colleagues (Institute for Research and Reform in Education, 1998).

THEORETICAL AND EMPIRICAL REVIEW OF THE LITERATURE

Theoretical Coherence

There is a high level of theoretical coherence for the element of trust, attachment, and relatedness. The idea that affectional bonds established early in life have significance for subsequent social and emotional well-being is well established in theories of personality development, including psychodynamic theories such as those of Erikson (1963, 1980), Mahler (Mahler, Pine, & Bergman, 1975), and Fraiberg (Fraiberg, Adelson, & Shapiro, 1987). The most influential theoretical approach to the study of early attachments and their influences on subsequent development is the model proposed by Bowlby (1969/1982, 1973, 1980) and further developed by Ainsworth and her colleagues (e.g., Ainsworth et al., 1978). Commonly referred to as an ethological model, the Bowlby/Ainsworth approach combines elements of both ethological/ evolutionary and psychodynamic theories.

Bowlby defined attachment as the tendency of infants (beginning in the second half of the first year of life) to maintain contact to one or a few caregivers—usually the mother and possibly one or two others. From an evolutionary perspective, proximity maintenance serves to promote the survival of the infant by promoting caregiving and protective behaviors on the part of the mother (or other caregiver). The tendency to attach is innate and powerful and infants will form an attachment bond with a caregiver provided a sufficient amount of contact. The quality, or security, of the attachment relationship is affected by the responsiveness of the caregiver.

Clearly, infants do not only seek proximity to caregivers. Locomotor infants, in fact, may actively move away from caregivers in order to explore the environment. Bowlby proposed that there is in fact a balance between proximity and exploration that is promoted by attachments to caregivers. This balance is affected by environmental conditions. For example, when infants are in familiar settings with their caregivers, they should feel secure and hence have little need for close proximity to the caregiver. In these conditions, when "felt security" is high, infants will move away from their caregivers in order to explore the environment, occasionally checking back with them, either physically or visually. Bowlby, Ainsworth, and others refer to this behavior as the infant's use of the caregiver as a "secure base" from which to explore the environment. In contrast, a change in the environment, such as the entrance of a stranger, or a change in the physiological state of the infant that produces discomfort, such as hunger or tiredness, may cause the infant to feel less secure and to seek closer proximity and assistance from the caregiver in order to reestablish felt security.

The idea that early attachments exert their influence on subsequent relationships through the development of internal working models of relationships and of self within relationships has been a key component of attachment theory from its inception. However, this element received relatively little attention until the focus of research began to shift away from predictors of individual differences in infant–parent attachment quality to the extent to which early differences in attachment security could predict subsequent individual differences in social, emotional, and cognitive development. Although there are a variety of perspectives on the exact nature of internal working models (e.g., Bretherton, 1985; Cicchetti & Toth, 1995), there is considerable convergence in the research and empirical attachment literature on the existence of internal working models. Further, there is some convergence in the view that these internal working models can be accessed through projective, semiprojective, and structured interview techniques in which both the content and style of responses are taken into consideration. Finally, there is convergence on the idea that the attachment security classifications derived on the basis of behaviors in infancy and early childhood (i.e., secure, avoidant, and anxious/ambivalent attachment classifications) are functionally equivalent to attachment classifications derived on the basis of the various measures designed to tap internal working models of attachment in childhood, adolescence, and beyond.

As noted earlier, the idea that early attachments have enduring impacts on social and personality development is well supported by a coherent theoretical perspective. Researchers and theorists have also been concerned with the associations between early attachments and aspects of cognitive development as well. The theoretical foundation for this is somewhat less coherent. The primary theoretical bases for expectations that early security of infant–parent attachments will directly affect cognitive development involve the impact of secure base behavior (i.e., exploration) and the establishment of secure internal working models of attachment.

Empirical Review

There is a huge body of research on attachment in infancy and later outcomes. Smaller but quickly growing literatures are developing on the relations between attachment and other measures of relatedness in childhood and adolescence and other concurrent and subsequent indicators of positive development. Due to the enormous and ever-growing body of literature on attachments in infancy and beyond, the focus of this review is on reports published since 1995. The primary emphases of this current research are exploring attachments beyond infancy, as well as the associations between security of attachment and concurrent and subsequent functioning in three general domains: cognitive and cognitive-affective development, relationship and social interaction characteristics, and positive and negative psychological functioning.

Associations Between Attachment, Cognitive, and Cognitive-affective Development.   Researchers have found that infants and toddlers classified as securely attached to their mothers demonstrate more positive cognitive performance than do insecurely attached infants. In a meta-analysis of studies examining the relations between attachment security and measures of intelligence and language development, van IJzendoorn, Dijkstra, and Bus (1995) found that there was evidence that secure infants and toddlers demonstrate more early language competence than do insecure infants and toddlers, but no evidence for associations with measures of intelligence in infancy or early childhood. Other researchers have found that security of infant–mother attachments are positively associated with measures of cognitive development in the preschool period, including memory (e.g., Belsky, Spritz, & Crnic, 1996; Kirsh & Cassidy, 1997; Meins, Fernyhough, Russell, & Clark-Carter, 1998), perspective-taking (Meins et al., 1998), and the sophistication of symbolic play (Meins et al., 1998). Security of attachments assessed later in childhood have also been found to be associated with concurrent and subsequent school-related outcomes, such as school engagement and grade point average (Jacobsen & Hoffmann, 1997).

Research by Connell and his colleagues (Connell & Wellborn, 1991; Institute for Research and Reform in Education, 1998) indicates that elementary- and middle-school students' self-reported emotional security with parents, peers, and teachers are significantly and positively associated with self- and teacher-reported school engagement. Emotional security with teachers also demonstrated some low but significant associations with composites of school-records indicators of student performance and commitment in school.

Attachment, Relationship and Social Interaction Characteristics. One of the most direct hypothesized links between attachment and later outcomes is that secure attachments promote social competence, resulting in more positive relationships. Consistent with this hypothesis, associations have been found between attachment security and friendship and social interaction characteristics in infancy and childhood. Security of attachment in toddlerhood has been found to be associated with more positive peer interactions (e.g., Fagot, 1997). Security of attachment in the preschool period assessed both observationally and through interview techniques has been found to be associated with concurrent peer social competence as rated by teachers (Bost, Vaughn, Washington, Cielinski, & Bradbard, 1998; Verschueren & Marcoen, 1999), and by direct observational techniques (Rose-Krasnor, Rubin, Booth, & Coplan, 1996). Of particular note is the work of Verschueren and Marcoen, who examined attachments to both mothers and fathers and found that both were predictive of peer social competence. Secure attachments in middle childhood have been found to be associated with a variety of positive friendship and peer interaction characteristics (Kerns, 1996; Kerns, Klepac, & Cole, 1996).

Secure attachments in the preschool years have also been found to be associated with higher levels of perceived social support concurrently (Bost et al., 1998) and in subsequent years (Anan & Barnett, 1999; Booth, Rubin, & Rose-Krasnor, 1998). Indeed, Booth and her colleagues (Booth et al., 1998) found that preschool attachment security was a better predictor of perceptions of maternal support at age 8 than was the mother's actual current behavior (observer-rated maternal warmth).

Attachment and Psychological Symptoms Versus Adaptive Functioning. A number of studies have found that children who are securely attached in infancy and toddlerhood are less likely to exhibit symptoms of psychological problems in early childhood than are insecurely attached infants (e.g., Lyons-Ruth, Easterbrooks, & Cibelli, 1997).

Concurrent and longitudinal associations have also been found between attachment security and perceptions of self and psychological symptoms (e.g., Anan & Barnett, 1999; Jacobsen & Hoffman, 1997; Moss, Rousseau, Parent, St.-Laurent, & Saintonge, 1998; Verschueren & Marcoen, 1999; Verschueren et al., 1996). Verschueren and her colleagues, for example, found that security of preschool children's attachments with mothers and fathers were positively associated with self-feelings and school adjustment, and negatively associated with teacher-rated anxious/withdrawn behavior. Elementary and middle school students' self-reported relatedness to parents, teachers, and peers have all been found to be positively correlated with positive self-feelings (Connell & Wellborn, 1991; Institute for Research and Reform in Education, 1998).

One additional area of interest to researchers assessing attachments in adolescence involves antisocial and delinquent behavior. Security of attachments to mothers, fathers, family, and peers have all been found to be negatively associated with self-reported antisocial and delinquent behavior among adolescents (e.g. Marcus & Betzer, 1996; Sokol-Katz, Dunham, & Zimmerman, 1997).

Summary of Attachment Research.   Overall, the very large and growing body of developmental research pertaining to the effects of childhood attachments on later social, emotional, and cognitive-affect outcomes suggests that attachment as variously assessed throughout childhood and adolescence is a key element of developmental well-being. The evidence for this appears to be particularly strong in the area of effects on social functioning in school and peer interaction settings.

There are some serious limitations to this body of research. Most of the studies reported have small samples, particularly for studies of younger children that rely on observational procedures that are costly and time-consuming to undertake.

Another general concern involves the demographic characteristics of the samples studied. Most attachment research is conducted with predominantly European American, middle-class samples. Indeed, in the studies reported above, more are international (e.g. Jacobsen & Hoffmann, 1997; Moss et al., 1998; Verschueren & Marcoen, 1999) than involve non-European-American samples in any substantial way. Of the studies reported, only Anan and Barnett (1999), and Bost et al. (1998) utilized African American samples (low income in both cases), and only Sokol-Katz et al. (1998) included a substantial number of Hispanic subjects.

DEVELOPMENTAL STABILITY OF TRUST OVER THE LIFE SPAN

Theoretically, the security of an attachment relationship is expected to remain somewhat stable across development. Changes in the quality of attachment relationship are expected to occur, however, when meaningful changes in the caregiving environment occur. Positive changes in characteristics of the caregiver or of the caregiving environment, such as improved financial or physical resources, or improved maternal mental or physical health, may lead to positive changes in attachment security. Negative changes in attachment quality may be expected under conditions that increase stress on parents and children, such as increased marital conflict, financial stress, or the birth of a second child to a parent whose resources are already taxed (Owen & Cox, 1997; Teti, Sakin, Kucera, Corns, & Das Eiden, 1996; Thompson, 2000; Vaughn, Egeland, Sroufe, & Waters, 1979).

Attachment security as assessed with the Strange Situation has frequently been found to be unstable across assessments spaced as little as 6 months apart (Belsky, Campbell, Cohn, & Moore, 1996; Thompson, 1998). Some researchers have been able to predict instability from positive or negative changes in maternal caregiving competence or affective styles (Egeland & Farber, 1984), or from changing life circumstances for the family (Thompson, Lamb, & Estes, 1982), although this has not always been the case (Belsky, Campbell, Cohn, & Moore, et al., 1996). To date there have been no studies that have been specifically designed to evaluate possible causes for individual differences in attachment stability across time (Thompson, 2000). Reasons for differences have been explored in a post hoc way following findings of substantial variability.

Some studies have found substantial stability in attachment quality ratings from infancy into early childhood (e.g., Main & Cassidy, 1988; Wartner, Grossmann, Bremmer-Bombik, & Suess, 1994). This has been particularly the case for studies that utilized highly similar assessments at both ages (e.g., observational measures used by Howes, Hamilton, & Philipsen, 1998; and Wartner et al., 1994; maternal interview measures used by Chisholm, 1998). Howes et al. (1998) did find, however, that infants with secure attachment relationships were likely to remain secure at 4 years of age, whereas insecure attachments were more likely to change.

Fewer studies have been able to demonstrate consistency in attachment security when using different types of assessment procedures at different time points. Chisholm (1998) included both maternal interview procedures and an in-home observation at a preschool-age assessment that included a separation/reunion procedure from which attachment security ratings were derived. She found that attachment security assessed through maternal interviews at either age was only marginally associated with attachment classifications based on home observations.

Howes et al. (1998) also included assessments of child–mother and child–teacher relationship quality when the children in the study were 9 years of age. They found evidence for consistency in relationship quality from the earlier ages to age 9. Children who were secure with their mothers at both the infant and the preschool attachment assessments had significantly more positive relationship perceptions at age 9 than did children who were insecure at both earlier time points. Children with nonconcordant security classifications at the two earlier ages had perceptions of maternal relationships that were intermediate.

Recently, a series of studies was published presenting information on longitudinal associations between infant–parent attachment quality and the security of attachment representations in late adolescence or young adulthood (Hamilton, 2000; Waters, Hamilton, & Weinfield, 2000; Waters, Merrick, Treboux, Crowell, & Albersheim, 2000; Waters, Weinfield, & Hamilton, 2000; Weinfield, Sroufe, & Egeland, 2000). Significant consistency appeared in two samples (Hamilton, 2000; Waters, Merrick, et al., 2000), but not in a third (Weinfield et al., 2000). Inconsistency was associated with the number of negative life events reported by the individual. Similarly, Lewis, Feiring, and Rosenthal (2000) found little consistency in attachment quality from infancy to late adolescence. Rather, these researchers found that insecure attachments in later adolescence were more strongly associated with parental divorce.

Overall, the attachment literature suggests that there is some continuity in attachment quality as assessed across time, although substantial numbers of children and adolescents exhibit change across different ages of assessment. Most research including true longitudinal assessment of attachment relationships has been conducted with young children. There is little longitudinal research on attachment and relatedness measures used with older children and adolescents. Finally, information on the linkages between childhood attachments and relatedness and adult positive functioning remains scant. Retrospective studies have demonstrated associations between observed maternal parenting and mothers' recollections of their own attachment experiences in childhood (e.g., Main, Kaplan, & Cassidy, 1985; Ricks, 1985). The extent to which such adult recollections might be associated with individual differences in attachment security as actually assessed in childhood has not been established, however.

POSSIBLE FACTORS AFFECTING THE DEVELOPMENT OR PROMOTION OF TRUST

Attachment theorists and researchers have proposed that secure attachments in infancy and childhood are promoted by sensitive parenting. The primary elements of sensitivity include consistency, contingency, appropriateness, and positive affectivity (Ainsworth et al., 1978). Sensitive caregivers are consistent in their responsiveness to children, thus creating a predictable caregiving environment for their children. Sensitive caregivers tailor their responses to the needs of their children and respond contingently to the signals, bids, or requests of their children. Sensitive caregivers are able to accurately interpret these signals, bids, or requests, and to respond appropriately. Finally, sensitive caregivers express positive feelings about, and in interactions with, their children. These positive feelings clearly predominate over negative feelings that may arise over the course of the normal stresses of childrearing.

A large body of research supports the view that characteristics of the caregiving environment do predict attachment security. Specifically, researchers have found support for the view that variations in parent characteristics included within the global construct of sensitivity are associated with differential outcomes for infants and children (see Bretherton & Waters, 1985; Thompson, 1998; Waters et al., 1995). For example, in one recent study, Teti and Gelfand (1997) found that mothers of secure preschoolers were more emotionally and verbally responsive (based on home observations) than were mothers of insecure children.

Researchers have also found links between family characteristics and child–parent attachments. For example, several studies have found that security of infant–parent attachment is predicted by parents' levels of marital adjustment and marital conflict. (e.g., Belsky & Isabella, 1988; Das Eiden, Teti, & Corns, 1995; Egeland & Farber, 1984; Teti et al., 1996). Although some of these effects may be due to the effects of stress on parental sensitivity, some may directly affect children's attachment security by placing excessive burdens on their abilities to cope with frightening experiences (Owen & Cox, 1997; see Davies & Cummings, 1994).

Finally, perceived relatedness has been found to be associated with characteristics of the home and school environment. Connell and Wellborn (1991) specifically proposed that relatedness should be most strongly associated with parental (or teacher, or other adult) involvement. Involvement is defined as the extent to which adults express warm feelings toward the child (or adolescent), and the extent to which they know the child—his or her activities and friends, and his or her feelings, wishes, and beliefs. These are, of course, very consistent with the characteristics of sensitive parenting described by attachment researchers. Connell, Spencer, and Aber (1994) and Connell, Halpern-Felsher, Clifford, Crichlow, and Usinger et al. (1995) found that parental involvement was positively associated with relatedness (a composite of relatedness to parents, to teachers, and to peers) in samples of urban, African American fifth- through ninth-grade students.

CONCLUSIONS

The empirical foundation for attachment as an important precursor of later positive development—particularly in the socioemotional domain but to some extent in the cognitive (or cognitive-affective) domain—is quite strong. The primary difficulty with attachment as an indicator of developmental well-being is the difficulty and costliness of assessment—particularly in infancy and very early childhood. Although the use of briefer, more direct self-report measures in later childhood and beyond has met with some skepticism among attachment theorists, some such measures have been found to be internally consistent and to predict expected outcomes. Thus, such measures could be considered for inclusion in a set of indicators of developmental well-being.

REFERENCES

Ainsworth, M. D. S., Blehar, M. C., Waters, E., & Wall, S. (1978). *Patterns of attachment: A psychological study of the Strange Situation*. Hillsdale, NJ: Lawrence Erlbaum Associates.

Anan, R. M., & Barnett, D. (1999). Perceived social support mediates between prior attachment and subsequent adjustment: A study of urban African-American children. *Developmental Psychology, 35*, 1210–1222.

Armsden, G. C., & Greenberg, M. T. (1987). The inventory of parent and peer attachment: Individual differences and their relationship to psychological well-being in adolescence. *Journal of Youth and Adolescence, 16*, 427–454.

Belsky, J., Campbell, S. B., Cohn, J. F., & Moore, G. (1996). Instability of infant–parent attachment security. *Developmental Psychology, 32*, 921–924.

Belsky, J., & Isabella, R. (1988). Maternal, infant, and social-contextual determinants of attachment security. In J. Belsky & T. Nezrowski (Eds.), *Clinical implications of attachment* (pp. 41–94). Hillsdale, NJ: Lawrence Erlbaum Associates.

Belsky, J., Spritz, B., & Crnic, K. (1996). Infant attachment security and affective-cognitive information processing at age 3. *Psychological Science, 7*, 111–114.

Booth, C. L., Rubin, K. H., & Rose-Krasnor, L. (1998). Perceptions of emotional support from mother and friend in middle childhood: Links with socio-emotional adaptation and preschool attachment security. *Child Development, 69*, 427–442.

Bost, K. K., Vaughn, B. E., Washington, W. N., Cielinski, K. L., & Bradbard, M. R. (1998). Social competence, social support, and attachment: Demarcation of construct domains, measurement, and paths of influence for preschool children attending Head Start. *Child Development, 69*, 192–218.

Bowlby, J. (1969/1982). *Attachment and loss: Vol. 1. Attachment*. New York: Basic.

Bowlby, J. (1973). *Attachment and loss: Vol. 2. Separation*. New York: Basic.

Bowlby, J. (1980). *Attachment and loss: Vol. 3. Loss*. New York: Basic.

Bretherton, I. (1985). Attachment theory: Retrospect and prospect. In I. Bretherton & E. Waters (Eds.), Growing points of attachment theory and research. *Monographs of the Society for Research in Child Development, 50*(1–2, Serial No. 209), pp. 3–35.

Bretherton, I., & Waters, E. (Eds.). (1985). Growing points of attachment theory and research. *Monographs of the Society for Research in Child Development, 50*(1–2, Serial No. 209).

Cassidy, J. (1988). Child–mother attachment and the self in six-year-olds. *Child Development, 59,* 121–134.

Cassidy, J., & Marvin, R. S. (1991). *Attachment organization in three- and four-year-olds: Coding guidelines.* Seattle, WA: MacArthur Working Group in Attachment.

Chisholm, K. (1998). A three year follow-up of attachment and indiscriminate friendliness in children adopted from Romanian orphanages. *Child Development, 69,* 1092–1106.

Cicchetti, D., & Toth, S. L. (Eds.). (1995). *Emotion, cognition, and representation: Rochester Symposium on Developmental Psychopathology* (Vol. 6). Rochester, NY: University of Rochester Press.

Connell, J. P., Halpern-Felsher, B. L., Clifford, E., Crichlow, W., & Usinger, P. (1995). Hanging in there: Behavioral, psychological, and contextual factors affecting whether African American adolescents stay in high school. *Journal of Adolescent Research, 10,* 41–63.

Connell, J. P., Spencer, M. B., & Aber, J. L. (1994). Educational risk and resilience in African-American youth: Context, self, action, and outcomes in school. *Child Development, 65,* 493–506.

Connell, J. P., & Wellborn, J. G. (1991). Competence, autonomy, and relatedness: A motivational analysis of self-system processes. In M. R. Gunnar & L. A. Sroufe (Eds.), *Self processes in development: Minnesota Symposium on Child Psychology* (Vol. 23), pp. 43–77. Chicago: University of Chicago Press.

Das Eiden, R., Teti, D. M., & Corns, K. M. (1995). Maternal working models of attachment, marital adjustment, and the parent-child relationship. *Child Development, 66,* 1504–1518.

Davies, P. T., & Cummings, E. M. (1994). Marital conflict and child adjustment: An emotional security hypothesis. *Psychological Bulletin, 116,* 387–411.

Egeland, B., & Farber, E. A. (1984). Infant–mother attachment: Factors related to its development and change over time. *Child Development, 55,* 753–771.

Erikson, E. H. (1963). *Childhood and society.* New York: Norton.

Erikson, E. H. (1980). *Identity and the life cycle.* New York: Norton.

Fagot, B. I. (1997). Attachment, parenting, and peer interactions of toddler children. *Developmental Psychology, 33,* 489–499.

Fraiberg, S., Adelson, E., & Shapiro, V. (1987). Ghosts in the nursery: A psychoanalytic approach to the problems of impaired infant–mother relationships. In L. Fraiberg (Ed.), *Selected writings of Selma Fraiberg* (pp. 100–136). Columbus, OH: State University Press.

Hamilton, C. E. (2000). Continuity and discontinuity of attachment from infancy through adolescence. *Child Development, 71,* 690–694.

Howes, C., Hamilton, C. E., & Philipsen, L. C. (1998). Stability and continuity of child–caregiver and child–peer relationships. *Child Development, 69,* 418–426.

Institute for Research and Reform in Education. (1998). Research Assessment Package for Schools (RAPS). Student supports and opportunities in school: Engagement, beliefs about self, and experiences of interpersonal support. Manual for elementary and middle school assessments. Philadelphia, PA: Author.

Jacobsen, T., & Hoffman, V. (1997). Children's attachment representations: Longitudinal relations to school behavior and academic competency in middle childhood and adolescence. *Developmental Psychology, 33,* 703–710.

Kerns, K. A. (1996). Individual differences in friendship quality: Links to child–mother attachment. In W. M. Bukowski, A. F. Newcomb, & W. W. Hartup (Eds.), *The company they keep. Friendship in childhood and adolescence* (pp. 137–157). Cambridge, UK: Cambridge University Press.

Kerns, K. A., Klepac, L., & Cole, A. (1996). Peer relationships and preadolescents' perceptions of security in the child–mother relationship. *Developmental Psychology, 32,* 457–466.

Kirsh, S., & Cassidy, J. (1997). Preschoolers' attention to and memory for attachment-relevant information. *Child Development, 68,* 1143–1153.

Lewis, M., Feiring, C., & Rosenthal, S. (2000). Attachment over time. *Child Development*, *71*, 707–720.

Lyons-Ruth, K., Easterbrooks, M. A., & Cibelli, C. D. (1997). Infant attachment strategies, infant mental lag, and maternal depressive symptoms: Predictors of internalizing and externalizing problems at age 7. *Developmental Psychology*, *33*, 681–692.

Main, M., & Cassidy, J. (1988). Categories of responses to reunion with the parent at age six: Predictable from infant attachment classification and stable over a one-month period. *Developmental Psychology*, *24*, 415–426.

Main, M., Kaplan, N., & Cassidy, J. (1985). Security in infancy, childhood, and adulthood: A move to the level of representations. In I. Bretherton & E. Waters (Eds.), Growing points of attachment theory and research. *Monographs of the Society for Research in Child Development*, *50*(1–2, Serial No. 209), 66–104.

Mahler, M. S., Pine, F., & Bergman, A. (1975). *The psychological birth of the human infant*. New York: Basic.

Marcus, R. F., & Betzer, P. D. S. (1996). Attachment and antisocial behavior in early adolescence. *Journal of Early Adolescence*, *16*, 229–248.

Meins, E., Fernyhough, C., Russell, J., & Clark-Carter, D. (1998). Security of attachment as a predictor of symbolic and mentalising abilities: A longitudinal study. *Social Development*, *7*, 1–24.

Moss, E., Rousseau, D., Parent, S., St.-Laurent, D., & Saintonge, J. (1998). Correlates of attachment at school age: Maternal reported stress, mother–child interaction, and behavior problems. *Child Development*, *69*, 1390–1405.

Oppenheim, D. (1997). The attachment doll-play interview for preschoolers. *International Journal of Behavioral Development*, *20*, 681–697.

Owen, M. T., & Cox, M. J. (1997). Marital conflict and the development of infant–parent attachment relationships. *Journal of Family Psychology*, *11*, 152–164.

Richters, J. E., Waters, E., & Vaughn, B. E. (1988). Empirical classification of infant–mother relationships from interactive behavior and crying during reunion. *Child Development*, *59*, 512–522.

Ricks, M. H. (1985). The social transmission of parental behavior: Attachment across generations. In I. Bretherton & E. Waters (Eds.), Growing points of attachment theory and research. *Monographs of the Society for Research in Child Development*, *50*(1–2, Serial No. 209), 211–227.

Rose-Krasnor, L., Rubin, K. H., Booth, C. L., & Coplan, R. (1996). The relation of maternal directiveness and child attachment security to social competence in preschoolers. *International Journal of Behavioral Development*, *19*, 309–3252.

Sokol-Katz, J., Dunham, R., & Zimmerman, R. (1997). Family structure versus parental attachment in controlling adolescent deviant behavior: A social control model. *Adolescence*, *32*, 199–215.

Teti, D. M., & Gelfand, D. M. (1997). The preschool assessment of attachment: Construct validity in a sample of depressed and nondepressed families. *Development and Psychopathology*, *9*, 517–536.

Teti, D. M., & McGourty, S. (1996). Using mothers versus trained observers in assessing children's secure base behavior: Theoretical and methodological considerations. *Child Development*, *67*, 597–605.

Teti, D. M., Sakin, W. J., Kucera, E., Corns, K. M., & Das Eiden, R. (1996). And baby makes four: Predictors of attachment security among preschool-age firstborns during the transition to siblinghood. *Child Development*, *67*, 579–596.

Thompson, R. A. (2000). The legacy of early attachments. *Child Development*, *71*, 145–152.

Thompson, R., Lamb, M., & Estes, D. (1982). Stability of infant–mother attachment and its relationship to changing life circumstances in an unselected middle-class sample. *Child Development*, *53*, 144–148.

van IJzendoorn, M. H., Dijkstra, J., & Bus, A. G. (1995). Attachment, intelligence, and language: A meta-analysis. *Social Development*, *4*, 115–128.

Vaughn, B. E., Egeland, B., Sroufe, L. A., & Waters, E. (1979). Individual differences in infant–mother attachment at twelve and eighteen months: Stability and change in families under stress. *Child Development*, *50*, 971–975.

Verschueren, K., & Marcoen, A. (1999). Representation of self and socioemotional competence in kindergartners: Differential and combined effects of attachment to mother and father. *Child Development*, *70*, 183–201.

Verschueren, K., Marcoen, A., & Schoefs, V. (1996). The internal working model of the self, attachment, and competence in five-year-olds. *Child Development*, *67*, 2493–2511.

Wartner, U. G., Grossmann, K., Fremmer-Bombik, E., & Suess, G. (1994). Attachment patterns at age six in south Germany: Predictability from infancy and implications for preschool behavior. *Child Development*, *65*, 1014–1027.

Waters, E., & Deane, K. E. (1985). Defining and assessing individual differences in attachment relationships: Q-methodology and the organization of behavior in infancy and early childhood. In I. Bretherton & E. Waters (Eds.), Growing points of attachment theory and research. *Monographs of the Society for Research in Child Development*, *50*(1–2, Serial No. 209), pp. 41–65.

Waters, E., Hamilton, C. E., & Weinfield, N. S. (2000). The stability of attachment security from infancy to adolescence and early adulthood: General introduction. *Child Development*, *71*, 678–683.

Waters, E., Merrick, S., Treboux, D., Crowell, J., & Albersheim, L. (2000). Attachment security in infancy and early adulthood: A twenty-year longitudinal study. *Child Development*, *71*, 684–689.

Waters, E., Vaughn, B. E., Posada, G., & Kondo-Ikemura, K. (Eds.). (1995). Caregiving, cultural, and cognitive perspectives on secure-base behavior and working models: New growing points of attachment theory and research. *Monographs of the Society for Research in Child Development*, *60*(2–3, Serial No. 244).

Waters, E., Weinfield, N.S., & Hamilton, C. E. (2000). The stability of attachment security from infancy to adolescence and early adulthood: General discussion. *Child Development*, *71*, 703–706.

Weinfield, N. S., Sroufe, L. A., & Egeland, B. (2000). Attachment from infancy to early adulthood in a high-risk sample: Continuity, discontinuity, and their correlates. *Child Development*, *71*, 695–702.

15

Parent–Child Relationships

Martha J. Cox

Kristina S. M. Harter
University of North Carolina at Chapel Hill

INTRODUCTION

Research on parenting has been central to efforts in psychology and other related sciences to understand how children become adults who are able to function well as members of society. In modern society, it is widely accepted that childhood social-ization takes place in at least three major contexts: families, out-of-home contexts like day care centers or schools, and peer groups. Although evidence suggests the contribution of all these contexts in shaping children's development, an enormous body of theoretical and empirical literature supports the significant role of parents (Collins, Maccoby, Steinberg, Hetherington, & Bornstein, 2000; Maccoby, 2000). In particular, research is converging on the idea that it is the quality of the parent–child relationship that seems particularly important in understanding the course of the child's emotional and social development. In this chapter, we review major work on the links between parent–child relationships and child emotional and so-cial well-being. We address issues of definition and measurement. We provide a brief theoretical and empirical review of the literature. We extract from this review a description of the characteristics of positive parent–child relationships and con-sider whether these characteristics change over time and with development. Finally, we conclude with a discussion of the factors that affect the development of relationships between parents and children.

TECHNICAL ISSUES

We have said that an enormous body of theoretical and empirical literature supports the significant role of parents. But we must consider specifically what is important about parenting. First, we submit that it is the quality of the parent–child relationship that seems particularly important in understanding the course of the child's development and that the parent–child relationship is co-constructed by the parent and the child and is not something that comes from the parent alone. Second, we make the case that parents must regulate parenting practices to fit the child and the context in which the child is being reared. For example, parent–child interaction differs with gender of the child and gender of the parent, the age of the child, the temperament of the child, whether the child is healthy or handicapped, as well as with aspects of context. Goals and expectations for children differ between cultures and among subgroups within a culture, and these differences in goals and expectations are reflected in interactions between parents and children.

Not only is defining what is specifically important about parenting a complex issue, but the issue of measurement of parent–child relationships also is not simple. The parenting and family literature has a long history of use of self-report measurement. As noted by Dix and Gershoff (in press), self-reports should be used when individuals' subjective experience is the issue, that is, when investigators are interested in parents' or children's attributions, perceptions, or beliefs about parent–child relationships. Problems arise when investigators confuse their level of measurement and treat these individual perceptions as a proxy for an assessment of the dyadic parent–child relationship. The assessment of qualities of the parent–child dyad may differ sharply from either the parent or the child's perceptions or beliefs about the parent–child relationship. Thus, self-report measures are not problematic when the level of measurement is recognized as that of individual perceptions; it is when they are interpreted as reflecting qualities of the dyad that they become problematic (Cox & Paley, 1997). The use of self-report allows investigators to collect information in a relatively timely and inexpensive fashion. It also can provide a valuable window into children's emotional experience and children's conceptualization of parents and parent–child relationships.

Whereas self-reports reveal subjective experience, observation of overt behaviors more objectively reveal how parents and children interact with each other (Floyd & Costigan, 1997). In general, direct observation methodologies are best used when one is concerned with describing the dyadic relationship between parents and children rather than individual perceptions and are particularly appropriate for phenomena that are difficult to obtain through self-report such as affective qualities of interactions. These methods are also especially useful for studying parents with young children who do not have the language skills to respond to questionnaires (Lindahl, 2001). These observational approaches, of course, pose problems of their own in that they are very costly and time consuming, and may be too brief or context bound to be representative of real-world relationships (Dix & Gershoff, in press; Lindahl, 2001).

THEORETICAL AND EMPIRICAL REVIEW OF THE LITERATURE

Many theorists take the view that to understand the mutual impact of the child and the parent, one must start at infancy and the preschool years when amazing growth in the child's capacity for self-control and self-regulation and in the internalization of standards for behavior occurs. Sroufe (1990) notes the challenge of understanding how the "self" or "personality" of the child develop so that the child comes to manage frustration; accept delays and disappointments, operate in the environment autonomously and effectively, cooperate and coordinate in give and take with others, emotionally engage and share fun with others, understand and respond to the feelings of others, and regulate tensions that are inevitable in complex social interactions. Organizational theories of development suggest that self or personality is best seen not as a set of traits that individuals possess, but as an inner organization of attitudes, beliefs, and values. Important features of this organization include the child's openness to the range of emotional experience, style of regulating arousal and emotion, confidence in their own regulating capacities, and their expectations about others and relationships (Sroufe, 1990).

Attachment theory (Ainsworth, Bell, & Stayton, 1974; Bowlby, 1969/1982) as well as a number of complementary theoretical views (e.g., Erikson, 1959, 1963; Mahler, Pine, & Bergman, 1975; Sander, 1975) combine to yield a developmental view of the emergence of the child's individual self that emphasizes the importance of the parent–child relationship. These theories suggest that the organization of self-regulation exists from the very beginning, but resides in the infant–caregiver system, which at first involves the caregiver's synchronization with and sensitive-responsiveness to the infant (Sander, 1975). The emerging self reflects the incorporation of this dyadic organization into the developing psyche of the child. That is, the parent's early sensitive responding to the child's signals is considered key to the development of self-regulation (Sroufe, 1995). As infants acquire the ability to self-regulate, they naturally exercise this ability, drawn by the motive for increased autonomous functioning (Sander, 1975). The emergence of a stable and self-regulatory core in the child is based on the entire history of harmonious regulation in interactions with the caregiver (parent) with the gradual transfer of regulatory functions to the child, as well as on the parent's acceptance of greater independence for the child. If the caregiver is threatened by this independence or punitive in response to the child's expressions of autonomy, important features of the inner self may be compromised. Acceptance by the parent of the child's explorations and continued availability for closeness and reassurance while sensitively following the child's lead promote flexible self-regulation in the child (Sroufe, 1995).

From an attachment theory perspective, Sroufe notes that the young child's confidence in the parent–child relationship becomes self-confidence; security within the attachment relationships becomes self-reliance. On the other hand, children who have experienced chaotic and inconsistent parenting do not have the positive regulatory experiences to guide their own efforts, nor the confidence in the caregiver (and consequently in themselves) required for flexible experimentation with regulation. Additionally, children who have been pushed to precocious independence because the parent is emotionally unavailable or harsh tend to adopt rigid regulatory strategies that they attempt to use on their own. In this scenario, children do not learn to access social resources to help them with regulation. Thus, normatively, the individual's sense of security can be thought of as the core of the self, their fundamental sense of others as caring, the self as worthy, and the world as safe. This arises from the history of sensitive and responsive care within the parent–child attachment relationship.

DEVELOPMENTAL STABILITY AND CONTINUITY OVER THE LIFE SPAN

Research with young children and their parents tends to support this theoretical view. Children whose interactions with their parents have been characterized by sensitive, responsive care from the parent as opposed to over-stimulating, dysregulating care have been found to be better able to handle frustration, be less hyperactive, and show better attention during the preschool years, and to do better academically and emotionally in the early elementary years (Carlson, Jacobvitz, & Sroufe, 1995; Egeland, Pianta, & O'Brien, 1993; Jacobvitz & Sroufe, 1987). In toddlerhood, willing compliance with parents is associated with parent interaction behaviors that are well coordinated with the child's. Parent's behaviors scaffold the child's efforts, fit with what the child is doing, and add to it (Edwards, 1995; Parpal & Maccoby, 1985; Westerman, 1990). In a large, longitudinal study currently underway, it has been found that maternal sensitivity to the child's signals is a consistently strong predictor of positive outcome for the child in terms of cognitive and social development (NICHD Early Child Care Research Network, 1997a, 1997b, 1998, 1999b). Children with a history of secure attachment relationships with their parents, having experienced responsive care, show greater self-reliance in the classroom, better ability to delay and less inclination to fall apart under stress, a greater curiousity and willingness to make a strong effort in the face of challenge, and a greater flexibility and complexity in their play (Rosenberg, 1984; Sroufe, Schork, Motti, Lawroski, & LaFrenier, 1984). Additionally, children with secure relationships show peer relationships with more commitment and emotional closeness, positive affect, and are more empathic and prosocial with other children when the partner is less able, injured, or distressed, but are assertive with aggressive partners (Kestenbaum, Farber, & Sroufe, 1989; Pancake, 1988; Sroufe, 1983; Troy & Sroufe, 1987).

In middle childhood, parents and children spend less time together and cognitive changes on the part of children greatly expand their capacity for solving problems and gaining necessary information on their own (Collins, Harris, & Susman, 1995). However, as with younger ages, the relationship between parent and child is critical (Collins, Harris, & Sussman, 1995; Darling & Steinberg, 1993; Maccoby, 1983). Attentive, responsive relationships between parents and their children in middle-childhood are associated with the development of self-esteem, competence, and social responsibility in the child (Collins et al., 1995). Parental monitoring of their children also seems to be particularly important as poor monitoring has been linked to antisocial behavior in middle childhood (Patterson, 1982, 1986; Pulkinnen, 1982; Tolan & Loeber, 1993). However, the ability of parents to monitor, guide and support their children when their children are not always near by depends very much on the relationship between them. Parents must not only be aware of children's whereabouts and behaviors, but children must be willing to inform their parents of their whereabouts, activities, and problems. Thus, the effectiveness of monitoring depends on an attentive, responsive, warm relationship between the parent and child.

The amount of responsiveness in the relationship between parent and child continues to be of major importance in predicting positive outcomes during the adolescent years and even into the adult years as parents continue to be sources of support for their children (Cooper, 1988; Cooper, Grotevant, & Condon, 1983; Hauser, Powers, & Noam, 1991; Maccoby & Martin, 1983). Warm and responsive relationships between adolescents and parents, for example, are associated with a variety of positive outcomes including self-esteem, identity formation, and prosocial behavior, better parent–adolescent communication, and less depression, anxiety, and behavior problems in adolescents (Armsden & Greenberg, 1987; Barnes & Olson, 1985; Dix, 1991; Hetherington & Martin, 1986; Holmbeck, Paikoff, & Brooks-Gunn, 1995; Maccoby & Martin, 1983; Papini, Micka, & Barnett, 1989; Papini & Roggman, 1992).

The challenge during adolescence is that warm, responsive, and involved relationships must be maintained at a time when the asymmetries in power that characterized earlier parent–child relationships are shifting to more equality in the face of the adolescent's more sophisticated social cognitive skills and broader contacts with the environment outside the family (Eccles et al., 1993; Holmbeck & Hill, 1991; Kidwell, Fischer, Dunham, & Baranowski,, 1983). The transition to adolescents involves biological, cognitive, social cognitive, emotional, self-definitional, peer relationship, and school context changes for the adolescent (Holmbeck et al., 1995). Increases in negative affect expression occur from preadolescent to middle adolescence (Brooks-Gunn, 1991; Brooks-Gunn & Paikoff, 1992; Peterson, Sarigiana, & Kennedy, 1991). Cognitive changes may result in more confrontations between parents and adolescents as adolescents increasingly begin to question and debate parental rules and expectations (Collins, 1990; Smetana, 1989a). In this context, it is still important that parents are involved and are providing supervision for their children (Fuligni & Eccles, 1993; Maccoby & Martin, 1983, Patterson, 1986; Patterson, Bank, & Stoolmiller, 1990). However, modifications in the degree and nature of supervision are necessary, and those modifications appear best achieved with the most positive outcomes when built on a foundation of close relations with parents (Fuligni & Eccles, 1993; Grotevant & Cooper, 1985; Hill & Holmbeck, 1986). Smetana (1989a, 1989b) suggests that differences arise between parents and children at adolescence regarding the legitimacy of parental authority in particular arenas. For parental authority to be intact, not only must parents assert it, but adolescents must also accept it. There is likely wide cultural and subgroup variation in what is considered to be appropriate and legitimate parental authority. However, across cultures and subgroups, the quality of parent–child relationships in terms of sensitivity and responsiveness are likely to be important in determining whether differences arise regarding parental authority and how well differences are resolved.

In this light, Collins and Laursen (1992) have noted that although parent–child conflict typically increases during adolescence, the conflict can serve as an important signal to parents that parenting behaviors need to be modified in response to the changing developmental needs of their children. Holmbeck and Hill (1991) similarly have argued that parent–adolescent conflict can serve an adaptive function as conflict can be an impetus to change, adaptation, and development. Conflicts that occur in the context of generally warm, supportive family relationships may be more likely to be facilitative of development (Cooper, 1988).

Thus, the construct of sensitive and responsive child-centered relationships between parents and children is generally stable, remaining key to positive development across childhood. The specific activities or behaviors of parents and children, however, must change in line with the developmental changes in the child. Namely, these changes involve a transition toward greater responsibility for children in regulating their own behavior and interactions with others (Collins et al., 1995).

FACTORS AFFECTING THE DEVELOPMENT AND PROMOTION OF POSITIVE PARENT–CHILD RELATIONSHIPS

Parent–child relationships do not occur in a vacuum and the context in which the relationships develop are likely to affect the nature of parent–child relationships (Cox & Paley, 1997). Family configuration, social support, social class, poverty, and culture are associated with differences in parenting perceptions and practices (Bornstein, 1995; McLoyd, 1998). The qualities of marital or adult relationships also are important predictors of parent–child relationships (Cox, Paley, & Harter, in press). Individual qualities of parents and infants also affect parenting (Bornstein, 1995). A major question has concerned whether "fathering" is different from "mothering;" in other words, whether fathers bring something different to the parent–child relationship than do mothers, so that children are put at a disadvantage if they are raised without the involvement of a father or a father-figure (Parke, 1996).

Bornstein (1995) notes that family configuration is related to parenting behaviors. Mothers of firstborns engage, respond to, stimulate, talk to and express positive affection to their babies more than mothers of laterborns, even when there are no differences in first and later born behavior (Belsky, Taylor, & Rovine, 1984). Firstborns are likely to experience different parent–child relationships than later-borns.

Financial and emotional stresses negatively affect the well being of parents and adversely affect their attentiveness and sensitivity to their children (Crnic & Acevedo, 1995; McLoyd, 1990, 1998). Social support networks are also important.

Well-supported mothers are less restrictive and punitive with their infants than are mothers without good social support, and improvements in social support are associated with improvements in parent–child relationships (Bornstein, 1995; Crnic, Greenberg, Ragozin, Robinson, & Basham, 1983). Parents' perceptions of supportive networks beyond the family are associated with more positive parenting and more positive child development (Cochran & Niego, 1995). Intimate support in the marital relationship seems particularly important to positive parent–child relationships (Crnic et al., 1983). In contrast, the existence of marital conflict that is unresolved seems to erode a parent's ability to be positive and warm with children and to be positively involved and attentive to the child (Cox, Paley, & Harter, in press; Grych & Fincham, 1990).

The education and income of parents has been associated in many studies with variations in parenting behavior. Mothers with higher education and higher incomes are observed to be more sensitive to the signals of their young children and their young children show more positive engagement with them (NICHD Early Child Care Research Network, 1999a).

Culture also influences parenting patterns. The types of values that parents wish to inculcate in their children and the goals that they have in socializing children may vary from group to group. For example, Demo and Cox (2000) note that mainstream American culture places a strong emphasis on individualism, competition, independence, self-development, and self-satisfaction. In contrast, ethnic minority children are more likely to be socialized to value cooperation, sharing reciprocity, obligation, and interdependence (Harrison et al., 1990). Cultural patterns influence parent practices and child development from infancy through such routes as when and how parents care for infants, the extent to which parents permit infants to explore, how nurturant and restrictive parents are, and which behaviors parents emphasize (Bornstein, 1995). For example, American mothers promote autonomy and foster physical and verbal assertiveness and independence in their children, whereas Japanese mothers consolidate and strengthen closeness and dependency within the parent–child relationship (Befu, 1986; Kojima, 1986). These differences are important and striking; however, it should be noted that there are also great similarities across cultures in the way parents interact with their children, and that within cultures there is great variability in the way in which parent and child relationships develop.

Individual differences in parents and children also are important to the development of parent–child relationships. Infant temperament clearly influences adults. Having a baby who is easily soothed leads mothers to perceive themselves as more competent parents (Deutsch et al., 1988; Sanson & Rothbart, 1995). Infant temperament may interact with other factors such as social support so as to make having good social support more important to the development of the parent–child relationship when infants are difficult to sooth (Crockenberg, 1981). Because the parent–child relationship is a co-construction of both parent and child, the input of the child (what the child brings to the relationship) is important at every point in development.

Parental personality and functioning also has been found to be important in predicting parent–child relationships (Belsky, 1984; Cox, Owen, Lewis, & Henderson, 1989; Lamb & Easterbrooks, 1981). Depression has perhaps been studied more than other parental characteristics. Field (1984) found that the interactions between depressed mothers and their infants were characterized by less positive and more negative affect, less infant vocalization, and more passivity on the part of the infant. In a recent study (NICHD Early Child Care Research Network, 1999b), mothers with high and chronic depressive symptoms were less sensitive with their infants, but only when they also had low income. Levels of parent psychopathology are related to qualities of the parent–child relationship and the child's adjustment (Dodge, 1990; Hauser & Bowlds, 1990; Rutter, 1990).

Gender of the parent may also be important. There has been a recent concern about fathering and whether children are disadvantaged if they do not experience the parenting of an involved and active father. Recent popular movements have tried to support the involvement of men in the lives of their children. Children in single mother homes are much more likely to live in poverty and, as cited earlier, McLoyd's work (1991, 1998) demonstrates the negative impact of poverty and its accompanying stresses on the parenting of mothers. But is there an effect of growing up without a father or with an uninvolved father on the development of children, or is it only the conditions such as poverty that are created by the absence of a father that are important? Do fathers provide parenting that is different or unique such that the child's development is hindered without an involved father? Parke (1996) summarizes research that suggests that the relationship of boys with fathers or available male figures is associated with competence with peers. Some of this effect seems to be due to the changes in family income that are associated with a father's departure from the home, whereas some of the effect may be due to interactions that fathers have with their children. Parke (1996) notes that games that mothers and fathers play with their young children may be important for the child's later social and cognitive development. Although mothers and fathers are both important play partners, in the United States and some other western cultures (e.g., England, Australia), father's play is more active and physical, whereas mother's play is more verbal. In each case, the sensitivity and reciprocal nature of the play is associated with more positive outcome, but the different styles may supplement each other in the development of the child's capacity to regulate emotion and arousal. Children who are popular with their peers had fathers who were able to sustain physical play for longer periods of time and were less directive and coercive (i.e., were more synchronized and responsive) with their children (Parke et al., 1989).

Differences in mothers' and fathers' interactions with their children can also be seen in adolescents, although it should be noted that at all ages there are more similarities than differences (Holmbeck et al., 1995). Mothers spend more time with their children than do fathers and are more likely to be involved in caregiving, while fathers are more likely to be involved in leisure activities. Adolescents' relationships with their mothers are closer than with their fathers (Collins & Russell, 1991).

However, Lamb (1997) notes that fathers may influence their children indirectly as well as directly by contributing in positive ways to the complex social system of the family in which the child develops. This could be through the father's relationship with the mother and the support for her parenting, through the income and opportunities the father brings into the family, as well as through the model of achievement and social contribution the father provides. From this point of view, it is much harder to quantify the way in which men contribute to their families and their children, but clearly these sources of influence are potentially important (Lamb, 1997).

CONCLUSIONS

A large amount of literature and theory converges on the notion that it is the relationship between the parent and child that is critical for the positive development of children. Specifically, a common theme during childhood is that the way in which parents are able to sensitively regulate their parenting behavior in interaction with their child based on the developmental needs of the children is a critical determinant of positive outcome. In infancy, the parent's early sensitive responding to the child's signals is considered key to the development of self-regulation. There is wide agreement that the role of the caregiver in soothing distress, enhancing alertness, and allowing the child the experience of self-regulation by sensitively responding to the child's signals of need for soothing or increased stimulation is critical to the development of infant adaptive self-organization (Sameroff, 1989; Sroufe, 1995; Tronick, 1989). As the child grows older, attentive, responsive relationships between parents and their children are associated with the development of self-esteem, competence, and social responsibility in the child. Monitoring of the child's behavior and whereabouts becomes very important as children become more autonomous and spend more time away from home, but the effectiveness of monitoring depends on an attentive, responsive, warm relationship between the parent and child (Collins et al., 1995; Darling & Steinberg, 1993; Maccoby, 1983). Although optimal childrearing practices may differ in different societies, relationships between parents and children in which there is responsiveness to children's needs and support for their development seems to foster competent, responsible behavior generally (Collins et al., 1995). The key component seems to be sensitive, responsive, child-centered parenting in which parents exert their influence by sensitively fitting their behavior to behavioral cues from children, rather than allowing their own needs to determine parent–child interaction (Maccoby & Martin, 1983). Thus, the construct of sensitive and responsive child-centered relationships between parents and children is a construct that is fairly stable across childhood as key to positive development, but the specific activities or behaviors of parents and children must change in line with the characteristics of the child, the contexts in which parents are raising the child, and the developmental changes in the child.

Parenting is influenced by many factors within and outside of the family. The individual characteristics and adjustment of the family members, the quality of adult relationships in the family, the quality of social support, and the level of stresses all seem to contribute to parenting. Fathering and mothering seem more alike than different, although fathers may bring some experiences to the child that supplement those that the mother brings.

REFERENCES

Ainsworth, M. D. S., Bell, S., & Stayton, D. (1974). Infant–mother attachment and social development: Socialization as a product of reciprocal responsiveness to signals. In M. Richards (Ed.), *The integration of the child into the social world*. Cambridge, OK: Cambridge University Press.

Armsden, G. C., & Greenberg, M. T. (1987). The Inventory of Parent and peer attachment: Individual differences and their relationship to psychological well-being in adolescence. *Journal of Youth and Adolescence, 16*, 427–454.

Barnes, H. L., & Olson, D. H. (1985). Parent–adolescent communication and the circumplex model. *Child Development, 56*, 438–447.

Belsky, J. (1984). The determinants of parenting: A process model. *Child Development, 55*, 83–96.

Belsky, J., Taylor, D., & Rovine, M. (1984). The Pennsylvania Infant and Family Development Project, II: The development of reciprocal interaction in the mother–infant dyad. *Child Development, 55*, 706–717.

Bornstein, M. H. (1995). Parenting infants. In Mark H. Bornstein (Ed.), *Handbook of parenting: Vol. 1. Children and parenting* (pp. 3–39). Mahwah, NJ: Lawrence Erlbaum Associates.

Bowlby, J. (1969/1982). *Attachment and loss* (2nd ed., Vol. 1). New York: Basic Books.

Brooks-Gunn, J. (1991). How stressful is the transition to adolescence for girls? In M. E. Colton & S. Gore (Eds.), *Adolescent stress: Causes and consequences* (pp. 131–149). New York: Aldine de Gruyter.

Brooks-Gunn, J., & Paikoff, R. L. (1992). Changes in self-feelings during the transition towards adolescence. In H. McGurk (Ed.), *Childhood social development: Contemporary issues* (pp. 63–97). Hillsdale, NJ: Lawrence Erlbaum Associates.

Carlson, E. A., Jacobvitz, D., & Sroufe, L. A. (1995). A developmental investigation of inattentiveness and hyperactivity. *Child Development, 66*, 37–54.

Cochran, M., & Niego, S. (1995). Parenting and Social Networks. In M. Bornstein (Ed.), *Handbook of Parenting, Vol. 3. Status and Social Conditions of Parenting* (pp. 393–418). Mahwah, NJ: Lawrence Erlbaum Associates.

Collins, W. A. (1990). Parent–child relationships in the transition to adolescence: Continuity and change in interaction, affect, and cognition. In R. Montemayor, G. Admas, & T. Gullota (Eds.), *Advances in adolescent development: From childhood to adolescence: A transitional period?* (Vol. 2, pp. 85–106). Beverly Hills, CA: Sage.

Collins, W. A., Harris, M. L., & Susman, A. (1995). Parenting during middle childhood. In Mark H. Bornstein (Ed.), *Handbook of parenting: Vol. 1. Children and parenting* (pp. 65–89). Mahwah, NJ: Lawrence Erlbaum Associates.

Collins, W. A., & Laursen, B. (1992). Conflict and relationships during adolescence. In C. U. Shantz & W. W. Hartup (Eds.), *Conflict in child and adolescent development* (pp. 216–341). New York: Cambridge University Press.

Collins, W. A., Maccoby, E. E., Steinberg, L., Hetherington, E. M., & Bornstein, M. H. (2000). Contemporary research on parenting: The case for nature and nurture. *American Psychologist, 55*(2), 218–232.

Collins, W. A., & Russell, G. (1991). Mother–child and father–child relationships in middle childhood and adolescence: A developmental analysis. *Developmental Review, 11*, 99–136.

Cooper, C. R. (1988). Commentary: The role of conflict in adolescent–parent relationships. In M. R. Gunnar & W. A. Collins (Eds.), *21st Minnesota symposium on child psychology* (pp. 181–187). Hillsdale, NJ: Lawrence Erlbaum Associates.

Cooper, C. R., Grotevant, H. D., & Condon, S. M. (1983). Individuality and connectedness in the family as a context for adolescent identity formation and role-taking skill. In H. D. Grotevant, & C. R. Cooper (Eds.), *Adolescent development in the family: New directions for child development* (No. 22, pp. 43–59). San Francisco: Jossey-Bass.

Cox, M. J., Owen, M., Lewis, J. M., & Henderson, V. K. (1989). Marriage, adult adjustment and early parenting. *Child Development*, *60*, 1015–1024.

Cox, M. J., & Paley, B. (1997). Families as systems. *Annual Review of Psychology*, *48*, 243–267.

Cox, M. J., Paley, B., & Harter, K. (in press). Interparental conflict and parent–child relationships. In J. Grych & F. Fincham (Eds.), *Child Development and Interparental Conflict*. Cambridge University Press.

Crnic, K., & Acevedo, M. (1995). Everyday stresses and parenting. In M. Bornstein (Ed.), *Handbook of Parenting, Vol. 4. Applied and Practical Parenting* (pp. 277–297). Mahwah, NJ: Lawrence Erlbaum Associates.

Crnic, K. A., Greenberg, M., Ragozin, A. S., Robinson, N. M., & Basham, R. B. (1983). Effects of stress and social support on mothers and premature and fullterm infants. *Child Development*, *54*, 209–217.

Crockenberg, S. B. (1981). Infant irritability, mother responsiveness, and social support influences on the security of the infant–mother attachment. *Child Development*, *52*, 857–865.

Darling, N., & Steinberg, L. (1993). Parenting style as context: An integrative model. *Psychological Bulletin*, *113*, 487–496.

Demo, D., & Cox, M. (2000). Families with young children: A review of research in the 1990s. (Special Decade in Review Issue entitled *Understanding families into the new millennium*), *Journal of Marriage and the Family*, *62*, 876–895.

Deutsch, F. M., Ruble, D. N., Fleming, A., Brooks-Gunn, J., & Stangor, C. (1988). Information-seeking and self-definition during the transition to motherhood. *Journal of Personality and Social Psychology*, *55*, 420–431.

Dix, T., & Gershoff, E. T. (in press). Measuring parent–child relations. To appear in J. Touliatos, B. Perlmutter, & G. W. Holden (Eds.), *Second handbook of family measurements techniques*. New Park, CA: Sage.

Dix, T. (1991). The affective organization of parenting: Adaptive and maladaptive processes. *Psychological Bulletin*, *110*, 3–25.

Dodge, K. A. (1990). Developmental psychopathology in children of depressed mothers. *Developmental Psychology*, *26*, 3–6.

Eccles, J. S., Midgley, C., Wigfield, A., Buchanan, C. M., Reuman, D., Flanagan, C., & MacIver, D. (1993). Development during adolescence: The impact of stage-environment fit in young adolescents' experiences in schools and in families. *American Psychologist*, *48*, 90–101.

Edwards, C. P. (1995). Parenting toddlers. In Mark. H. Bornstein (Ed.), *Handbook of parenting: Vol. 1. Children and parenting* (pp. 41–63). Mahwah, NJ: Lawrence Earlbaum Associates.

Egeland, B., Pianta, R., & O'Brien, M. (1993). Maternal intrusiveness in infancy and child maladaptation in the early school years. *Development and Psychopathology*, *81*, 359–370.

Erickson, E. (1959). Identity and the life cycle: Selected papers. *Psychological Issues*, *1*, 5–165.

Erickson, E. (1963). *Childhood and society* (2nd ed.). New York: Norton.

Floyd, F. J., & Costigan, C. (1997). Family interactions and family adaptation. *International Review of Research in Mental Retardation*, *20*, 47–74.

Fuligni, A. J., & Eccles, J. S. (1993). Perceived parent–child relationships and early adolescents' orientation toward peers. *Developmental Psychology*, *29*, 622–632.

Grotevant, H. D., & Cooper, C. R. (1985). Patterns of interaction in family relationships and the development of identity exploration in adolescence. *Child Development*, *56*, 415–428.

Grych, J. H., & Fincham, F. D. (1990). Marital conflict and children's adjustment: A cognitive-contextual framework. *Psychological Bulletin*, *108*, 267–290.

Gunnar, (?), & Thelen, E. (Eds.). (????). *Systems and Development. The Minnesota Symposium on Child Psychology*, *22*, 219–235. Hillsdale, NJ: Lawrence Erlbaum Associates.

Harrison, A. O., Wilson, M. N., Pine, C. J., Chan, S. Q., & Buriel, R. (1990). Family ecologies of ethnic minority children. *Child Development*, *61*, 347–362.

Hauser, S. T., & Bowlds, M. K. (1990). Stress, coping, and adaptation. In S. S. Feldman & G. L. Elliott (Eds.), *At the threshold: The developing adolescent* (pp. 388–413). Cambridge: MA: Harvard University Press.

Hauser, S. T., Powers, S. I., & Noam, G. G. (1991). *Adolescents and their families: Paths of ego development.* New York: Free Press.

Hetherington, E. M., & Martin, B. (1986). Family factors and psychopathology in childhood. In H. C. Quay (Ed.), *Psychopathological disorders of childhood* (3rd ed., pp. 332–390). New York: Wiley.

Hill, J. P., & Holmbeck, G. N. (1986). Attachment and autonomy during adolescence. In M. R. Gunnar & W. A. Collins (Eds.), *21st Minnesota symposium on child psychology* (pp. 43–77). Hillsdale, NJ: Lawrence Erlbaum Associates.

Hinde, R. A. (1995). Foreword. In M. H. Bornstein (Ed.), *Handbook of Parenting, Vol. 1. Children and Parenting* (pp. xi–xii). Mahwah, NJ: Lawrence Erlbaum Associates.

Hoffman, M. L. (1970). Moral development. In P. H Mussen (Ed.), *Carmichael's manual of child psychology* (Vol. 2, pp. 261–359). New York: Wiley.

Holmbeck, G. N., & Hill, J. P. (1991). Conflictive engagement, positive affect, and menarche in families with seventh-grade girls. *Child Development, 62,* (1030–1048).

Holmbeck, G. N., Paikoff, R. L., & Brooks-Gunn, J. (1995). Parenting adolescents. In Mark H. Bornstein (Ed.), *Handbook of parenting: Vol. 1. Children and parenting* (pp. 91–118). Mahwah, NJ: Lawrence Erlbaum Associates.

Jacobvitz, E., & Sroufe, L. A. (1987). The early caregiver–child relationship and attention deficit disorder with hyperactivity in kindergarten. *Child Development, 58,* 1488–1495.

Kestenbaum, R., Fauber, E., & Sroufe, L. A. (1989). Individual differences in empathy among preschoolers: Concurrent an predictive validity. In N. Eisenberg (Ed.), *Empathy and related emotional responses: New directions for child development* (pp. 51–56). San Francisco: Jossey-Bass.

Kidwell, J., Fischer, J. L., Dunham, R. M., & Baranowski, M. (1983). Parents and adolescents: Push and pull of change. In H. I. McCubbin & C. R. Figley (Eds.), *Stress and the family: Vol 1. Coping with normative transitions* (pp. 74–89). New York: Brunner/Mazel.

Lamb, M. E. (1997). Fathers and child development: An introductory overview and guide. In M. E. Lamb (Ed.), *The role of the father in child development* (3rd ed., pp. 1–18). New York: Wiley.

Lamb, M. E., & Easterbrooks, M. A. (1981). Individual differences in paternal sensitivity: Origins, components, and consequences. In M. E. Lamb & L. R. Sherrod (Eds.), *Infant social cognition: Empirical and theoretical considerations* (pp. 127–153). Hillsdale, NJ: Lawrence Erlbaum Associates.

Lindahl, K. M. (2001). Methodological issues in family observational research. In P. K. Kerig & K. M. Lindahl (Eds.), *Family observational coding systems: Resources for systematic research* (pp. 23–32). Mahwah, NJ: Lawrence Erlbaum Associates.

Maccoby, E. E. (1983). Social-emotional development and response to stressors. In N. Garmezy & M. Rutter (Eds.), *Stress, coping, and development in children* (pp. 217–234). New York: McGraw-Hill.

Maccoby, E. E. (1992). The role of parents in the socialization of children: An historical overview. *Developmental Psychology, 28,* 1006–1017.

Maccoby, E. E., & Martin, J. A. (1983). Socialization in the context of the family: Parent–child interaction. In P. H. Messen & E. M. Hetherington (Eds.), *Handbook of Child Psychology.* (Vol. 4, pp. 1–102). New York: Wiley.

Maccoby, E. E. (2000). Parenting and its effects on children: On reading and misreading behavior genetics. *Annual Review of Psychology, 51,* 1–27.

Mahler, M., Pine, A., & Bergman, F. (1975). *The psychological birth of the human infant.* New York: Basic.

McLoyd, V. C. (1990). The impact of economic hardship on black families and children: Psychological distress, parenting, and socioemotional development. *Child Development, 61,* 311–346.

McLoyd, V. C. (1998). Children in poverty: Development, public policy, and practice. In W. Damon, I. E. Sigel, & K. A. Renninger (Eds.), *Handbook of Child Psychology* (Vol. 4, pp. 135–208). New York: Wiley.

NICHD Early Child Care Research Network. (1997a). Infant child care and attachment security: Results of the NICHD Study of Early Childcare. *Child Development, 68,* 860–879.

NICHD Early Child Care Research Network. (1997b, April). *Mother–child interaction and cognitive outcomes associated with early child care: Results from the NICHD Study.* Paper presented at the Workshop on Longitudinal Research on Children, Washington, DC.

NICHD Early Child Care Research Network. (1998). Early child care and self control, compliance, and problem behavior at 24 and 36 months. *Child Development, 69,* 1145–1170.

NICHD Early Child Care Research Network. (1999a). Child care and mother–child interaction in the first 3 years of life. Developmental Psychology, *35,* 1399–1413.

NICHD Early Child Care Research Network. (1999b). Chronicity of depressive symptoms, maternal sensitivity, and child functioning at 36 months: Results from the NICHD Study of Early Child Care. *Developmental Psychology, 35,* 1297–1310.

Osofsky, J. D., Wewers, S., Aann, D. M., & Fick, A. C. (1993). Chronic community violence: What is happening to our children? *Psychiatry, 56*, 36–45.

Pancake, V. R. (1988). *Quality of attachment in infancy as a predictor of hostility and emotional distance in preschool peer relationships*. Unpublished doctoral dissertation, University of Minnesota, Minneapolis.

Papini, D. R., Micka, J., & Barnett, J. (1989). Perceptions of intrapsychic and extrapsychic functioning as bases of adolescent ego identity statuses *Journal of Adolescent* Research, *4*, 460–480.

Papini, D. R., & Roggman, L. A. (1992). Adolescent perceived attachment to parents in relation to competence, depression, and anxiety: A longitudinal study *Journal of Early Adolescence, 12*, 420–440.

Parke, R. D. (1996). *Fatherhood*. Cambridge, MA: Harvard University Press.

Parke, R. D., MacDonald, K., Burks, V., Carson, J., Bhavnagri, N., Barth, J., & Beitel, A. (1989). Family-peer systems: In search of linkages. In K. Kreppner & R. M. Lerner (Eds.), *Family systems and life span development*. Hillsdale, NJ: Lawrence Erlbaum Associates.

Parpal, M., & Maccoby, E. E. (1985). Maternal responsiveness and subsequent child compliance. *Child Development, 56*, 1326–1334.

Patterson, G. R. (1982). *Coercive family processes*. Eugene, OR: Castalia Press.

Patterson, G. R. (1986). Performance models for antisocial boys. *American Psychologist, 41*, 432–444.

Patterson, G. R., Bank, L., & Stoolmiller, M. (1990). The preadolescent's contributions to disrupted family process. In R. Montemayor, G. R. Adams, & T. P. Gullotta (Eds.), *From childhood to adolescence: A transitional period?* (pp. 107–133). Newbury Park, CA: Sage.

Peterson, A. C., Sarigiani, P. A., & Kennedy, R. E. (1991). Adolescent depression: Why more girls? *Journal of Youth and Adolescence, 20*, 247–271.

Pulkinnen, L. (1982). Self-control and continuity from childhood to adolescence. In P. B. Balter & O.G. Brim (Eds.), *Life-span development and behavior* (Vol. 4, pp. 64–105). New York: Academic Press.

Rosenberg, D. (1984). *The quality and content of preschool fantasy play: Correlates in concurrent social-personality function and early mother–child attachment relationships*. Unpublished doctoral dissertation, University of Minnesota, Minneapolis.

Rutter, M. (1990). Commentary: Some focus and process considerations regarding effects of parental depression on children. *Developmental Psychology, 26*, 60–67.

Sameroff, A. J. (1989). General systems and the regulation of development. In M. R. Gunnar & E. Thelen (Eds.), Systems and development. *The Minnesota Symposium on Child Psychology, 22*, 219–235. Hillsdale, NJ: Lawrence Erlbaum Associates.

Sander, L. (1975). Infant and caretaking environment. In E. J. Anthony (Ed.), *Explorations in child psychiatry* (pp. 129–165). New York: Plenum.

Sanson, A. V., & Rothbart, M. K. (1995). Child Temperament and Parenting. In M. H. Bornstein (Ed.), *Handbook of Parenting, Vol. 4. Applied and Practical Parenting* (pp. 299–321). Mahwah, NJ: Lawrence Erlbaum Associates.

Smetana, J. G. (1989a). Adolescents' and parents' conceptions of parental authority. *Child Development, 59*, 321–335.

Smetana, J. G. (1989b). Concepts of self and social convention: Adolescents' and parents' reasoning about hypothetical and actual family conflicts. In M. R. Gunnar & W. A. Collins (Eds.), *Minnesota Symposia on child psychology* (Vol. 21, pp. 123–150). Hillsdale, NJ: Lawrence Erlbaum Associates.

Sroufe, L. A. (1983). Infant–caregiver attachment and patterns of adaptation in preschool: The roots of maladaptation and competence. In M. Perlmutter (Ed.), *Minnesota Symposia on child psychology* (Vol. 16, pp. 41–83). Hillsdale, NJ: Lawrence Erlbaum Associates.

Sroufe, L. A. (1990). An organizational perspective on the self. In D. Cicchetti & M. Beeghly (Eds.), *Transitions from infancy to childhood: The self* (pp. 281–307). Chicago: University of Chicago Press.

Sroufe, L. A. (1995). *Emotional development: The organization of emotional life in the early years*. New York: Cambridge University Press.

Sroufe, L. A., Schork, E., Motti, F., Lawroski, N., & LaFrenier, P. (1984). The role of affect in social competence. In C. Izard, J. Kagan, & R. Zajonc (Eds.), *Emotions, cognition, and behavior* (pp. 289–319). New York: Cambridge University Press.

Tolan, P. A., & Loeber R. (1993). Antisocial behavior. In P. H. Tolan & B. Cohler (Eds.), *Handbook of Clinical Research and Practice with Adolescents* (pp. 307–331). NY: Wiley.

Tronick, E. (1989). Emotions and emotional communication in infants. *American Psychologist*, *44*(22), 112–119.

Troy, M., & Sroufe, L. A. (1987). Victimization among preschoolers: Role of attachment relationship history. *Journal of the American Academy of Child and Adolescent Psychiatry*, *26*, 166–172.

Walker, L. J., & Taylor, J. H. (1991). Family interactions and the development of moral reasoning. *Child Development*, *62*, 264–283.

Westerman, M. A. (1990). Coordination of maternal directives with preschoolers' behavior in compliance-problems and healthy dyads. *Developmental Psychology*, *26*, 621–630.

16

Sibling Relationships

Brenda L. Volling
University of Michigan, Lansing

INTRODUCTION

The close supportive relationships children form with family members are essential for the optimal development of children. Research addressing children's development and family relationships has focused predominantly on the mother–child relationship as the major socializing influence on children. Yet, most children in the United States grow up in families with at least one brother or sister and there is growing evidence that the sibling relationship provides a positive socialization context for children throughout childhood and adolescence (Dunn, 1987, 1998). Although many parenting handbooks often discuss the rivalrous and competitive nature of sibling relationships (e.g., Faber & Mazlish, 1987), the relationship a child has with her sibling can also be an important source of companionship and support (Furman & Buhrmester, 1985). Early developments in the quality of children's sibling relationships are significant for the child's development, as sibling relationships are one of the longest lasting relationships of an individual's life (Lamb & Sutton-Smith, 1982). It is true that intense sibling rivalries can originate in the early years of childhood, be long-lived, and affect the closeness of adult sibling relationships decades later (Ross & Milgram, 1982). Siblings in later life, however, may be some of the last remaining members of the family of origin and close sibling relationships in late adulthood are often a source of companionship and support for the elderly (Gold, 1987).

This review begins by briefly identifying various qualitative dimensions of children's sibling relationships and the development of sibling relationships from early childhood into late adolescence. The developmental consequences for children's well-being when sibling relationships are characterized as warm and nurturant is also addressed, as is the positive developmental outcomes of children's involvement in sibling conflict and rivalry, long considered to be negative aspects of social relationships. Finally, those family and child characteristics that appear to foster positively affectionate and supportive sibling relationships are briefly presented.

DEFINING SIBLING RELATIONSHIP QUALITY

Developmental research indicates that in the early and middle childhood years, children spend more time in the company of their siblings than with their parents (Dunn & Kendrick, 1982; McHale & Crouter, 1996). Even so, the quality of a child's significant relationships is often a far better predictor of children's developmental outcomes than the sheer quantity of time spent with another (Parke, 2000). Several relationship dimensions have been identified as indicators of sibling relationship quality across different periods of childhood.

Furman and Buhrmester (1985) were one of the first to address specifically the qualitative dimensions of children's sibling relationships and to describe age differences in sibling relationship quality. Elementary school-age children were queried about what they thought were the most important dimensions of sibling relationships. The most frequently cited positive relationship qualities were companionship (93%), admiration of the sibling (81%), prosocial behavior (77%), and affection (65%), whereas the most frequently cited negative relationship qualities included antagonism (91%) and quarreling (79%). Based on follow-up research, Furman and Buhrmester (1985) eventually concluded that there were four qualitative dimensions of sibling relationships among school-age children: (1) warmth/closeness, (2) conflict, (3) rivalry, and (4) relative status/power. Similar dimensions of warmth/affection, rivalry/competition, and conflict/hostility in sibling relationship quality have been reported by others using parents' reports of sibling relationship quality in early childhood (Kramer & Baron, 1995) and preadolescents' reports of their sibling relationships (Hetherington & Clingempeel, 1992; Stocker & McHale, 1992). Few would question the developmental significance of a warm and close sibling relationship for children's well-being, but what about the conflict, rivalry, and power seen between siblings?

A Word About Sibling Conflict and Rivalry

A discussion about conflict and rivalry may not immediately seem appropriate for a paper devoted to the positive aspects of sibling relationships. However, accumulating evidence reveals that children learn important life-long skills while navigating conflict between family members, including conflicts with a sibling. Dunn and Munn (1985), for instance, have argued that children develop an understanding of the feelings and intentions of others as they engage in disputes with their mothers and siblings. Even though destructive conflicts and aggression between siblings have been linked to poor adjustment outcomes and conduct problems (Garcia, Shaw, Winslow, & Yaggi, 2000; Patterson, 1986), young children also learn constructive conflict resolution skills while in conflict with mothers and siblings and these, in turn, predict these children's abilities to settle conflicts with their friends years later (Herrera & Dunn, 1997).

Rivalry between siblings can vary from mild and friendly competition to fierce feelings of hatred and a desire to do harm against the sibling. Ross & Milgram (1982) reported that intense rivalries between many of the adult siblings they interviewed had their origins in the childhood years. Sibling rivalry often involves competition between siblings for favorable rewards such as parental love, approval, and recognition. Often social comparison processes are at work and siblings make evaluations of the self with other siblings in the family (Tesser, 1980). According to Cicirelli (1985), rivalry often involves a sibling weakness on some valued dimension (e.g., achievement, appearance, performance) with the rival's strength on the same dimension, along with an evaluative comparison of the two. Intense rivalries based on discrepant performance or talents can lead to negative evaluations of self and lower self-esteem. On the other hand, friendly competition in an otherwise amiable sibling relationship might actually promote the development of skills by creating the type of stimulating and challenging environment that promotes learning and achievement (Cicirelli, 1985; Bryant, 1982). When interviewed about their sibling relationships, older adults often reported that sibling rivalries and social comparisons with one's sibling in childhood were the source of positive growth experiences and achievement outcomes in later life (Bedford, Volling, & Avioli, 2000). To date, no study has examined whether positive intellectual or academic benefits might accrue for children as a result of friendly and challenging "rivalry" between siblings.

Significance of Status and Power

Unless one's sibling is a twin, brothers and sisters in the same family are of different ages, and the age space between siblings may be relatively close or quite wide. Age differences between siblings mean that one sibling, usually the oldest, has more power and status in the sibling relationship than the other. These differences across age in the older and younger siblings' power in the relationship underscore that siblings experience their sibling relationships differently depending on whether they are the older or younger child. Older siblings often manage the interaction and teach younger siblings, whereas the younger is more likely to be the recipient of teaching and caregiving (Brody, Stoneman, MacKinnon, & MacKinnon, 1985). Such differences in sibling roles as a function of age and sibling position have important implications for the children's socialization experiences within the family, as well as for the developmental outcomes of both siblings (Dunn & Plomin, 1991).

THEORETICAL AND EMPIRICAL REVIEW OF THE LITERATURE

Sibling Relationships in Early Childhood

What are the positive benefits for children with a warm and supportive sibling relationship? Several lines of research indicate that early sibling relationships provide a developmental context that can promote moral reasoning, conflict-resolution skills, and social understanding in very young children. Dunn and Munn (1986a), for instance, argued that observations of young children interacting with an older sibling provide a window onto the nature of young children's social understanding during the second and third years of life. According to these authors, children demonstrate powers of social understanding during emotionally charged interactions with family members that are not revealed in standard experimental paradigms of children's social-cognitive skills. Sibling relationships are emotionally intense, and both positive and negative emotional exchanges are observed frequently between siblings. This emotional intensity and ambivalence characteristic of the sibling relationship, in addition to the familiarity and uninhibited interaction between siblings, may provide a unique context for learning about other's emotions, intentions, and thoughts (Dunn, Brown, Slomkowski, Tesla, & Youngblade, 1991). Indeed, Dunn and her colleagues (Dunn & Dale, 1984; Slomkowski & Dunn, 1992) have demonstrated that young children's pretend play and conflict differ across mother–child and sibling–child interaction, and individual differences in conflict management skills and involvement in joint pretense with mothers and siblings predict individual differences in the preschool child's understanding of others' emotions and minds (Dunn et al., 1991, Youngblade & Dunn, 1995), later conflict resolution skills with a friend at 6 years (Herrera & Dunn, 1997), and children's adjustment to first grade (Donelan-McCall & Dunn, 1997).

Family conflict can be aggressive, leading to more aggression inside and outside of the home (Garcia et al., 2000; MacKinnon-Lewis, Starnes, Volling, & Johnson, 1997), but conflict is not synonymous with aggression (Shantz & Hobart, 1989). Conflict involves opposition to another and conflict situations can provide children with an important context for social-cognitive growth. Indeed, exposure to sophisticated argument skills and constructive negotiation in sibling relationships may allow the child to learn to argue effectively in other social relationships with friends and schoolmates (Herrera & Dunn, 1997).

Conflict resolution skills may facilitate young children's social understanding and their cooperation with others. Dunn and Munn (1986b) reported that relatively mature conflict behaviors on the part of 2 year olds (e.g., teasing, conciliation) were correlated with mature prosocial behaviors (e.g., sharing, comforting). The young child's use of physical aggression toward the older sibling was unrelated to their use of prosocial behavior. Thus, not only were very young children capable of sharing, comforting, and cooperating with their older siblings, but the child's social understanding was revealed in their use of sophisticated prosocial and conflict behaviors. In sum, conflict and cooperation between siblings may provide unique opportunities for children to learn conflict negotiation skills, emotion regulation, and social understanding.

Sibling Relationships in Middle Childhood

Unlike the period of early childhood, there is far less research devoted to understanding the links between children's sibling relationships in middle childhood and positive developmental outcomes, although more research has recently addressed this developmental period (e.g., Brody, Stoneman, & McCoy, 1994b, 1994a; Buhrmester, 1992; Dunn, 1996). Considering that siblings in middle childhood spend more time with each other than with mothers, fathers, and friends (McHale & Crouter, 1996), it is quite likely that siblings continue to exert a strong socializing influence on children's developmental outcomes. As children move into middle childhood, significant developmental changes occur in children's sociocognitive understanding and their abilities to engage social partners, and this may explain, in part, why the balance of power in sibling relationships begins to equalize. This time period also marks the beginning of elementary school and newfound relationships with classmates. These changes and the close contact still evident between siblings may lead to increases in both conflict and cooperation between siblings. Again, even though coercive and aggressive sibling interaction in middle childhood has been linked to antisocial behavior, delinquency, and difficulties with peers in school (Bank, Patterson, & Reid, 1996; Lewin, Hops, Davis, & Dishion, 1993; Patterson, 1986), both the "negative" (e.g., conflict, competition) as well as the "positive" (e.g., warmth, support) aspects of sibling relationships in middle childhood have been associated with positive developmental outcomes (e.g., Hetherington, 1988; Stormshak, Bellanti, Bierman, & the Conduct Problems Prevention Research Group, 1996). Conflict not involving aggression or occurring in the context of a warm and supportive sibling relationship may actually foster the development of children's behavioral and emotional regulation, as well as social competence with peers, even for aggressive children. In a sample of aggressive first- and second-grade children, Stormshak and her colleagues found that aggressive children in involved sibling relationships (i.e., moderate on conflict and warmth) were rated by their elementary-school teachers as more socially competent, more emotionally controlled, and more attentive at school than children in conflictual sibling relationships (i.e., high conflict, low warmth). Similarly, Hetherington (1988) examined sibling relationships in both remarried and nonremarried families and found that when children in the nonremarried families had an ambivalent (i.e., high on conflict and warmth) sibling relationship, they also had positive relationships with peers at school. Finally, McGuire, McHale, and Updegraff (1996) examined the self-reports of elementary school-age siblings between 6 and 11 years of age and found that siblings in affect-intense relationships (i.e., high warmth, high conflict) were more satisfied with the sibling relationship and reported greater intimacy between siblings than siblings in hostile relationships (i.e., high conflict, low warmth). It appears, then, that while extreme forms of sibling conflict involving destructive behavior and aggression are related to social and emotional difficulties in the period of middle childhood, there is also evidence, as was the case with children in early childhood, that conflict between siblings, when accompanied by warmth and support, may also facilitate positive developmental outcomes, most notably children's social competence with peers. As such, involvement in sibling conflict may have very different meanings for children depending on whether conflict occurs in the presence or absence of sibling warmth.

In addition to children's social and emotional development, siblings may have a beneficial effect on children's cognitive development and achievement in the middle childhood years. In an examination of second- and third-grade older siblings teaching their younger kindergarten and first-grade siblings, Azmitia and Hessor (1993) reported that sibling relationships provided unique experiences for younger siblings with respect to learning and task mastery. Younger children were more likely to observe, imitate, and consult with their older siblings than with an older peer in an unstructured building task, and the older siblings were more inclined to give explanations, provide spontaneous guidance, give positive feedback, and let the younger sibling have more control over the teaching task than were older peers. The children taught by their siblings also performed better on a posttest than did those taught by an older peer. Younger children were also more active learners with their older siblings, prompting their older siblings for explanations and often demanding that the older turn more control of the task over to them. Thus, features that were unique to the teaching and learning interaction occurring between siblings appeared to facilitate the younger sibling's cognitive development.

Sibling Relationships in Adolescence

The research base for sibling relationships in adolescence is sparse compared to other developmental periods. Although some have noted that there is a decrease in warmth and an increase in conflict as adolescence approaches (e.g., Brody et al., 1994b), there are striking individual differences in the quality of adolescents' sibling relationships (Dunn et al., 1994), and sibling relationships continue to remain close during adolescence (Buhrmester & Furman, 1990). Amato (1989) found that the positive quality of sibling relationships in adolescence (i.e., how well they got along with one another) was significantly related to adolescent competence as reflected in self-esteem, social competence, self-control, and independence. The quality of the sibling relationship was a stronger predictor of these outcomes for adolescents than children in middle childhood, leading the author to conclude that general competence may be influenced more by sibling relationship quality as children enter adolescence. Seigner (1998) in a study of 11th grade adolescents reported that a positive sibling relationship with an older sibling predicted a greater sense of emotional support above the contribution of mother, father, and peer acceptance. Older siblings and the quality of the sibling relationship also played a role in the younger siblings' empathy development in the preadolescent period (Tucker, Updegraff, McHale, & Crouter, 1999). Younger brothers were more empathic if they had an empathic older brother and their relationship was warm and close. For younger sisters, the association between empathy development and sibling relationship quality was moderated by the gender of the older sibling, with younger sisters reporting the highest levels of empathy when their older brother displayed more positive behaviors and the sibling relationship between brother and sister was warm and close, and more empathy when their older sister was also empathic. Older siblings' empathy, in general, was not predicted by the younger siblings' empathy indicating that interacting with an empathic older sibling in the context of a warm and nurturant sibling relationship may indeed foster the development of the younger siblings' empathy, but the opposite does not appear to be the case.

Older adolescent siblings' academic achievement was associated, over a two-year period, with teaching their younger siblings (Smith, 1993), indicating some benefits do accrue for older siblings when interacting with a younger sibling. In summary, decreases in the positive aspects of sibling relationships across middle childhood and adolescence may reflect normative changes as children mature and enter the world of peers, but the positive nature of sibling relationships during this developmental period appears to exert a strong and, in some cases, unique influence on adolescents' competence.

Sibling Relationships as Protective Factors

There is some evidence suggesting that sibling relationships may protect children from adverse life circumstances. For instance, Jenkins and Smith (1990) reported that in homes with marital discord, children were protected from negative outcomes if they had a positive sibling relationship. Similarly, Dunn and her colleagues (1994), in a longitudinal study following children from preschool through adolescence, found a positive association between negative life events experienced during the middle-childhood to adolescent years, and the warmth and intimacy in the adolescent sibling relationship. As a final example, East and Rook (1992) found that children who were isolated by their peer group were less anxious and immature, as rated by their classroom teachers, if they had high support in their favorite sibling relationship. In these few available studies, it was not the case that children experiencing more negative life events had a positive relationship with a sibling that protected them from future maladjustment. Rather, children were not as detrimentally affected if they were fortunate enough to have a positive and supportive relationship with a sibling during times of stress. Jenkins (1992) stated that, in general, marital discord and sibling aggression were highly correlated; it was the children who had a positive sibling relationship in the martially discordant homes who were protected.

DEVELOPMENTAL STABILITY OF CHILDREN'S SIBLING RELATIONSHIPS

Several cross-sectional studies have examined age differences in sibling relationship quality (i.e., warmth, conflict, rivalry, power). Few longitudinal studies following children's sibling relationships across different periods of childhood are currently available. The cross-sectional research finds, in some cases, that sibling relationships become less emotionally intense over the middle childhood and adolescent years, with less warmth and closeness as well as less conflict reported by older adolescents than elementary school-age and preadolescent children (Buhrmester & Furman, 1990). Sibling relationships also become more egalitarian as children approach adolescence (Buhrmester & Fuhrman, 1990; Vandell, Minnett, & Santrock, 1987), with older siblings yielding less power and status over their younger siblings along with a corresponding increase in the younger siblings' power over the older sibling.

Longitudinal research following children from childhood into adolescence, however, indicates that there are increases in sibling conflict and decreases in positive sibling relationships from middle childhood into adolescence (Brody et al., 1994b). These changes are most likely due to the increasing autonomy and involvement of adolescents with peers outside the home. Indeed, reports from children and mothers in a longitudinal study by Dunn, Slomkowski, and Beardsall (1994) indicated that declines in positive behavior over time from middle childhood into adolescence appeared to be due to the older sibling establishing new friendships in the peer group. Thus, normative developmental changes occurring over this period, wherein older children begin to establish themselves in a wider social network outside the family, have significant effects on the developing sibling relationship. Rather than focusing on whether these changes indicate deterioration of the sibling relationship over time, it may be best to consider how changes in sibling relationships co-occur with other significant developments in children's lives by noting that normative changes in one social arena will bring about changes in another.

Although average declines in the emotional intensity of the sibling relationship were documented from the middle childhood to adolescent years, Buhrmester and Furman (1990) also noted that these decreases were relatively modest and the emotional closeness between siblings, as seen in their ratings of intimacy, affection, and admiration, remained relatively high. There are also marked individual differences in sibling relationship quality in early childhood (Dunn & Kendrick, 1982; Dunn & Munn, 1986a), middle childhood (Brody et al., 1992; Stocker, Dunn, & Plomin, 1989), and adolescence (Dunn, Slomkowski, & Beardsall, 1994; McHale & Crouter, 1996), with some children having close and intimate relationships with their siblings and others with sibling relationships characterized by hostility, destructive rivalry, and aggression.

In their examination of the stability of individual differences in the quality of children's sibling relationships from preschool to adolescence, Dunn et al. (1994) noted that even though both the negative and positive dimensions remained relatively stable over time, this was especially clear in the case of the positive aspects of the relationship. In fact, significant variance in the positive aspects of the sibling relationship in adolescence based on older sibling's reports (i.e., warmth and intimacy) were predicted from the earlier preschool measures of sibling relationship quality (e.g., mother's reports of admiration, care, and nurturance) above and beyond the effects of gender and socioeconomic status (SES). Negative aspects of the sibling relationship (e.g., aggression, destructive conflict, and hostility), the stability of aggression over time, and the detrimental effects of sibling aggression and hostility on children's social-emotional development have been the focus of numerous studies (Bank et al., 1996; Patterson, 1986; Garcia et al., 2000). Dunn et al.'s findings, however, indicate that intimacy, warmth, and closeness between siblings are also stable over childhood and may be even more stable than the conflict and hostility seen between siblings.

The stability of individual differences in children's sibling relationships is evident even in the toddler to early school years. Stillwell and Dunn (1985) found that the initial positive interest of the older preschool child toward their newborn sibling at 2 to 3 weeks after the birth predicted positive comments made by the older about the younger sibling when the older child was 6 years of age. In sum, individual differences in children's sibling relationships are quite varied in childhood and adolescence, and even though mean group differences in relationship quality have been noted across developmental periods, both the positive and negative dimensions of sibling relationship quality are relatively stable over time.

FACTORS AFFECTING DEVELOPMENT AND PROMOTION OF SIBLING RELATIONSHIP QUALITY

Brody (1998) recently presented one of the most comprehensive models of the family and individual factors that predict positive and negative sibling relationship quality. Brody's model considers the sibling relationship as part of the family system and as such, it should be investigated as an interrelated component with other family relationships. The quality of the marital relationship as well as the children's relationships with each parent, are influential in predicting sibling relationship quality. In addition, parental differential treatment, that is, the difference in how parents treat one child in relation to the other, is hypothesized to induce rivalry and jealousy between siblings, which then results in increased conflict and decreased positive interactions between siblings. Finally, individual characteristics of the parents (e.g., depressed affect, well-being) and the children (e.g., temperament) have been implicated as determinants of sibling relationship quality. Each of these areas will be considered briefly next.

Parent–Child Relationships and Siblings

Much of the early research on sibling relationships focused on mothers and their interactions with both siblings (e.g., Brody, Stoneman, & MacKinnon, 1986; Dunn & Kendrick, 1982; Bryant & Crockenberg, 1980). Not surprisingly, warm and affectionate mother–child interactions were related to affectionate and prosocial exchanges between preschool and school-age siblings (e.g., Brody, Stoneman, & McCoy, 1992a, 1994b; Stocker, Dunn, & Plomin, 1989).

Far less research has investigated the role of fathers for the development of children's sibling relationships and positive well-being. In those few studies that have included fathers, paternal positivity with children is associated with positivity in the sibling relationship (Brody, Stoneman, & McCoy, 1992a; Volling & Belsky, 1992). In addition, fathers may provide unique experiences for children that may be particularly important for the development of positive sibling behavior during early childhood and middle childhood (Brody et al., 1992a, Stocker & McHale, 1992; Volling & Belsky, 1992). In a longitudinal investigation of family relationships from infancy through the preschool years, Volling and Belsky reported that a supportive and affectionate father-child relationship with the older sibling at 3 years of age was later associated with prosocial sibling behavior when the older sibling was 6 years old. Similarly, in a study of elementary school-age children, Stocker and McHale reported that children who spent more time in dyadic activities with their fathers and reported warmer father–child relationships had the most affectionate and least hostile sibling relationships. Finally, Brody et al. (1992a) found that paternal behavior continued to predict unique variance in sibling relationship quality once maternal behavior had been controlled.

Parental Differential Treatment

When one child is treated preferentially over the other (i.e., more affection, less control) by either mothers or fathers, sibling relationships, in general, are more negative and less positive (Brody et al., 1992a, 1994a; Hetherington, 1988; McHale, Crouter, McGuire, & Updegraff, 1995; Stocker et al., 1989; Volling & Belsky, 1992). Some have recently suggested that parents are sensitive to the age differences between their children, and therefore, differential treatment may be the norm during particular periods of childhood (Brody, 1998; Volling & Elins, 1998). Parents may be reacting differentially to sibling differences in size, strength and maturity that coincide with age differences. McHale and her colleagues (1995) also reported that older and younger siblings in the family do not react to differential parental treatment in the same manner. Younger middle-school siblings were seemingly more sensitive to differences in parenting. The authors concluded that children's perceptions of the meaning of differential treatment may change across developmental periods, with adolescents far more likely to justify the unequal treatment as due to age differences or differences in personal attributes of the children. This conclusion seems warranted in light of Kowal and Kramer's (1997) findings that parental differential treatment was related to poor sibling relationships, only if the children interpreted the differences as unfair. Those children who attributed differential treatment to differences in the children's ages, personalities, or relationship needs were far more likely to report satisfying sibling relationships. Therefore, parental differential treatment does not always have negative consequences for children and additional research is needed to understand under what conditions differential treatment poses a risk for children and under what conditions it may reflect age-related family processes (Volling & Elins, 1998).

Marital Relationships and Siblings

Given the consistent association reported between marital conflict and children's adjustment difficulties (Cummings & Davies, 1994), it is noteworthy that so few studies have addressed the association between marital relationship quality and sibling relationship quality. Marital dissatisfaction or marital conflict has been related to sibling conflict and negativity (Brody, Stoneman, McCoy, & Forehand, 1992; Erel, Margolin, & John, 1998; Jenkins, 1992; MacKinnon, 1989; Stocker, Ahmed, & Stall, 1997). Even though these studies find a link between marital and sibling relationships, they have overwhelmingly focused on marital conflict and discord as predictors of conflict, hostility, and rivalry between siblings. Few studies have looked at the positive side of marital life, such as expressions of love, communication styles, or conflict-resolution strategies, and how these marital qualities may impinge on sibling relationship quality. In both McHale et al. (1995) and Volling (1997), parents were less likely to treat their children differently when they reported more love in their marriages. The emphasis on marital discord and its relation to children's maladjustment is prevalent in the study of child development, and the lack of sibling studies focused on loving marital relationships as opposed to discordant marriages reflects this overarching tendency. We do not have much in the way of evidence to show how positive marital communication and loving emotions benefit children's sibling relationship quality and their well-being. Needless to say, there is substantial room for more investigations into the manner in which marriages can positively influence children's sibling relationships.

Siblings and Temperamental Differences

In addition to family relationship dynamics, individual characteristics of both parents and children have been considered in sibling relationship studies. Temperamental differences between children have received the most attention by sibling researchers. Indeed, children who are highly active and emotionally intense have more conflicted sibling relationships than less active and less intense children (Brody et al., 1987, 1994b; Stocker et al., 1989). Moreover, the behavior of the nonactive sibling is related to the temperamental style of the active sibling. For instance, younger siblings directed more antagonism toward highly active older siblings during sibling interaction than to less active older siblings (Brody et al., 1987).

Even though active and emotionally intense children have more conflict with their siblings, it is notable that all studies to date have focused on temperamental characteristics that were once considered characteristic of the "difficult" child

(Rothbart, 1982). Temperament also includes the child's capacity to be soothed, to express pleasure, and to adapt to change (Rothbart, 1986). As these temperamental characteristics have not been studied as extensively as the cluster of difficult temperamental characteristics, one cannot ascertain how these more positive temperamental tendencies may affect sibling relationship quality. One study by Stoneman and Brody (1993), however, provides some insight into the importance of positive temperamental characteristics for sibling relationships. Siblings may be similar (e.g., both active) or dissimilar (e.g., one active and the other not) with respect to their temperamental styles. Stoneman and Brody (1993) hypothesized that when siblings had dissimilar temperaments, the positive temperamental characteristics of one child would protect the sibling relationship from increased conflict associated with difficult temperament in the sibling. As expected, the lowest levels of sibling conflict occurred in dyads in which both children had low activity levels and the highest levels of conflict occurred in dyads with two highly active children. Contrary to expectations, the protective function of positive temperamental characteristics was evident only in the dyads consisting of a highly active younger sibling and a less active older sibling. In fact, those sibling dyads wherein the older sibling was highly active and the younger sibling was not actually had relatively high levels of conflict. Because older siblings have a more dominant role in the sibling relationship, highly active older siblings may set the emotional tone of the relationship and override the more positive characteristics of the younger sibling. These findings underscore the importance not only of children's temperament for the developing sibling relationship, but also the fact that temperament interacts with sibling position to create different relationship environments, one offering possible protection and the other increasing risk.

Parent Characteristics

Few studies have examined the impact of parents' mental health on the sibling relationship, even though it is hypothesized to be a contributing factor to the quality of sibling relationships in the family. Brody and his colleagues (1994a) examined parental depression and hostility and their relations with sibling relationship quality, and not surprisingly, found that maternal depression and paternal hostility were negatively related to positive sibling interaction. A similar study with African American families indicated that maternal psychological resources (i.e., more depressive symptoms and lower self-esteem) affected sibling relationship quality indirectly (Brody, Stoneman, Smith, & Gibson, 1999). That is, children of more depressed parents reported less support in the mother–child relationship, which was linked directly to the child's self-regulation, and this, in turn, was related to sibling relationship quality. Even though these initial studies indicated that parental psychological resources were related to sibling relationship quality indirectly by altering parenting practices, parental depression and hostility, rather than indicators of parental mental health, have received the most attention. Several recent studies have included measures of parents' positive and negative emotional expressiveness (Garner, Jones, & Miner, 1994; Stocker, Ahmed, & Stall, 1997). In a sample of low-income preschoolers, for instance, maternal positive emotional expressiveness was related to more sibling caregiving by preschoolers (Garner et al. 1994). These studies are suggestive of a link, albeit indirect in some cases, between parent characteristics and sibling relationship quality, although there is still much to be explored in this area.

CONCLUSIONS

In general, the extant research is suggestive in providing evidence that positive dimensions of sibling relationships (e.g., warmth, closeness, affection, caregiving) are associated with warm and affectionate parent–child relationships, less difficult child temperament, and more equal treatment of siblings. Additional work, though limited, also suggests that early developments in conflict resolution may also promote children's social competence in other social relationships (e.g., peers). The terms *positivity* or *positive relationships* are used frequently to describe the close, nurturant, and warm relationships siblings enjoy with one another. Use of such terms to describe relationship quality, however, is too global and future work needs to be more specific as to what positivity or a positive relationship is. Put simply, using positivity and negativity as global characteristics of relationship quality inherently divides the world into "good" and "bad," and this might lead some researchers to dismiss "negative" dimensions such as conflict and rivalry as having potential positive consequences for children. As the work with preschool children has clearly demonstrated, conflict and the skills of negotiation and resolution that young children learn in these circumstances may be critically important for how children later manage conflicts with their peers in school. Thus, there is really nothing inherently "negative" about conflict, and indeed, there may be many positive benefits for children when conflict is handled in a constructive manner. It becomes harmful to children's well-being when it involves coercion, destruction, and physical aggression. In sum, we must refine our conceptualization and measurement of positivity and negativity in order to understand precisely how specific behaviors displayed by siblings either enhance or undermine children's well-being in the context of their sibling relationships.

REFERENCES

Amato, P. R. (1989). Family processes and the competence of adolescents and primary school children. *Journal of Youth and Adolescence*, *18*, 39–53.

Azmitia, M., & Hessor, J. (1993). Why siblings are important agents of cognitive development: A comparison of siblings and peers. *Child Development*, *64*, 430–444.

Bank, L., Patterson, G. R., & Reid, J. B. (1996). Negative sibling interaction patterns as predictors of later adjustment problems in adolescent and young adult males. In G. H. Brody (Ed.), *Sibling relationships: Their causes and consequences* (pp. 197–230). Norwood, NJ: Ablex.

Bedford, V. H., Volling, B. L., & Avioli, P. S. (2000). Positive consequences of sibling conflict in child-hood and adulthood. *International Journal of Aging and Human Development*, *51*, 53–69.

Brody, G. H. (1998). Sibling relationship quality: Its causes and consequences. *Annual Review of Psychology*, *49*, 1–24.

Brody, G. H., Stoneman, Z., & Burke, M. (1987). Child temperaments, maternal differential behavior, and sibling relationships. *Developmental Psychology*, *23*, 354–362.

Brody, G. H., Stoneman, Z., & MacKinnon, C. E. (1986). Contributions of maternal child–rearing practices and play contexts to sibling interactions. *Journal of Applied Developmental Psychology*, *7*, 225–236.

Brody, G. H., Stoneman, Z., MacKinnon, C. E., & MacKinnon, R. (1985). Role relationships and behavior between preschool-aged and school-aged sibling pairs. *Developmental Psychology*, *21*, 124–129.

Brody, G. H., Stoneman, Z., & McCoy, J. K. (1994a). Forecasting sibling relationships in early adolescence from child temperaments and family processes in middle childhood. *Child Development*, *65*, 771–784.

Brody, G. H., Stoneman, Z., & McCoy, J. K. (1992a). Associations of maternal and paternal direct and differential behavior with sibling relationships: Contemporaneous and longitudinal analyses. *Child Development*, *63*, 82–92.

Brody, G. H., Stoneman, Z., & McCoy, J. K. (1994b). Contributions of family relationships and child temperaments to longitudinal variations in sibling relationship quality and sibling relationship styles. *Journal of Family Psychology*, *8*, 274–286.

Brody, G. H., Stoneman, S., McCoy, J. K., & Forehand, R. (1992b). Contemporaneous and longitudinal associations of sibling conflict with family relationship assessments and family discussions about sibling problems. *Child Development*, *63*, 391–400.

Brody, G. H., Stoneman, Z., Smith, T. S., Gibson, N. M. (1999). Sibling relationships in rural African American families. *Journal of Marriage and the Family*, *61*, 1046–1057.

Bryant, B. K. (1982). Sibling relationships in middle childhood. In M. E. Lamb & B. Sutton-Smith (Eds.), *Sibling relationships: Their nature and significance across the life span* (pp. 87–121). Hillsdale, NJ: Lawrence Erlbaum Associates.

Bryant, B. K., & Crockenberg, S. B. (1980). Correlates and dimensions of prosocial behavior: A study of female siblings with their mothers. *Child Development*, *51*, 529–544.

Buhrmester, D. (1992). The developmental course of sibling and peer relationships. In F. Boer & J. Dunn (Eds.), *Children's sibling relationships: Developmental and clinical issues* (pp. 19–40). Hillsdale, NJ: Lawrence Erlbaum Associates.

Buhrmester, D., & Furman, W. (1990). Perceptions of sibling relationships during middle childhood and adolescence. *Child Development*, *61*, 1387–1398.

Cicirelli, V. G. (1982). Sibling influence throughout the life span. In M. E. Lamb & B. Sutton-Smith (Eds.), *Sibling relationships: Their nature and significance across the life span* (pp. 267–284). Hillsdale, NJ: Lawrence Erlbaum Associates.

Cicirelli, V. G. (1985). Sibling relationships throughout the life cycle. In L. L'Abate (Ed.), *The handbook of family psychology and therapy* (pp. 177–214). Homewood, IL: Dorsey Press.

Cummings, E. M., & Davies, P. (1994). *Children and marital conflict: The impact of family dispute and resolution*. New York: Guilford Press.

Donelan-McCall, N., & Dunn, J. (1997). School work, teachers, and peers: The world of first grade. *International Journal of Behavioral Development*, *21*, 155–178.

Dunn, J. (1987). The beginnings of moral understanding: Development in the second year. In J. Kagan & S. Lamb (Eds.), *The emergence of morality in young children* (pp. 91–112). Chicago, IL: University of Chicago Press.

Dunn, J. (1996). Brothers and sisters in middle childhood and early adolescence: Continuity and change in individual differences. In G. H. Brody (Ed.), *Sibling relationships: Their causes and consequences* (pp. 31–46). Norwood, NJ: Ablex.

Dunn, J. (1998). Siblings, emotion and the development of understanding. In S. Braten (Ed.), *Intersubjective communication and emotion in early ontogeny*. Cambridge, England: Cambridge University Press.

Dunn, J., Brown, J., Slomkowski, C., Tesla, C., & Youngblade, L. (1991). Young children's understanding of other people's feelings and beliefs: Individual differences and their antecedents. *Child Development*, *62*, 1352–1366.

Dunn, J., & Dale, N. (1984). I a Daddy: 2-year olds' collaboration in joint pretend with sibling and mother. In I. Bretherton (Ed.), *Symbolic play: The development of social understanding* (pp. 131–158). New York: Academic Press.

Dunn, J., & Kendrick, C. (1982). *Siblings: Love, envy, and understanding.* Cambridge, MA: Harvard University Press.

Dunn, J., & Munn, P. (1985). Becoming a family member: Family conflict and the development of social understanding in the second year. *Child Development, 56,* 480–492.

Dunn, J., & Munn, P. (1986a). Sibling quarrels and maternal intervention: Individual differences in understanding and aggression. *Journal of Child Psychology and Psychiatry, 27,* 583–595.

Dunn, J., & Munn, P. (1986b). Siblings and the development of prosocial behavior. *International Journal of Behavioral Development, 9,* 265–284.

Dunn, J., & Plomin, R. (1991). Why are siblings so different? The significance of differences in sibling experiences within the family. *Family Process, 30,* 271–283.

Dunn, J., Slomkowski, C., & Beardsall, L. (1994). Sibling relationships from the preschool period through middle childhood and early adolescence. *Developmental Psychology, 30,* 315–324.

East, P. L., & Rook, K. S. (1992). Compensatory patterns of support among children's peer relationships: A test using school friends, nonschool friends, and siblings. *Developmental Psychology, 28,* 163–172.

Erel, O., Margolin, G., & John, R. S. (1998). Observed sibling interaction: Links with the marital relationship and the mother–child relationship. *Developmental Psychology, 34,* 288–298.

Faber, A., & Mazlish, E. (1987). *Siblings without rivalry.* New York: Avon.

Furman, W., & Buhrmester, D. (1985). Children's perceptions of the qualities of sibling relationships. *Child Development, 56,* 448–461.

Garcia, M. M., Shaw, D. S., Winslow, E. B., & Yaggi, K. E. (2000). Destructive sibling conflict and the development of conduct problems in young boys. *Developmental Psychology, 36,* 44–53.

Garner, P. W., Jones, D. C., & Miner, J. F. (1994). Social competence among low-income preschoolers: Emotion socialization practices and social cognitive correlates. *Child Development, 65,* 622–637.

Gold, D. T. (1987). Siblings in old age: Something special. *Canadian Journal on Aging, 6,* 199–215.

Herrera, C., & Dunn, J. (1997). Early experiences with family conflict: Implications for arguments with a close friend. *Developmental Psychology, 33,* 869–881.

Hetherington, E. M. (1988). Parents, children, and siblings: Six years after divorce: In R. H. Hinde & J. Stevenson-Hinde (Eds.), *Relationships within families: Mutual influences* (pp. 311–331). New York: Oxford University Press.

Hetherington, E. M., & Clingempeel, W. G. (1992). Coping with marital transitions: A family systems approach. *Monographs of the Society for Research in Child Development, 57,* (2–3, Serial No. 227).

Jenkins, J. (1992). Sibling relationships in disharmonious homes: Potential difficulties and protective effects. In F. Boer & J. Dunn (Eds.), *Children's sibling relationships: Developmental and clinical issues* (pp. 125–138). Hillsdale, NJ: Lawrence Erlbaum Associates.

Jenkins, J., & Smith, M. A. (1990). Factors protecting children in disharmonious homes. *Journal of the American Academy of Child and Adolescent Psychiatry, 28,* 182–189.

Lamb, M. E., & Sutton-Smith, B. (1982). *Sibling relationships: Their nature and significance across the life span.* Hillsdale, NJ: Lawrence Erlbaum Associates.

Kowal, A., & Kramer, L. (1997). Children's understanding of parental differential treatment. *Child Development, 68,* 113–126.

Kramer, L., & Baron, L. A. (1995). Parental perceptions of children's sibling relationships. *Family Relations, 44,* 95–103.

Lewin, L. M., Hops, H., Davis, B., & Dishion, T. J. (1993). Multimethod comparison of similarity in school adjustment of siblings and unrelated children. *Developmental Psychology, 29,* 963–969.

MacKinnon, C. E. (1989). An observational investigation of sibling interactions in married and divorced families. *Developmental Psychology, 25,* 36–44.

MacKinnon-Lewis, C. E., Starnes, R., Volling, B. L., & Johnson, S. (1997). Perceptions of parenting as predictors of boys' sibling and peer relations. *Developmental Psychology, 33,* 1024–1031

McGuire, S., McHale, S. M., & Updegraff, K. (1996). Children's perceptions of the sibling relationship in middle childhood: Connections within and between family relationships. *Personal Relationships, 3,* 229–239.

McHale, S. M., & Crouter, A. C. (1996). The family contexts of children's sibling relationships. In G. H. Brody (Ed.), *Sibling relationships: Their causes and consequences* (pp. 173–196). Norwood, NJ: Ablex.

McHale, S. M., Crouter, A. C., McGuire, S. A., & Updegraff, K. A. (1995). Congruence between mothers' and fathers' differential treatment of siblings: Links with family relations and children's well-being. *Child Development, 66*, 116–128.

Parke, R. D. (2000). Father involvement: A developmental psychological perspective. *Marriage and Family Review, 29*, 43–58.

Patterson, G. R. (1986). The contribution of siblings to training for fighting: A microsocial analysis. In D. Olweus, J. Block, & M. Radke-Yarrow (Eds.), *Development of antisocial and prosocial behavior* (pp. 235–261). New York: Academic Press.

Ross, H. G., & Milgram, J. I. (1982). Important variables in adult sibling relationships: A qualitative study. In M. E. Lamb & B. Sutton-Smith (Eds.), *Sibling relationships: Their nature and significance across the life span* (pp. 225–249). Hillsdale, NJ: Lawrence Erlbaum Associates.

Rothbart, M. (1982). The concept of difficult temperament: A critical analysis of Thomas, Chess, & Korn. *Merrill-Palmer Quarterly, 28*, 35–40.

Rothbart, M. (1986). Longitudinal observation of infant temperament. *Developmental Psychology, 22*, 356–365.

Seigner, R. (1998). Adolescents' perceptions of relationships with older sibling in context of other close relationships. *Journal of Research on Adolescence, 8*, 287–308.

Shantz, C. U., & Hobart, C. J. (1989). Social conflict and development: Peers and siblings. In T. J. Berndt & G. W. Ladd (Eds.), *Peer relationships in child development* (pp. 71–94). New York: Wiley.

Slomkowski, C. L., & Dunn, J. (1992). Arguments and relationships within the family: Differences in young children's disputes with mother and sibling. *Developmental Psychology, 28*, 919–924.

Smith, T. E. (1993). Growth in academic achievement and teaching younger siblings. *Social Psychology Quarterly, 56*, 77–85.

Stillwell, R., & Dunn, J. (1985). Continuities in sibling relationships: Patterns of aggression and friendliness. *Journal of Child Psychology and Psychiatry, 26*, 627–637.

Stocker, C., Ahmed, K., & Stall, M. (1997). Marital satisfaction and maternal emotional expressiveness: Links with children's sibling relationships. *Social Development, 3*, 373–385.

Stocker, C. M., Dunn, J., & Plomin, R. (1989). Sibling relationships: Links with child temperament, maternal behavior, and family structure. *Child Development, 60*, 715–727.

Stocker, C. M., & McHale, S. M. (1992). The nature and family correlates of preadolescents' perceptions of their sibling relationships. *Journal of Social and Personal Relationships, 9*, 179–195.

Stoneman, Z., & Brody, G. H. (1993). Sibling temperaments, conflict, warmth, and role asymmetry. *Child Development, 64*, 1786–1800.

Stormshak, E. A., Bellanti, C. J., Bierman, K. L., & Conduct Problems Prevention Research Group. (1996). The quality of sibling relationships and the development of competence and behavioral control in aggressive children. *Developmental Psychology, 32*, 79–89.

Tesser, A. (1980). Self-esteem maintenance in family dynamics. *Journal of Personality and Social Psychology, 39*, 77–91.

Tucker, C. J., Updegraff, K. A., McHale, S. M., & Crouter, A. C. (1999). Older siblings as socializers of younger siblings' empathy. *Journal of Early Adolescence, 19*, 176–198.

Vandell, D. B., Minnett, A. M., & Santrock, J. W. (1987). Age differences in sibling relationships in middle childhood. *Journal of Applied Developmental Psychology, 8*, 247–257.

Volling, B. L. (1997). The family correlates of maternal and paternal perceptions of differential treatment in early childhood. *Family Relations, 46*, 227–236.

Volling, B. L., & Belsky, J. (1992). The contribution of mother–child and father–child relationships to the quality of sibling interaction: A longitudinal study. *Child Development, 63*, 1209–1222.

Volling, B. L., & Elins, J. (1998). Family relationships and children's emotional adjustment as correlates of maternal and paternal differential treatment: A replication with toddler and preschool siblings. *Child Development, 63*, 1209–1222.

Youngblade, L. M., & Dunn, J. (1995). Individual differences in young children's pretend play with mother and sibling: Links to relationships and understanding of other people's feelings and beliefs. *Child Development, 66*, 1472–1492.

17

Peer Relationships

William M. Bukowski
Concordia University, Montréal, Québec

INTRODUCTION

For over a century, child psychologists have been interested in the effects that experiences with peers have on development. This interest has been especially intense during the past 25 years when a broad range of topics regarding the effects of peer relationships have been studied. It is probably safe to say that during this period more has been learned about peer relationships than had been learned in the previous 75 years. Interest in peer relationships has been typically motivated by a single powerful idea that is drawn from several conceptual perspectives and from a large database regarding the precursors of adjustment. This idea is that peers provide essential socialization experiences that are necessary for the acquisition of several fundamental skills, for healthy personality development, and for psychosocial adjustment. According to this idea, peers are not a luxury but are instead a necessity for healthy development and adjustment.

TECHNICAL ISSUES

The theoretical support comes from several sources indicating that the unique characteristics of peer relationships are needed to stimulate particular forms of development that cannot result from experiences with adults or siblings. The basic point of these models is that experiences with a co-equal are necessary for some forms of psychological growth. (See Rubin, Bukowski, & Parker, 1998, for a discussion.) The empirical support for this idea was initially taken from studies reported in the

1970s (e.g., Cowen, Pedersen, Bagigian, Izzo, & Trost, 1973; Roff, Sells, & Golden, 1972) indicating that childhood experiences with peers could be used to predict subsequent adjustment in several domains of functioning. Indeed, measures of peer relationships could be used to predict criminality, academic failure, mental health, and success in adjusting to adult roles. In spite of the pervasiveness of the empirical demonstrations that peer measures could predict outcomes, this support was more intriguing than it was compelling. It was intriguing in its clear demonstration of associations between measures of peer experience and measures of outcome. These findings were not compelling, however, as they were limited both conceptually and methodologically.

Conceptual Limitations in the Study of Peer Relationships and Health

There were two important conceptual limitations to these initial studies. First, adjustment and well-being were measured via negative outcomes such as psychiatric hospitalizations, criminality, unemployment, or high school dropout (Parker & Asher, 1987). These findings were focused on the deficits that would result if a child's peer relationships had been inadequate. That so much emphasis had been placed on negative outcomes is ironic considering that the emphasis of most theory had been on the value of adequate peer relationships rather than on the problems that would be posed by inadequate experiences. That is, theory emphasized healthy outcomes that would result from peer relationships; the empirical literature emphasized deficits. Second, researchers failed to distinguish between the many experiences that fall within the general rubric of "peer relationships." Many variables that reflect components of children's experiences with peers were used interchangeably or without regard for the differences between them. Researchers treated the concept of peer relationships as if it were a monolithic entity. As a result, in many studies it was difficult to determine which aspect of peer relationships was most critical to which aspects of development.

Methodological Limitations in the Study of Peer Relationships and Maladjustment

Studies of peer relationships have been typically limited by problems in the design of studies. Although studies have repeatedly demonstrated associations between experiences with peers and indices of well-being and adjustment, the evidence of these associations has been largely correlational. Certainly many studies have adopted prospective designs and have controlled for some factors. For the most part, however, the goal of these studies was to demonstrate predictive associations among variables rather than to test particular process-oriented hypotheses about how peer relationships affect development. This criticism cannot be applied to all studies of peer relationships. A group of experimental studies of the origins of popularity in children's playgroups are not entirely correlational in nature but they nevertheless lacking in clear evidence of causality (e.g., Coie & Kupersmidt, 1983).

Aside from issues of design, a further limitation is the failure to control for confounds among variables. Peer researchers have at their disposal a broad range of concepts and measures that index many different forms of experience. Often the differences between these concepts or between measures have not been fully recognized and investigators have not always resolved the empirical entanglements among measures. As a result, measures have been employed without a clear rationale. For example, the techniques used to measure friendship and popularity have typically relied on very similar forms of data, leading to empirical confounds due to shared method variance.

THEORETICAL AND EMPIRICAL BACKGROUND

In spite of these problems, however, the study of peer relationships has never suffered from a lack of ideas. To the contrary, peers have been implicated, often centrally, in several theoretical models designed to explain adaptation and adjustment. Use of these theories has been slow as researchers have been motivated instead by the broad concern with the association between peer relationships and maladaptive outcomes. In the past decade, however, the adoption of these theoretical models has become more widespread, especially as researchers have had a clearer idea of how to conceptualize the multiple levels of experience that comprise the peer system. As a result, research on peer relationships has become more focused and conceptually driven. The theoretical accounts of how peer relationships contribute to healthy development can be divided into four types: self-perceptual models, skills models, co-construction, and behavioral. These views differentially invoke experiences that occur at different levels of social complexity, that is at the level of the individual, the dyad, and the group (see Rubin, Bukowski, & Parker, 1998).

Peers and the Perception of Self

Models of peer relationships that fall within the self-perceptual domain emphasize experiences that typically occur at the dyadic level. These models have been proposed by Sullivan (1953) and by a group of thinkers collectively known as the symbolic interactionists (e.g., Cooley, 1909; Mead, 1934). They argue that in interactions and relationships with specific peers, most notably with friends, children have their first opportunities to experience a sense of self-validation. This validation would result from the recognition of the positive regard and care that their chums hold for them. Sullivan went so far as to argue that the positive experiences of having a "chum" in early adolescence would be so powerful so as to enable early adolescents to overcome the "warps" that may have resulted from social experiences in the family. In parallel to this view, the symbolic interactionists argued that people defined themselves according to the "information" they derive from their interactions with others. According to Mead (1934), for example, the ability to self-reflect, to consider the self in relation to others, and to understand the perspectives of others was largely a function of participation in organized, rule-governed activities with peers. He suggested that exchanges among peers, whether experienced in the arenas of cooperation or competition, conflict or friendly discussion, allowed the child to gain an understanding of the self as both a subject and an object. In this way, experiences with peers were critical for the development of a healthy self-concept.

Skill Models

Skill models propose that the social competencies needed for adjustment in adulthood need derive from experiences with peers. Whereas infants, preschoolers, and children certainly acquire many abilities in interactions with parents, the vertical nature of the parent–child relationship prevents them from having the sort of equal one-to-one needed for particular skills. It is for this reason that experience with peers has been identified as critical for the development of several basic skills such as (a) the ability to coordinate play behavior with that of the play partner (e.g., Baudonnière, Garcia-Werebe, Michel, & Liegois, 1989); (b) imitation (Eckerman, 1993); (c) turn-taking that involves complex observe-and-respond sequences (Howes, 1988); (d) prosocial behaviors (Zahn-Waxler & Smith, 1992); and (e) the ability to respond appropriately to the peer partner's characteristics (Brownell, 1990). Perhaps the most critical skill learned in interaction with peers is conflict resolution (Hartup, 1992). It has been argued that experiences with peers promote the perspective-taking, communication, and negotiation skills needed for productive conflict resolution (Dunn & Slomkowski, 1992).

Peers and Co-construction

Theory regarding peer relationships and children's construction of a sense of their social and nonsocial worlds is also predicated on the importance of interaction with agemates as a critical antecedent of development. Piaget (1926, 1932) implicated peer interaction, discourse, and negotiation as crucial elements that underlie the emergence of operational thinking. To Piaget, peer exchange allowed children to actively explore their ideas rather than to risk their devaluation and criticism by adult authority figures. In short, it was posited that children come to accept adults' notions, thoughts, beliefs, and rules, not necessarily because they understand them, but rather because obedience is viewed as required. With their peers, however, Piaget believed that children could experience opportunities to examine conflicting ideas and explanations, to negotiate and discuss multiple perspectives, to decide to compromise with, or to reject, the notions held by peers. These peer interactive experiences were believed to result in positive and adaptive developmental outcomes for children, such as the ability to understand others' thoughts, emotions, and intentions. According to this view, developmental change results from the exchange of differences of opinion. Such differences lead to cognitive disequilibrium that can be so uncomfortable that the child is motivated to find a solution. As a result, each interactant must construct, or reconstruct, a coordinated perspective so as to return to a state of cognitive equilibrium. An alternative view is seen in Vygotsky's (1978) argument that cognitive growth and development result from cooperative interpersonal exchanges. Vygotsky proposed that peers often provided the sort of collaboration and assistance that could elevate a child's level of cognitive functioning. That is, by providing opportunities for cooperative constructive action, peers would stimulate each other's functioning and development.

Behavioral Models

A fourth model of the processes by which peer relationships affect healthy development has received the least direct attention but is implicit in a large number of studies (Hartup, 1970; Berndt, 1979). The behavioral approach to the study of peer relationships implies that peers shape each other's behaviors through observational learning or even via direct reinforcement. According to these views, the peer group sets standards or norms that guide children's behaviors and attitudes. In these approaches, children are regarded as highly responsive to the expectations of their peers and they organize their behavior accordingly.

Summary

Broad theoretical positions state explicitly that experience with peers is important, if not necessary, for healthy affective and behavioral development. Without adequate relationships with peers, the development of a positive self-concept, the acquisition of social and cognitive skills, and the formation of a competent behavioral profile would be impossible. Some theory (e.g., Sullivan, 1953) goes so far as to claim the relationships with peers can "buffer" a child from non-optimal conditions or experiences in other domains. This emphasis on the positive consequents of peer relationships stands in contrast to the emphasis in many, if not most, empirical studies on outcomes that are indicative of maladjustment. This concern with risk and maladjustment is, to some extent, the flip side of the argument that peer relationships promote health. But research has, for the most part, overlooked the importance of peer relationships for the emergence of competence and well-being.

WHAT PROMOTES POSITIVE PEER RELATIONSHIPS: LEVELS OF SOCIAL COMPLEXITY

The four broad models previously discussed emphasize aspects of peer experiences drawn from different levels of social complexity. Whereas the self-perceptual models typically emphasize dyadic experiences, the ideas of Sullivan (1953) are more specifically focused on friendship than are the ideas of Mead (1934) and Cooley (1909), who emphasized dyadic relationships more broadly than just friendships. The skill models also take a broad view, essentially emphasizing dyadic interactions in general (e.g., Hartup, 1992). Nevertheless, they recognize that interactions with friends may be more critical for skill development than are interactions with other peers (Dunn & Slomkowski, 1992). Similar remarks can be made about models of co-construction. Although the models of Piaget and Vygotsky emphasize general interactional experiences with peers, they emphasize patterns of interaction that are more characteristic of interactions between friends than among non-friends. For example, in his conceptualization of peer interaction as the basis of moral development, Piaget refers to the sort of exchanges and involvement that are seen more often among friends than non-friends (e.g., Newcomb & Brady, 1982). The behavioral models have also ascribed particular power to the dyad in the sense that reinforcements are more frequent and more salient between friends than non-friends (Charlesworth & Hartup, 1967; Masters, 1971; Masters & Furman, 1981). Nevertheless, some behavioral models ascribed a great deal of power to the group in general. Harris (1995) argues in particular that the group has a nearly tyrannical influence over the individual as children and adolescents are highly motivated to organize their behavior in order to conform to group expectations and standards.

Although different models ascribe significance to different aspects of children's experiences with peers, they all emphasize phenomena from the level of the individual as the consequents of peer experience (e.g., self-perceptions, skills, and behaviors). The level of the individual has been emphasized also in research on the concept of risk. This emphasis appears in two broad ways. First, the major purpose of a large number of studies has been the association between individual characteristics and experiences at the group and dyadic levels (see Newcomb, Bukowski, & Pattee, 1993). These studies have shown that children with characteristics indicating competence (see Bukowski, Rubin, & Parker, in press; Bukowski, Bergevin, Sabongui, & Serbin, 1998) are more likely than other children to be liked by peers (i.e., to be generally accepted by peers) and to be involved in friendship. Second, it has been argued that the effect of peers will vary as a function of a child's individual characteristics (Rubin et al., 1998). For example, one hypothesis is that the effects of having a friend will vary as a function of individual characteristics such as tendencies to be aggressive or withdrawn (Hoza, Molina, Bukowski, & Sippola, 1995).

Distinguishing Between and Accounting for Different Levels of Social Complexity

The differential emphasis across theories on different levels of social complexity and the proposal that the effects of peer experience will vary as a function of individual characteristics require that clear distinctions are made between these levels. A major advance in the past decade has been the articulation of constructs and measurement procedures for each level. As a result of this more careful description of the types of experiences children have within the peer system, researchers have been able to make more precise measurement and they have been able to see how these different experiences account uniquely and as a group for development outcomes. (As these techniques are the focus of the attached discussion of measurement, only a brief description is provided here for each of the three levels.)

The Level of the Individual.   The level of the individual consists of the behavioral, affective, and cognitive characteristics and dispositions that a child brings to his/her social interactions. They are unique to the child per se. These characteristics include behavioral tendencies, either derived from experience or temperament, cognitions about self and other, motivations and goals, relationship history, and affective states and traits. The level of the individual is the most basic level of social complexity. Although it might appear that the level of the individual has no social complexity, such complexity can exist in a child's representations of self and other (e.g., in internal working models) as well as in their planning for social interactions and relationships. The two features from the level of individual that have been studied most broadly concern individuals' general social behaviors and their social cognitions.

The Level of the Dyad.   Peer experiences at the level of the dyad can be conceptualized as reflecting either interactions or relationships. According to Hinde (e.g., 1976, 1979, 1987), interactions are the series of interchanges that occur between individuals over a limited time span. Interactions are defined as interdependencies in behavior (Hinde, 1979). That is, two persons are interacting when their behaviors are mutually responsive. If a person addresses someone (e.g., says "Have a nice day") and the other person responds ("Thank you"), they have had an interaction, albeit a rather primitive one. Relationships are based on these patterns of interaction. The relationship consists of the cognitions, emotions, internalized expectations, and qualifications that the relationship partners construct as a result of their interactions with each other. The relationship that has been studied most widely is friendship. Researchers have examined dyadic relationships, such as friendship, according to (a) what the partners do together (i.e., the content of the relationship), (b) the number of different activities in which the partners engage (i.e., the breadth of their interactions), (c) whether the child has a stable relationship with a particular peer based on mutual liking and shared activities and closeness (i.e., a friendship), and (d) the quality of the interactions within the relationship (e.g., reciprocal, complementary, positive, negative).

The Level of the Group.   Group experiences refer to experiences among a set of individuals who have been organized by either formal or informal means. Group phenomena do not refer to individuals but instead refer to (a) the links that exist among the persons in the group and (b) the features that characterize the group. Groups can be measured according to (a) their structure and size (cf.,

Bennenson, 1990) and (b) the themes or the content around which groups are organized (cf., Brown, 1989). Many of the best known studies of children and their peers were concerned with the group per se, including Lewin, Lippit and White's (1938) study of group climate and Sherif, Harvey, White, Hood, and Sherif's (1961) study of intragroup loyalty and intergroup conflict.

Individual and Group: Acceptance and Rejection as the Interface Between Two Levels. Ironically, in spite of the apparent clarity of this multiple levels approach to conceptualizing the peer group, two of the most widely studied variables defy categorization at particular levels. These variables are acceptance and rejection. Whereas acceptance refers to how much a child is liked by group members, rejection refers to how much a child is disliked by group members. To a large extent these measures tell us about the child as an individual. They also, however, tell us about the group's view toward the individual. This difficulty in disentangling group from individual and individual from group underscores the importance of recognizing the distinctions between different levels of social complexity as well as the inextricable associations between them.

WHAT PROMOTES POSITIVE PEER RELATIONSHIPS: RECENT RESEARCH ON PEER EXPERIENCE AND WELL-BEING

In this final section, a small set of recent studies regarding the association between peer experience and adaptive outcomes is presented. Already, large review papers are available to cover the vast literature on peer relationships (Rubin et al., 1998). Here, five types of "outcomes" are presented: (a) self-perceptions of well-being, (b) school performance, (c) cognitive skills, (d) altruism, and (e) protection from conditions of risk.

Peer Relationships and Self-Perceptions

Studies have consistently revealed an association between children's self-perceptions and their peer relationships. Popular or accepted children have been shown to be more likely to feel and think positively about themselves and their social competencies, and to perceive social situations as relatively comforting and easy to deal with (Harter, 1982; Kurdek & Krile, 1982; Ladd & Price, 1986; Rubin, 1985; Wheeler & Ladd, 1982). This association is probably most salient for children who are otherwise withdrawn from their peers. That is, being popular can help withdrawn children to have a more positive view of themselves (Boivin & Begin, 1989; Boivin, Thomassin, & Alain, 1989; Hymel, Bowker, & Woody, 1993). Friendship experiences also appear to be related to more positive views of self. Regardless of their popularity status, children with friends are less lonely than are other children (Parker & Asher, 1993). In parallel to these results, Bukowski and Hoza (1989) reported that having one mutual friend in one's elementary school class was related to more positive self-perception, even for unpopular children.

These studies show that the self and experience with peers are interrelated. These studies, however, are almost always correlational "snapshot" studies that preclude even weak interpretations regarding causal influence. Accordingly, a critical need exists for studies that will examine this association in designs that will allow for causal interpretations.

Peer Relationships and School Performance

Studies of the association between peer relationships and school performance provide clearer evidence of causal effects of peer experience. Ladd (1990), for example, reported that children with many friends at school entrance developed more favorable school perceptions in the early months than children with fewer friends. Those who maintained these friendships also liked school better as the year went by. Making new friends in the classroom also predicted gains in school performance. By comparison, measures of school performance at the start of the transition to kindergarten did not generally forecast gains in social adjustment. Positive, harmonious close friendships also have been found to facilitate the school adjustment of Head Start preschoolers (Taylor & Machida, 1993) and adolescents' transitions to middle school (Berndt & Keefe, 1993; Terry, Coie, Lochman, & Jacobs, 1992). At the group level, Kindermann (1993) reported that children's motivation for school performance reflected the attitudes of the peers with whom they associated. In his longitudinal study, this effect of a child's peers' motivations was seen even after the child's initial level of motivation had been accounted for. Together these longitudinal studies show that both dyadic and group experience can affect school performance.

Peer Relationships and Cognition

Following the initial argument of Piaget and Vygotsky, co-constructivist thinkers such as Azmitia (1988; Azmitia & Montgomery, 1993) and Hartup (1995) proposed that the quality of the relationship between the peers who are interacting with each other may contribute to cognitive and social-cognitive growth and development. For example, friends can challenge each other with relative impunity. Given that friends are more sensitive to each other's needs and more supportive of each other's thoughts and well-being than non-friends, it may be that children would be more likely to talk openly and challenge each other's thoughts and deeds in the company of friends than non-friends. Accordingly, exchanges between friends should be more likely than exchanges between nonfriends to promote cognitive and social-cognitive growth. Their studies have shown that children can, and do, make cognitive advances when they exchange and cooperatively discuss conflicting perspectives on various issues (see Hartup, 1996). It has been shown also that interactions during which children openly criticize each other's ideas and clarify and elaborate their own ideas are more often observed in the company of friends than of non-friends (e.g., Azmitia & Montgomery, 1993).

Altruism.   Although there have been several studies indicating that peers influence each other's aggressive behaviors, only weak and indirect evidence indicates similar effects for prosocial behavior. There is, of course, plenty of evidence that children treat their friends in more prosocial ways than they treat others (Berndt, 1986; Newcomb & Bagwell, 1995). Nevertheless, evidence that such experiences have an enduring impact on children's subsequent behaviour however is currently lacking. Studies of conformity (e.g., Berndt, 1979) have shown that children will alter their behaviors so as to match the expectations of their peers. These studies have typically been self-report in nature and have not looked at actual behavioral patterns.

Eisenberg and Fabes (1998) have pointed out that the lack of empirical evidence of peer influence on prosocial behavior is surprising for several reasons. Most importantly, peers are salient entities in a child's social environment. Studies have shown clearly that they dispense frequent reinforcements to each other. Also, given their similarity to each other, one would expect peers to be powerful models for each other. These issues are certainly ripe for some empirical attention.

Friendships as Protective Forces.   Sullivan and others (e.g., Davies, 1984) have stated explicitly that friendship can protect children from the negative consequences associated with high risk conditions. Several studies have provided support for this view. In two studies, Hodges (Hodges, Malone, & Perry, 1997; Hodges, Boivin, Vitaro, & Bukowski, 1999), showed that children who were at risk for victimization by peers were protected from such victimization if they were engaged in a friendship. In a study that integrated experiences from the family and peer systems, Gauze, Bukowski, Sippola, and Aquan-Assee (1996) revealed that the experience of having a friend and having a high quality friendship protects children from the effects of coming from a nonadaptive or chaotic family. Specifically, using a measure of self-perception as their dependent measure, they showed that friended children from non-optimal families did not differ from children from optimal families. Previous studies have shown that friendships can be a source of resilience at times of potential developmental disruption (Hetherington, 1989).

CONCLUSIONS

Theory and data point to the role of peers as a positive force in development. Typically, peer researchers have approached the study of the peer system via the concept of risk, often using indices of maladjustment as measures of outcome. There is reason to expect that peer relationships can have powerful influences on children's functioning in several domains indicative of health and well-being, including self-perceptions, social skills, cognitive abilities, school, and behavior. These theoretical accounts have invoked experiences and processes at the individual, dyadic, and group levels of social complexity. Current research on peer relationships is more theoretically focused and more health oriented than it has been in the past. Moreover, the use of designs that reveal associations between peer relationships and outcome but which preclude the analysis of causal patterns has been replaced by multiple variable longitudinal studies that allow for the precise analysis of theoretically derived hypotheses. The next wave of peer research is likely to show the ways that peers influence children's healthy development.

REFERENCES

Azmitia, M. (1988). Peer interaction and problem solving: When are two heads better than one? *Child Development, 59*, 87–96.

Azmitia, M., & Montgomery, R. (1993). Friendship, transactive dialogues, and the development of scientific reasoning. *Social Development, 2*, 202–221.

Baudonnière, P., Garcia-Werebe, M., Michel, J., & Liegois, J. (1989). Development of communicative competencies in early childhood: A model and results. In B. H. Schnieder, G. Attili, J. Nadel, & R. P. Weissberg (Eds.), *Social competence in developmental perspective.* Boston: Kluwer Academic Publishers.

Benenson, J. F. (1990). Gender differences in social networks. *Journal of Early Adoloescence, 10*, 472–495.

Berndt, T. J. (1979). Developmental changes in conformity to peers and parents. *Developmental Psychology, 15*, 608–616.

Boivin, M., & Begin, G. (1989). Peer status and self-perception among early elementary school children: The case of rejected children. *Child Development, 60*, 591–596.

Boivin, M., Thomassin, L., & Alain, M. (1989). Peer rejection and self-perceptions among early elementary school children: Aggressive rejectees versus withdrawn rejectees. In B. H. Schneider, G. Attili, J. Nadel, & R. P. Weissberg (Eds.), *Social competence in developmental perspective* (pp. 392–393). Boston: Kluwer Academic Publishing.

Brown, B. B. (1989). The role of peer groups in adolescents' adjustment to secondary school. In T. J. Berndt & G. W. Ladd (Eds.), *Peer relationships in child development* (pp. 188–216). New York: Wiley.

Brownell, C. (1990). Peer social skills in toddlers: Competence and constraints illustrated by same-age and mixed-age interaction. *Child Development, 61*, 838–848.

Bukowski, W., & Hoza, B. (1989). Popularity and friendship: Issues in theory, measurement and outcome. In T. J. Berndt & G. W. Ladd (Eds.), *Peer relations in child development* (pp. 15–45). New York: Wiley.

Bukowski, W. M., Bergevin, T., Sabongui, A., & Serbin, L. (1998). Competence: The short history of the future of an idea. In D. Pushkar, W. Bukowski, A. Schwartzman, D. Stack, & D. White (Eds.), *Improving competence across the life span* (pp. 91–100). New York: Plenum.

Bukowski, W. M., Hoza, B., & Boivin, M. (1994). Measuring friendship quality during pre- and early adolescence: The development and psychometric properties of the friendship qualities scale. *Journal of Social and Personal Relationships, 11*, 471–484.

Bukowski, W. M., Rubin, K. H., & Parker, J. G. (in press). Social competence during childhood and adolescence. In N. Smelser & P. Baltes (Eds. in chief) & N. Eisenberg (Vol. Ed.), *Encyclopedia of the social and behavioral sciences.* New York: Pergamon.

Charlesworth, R., & Hartup, W. W. (1967). Positive social reinforcement in the nursery school peer group. *Child Development, 38*, 993–1002.

Coie, J. D., & Kupersmidt, J. (1983). A behavioral analysis of emerging social status in boys' groups. *Child Development, 54*, 1400–1416.

Cooley, C. H. (1902). *Human nature and the social order.* New York: Scribner.

Cowen, E. L., Pedersen, A., Bagigian, H., Izzo, L. D., & Trost, M. A. (1973). Long-term follow-up of early detected vulnerable children. *Journal of Consulting and Clinical Psychology, 41*, 438–446.

Davies, B. (1984). *Life in the classroom and playground.* London: Routledge.

Dunn, J., & Slomkowski, C. (1992). Conflict and the development of social understanding. In C. U. Shantz & W. W. Hartup (Eds.), *Conflict in child and adolescent development* (pp. 70–92). Cambridge, England: Cambridge University Press.

Eckerman, C. O. (1993). Imitation and toddlers' achievement co-ordinated action with others. In J. Nadel & L. Camaioni (Eds.) *New perspectives in early communicative development* (pp. 116–156). New York: Routledge.

Eckerman, C. O., Davis, C. C., & Didow, S. M. (1989). Toddlers' emerging ways of achieving social coordinations with a peer. *Child Development, 60,* 440–453.

Eisenberg, N., & Fabes, R. (1998). Prosocial development. In W. Damon (Series Ed.) & N. Eisenberg (Vol. Ed.), *The handbook of child psychology* (pp. 701–778). New York: Wiley.

Gauze, C., Bukowski, W. M., Aquan-Assee, J., & Sippola, L. K. (1996). Interactions between family environment and friendship and associations with self-perceived well-being during early adolescence. *Child Development, 67,* 2201–2216.

Harris, J. (1995). Where is the child's environment? A group socialization theory of development. *Psychological Review, 102,* 458–489.

Harter, S. (1982). The perceived competence scale for children. *Child Development, 53,* 89–97.

Hartup, W. W. (1970). Peer interaction and social organization. In P. H. Mussen (Ed.), *Carmichael's manual of child psychology* (Vol. 2, pp. 361–456). New York: Wiley.

Hartup, W. W. (1992). Conflict and friendship relations. In C. U. Shantz & W. W. Hartup (Eds.), *Conflict in child and adolescent development* (pp. 185–215). Cambridge, England: Cambridge University Press.

Hartup, W. W. (1996). Cooperation, close relationships, and cognitive development. In W. M. Bukowski, A. F. Newcomb, & W. W. Hartup (Eds.), *The company they keep: Friendship during childhood and adolescence* (pp. 213–237). New York: Cambridge University Press.

Hetherington, E. M. (1989). Coping with family transitions: winners, losers and survivors (Presidential Address). *Child Development, 60,* 1–14.

Hinde, R. A. (1976). On describing relationships. *Journal of Child Psychology and Psychiatry, 17,* 1–19.

Hinde, R. A. (1979). *Towards understanding relationships.* London: Academic Press.

Hinde, R. A. (1987). *Individuals, relationships and culture.* Cambridge, England: Cambridge University Press.

Hodges, E., Boivin, M., Vitaro, F., & Bukowski, W. M. (1999). The power of friendship: Friendship as a factor in the cycle of victimization and maladjustment. *Developmental Psychology, 35,* 94–101.

Hodges, E., Malone, M., & Perry, D. (1997). Individual risk and social risk as interacting determinants of victimization in the peer group. *Developmental Psychology, 33,* 1032–1039.

Howes, C. (1988). Peer interaction of young children. *Monographs of the Society for Research in Child Development, 53,* (Serial No. 217).

Hoza, B., Molina, B., Bukowski, W. M., & Sippola, L. K. (1995). Aggression, withdrawal and measures of popularity and friendship as predictors of internalizing and externalizing problems during early adolescence. *Development and Psychopathology, 7,* 787–802.

Hymel, S., Bowker, A., & Woody, E. (1993). Aggressive versus withdrawn unpopular children: Variations in peer and self-perceptions in multiple domains. *Child Development, 64,* 879–896.

Kinderman, T. (1993). Natural peer groups as contexts for individual development: The case of children's motivation in school. *Developmental Psychology, 29,* 970–977.

Kurdek, L. A., & Krile, D. (1982). A developmental analysis of the relation between peer acceptance and both interpersonal understanding and perceived social self-competence. *Child Development, 53,* 1485–1491.

Ladd, G. W. (1990). Having friends, keeping friends, making friends, and being liked by peers in the classroom: Predictors of children's early school adjustment? *Child Development, 61,* 312–331.

Ladd, G. W., & Price, J. M. (1986). Promoting children's cognitive and social competence: The relation between parents' perceptions of task difficulty and children's perceived and actual competence. *Child Development, 57,* 446–460.

Lewin, K., Lippit, R., & White, R. K. (1938). Patterns of aggressive behavior in experimentally created "social climates." *Journal of Social Psychology, 10,* 271–299.

Masters, J. C. (1971). Effects of social comparison on children's self-reinforcement and altruism toward competitors and friends. *Developmental Psychology, 5,* 64–72.

Masters, J. C., & Furman, W. (1981). Popularity, individual friendship selection, and specific peer interaction. *Developmental Psychology, 17,* 344–350.

Mead, G. H. (1934). *Mind, self, and society.* Chicago: University of Chicago Press.

Newcomb, A. F., & Bagwell, C. (1995). Children' friendship relations: A meta-analytic review. *Psychological Bulletin*, *117*, 306–347.

Newcomb, A. F., & Brady, J. E. (1982). Mutuality in boys' friendship relations. *Child Development*, *53*, 392–395.

Newcomb, A. F., Bukowski, W. M., & Pattee, L. (1993). Children's peer relations: A meta-analytic review of popular, rejected, neglected, controversial, and average sociometric status, *Psychological Bulletin*, *113*, 99–128.

Parker, J. G., & Asher, S. R. (1993). Friendship and friendship quality in middle childhood: Links with peer group acceptance and feelings of loneliness and social dissatisfaction. *Developmental Psychology*, *29*, 611–621.

Parker, J. G., & Asner, S. R. (1987). Peer relations and later personal adjustment: Are low-accepted children "at risk"? *Psychological Bulletin*, *102*, 357–389.

Piaget, J. (1932). *The moral judgment of the child*. Glencoe, IL: Free Press.

Roff, M., Sells, S. B., & Golden, M. M. (1972). *Social adjustment and personality development in children*. Minneapolis, MN: University of Minnesota Press, 1972.

Rubin, K. H., Bukowski, W. M., & Parker, J. G. (1998). Peer interactions, relationships and groups. In W. Damon (Series Ed.) & N. Eisenberg (Vol. Ed.), *The handbook of child psychology* (pp. 619–700). New York: Wiley.

Sherif, M., Harvey, O. J., White, B. J., Hood, W. R., & Sherif, C. (1961). *Inter-group conflict and cooperation: The Robbers Cave experiment*. Norman, OK: University of Oklahoma Press.

Sullivan, H. S. (1953). *The interpersonal theory of psychiatry*. New York: Norton.

Taylor, A. R., & Machida, S. (1993). *The contribution of peer relations to social competence in low-income children*. Paper presented at the biennial meeting of the Society for Research in Child Development, New Orleans, LA.

Terry, R. A., Coie, J. D., Lochman, J. E., & Jacobs, M. (1992, August). *Dynamic social development and its relation to middle school adjustment*. In J. B. Kupersmidt (Chair), *Longitudinal research in child psychopathology: Peer rejection and children's behavioral adjustment*. Symposium conducted at the Centennial Convention of the American Psychological Association, Washington, DC.

Vygotsky, L. S. (1978). *Mind in society: The development of higher psychological processes*. Cambridge, MA: Harvard University Press.

Wheeler, V. A., & Ladd, G. W. (1982). Assessment of children's self-efficacy for social interactions with peers. *Developmental Psychology*, *18*, 795–805.

18

Positive Development of the Self: Self-Concept, Self-Esteem, and Identity

Jonathan F. Zaff

Elizabeth C. Hair
Child Trends, Washington, DC

INTRODUCTION

The self is an important element of individual development. This paper focuses on self-concept, self-esteem, and identity as the components that comprise the self, and which are intuitively integral to the healthy formation of the child and adolescent. These three components can be considered, respectively, the cognitive, affective, and self-evaluative aspects of the self. Through socialization by parents and peers and by other factors within the environment the self is formed. There are also data to support the effect of the positive development of the self on other positive outcomes such as academic achievement and positive interpersonal relationships. However, conclusions should be tempered by the fact that there is a dearth of longitudinal data. The present paper (a) defines the components of the self, including how self-concept, self-esteem, and identity are measured; (b) reviews the theoretical and empirical evidence to support the self as a positive construct of positive development; (c) provides data to suggest the developmental stability of the construct; and (d) describes the factors that affect the development and promotion of the components of the self.

How people develop the self can be a complex process. The first to try to resolve this issue in modern times, James (1890, 1892) developed the distinction between the "I" and the "Me" aspects of the self. The "I" self is concerned with an individual's continuity across time and the distinctiveness of oneself as a person. The "Me" self refers to the ideas that an individual has about who they are and what they are like. Symbolic interactionists believe the self is primarily a social construction made up of interactions with others in which an individual imagines how others perceive him or her, imagines how he or she is being evaluated, and how he or she feels about that evaluation (e.g., Cooley, 1922; Mead, 1934).[1]

TECHNICAL ISSUES

Defining the Self

Self-concept.   Around the age of 18 to 24 months, babies begin to recognize their image in the mirror as their own (Lewis & Brooks-Gunn, 1979). This self-recognition is presumed to be the beginning of the self-concept (Povinelli, Rulf, & Bierschwale, 1994). The self-concept is the sum of an individual's beliefs about their own attributes such as their personality traits, cognitive schemas, and their social roles and relationships (Franzoi, 1996).

There are several theories concerning self-discovery of an individual's beliefs. Introspection—gaining insight into one's own attitudes and beliefs—may not always be accurate (Wilson, 1985; Wilson & LaFleur, 1995; Wilson & Schooler, 1991), but it may not be futile. Behaviors that are cognitively driven may increase in accuracy after introspection, whereas behaviors that are affectively driven may not (Millar & Tesser, 1989).

In self-perception theory, in which we watch our own behaviors, people determine what they feel or think by observing their own behaviors and the situation in which the behavior occurred (Bem, 1972). When people are coaxed into doing something, and when they are not otherwise sure of how they feel, they will view themselves in ways that are consistent with their behavior (Chaiken & Baldwin, 1981; Fazio, 1987; Schlenker & Trudeau, 1990). Cognitive processes have also been theorized as important for the development of self-concept. For instance, an individual would have no self-concept without autobiographical memories that link the past with the present (Brown & Kulik, 1977; Conway, 1990; Friedman, 1993; Rubin, 1986).

Individuals may form modules of information or self-schemas that guide them in processing information that is self-relevant (Markus, 1977). In this approach, self-schemas are important because they let individuals interpret and recall life experiences in personally relevant terms or themes (Kihlstrom & Cantor, 1984). Individuals think about their current self and their possible selves: what they might

---

[1]Cooley used the term "looking glass self" to describe how individuals see themselves as reflected in the eyes of other people.

become, would like to become, and are afraid of becoming (Markus & Nurius, 1986). The possible selves provide individuals with an imaginary blueprint for their future goals and plans (Ruvolo & Markus, 1992).

Identity.   While self-concept refers to an awareness, identity refers to a commitment to that awareness. Concisely, identity refers to "having a clearly delineated self-definition … comprised of those goals, values, and beliefs which the person finds personally expressive, and to which he or she is unequivocally committed" (Waterman, 1985, p. 6). There are two major theories that drive most identity research: ego identity development and social identity development.

Erikson's (1959, 1968) original ego identity theory posited that the search for identity in adolescence is one of life's major crises. Although he stated that identity is an ongoing process from the time that a child is born, adolescence marks the point at which the individual must integrate the various components of the self-concept into one general identity. This is a time of exploration that will hopefully lead to a definitive meaning of the self. Several content areas were defined by Erikson as necessary for commitment in order for life to continue on a positive path: vocation, political ideology, religion/morals, and social roles. However, the content of these areas possibly do not cover the important components of all ethnicities and both genders (e.g., Gilligan, 1982).

Other theorists have operationalized and placed identity theory within a developmental process. Marcia (1966) created four statuses of identity development that describe statuses of identity search and commitment: *Diffusion* is a status in which no exploration has occurred and no commitment has been made to an identity; *foreclosure* is defined as a point at which a commitment has been made, but without any exploration having taken place; *moratorium* is the time of exploration, when the adolescent is actively searching for an identity and possibly trying on several different masks; *identity achieved*, or commitment, is the status in which the individual has committed to a particular identity.

Waterman (1985) has expanded on Marcia's constructs, by theorizing that there was a developmental trajectory. For example, an achieved identity could only be attained through active exploration (i.e., through the moratorium phase), while a person could go directly from a diffuse status to a foreclosed one.

A second theory of identity development is social identity theory (Tajfel & Turner, 1986), which is based on the premise that an individual has the need to identify with and achieve a positive self-image from a social group. This theory is divided into three main components: categorization, identification, and social comparison (respectively, the individual places himself or herself into a social group, feels a part of that group, and then compares himself or herself to others in that group, usually in a favorable light).[2] Such comparison usually leads to in-group biases, which have been used to explain prejudice

---

[2]However, identifying with a group that has a low status in society (e.g., an oppressed ethnic minority) may lead to a preference for a higher status out-group (Tajfel, 1978).

within society (Gaertner, Rust, Dovidio, Bachman, & Anastasio, 1996; van Hippel, Sekaquaptewa, & Vargas, 1997; Williams & Giles, 1992).

Identity theories related to specific subpopulations, such as ethnic groups, have generally combined the social identity and ego identity theories (e.g., Atkinson, Morton, & Sue, 1973; Cross, 1991; Phinney, 1989). The theories generally surmise that an individual must go through a period of exploration before an achieved identity state can be reached. However, the exploration is based on the identification with a particular categorical group and may involve a comparison with other groups. The comparison is based on the premise of being an ethnic minority member (e.g., African American, Asian American, or Hispanic American) in a majority (i.e., Caucasian American) society. In regard to ethnicity, identity has been defined as "one's sense of belonging to an ethnic group and the part of one's thinking, perceptions, feelings, and behaviors that is due to ethnic group membership" (Rotheram-Boras & Phinney, 1989, p. 13). There have also been more culturally specific theories that define identity by commitment to particular tenets of a culture, but do not deal with exploration, as defined by ego identity theory (e.g., Baldwin, 1981; Nobles, 1973).

Self-esteem.   Self-esteem is the affective assessment of both self-concept and identity. A person's positive and negative self-evaluations contribute to how a person feels about him or herself (Coopersmith, 1967). Individuals with positive self-esteem are normally not afraid to speak their opinion in a polite and appropriate fashion, seek opportunities for self-development, and are not threatened by other's successes and use positive self-statements. These individuals appear to be self-assured without being overconfident (Brown, 1991; Heatherton & Polivy, 1991). As a youth reaches middle childhood, measurement of the child's self-concept and self-esteem are indistinguishable. Therefore, the research literature after this time period uses the terms *self-concept* and *self-esteem* interchangeably.

A controversy surrounding self-esteem focuses on the multiplicity of the self-concept; whether there are multiple selves or a single unified self (Harter, 1998; Kihlstrom, 1993; McAdams, 1995). Historically, researchers have believed that individuals have a unified self (Allport, 1961; Epstein, 1981; Maslow, 1954; Rogers, 1951), arguing that a basic need of individuals is to preserve the coherence of the system that defines them. They develop a life-story or self-narrative that creates a sense of continuity across time and settings (Freeman, 1992; Gergen & Gergen, 1988). However, there is considerable evidence for the development of multiple selves. Beginning in childhood, children can evaluate themselves differently across a variety of domains (Harter, 1998). The number of domains on which children can differentiate themselves increases across the child's development (early childhood through adulthood) (Braken, 1996). Although there has been a shift to multidimensional models of the self, the concept of global self-esteem (often called "self-worth") has been retained (Harter, 1998; Marsh & Hattie, 1996; Shavelson, Hubner, & Stanton, 1976). This move to multidimensional models of the self has been reflected in the development of instruments to measure the self.

Instruments to Measure the Self

Instruments for Self-concept/Self-esteem.   There are many different methods for measuring self-concept or self-esteem. Projective tests, such as the Rorshach and the Thematic Apperception Test (TAT), have been used in the assessment of the self-concept, but are generally considered peripheral measures of the self (Wylie, 1989). The most commonly used method for assessing self-concept or self-esteem is the self-report inventory (see Keith & Bracken, 1996, for review of self-concept instruments). One of the earliest measures of global self-esteem is the Rosenberg Self-esteem Scale (RSES; Rosenberg, 1979). Although the RSES laid the groundwork for the self-report measurement of the self-esteem, it is no longer considered the most appropriate instrument to use (Keith & Bracken, 1996). It only measures global self-esteem and it was initially validated on an adult sample and therefore may not be appropriate for measuring the self in children.

The Self-perception Profile for Children (SPPC; Harter, 1985) includes six domains: Scholastic Competence, Social Acceptance, Athletic Competence, Physical Appearance, Behavioral Conduct, and Global Self-worth. Harter's 36-item scale is a significant improvement in the measurement of self-esteem, because the SPPC has its foundation on a strong theoretical model (Keith & Bracken, 1996). The Harter scale also has the children identify the domains that they considered important to their self-esteem.

More recent measures of self-esteem include subscales to reflect the multifaceted nature of the self. The Self-Description Questionnaire, II (SDQII; Marsh, 1990) is based on the multidimensional and hierarchical theoretical model of self-concept proposed by Shavelson et al., (1976). It measures the general self, as well as four nonacademic domains (Physical Abilities, Physical Appearance, same and opposite sex Peer Relations, and Parent Relations) and three academic domains (Reading, Mathematics, and General School) of the self. Although the scale was normed in Australian, using some terms that are specific to that society, a version has been used in a nationally representative study of American youth.

Instruments for Identity.   Measures that have been used to assess ego identity have been derived from Marcia's (1966) Identity Status Interview (ISI). Meeus (1996) conducted a literature review of general identity measures, and found that, along with the ISI, other predominant measures include the Objective Measure of Ego Identity (OM-EIS) and the Extended Objective Measure of Ego Identity Status (EOM-EIS; Grotevant & Adams, 1984). Space is too limited to describe these scales or other scales that are specific to one domain of identity (e.g., Vocational Identity; Holland, Gottfredson, & Power, 1980). Ego identity scales tend to be psychometrically sound, but only tap indices based on Erikson's model, which is based on Western male norms, thus neglecting interdependent constructs important to women and more communal cultures (Gilligan, 1982). These measures also have not been used many times in longitudinal analyses, meaning that they have not been

validated as instruments that measure the development of identity, only the usefulness of placing people into particular identity statuses.

Social identity researchers have employed several different methods for measurement, usually focusing on each of the three components of social identity, one
at a time, such as using Social Identity Maps (e.g., Hamid, 1996) and self-identity
social-similarity grids (e.g., Ganiere & Enright, 1989) to approximate the social
distance that an individual feels from particular groups. These measures are generally effective in identifying group identification and social comparison. However,
social identity was originally conceived as being dichotomous; that is, someone either is a part of a group or is not (Turner, 1982). Thus these measures examine group
membership, not identity.

Ethnic identity measures are plentiful (e.g., Baldwin & Bell, 1985; Parham &
Helms, 1981; Phinney, 1992). These measures are generally effective in identifying
group identification and social comparison, but there has been much criticism
about the ability of the measures to capture all aspects of ethnic identity, specifically the content and quality of ethnic identity.

THEORETICAL AND EMPIRICAL REVIEW OF THE LITERATURE

Self-Esteem

Most research to date on the self has viewed self-esteem as an outcome measure
(Bracken, 1996). The research has focused mainly on the causes or correlates of
self-esteem, such as psychopathology, disabilities, health problems, and life history
problems (i.e., family structure, child abuse, and adolescent pregnancy; Prout &
Prout, 1996). The limited and recent evidence supports self-esteem as a predictor of
positive outcomes.

These programs have not succeeded in increasing the students' performance academically. Domain specific research on self-esteem indicates that programs that
target specific domains such as academic competence may be more successful in
enhancing academic performance. For instance, specific domains, such as aca-
demic/scholastic self-esteem, have been linked to positive outcomes, such as
higher scores on standardized tests of achievement (Bryne, 1984). A major limitation in most of these studies is that they are cross-sectional and causality cannot be
concluded (Cook & Campbell, 1979; Kenny, 1979). A longitudinal research design
is required. There are not very many studies available that assess the relationship of
self-esteem and positive outcomes over time. For example, there is a dearth of longitudinal research documenting a causal relationship between academic
self-esteem and academic achievement (Marsh, 1990; Shavelson & Bolus, 1982).
A second limitation of these studies is that they have focused primarily on standardized test scores as outcomes. Research has found longitudinal results showing a relationship of self-esteem in middle school to grade point average, and to positive
measures of the students' functioning or adjustment in high school (Hair, 1999).

Identity

Theoretically, the definition of identity—commitment to a set of values and beliefs—is in itself a reason to include it as a component of child and adolescent well-being. An achieved identity gives a person a life path to follow which intuitively can be considered an integral part of development. For instance, having a strong vocational identity would theoretically mean that an individual has committed to a particular occupational course. Erikson (1968) also theorized that attaining a solid identity would enable an individual to integrate various aspects of his or her life, including relationships with peers and family, and allow the individual to deal with temporary, but sudden, changes in the individual's life. Social identity theory is also based in the premise that identity is a prerequisite for positive development: Humans need to feel a part of or identity with a group in order to have a solid sense of well-being (Tajfel, 1978). For instance, identifying with one's own ethnic group can give the individual a strong sense of belonging. (See Phinney, 1990, and Spencer & Markstrom-Adams, 1990, for a discussion of the unique experiences of members of ethnic groups as they explore their identities.) The strong theoretical basis that supports identity as an element of positive development has resulted in identity, in its various forms, being used as an outcome measure instead of a predictor, such as studying the effects of a high or low self-esteem on the attainment of an identity (Munson, 1992). However, there is currently limited empirical support for identity being including as an element of positive development that predicts future or concurrent positive outcomes.

Identity research has mainly dealt with ethnic minority groups or with gender issues. However, the outcome measures that are seen throughout most of the literature have not been normed on subpopulations. This even includes the basic notions of what achievement or success means within subpopulations, as these definitions can vary by culture and by gender (e.g., Duda, 1980; Fan & Karnilowicz, 1997; Gilligan, 1982; Matute-Bianchi, 1986; Zaff, 1999). The studies that are not specifically focused on ethnic minority groups generally use samples that are predominantly Caucasian American.

Identity, as a general construct, has been found to act as a mediator between poverty and behavioral outcomes such as GPA, delinquency, and psychological well-being (DeHaan & MacDermind, 1998, 1999), and to be associated with greater self-awareness (Adams, Abraham, & Markstrom, 1987), a more positive self-esteem (Coover & Murphy, 2000; Meeus, 1996; Meeus, Iedema, Helsen, & Vollebergh, 1999), and greater academic achievement (Streitmatter, 1989). In other words, a more developed identity is related to more positive outcomes.

The much larger ethnic identity literature points to a relationship between identity and positive outcomes. Once reaching an achieved phase, according to many ethnic identity models (e.g., Atkinson et al., 1983; Cross, 1991; Phinney, 1989), the individual is considered to have comfort and acceptance within and outside of his or her ethnic group. This is an important component of positive inter-group relations

(Phinney, Ferguson, & Tate, 1997). Positive in-group and out-group relations are also important because they enable an individual to traverse among and function within different ethnic and cultural worlds within society (Boykin, 1985; Phelan, Davidson, & Cao, 1991). Without this ability, children and adolescents from ethnic minority groups may succeed in one of the worlds, but fail in the others, either because of psychological or social maladaptation or because of a lack of academic achievement (Arroyo & Zigler, 1995; Fordham, 1989). Having a positive ethnic identity has also been associated with indicators of psychological well-being, such as a positive association with global self-esteem and optimism and a negative association with loneliness and depression (Martinez & Dukes, 1997; Phinney, 1989; Phinney, 1992; Phinney & Tarver, 1987; Roberts et al., 1999). Identity achievement has also been shown to be related to academic success (Ford & Harris, 1997; Witherspoon, Speight, & Thomas, 1997).

Aside from a few longitudinal studies, such as ones conducted by Meeus and his colleagues (1996, 1999), most examinations have been cross-sectional (e.g., Ford & Harris, 1997; Phinney, Ferguson, & Tate, 1997; Witherspoon et al., 1997). Therefore, the reader should use caution when interpreting the mostly correlational results because of the lack of evidence regarding direction of causation.

In summary, there appears to be evidence that identity is related to positive child and adolescent outcomes such as scholastic achievement and psychological well-being. However, the evidence was gathered through predominantly correlational methods and causation could not be well supported, only suggested. This information is nevertheless informative and can lead to substantial hypothesis and theory building.

DEVELOPMENTAL STABILITY OF THE SELF OVER THE LIFE SPAN

Self-Esteem

As children move into middle childhood, research indicates a drop in self-esteem (Frey & Ruble, 1985, 1990; Harter, 1982; Harter & Pike, 1984). Most of these researchers attribute the decline in self-esteem to be associated with the child relying on social comparison information and external feedback. This information provides the child with more accurate information about his or her own capabilities (Crain, 1996; Marsh, 1989). There appears to be another decline in self-esteem in early adolescence (ages 11–13). The declines appear to be associated with the transition from elementary to junior high school and puberty (Eccles & Midgley, 1989; Simmons & Blyth, 1987).

After these declines, self-esteem gradually becomes more positive across the period of adolescence (Dusek & Flaherty, 1981; Harter, 1998; Marsh, Parker, & Barnes, 1985; Rosenberg, 1986). These increases could be associated with (a) a gain in personal autonomy that allows the adolescent to choose domains of competency, (b) increasing freedom that allows the adolescent to choose support groups that are self-esteem enhancing, and/or (c) increased role-taking that allows the teenager to behave in more socially acceptable ways (Hart, Fegeley, & Brengelman, 1993; McCarthy & Hoge, 1982).

There is a growing consensus to support James' original idea that individuals possess both a "baseline" self and a "barometric" self (see review by Demo & Savin-Williams, 1992). According to this view, people have a core sense of self that is consistent over time, but that there is situational variation surrounding this core (Heatherton & Polivy, 1991). Within the framework of the hierarchical models of the self, global self-esteem is more stable than the situation-specific domains (Epstein, 1991; Hattie, 1992), with research suggesting that self-esteem is not stable during the transition from middle to high school (Hair, 1999). It is possible that during this critical transition period, adolescents are developing the domain-specific areas that are relevant to them. Before this time, adolescents may focus more on global self-esteem than on domain-specific self-esteem.

Identity

The findings from the majority of studies on the developmental trajectory of identity are based on cross-sectional designs. In fact, in a review by Meeus (1996), only six longitudinal studies examining the developmental trajectory of identity were found between 1966 and 1993. This sample of studies includes those conducted with college students, and young and old adults, not just children. However, the cross-sectional data provide compelling evidence for developmental trends. They suggest that as young adolescents age, they move out of the foreclosed and diffused statuses of identity and into the moratorium and achieved statuses. These changes have been seen when comparing seventh and eighth graders (Streitmatter, 1988), early-, mid-, late-, and post-adolescents (Meeus, 1996; Meeus & Dekovic, 1995), and eighth and eleventh graders (Phinney et al., 1997). Limited longitudinal data support this trajectory. Perron, Vondtracek, Skorikov, Tremblay, and Corbiere (1998) assessed the vocational maturity and ethnic identity of high school students three times over a 15-month time period. The results demonstrated that minority students were more vocationally mature and had a more advanced ethnic identity as time progressed. Majority group students' ethnic identity decreased over this same period, possibly because of the low salience of ethnicity in their lives. Another study, of seventh and eighth grades over a 3-year period, found that at the follow-up in 10th and 11th grades, students showed an increase in identity search, but no increase in identity achievement, thus supporting the theory that adolescence is a time of identity exploration, not commitment (Erikson, 1968).

There are problems with drawing definitive conclusions from these data. The samples that have been used were diverse. Samples were drawn from different countries and different ethnicities. Although one could argue that using diverse samples would add credibility to the ego identity theory, all scales have not been normed on all populations and subpopulations and the scales that were used for assessment were not necessarily comparable across studies. To confound the findings further, there have been other studies which have not shown a linear developmental progression throughout adolescence (e.g., Archer, 1989). Such results are cosistent with theory and research that has argued and demonstrated that identity development may begin later than early adolescence and may not end until adulthood.

FACTORS AFFECTING DEVELOPMENT AND PROMOTION OF THE SELF

Self-Esteem

There is a general consensus among researchers that support from significant others is critical in the development of the self (Harter, 1999). There is some debate with regard to the sources of social support (e.g., parent, teachers, or peers) and their influence in either public or private domains. To date, research has found that an individual's perceptions of support are more predictive of self-esteem than more objective measures of support (Berndt & Burgy, 1996; Felson, 1993; John & Robbins, 1994; Rosenberg, 1979).

From a life span perspective, perceived approval from parents has been found to be more predictive of self-esteem than perceived approval from peers in younger children (Nikkari & Harter, 1993; Rosenberg, 1979). This appears to be related to young children's need to draw information from individuals of high importance in their lives, such as their parents. The relationship between perceived peer approval and self-esteem has been found to increase with development through adolescence, though the importance of perceived parental support does not appear to diminish (Harter, 1990; Oosterwegel & Oppenheimer, 1993).

The perceived perceptions of support from classmates in adolescence are more predictive of the adolescent's self-esteem than is perceived support from close friends (Harter, 1990). It is possible that perceived support from classmates may better represent acceptance from the "generalized other" or is considered more objective and credible than support from close friends. Perceived support from close friends seems to function as a secure psychological base to maintain a positive sense of self, but from which the adolescent can emerge to face the challenges of everyday life.

As youth move into adolescence, the opinions and support of specific subgroups become critical to their self-definition (Bynner, O'Malley, & Bachman, 1981; Kaplan, 1980). For example, if an adolescent fails to meet the standards or expectations of his or her dominant group, it may produce negative self-attitudes for the youth. In such cases, the adolescent may try to seek the approval of the group by performing behaviors that are admired by the group (e.g., delinquent behaviors in a gang; Kaplan, 1980).

Identity

The factors promoting identity development is another under-researched area, but there is enough evidence to suggest what may be important in promoting a positive identity. The greater part of the literature is based in the ethnic identity area.

Stevenson (1995) postulated that racial socialization is a construct that contributes to ethnic awareness and ethnic identity development over the life span. He found that greater racial socialization was inversely related to less rejection and more acceptance of the African American community (Cross, 1991). Other researchers have found similar linkages between parents' socialization of their children and identity, such as a relation between a more assertive/integrative socialization style or an authoritative parenting style and children who feel a stronger attachment and pride to their ethnic group (Demo & Hughes, 1990; Rosenthal & Feldman, 1992). Also, parents who reported that they prepared their children for a world in which race matters had children who were significantly more likely to be characterized as having been attuned to racial experiences (Marshall, 1995).

Factors that affect parents' ethnic identity will have an indirect effect on the ethnic socialization of the child (Hurtado, Gurin, & Peng, 1994). The language that is spoken by the family exemplifies this. Hurtado and Gurin (1987) examined the ethnic identity and bilingual attitudes of Mexican Americans from across the United States. The researchers found that speaking Spanish was a major way for the participants to retain their Chicano/a identity.

The evidence regarding the effects of peers on identity development is not conclusive. For instance, some have found that in the African American community, students may believe that they cannot achieve success if they have a strong association with their ethnic community. Racelessness, in which the individual rejects the African American community and takes on the norms of the majority culture, results (Arroyo & Zigler, 1995; Fordham, 1988). However, others have rejected this conclusion, finding that successful African American students have positive relationships with other African Americans and have a positive sense of self (Cook & Lugwig, 1997; Hemmings, 1998).

Aside from socialization affecting one's identity development, the way ethnic groups are labeled can also be important. For instance, the national census uses discrete racial variables to classify members of various ethnic groups for accounting purposes. By design, the census lumps new immigrants to the United States with those who have lived here for decades (Gimenez, 1992). The result would be a Mexican family that just immigrated to the United States being matched with that of members of a Mexican American family who were all born in the United States. Both of the groups, in turn, are placed within the domain of Hispanic to describe those from all of South and Central America and Mexico; many from these countries have never spoken Spanish, such as Brazilians who speak Portuguese or the various South and Central American Mayan and Zapotec groups that speak other languages. This would be analogous to placing all native speaking English speakers, such as European Americans and African Americans, into the same group (Forbes, 1992).

CONCLUSIONS

The self falls within the definition of a core element of developmental well-being. Aside from the theories that have been proposed over the past century or more, the empirical evidence of self-concept, self-esteem, and identity demonstrates the need for a strong sense of self in order for an individual to develop positively throughout life. There is also empirical evidence that demonstrates the malleability of each component of the self. Considering the theoretical effect that others have on an individual's identity and self-concept, it is not surprising to see that socialization by parents and social relationships with peers appear to affect the individual's sense of self. However, the one problem with this area of study is that much of the research is based on less than suitable designs. Nonetheless, there is enough substantial evidence to bring us to the conclusion that a strong and favorable sense of self, comprising self-concept, self-esteem, and identity, is one important component of positive development.

REFERENCES

Allport, G. W. (1961). *Pattern and growth in personality.* New York: Holt, Rinehart, and Winston.

Archer, S. L. (1989). Gender differences in identity development: Issues of process, domain, and timing. *Journal of Adolescence, 12,* 117–138.

Arroyo, C. G., & Zigler, E. (1995). Racial identity, academic achievement and the psychological well-being of economical disadvantages adolescents. *Journal of Personality and Social Psychology, 69,* 903–914.

Atkinson, D. R., Morten, G., & Sue, D. W. (1983). Proposed minority identity development model. In D. R. Atkinson, G. Morten, & D. W. Sue (Eds.), *Counseling American minorities: A cross cultural perspective* (pp. 32–42). Dubuque, IA: Brown.

Baldwin, J. A. (1981). Notes on an Africentric theory of Black personality. *The Western Journal of Black Studies, 5,* 172–179.

Baldwin, J. A., & Bell, Y. R. (1985). The African self-consciousness scale: An Africentric personality questionnaire. *Western Journal of Black Studies, 9,* 61–68.

Bem, D. J. (1972). Self-perception theory. In L. Berkowitz (Ed.), *Advances in experimental social psychology* (Vol. 6, pp. 1– 62). New York: Academic Press.

Berndt, T. J., & Burgy, L. (1996). The social self-concept. In B. A. Bracken (Ed.), *Handbook of self-concept* (pp. 171–209). New York: Wiley.

Boykin, A. W. (1985). The triple quandary and the schooling of Afro-American children. In U. Neisser (Ed.), *The school achievement of minority children: New perspectives.* Hillsdale, NJ: Lawrence Erlbaum Associates.

Bracken, B. (1996). Clinical applications of a context-dependent multi-dimensional model of self-concept. In B. Bracken (Ed.), *Handbook of self-concept* (pp. 463–505). New York: Wiley.

Brown, J. D. (1991). Accuracy and bias in self-knowledge. In C. R. Snyder & D. F. Forsyth (Eds.), *Handbook of social and clinical psychology: The health perspective* (pp. 158–178). New York: Pergamon Press.

Brown, R., & Kulik, J. (1977). Flashbulb memories. *Cognition, 5,* 73–99.

Bryne, B. M. (1984). The general/academic self-concept nomological network: A review of the construct validation research. *Review of Educational Research, 54,* 427–456.

Bynner, J. M., O'Malley, P. M., & Bachman, J. C. (1981). Self-esteem and delinquency revisited. *Journal of Youth and Adolescence, 10,* 407–441.

Chaiken, S., & Baldwin, M. W. (1981). Affective-cognitive consistency and the effect of salient behavioral information on the self-perception of attitudes. *Journal of Personality and Social Psychology, 41,* 1–12.

Conway, M. A. (1990). *Autobiographical memory: An introduction.* Philadelphia, Open University Press.

Cook, P. J., & Ludwig, J. (1997). Weighing the burden of acting White: Are there race differences in attitudes toward education. *Journal of Policy Analysis and Management, 16,* 356–278.

Cook, T. D., & Campbell, D. T. (1979). *Quasi-experimentation: Design and analysis issues for field settings*. Chicago: Rand McNally.

Cooley, C. H. (1922). *Human nature and the social order*. New York: Schribner.

Coopersmith, S. (1967). *The antecedents of self-esteem*. San Francisco: Freeman.

Coover, G. E., & Murphy, S. T. (2000). The communicated self: Exploring the interaction between self and social context. *Human Communication Research, 26*, 125–147.

Crain, R. M. (1996). The influences of age, race, and gender on child and adolescent multidimensional self-concept. In B. A. Bracken (Ed.), *Handbook of self-concept* (pp. 395–420). New York: Wiley.

Cross, W. E. (1991). *Shades of Black: Diversity in African-American identity*. Philadelphia: Temple University Press.

De Haan, L. G., & MacDermid, S. (1998). The relationship of individual and family factors to the psychological well-being of junior high school students living in urban poverty. *Adolescence, 33*, 73–89.

DeHaan, L. G., & MacDermid, S. M. (1999). Identity development as a mediating factor between urban poverty and behavioral outcomes for junior high school students. *Journal of Family and Economic Issues, 20*, 123–148.

Demo, D. H., & Savin-Williams, R. C. (1992). Self-concept stability and change during adolescence. In R. P. Lipka & T. M. Brinthaupt (Eds.), *Self-perspectives across the life span* (pp. 116–150). Albany, NY: State University of New York Press.

Duda, J. L. (1980). Achievement motivation among Navajo students. *Ethos, 8*, 316–331.

Dusek, J. B., & Flaherty, J. (1981). The development of the self during the adolescent years. *Monograph of the Society for Research in Child Development, 46*, 1–61.

Eccles, J. S., & Midgley, C. (1989). Stage/environment fit: Developmentally appropriate classrooms for early adolescents. In R. Ames & C. Ames (Eds.), *Research on motivation in education* (Vol. 3, pp. 139–181). San Diego, CA: Academic Press.

Epstein, S. (1981). The unity principle versus the reality and pleasure principles, or the tale or the scorpion and the frog. In M. D. Lynch, A. A. Norem-Hebeisen, & K. Gergen (Eds.), *Self-concept: Advances in theory and research* (pp. 82–110). Cambridge, MA: Ballinger.

Epstein, S. (1991). Cognitive-experiential self-theory: Implications for developmental psychology. In M. R. Gunnar & L. A. Sroufe (Eds.), *Self processes and development: The Minnesota Symposium on Child Development* (Vol. 23, pp. 111–137). Hillsdale, NJ: Lawrence Erlbaum Associates.

Erikson, E. H. (1959). Identity and the life cycle. *Psychological issues, Monograph 1*. New York: International University Press.

Erikson, E. H. (1968). *Identity: Youth and crisis*. New York: Norton.

Fan, C., & Karnilowicz, W. (1997). Measurement of definitions of success among Chinese and Australian girls. *Journal of Cross-Cultural Psychology, 28*, 589–599.

Fazio, R. H. (1987). Self-perception theory: A current perspective. In M. P. Zanna, J. M. Olson, & C. P. Herman (Eds.), *Social influence: The Ontario Symposium* (Vol. 5, pp. 129–150). Hillsdale, NJ: Lawrence Erlbaum Associates.

Felson, R. B. (1993). The (somewhat) social self: How other affect self-appraisals. In J. Suls (Ed.), *Psychological perspectives on the self* (Vol. 4, pp. 1–26). Hillsdale, NJ: Lawrence Erlbaum Associates.

Forbes, J. D. (1992). The Hispanic spin: Party politics and governmental manipulation of ethnic identity. *Latin American Perspectives, 19*, 59–78.

Ford, D. Y., & Harris, J. J. (1997). A study of the racial identity and achievement of Black males and females. *Roeper Review, 20*, 105–110.

Fordham, S. (1988). Racelessness as a factor in Black students' school success: Pragmatic strategy or pyrrhic victory? *Harvard Educational Review, 58*, 54–85.

Franzoi, S. L. (1996). *Social psychology*. Chicago: Brown & Benchmark Publishers.

Freeman, M. (1992). Self as narrative: The place of life history in studying the life span. In T. M. Brinthaupt & R. P. Lipka (Eds.), *The self: Definitional and methodological issues* (pp. 15–43). Albany, NY: State University of New York Press.

Frey, K. S., & Ruble, D. N. (1985). What children say when the teacher is not around: Conflicting goals in social comparison and performance assessment in the classroom. *Journal of Personality and Social Psychology, 48*, 550–562.

Frey, K. S., & Ruble, D. N. (1990). Strategies for comparative evaluation: Maintaining a sense of competence across the life span. In R. J. Sternberg & J. Kolligan, Jr. (Eds.), *Competence considered* (Vol. 7, pp. 167–189). New Haven, CT: Yale University Press.

Friedman, W. J. (1993). Memory for the time of past events. *Psychological Bulletin, 113,* 44–66.

Gaertner, S. L., Rust, M. C., Dovidio, J. F., Bachman, B. A., & Anastasio, P. A. (1996). The contact hypothesis: The role of a common ingroup identity on reducing intergroup bias among majority and minority group members. In J. L. Nye & A. M. Brower (Eds.), *Research on shared cognition in small groups* (pp. 230–259). Thousand Oaks, CA: Sage.

Gergen, K. J, & Gergen, M. M. (1988). Narrative and the self as relationship. In L. Berkowitz (Ed.), *Advances in experimental social psychology* (Vol. 21, pp. 17–56). New York: Academic Press.

Gilligan, C. (1982). *In a different voice: Psychological theory and women's development.* Cambridge, MA: Harvard University Press.

Gimenez, M. E. (1992). U.S. ethnic politics: Implications for Latin Americans. *Latin American Perspectives, 19,* 7–17.

Hair, E. C. (1999). *Longitudinal analysis of the self and personality.* Unpublished doctoral dissertation, Texas A&M University, College Station.

Hart, D., Fegeley, S., & Brengelman, D. (1993). Perceptions of past, present, and future selves among children and adolescents. *British Journal of Developmental Psychology, 11,* 265–282.

Harter, S. (1982). The perceived competence scale for children. *Child Development, 53,* 87–97.

Harter, S. (1985). *Manual for the Self-Perception Profile for Children (Revision of the Perceived Competence Scale for Children).* Denver, CO: University of Denver.

Harter, S. (1990). Causes, correlates, and the functional role of global self-worth. A life-span perspective. In R. Sternberg & J. Kolligan, Jr., (Eds.), *Competence considered* (pp. 67–98). New Haven, CT: Yale University Press.

Harter, S. (1998). The development of self-representations. In N. Eisenberg (Ed.), *Handbook of child psychology: Vol. 4, Social and personality development* (5th ed., pp. 553–600). New York: Wiley.

Harter, S. (1999). *The construction of the self: A developmental perspective.* New York: Guilford Press.

Harter, S., & Pike, R. (1984). The pictorial scale of perceived competence and social acceptance for younger children. *Child Development, 55,* 1969–1982.

Hattie, J. (1992). *Self-concept.* Hillsdale, NJ: Lawrence Erlbaum Associates.

Heatherton, T. F., & Polivy, J. (1991). Development and validation of a scale for measuring state self-esteem. *Journal of Personality and Social Psychology, 60,* 895–910.

Hemmings, A. (1998). The self-transformation of African-American achievers. *Youth & Society, 29,* 330–368.

Hurtado, A., & Gurin, P. (1987). Ethnic identity and bililngualism attitudes. *Hispanic Journal of Behavioral Sciences, 9,* 1–18.

Hurtado, A., Gurin, P., & Peng, T. (1994). Social identities: A framework for studying the adaptations of immigrants and ethnics: The adaptations of Mexicans in the United States. *Social Problems, 41,* 129–151.

James, W. (1890). *Principles of psychology.* Chicago: Encyclopedia Britannica.

James, W. (1892). *Psychology: The briefer course.* New York: Holt.

John, O. P., & Robins, R. W. (1994). Accuracy and bias in self-perception: Individual differences in self-enhancement and the role of narcissism. *Journal of Personality and Social Psychology, 66,* 206–219.

Kaplan, H. (1980). Self-management methods. In F. H. Kanfer & A. P. Goldstein (Eds.), *Helping people change: A textbook of methods* (2nd ed., pp. 232–258). New York: Pergamon Press.

Keith, L. K., & Bracken, B. A. (1996). Self-concept instrumentation; An historical and evaluative review. In B. A. Bracken (Ed.), *Handbook of self-concept* (pp. 91–170). New York: Wiley.

Kenny, D. A. (1979). *Correlation and causality.* New York: Wiley.

Kernis, M. H., & Waschull, S. B. (1995). The interactive roles of stability and level of self-esteem: Research and theory. In M. Zanna (Ed.), *Advances in Experimental Social Psychology* (Vol. 27, pp. 93–141).

Kihlstrom, J. F. (1993). What does the self look like? In T. K. Srull & R. S. Wyer, Jr. (Eds.), *The mental representation of trait and autobiographical knowledge about the self: Advances in social cognition* (Vol. 5, pp. 79–90). Hillsdale, NJ: Lawrence Erlbaum Associates.

Lewis, M., & Brooks-Gunn, J. (1979). *Social cognition and the acquisition of self.* New York: Plenum.

Marcia, J. E. (1966). Development and validation of ego identity status. *Journal of Personality and Social Psychology, 3,* 551–558.

Markus, H. (1977). Self-schemata and processing information about the self. *Journal of Personality and Social Psychology, 35,* 63–78.

Markus, H., & Nurius, P. (1986). Possible selves. *American Psychologist, 41,* 954–969.

Marsh, H. W. (1989). Age and sex effects in multiple dimensions of self-concept: Preadolescence to early adulthood. *Journal of Educational Psychology, 81,* 417–430.

Marsh, H. W. (1990). Confirmatory factor analysis of multitrait-multimethod data: The construct validation of multidimensional self-concept responses. *Journal of Personality, 58,* 661–692.

Marsh, H. W., & Hattie, J. (1996). Theoretical perspectives on the structure of self-concept. In B. A. Bracken (Ed.), *Handbook of self-concept* (pp. 38–90). New York: Wiley.

Marsh, H. W., Parker, J., & Barnes, J. (1985). Mulitdimensional adolescent self-concept: Their relationship to age, sex, and academic measures. *American Educational Research Journal, 22,* 422–444.

Marshall, S. (1995). Ethnic socialization of African American children: Implications for parenting, identity development, and academic achievement. *Journal of Youth and Adolescence, 24,* 377–396.

Martinez, R. O., & Dukes, R. L. (1997). *Journal of Youth and Adolescence, 26,* 503–516.

Maslow, A. H. (1954). *Motivation and personality.* New York: Harper & Row.

Matute-Bianchi, M. E. (1986). Ethnic identities and patterns of school success and failure among Mexican-decent and Japanese-American students in a California high school: An ethnographic analysis. *American Journal of Education, 95,* 233–255.

McAdams, D. P. (1995). What do we know when we know a person? *Journal of Personality, 63,* 365–396.

McCarthy, J., & Hoge, D. (1982). Analysis of age effects in longitudinal studies of adolescent self-esteem. *Developmental Psychology, 18,* 372–379.

Mead, G. H. (1934). *Mind, self, and society from the standpoint of a social behaviorist.* Chicago: University of Chicago Press.

Meeus, W. (1996). Studies on identity development in adolescence: An overview of research and some new data. *Journal of Youth and Adolescence, 25,* 569–598.

Meeus, W., & Dekovic, M. (1995). Identity development, parental and peer support in adolescence: Results of a national Dutch survey. *Adolescence, 30,* 931–944.

Meeus, W., Iedema, J., Helsen, M., & Vollebergh, W. (1999). Patterns of adolescent identity development: Review of literature and longitudinal analysis. *Developmental Review, 19,* 419–461.

Millar, M. G., & Tesser, A. (1989). The effects of affective-cognitive consistency and thought on the attitude-behavior relation. *Journal of Experimental Social Psychology, 25,* 189–202.

Munson, W. W. (1992). Self-esteem, vocational identity and career salience in high school students. *The Career Development Quarterly, 40,* 361–368.

Nobles, W. W. (1973). Psychological research and Black self-concept: A critical review. *Journal of Social Issues, 29,* 11–51.

Oosterwegel, A., & Oppenheimer, L. (1993). *The self-system: Developmental changes between and with self-concepts.* Hillsdale, NJ: Lawrence Erlbaum Associates.

Parham, T., & Helms, J. (1981). The influences of a Black student's racial identity attitudes on preference for counselor's race. *Journal of Counseling Psychology, 28,* 250–256.

Peevers, B., & Secord, P. (1973). Developmental changes in the attribution of descriptive concepts to persons. *Journal of Personality and Social Psychology, 27,* 120–128.

Perron, J., Vondracek, F. W., Skorikov, V. B., Tremblay, C., & Corbiere, M. (1998). A longitudinal study of vocational maturity and ethnic identity development. *Journal of Vocational Behavior, 52,* 409–424.

Phelan, P., Davidson, A. L., & Cao, H. T. (1991). Students' multiple worlds: Negotiating the boundaries of family, peer, and school cultures. *Anthropology and Education Quarterly, 22,* 224–250.

Phinney, J. (1989). Stages of ethnic identity development in minority group adolescents. *Journal of Early Adolescence, 9,* 34–49.

Phinney, J. (1990). Ethnic identity in adolescents and adults: Review of research. *Psychological Bulletin, 108,* 499–514.

Phinney, J. (1992). The multigroup ethnic identity measure: A new scale for use with diverse groups. *Journal of Adolescent Research, 7,* 156–176.

Phinney, J. S., Ferguson, D. B., & Tate, J. D. (1997). Intergroup attitudes among ethnic minority adolescents: A causal model. *Child Development, 68,* 955–969.

Phinney, J., & Tarver, S. (1988). Ethnic identity search and commitment in Black and White eighth graders. *Journal of Early Adolescence, 8,* 265–277.

Povinelli, D. J., Rulf, A. B., & Bierschwale, D. T. (1994). Absence of knowledge attribution and self-recognition in young chimpanzees. *Journal of Comparative Psychology, 108,* 74–80.

Prout, H. T., & Prout, S. M. (1996). Global self-concept: Its structure, measurement, and relation to academic achievement. In B. A. Bracken (Ed.), *Handbook of self-concept* (pp. 259–286). New York: Wiley.

Roberts, R. E., Phinney, J. S., Masse, L. C., Chen, Y. R., Roberts, C. R., & Romero, A. (1999). The structure of ethnic identity of young adolescents from diverse ethnocultural groups. *Journal of Early Adolescence, 19,* 301–322.

Rogers, C. R. (1951). *Client centered therapy.* Boston: Houghton Mifflin.

Rosenberg, M. (1979). *Conceiving the self.* New York: Basic Books.

Rosenberg, M. (1986). Self-concept from middle childhood through adolescence. In J. Suls & A. G. Greenwald (Eds.), *Psychological perspectives on the self* (Vol. 3, pp. 107–135). Hillsdale, NJ: Lawrence Erlbaum Associates.

Rosenthal, D., & Feldman, S. (1992). The relationship between behavior and ethnic identity in Chinese-American and Chinese-Australian adolescents. *International Journal of Psychology, 27,* 19–31.

Rotheram, M. J., & Phinney, J. (1989). Introduction: Definitions and perspectives in the study of children's ethnic socialization. In J. Phinney & M. J. Rotheram (Eds.), *Children's ethnic socialization: Pluralism and development* (pp. 10–28). Newbury Park, CA: Sage.

Rubin, D. C. (1986). *Autobiographical memory.* New York: Cambridge University Press.

Ruvolo, A., & Markus, H. (1992). Possible selves and performance: The power of self-relevant imagery. *Social Cognition, 9,* 95–124.

Schlenker, B. R., & Trudeau, J. V. (1990). The impact of self-presentations on private self-beliefs: Effects of prior self-beliefs and misattribution, *Journal of Personality and Social Psychology, 58,* 22–32.

Shalveson, R. J., & Bolus, R. (1982). Self-concept: The interplay of theory and methods. *Journal of Educational Psychology, 74,* 3–17.

Shavelson, R. J., Hubner, J. J., & Stanton, J. C. (1976). Self-concept: Validation of construct interpretations. *Review of Educational Research, 46,* 407–441.

Simmons, R. G., & Blyth, D. A. (1987). *Moving into adolescence: The impact of pubertal change and school context.* New York: Aldine de Gruyter.

Spencer, M. B., & Markstrom-Adams, C. (1990). Identity processes among racial and ethnic minority children in America. *Child Development, 61,* 290–310.

Stevenson, H. (1995). Relationship of adolescent perceptions of racial socialization to racial identity. *Journal of Black Psychology, 21,* 49–70.

Streitmatter, J. L. (1989). Identity development and academic achievement in early adolescence. *Journal of Early Adolescence, 9,* 99–116.

Stretmatter, J. L. (1988). Ethnicity as a mediating variable of early adolescent identity development. *Journal of Adolescence, 11,* 335–346.

Tajfel, H. (1978) *Differententiation between social groups: Studies in the psychology of inter-group relations.* London: Academic Press.

Tajfel, H., & Turner, J. (1986). The social identity theory of intergroup behavior. In S. Worchel & W. Austin (Eds.), *Psychology of intergroup relations* (pp. 7–24). Chicago: Nelson-Hall.

von Hippel, W., Sekaquaptewa, D., & Vargas, P. (1997). The linguistic intergroup bias as an implicit indicator of prejudice. *Journal of Experimental Social Psychology, 33,* 490–509.

Waterman, A. S. (1985). Identity in the context of adolescent psychology. In A. S. Waterman (Ed.), *Identity in adolescence: Processes and contents.* San Francisco: Jossey-Bass.

Wilson, T. D. (1985). Strangers to ourselves: The origins and accuracy of beliefs about one's own mental states. In J. H. Harvey & G. Weary (Eds.), *Attribution: Basic issues and applications* (pp. 9–36). New York: Academic Press.

Wilson, T. D., & LaFleur, S. J. (1995). Knowing what you'll do: Effects of analyzing reasons on self-prediction. *Journal of Personality and Social Psychology, 68,* 21–35.

Wilson, T. D., & Schooler, J. W. (1991). Thinking too much: Introspection can reduce the quality of preferences and decisions. *Journal of Personality and Social Psychology, 60*, 181–192.

Witherspoon, K. M., Speight, S. L., & Thomas, A. J. (1997). Racial identity attitudes, school achievement, and academic self-efficacy among African American high school students. *Journal of Black Psychology, 23*, 344–357.

Wylie, R. C. (1989). *Measures of self-concept*. Lincoln, NE: University of Nebraska Press.

Zaff, J. F. (1999). *Ethnic identity development and the definitions of success among African American men: An ecological model*. Unpublished doctoral dissertation.

19

Prosocial Behavior, Empathy, and Sympathy

Nancy Eisenberg
Arizona State University, Tempe

INTRODUCTION

Empathy-related responding and prosocial behavior are considered important aspects of social competence and positive development. This is because they are believed to promote positive interactions and relationships among people and, in many cases, to reflect caring or compassion for others.

OPERATIONAL DEFINITIONS AND DESCRIPTION
OF THE CONSTRUCT

Prosocial behavior is defined as voluntary behavior intended to benefit another. Prosocial behavior is not necessarily other-oriented; indeed, helpful actions may be enacted for selfish reasons, such as the desire to gain approval or material compensation. However, a subtype of prosocial behavior—*altruism*—is viewed as especially positive and moral. A representative definition of altruism is intrinsically motivated voluntary behavior intended to benefit another; that is, prosocial behaviors motivated by internal motives, such as concern for others or internalized values, goals, and self-rewards, rather than by the expectation of concrete or social rewards or the avoidance of punishment (Eisenberg & Mussen, 1989). There is some debate, in both the philosophical and social psychological literature, regarding if any prosocial behavior is ever truly selfless or altruistic, or if all prosocial be-

253

havior is based on selfish motives (e.g., avoidance of guilt; Batson, 1991; Cialdini, Brown, Lewis, Luce, & Neuberg, 1997).

It has been argued repeatedly that much (but not necessarily all) altruistic behavior—especially that which is most clearly selfless—is motivated by sympathy or empathy (Batson, 1998; Eisenberg & Fabes, 1998; Hoffman, 1982). However, in recent theory, empathy and sympathy have been differentiated. *Empathy* can be defined as an affective response that stems from the apprehension or comprehension of another's emotional state or condition, and which is identical or very similar to what the other person is feeling or would be expected to feel. It has been argued that empathy sometimes, but not always, leads to sympathy. *Sympathy* is defined as an affective response that frequently stems from empathy (but can derive directly from perspective taking or other cognitive processing), and consists of feelings of sorrow or concern for the distressed or needy other (rather than the same emotion as the other person). Sympathetic concern or compassion, more than empathy, would be expected to motivate altruistic behavior because empathy may dissipate before an individual experiences sympathy or may be experienced as aversive and lead to a self-focus (Eisenberg & Fabes, 1998). Unfortunately, in much of the research, it is difficult to differentiate empathy from sympathy.

Prosocial and altruistic behaviors have been assessed in many ways, including self- or other-reports or observed behavior (either observed in experimental contexts or in natural settings). Most of the time it is difficult to ascertain the motives behind prosocial actions, so it is difficult to know if prosocial behaviors are altruistic or not. Similarly, sympathy (or empathy) has been assessed with self-reports, other-reports, and facial or physiological reactions to viewing others in distress (Losoya & Eisenberg, 2001). Self- or other-reports of prosocial or empathy-related responding can be obtained in reaction to specific situations or stimuli (e.g., in a situation in which a distressed child needs help) or with questionnaire measures that tap dispositional prosocial behavior, altruism, sympathy, or empathy. Self- and other-report measures often are internally reliable, and adequate inter-rater reliabilities often have been obtained for observed indexes of prosocial behavior or empathy/sympathy. Evidence of validity of the many measures of these constructs varies considerably, depending on the specific measure.

CONCEPTUAL BASE FOR THE ELEMENTS

As previously noted, Batson (1991), Hoffman (1982), and others have hypothesized that sympathy (or empathy) is closely related to altruism because it often motivates selfless, other-oriented prosocial acts. According to this view, it is important to try to differentiate truly altruistic behavior from prosocial behavior motivated by baser motives and to differentiate sympathy from empathic reactions that either do not turn into sympathy and/or become so arousing that they motive the individual to attend to his or her own needs rather than the needs of others (i.e., personal distress; see Eisenberg et al., 1994; Eisenberg & Fabes, 1998). In studies in which investigators try to assess altruism and sympathy, there tends to be a positive relation between situational or dispositional sympathy and prosocial actions, such as helping or sharing, that are likely altruistic in motive (e.g., Batson, 1991, 1998; Eisenberg & Fabes, 1998; Eisenberg et al., 1991, 1999; Zahn-Waxler, Radke-Yarrow, Wagner, & Chapman, 1992). For example, children who show facial concern and heart rate deceleration (an index of outwardly directed attention) when they see a needy or distressed person in a videotape are more likely to assist this individual or others who are in a similar situation than are other children (Eisenberg & Fabes, 1990, 1998; Zahn-Waxler, Cole, Welsh, & Fox, 1995). Relations between measures of prosocial behavior and empathy-related responding vary considerably across studies, probably because nonaltruistic prosocial behaviors are unlikely to be consistently associated with sympathy or empathy.

ARE PROSOCIAL BEHAVIOR/ALTRUISM AND EMPATHY/SYMPATHY POSITIVE CHARACTERISTICS?

By definition, altruism is a positive characteristic valued in most societies. Moreover, prosocial behaviors, even when they are not altruistically motivated, often may be valued by others due to the benefits they provide. However, prosocial behaviors that are altruistic probably are more likely than prosocial actions that are not altruistic to be associated with positive adjustment.

In any case, there does appear to be a positive relation between prosocial behavior (generally undifferentiated in research in regard to altruistic motives) and children's self-esteem, especially for older children (see review in Eisenberg & Fabes, 1998). In addition, prosocial individuals tend to be viewed by others as relatively socially competent and as constructive copers (e.g., Eisenberg, Fabes, Karbon, et al., 1996), and they are high in positive social interactions with peers (e.g., Farver & Branstetter, 1994) and are low in aggression (e.g., Ladd & Profilet, 1996) and other types of externalizing behavior (Murphy, Shepard, Eisenberg, Fabes, & Guthrie, 1999). In general, prosocial children tend to be relatively popular with peers (Coie, Dodge, & Kupersmidt, 1990; Wentzel & McNamara, 1999), which suggests that prosocial behavior is associated with positive social outcomes in development.

As noted previously, sympathy is related to prosocial behavior and is viewed as a motivator of other-oriented actions; thus, it can be viewed as leading to, or associated with, positive development. Children's sympathy (and sometimes empathy) also has been positively related to social competence (Eisenberg, Fabes, Murphy, et al., 1996; Eisenberg & Miller, 1987; Murphy et al., 1999), as well as children's attentional and behavioral regulation (Eisenberg, Fabes, Murphy, et al., 1996; Eisenberg et al., 1998; Murphy et al., 1999), sometimes even when predicting across time. Thus, sympathy generally would be expected to predict positive development. However, nearly all the extant research is correlational, so it is impossible to verify cause and effect (although some research linking sympathy to prosocial behavior in adults is experimental; Batson, 1991, 1998).

DEVELOPMENTAL STABILITY OF PROSOCIAL BEHAVIOR
AND EMPATHY/SYMPATHY

There is considerable evidence that prosocial behavior is moderately consistent across time and contexts (Graziano & Eisenberg, 1997). Evidence of consistency is weakest for infants and preschoolers (e.g., Dunn & Munn, 1986; Eisenberg, Wolchik, Goldberg, & Engel, 1992), although some evidence of consistency has been found in the early years (Radke-Yarrow & Zahn-Waxler, 1984). There seems to be at least modest consistency by the late preschool years; for example, Baumrind (reported in Eisenberg & Mussen, 1989) found that social responsible, prosocial behavior in the preschool years (as rated by observers) was significantly correlated with similar behavior when in elementary school 5 to 6 years later. By elementary school and early adolescence, there is considerable evidence of consistency over a year or more in self- or other-reports of prosocial behavior or sympathy (Eisenberg, Shell et al., 1987; Eisenberg, Miller, Shell, McNalley, & Shea, 1991; Tremblay, Vitaro, Gaganon, Piche, & Royer, 1992; Vitaro, Gagnon, & Tremblay, 1991). For example, Eisenberg, Shell et al., (1987) found that donating to charity was consistent from age 7–8 years to age 9–10, and from age 9–10 to 11–12. Helping (e.g., helping pick up paper clips or spilled papers), which was assessed at ages 9 to 10 and 11 to 12, also was relatively stable over this 2-year time period. Further, self- and mother-reported prosocial behaviors were both consistent over years, as was helping by doing extra tasks for the experimenter such as filling out extra questionnaires (Eisenberg et al., 1991; Eisenberg, Carlo, Murphy, & Van Court, 1995). In adolescence, there is additional evidence of stability over weeks or years in both prosocial behavior (Eisenberg et al., 1995) and sympathy (Davis & Franzoi, 1991; Eisenberg et al., 1995).

Evidence of stability over more than 4 years of time is scarce. However, Eisenberg et al. (1999) found that preschoolers' naturally occurring, spontaneously emitted sharing behavior (which is viewed as likely to reflect altruism because such behaviors were not due to mere compliance and entailed a cost) predicted prosocial behavior—observed and reported—years later, as well as self-reported prosocial tendencies in early adulthood. In addition, spontaneous sharing predicted self- or friend-reported dispositional sympathy in early adulthood. Thus, early altruistic behavior in early childhood predicted prosocial tendencies into early adulthood. In contrast, there were few relations with sympathy or prosocial behavior in adolescence and adulthood for preschoolers' prosocial behaviors that were not viewed as altruistic (i.e., low cost prosocial acts or acts in response to verbal or nonverbal requests from peers, which likely reflected compliance more than altruism). One exception to this pattern was a relation between early compliant sharing and later self-reported helping behavior (but not actual prosocial behavior or other-reported prosocial tendencies). Consequently, it appeared that continuity over time was limited to prosocial behaviors that were most like to be relatively altruistic.

There also is evidence of continuity in prosocial responding in adulthood. Oliner and Oliner (1988), in a retrospective study of Europeans who had previously rescued Jews from the Nazis in World War II, found that rescuers were more likely than peers who did not engage in rescuing activities to report involvement in a number of prosocial activities during the year prior to their interview (e.g., feeding the sick or aged or visiting the ill, making telephone calls on behalf of a group or cause, or helping raise money for a group or cause). Thus, using a sample of verified altruists, the Oliners obtained evidence of consistency in prosocial responding across 3 to 4 decades.

Although some of the research on consistency has involved laboratory procedures that might lack generalizability, other studies have involved observation of children in real-life interactions (e.g., Eisenberg et al., 1999) or real-life, significant acts of prosocial behavior (e.g., Oliner & Oliner, 1988). Thus, at least some of the data indicating consistency reflect responding in real world contexts.

LINKAGES TO ADULT POSITIVE FUNCTIONING

There is little research linking prosocial behavior or empathy/sympathy in childhood to positive outcomes in adulthood. The most relevant data are probably those in the longitudinal study previously discussed. Eisenberg et al. (1999) found that preschoolers' spontaneously emitted sharing behaviors were related to the self-reported tendency to take others' perspectives in adolescence and early adulthood, as well as to other prosocial characteristics such as social responsibility and suppression of aggression. Although it is likely that childhood prosocial behavior predicts social competence in adulthood, this hypothesis has not, to my knowledge, been tested.

FACTORS ASSOCIATED WITH THE DEVELOPMENT OR PROMOTION OF PROSOCIAL BEHAVIOR AND EMPATHY/SYMPATHY

Numerous variables have been found to predict both prosocial behavior and sympathy. These variables pertain to heredity, temperament, sociocognitive development, and socialization. Demographic variables such as age and sex also are related to prosocial responding. In most of the research, findings reflect correlations and indicate associations rather than causal relations.

The Role of Biology

Evidence from well designed twin studies suggests that heredity contributes to the development of sympathy and prosocial behavior. Zahn-Waxler, Emde, and colleagues (Plomin et al., 1993; Zahn-Waxler, Robinson, & Emde, 1992) examined twin toddlers' reactions to simulations of distress in others (in both home and laboratory settings). Estimates of heritability indicated a genetic component for empathic concern (sympathy), prosocial acts, and maternal reports of prosocial acts at 14 months of age; however, the variance accounted for by heredity was much less than 50% for all measures but maternal reports. When the toddlers were 20 months old, empathic concern during simulations of distress and maternal reports of prosocial acts (but not prosocial acts) continued to show genetic contributions. Unresponsiveness and active indifference in response to another's distress also showed genetic influence at both time periods (Zahn-Waxler, Robinson et al., 1992). Moreover, Plomin et al. (1993) found that genetic factors partially accounted for stability from 14 to 20 months in empathy. These findings are consistent with twin studies in adulthood, which indicate that self-reports of sympathy and prosocial behavior have a genetic basis (e.g., Rushton, Fulker, Neale, Nias, & Eysenck, 1986). They suggest that empathy-related responding and prosocial behavior have a genetic basis, but that the environment also contributes substantially to the development of these aspects of functioning. However, given that there are few studies with children or studies involving measures other than self-report, replication of these findings is desirable.

Temperament

Temperament is believed to be influenced by constitutional as well as environmental factors. Recent evidence suggests that some aspects of children's temperament are related to individual differences in their prosocial behavior and sympathy. Prosocial children tend to be temperamentally well-regulated (Eisenberg, Fabes, Karbon et al., 1996; see Eisenberg & Fabes, 1998), as are sympathetic children (Eisenberg & Fabes, 1995; Eisenberg, Fabes, Murphy, et al., 1996; Eisenberg et al., 1998; Murphy et al., 1999). In addition, resilient children, who appear to be optimally regulated, tend to be prosocial and empathic (Strayer & Roberts, 1989). Eisenberg and colleagues have argued that children who are well regulated can manage their empathic arousal so that they do not become over-aroused in empathy inducing contexts and, thus, are likely to experience sympathy and behave in an altruistic manner.

In general, prosocial behavior and sympathy/empathy have been linked to dispositional positive emotionality (Robinson, Zahn-Waxler, & Ernde, 1994; see Eisenberg & Fabes, 1998, for a review). Further, prosocial behavior has been consistently associated with low negative emotionality, as has children's, but not infants' or adults', sympathy (e.g., Eisenberg, Fabes, Karbon, et al., 1996; Wentzel & McNamara, 1999; see Eisenberg & Fabes, 1998). It is likely that sympathy is especially negatively related to externalizing types of negative emotion such as anger, which often are salient to adults when they rate children's negative emotionality. In contrast, relations of negative emotionality to empathy have been quite inconsistent (Eisenberg & Fabes, 1998). However, children who are prone to intense emotions but also are well regulated appear to be prone to sympathy (Eisenberg, Fabes, Murphy, et al., 1996; Eisenberg et al., 1998). Such children are likely to experience another's distress but can adequately regulate it so that they are likely to feel sympathy.

Sociocognitive Functioning

Children who are skilled at understanding others' emotions and thoughts are relatively likely to be prosocial (e.g., Carlo et al., 1991; Roberts & Strayer, 1996). In addition, children who are relatively mature in their moral reasoning about prosocial moral conflicts are relatively likely to engage in prosocial behavior (e.g., Eisenberg & Fabes, 1998; Eisenberg et al., 1987; Eisenberg, et al., 1991). Further, prosocial children report being less likely than other children to attribute hostile intentions to others in situations involving provocation and are more likely to evaluate the use of aggressive responses in such situations negatively (Nelson & Crick, 1999). Thus, prosocial children appear to be relatively sophisticated in their social cognitive skills. Further, children high in perspective taking or moral judgment are especially likely to be prosocial if they also are high in sympathy (Knight, Johnson, Carlo, & Eisenberg, 1994; Miller, Eisenberg, Fabes, & Shell, 1996).

Socialization

There is a substantial body of literature linking children's prosocial behavior or sympathy to caregivers' socialization practices. However, because most of the research on the socialization of prosocial responding is correlational in design, it is impossible to draw firm conclusions about cause-and-effect relations from extant research.

Parental Disciplinary Practices.   Parents who are supportive *and* expect and demand appropriate behavior from their children (i.e., authoritative parents) tend to have children who are high in prosocial behavior. In contrast, a parenting style that typically involves physical punishment, threats, and an authoritarian style of parenting tends to be associated low prosocial behavior and sympathy in children (Dekovic & Janssens, 1992; Krevans & Gibbs, 1996; Robinson et al., 1994).

An aspect of authoritative parenting that appears to play an important role in prosocial development is parental use of reasoning (inductions) as discipline. Although the results of studies are not entirely consistent (e.g., McGrath & Power, 1990), generally high parental use of inductive discipline is related to both high prosocial behavior and sympathy in offspring (Krevans & Gibbs, 1996; Miller, Eisenberg, Fabes, Shell, & Gular, 1989; also see McGrath, Wilson, & Frassetto, 1995, for experimental laboratory evidence). Parental inductions appear to be useful in fostering prosocial behavior even with toddlers if mothers deliver them with affective force (Zahn-Waxler, Radke-Yarrow, & King, 1979). It is likely that parents' use of inductions helps children to understand and take others' perspectives and, consequently, sympathize with them (Hoffman, 1983). Parental use of reasoning also may help children to understand the consequences of their behavior and can provide reasons that children can use to guide their behavior in future situations.

Cold, punitive parenting generally has been either unrelated (Janssens & Gerris, 1992) or negatively related (Dekovic & Janssens, 1992) to children's prosocial behavior and empathy (see Eisenberg & Fabes, 1998, for a review). Similarly, high levels of familial or maternal dominant negative emotion (e.g., anger) have been linked to low levels of sympathetic concern and high levels of self-focused personal distress (Crockenberg, 1985; Eisenberg, Fabes, et al., 1992). If children are regularly punished for failing to engage in prosocial behavior, they may start to believe that the reason for helping others is primarily to avoid punishment (Hoffman, 1983).

The combination of parental warmth and parenting practices that promote prosocial behavior—not parental warmth by itself—seems to be especially effective for fostering prosocial tendencies in children. Thus, children tend to be more prosocial when parental warmth and support are combined with the use of reasoning for discipline and demands for mature behavior (Dekovic & Janssens, 1992; Janssens & Dekovic, 1997). In a study in which inductions were not correlated with prosocial behavior, maternal and paternal use of induction, combined with parental demands for mature behavior and low power assertion, was linked to children's self-reported empathy, which in turn was associated with teachers' reports of the children's prosocial behavior (Janssens & Gerris, 1992).

Modeling and the Communication of Values. Children tend to imitate other people's helping and sharing behaviors, even those of peers or unknown adults (see Eisenberg & Fabes, 1998). They are especially likely to imitate adults with whom they have a positive relationship (Hart & Fegley, 1995; Yarrow, Scott, & Waxler, 1973). This may be why parents and children tend to be similar in their levels of prosocial behavior and sympathy (Clary & Miller, 1986; Eisenberg, Fabes, et al., 1992).

In a study of real-life altruistic exemplars, people who had risked their lives to rescue Jews from the Nazis in Europe during World War II were interviewed many years later. When they were asked to recall the values that they had learned from their parents and other influential adults, 44% of the rescuers mentioned generosity and caring for others compared with only 21% of bystanders, that is, adults from the same communities who had not been involved in rescue activities (Oliner & Oliner, 1988). Rescuers also were six times more likely than bystanders to report that their parents taught them that values related to caring should be applied to all human beings. Thus, parental teachings may determine whether children are prosocial with only those in their own group or with people from other groups.

Opportunities for Prosocial Activities. Providing children with opportunities to engage in helpful activities can increase their willingness to engage in prosocial tasks at a later time (Eisenberg, Cialdini, McCreath, & Shell, 1987; Staub, 1979). In the home, opportunities to help others that seem to be linked to prosocial behavior include household tasks that are performed on a routine basis and benefit others (Richman, Berry, Bittle, & Himan, 1988), although performance of household tasks may foster prosocial actions primarily toward family members (Grusec, Goodnow, & Cohen, 1996). Adolescents' voluntary community service, such as working in homeless shelters or other community agencies, also can be a way of gaining experience in helping others and increasing their feelings of commitment to helping others (Yates & Youniss, 1996).

Socialization in the School Context

This is initial evidence that school-based programs designed to foster prosocial behavior can be effective. An example is the Child Development Project in the East Bay of the San Francisco area (Battistich, Solomon, Watson, & Schaps, 1997; Battistich, Watson, Solomon, Schaps, & Solomon, 1991). This 7-year longitudinal intervention included some parent involvement and school-wide activities, but its primary intervention component was training teachers to provide opportunities for children to (a) engage in cooperative learning activities; (b) practice important social skills such as understanding of others' thoughts and feelings; (c) provide meaningful help to others (e.g., school and community service and helping peers); and (d) discuss and reflect on their own and others' behaviors as they relate to the values of fairness, concern and respect for others, and social responsibility. In addition, teachers were trained to use reasoning in their disciplinary actions whenever possible. The program led to increases in elementary-school students' prosocial behavior, conflict-resolution skills, and prosocial moral reasoning (Solomon, Watson, Delucchi, Schaps, & Battistich, 1988; Solomon, Battistich, & Watson, 1993). Such evidence, because of the experimental design, supports the notion that the intervention procedures actually caused children's in prosocial responding.

In recent years, the concept of the school as a caring community has become a central part of similar interventions (Battistich, Solomon, Watson, & Schaps, 1994; Battistich et al., 1997). The caring school community is one in which teachers and students are concerned about and support one another, share common values, norms, goals, and a sense of belonging, and participate in group decisions. Initial findings suggest that enhancing a sense of community promotes children's concern for others and prosocial behavior.

AGE AND SEX DIFFERENCES

Age-related Changes in Prosocial Behavior and Empathy/Sympathy

In a recent meta-analysis, Eisenberg and Fabes (1998) found a significant, positive effect for age differences in prosocial behavior; as children get older, prosocial behaviors are more likely to occur. This pattern was found for all cross-age group comparisons from preschool onward, although there was considerable variation in the magnitude of effect sizes across different age group comparison. Many factors could account for this age-related change, including advances in perspective-taking skills, moral judgment, self-regulation, and sympathy (which also increases with age; Eisenberg & Fabes, 1998), as well as socialization influences.

Sex Differences in Prosocial Behavior and Empathy/Sympathy

A recent meta-analysis indicates that girls are slightly more likely to engage in prosocial behavior than are boys. This sex difference appears to be greater for kindness/consideration than for instrumental modes of prosocial behavior (Eisenberg & Fabes, 1998). In addition, females, including girls, tend to report more sympathy/empathy than do males and score higher on observational measures of empathy (involving facial and gestural reactions); they did not differ significantly on nonverbal facial or physiological measures (Eisenberg & Fabes, 1998). It is unclear if females actually are more empathic or sympathetic, or merely believe themselves to be. Clearly, the feminine gender role is more consistent with sympathetic responding than is the masculine gender role; thus, females may be more likely than males to interpret their emotional responses to others' emotion or need as empathy or sympathy. It is also likely that girls are socialized to be more concerned with others' needs than are boys and, thus, are more likely than boys to process their empathic responses as sympathy.

CONCLUSIONS

Currently, there is considerable evidence that empathy-related and prosocial responding are related not only to each other but also to other positive aspects of human functioning. However, there currently is little longitudinal research examining either the long-term stability of these aspects of functioning or their correlates in adulthood. Moreover, most of the research on variables related to the existence and socialization of empathy-related and prosocial responding is correlational, so it is impossible to draw firm conclusions regarding causal relations. More experimental interventions designed to promote empathy-related responding and prosocial behavior, as well as prospective longitudinal studies, are needed to tease out cause-and-effect relationships.

REFERENCES

Batson, C. D. (1991). *The altruism question: Toward a social-psychological answer.* Hillsdale, NJ: Lawrence Erlbaum Associates.

Batson, C. B. (1998). Altruism and prosocial behavior. In D. T. Gilbert, S. T. Fiske, & G. Lindzey (Eds.), *The handbook of social psychology.* (Vol. 2, pp. 282–316). Boston: McGraw-Hill.

Battistich, V., Solomon, D., Watson, M., & Schaps, E. (1994, April). *Students and teachers in caring classrooms and school communities.* Paper presented at the meeting of American Educational Research Association, New Orleans, LA.

Battistich, V., Solomon, D., Watson, M., & Schaps, E. (1997). Caring school communities. *Educational Psychologist, 32,* 137–151.

Battistich, V., Watson, M., Solomon, D., Schaps, E., & Solomon, J. (1991). The Child Development Project: A comprehensive program for the development of prosocial character. In W. M. Kurtines & J. L. Gerwirtz (Eds.), *Handbook of moral behavior and development: Vol. 3. Application* (pp. 1–34). Hillsdale, NJ: Lawrence Erlbaum Associates.

Carlo, G., Knight, G., Eisenberg, N., & Rotenberg, K. (1991). Cognitive processes and prosocial behaviors among children: The role of affective attributions and reasoning. *Developmental Psychology*, *27*, 456–461.

Cialdini, R. B., Brown, S. L., Lewis, B. P., Luce, C., & Neuberg, S. L. (1997). Reinterpreting the empathy-altruism relationship: When one into one equals oneness. *Personality and Social Psychology*, *73*, 481–494.

Clary, E. G., & Miller J. (1986). Socialization and situational influences on sustained altruism. *Child Development*, *57*, 1358–1369.

Coie, J. D., Dodge, K. A., & Kupersmidt, J. B. (1990). Peer group behavior and social status. In S. R. Asher & J. D. Coie (Eds.), *Peer rejection in childhood* (pp. 17–59). Cambridge, England: Cambridge University Press.

Crockenberg, S. (1985). Toddlers' reactions to maternal anger. *Merrill-Palmer Quarterly*, *31*, 361–373.

Davis, M. H., & Franzoi, S. (1991). Stability and change in adolescent self-consciousness and empathy. *Journal of Research in Personality*, *25*, 70–87.

Dekovic, M., & Janssens, J. M. A. M. (1992). Parents' child-rearing style and children's sociometric status. *Developmental Psychology*, *28*, 925–932.

Dunn, J., & Munn, P. (1986). Siblings and the development of prosocial behavior. *International Journal of Behavioral Development*, *9*, 265–284.

Eisenberg, N., Carlo, G., Murphy, B., & Van Court, P. (1995). Prosocial development in late adolescence: A longitudinal study. *Child Development*, *66*, 1179–1197.

Eisenberg, N., Cialdini, R., McCreath, H., & Shell, R. (1987). Consistency-based compliance: When and why do children become vulnerable? *Journal of Personality and Social Psychology*, *52*, 1174–1181.

Eisenberg, N., & Fabes, R. A. (1990). Empathy: Conceptualization, assessment, and relation to prosocial behavior. *Motivation and Emotion*, *14*, 131–149.

Eisenberg, N., & Fabes, R. A. (1995). The relation of young children's vicarious emotional responding to social competence, regulation, and emotionality. *Cognition and Emotion*, *9*, 203–228.

Eisenberg, N., & Fabes, R. A. (1998). Prosocial development. In W. Damon (Series Ed.) & N. Eisenberg (Vol. Ed.), *Handbook of child psychology: Vol. 3. Social, emotional, and personality development* (5th ed., pp. 701–778). New York: Wiley.

Eisenberg, N., Fabes, R. A., Carlo, G., Troyer, D., Speer, A. L., Karbon, M., & Switzer, G. (1992). The relations of maternal practices and characteristics to children's vicarious emotional responsiveness. *Child Development*, *63*, 583–602.

Eisenberg, N., Fabes, R. A., Karbon, M., Murphy, B. C., Wosinski, M., Polazzi, L., Carlo, G., & Juhnke, C. (1996). The relations of children's dispositional prosocial behavior to emotionality, regulation, and social functioning. *Child Development*, *67*, 974–992.

Eisenberg, N., Fabes, R. A., Murphy, B., Karbon, M., Maszk, P., Smith, M., O'Boyle, C., & Suh, K. (1994). The relations of emotionality and regulation to dispositional and situational empathy-related responding. *Journal of Personality and Social Psychology*, *66*, 776–797.

Eisenberg, N., Fabes, R. A., Murphy, B., Karbon, M., Smith, M., & Maszk, P. (1996). The relations of children's dispositional empathy-related responding to their emotionality, regulation, and social functioning. *Developmental Psychology*, *32*, 195–209.

Eisenberg, N., Fabes, R. A., Shepard, S. A., Murphy, B. C., Jones, J., & Guthrie, I. K. (1998). Contemporaneous and longitudinal prediction of children's sympathy from dispositional regulation and emotionality. *Developmental Psychology*, *34*, 910–924.

Eisenberg, N., Guthrie, I. K., Murphy, B. C., Shepard, S. A., Cumberland, A., & Carlo, G. (1999). Consistency and development of prosocial dispositions: A longitudinal study. *Child Development*, *70*, 1360–1372.

Eisenberg, N., & Miller, P. (1987). The relation of empathy to prosocial and related behaviors. *Psychological Bulletin*, *101*, 91–119.

Eisenberg, N., Miller, P. A., Shell, R., McNalley, S., & Shea, C. (1991). Prosocial development in adolescence: A longitudinal study. *Developmental Psychology*, *27*, 849–857.

Eisenberg, N., & Mussen, P. (1989). *The roots of prosocial behavior in children*. Cambridge, England: Cambridge University Press.

Eisenberg, N., Shell, R., Pasternack, J., Lennon, R., Beller, R., & Mathy, R. M. (1987). Prosocial development in middle childhood: A longitudinal study. *Developmental Psychology, 24*, 712–718.

Eisenberg, N., Wolchik, S., Goldberg, L., & Engel, I. (1992). Parental values, reinforcement, and young children's prosocial behavior: A longitudinal study. *Journal of Genetic Psychology, 153*, 19–36.

Farver, J. A. M., & Branstetter, W. H. (1994). Preschoolers' prosocial responses to their peers' distress. *Developmental Psychology, 30*, 334–341.

Graziano, W. G., & Eisenberg, N. H. (1997). Agreeableness: A dimension of personality. In R. Hogan, J. Johnson, & S. Briggs (Eds.), *Handbook of personality psychology* (pp. 795–824). San Diego: Academic Press.

Grusec, J. E., Goodnow, J. J., & Cohen, L. (1996). Household work and the development of concern for others. *Developmental Psychology, 32*, 999–1007.

Hart, D., & Fegley, S. (1995). Altruism and caring in adolescence: Relations to self-understanding and social judgment. *Child Development, 66*, 1346–1359.

Hoffman, M. L. (1982). Development of prosocial motivation: Empathy and guilt. In N. Eisenberg (Ed.), *The development of prosocial behavior* (pp. 281–313). New York: Academic Press.

Hoffman, M. L. (1983). Affective and cognitive processes in moral internalization. In E. T. Higgins, D. N. Ruble, & W. W. Hartup (Eds.), *Social cognition and social development: A sociocultural perspective* (pp. 236–274). Cambridge, England: Cambridge University Press.

Janssens, J. M. A. M., & Dekovic, M. (1997). Child rearing, prosocial moral reasoning, and prosocial behaviour. *International Journal of Behavioral Development, 20*, 509–527.

Janssens, J. M. A. M., & Gerris, J. R. M. (1992). Child rearing, empathy and prosocial development. In J. M. A. M. Janssens & J. R. M. Gerris (Eds.), *Child rearing: Influence on prosocial and moral development* (pp. 57–75). Amsterdam: Swets & Zeitlinger.

Knight, G. P., Johnson, L. G., Carlo, G., & Eisenberg, N. (1994). A multiplicative model of the dispositional antecedents of a prosocial behavior: Predicting more of the people more of the time. *Journal of Personality and Social Psychology, 66*, 178–183.

Krevans, J., & Gibbs, J. C. (1996). Parents' use of inductive discipline: Relations to children's empathy and prosocial behavior. *Child Development, 67*, 3263–3277.

Ladd, G. W., & Profilet, S. M. (1996). The Child Behavior Scale: A teacher-report measure of young children's aggressive, withdrawn, and prosocial behaviors. *Developmental Psychology, 32*, 1008–1024.

Losoya, S. H., & Eisenberg, N. (2001). Affective empathy. In J. A. Hall & F. J. Bernerei (Eds.), *Interpersonal sensitivity: Theory and measurement*. Mahwah, NJ: Lawrence Erlbaum Associates.

McGrath, M. P., & Power, T. G. (1990). The effects of reasoning and choice on children's prosocial behaviour. *International Journal of Behavioral Development, 13*, 345–353.

McGrath, M. P., Wilson, S. R., & Frassetto, S. J. (1995). Why some forms of inductive reasoning are better than others: Effects of cognitive focus, choice, and affect on children's prosocial behavior. *Merrill-Palmer Quarterly, 41*, 346–360.

Miller, P. A., Eisenberg, N., Fabes, R. A., & Shell, R. (1996). Relations of moral reasoning and vicarious emotion to young children's prosocial behavior toward peers and adults. *Developmental Psychology, 32*, 210–219.

Miller, P. A., Eisenberg, N., Fabes, R. A., Shell, R., & Gular, S. (1989). Socialization of empathic and sympathetic responding. In N. Eisenberg (Ed.), *The development of empathy and related vicarious responses* (pp. 65–83). San Francisco: Jossey-Bass.

Nelson, D. A., & Crick, N. R. (1999). Rose-colored glasses: Examining the social information-processing of prosocial young adolescents. *Journal of Early Adolescence, 19*, 17–28.

Oliner, S. P., & Oliner, P. M. (1988). *The altruistic personality: Rescuers of Jews in Nazi Europe*. New York: Free Press.

Murphy, B. C., Shepard, S. A., Eisenberg, N., Fabes, R. A., & Guthrie, I. K. (1999). Contemporaneous and longitudinal relations of young adolescents' dispositional sympathy to their emotionality, regulation, and social functioning. *Journal of Early Adolescence, 19*, 66–97.

Plomin, R., Emde, R. N., Braungart, J. M., Campos, J., Kagan, J., Reznick, J. S., Robinson, J., Zahn-Waxler, C., & DeFries, J. C. (1993). Genetic change and continuity from fourteen to twenty months: The MacArthur Longitudinal Twin Study. *Child Development, 64*, 1354–1376.

Radke-Yarrow, M., & Zahn-Waxler, C. (1984). Roots, motives, and patterns in children's prosocial behavior. In E. Staub, D. Bar-Tal, J. Karylowski, & J. Reykowski (Eds.), *Development and maintenance of prosocial behavior: International perspectives on positive behavior* (pp. 81–99). New York: Plenum.

Richman, C. L., Berry, C., Bittle, M., & Himan, M. (1988). Factors related to helping behavior in preschool-age children. *Journal of Applied Developmental Psychology, 9*, 151–165.

Roberts, W., & Strayer, J. (1996). Empathy, emotional expressiveness, and prosocial behavior. *Child Development, 67*, 449–470.

Robinson, J. L., Zahn-Waxler, C., & Emde, R. N. (1994). Patterns of development in early empathic behavior: Environmental and child constitutional influences. *Social Development, 3*, 125–145.

Rushton, J. P., Fulker, D. W., Neal, M. C., Nias, D. K. B., & Eysenck, H. J. (1986). Altruism and aggression: The heritability of individual differences. *Journal of Personality and Social Psychology, 50*, 1192–1198.

Solomon, D., Battistich, & Watson, M. (1993, March). *A longitudinal investigation of the effects of a school intervention program on children's social development.* Paper presented at the biennial meeting of the Society for Research in Child Development, New Orleans, LA.

Solomon, D., Watson, M. S., Delucchi, K. L., Schaps, E., & Battistich, V. (1988). Enhancing children's prosocial behavior in the classroom. *American Educational Research Journal, 25*, 527–554.

Strayer, J., & Roberts, W. (1989). Children's empathy and role taking: Child and parental factors, and relations to prosocial behavior. *Journal of Applied Developmental Psychology, 10*, 227–239.

Staub, E. (1979). *Positive social behavior and morality: Vol 2: Socialization and development.* New York: Academic Press.

Tremblay, R. E., Vitaro, F., Gagnon, C., Piche, C., & Royer, N. (1992). A prosocial scale for the preschool behavior questionnaire: Concurrent and predictive correlates. *International Journal of Behavioral Development, 15*, 227–245.

Vitaro, F., Gagnon, C., & Tremblay, R. E. (1991). Teachers' and mothers' assessment of children's behaviors from kindergarten to grade two: Stability and change within and across informants. *Journal of Psychopathology and Behavioral Assessment, 13*, 325–343.

Wentzel, K. R., & McNamara, C. C. (1999). Interpersonal relationships, emotional distress, and prosocial behavior in middle school. *Journal of Early Adolescence, 19*, 114–125.

Yarrow, M. R., Scott, P. M., & Waxler, C. Z. (1973). Learning concern for others. *Developmental Psychology, 8*, 240–260.

Yates, M. & Youniss, J. (1996). A developmental perspective on community service in adolescence. *Social Development, 5*, 85–111.

Zahn-Waxler, C., Cole, P. M., Welsh, J. D., & Fox, N. A. (1995). Psychophysiological correlates of empathy and prosocial behaviors in preschool children with problem behaviors. *Development and Psychopathology, 7*, 27–48.

Zahn-Waxler, C., Radke-Yarrow, M., King, R. A. (1979). Child rearing and children's prosocial initiations toward victims of distress. *Child Development, 50*, 319–330.

Zahn-Waxler, C., Radke-Yarrow, M., Wagner, E., & Chapman, M. (1992). Development of concern for others. *Developmental Psychology, 28*, 126–136.

Zahn-Waxler, C., Robinson, J., & Emde, R. N. (1992). The development of empathy in twins. *Developmental Psychology, 28*, 1038–1047.

PART III

COGNITIVE DOMAIN

Edited by

Marc H. Bornstein
*National Institute of Child Health
and Human Development, Bethesda, MD*

D. Camille Smith
Centers for Disease Control and Prevention, Atlanta, GA

20

Information Processing and Memory

Robert V. Kail

Purdue University, West Lafayette, IN

INTRODUCTION

From infancy to adulthood, children acquire ever-greater cognitive skill, in domains ranging from reasoning to mathematics to wayfinding (DeLoache, Miller, & Pierroutsakos, 1998). For many years, the best account of this widespread cognitive growth was provided by Piaget's theory, with its emphasis on qualitatively different stages of thought. Today, however, we know that cognitive development is not as rigidly stage-like as Piaget envisioned but *is* coordinated across domains. To explain how cognitive growth can be coordinated yet still progress unevenly across different domains, theorists have proposed general processing mechanisms that are implicated in performance across a wide range of tasks. Because the impact of these mechanisms is pervasive, developmental change therein can account for coordinated cognitive growth. Heterogeneity is expected because the general mechanisms are not implicated in all tasks and, when implicated, the extent of their contribution may vary.

Although the details differ, many theories (e.g., Case, 1998; Demetriou & Valanides, 1998; Kail, 1996) include processing speed (or efficiency) as one of the general mechanisms and working memory as the other. The remainder of this chapter concerns the nature, development, and impact of these two mechanisms.

THE NATURE AND MEASUREMENT OF PROCESSING SPEED AND WORKING MEMORY

Most researchers studying general mechanisms of cognitive development adhere to an information- processing approach (Kail & Bisanz, 1992; Klahr & MacWhinney, 1998), which draws heavily on computer functioning to explain thinking and how it develops. Just as computers consist of both hardware (disk drives, random-access memory, and a central processing unit) and software (the programs we use), information-processing approaches assume that human cognition consists of mental hardware[1] (cognitive structures, including different memories where information is stored) and mental software (organized sets of cognitive processes that allow people to complete specific tasks, such as reading a sentence). In the information-processing approach, processing speed is analogous to the speed of a computer's central processing unit and denotes the amount of time required for a person to execute fundamental cognitive processes. Working memory is analogous to a computer's random-access memory and denotes a structure that includes ongoing cognitive processes and the information required for those processes.

In the remainder of this section, I describe tasks used to assess processing speed and working memory. The appropriate tasks are age-specific; I begin with tasks for children and adolescents.

Tasks for Children and Adolescents

Beginning during the preschool years, investigators assess processing speed and working memory with tasks devised originally for adults. In studying processing speed, most investigators initially relied on tasks in which a stimulus is presented and participants respond by selecting one of two alternatives, typically by pressing a button or a key on a keyboard (Kail & Bisanz, 1982). Tasks were usually constructed to include different within-participant conditions to isolate speeds of specific processes. For example, in the simplest version, there would be two conditions. In one, participants would press a button as rapidly as possible whenever any number appears on a computer monitor. In a second condition, they press one button for odd numbers and another button for even numbers. The time to respond to the stimulus (response time or RT) would typically be greater in the second condition and the difference apparently reflects the additional time for participants to decide whether the number was odd or even, then program the appropriate motor response.

Tasks built on this logic are still used today when investigators wish to focus on particular processes. However, these tasks are time-consuming: many trials are needed within each condition to estimate RTs accurately. Even then, the data rarely achieve accepted psychometric levels of reliability. In addition, children

---

[1]In the present context, mental hardware refers to functional aspects of mind, not to actual neural structures in the brain.

are often bored by the repetitive nature of these tasks, which can cause their performance to deteriorate.

Because of these limits, to estimate general processing speed in children, adolescents, and adults, many investigators rely upon psychometric measures. The Cross Out task from the Woodcock-Johnson Tests of Cognitive Ability is illustrative. Thirty rows consist of a geometric figure at the left end of a row and 19 similar figures to the right. One row, for example, consists of a triangle enclosing a single dot; the 19 figures are triangles with various objects in the interior (e.g., a single dot, three dots, a plus, a square). The participant places a line through the 5 figures of the 19 that are identical to the one at the left. The performance measure is the number of rows completed in 3 minutes.

Performance on these and other similar tasks is highly reliable (e.g., test–retest reliabilities for the Cross Out tasks are .64–.73, for children and adolescents). In addition, performance is highly correlated with performance on the information-processing tasks described previously.

To measure memory in children and adolescents, researchers have used span tasks for more than a century. In these tasks, digits, letters, or words are presented to participants, who must repeat them in order (usually aloud but sometimes in writing). Testing typically begins with 1 or 2 stimuli, then increases until participants are no longer able to recall the sequence accurately.

Strictly speaking, these "simple span" tasks are thought to measure short-term memory, not working memory. Although the exact relation between these constructs is still debated, one view (Cowan, 1995) is that short-term memory refers to information in long-term memory that is activated above some threshold; working memory includes short-term memory as well as the attentional processes used to keep some elements in short-term memory in an activated state. To measure working memory, investigators often use complex span tasks in which participants remember information while concurrently performing other processing tasks. In the prototypic complex span task, devised by Daneman and Carpenter (1980), participants read sets of sentences and concurrently remember the last word from each sentence in the set. Testing begins with 1 or 2 sentences (hence, participants must remember 1 or 2 sentence-ending words) and continues until participants are no longer able to recall the sentence-ending words in the correct sequence. In other complex span tasks, participants perform arithmetic tasks and remember the products of the arithmetic operations (Engle, Tuholski, Laughlin, & Conway, 1999).

Both simple and complex span tasks are reliable. For example, Engle et al. (1999) reported reliability coefficients of .61–.74 for simple span tasks and .53–.75 for complex span tasks.

Tasks for Infants

For many years, researchers have studied infant memory using novelty-preference tasks. Although there are many variants of these tasks, all are based on the fact that infants usually orient to novel but not familiar stimuli (Bornstein, 1998; Fagan, 1971). In the simplest form of the paradigm, infants might be shown a picture; their looking time is recorded. Immediately thereafter, infants are shown the same picture with a picture not shown previously. Infants typically look longer at the novel picture, suggesting that they recognize the other picture from its prior presentation.

Another method of assessing infant memory relies on conjugate reinforcement (Rovee-Collier, 1997, 1999). A mobile is mounted temporarily above an infant's crib and a ribbon connects the mobile to the infant's leg. Within a few minutes, 2- to 3-month-olds learn to kick to make the mobile move. The mobile is then removed but, at various intervals, reattached. Infants often kick spontaneously, suggesting that they remember the contingency between leg movement and the mobile's motion.

Both of these paradigms have been used successfully to study many aspects of memory during infancy. It should be noted, however, each technique measures a broad collection of memory processes, not simply working memory. Measures of infant memory typically have not included the concurrent processing component that is the hallmark of working memory tasks for older children, adolescents, and adults.

Processing speed has been studied less extensively than memory in infants. Consequently, suitable tasks are still emerging. One approach relies on the novelty-preference paradigm and simply records the amount of time that infants spend looking at a novel stimulus. Infants differ substantially in their average looking, and, when tested on other cognitive tasks, "short-looking" infants tend to perform better than "long-looking" infants (e.g., Colombo, Mitchell, Coldren, & Freeseman, 1991). These results suggest that infants who look at novel stimuli briefly are processing them more rapidly than infants who look longer.

Another method, known as the visual expectation paradigm, involves rapid presentation of pictures to an infant's peripheral visual field (Haith, Hazan, & Goodman, 1988; Canfield, Smith, Brezsnyak, & Snow, 1997). Typically, the infant's eye moves rapidly and directly toward the picture, a motion known as a saccade. These eye movements are videotaped, and these tapes are scored to measure saccade RT, the time elapsed from the appearance of a picture until the start of the eye's movement toward the picture.

Several caveats are associated with these methods for estimating processing speed: (1) both methods, but particularly the visual expectation paradigm, require elaborate apparatus and complex scoring, (2) the saccade RTs from the visual expectation paradigm can be interpreted in much the same way in infants, children, and adolescents, but this not likely to be true for looking times obtained from novelty-preference tasks, and (3) estimates of processing speed from novelty-preference and visual-expectation paradigms are related, but not substantially (Jacobson et al., 1992).

REVIEW OF THE LITERATURE

In this section, I begin with research on processing speed, then examine working memory. Within each area, I first consider work with children and adolescents, then move to work with infants and, where appropriate, toddlers.

Processing Speed

On most tasks in which participants must respond rapidly, speed of response increases steadily throughout childhood and adolescence (Kail, 1991). Because this finding is consistent across many diverse tasks, the age differences might reflect a global mechanism that limits the speed with which children and adolescents process information. In fact, considerable research provides support for a global mechanism that is not specific to particular tasks or domains but is, instead, a fundamental characteristic of the developing information-processing system.

One relevant line of evidence comes from studies of developmental functions. If speeds of different processes are limited by a common, global mechanism, then the same pattern of developmental change in processing speed is expected for these processes. If, instead, the speed of each process reflects experiences or practice specific to that process, then patterns of developmental change should vary across processes. In reality, speeds for processes such as mental addition, mental rotation, memory search, and simple motor skills all change at a common rate that is well described by an exponential function (Kail, 1995).

Another line of evidence comes from studies examining relations between children's RTs and adults' RTs. If children at a given age execute cognitive processes more slowly than adults, by a constant factor, m, then children's RTs should always be a multiple (m) of adults' RTs from the same experimental conditions. This prediction has been supported repeatedly (Kail, 2000). For example, Kail (1991) analyzed RTs for 4- to 14-year-olds and adults. At each age, children's RTs could be expressed as a simple multiple of adults' RTs. Furthermore, the value of the multiple (m) decreased exponentially across childhood and adolescence.

Little is known about the nature of change in processing speed during infancy. However, Canfield et al. (1997) tested 13 infants longitudinally on the visual expectation paradigm. Saccade RTs declined from 440 ms at 2 months to 354 ms at 6 months to 285 ms at 12 months. Furthermore, when the Canfield et al. data are compared with saccade RTs for older children and adolescents, they suggest nonlinear developmental change like that observed on cognitive tasks.

A number of lines of evidence suggest that developmental change in speed of processing can be attributed, at least in part, to biological causes, probably those linked to the functioning of the central nervous system:

- During the years in which processing speed changes most rapidly, there are age-related changes in the number of transient connections in the central nervous system (e.g., Huttenlocher, 1979) as well as age-related increases in myelinization (e.g., Yakovlev & Lecours, 1967).
- Children and adults with impairments to the nervous system often have slower processing rates (Kail, 1992, 1998).
- Twin studies (e.g., Ho, Baker, & Decker, 1988) indicate that approximately half the variability in processing speed reflects genetic influences (i.e., a heritability coefficient of approximately .5).

- The achievement of adult-like processing speed in adolescence is linked to pubertal change (Eaton & Ritchot, 1995).

Thus, although the evidence is often indirect and sometimes speculative, I believe it is reasonable to view processing speed as a basic parameter of cognitive functioning that changes with development, due, at least in part, to underlying biological factors.

Memory

Performance on span tasks shows the same pattern of nonlinear change seen for processing speed. That is, change is large during the preschool and elementary school years but much smaller during adolescence (Dempster, 1981). Furthermore, this pattern occurs on both simple and complex span tasks and, within each task, across a variety of stimuli. For example, digit span increases from approximately 2.5 digits at age 2 years to 5 digits at age 7 to 6.5 digits at age 12 (Dempster, 1981).

Nonlinear developmental change in memory is reminiscent of nonlinear change in processing speed, and for good reason: Much of the age-related change in working memory is due to increases in processing speed (Kail & Park, 1994). That is, as children develop, their processing speed increases, which allows them to execute the various updating functions of working memory more rapidly. For example, Cowan et al. (1998) found that age differences in digit span between 7 and 11 years reflected more rapid rehearsal and more rapid retrieval of items in working memory.

Less is known concerning the early development of memory, largely because few memory tasks are appropriate throughout infancy. However, Rovee-Collier (1999) has created a task for older infants like the mobile task (which is most appropriate for 2- to 6-month-olds). Infants seated in a parent's lap learn to press a lever, which moves a toy train. At various intervals, infants are returned to the toy train and spontaneous level-pressing is recorded. Testing 2- to 6-month-olds on the mobile task and 6- to 18-month-olds on the train task reveals a steady increase in the length of time that infants remember the appropriate response (kicking or pushing the lever). With the typical training procedures, 2-month-olds remember a few days but 18-month-olds remember for 3 months. (The absolute levels of performance depend critically upon the exact procedures used and, consequently, are less important than the developmental trend, which is quite general.) These results show that infants can remember over increasingly long intervals, but they do not assess whether the capacity of working memory actually increases in infancy. This question remains unanswered because, as noted previously, investigators have not created measures of working memory for infants that are analogous to the complex span tasks used with adults.

COGNITIVE CONSEQUENCES OF INCREASES IN PROCESSING SPEED AND WORKING MEMORY

Many theorists believe that cognitive development during infancy, childhood, and adolescence reflects, in part, increases in speed of processing and working memory. For example, Fry and Hale (1996) argued that "… processing speed becomes faster, leading to improvements in working memory, and improved working memory, in turn leads to increases in [reasoning and problem solving]" (p. 237). They evaluated this hypothesis by administering measures of processing speed and working memory to 7- to 19-year-olds. They also measured fluid intelligence, which denotes processes involved in making inferences and in identifying relations among concepts. Consistent with their hypothesis, age-related increases in speed were associated with increases in working memory capacity, which, in turn, were associated with higher scores on the test of fluid intelligence. Thus, as children process information more rapidly, they can use working memory more effectively, which allows them to solve problems like those on the test of fluid intelligence more successfully.

Research also links processing speed and working memory to academic skills. For example, Kail and Hall (1999) determined that two factors independently contributed to 8- to 12-year-olds' success in solving simple arithmetic word problems (e.g., "If Marc has 4 apples and Bob has 2, how many more apples does Marc have?"). One factor was children's skill at the relevant addition and subtraction operations; the second was general information processing skill, defined by processing speed and working memory. Similarly, Kail and Hall (2001) found that children's reading skill was predicted by working memory, which, in turn, was predicted by processing speed. These findings are typical (e.g., Allen & Ondracek, 1995) of work implicating processing speed and working memory in a broad array of higher-order cognitive changes during childhood and adolescence.

Longitudinal research conducted with infants and preschoolers demonstrates a similar link. Dougherty and Haith (1997) tested 3½-month-olds on the visual expectation paradigm. At approximately 4 years of age, the children were tested on the Wechsler Preschool and Primary Scale of Intelligence—Revised. The correlation between saccade RT and childhood IQ was −.44: infants with more rapid processing tended to have higher IQ scores as 4-year-olds.

Other research shows that processing speed and memory are often affected in children with cognitive impairments. For example, slower processing speed or reduced memory capacity has been demonstrated in such diverse groups as children with depression (Lauer, Giordani, Boivin, & Halle, 1994), children with leukemia (Cousens, Ungerer, Crawford, & Stevens, 1991), and children with specific language impairment (Miller, Kail, Leonard, & Tomblin, 2001). Although the causal connections between these impairments and reduced information processing are often unclear, it is the case that the reduced information processing is sometimes associated with delayed cognitive development in children with impairments (Kovacs, Ryan, & Obrosky, 1994).

These results suggest that increases in processing speed and working memory capacity may contribute to cognitive growth in many settings. In addition, they indicate that processing speed may influence cognitive development directly (by allowing processes to be performed more rapidly) and indirectly (by increasing the functional capacity of working memory).

FOSTERING PROCESSING SPEED AND WORKING MEMORY

Because processing speed and working memory are typically viewed as fundamental features of a child's cognitive architecture, many theorists have assumed that processing speed and working memory per se are not likely to be strongly influenced by experience or culture. Consequently, investigators interested in fostering children's development have focused on ways of bypassing fundamental limitations imposed by processing speed and working memory. In this last section, I describe three ways to bypass these limitations and thereby improve children's cognitive skills.

Base Performance On Retrieval, Not Algorithms

In the early phases of mastering a new skill, children and adolescents often rely upon task-specific algorithms. For example, in determining simple sums (e.g., 2 + 3 = ?), young children often extend fingers on each hand, then count the number of extended fingers (Siegler & Jenkins, 1989). As the task is performed repeatedly, the stimulus ("2 + 3 =") and the child's response are stored together in memory, so that on subsequent trials the answer is retrieved directly from memory, not computed. Computing an answer (or, more generally, any type of attention-demanding processing) requires substantial working memory capacity, but retrieving an answer does not. Consequently, in learning a new skill, children should continue practicing beyond the point where they answer correctly, until they have mastered the new skill. Additional practice strengthens the representation of the problem solution in memory, thereby allowing performance to be based on retrieval and allowing working memory capacity to be allocated to other activities (Kail & Park, 1990). For example, in solving arithmetic word problems like those described previously, children who have not mastered their arithmetic facts are often less successful because computing an answer (rather than retrieving one) consumes working memory capacity that might otherwise be allocated to other aspects of problem solving (Kail & Hall, 1999).

Adjust Rate of Presentation

Just as we often better understand someone else speaking in a foreign language when they talk slowly, many researchers have demonstrated that children's performance on cognitive tasks improves when information is presented more slowly. Usual presentation rates are often too rapid for children to process the information completely; by slowing presentation to a rate more suited to the child's processing speed, cognitive processing is often enhanced (Pezdek & Miceli, 1982).

Use Strategies to Increase the Functional Capacity of Working Memory

Another way to reduce the impact of capacity limits of working memory is through strategies. That is, children can be taught strategies to increase the functional capacity of working memory. The capacity of working memory is usually measured in chunks, which are better illustrated than defined: The three letters—S B C—are three chunks (for most people) but the same three letters reversed—C B S—are a single chunk (again, for most people living in the United States). Many adolescents could remember five familiar 3-letter acronyms but only five randomly selected letters. By training and encouraging children to create larger chunks of information, the influence of limited capacity working memory can be reduced. Pressley, Borkowski, and Schneider (1989; Pressley, 1995) have developed a Good Information-Processing model that describes, in detail, how adults can teach children to use different strategies to enhance memory and to recognize when each strategy would be most appropriate for a task.

CONCLUSIONS

More efficient information processing helps to explain the coordinated cognitive growth that typifies childhood and adolescence. That is, more rapid processing and greater working memory capacity help to set the stage for developmental increases in cognitive power. Better information processing can be fostered with methods that help children to bypass the limits imposed by processing speed and memory and with methods that help them to use working memory more effectively.

ACKNOWLEDGMENT

The author's research described in this chapter was supported by grants from the National Science Foundation and the National Institute of Child Health and Human Development.

REFERENCES

Allen, G. L., & Ondracek, P. J. (1995). Age-sensitive cognitive abilities related to children's acquisition of spatial knowledge. *Developmental Psychology, 31,* 934–945.

Bornstein, M. H. (1998). Stability in mental development from early life: Methods, measures, models, meanings, and myths. In G. E. Butterworth & F. Simion (Eds.), *The development of sensory, motor, and cognitive capacities in early infancy: From sensation to cognition* (pp. 301–332). Hove, England: Psychology Press.

Canfield, R. L., Smith, E. G., Brezsnyak, M. P., & Snow, K. L. (1997). Information processing through the first year of life: A longitudinal study using the visual expectation paradigm. *Monographs of the Society for Research in Child Development* (Serial No. 250).

Case, R. (1998). The development of conceptual structures. In W. Damon (Ed.), *Handbook of child psychology* (Vol. 2, pp. 745–800). New York: Wiley.

Colombo, J., Mitchell, D. W., Coldren, J. T., & Freeseman, L. J. (1991). Individual differences in infant visual attention: Are short lookers faster processors or feature processors? *Child Development, 62,* 1247–1257.

Cousins, P., Ungerer, J. A., Crawford, J. A., & Stevens, M. M. (1991). Cognitive effects of childhood leukemia therapy: A case for four specific deficits. *Journal of Pediatric Psychology, 16,* 475–488.

Cowan, N. (1995). *Attention and memory: An integrated framework.* Oxford, England: Oxford University Press.

Cowan, N., Wood, N. L., Wood, P. K., Keller, T. A., Nugent, L. D., & Keller, C. V. (1998). Two separate verbal processing rates contributing to short-term memory span. *Journal of Experimental Psychology: General, 127*, 141–160.

Daneman, M., & Carpenter, P. A. (1980). Individual differences in working memory and reading. *Journal of Verbal Learning and Verbal Behavior, 19*, 450–466.

DeLoache, J. S., Miller, K. F., & Pierroutsakos, S. L. (1998). Reasoning and problem solving. In W. Damon (Ed.), *Handbook of child psychology.* (Vol. 2, pp. 801–850). New York: Wiley.

Demetriou, A., & Valanides, N. (1998). A three-level theory of the developing mind: Basic principles and implications for instruction and assessment. In R. J. Sternberg & W. M. Williams (Eds.), *Intelligence, instruction, and assessment: Theory into practice* (pp. 149–199). Mahwah, NJ: Lawrence Erlbaum Associates.

Dempster, F. N. (1981). Memory span: Sources of individual and developmental differences. *Psychological Bulletin, 89*, 63–100.

Doughtery, T. M., & Haith, M. M. (1997). Infant expectations and reaction time as predictors of childhood speed of processing and IQ. *Developmental Psychology, 33*, 146–155.

Eaton, W. O., & Ritchot, K. F. M. (1995). Physical maturation and information-processing speed in middle childhood. *Developmental Psychology, 31*, 967–972.

Engle, R. W., Tuholski, S. W., Laughlin, J. E., & Conway, A. R. A. (1999). Working memory, short-term memory, and general fluid intelligence: A latent-variable approach. *Journal of Experimental Psychology: General, 128*, 309–331.

Fagan, J. (1971). Infant recognition memory for a series of visual stimuli. *Journal of Experimental Child Psychology, 11*, 244–250.

Fry, A. F., & Hale, S. (1996). Processing speed, working memory, and fluid intelligence: Evidence for a developmental cascade. *Psychological Science, 7*, 237–241.

Haith, M. M., Hazan, C., & Goodman, G. S. (1988). Expectation and anticipation of dynamic visual events by 3.5-month-old babies. *Child Development, 59*, 467–479.

Ho, H., Baker, L. A., & Decker, S. N. (1988). Covariation between intelligence and speed of cognitive processing: Genetic and environmental influences. *Behavior Genetics, 18*, 247–261.

Huttenlocher, P. R. (1979). Synaptic density in human frontal cortex—Developmental changes and effects of aging. *Brain Research, 163*, 195–205.

Jacobson, S. W., Jacobson, J. L., O'Neill, J. M., Padgett, R. J., Frankowski, J. J., & Bihun, J. T. (1992). Visual expectation and dimensions of infant information processing. *Child Development, 63*, 711–724.

Kail, R. (1991). Developmental change in speed of processing during childhood and adolescence. *Psychological Bulletin, 109*, 490–501.

Kail, R. (1992). General slowing of information processing by persons with mental retardation. *American Journal of Mental Retardation, 97*, 333–341.

Kail, R. (1995). Processing speed, memory, and cognition. In W. Schneider & F. E. Weinert (Eds.), *Memory performance and competencies: Issues in growth and development* (pp. 71–88). Hillsdale, NJ: Lawrence Erlbaum Associates.

Kail, R. (1996). Nature and consequences of developmental change in speed of processing. *Swiss Journal of Psychology, 55*, 133–138.

Kail, R. (1998). Speed of information processing in patients with multiple sclerosis. *Journal of Clinical and Experimental Neuropsychology, 20*, 1–9.

Kail, R. (2000). Speed of information processing: Developmental change and links to intelligence. *Journal of School Psychology, 38*, 51–61.

Kail, R., & Bisanz, J. (1982). Cognitive development: An information-processing perspective. In R. Vasta (Ed.), *Strategies and techniques of child study* (pp. 209–243). New York: Academic Press.

Kail, R., & Bisanz, J. (1992). The information-processing perspective on cognitive development in childhood and adolescence. In R. J. Sternberg & C. A. Berg (Eds.), *Intellectual development* (pp. 229–260). New York: Cambridge University Press.

Kail, R., & Hall, L. K. (1999). Sources of developmental change in children's word-problem performance. *Journal of Educational Psychology, 91*, 660–668.

Kail, R., & Hall, L. K. (2001). Distinguishing short-term from working memory. *Memory & Cognition, 29*, 1–9

Kail, R., & Park, Y. (1990). Impact of practice on speed of mental rotation. *Journal of Experimental Child Psychology*, *49*, 227–244.

Kail, R., & Park, Y. (1994). Processing time, articulation time, and memory span. *Journal of Experimental Child Psychology*, *57*, 281–291.

Klahr, D., & MacWhinney, B. (1998). Information processing. In W. Damon (Ed.), *Handbook of child psychology* (Vol. 2, pp. 631–678). New York: Wiley.

Kovacs, M., Ryan, C., & Obrosky, D. S. (1994). Verbal intellectual and verbal memory performance of youths with childhood-onset insulin-dependent diabetes mellitus. *Journal of Pediatric Psychology*, *19*, 475–483.

Lauer, R. E., Giordani, B., Boivin, M. J., & Halle, N. (1994). Effects of depression on memory performance and metamemory in children. *Journal of the American Academy of Child and Adolescent Psychiatry*, *33*, 679–685.

Miller, C. A., Kail, R., Leonard, L. B., & Tomblin, J. B. (2001). Speed of processing in children with specific language impairment. *Journal of Speech, Language, and Hearing Research*, *44*, 2, 416–433.

Pezdek, K., & Miceli, L. (1982). Life-span differences in memory integration as a function of processing time. *Developmental Psychology*, *18*, 485–490.

Pressley, M. (1995). What is intellectual development about in the 1990s? Not strategies!: Good information processing, not strategies instruction!: Instruction cultivating good information processing. In W. Schneider & F. E. Weinert (Eds.), *Memory performance and competencies: Issues in growth and development* (pp. 375–404). Hillsdale, NJ: Lawrence Erlbaum Associates.

Pressley, M., Borkowski, J. G., & Schneider, W. (1989). Good information processing: What is it and what education can do to promote it. *International Journal of Educational Research*, *13*, 857–867.

Rovee-Collier, C. (1997). Dissociations in infant memory: Rethinking the development of implicit and explicit memory. *Psychological Review*, *104*, 467–498.

Rovee-Collier, C. (1999). The development of infant memory. *Current Directions in Psychological Science*, *8*, 80–85.

Siegler, R. S., & Jenkins, E. (1989). *How children discover new strategies*. Hillsdale, NJ: Lawrence Erlbaum Associates.

Yakovlev, P. I., & Lecours, A. R. (1967). The myelogenetic cycles of regional maturation of the brain. In A. Minkowski (Ed.), *Regional development of the brain in early life* (pp. 3–64). Oxford: Blackwell.

21

Curiosity, Exploration, and Novelty-Seeking

Naomi Wentworth
Lake Forest College, Lake Forest, IL

Sam L. Witryol
University of Connecticut, Storrs

INTRODUCTION

Curiosity, quite simply, is the desire to learn more. Like other motivational concepts, it entails two important properties: the capacity to energize behavior and the power to control its direction. Typically, curiosity is aroused when we are exposed to an object or event that is outside the realm of customary experience, but it can also be aroused when we reconsider, from a new perspective, that which has become customary. A curious person is one who is open to new information or new ways of looking at what has become familiar. Environments that foster curiosity are complex and varied enough to engender a range of expectations for what might occur, while still offering enough structure to support the development of these expectations.

Exploration is the behavior that is energized and directed by curiosity. Exploratory behavior can take many forms including visual search and attention, object manipulation, concept formation, hypothesis testing, and so forth. Thus, exploratory behavior relies on (and exercises) perceptual, motor, and cognitive systems. As is apparent in infancy, our capacity to explore is constrained by the state of our perceptual, motor, and cognitive systems. As many developmental psychologists have noted (e.g., Gibson, 1988; Rheingold, 1985), there is a clear progression in the type of exploration that is activated at each age. A young infant, recently fed, diapered, and cuddled against a parent's shoulder, will scan the wallpaper, curtains, ceiling tiles, rug pattern, and all other features of this new world that contrasts so sharply with the uterine environment. With the development of prehension, looking is no longer enough; older infants must explore the properties of objects by hand, eyes, and mouth. With the onset of crawling, infants gain a new means of exploring the familiar environment, enabling them to discover new properties of the world. Similarly, with advances in cognitive development, children begin to explore an ever expanding range of concepts and relations in their physical and social worlds.

Finally, novelty-seeking provides a bias in the direction toward which curiosity aims. Exploration serves to make various aspects of the world familiar, and this familiarity provides a backdrop against which novel elements are highlighted (Rheingold, 1985). Thus, in order to define novelty, we must put it into a context that depends on the person's past experience; novelty, like beauty, is in the eye of the beholder. When curiosity is directed toward novelty, and exploratory behavior follows, the end product is to make familiar what was formerly unknown. Obviously, an organism with a stronger bias toward novelty is likely to learn more than one with a weaker bias, or one who is biased toward the familiar. In fact, several studies suggest that there is a correlation between early novelty preference and later intelligence (e.g., Berg & Sternberg, 1985; Fantz, Fagan, & Miranda, 1975; Jacobson et al., 1992).

THEORETICAL AND EMPIRICAL REVIEW OF THE LITERATURE

In an early account of the psychological mechanics underlying exploration, Berlyne (1960) proposed that certain situations can generate an arousal-producing conflict by simultaneously activating incompatible responses. The person must then seek information to resolve the conflict. Once the conflict is resolved, arousal dissipates, and exploration is turned toward another target. According to Berlyne, situations with the capacity to arouse conflict, and hence to activate exploratory behavior, require the person to "collate" or compare information from several sources. Although Berlyne nominated many stimulus properties as candidates for generating curiosity such as novelty, change, ambiguity, surprise, incongruity, and others, each can be subsumed under three superordinate classes—novelty, complexity, and uncertainty.

Nunnally and Lemond (1973) proposed that arousal increases linearly with progressive levels of novelty, whereas Berlyne (1960) predicted that *preference* for novelty, as indicated by attention to and engagement with novel stimuli, follows an inverted-U shaped function of the amount of novelty. For each individual, there should be an optimal level of novelty where curiosity and exploration are maximal. Levels of novelty below this amount would be too low to foster curiosity, and higher levels of novelty would be too high, overwhelming the individual and precluding exploration. Many variants of this "optimal level" hypothesis have been proposed (e.g., McCall & Kagan, 1970).

Another of Berlyne's distinctions concerned the difference between specific exploration and diversive exploration, with the former directed toward a particular target and the latter a more general search for something "new and interesting." Exploration can move from specific to diversive (or vice versa) over time. Thus, children's activity with a new toy might begin with specific exploration, marked by attempts to discover what the toy does and how it works. After a while, children may then switch to diversive exploration, marked by a more playful attitude and an attempt to incorporate the toy into a wide range of activities (e.g., Hutt, 1970).

Research has generally confirmed that the variables Berlyne nominated as potential sources of curiosity are associated with eliciting and maintaining exploratory activity (e.g., Hutt, 1970; Nunnally & Lemond, 1973). Unfortunately, defining terms such as novelty, ambiguity, and uncertainty with sufficient precision to enable rigorous study has proven surprisingly difficult. One strategy to overcome this measurement problem has been to use the metrics of information theory (e.g., Shannon & Weaver, 1949) to quantify the collative variables identified by Berlyne. The utility of this strategy has been demonstrated in a diverse array of studies into topics such as children's visual exploration (e.g., Cancelli, Duley, & Meredith, 1980), material reward choices (e.g., Wentworth & Witryol, 1984), exploratory play with construction toys (Cahill-Solis & Witryol, 1994), guessing game preferences (Eckblad, 1964), and selection of stimuli after sensory deprivation (Wood, 1977).

In addition to Berlyne's early theorizing, and the subsequent attempts to verify and quantify the variables that Berlyne identified, our current framework has its foundation in empirical work that has explored the cognitive consequences of curiosity and novelty-seeking. An early study by Fantz (1964) laid the groundwork for an enormous body of literature on the consequences of curiosity and novelty-seeking. Fantz discovered that when new pictures were paired with familiar pictures, young infants looked longer at the pictures they had not previously seen. Although Fantz's initial interest was in measuring the perceptual properties of the young infant's visual system, his discovery paved the way for a long line of studies on infant visual capabilities, learning processes, and recognition memory. Eventually, research using modifications of Fantz's preferential looking paradigm demonstrated that (a) infants at risk for later intellectual deficits were less likely to look at novel pictures (e.g., Fantz, Fagan, & Miranda, 1975; Singer & Fagan, 1984), (b) there was a significant correlation between novelty preference in infancy and later IQ in childhood (e.g., Berg & Sternberg, 1985; Jacobson, et al., 1992), and (c) selective attention to novelty is related to information processing across the life span (Fagan & Haiken-Vasen, 1997).

A great deal of research has shown that curiosity and novelty-seeking are quite ubiquitous, both over the life span and across species. Rats, for example, will learn to press a bar in order to obtain a change in visual brightness (Myers & Miller, 1954; Levin & Forgays, 1959), and monkeys will learn a color discrimination problem in order to obtain a brief look outside the confines of their cage (Butler, 1953). These observations of the potent motivational properties of novelty and exploration were somewhat surprising to the generation of researchers who struggled to understand the workings of memory and learning processes from within a theoretical perspective that emphasized the reduction of biological needs as the prime motivator of learned behavior. But the ubiquity of novelty-familiarity effects forced the expansion of these early psychological theories so that they could accommodate the role that novelty plays in attention and learning. As David Zeaman (1976) put it, "… I never planned to study habituation, but I have been continually plagued throughout my research career by a problem closely related to, if not identified with, habituation: differential responsiveness to new and old stimuli" (p. 297). On the basis of an influx of reports on the widespread effects of novelty, complexity, and violations in expectations, theories of learning and motivation were modified (e.g., White, 1959), and many empirical studies into the nature and operation of novelty-seeking, curiosity, and exploration were undertaken.

Over the past three decades, Witryol and a number of his associates have undertaken a uniquely long-term and systematic program of research directed toward understanding the nature and operation of curiosity motivation in children. In particular, studies from the Witryol laboratory have focused on (a) the development of paradigms to translate Berlyne's collative variables into operations that are amenable to experimental study, (b) application of these paradigms to explore developmental trends in the motivational properties of collative variables, (c) comparison of the relative attractiveness of complexity, variety, novelty, and uncertainty, and (d) studies of the dispositional and cognitive correlates of individual differences in curiosity motivation.

Studies of Novelty

Many studies have shown that across species, and across developmental levels, novel stimuli are typically responded to more quickly, inspected for longer periods of time, chosen more often, and rated more highly than more familiar alternatives (for reviews see Cantor, 1963; Hutt, 1970; Nunnally & Lemond, 1973). However, in most of these studies, the novel stimuli were either of neutral reward value or their incentive properties were unknown. Is it the case that the value of material rewards can be modified by manipulating their relative novelty? To explore this question, Skidgell, Witryol, and Wirzbicki (1976) manipulated the short-term novelty of bubble gum and M&M candy, stimuli that were often used as rewards in studies of children's learning. A prior paired-comparisons study had established that bubble gum has a markedly higher reward value for children. With this in mind, Skidgell et al. (1976) used a familiarization sequence to create four levels of short-term novelty for the bubble gum reward. At the end of the 3-trial familiarization sequence, the 6-year-old children had amassed three rewards which might include zero, one, two, or three pieces of the highly valued bubble gum. Following familiarization, children chose between a piece of bubble gum and an M&M. The familiarization procedure had a significant effect on children's choices; choice of the higher valued bubble gum reward declined in a significant linear trend as the gum's relative novelty decreased. Further studies have found the same monotonic function between preference and novelty level across an impressive developmental range from 4-year-old preschoolers (Witryol & Wanich, 1983) to 11-year-old fifth-graders (Witryol & Valenti, 1980), despite the use of plastic trinket incentives rather than edible rewards in the more recent studies.

Using an extension of Skidgell et al.'s (1976) method, Valenti and Witryol (1982) tested the generality of the finding that short-term novelty enhances the attractiveness of material rewards. Following the familiarization sequence, children chose between two rewards that were either of approximately equal value, had markedly unequal values (i.e., a highly valued reward paired with reward of low value), or had a moderate difference in reward value. Although reward differential affected the overall rate at which children chose the higher reward, novelty level had the predicted effect on choice regardless of reward differential: The likelihood of children's choices for any reward increased as the reward's novelty level increased.

As Valenti and Witryol (1982) suggested, novelty is a concept with multiple dimensions. In addition to its recency and frequency effects, novelty also introduces greater variety into life. Is novelty preferred simply because it adds variety to experience? Analyses of children's choices for heterogeneous and homogeneous sets of novel and familiar trinkets indicated that although variety adds incentive value to novelty, novelty's appeal cannot be reduced to simple variation in experience (Wentworth & Witryol, 1983). In a follow-up study, Wentworth and Witryol (1986) found that low recency and low probability of occurrence enhanced choice of a high reward, and both recency and probability added independent variance to novelty's incentive value. Moreover, the *relative* frequency (i.e., probability) of the reward was more closely related to its appeal than was the reward's absolute frequency.

In certain training situations, the appeal of novelty can distract children from the correct response. Consider, for example, a child who notices the novel spellings of words that are often seen on billboards or commercial signs. A child who is trying to learn how to spell *tonight* may be led astray by attending to *tonite* or *2-nite* or other novel spellings. As children become more effective learners, they must channel their novelty preferences into appropriate situations. Valenti (1985) used a standard selective learning task to see whether preschool, kindergarten, and first-grade children modified their novelty preferences when choice of the novel alternative interfered with obtaining the correct answer. Children received three demonstrations during which the correct choice was associated with a highly valued horse trinket or the incorrect choice was associated with a lower valued reward (a dried bean). During choice tests, if children chose the correct object, they received the trinket; if they chose the incorrect object, they received the bean. Choice of the correct object was highly dependent on whether it was novel or familiar: In the positive condition, the correct object was familiar and it was chosen on only 33% of the test trials; in the negative condition, the correct object was novel and it was chosen on 86% of the test trials. This bias in choice of the novel alternative occurred for all ages. As is clear from this experiment, children's predisposition to explore the novel alternative can compete with mastery of correct responses in a learning task.

Studies of Uncertainty

To study the incentive value of uncertainty, Feldstein and Witryol (1971) let 10-year-olds chose between a high value bubble gum reward and an opaque package containing one of four possible rewards of equal or lower value. Children who were allowed to open their packages immediately, or after short delays, chose the uncertain packaged reward more than the constantly available, higher valued, bubble gum reward. For children who had longer delays before they were given the chance to open their packages, package choices increased immediately after the opportunity to open packages, as would be expected if the opportunity to *reduce* uncertainty motivated package choice.

In a similar vein, Wentworth and Witryol (1984) examined 6- and 10-year-old children's preference for uncertainty and the relative capacity of uncertainty and novelty to stimulate curiosity. Children chose between a moderately valued marble and a small package, either opaque, creating uncertainty about its contents, or transparent, conveying information by revealing its contents. Familiarization trials prior to choice manipulated the relative novelty of the reward in the package. Analyses of children's package choices confirmed that packages were chosen more often when their contents were uncertain. Also, uncertainty generated far greater curiosity than did novelty: regardless of age, children were more likely to choose the uncertainty package, even when it contained a familiar reward, than the no uncertainty package, even when a novel reward was visible inside.

Studies of a Curiosity Hierarchy

Building on earlier research and theorizing, Wentworth and Witryol (1990) outlined a curiosity hierarchy ranging from simple variation in experience, to novelty, to uncertainty. Variety, novelty, and uncertainty all introduce variation into experience, but each variable differs according to how this variation occurs. Variety, defined as simple concurrent variation in experience, was placed at the lowest level. Novelty, defined as variation in current experience compared to the past, was placed at a higher level because it compels the individual to integrate experience over time. Uncertainty, defined as simultaneous anticipation of multiple alternatives, was placed at the highest level because it requires continued engagement in order for the uncertainty to be reduced. To test this hierarchy, Wentworth and Witryol gave 6- and 10-year-olds a preference task in which a constantly available, high value trinket was placed in competition with the contents of a covered well. The well cover was either opaque, creating uncertainty about the well's contents, or transparent. Children's choices generally confirmed the proposed collative hierarchy for both ages: variety had a relatively weak effect, novelty was more compelling, and uncertainty clearly occupied the highest position.

Studies of Complexity and Variety

Although variety has not received much attention, a related construct, complexity, has. Complexity is typically defined in terms of numerosity. For example, studies have varied complexity by increasing the number of sides in random polygons and shapes (e.g., Attneave, 1957; Munsinger & Kessen, 1966) or the number of dots in a random array (e.g., Panek, Stern, Barrett, & Alexander, 1978). Variety's appeal may be related to the fact that it introduces *more stimuli* into experience, as does complexity, or to the fact that it introduces *different stimuli*. In a test of these alternatives, O'Neill and Witryol (1985) found that variety had a generally positive effect on 4-, 7-, and 10-year-old children's choices regardless of age, and generated significantly more curiosity than alternatives that simply offered a greater number of identical elements. Similarly, Alberti and Witryol (1990) found that 7- and 11-year-old children preferred patterns with increasing perceptual elements, even when the number of items was held constant. No age differences were found, once again pointing to developmental invariance of curiosity effects. Although children generally prefer variety and complexity, studies by Werner and Witryol (1988, 1990) suggest that individual differences may also exist.

Correlates of Curiosity Motivation

David and Witryol (1990) correlated novelty preference scores of 8- and 11-year-old children with scores on Harter's (1980) Intrinsic–Extrinsic Orientation scale. For the boys, significant positive correlations were found between novelty preference scores and Harter's Curiosity subscale, and marginal correlations were found between novelty preference scores and Harter's Challenge subscale. For the girls, there was a significant correlation between novelty preference scores and Harter's Independent Judgment subscale. These findings are remarkable, given the low standard deviations in novelty preference that are typically obtained, which would tend to attenuate any correlation between novelty preference and other variables. The results also suggested that boys and girls may express their curiosity in different ways when it comes to classroom attitudes and behavior. Boys may emphasize an action-oriented form of curiosity that is less dependent on school rules and teacher expectations, whereas girls may emphasize a thought-oriented form of curiosity that does not conflict with teachers' expectations.

Two studies related children's novelty preference scores to scholastic achievement of third- and fifth-grade children in Connecticut (Alberti & Witryol, 1994) and to second- and fifth-grade children in California (Cahill-Solis & Witryol, 1994). In the Alberti and Witryol study, novelty preference scores were correlated with teacher ratings of children's curiosity and performance on standardized measures of scholastic achievement. Overall, novelty preference was correlated with academic performance ($r = .35$, $p = .002$) although there were substantial differences for gender–grade subgroups. Teacher ratings of curiosity were generally correlated with student performance on scholastic achievement tests but not with choices on the novelty preference task.

In the Cahill-Solis and Witryol (1994) study, relative novelty of Tinker toy constructions was manipulated and the child's preference for constructing the more novel toy was assessed. At the start of the study, the experimenter demonstrated how to construct two different Tinker toy models, one was of intermediate complexity (4 elements) and the other was more complex (7 elements). On each of three familiarization trials, the child received the relevant materials and a model of one of the toy constructions that the experimenter had demonstrated. The child was then asked to build the toy in the model. After three familiarization trials, the child chose to construct either the intermediate complexity toy or the high complexity toy. Novelty level of the high complexity toy was manipulated by the number of times it had been built during the preceding familiarization sequence. Novelty preference scores from this procedure were correlated with individual scores on the California Achievement Test. First, it is important to note that the novelty preference functions obtained in this study were remarkably similar to those obtained by studies in which children accumulated edible (Skidgell et al., 1976) or material rewards (Witryol & Valenti, 1980; Witryol & Wanich, 1983), despite the substantial difference in procedure. Second, the correlation between novelty preference and scholastic achievement in this study ($r = .31, p = .01$) was nearly identical to that obtained by Alberti and Witryol (1994) within their sample of third- and fifth-grade children from Connecticut ($r = .35$). Moreover, correlations for the younger children in both samples were smaller than those for the older children.

DEVELOPMENTAL STABILITY AND CONTINUITY

Regardless of whether we speak of sensory-motor learning in infancy, play in the preschool period, achievement during formal schooling, competence in job training and performance, or adjustment to retirement, we must consider the importance to optimal development of curiosity, exploration, and novelty-seeking. A great deal of evidence suggests that curiosity, exploration, and novelty-seeking are important features of cognitive growth across the life span. Consider novelty, for example. Studies from the Witryol laboratory have shown remarkable stability in novelty preference functions across the period from 4 to 11 years old. Studies of information processing, summarized by Fagan and his associates (for a recent review, see Fagan & Haiken-Vasen, 1997), find similar developmental constancy in the attractiveness of novelty over an even wider developmental range. Studies also suggest that individual differences in attention to novelty early in life are related to later intellectual functioning (e.g., Bornstein & Sigman, 1986; Columbo, 1993; Fagan & Singer, 1983; McCall & Carriger, 1993), with correlations on the order of .45. Moreover, visual attention to novel stimuli is depressed in infants who have been exposed in utero to alcohol (Jacobson, Jacobson, & Sokol, 1994) and other teratogens that are likely to have adverse effects on later school performance, such as PCBs (Jacobson, 1998). Finally, as the Alberti and Wityrol (1994) and the Cahill-Solis and Wityrol (1994) studies show, novelty preferences in material reward choices and in toy construction, respectively, are related to measures of concurrent scholastic achievement.

Selective attention to novelty has been studied more extensively than other forms of curiosity. However, recent studies using Haith's Visual Expectation paradigm (e.g., Benson, Cherny, Haith, & Fulker, 1993; DiLalla et al., 1990; Dougherty & Haith, 1997; Jacobson, 1998; Jacobson et al., 1992) suggest that other variables may also prove useful in understanding individual differences in intellectual functioning and in predicting these differences from infancy. In Haith's Visual Expectation paradigm (Haith, Hazan, & Goodman, 1988), infants view brief picture presentations at two locations (usually left and right of visual center). A pattern (e.g., simple alternation) governs picture presentations. To the extent that infants can extract the structure of the pattern that underlies picture presentations, they can anticipate upcoming pictures or react to unanticipated pictures more quickly when they appear. The role that uncertainty reduction plays in this task is clear; at the start of the session, two possible picture locations must be entertained. Until the rule is mastered, there is uncertainty about where the next picture will appear. Infants who are motivated to reduce uncertainty, and who have the basic information processing skills that this task requires, will learn the rule, form appropriate expectations based on the rule, and implement their expectations as anticipations or speeded reactions. The studies that have been conducted, to date, indicate that the Visual Expectation paradigm taps important motivational and cognitive components in infancy that are related to current developmental status (Jacobson, 1998; Jacobson et al., 1992) and that predict later cognitive outcome in childhood (Dougherty & Haith, 1997) and perhaps beyond (Benson et al., 1993; DiLalla et al., 1990).

FACTORS AFFECTING DEVELOPMENT
AND FOSTERING CURIOSITY

Fagan's (1992) theory on the nature of cognition provides a useful starting place for a discussion of the factors that might affect the development and fostering of curiosity. Fagan has proposed that an individual's information processing activity and the type of information that is processed act, in concert, to determine what a person knows. The quality of an individual's information processing is affected by genetic factors and environmental exposure to positive experiences (e.g., adequate nutrition) or deleterious events (e.g., starvation, teratogens). The amount and type of information that is available to be processed will be influenced by cultural factors, both at a global level, such as socioeconomic status, and at a local level, such as birth order. To this model, we would add motivational factors, such as novelty preference, interest in the reduction of uncertainty, selective attention to incongruity, and so forth. Clearly, these dispositions will affect the amount and type of information to which the individual is exposed (or seeks out). And, we can expect that exposure to such information will certainly affect what is learned and, possibly, the efficiency with which that information is processed. Thus, curiosity plays an important role in determining the amount and nature of what is learned, and in exercising many intellectual abilities such as acquisition of information to reduce uncertainty, detection of stimulus incongruity, complexity, and novelty, resolution of conflicting explanations, hypothesis formation, and the testing of these hypotheses.

One important question that remains is: How can we enhance the development and expression of curiosity throughout the life span? Fagan's (1992) model suggests some answers to this question. First, the environment should be designed so that it is varied enough, dynamic enough, and structured enough to stimulate curiosity and support exploration, but not so varied or dynamic that it overwhelms the child's attempts to process it. Many studies (e.g., Kunst-Wilson & Zajonc, 1980; Richards, 1997) have shown that there are situations when individuals prefer familiar stimuli to novel. Typically, although certainly not exclusively, familiarity preferences are found when the novel alternatives are difficult to process, given the individual's current experience or information processing capacity. Thus, in designing an appropriate environment, we should consider the child's past experience and current information processing capabilities. Otherwise, children may be faced with stimulation that interferes with curiosity and exploration.

Acting in concert with a proper environment, the factors that promote social-emotional well-being will also play a critical role in fostering the expression of curiosity in exploratory behavior and novelty-seeking. The literatures on secure attachment in infants (e.g., van den Boom, 1994) and adults (e.g., Johnston, 1999) suggest that individuals who have formed secure attachments are more likely to explore novel environments than those whose attachments are less secure. Thus, factors that promote secure attachment are also likely to support appropriate exploratory behavior and interest in novelty. In addition, the way that infants and children are nurtured must be sensitive to the individual's temperament in order to promote optimal exploratory behavior and attention to novel stimulation (e.g., Kagan, 1997; Miceli, Whitman, Borkowski, Braungart-Rieker, & Mitchell, 1998).

Finally, factors that ensure normal physical development and promote the acquisition of sensory and motor skills are also important in enabling exploration and novelty-seeking. As Fagan's model makes clear, a properly functioning nervous system is a prerequisite for information processing and the knowledge that results. In addition, the type of information that can serve as input to the information processing system depends critically on the quality of the incoming sensory information, as well as the nature of the exploratory behaviors that are within the organism's repertoire. Thus, individuals who experience sensory loss or deficit may have more difficulty in perceiving, and hence exploring, novel stimuli (e.g., Bigelow, 1992); similarly, individuals who experience loss of mobility, are likely to have difficulty in exploring the novel features of their environment (e.g., Butler, 1986). When sensory or motor deficits occur, compensatory strategies need to be developed to enhance the individual's ability to exercise their curiosity and exploratory behavior.

CONCLUSIONS

Human infants are so incompletely developed at birth that much remains to be specified by experience. Because of this malleability, a selective orientation toward novelty and exploration can play a crucial role in the ultimate form that the intellect will take, both in terms of its breadth and depth. In addition, human cultures can change so dramatically within one's life time, that an interest in novelty and the adequate physical and intellectual resources for exploring new, unusual, or unpredictable occurrences are crucial for human adaptation. Clearly, it is advantageous to foster curiosity, exploration, and novelty-seeking, in appropriate ways, at all points along the life span.

Having extolled the virtues of curiosity, exploration, and novelty-seeking, we would be remiss if we did not mention some important caveats. Simple arousal and curiosity is not necessarily good, in and of itself; the value of curiosity and exploration depends critically on the nature of the stimulation that is the object of the individual's attention. Children's innate curiosity can as easily direct them to explore novel pornographic Web sites as it can direct them to the marvels inside a museum. Thus, careful guidance from parents and teachers is necessary in choosing the information that will be explored. Relatedly, some of the information that children must master in their school work, such as trigonometric functions or the nuances of literature, may be complex or novel enough to extend beyond the range that is appealing to them. When children must explore topics that are beyond the range that is optimal for their spontaneous interest, careful guidance by a teacher or parent is again required. It is also important to coordinate incentives from a variety of sources, both internal to the child and external, to optimally support and guide children's curiosity, exploration, and novelty-seeking.

REFERENCES

Alberti, E. T., & Witryol, S. L. (1990). Children's preference for complexity as a function of perceived units in collative motivation. *Journal of Genetic Psychology, 151,* 91–101.

Alberti, E. T., & Witryol, S. L. (1994). The relationship between curiosity and cognitive ability in third- and fifth-grade children. *Journal of Genetic Psychology, 155,* 129–145.

Attneave, F. (1957). Physical determinants of the judged complexity of shapes. *Journal of Experimental Psychology, 53,* 221–227.

Benson, J. B., Cherny, S. S., Haith, M. M., & Fulker, D. W. (1993). Rapid assessment of infant predictors of adult IQ: The midtwin-midparent approach, *Developmental Psychology, 29,* 434–447.

Berg, C. A., & Sternberg, R. J. (1985). Response to novelty: Continuity versus discontinuity in the developmental course of intelligence. In H. W. Reese (Ed.), *Advances in child development and behavior* (Vol. 19, pp. 1–47). New York: Academic Press.

Berlyne, D. E. (1960). *Conflict, arousal and curiosity.* New York: McGraw-Hill.

Bigelow, A. E. (1992). Locomotion and search behavior in blind infants. *Infant Behavior & Development, 15,* 179–189.

Bornstein, M. H., & Sigman, M. D. (1986). Continuity in mental development from infancy. *Child Development, 57,* 251–274.

Butler, C. (1986). Effects of powered mobility on self-initiated behavior of very young children with locomotor disability. *Developmental Medicine & Clinical Neurology, 28,* 325–332.

Butler, R. A. (1953). Discrimination learning by rhesus monkeys to visual exploration motivation. *Journal of Comparative and Physiological Psychology, 46,* 95–98.

Cahill-Solis, T. L., & Witryol, S. L. (1994). Children's exploratory play preferences for four levels of novelty in toy constructions. *Genetic, Social, and General Psychology Monographs, 120*, 393–408.

Cancelli, A. A., Duley, S. M., & Meredith, K. E. (1980). Subjective uncertainty as a predictor of specific exploration. *Journal of Psychology, 104*, 3–9.

Cantor, G. N. (1963). Responses of infants and children to complex and novel stimulation. In H. W. Reese & L. P. Lipsitt (Eds.), *Advances in child development and behavior* (Vol. 1, pp. 2–30). San Diego, CA: Academic Press.

Colombo, J. (1993). *Infant cognition: Predicting later intellectual functioning.* Thousand Oaks, CA: Sage.

David, D. B., & Witryol, S. L. (1990). Gender as a moderator variable in the relationship between an intrinsic motivation scale and short-term novelty in children. *Journal of Genetic Psychology, 151*, 153–167.

DiLalla, L. F., Thompson, L. A., Plomin, R., Phillips, K., Fagan, J. F., Haith, M. M., Cyphers, L. H., & Fulker, D. W. (1990). Infant predictors of preschool and adult IQ: A study of infant twins and their parents. *Developmental Psychology, 26*, 759–769.

Dougherty, T. M., & Haith, M. M. (1997). Infant expectations and reaction time as predictors of childhood speed of processing and IQ. *Developmental Psychology, 33*, 146–155.

Eckblad, G. (1964). The attractiveness of uncertainty. II: Effect of different rates of reduction in the level of subjective uncertainty. *Scandinavian Journal of Psychology, 5*, 33–49.

Fagan, J. F. (1992). Intelligence: A theoretical viewpoint. *Current Directions in Psychological Science, 1*, 82–86.

Fagan, J. F. (2000). A theory of intelligence as processing: Implications for society. *Psychology, Public Policy, & Law, 6*, 168–179.

Fagan, J. F., & Haiken-Vasen, J. (1997). Selective attention to novelty as a measure of information processing across the life span. In J. A. Burack & J. T. Enns (Eds.), *Attention, development, and psychopathology* (pp. 55–73). New York: Guilford.

Fagan, J. F., & Singer, L. T. (1983). Infant recognition memory as a measure of intelligence. In L. P. Lipsitt (Ed.), *Advances in infancy research* (Vol. 2, pp. 31–78), Norwood, NJ: Ablex.

Fantz, R. L. (1964). Visual experience in infants: Decreased attention to familiar patterns relative to novel ones. *Science, 146*, 668–670.

Fantz, R. L., Fagan, J. F., & Miranda, S. B. (1975). Early visual selectivity. In L. B. Cohen & P. Salapatek (Eds.), *Infant Perception: From Sensation to Cognition. Vol. 1: Basic Visual Processes* (pp. 249–345). New York, NY: Academic Press, Inc.

Feldstein, J. H., & Witryol, S. L. (1971). The incentive value of uncertainty reduction for children. *Child Development, 42*, 793–804.

Gibson, E. J. (1988). Exploratory behavior in the development of perceiving, acting, and the acquiring of knowledge. *Annual Review of Psychology, 39*, 1–41.

Haaf, R. A., Feldstein, J. H., & Witryol, S. L. (1970). A developmental study of children's incentive-object preferences. *Developmental Psychology, 3*, 275.

Haith, M. M., Hazan, C., & Goodman, G. G. (1988). Expectation and anticipation of dynamic visual events by 3.5-month-old babies. *Child Development, 59*, 467–479.

Harter, S. *A scale of intrinsic versus extrinsic orientation in the classroom.* Unpublished manuscript. (Available from Susan Harter, Department of Psychology, University of Denver, Denver, CO 80208).

Hutt, C. (1970). Specific and diversive exploration. In H. W. Reese (Ed.), *Advances in child development and behavior* (Vol. 5, pp. 119–180). New York: Academic Press.

Jacobson, S. W. (1998). Specificity of neurobehavioral outcomes associated with prenatal alcohol exposure. *Alcoholism: Clinical & Experimental Research, 22*, 313–320.

Jacobson, S. W., Jacobson, J. L., O'Neill, J. M., Padgett, R. J., Frankowski, J. J., & Bihun, J. T. (1992). Visual expectation and dimensions of infant information processing. *Child Development, 63*, 711–724.

Jacobson, S. W., Jacobson, J. L., & Sokol, R. J. (1994). Effects of fetal alcohol exposure on infant reaction time. *Alcoholism: Clinical & Experimental Research, 18*, 1125–1132.

Johnston, M. A. (1999). Influences of adult attachment in exploration. *Psychological Reports, 84*, 31–34.

Kagan, J. (1997). Temperament and the reactions to unfamiliarity. *Child Development, 68*, 139–143.

Kunst-Wilson, W. R., & Zajonc, R. B. (1980). Affective discrimination of stimuli that cannot be recognized. *Science, 207*(4430), 557–558.

Levin, H., & Forgays, D. G. (1959). Learning as a function of sensory stimulation of various intensities. *Journal of Comparative and Physiological Psychology, 52*, 195–201.

McCall, R. B., & Carriger, M. S. (1993). A meta-analysis of infant habituation and recognition memory performance as predictors of later IQ. *Child Development, 64*, 57–59.

McCall, R. B., & Kagan, J. (1970). Individual differences in the infant's distribution of attention to stimulus discrepancy. *Developmental Psychology, 2*, 90–98.

Miceli, P. J., Whitman, T. L., Borkowski, J. G., Braungart-Rieker, J. M., & Mitchell, D. W. (1998). Individual differences in infant information processing: The role of temperamental and maternal factors. *Infant Behavior & Development, 21*, 119–136

Munsinger, H., & Kessen, W. (1966). Stimulus variability and cognitive change. *Psychological Review, 73*, 164–178.

Myers, A. K., & Miller, N. E. (1954). Failure to find learned drive based on hunger: Evidence for learning motivated by "exploration." *Journal of Comparative and Physiological Psychology, 47*, 428–436.

Nunnally, J. C., & Lemond, L. C. (1973). Exploratory behavior and human development. In H. W. Reese (Ed.), *Advances in child development and behavior* (Vol. 8, pp. 59–109). New York: Academic Press.

O'Neill, J. M., & Witryol, S. L. (1985). A developmental investigation of collative preference for variety. *Genetic, Social, and General Psychology Monographs, 111*, 83–99.

Panek, P. E., Stern, H. L., Barrett, G. V, & Alexander, R. A. (1978). Note on preference for stimulus complexity across the life-span. *Perceptual and Motor Skills, 46*, 393–394.

Rheingold, H. L. (1985). Development as the acquisition of familiarity. *Annual Review of Psychology, 36*, 1–17.

Richards, J. E. (1997). Effects of attention on infants' preference for briefly exposed stimuli in the paired-comparison recognition-memory paradigm. *Developmental Psychology, 31*, 22–31.

Shannon, C. E., & Weaver, W. (1949). *The mathematical theory of communication.* Urbana, IL: University of Illinois Press.

Singer, L. T., & Fagan, J. F. (1984). Cognitive development in the failure-to-thrive infant: A three-year longitudinal study. *Journal of Pediatric Psychology, 9*, 363–383.

Skidgell, A. C., Witryol, S. L., & Wirzbicki, P. J. (1976). The effect of novelty-familiarity levels on material reward preference of first-grade children. *Journal of Genetic Psychology, 128*, 291–297.

Valenti, S. S. (1985). Children's preference for novelty in selective learning: Developmental stability of change? *Journal of Experimental Child Psychology, 40*, 406–419.

Valenti, S. S., & Witryol, S. L. (1982). The effects of short-term novelty on children's preferences for incentive objects. *Genetic Psychology Monographs, 105*, 155–178.

van den Boom, D. C. (1994). The influence of temperament and mothering on attachment and exploration: An experimental manipulation of sensitive responsiveness among lower-class mothers with irritable infants. *Child Development, 65*, 1457–1477.

Wentworth, N., & Witryol, S. L. (1983). Is variety the better part of novelty? *Journal of Genetic Psychology, 142*, 3–15.

Wentworth, N., & Witryol, S. L. (1984). Uncertainty and novelty as collative motivation in children. *Journal of Genetic Psychology, 144*, 3–17.

Wentworth, N., & Witryol, S. L. (1986). What's new? Three dimensions for defining novelty. *Journal of Genetic Psychology, 147*, 209–218.

Wentworth, N., & Witryol, S. L. (1990). Information theory and collative motivation: Incentive value of uncertainty, variety, and novelty for children. *Genetic, Social, and General Psychology Monographs, 116*, 299–322.

Werner, A. B., & Witryol, S. L. (1988). Sex differences in collative preference for complexity in kindergarten and elementary school children. *Genetic, Social, and General Psychology Monographs, 114*, 463–475.

Werner, A. B., & Witryol, S. L. (1990). Complexity discrimination as a determinant of children's preferences in collative motivation. *Journal of Genetic Psychology, 151*, 231–243.

White, R. W. (1959). Motivation reconsidered: The concept of competence. *Psychological Review, 66*, 297–333.

Witryol, S. L., & Valenti, S. S. (1980). A developmental comparison of novelty-familiarity levels in first- and fifth-grade children. *Journal of Genetic Psychology, 136*, 281–284.

Witryol, S. L., & Wanich, G. A. (1983). Developmental invariance of novelty functions contrasted to age differences in the Moss-Harlow effect. *Journal of Genetic Psychology, 143*, 3–8.

Wood, R. I. (1977). Drive and incentive properties of stimulus variability in young children (Doctoral dissertation, Arizona State University, 1977). *Dissertation Abstracts International, 38*, 1430B.

Zeaman, D. (1976). The ubiquity of novelty-familiarity (habituation?) effects. In T. J. Tighe & R. N. Leaton (Eds.), *Habituation: Perspectives from Child Development, Animal Behavior, and Neurophysiology* (pp. 297–320). Hillsdale, NJ: Lawrence Erlbaum Associates.

22

Mastery Motivation and Goal Persistence in Young Children

Kay Donahue Jennings

Laura J. Dietz
University of Pittsburgh

INTRODUCTION

Mastery motivation is an intrinsic desire to master one's environment, especially one's physical environment. Although mastery motivation is associated with cognitive competence, it is a distinct construct. Competence represents what one already knows how to do, whereas mastery motivation is the disposition to persistently acquire competence. Controlling the environment and achieving a goal are inherently (i.e., intrinsically) pleasurable and rewarding. Thus, mastery motivation is a self-directed behavior that can best be inferred when extrinsic rewards are absent. Still, extrinsic rewards, especially social rewards, influence the development of mastery motivation and the amount of motivation shown in a given circumstance.

Motivation cannot, of course, be directly observed. Instead, it must be inferred from behavior. In infants and very young children, it must be inferred from action because verbal behavior (and metacognition) are insufficiently developed. A motivational perspective on behavior focuses on the intent of action, the accompanying affect, and the persistence of effort rather than the skills needed to carry out the intentional action (Atkinson, 1964).

Robert White (1959) brought attention to this motivational construct in a seminal paper, "Motivation reconsidered: The Concept of Competence." He used the term *effectance motivation* to draw attention to behaviors with an underlying goal of affecting one's environment. He argued that such motivation was necessary for the young of higher species, including humans, to become competent in their environment. He wrote this paper at the same time that Bowlby (1958) was writing on attachment. Both theorists questioned the usefulness of social learning theory that was then the dominant theoretical framework for understanding origins of human behavior and development. Instead, both used an ecological prospective to argue that predispositions to certain behaviors were biologically useful, and even necessary, for survival. Bowlby argued that two motivational systems are needed for the young to survive: attachment and exploration. Bowlby's work focused on the attachment motivational system. White and his successors have focused on understanding the other motivational system: exploratory or mastery motivation.

White (1959) argued that it was advantageous for humans and other higher species to have an inborn inclination to explore and master their environment. Such motivation encourages a wide range of learning about the environment. If the young only learned about the specific aspects of the environment that had proved useful in the past (as would be the case if all learning was governed by extrinsic rewards), they would be ill equipped for new environments or changes in environments. Instead, mastery motivation encourages adaptive functioning in a broad range of environments and leads to a broad range of competence.

Although a variety of terms have been used to describe this motivation, including *effectance motivation* and *competence motivation*, *mastery motivation* is the dominant term currently used to describe this motivation in young children. Use of the term mastery motivation stems in part from a more differentiated view of infants' and young children's motivation that has arisen from research on the early development of goal-directed behavior. As infants develop, they become able to form specific goals for their actions and are no longer content to simply make something happen. Rather, they focus on achieving particular desired outcomes. Consequently, the term mastery motivation appears more appropriate because it is more comprehensive and can include motivation to simply explore objects as well as motivation to attain a desired effect. Mastery motivation is a construct that is typically reserved for infants and preschoolers, although it is closely related to task-persistence, achievement motivation, self-efficacy and other motivational constructs used for older children and adults.

In this chapter we first describe the early development of mastery motivation, including its differentiation and integration with affect, the self-system, and action regulation. We then describe frequently used methods to operationalize the construct. Finally, we summarize empirical evidence on mastery motivation with an emphasis on its stability over time, its relationship to other child characteristics, and factors influencing its development.

DEVELOPMENT OF MASTERY MOTIVATION

Mastery motivation undergoes transformations as infants mature. Earlier phases are retained, leading to an increasingly differentiated system with multiple components. Depending on the demands of a particular environmental task, children can use whichever mastery motivational component is most appropriate (assuming they have mastered the component). Jennings (1991, 1993), Barrett and Morgan (1995), and Messer (1995) have outlined fairly similar conceptualizations of the development of mastery motivation. We present the developmental phases as outlined by Jennings.

Development in Infancy

Attend to the Novel. Shortly after birth, infants can process information in their environment at a rudimentary level. Even very young infants visually attend to novel objects (Fantz, Fagan, & Miranda, 1975). Later they explore novel objects both orally and manually—preferring them to familiar objects (Keller, Scholmerich, Miranda, & Gauda, 1987).

Influence the Environment. By about 2 months of age, infants become aware of contingency between their actions and environmental events. They increase the frequency of actions that have interesting contingent feedback but do not increase the frequency of actions with noncontingent feedback (DeCasper & Carstens, 1981; Rovee-Collier & Lipsitt, 1982). In addition, they smile and show excitement when their actions produce interesting contingent feedback but not when the same interesting feedback is made noncontingent (Barrett, Morgan, & Maslin-Cole, 1993; Watson & Ramey, 1972). This positive affect and excitement strongly suggest that exercising control over the environment is intrinsically pleasurable.

Control the Environment (Achieve a Simple Goal). Beginning at about 9 months of age, means and end can be separated so that infants can maintain a salient goal and engage in an action separate from the goal to obtain the goal (Messer, Rachford, McCarthy, & Yarrow, 1987; Piaget, 1954). At the simplest level, this means that infants can reach around an obstacle to obtain an attractive object. Later infants are able to maintain a simple process-oriented goal, that is, a temporary endpoint that can be endlessly repeated (Fenson, Kagan, Kearsley, & Zelazo, 1976; McCall, Eichorn, & Hogarty, 1977). For example, an infant putting blocks in a bucket can focus on the process-goal of putting each block in the bucket. The fact that the infant's goal is simply to put in blocks becomes clear when the infant runs out of blocks and empties the bucket to continue the activity.

Focus on Outcome of Action Chains. Beginning at about 18 months of age, toddlers are capable of maintaining constructs that are relatively independent of action and context. As a result, toddlers become able to conceptualize true endpoints, or outcomes, for their activities. Thus, returning to the bucket example, the toddler is now able to focus on the endpoint of filling the bucket rather than merely the process-goals of putting each piece in the bucket. This ability to conceptualize true endpoints can also be thought of as the ability to form standards to evaluate the outcome of actions (Kagan, 1981). As children become able to form standards for outcomes, they also become aware of external standards for their behavior, which then influence their evaluations of themselves (Kagan, 1981; Stipek, Recchia, & McClintic, 1992). Thus, toddlers begin to evaluate themselves and become aware that others can also evaluate them. Toddlers smile more when completing an activity (Bullock & Lutkenhaus, 1988; Kagan, 1981; Morgan, Harmon, & Maslin-Cole 1990), begin to show pride, and call attention to their successful outcomes (Heckhausen, 1982, 1987; Jennings, 1992; Kagan, 1981; Stipek et al., 1992). In addition, they also begin to focus on their own agency. They begin protesting unneeded help because it is a threat to their own sense of agency and accomplishment (Dietz, Hungerford, Yaggi, & Jennings, 1999; Geppert & Kuster, 1983; Heckhausen, 1982; Jennings, 1992).

Beginning about 3 Years

Focus on Difficulty Level and Challenge.   As they mature, children understand more task-relevant information. Prior to age 3, children focus mainly on (a) whether the desired outcome was successfully reached, and (b) whether the outcome was achieved by themselves. Older children can also focus on whether the task is challenging or requires some skill. Although some implicit awareness of task difficulty is sometimes seen at earlier ages (Barrett et al., 1993), not until age 3 do children persist more on moderately difficult tasks than easy tasks (Redding, Morgan, & Harmon, 1988). Furthermore, after age 3, children begin to use the words *easy* and *hard* with some accuracy to describe task difficulty (Heckhausen, 1982; Bird & Thompson, 1986; Schneider, Hanne, & Lehmann, 1989). Children also show more pride when succeeding on difficult rather than easy tasks and show more shame when failing easy tasks than difficult tasks (Alessandri & Lewis, 1996). In addition, 3-year-old children begin to compare their performance against that of others (Heckhausen, 1982; Stipek et al., 1992). By the end of the preschool period, children are beginning to understand that their self-efficacy depends on both qualities of the task and qualities of the self. Constructs of achievement motivation, beliefs about self-control, and implicit theories of intelligence then become important in explaining children's behavior in mastery situations.

OPERATIONAL DEFINITIONS OF MASTERY MOTIVATION AND PERSISTENCE

A variety of methods for operationalizing mastery motivation have been developed. We describe the primary ones. A more detailed review can be found in MacTurk, Morgan, and Jennings (1995).

Persistence and Other Behavior on Solvable Tasks

Yarrow and his colleagues conceptualized mastery motivation as multi-faceted, and they developed tasks to assess the most important facets including problem solving and effectance (e.g., Yarrow et al., 1983; Yarrow, Morgan, Jennings, Harmon, & Gaiter, 1982). This continues to be the most common approach to assessing mastery motivation. Tasks have been developed for a broad age range from 6 months of age (e.g., Messer et al., 1986) to 4½ years (e.g., Jennings, Connors, & Stegman, 1988). In this approach, each task assesses a particular aspect of mastery motivation; for example, puzzles and shape-sorters assess mastery motivation on problem-solving tasks whereas cause-effect toys assess mastery motivation on effectance. Tasks are designed to be moderately challenging for a given-aged child. An important part of the format is that the child is asked to work independently while the examiner and mother are "busy." The intent is to observe the child's motivation for independently mastering the task. Persistence of task-directed behavior is typically the primary measure of motivation. In addition, the sophistication of the task behavior is noted (from exploratory to goal-directed). Barrett and Morgan have conceptualized persistence and related behaviors as instrumental aspects of mastery motivation. Affect while engaged in the task or at completion of the task is also an important indicator of motivation. Affect, typically coded, includes mastery smiles and displays of pride and shame. Barrett and Morgan (1995) have conceptualized affect as the expressive aspect of mastery motivation. Finally, social bids, including help-seeking and drawing attention to success, are also indicators of motivation and are sometimes the main focus of interest (Wachs & Comb, 1995).

A variant of this approach is using pretesting to determine a task that is optimally challenging to the particular child (neither too easy nor too difficult; Morgan, Busch-Rossnagel, Maslin-Cole, & Harmon, 1992). Morgan and his colleagues have argued that using the same tasks for all children of a given age means that the tasks are too easy for some children and too difficult for others. Using a series of graded difficulty tasks, such as puzzles, they code mastery motivation on the task (e.g., puzzle) that the child requires between 1 and 3 minutes to solve.

Persistence and Other Behavior on Impossible Tasks and Other Contrived Tasks

Different formats have been developed to assess children's response to failure and their investment in completing tasks by themselves. Tasks designed to assess failure are contrived to be subtly impossible (puzzle pieces may be slightly the wrong shape or not enough time is allowed). Displays of shame at failure and persistence shown at the next task presented assess helplessness (e.g., Alessandri & Lewis, 1996; Heckhausen, 1987; Kelley & Jennings, in press). In other tasks, the examiner offers unneeded "help" or attempts to take over the task, especially the last step (e.g., Dietz et al., 1999; Geppert & Kuster, 1983; Jennings, 1992). Children's attempts to resist help and complete the task on their own are coded.

Ratings During Administration of Developmental Tests

The Behavior Rating Scale (BRS) is part of the Bayley Scales of Infant Development (Bayley, 1993) and has been widely used to rate children's test behavior. Ratings pertinent to mastery motivation include persistence in attempting to complete tasks and enthusiasm toward tasks. These scales show good short-term stability (r's = .57 to .96) and good inter-observer agreement (r's = .83 to .97; Bayley, 1993). The BRS and its predecessor, the Infant Behavior Record, have been used to assess mastery motivation and emotion regulation during mastery situations (e.g., McGowan, Johnson, & Maxwell, 1981; Yarrow & Messer, 1983; Yarrow et al., 1982).

Observations of Naturally Occurring Play Behavior

Interest in assessing children's motivation during free play stems from the assumption that such assessments may index more typical levels of motivation than that observed during structured tasks. Children are observed while playing on their own with a variety of toys that offer some challenge and require some problem solving. Children's efforts at sustained, cognitively mature play are usually the primary measure of mastery motivation (Morgan, Maslin-Cole, Biringen, & Harmon, 1991; Jennings, Harmon, Morgan, Gaiter, & Yarrow, 1979), but sometimes the highest level of play observed is used as the index of mastery motivation (Hrncir, Speller, & West, 1985).

Mastery Motivation Questionnaire

The Dimensions of Mastery Questionnaire (DMQ) was developed by Morgan and colleagues (1992) to assess mastery motivation in children from ages 1 to 5. It can be completed by parents or teachers. The questionnaire produces five scales: mastery pleasure, object-oriented mastery motivation, social/symbolic mastery motivation, gross motor persistence, and competence. The last scale, competence, is not considered to be a measure of motivation. Internal consistency of the scales is good and scores are stable over time (median correlation of .60 for ratings more than one year apart; Morgan et al., 1993). In addition, some agreement has been found across raters and between ratings and children's observed behavior (summarized in MacTurk et al., 1995).

EMPIRICAL EVIDENCE SUPPORTING THE ADAPTIVE FUNCTION OF MASTERY MOTIVATION

Despite a theoretical orientation that mastery motivation should promote both cognitive and social competencies, empirical attention has focused almost exclusively on cognitive competence. Also, the few existing longitudinal studies have followed children over relatively brief time periods. No study has examined the influence of early mastery motivation on children's development beyond the preschool period. In the absence of broad longitudinal research, conclusions about the effects of early mastery motivation on children's later adaptive functioning and well-being across multiple domains remain largely theory based rather than empirically based. Seifer and Vaughn (1995) have outlined how mastery motivation should relate to other domains of competence including attachment, affect regulation, and peer relations. They too lament the lack of empirical work linking mastery motivation to competencies other than cognitive competence.

Mastery Motivation and Cognitive Competence

Most research on mastery motivation and adaptive functioning has focused on children's cognitive development, as measured by standardized tests, such as the Bayley Scales of Infant Development and the McCarthy Scales of Children's Achievement. However, some studies have used successful task completion or complexity of play as an index of competence. We first present evidence suggesting that mastery motivation and persistence relate to concurrent measures of competence, especially when competence is conceptualized as success on tasks. Then we present evidence suggesting that early motivation relates to later competence.

Considerable evidence suggests that persistence on a particular task is likely to lead to success (competence) on that task. For example, MacTurk and colleagues (1987) used sequential analysis to show that persistence on a task at 6 and 12 months of age was more likely to be followed by success than other behaviors. Also, 18- and 25-month-old children who persisted more on a task were more likely to succeed at the task than were children who persisted less (Maslin-Cole, Bretherton, & Morgan, 1993). Similarly, children who were more engrossed in their free play (thereby demonstrating higher motivation) were more likely to exhibit cognitively sophisticated play than were children who were less engrossed (Maslin-Cole et al., 1993). This work suggests that higher levels of mastery motivation should lead to higher future competence.

Yarrow and colleagues postulated that high mastery motivation in infancy, as evidenced by increased interest and exploration of the environment, would directly stimulate cognitive growth by providing young children with a wide range of experiences. Early work supported this connection. Infants showing high task persistence and mastery behaviors in the first year of life had higher IQs in the preschool years (Yarrow, Rubenstein, & Pedersen, 1975). Furthermore, early mastery motivation was found to be a better predictor of children's IQ at age 3 than was early cognitive development (Bayley Mental Developmental Index).

Later studies conducted in Yarrow's laboratory continued to demonstrate moderate relationships between early mastery motivation and later cognitive functioning. In two different samples of children, persistence and goal-directed behaviors during infancy predicted cognitive competence at preschool age (Jennings, Yarrow, & Martin, 1984; Messer et al., 1986, 1987). In both studies, however, expected relationships were found only for girls. Messer attributed this gender discrepancy to variability in boys' behavior during cognitive testing that could have interfered with their performance. The study by Messer and colleagues (1986) also provided evidence supporting the discriminant validity (i.e., uniqueness) of early mastery motivation in predicting later cognitive competence. In this study, early measures of cognitive competence (success at task completion and Bayley scores) were not strongly correlated with later McCarthy scores. Instead, early indices of mastery motivation predicted later developmental competence.

These studies suggest that mastery motivation is an important factor in children's well-being. Although engaging in mastery-related behaviors does not necessarily ensure competence, children who develop strategies for controlling and mastering their external environment and their internal mental and emotional states are more likely to become competent than children who have not developed these skills. They are also more likely to have a sense of self-efficacy.

Developmental Stability of Mastery Motivation Over the Life Span

Because of the lack of longitudinal research beyond the preschool years, little is known about how early mastery motivation influences later motivational development or how it may be transformed into more complex personality constructs that contribute to individual differences in well-being. However, the existing literature on mastery motivation in children under 5 years of age has informed our understanding of continuity across early developmental epochs during which new skills and concepts are emerging and being consolidated.

Empirical literature on individual differences in early mastery motivation has demonstrated moderate stability for relatively brief periods across infancy and toddlerhood (Jennings et al., 1984; Yarrow et al., 1983). Task persistence at 6 months related to task persistence at 12 months; continuities in visual attention to tasks and exploratory behavior were also found (Yarrow et al., 1983). Likewise, modest stability of persistence and task pleasure was found between 18 and 25 months (Maslin-Cole et al., 1993).

Empirical work also has identified discontinuities in mastery motivation. Several studies have demonstrated that specific aspects of mastery motivation in younger children do not directly relate to these constructs as measured in older children (DiLalla et al., 1990; Maslin-Cole et al., 1993). These findings have been largely attributed to developmental transformations in children's skills and capabilities. Early, more rudimentary skills that demonstrate infants' awareness and exploration of their external world are later replaced by more complex skills, that make direct comparisons problematic.

Thus, empirical results on the stability of early mastery motivation suggest both continuity in the general construct but discontinuity in more specific aspects of motivation across the infancy and toddler period. These findings illustrate the problem of assessing the stability of constructs, such as mastery motivation, during periods of rapid developmental change. They also present challenges to our ways of thinking about the developmental progression of children's mastery motivation skills—questions of which skills would be expected to remain stable across development and which early skills would be transformed into newer, more complex abilities.

Factors Promoting the Development of Mastery Motivation

Research has begun to clarify genetic and socialization influences on the development of mastery motivation.

Genetic Influences. As with most areas of development, genetic influences are important contributors to individual differences in mastery motivation. The re-emergence of the discipline of behavioral genetics has enhanced our understanding of how biologically based traits influence development. Through twin and adoption studies, assessments of genetic contributions to behavior and personality traits are possible. Several studies have examined the genetic contribution to task orientation (i.e., persistence, attention, and goal-directed activity) as assessed on the Bayley's Infant Behavior Record (IBR). Findings are consistent in suggesting a significant genetic influence on task-orientation by the end of the second year of life (Braungart, Plomin, DeFries, & Fulker, 1992; Emde et al., 1992; Matheny, 1980; Plomin et al., 1993). Less information is available for older children, but some evidence again suggests a genetic component to persistence and planfulness (Loehlin, 1992). This body of research indicates that genetic influences contribute to individual differences in children's mastery motivation.

Socialization Influences. Other influences on the development of children's mastery motivation are included under the rubric of socialization (i.e., relatively consistent experiences in the child's external world that come to shape behavior and beliefs about the self and others). In early childhood, the main socialization influences come from interactions with a primary caregiver or parent. Caregiver influences can be characterized as direct or indirect. Caregivers directly influence the child by their interactions with the child, including interactions that facilitate mastery of toys and tasks. Caregivers also indirectly influence the child by how they structure the physical environment for the child and how much access they provide the infant.

Attachment theorists have long been interested in how the quality of infants' attachment relationships with their mothers relates to infants' confidence and willingness to explore and master things in their environments. Attachment theory suggests that infants with secure attachments should explore more and show more mastery motivation. Several studies support a relationship between attachment and mastery motivation when measured contemporaneously (Frodi, Bridges, & Grolnick, 1985; Maslin-Cole et al., 1993; Roggman & Lee, 1992). However, studies have failed to find evidence for a longitudinal relationship between attachment and later mastery motivation (Maslin-Cole et al., 1993; Riksen-Walraven, Meij, van Roozendaal, & Koks, 1993). Thus, research to date suggests that a secure attachment to the mother supports children's current interest in exploring and mastering the environment but does not ensure increased mastery motivation later.

Aside from attachment, other aspects of the parent–child relationship have been demonstrated to promote young children's mastery motivation. First, the variety and amount of stimulation have been found to be important. Provision of challenging toys and other material at home relates to task persistence on similar toys (Barrett et al., 1993), suggesting that opportunities to play with challenging toys promotes further interest in such toys. In addition, the variety of cognitively oriented caregiver activities in infancy predicts later persistence at tasks (Gaiter, Morgan, Jennings, Harmon & Yarrow, 1982; Jennings et al., 1979; Yarrow et al., 1982). Thus, the provision of a broad range of mastery opportunities and experiences enhances the development of mastery motivation.

Parents' interactional style with their children has also been shown to relate to children's mastery motivation. Research to date (other than attachment research) has focused on parental style in mastery situations with objects, although Messer (1993) argues that in the first few months of life, parent–infant social interaction are crucial in the development of mastery motivation. Findings suggest that a parental style during object play that is characterized by warmth, minimal control, and appropriate scaffolding is most likely to promote the development of mastery motivation. Positive affect exchanges, or warmth, relates to higher task directedness and more pride in children (Morgan, Maslin-Cole, Ridgeway, & Kang-Park, 1988) and to better organized and more sustained play (i.e., persistence in play; Jennings & Connors, 1989). A less directive interactive style in play with objects has also been found to relate to more task persistence and higher maternal perceptions of mastery motivation (Jennings & Connors, 1989). Finally, appropriate scaffolding as needed to enhance success with objects relates to persistence on mastery tasks (Frodi et al., 1985; Grolnick, Frodi, & Bridges, 1984; Maslin-Cole et al., 1993). Together, these studies suggest that the most effective parenting style for enhancing mastery motivation is one that is characterized by warmth and fosters autonomy by diminishing unnecessary control while providing appropriate scaffolding (Busch-Rossnagel, Knauf-Jensen, & DesRosiers, 1995).

Finally, empirical work on developmental psychopathology further supports the importance of parental interaction style on children's developing mastery motivation. Impaired levels of mastery motivation have been documented in maltreated preschool children (Vondra, Barrett, & Cicchetti, 1990) and in children with depressed mothers (Jennings, Popper, & Dran, 1999; Redding, Morgan, & Harmon, 1990). These studies suggest that atypical styles of parental interaction (those involving parental depression or maltreatment) negatively affect the development of mastery motivation in young children.

CONCLUSIONS

The existing research has expanded our conceptualization of young children's mastery motivation. The concept has become multifaceted, including an action-on-objects component (e.g., persistence), an affective component (e.g., pleasure in producing outcomes), a social component (e.g., desire for autonomy[1]), and a self-concept component (e.g., experiencing pride in accomplishments). Research to date has focused on each of these components; however, few studies have looked at multiple components of mastery motivation.

Existing research also supports the idea that mastery motivation promotes cognitive competence. The relationship between mastery motivation and competence is seen as dynamic and reciprocal: Each influences the development of the other. Mastery motivation leads to increased competence. Conversely, increased cognitive competence modifies mastery motivation (e.g., cognitive understanding of task difficulty leads to increased motivation to accomplish challenging rather than easy tasks). Empirical research has also increased our understanding of factors that contribute to the development of mastery motivation.

Empirical research is notably lacking in two areas. First, we know little about how mastery motivation relates to competencies in domains other than cognitive competence or how mastery motivation relates to general well-being. Second, we do not know how early mastery motivation relates to motivation, competencies, and well-being beyond the preschool years. Broad-based longitudinal studies are needed if we are to better understand the mechanisms by which early mastery motivation influences the development of children's orientation toward achievement in school and their feelings of well-being.

ACKNOWLEDGMENT

This work was supported by grant RO1MH49419 from the National Institute of Mental Health.

REFERENCES

Alessandri, S. M., & Lewis, M. (1996). Differences in pride and shame in maltreated and nonmaltreated preschoolers. *Child Development, 67*, 1857–1869.

Atkinson, J. W. (1964). *An introduction to motivation.* Princeton, NJ: Van Nostrand.

Barrett, K. C., & Morgan, G. A. (1986). *Is task-directed persistence an index of mastery motivation during infancy?* Unpublished manuscript, Colorado State University, Fort Collins.

Barrett, K. C., & Morgan, G. A. (1995). Continuities and discontinuities in mastery motivation during infancy and toddlerhood: A conceptualization and review. In R. H. MacTurk & G. A. Morgan (Eds.), *Mastery motivation: Origins, conceptualizations, and applications. Advances in applied developmental psychology* (Vol. 12, pp. 57–93). Norwood, NJ: Ablex.

Barrett, K. C., Morgan, G. A., & Maslin-Cole, C. (1993). Three studies on the development of mastery motivation in infancy and toddlerhood. In D. J. Messer (Ed.), *Mastery Motivation in Early Childhood: Development, Measurement, and Social Processes* (pp. 83–108). London: Routledge.

Bayley, N. (1993). *Bayley Scales of Infant Development (2nd ed.): Manual.* San Antonio, TX: Harcourt Brace.

---

[1]For a detailed review of autonomy as an essential component of social-emotional development and well-being, see Bridges' chapter, "Autonomy," pp. 167–176, in this text.

Bird, J. E., & Thompson, G. B. (1986). Understanding of the dimensional terms 'easy' and 'hard' in the self-evaluation of competence. *International Journal of Behavioral Development*, *9*, 343–357.

Bowlby, J. (1958). The nature of the child's tie to his mother. *Internal Journal of Psycho-Analysis*, *39*, 350–373.

Braungart, J. M., Plomin, R., DeFries, J. C., & Fulker, D. W. (1992). Genetic influence on test-rated infant temperament as assessed by Bayley's Infant Behavior Record: Nonadoptive and adoptive siblings and twins. *Developmental Psychology*, *28*, 40–47.

Bullock, M., & Lutkenhaus, P. (1988). The development of volitional behavior in the toddler years. *Child Development*, *59*, 664–674.

Busch-Rossnagel, N. A., Knauf-Jensen, D. E., & DesRosiers, F. S. (1995). Mothers and others: The role of the socializing environment in the development of mastery motivation. In R. H. MacTurk & G. A. Morgan (Eds.), *Mastery motivation: Origins, conceptualizations, and applications. Advances in applied developmental psychology* (Vol. 12, pp. 117–145). Norwood, NJ: Ablex.

DeCasper, A. J., & Carstens, A. A. (1981). Contingencies of stimulation: Effects on learning and emotion in neonates. *Infant Behavior and Development*, *4*, 19–35.

Dietz, L. J., Hungerford, M. S., Yaggi, K., & Jennings, K. D. (1999, April). *Toddlers' self-concept development and their understanding of others as active agents.* Poster presented at the Society for Research in Child Development, Albuquerque, NM.

DiLalla, L. F., Thompson, L. A., Plomin, R., Phillips, K., Fagan, J. F., Haith, M. M., Cyphers, L. H., & Fulker, D. W. (1990). Infant predictors of preschool and adult IQ: A study of infant twins and their parents. *Developmental Psychology*, *26*, 759–769.

Emde, R. N., Plomin, R., Robinson, J., Corley, R., DeFries, J., Fulker, D.W., Reznick, J. S., Campos, J., Kagan, J., & Zahn-Waxler, C. (1992). Temperament, emotion, and cognition at fourteen months: The MacArthur Longitudinal Twin Study. *Child Development*, *63*, 1437–1455.

Fantz, R. L., Fagan, J. F., & Miranda, S. B. (1975). Early visual selection. In L. B. Cohen & P. Salapatek (Eds.), *Infant perception: From sensation to cognition* (Vol. 1, pp. XX–XX). New York: Academic Press.

Fenson, L., Kagan, J., Kearsley, R. B., & Zelazo, P. R. (1976). The developmental progression of manipulative play in the first two years. *Child Development*, *47*, 232–236.

Frodi, A., Bridges, L., & Grolnick, W. (1985). Correlates of mastery-related behavior: A short-term longitudinal study of infants in their second year. *Child Development*, *56*, 1291–1298.

Gaiter, J. L., Morgan, G. A., Jennings, K. D., Harmon, R. J., & Yarrow, L. J. (1982). Variety of cognitively oriented caregiver activities: Relationships to cognitive and motivational functioning at one and 3½ years of age. *Journal of Genetic Psychology*, *141*, 49–56.

Geppert, U., & Kuster, U. (1983). The emergence of 'wanting to do it oneself': A precursor of achievement motivation. *International Journal of Behavioral Development*, *6*, 355–369.

Grolnick, W., Frodi, A., & Bridges, L. (1984). Maternal control style and mastery motivation of one-year-olds. *Infant Mental Health Journal*, *5*, 72–82.

Heckhausen, H. (1981). Developmental precursors of success and failure experience. In G. d'Ydewalle & W. Lens (Eds.), *Cognition in Human Motivation and Learning* (pp. 15–32). Hillsdale, NJ: Lawrence Erlbaum Associates.

Heckhausen, H. (1982). The development of achievement motivation. In W. W. Hartup (Ed.), *Review of Child Development Research* (Vol. 6, pp. 600–668). Chicago: University of Chicago Press.

Heckhausen, H. (1987). Emotional components of action: Their ontogeny as reflected in achievement behavior. In D. Gorlitz & J. F. Wohlwill (Eds.), *Curiosity, imagination, and play: On the development of spontaneous cognitive and motivational processes* (pp. 326–348). Hillsdale, NJ: Lawrence Erlbaum Associates.

Hrncir, E. J., Speller, G. M., & West, M. (1985). What are we testing? *Developmental Psychology*, *21*, 226–232.

Jennings, K., Harmon, R., Morgan, G., Gaiter, J., & Yarrow, L. (1979). Exploratory play as an index of mastery motivation: Relationships to persistence, cognitive functioning, and environmental measures. *Developmental Psychology*, *15*, 386–394.

Jennings, K. D. (1991). Early development of mastery motivation and its relation to the self-concept. In M. Bullock (Ed.), *The development of intentional action: Cognitive, motivational, and interactive process. Contributions to human development.* Basel, Switzerland: Karger.

Jennings, K. D. (1992, May). *Development of mastery motivation and sense of agency in toddlers*. Presented at the International Conference of Infant Studies, Miami Beach, FL.

Jennings, K. D. (1993). Mastery motivation and the formation of self-concept from infancy through early childhood. In D. Messer (Ed.), *Mastery motivation in early childhood: Development, measurement, and social processes* (pp. 36–64). London: Routledge.

Jennings, K. D., & Connors, R. E. (1989). Mothers' interactional style and children's competence at 3 years. *International Journal of Behavioral Development, 12*, 155–175.

Jennings, K. D., Connors, R. E., & Stegman, C. E. (1988). Does a physical handicap alter the development of mastery motivation during the preschool years? *Journal of the American Academy of Child and Adolescent Psychiatry, 27*, 312–317.

Jennings, K. D., Popper, S. D., & Dran, A. J. (1999). *Toddlers' regulation of action: Associations with maternal depression and toddler psychopathology*. Poster presented at the Society for Research in Child Development, Albuquerque, NM.

Jennings, K. D., Yarrow, L. J., & Martin, P. P. (1984). Mastery motivation and cognitive development: A longitudinal study from infancy to 3½ years of age. *International Journal of Behavioral Development, 7*, 441–461.

Kagan, J. (1981). *The second year: The emergence of self-awareness*. Cambridge, MA: Harvard University Press.

Keller, H., Scholmerich, A., Miranda, K., & Gauda, G. (1987). The development of exploratory behavior in the first four years of life. In D. Gorlitz & J. F. Wohlwill (Eds.), *Curiosity, imagination, and play: On the development of spontaneous cognitive and motivational processes* (pp. 126–150). Hillsdale, NJ: Lawrence Erlbaum Associates.

Kelly, S., & Jennings, K. D. (in press). Putting the pieces together: Maternal depression, maternal behavior, and toddler helplessness. *Infant Mental Health Journal*.

Loehlin, J. C. (1992). *Genes and environment in personality development*. Newbury Park, CA: Sage.

MacTurk, R. H., McCarthy, M. E., Vietze, P. M., & Yarrow, L. J. (1987). Sequential analysis of mastery behavior in 6- and 12-month-old infants. *Developmental Psychology, 23*, 199–203.

MacTurk, R. H., Morgan, G. A., & Jennings, K. D. (1995). The assessment of mastery motivation in infants and young children. In R. H. MacTurk & G. A. Morgan (Eds.), *Mastery motivation: Origins, conceptualizations, and applications. Advances in applied developmental psychology* (Vol. 12, pp. 19–56). Norwood, NJ: Ablex.

Maslin-Cole, C., Bretherton, I., & Morgan, G. A. (1993). Toddler mastery motivation and competence: Links with attachment security, maternal scaffolding and family climate. In D. Messer (Ed.), *Mastery motivation in early childhood: Development, measurement, and social processes* (pp. 205–229). London: Routledge.

Matheny, A. P., Jr. (1980). Bayley's Infant behavior record: Behavioral components and twin analyses. *Child Development, 51*, 1157–1167.

McCall, R. B., Eichorn, D. H., & Hogarty, P. S. (1977). Transitions in early mental development. *Monographs of the Society for Research in Child Development, 42*, 3, (Serial No. 171).

McGowan, R. J., Johnson, D. L., & Maxwell, S. E. (1981). Relations between infant behavior ratings and concurrent and subsequent mental scores. *Developmental Psychology, 17*, 542–553.

Messer, D. J. (1993). Mastery, attention, IQ, and parent-infant social interaction. In D. Messer (Ed.), *Mastery motivation in early childhood: Development, measurement, and social processes* (pp. 19–35). London: Routledge.

Messer, D. J. (1995). Mastery motivation: Past, present and future. In R. H. MacTurk & G. A. Morgan (Eds.), *Mastery motivation: Origins, conceptualizations, and applications. Advances in applied developmental psychology* (Vol. 12, pp. 295–316). Norwood, NJ: Ablex Publishing.

Messer, D. J., McCarthy, M. E., McQuinton, S., MacTurk, R. H., Yarrow, L. J., & Vietze, P. M. (1986). Relation between mastery behavior in infancy and competence in early childhood. *Developmental Psychology, 22*, 366–372.

Messer, D. J., Rachford, D., McCarthy, M. E., & Yarrow, L. J. (1987). Assessment of mastery behavior at 30 months: Analysis of task-directed activities. *Developmental Psychology, 23*, 771–781.

Morgan, G. A., Busch-Rossnagel, N. A., Maslin-Cole, C. A., & Harmon, R. J. (1992). *Mastery motivation tasks: Manual for 15- to 36-month-old children*. Bronx, NY: Fordham University.

Morgan, G. A., Harmon, R. J., & Maslin-Cole, C. A. (1990). Mastery motivation: Definition and measurement. *Early Education and Development, 1*, 318–339.

Morgan, G. A., Harmon, R. J., Maslin-Cole, C. A., Busch-Rossnagel, N. A., Jennings, K. D., Hauser-Cram, P., & Brockman, L. M. (1992). *Assessing perceptions of mastery motivation: The dimensions of mastery questionnaire, its development, psychometrics and use.* Ft. Collins: Colorado State University, Human Development and Family Studies Department.

Morgan, G. A., Maslin-Cole, C. A., Biringen, Z., & Harmon, R. J. (1991). Play assessment of mastery motivation in infants and young children. In C. E. Schaefer, K. Gitlin, & A. Sandgrund (Eds.), *Play diagnosis and assessment* (pp. 263–291). New York: Plenum.

Morgan, G. A., Maslin-Cole, C., Harmon, R. J., Busch-Rossnagel, N. A., Jennings, K. D., Hauser-Cram, P., & Brockman, L. (1993). Parent and teacher perceptions of young children's mastery motivation: Assessment and review of research. In D. Messer (Ed.), *Mastery motivation in early childhood: Development, measurement, and social processes* (pp. 109–131). London: Routledge.

Morgan, G. A., Maslin, C. A., Ridgeway, D., & Kang-Park, J. (1988). Toddler mastery motivation and aspects of mother-child affect communication. *Program and Proceedings of the Developmental Psychobiology Research Group Retreat, 5*, 15–16.

Piaget, J. (1954). *Construction of reality in the child.* New York: Basic Books.

Plomin, R., Emde, R. N., Braungart, J. M., Campos, J., Corely, R., Fulker, D. W., Kagan, J., Reznick, J. S., Robinson, J., Zahn-Waxler, C., & DeFries, J. C. (1993). Genetic change and continuity from fourteen to twenty months: The MacArthur longitudinal twin study. *Child Development, 64*, 1354–1376.

Redding, R. E., Morgan, G. A., & Harmon, R. J. (1988). Mastery motivation in infants and toddlers: Is it greatest when tasks are moderately challenging? *Infant Behavior and Development, 11*, 419–30.

Redding, R. E., Morgan, G. A., & Harmon, R. J. (1990). Relationships between maternal depression and infants' mastery behaviors. *Infant Behavior and Development, 13*, 391–395.

Riksen-Walraven, J. M., Meij, J. T., van Roozendaal, J., & Koks, J. (1993). Mastery motivation in toddlers as related to quality of attachment. In D. Messer (Ed.), *Mastery motivation in early childhood: Development, measurement, and social processes.* (pp. 189–204). London: Routledge.

Roggman, L. A., & Lee, J. L. (1992, May). *Attachment and mastery motivation.* Paper presented at the International Conference on Infant Studies, Miami, FL.

Rovee-Collier, C., & Lipsitt, L. (1982). Learning, adaptation, and memory. In P. Stratton (Ed.), *Psychobiology of the human newborn* (**pp. XX–XX**). London: Wiley.

Schneider, K., Hanne, K., & Lehmann, B. (1989). The development of children's achievement-related expectancies and subjective uncertainty. *Journal of Experimental Child Psychology, 47*, 160–174.

Seifer, R., & Vaughn, B. (1995). Mastery motivation within a general organizational model of competence. In R. H. MacTurk & G. A. Morgan (Eds.), *Mastery motivation: Origins, conceptualizations, and applications. Advances in applied developmental psychology* (Vol. 12, pp. 95–115). Norwood, NJ: Ablex.

Stipek, D., Recchia, S., & McClintic, S. (1992). Self-evaluation in young children. *Monographs of the Society for Research in Child Development, 57*(1, Serial No. 226).

Vondra, J. I., Barrett, D., & Cicchetti, D. (1990). Self-concept, motivation and competence among preschoolers from maltreating and comparison families. *Child Abuse and Neglect, 14*, 525–540.

Wachs, T. D., & Combs, T. T. (1995). The domains of infant mastery motivation. In R. H. MacTurk & G. A. Morgan (Eds.), *Mastery motivation: Origins, conceptualizations, and applications. Advances in applied developmental psychology* (Vol. 12, pp. 147–164). Norwood, NJ: Ablex.

Watson, J. S., & Ramey, C. T. (1972). Reactions to response contingent stimulation early in infancy. *Merrill-Palmer Quarterly, 18*, 219–227.

White, R. W. (1959). Motivation reconsidered: The concept of competence. *Psychological Review, 66*, 297–333.

Yarrow, L. J., McQuinton, S., MacTurk, R. H., McCarthy, M. E., Klein, R. P., & Vietze, P. M. (1983). Assessment of mastery motivation during the first year of life: Contemporaneous and cross-age relationships. *Developmental Psychology, 19*(2), 159–171.

Yarrow, L. J., & Messer, D. J. (1983). Motivation and cognition in infancy. In M. Lewis (Ed.), *Origins of intelligence: Infancy and early childhood* (2nd ed.). New York, Plenum Press.

Yarrow, L. J., Morgan, G. A., Jennings, K. D., Harmon, R. J., & Gaiter, L. J. (1982). Infants' persistence at tasks: Relationships to cognitive functioning and early experience. *Infant Behavior and Development*, *5*, 131–141.

Yarrow, L. J., Rubenstein, J., & Pedersen, F. A. (1975). *Infant and environment: Early cognitive and motivational development*, Washington, DC: Hemisphere, Halsted, Witney.

23

Thinking and Intelligence

Robert S. Siegler
Carnegie Mellon University, Pittsburgh, PA

INTRODUCTION

Human cognition develops over a very long period. By the third month of the prenatal period, electrical activity in the fetal brain elicits kicks, toe curls, arm bends, and other activities. By the fifth month of the prenatal period, essentially all neurons are in place. Yet the brain continues developing on a large scale well into adolescence, and smaller changes in response to experience occur throughout life. Thus, cognitive development is a protracted process.

Although everyone would agree that thinking changes greatly from birth to adolescence, defining thinking is surprisingly difficult. The reason is that no sharp boundary divides activities that involve thinking from ones that do not. Thinking clearly involves high-level mental processes: solving problems, reasoning, symbolizing, planning, and so on. Other examples of thinking involve more basic processes, processes at which even young children are proficient: perceiving objects and events in the external environment and expressing oneself in language, to name two. Still other activities might or might not be viewed as examples of thinking. These include being socially skillful, having a keen moral sense, and understanding one's own strengths and weaknesses. The capabilities in this last group involve thought processes, but they also involve many other, nonintellectual, qualities.

Traditional global measures of thinking, notably intelligence tests, have tended to focus on the first set of activities, with some attention to the second set. However, some contemporary approaches to intelligence, notably those of Sternberg (e.g., 1999) and Gardner (e. g., 1999) have adopted a broader view of intelligence that in-

311

cludes understanding of oneself and others, creativity, musical ability, and other nonprototypic forms of intelligence. These broader definitions have the advantage of forcing us to consider what we mean by intelligence. Are intellectual capabilities those qualities that correlate positively with present and future academic performance? Are they qualities that correlate positively with later occupational success? Are they capabilities that correspond to everyday meanings of the term *intelligence*? There are no objectively correct answers to these questions, but it is useful to realize that intelligence can be conceptualized in alternative ways.

Thinking has been studied from two main perspectives, the one identified with the label *cognitive development*, the other identified with the label *intelligence*. The main difference is that cognitive developmentalists tend to emphasize changes in thinking that occur with age, whereas intelligence researchers emphasize individual differences at a given age and stability of those differences over time. The distinction is not absolute; for example, cognitive developmentalists have demonstrated that the rates at which infants stop looking at familiar displays (habituation) and resume looking when the display changes (dishabituation) are predictive of later differences in IQ scores (Bornstein & Sigman, 1986; Fagan & Singer, 1983; Rose & Feldman, 1995). For the most part, however, cognitive developmentalists focus on how the thinking of children in general changes with age, and intelligence researchers focus on how the thinking of individual children of a given age differs from that of other children of that age. The evidence most relevant to the questions posed for this paper comes from intelligence research; this evidence is the main focus in the remainder of this paper.

TECHNICAL ISSUES: THE MEASUREMENT OF INTELLIGENCE

Intelligence is measured through use of standardized tests, such as the WISC (Wechsler Intelligence Test for Children) and the Stanford-Binet. These tests assess intelligence by sampling numerous types of knowledge and abilities. For example, the WISC includes subtests on general information, vocabulary, arithmetic, comprehension, memory, and so on. Performance on the various subtests is combined into a single composite score, the IQ (intelligence quotient). The IQ score is based on each individual's score relative to that of age peers. The tests are designed so that the average score is 100, with higher scores indicating greater intelligence and lower scores indicating lower intelligence. Thus, at the time the test is constructed, a score of 115 is in the top 16% of scores and a score of 85 is in the bottom 16%.

Intelligence test items are selected in part because they measure inherently important parts of intelligence, in part because they predict school achievement and other intellectual outcomes, and in part because scores on them are positively related to scores on other items on the test. The technology involved in selecting items and constructing IQ tests is quite complex and is well beyond the scope of this brief introduction. For clear and comprehensive descriptions of test construction and the controversies surrounding it, see Brody (1992) and Neisser et al. (1996).

One of the main advantages of IQ scores is that they are easy to compare across different ages, despite the great increases in knowledge that accompany development in all children. A score of 130 at age 5 means that a child's performance exceeded that of 98% of age peers; a score of 130 at age 10 means exactly the same thing. This property has facilitated examination of the stability of intelligence over age, a topic that is examined next.

Stability of Intelligence Over Time

Longitudinal studies that have measured the same children's IQ scores at different ages have shown impressive stability from age 4 or 5 years onward. For example, IQs at ages 5 and 15 years are highly correlated (Humphreys, 1989). Few if any psychological qualities show as much stability over long stretches of time as does intelligence (Brody, 1992).

The fact that a person's IQ scores at different ages are highly correlated does not mean that the scores are likely to be identical. Children who take an IQ test at 4 years and again at 17 years show an average change of 13 points (up or down), those who take the test at 8 and 17 years show an average change of 9 points, and those who take it at 12 and 17 years show an average change of 7 points (Brody, 1992). These differences are due in part to random variation in children's day-to-day functioning and in their knowledge of the particular items on the tests. However, McCall, Applebaum, and Hogarty (1973) found that changes in IQ scores also reflect changes in children's lives and circumstances. For example, they found that scores tend to increase over time among children who believe that it is very important to do well in school. They also found that parental interest in their children's learning, emphasis on success, and use of rational disciplinary procedures also are associated with increases over time in children's IQs. However, they also found that IQ scores tend to decrease among children whose parents use very stern or very lax disciplinary procedures and who show little interest in their children's performance in school. Thus, both random and systematic factors contribute to changes in children's IQs over time.

IQ Scores as Predictors of Important Outcomes

IQ scores correlate positively and fairly strongly with school grades and achievement test performance, both at the time of the test and in later years (Brody, 1992). They also are positively related to long-term educational and occupational success. In the United States, IQ in sixth grade correlates about .60 with the number of years of education that a person will eventually obtain (Duncan, Featherman, & Duncan, 1972; Jencks, 1979). IQ also is positively related to income. In part, this positive relation is due to standardized test scores serving as a gatekeeper, determining which students will be allowed to go into law, medicine, and other lucrative professions. Even among people who initially have the same job, however, those with higher IQs tend to perform better (Hunter, 1986), earn more money (Jencks, 1979), and receive larger promotions (Wilk, Desmarais, & Sackett, 1995).

The strength of the relation between IQ scores and occupational success can be viewed either as the glass being half full or half empty. Consistent with the glass-half-full perspective, Brody (1992) noted, "IQ is the most important predictor of an individual's ultimate position within American society" (p. 255). A child's IQ is more closely related to the child's later occupational success than is the socioeconomic status of the family within which the child grows up, the family's income, the school the child attends, or any other variable that has been studied (Ceci, 1993; Duncan, Featherman, & Duncan, 1972). On the other hand, IQ is far from the whole story in occupational success. Motivation to succeed, creativity, emotional stability, health, social skills, and a host of other qualities also exert important influences (Feldman, 1986; Tannenbaum, 1986).

FACTORS THAT INFLUENCE THE DEVELOPMENT OF INTELLIGENCE

Genetic Contributions

Children's genetic inheritance exerts a substantial influence on their intelligence. About 50% of the variation in IQ among Caucasians in the United States is attributable to genetic variation.

A common stereotype is that the relative influence of heredity is greatest early in life, when children's experience is limited, and that it decreases as they gain experience. This stereotype has it backward. The genetic contribution to intelligence becomes larger, not smaller, as children develop. Correlations between adopted children's IQs and those of their biological parents (with whom they are not living) *increase* with age (Honzik, MacFarlane, & Allen 1948). In contrast, correlations between adopted children's IQs and those of their rearing parents *decrease* with age (Brody, 1992; DeFries, Ploman, & LaBuda, 1987; McGue, Bouchard, Iacono, & Lykken, 1993). The increasing genetic influence on intelligence is attributable to some genetic processes not having their effects until later childhood or adolescence (Loehlin, 1989) and also to adopted children increasingly choosing intellectual environments like those their biological parents would have provided (Scarr, 1992).

Genotype → Environment Interactions

At all ages, children's genotypes are related to the types of environments they encounter. The relation emerges through three types of processes: passive, evocative, and active (Scarr, 1992). Passive effects of children's genotypes arise not because of anything that children do but because most are reared by their biological parents whose genes overlap with their own. Thus, children whose genotypes predispose them to enjoy reading are likely to be reared in homes where reading materials are prominent, because their parents also like to read. Evocative effects of the genotype emerge through children influencing other people's behavior. Even if a child's parents are not avid readers, they will read more bedtime stories if their daughter seems interested than if she seems bored. Active effects of the genotype involve children choosing environments that they enjoy. A teenager who likes reading will check out books from the library and obtain books in other ways, regardless of whether her parents read much.

Family Environment

The quality of the home environment correlates positively with children's IQs when both are measured at the same time. The intellectual stimulation offered by parents, whether children have books of their own, the amount of parent–child interaction, and the parents' emotional support for the child all are related to children's IQs (Bradley, 1995). Quality of the home environment also is predictive of future IQ scores. For example, the quality of family environments of 6-month-olds correlate positively with the children's IQs when they are 4-year-olds (Bradley & Caldwell, 1984). Similarly, quality of home environments of 2-year-olds correlate positively with the children's IQ scores and school achievement at 11 years (Bradley, 1989; Olson, Bates, & Kaskie, 1992). When the family environment is relatively stable over time, IQ scores also tend to be stable; when the environment changes, IQ scores also tend to change in the same direction (Bradley, 1989).

Shared and Non-shared Family Environments

Homes are often quite different places for children within the same family. The fact that one child is the oldest in a family means that no one else can be the oldest. Children occupy niches within families, and the fact that one child is "the smart one" may lead siblings to withdraw from intellectual activity and instead become "the popular one," "the athletic one," or even "the bad one."

Such within-family differences affect the development of intelligence. For example, children born early within a family do a little better on IQ tests than do siblings born later (Zajonc & Markus, 1975). More generally, if we exclude very deficient homes from consideration, within-family variations in children's environment seem to have a greater impact on the development of their intelligence than do variations across different families (Plomin & Daniels, 1987).

Effects of Poverty

Although all societies have richer and poorer people, the degree of economic inequality varies a great deal from society to society. At one extreme are societies in which a family's wealth determines whether they can afford basic necessities such as adequate nutrition, basic health care, an elementary education, and decent housing. At the other extreme are societies in which all citizens have access to these and other necessities; affluent families can afford luxuries and better versions of necessities, such as nicer houses and choicer foods, but everyone has access to the basics. Growing up poor is a very different experience in the first type of society than in the second.

Nations vary considerably in degree of income inequality. The United States has a much higher degree of inequality than do Scandinavian countries, with countries such as Germany, Canada, and Great Britain in between. Amount of income inequality is closely linked to amount of difference in academic achievement between children from rich and poor homes within each society. In all countries that have been studied, children from wealthier homes score higher on IQ and achievement tests than do children from poorer homes (Case, Griffin, & Kelly, 1999). However, in developed countries where incomes are relatively unequal, such as the United States, the difference between the intellectual achievement of children from rich and poor homes is larger than in countries with greater equality of incomes.

The percentage of children living in poor families is much higher among African Americans and Latinos than among European Americans and Asians. In 1998, 26% of African American and Hispanic children lived in families with incomes below the poverty line versus 8% of European American children (U.S. Census Bureau, 2000). This means that the effects of poverty are not randomly distributed among families in the United States; they are concentrated in African American and Latino families.

Growing up in impoverished circumstances influences children's IQ scores. Even after taking into account mother's education, whether the home is headed by a single mother, and race, the adequacy of family income for meeting family needs is related to children's IQs (Duncan et al., 1994). Further, the more years children spend in poverty, the lower their IQs tend to be.

Poverty exerts its negative effect on intellectual development through several mechanisms: inadequate diet, lack of timely access to health services, parental preoccupation with other problems, and insufficient intellectual stimulation and support in the home. Thus, part of the effect of family income on IQ reflects families with higher incomes providing more stimulating and supportive intellectual environments for their children (Duncan et al., 1994).

Some children are resilient and do well in school and in life despite growing up in impoverished circumstances (Werner, 1993). What distinguishes such children from others? Bradley et al. (1994) identified a group of children, who despite being born into poor families and also being born prematurely, functioned in the normal or superior range on cognitive, social, health, and growth measures at age 3 years. The parents of these children were found to protect their children in varied ways from the usual deleterious effects of poverty. They were more likely than other parents to provide a variety of learning materials and safe play areas, to be responsive to their children, and to accept their behavior without disapproval. Thus, high-quality parenting can help children meet the challenges imposed by poverty.

EARLY INTERVENTIONS AND INTELLIGENCE

Reflecting both political attitudes of the time and research findings, many intervention programs designed to enhance the intellectual development of poor children were initiated during the 1960s. Most of these interventions were small-scale, experimental programs, intended to test ideas about the types of intervention that would be most beneficial. These intervention programs reflected a variety of ideas about how best to help children from impoverished backgrounds. Some were home-based programs that focused their educational efforts primarily on parents, especially mothers. The logic was that parents were the major influence on children's early development, and that improving parenting would help all children in the family. Others were center-based programs, which operated at separate sites, much like traditional nursery schools, and in which teachers interacted directly with children. Some programs were based on behaviorist theories, others on Piagetian theory, others on an eclectic mix of ideas from several theories.

Lazar, Darlington, Murray, Royce, and Snipper (1982) performed an in-depth analysis of the effects on intellectual development of 11 of the most prominent early intervention programs. All of the programs focused on 2- to 5-year-old African American children from low-income families. Despite substantial differences in the particulars of the programs, they tended to exert similar effects on intellectual development. By the time children completed the programs, their IQ scores had increased substantially—10 to 15 points. Smaller gains persisted for one to three years beyond the end of the programs. However, four years or more after the end of the program, no differences in IQ were apparent between participants and nonparticipants from the same neighborhoods and backgrounds. Similar patterns emerged for mathematics and reading achievement (McKey et al., 1985). A program that extended the special help through the end of third grade produced similar initial gains and similar fading of the gains a few years after the program ended (Becker & Gersten, 1982).

Fortunately, other effects of these experimental programs were more enduring than their effects on IQ and achievement test scores. Only half as many participants as non-participants were later assigned to special education classes—14% versus 29%. Similarly, fewer participants were held back in school, and more participants subsequently graduated from high school.

This combination of findings may seem puzzling. If the intervention programs do not increase IQs or school achievement, why would they lead to fewer children being assigned to special education classes or being held back in school? The likely reason is that the interventions have long-term effects on children's self-esteem, motivation, and classroom behavior. Interventions that focus on families also may improve mothers' parenting skills and ability to work effectively with teachers (Lazar et al., 1982). These effects would help participants make favorable impressions on teachers, principals, and school psychologists and thus convince them that the children were benefiting from their education in the classroom and that they should be promoted along with their classmates.

Participation also led to benefits after children finished school. Participants, in at least some of the programs, tended to use the welfare system less and to earn larger salaries (Haskins, 1989; McLoyd, 1998). Such positive effects suggest that early intervention programs not only can help participants lead more successful lives, they also may more than repay their costs by reducing the need for social services.

Yet greater gains in intellectual development are possible if intervention starts in infancy and affects more aspects of children's lives. Children in the Abcedarian Project (Campbell & Ramey, 1995) attended optimally staffed, educationally oriented daycare facilities from the time they were 6 months old to the time they were 5 years old. During this time, they and their families received health and nutritional supplements, and staff members worked with their mothers to help them understand basic principles of child development. The result was gains in IQ and achievement test scores that endured throughout adolescence and into adulthood. Thus, interventions can have substantial, lasting positive effects on poor children's intellectual development.

CONCLUSIONS

Individual differences in intelligence are already present in the first half year of life. These individual differences are fairly stable for years thereafter, though changes also occur, due to changes in children's lives and circumstances. Genes, environment, and the interaction between genes and environment all influence IQs. Poverty adversely affects many children's intelligence, particularly in societies that have substantial income inequality. Inadequate diet, lack of timely access to health services, parental preoccupation with other problems, and insufficient intellectual stimulation in the home all contribute to the adverse effects of poverty. Intervention programs with preschoolers that have been intended to counter these effects have been successful in raising IQ scores by the end of the programs, but the effects usually disappear over time. However, the interventions have produced other positive effects, such as reducing the frequency of dropping out of school or being assigned to special education classes. In addition, even greater gains in intellectual development are possible if interventions start in infancy.

REFERENCES

Becker, W. C., & Gersten, R. (1982). A follow-up of Follow Through: The later effects of the direct instruction model children in fifth and sixth grades. *American Educational Research Journal, 19*, 75–92.

Bornstein, M. H., & Sigman, M. D. (1986). Continuity in mental development from infancy. *Child Development, 57*, 251–274.

Bradley, R. H. (1989). The use of the HOME inventory in longitudinal studies of child development. In M. H. Bornstein & N. A. Krasnegor (Eds.), *Stability and continuity in mental development: Behavioral and biological perspectives* (pp. 191–215). Hillsdale, NJ: Lawrence Erlbaum Associates.

Bradley, R. H. (1995). Environment and parenting. In M. H. Bornstein (Ed.), *Handbook of parenting* (Vol. 2, 235–261). Mahwah, NJ: Erlbaum.

Bradley, R. H., & Caldwell, B. M. (1984). The relation of infants' home environments to achievement test performance in first grade: A follow-up study. *Child Development, 55*, 803–809.

Bradley, R. H., Whiteside, L., Mundfrom, D. J., Casey, P. H., Kelleher, K. J., & Pope, S. K. (1994). Contribution of early intervention and early caregiving experiences to resilience in low-birthweight, premature children living in poverty. *Journal of Clinical Child Psychology, 23*, 425–434.

Brody, N. (1992). *Intelligence* (2nd ed.). San Diego, CA: Academic Press.

Campbell, F. A., & Ramey, C. T. (1995). Cognitive and school outcomes for high risk African-American students at middle adolescence: Positive effects of early intervention. *American Educational Research Journal, 32*, 743–772.

Case, R., Griffin, S., & Kelly, W. M. (1999). Socioeconomic gradients in mathematical ability and their responsiveness to intervention during early childhood. In D. P. Keating & C. Hertzman (Eds.), *Developmental health and the wealth of nations: Social, biological, and education dynamics* (pp. 125–152). New York: Guilford Press.

Ceci, S. J. (1993). Contextual trends in intellectual development. *Developmental Review, 13*, 403–435.

DeFries, J. C., Plomin, R., & LaBuda, M. C. (1987). Genetic stability of cognitive development from childhood to adulthood. *Developmental Psychology, 23*, 4–12.

Duncan, G. J., Brooks-Gunn, J., & Klebanov, P. K. (1994). Economic deprivation and early childhood development. *Child Development, 65*, 296–318.

Duncan, O. D., Featherman, D. L., & Duncan, B. (1972). *Socioeconomic background and achievement.* New York: Seminar Press.

Fagan, J. F., III, & Singer, L. T. (1983). Infant recognition memory as a measure of intelligence. In L. P. Lipsitt (Ed.), *Advances in infancy research* (Vol. 2, pp. 31–78). Norwood, NJ: Ablex.

Feldman, D. H. (1986). *Nature's gambit: Child prodigies and the development of human potential.* New York: Basic Books.

Gardner, H. (1999). Are there additional intelligences? The case for naturalist, spiritual, and existential intelligences. In J. Kane (Ed.), *Education, information, and transformation* (pp. 111–131). Englewood Cliffs, NJ: Prentice-Hall.

Haskins, R. (1989). Beyond metaphor: The efficacy of early childhood education. *American Psychologist, 44*, 274–282.

Honzik, M. P., MacFarlane, J. W., & Allen, L. (1948). The stability of mental test performance between two and eighteen years. *Journal of Experimental Education, 17*, 309–329.

Humphreys, L. G. (1989) Intelligence: Three kinds of instability and their consequences for policy. In R. L. Linn (Ed.), *Intelligence* (pp. 193–216). Urbana, IL: University of Illinois Press.

Hunter, J. E. (1986). Cognitive ability, cognitive aptitudes, job knowledge, and job performance. *Journal of Vocational Behavior, 29*, 340–362.

Jencks, C. (1979). *Who gets ahead? The determinants of economic success in America.* New York: Basic Books.

Lazar, I., Darlington, R., Murray, H., Royce, J., & Snipper, A. (1982). Lasting effects of early education: A report from the Consortium for Longitudinal Studies. *Monographs of the Society for Research in Child Development, 47* (Serial No. 195).

McCall, R. B., Applebaum, M. I., & Hogarty, P. S. (1973). Developmental changes in mental performance. *Monographs of the Society for Research in Child Development, 38* (Serial No. 150).

McGue, M., Bouchard, T. J., Jr., Iacono, W. G., & Lykken, D. T. (1993). Behavioral genetics of cognitive ability: A life-span perspective. In R. Plomin & G. E. McClearn (Eds.), *Nature, nurture, and psychology* (pp. 59–76). Washington, DC: American Psychological Association.

McKey, R. H., Condelli, L., Ganson, H., Barrett, B. J., McConkey, C., & Plantz, M. C. (1985). *The impact of Head Start on children, families, and communities.* Washington, DC: U.S. Government Printing Office.

McLoyd, V. C. (1998). Children in poverty: Development, public policy, and practice. In W. Damon (Series Ed.), I. E. Sigel, & K. A. Renninger (Vol. Eds.), *Handbook of child psychology: Vol. 4. Child psychology in practice* (5th ed., pp. 135–208). New York: Wiley.

Neisser, U., Boodoo, G., Bouchard, T. J., Jr., Boykin, A. W., Brody, N., Ceci, S. J., Halpern, D. F., Loehlin, J. C., Perloff, R., Sternberg, R. J., & Urbana, S. (1996). Intelligence: Knowns and unknowns. *American Psychologist, 51*, 77–101.

Olson, S. L., Bates, J. E., & Kaskie, B. (1992). Caregiver-infant interaction antecedents of children's schoolage cognitive ability. *Merrill-Palmer Quarterly, 38*, 309–330.

Plomin, R., & Daniels, D. (1987). Why are children in the same family so different from each other? *Behavioral and Brain Sciences*, *10*, 1–16.

Rose, S. A., & Feldman, J. F. (1995). Prediction of IQ and specific cognitive abilities at 11 years from infancy measures. *Developmental Psychology*, *31*, 685–696.

Scarr, S. (1992). Developmental theories for the 1990s: Development and individual differences. *Child Development*, *63*, 1–19.

Sternberg, R. J. (1999). The theory of successful intelligence. *Review of General Psychology*, *3* (4), 292–316.

Tannenbaum, A. J. (1986). Giftedness: A psychosocial approach. In J. Sternberg & J. E. Davidson (Eds.), *Conceptions of giftedness* (pp. 21–52). Cambridge, England: Cambridge University Press.

U.S. Census Bureau. (2000). Percent of people in poverty by definition of income and selected characteristics: 1998. Available: http://www.census.gov/hhes/poverty/poverty98/table5.html

Werner, E. E. (1993). Risk, resilience, and recovery: Perspectives from the Kauai Longitudinal Study. *Development and Psychopathology*, *5*, 503–515.

Wilk, S. L., Desmarais, L. B., & Sackett, P. R. (1995). Gravitation to jobs commensurate with ability: Longitudinal and cross-sectional tests. *Journal of Applied Psychology*, *80*, 79–85.

Zajonc, R. B., & Markus, G. B. (1975). Birth order and intellectual development. *Psychological Review*, *82*, 74–88.

24

Problem Solving as an Element of Developmental Well-Being

D. Camille Smith

Centers for Disease Control and Prevention, Atlanta, GA

INTRODUCTION

Problem solving can be described as the use of a sequence of steps that attempt to identify and create alternate solutions for both cognitive and social problems. These steps include the ability to plan, resourcefully seek help from others, and think critically, creatively, and reflectively.

Problem solving, reasoning, and intelligence are highly interrelated constructs. Terman and Merrill (1932) provide the following example of a word problem:

> I planted a tree that was 8" inches tall. At the end of the first year it was 12" tall; at the end of the second year it was 18" tall; and at the end of the third year it was 27" tall. How tall was it at the end of the fourth year? (p. 25)

This word problem clearly demands problem-solving capabilities for its solution. The problem is labeled as one of *reasoning* on the Stanford Binet intelligence test (Sternberg, 1982).

Pintner (1921) defined intelligence in terms of problem solving as the ability "to adapt one self adequately to relatively new situations in life" (p. 139). Although definitions of intelligence are quite diverse, results from a survey of over 1,000 professionals indicated that the attributes (i.e., abstract thinking or reasoning, the capacity to acquire knowledge, and problem solving) were rated as important elements by nearly all respondents (Sattler, 1992). Historically, in whatever way intelligence has been defined, problem solving has been viewed as an important part of the definition and as a fundamental element of cognitive well-being.

Problems are met within a social context, whether they happen in the home, in the classroom, on the streets, or in a profession, and intelligence consists, in large part, of the ability to solve these problems. A crucial aspect of such intelligent functioning is understanding that there is a problem to be solved, defining it, and attempting to solve it, whether it be in everyday life or in abstract or academic problems/situations/applications. Authors use a variety of terms for solving problems within a social context: These include *social problem solving* (D'Zurilla & Nezu, 1982), *interpersonal problem solving* (Shure, 1981), *interpersonal cognitive problem solving* (Spivack, Platt, & Shure, 1976), and *personal problem solving* (Heppner & Peterson, 1982). Goldfried and D'Zurilla (1969) maintain that cognitive, behavioral and affect factors interact to produce effective problem solving. Sternberg (1982) stated that "solving the problems of life is placed at the center of the conception of intelligence" (p. 27).

Studies on resilient children repeatedly find the presence of problem-solving skills in the children studied. Even though there is little evidence that high intelligence alone promotes more effective coping, most longitudinal studies of resilient children and youths report that intelligence (especially communication and problem-solving skills) is associated positively with the ability to overcome difficulty and adversity in one's life (Block & Kremen, 1996). S. J. Wolin and S. Wolin (1994, p. 136) link problem-solving abilities with initiative—"Initiative: The Pleasure of Problems." They define initiative as "the determination to assert yourself and master your environment." The Wolins state that resilient people "prevail by carving out a part of life they can control," and that "as pieces of the world bend to their will, successful survivors build competence and a sense of power." Initiative, according to the Wolins, is first evident when children follow

> the call to go exploring. Opening and closing drawers, poking around and conducting trial-and-error experiments that often succeed, resilient children find tangible rewards and achieve a sense of effectiveness. By school age, exploring evolves into working. Though not all resilient children become outstanding students, the random activities of their earlier years become focused, organized, and goal-directed over a wide range of activities. In adults, the gratifications and self-esteem associated with completing jobs and solving problems becomes a lifelong attraction to generating projects that stretch the self and promote a cycle of growth.

Rutter and Quinton (1984) examined how and why some women who had been abused and neglected as girls were able to find men who were neither criminal nor mentally ill and went on to make successful marriages. The most important variable in the resilient women's marital and vocational success was their capacity to plan, problem-solve, exercise foresight, and take active steps to deal with the challenges in their environment. This capacity was correlated with a lower rate of teenage pregnancy and a lack of pressure to make hasty decisions about husbands (Rutter, 1987).

DEVELOPMENT OF PROBLEM SOLVING

Problem-solving capabilities are a product of both individual and contextual factors. There appears to be a reciprocal influence between the context and individual over time, with individuals helping to create their environment and their environment shaping the individual (Bandura, 1986; Vygotsky, 1978). Individual characteristics include differences in goals and aspirations (Ames, 1992; Bandura, 1986; Dweck & Leggett, 1989); attitudes, values, interests, and experiences (Charness & Bieman-Copland, 1992; Chi & Ceci, 1987); and perceived and actual control (Baltes & Baltes, 1985; Sternberg & Kolligan, 1990). Contextually, cultures and subgroups within the same culture may differ in what they label as a problem, in what is considered a successful resolution to the problem, and in the value put on that success. These individual and contextual or environmental characteristics appear to impact many aspects of the problem-solving process, including whether individuals plan (Friedman, Scholnik, & Cocking, 1987) and their choice of strategies used to solve problems (Berg, 1989; Ceci & Bronfenbrenner, 1985). These characteristics seem to affect the individuals' task choices, the degree of persistence on a task, and their willingness to engage in similar tasks in the future (Deci & Ryan, 1985; Harackiewicz, 1989). According to contextual perspectives on cognition, competence—including the ability to problem-solve—is produced through transactions of the individual with his or her social, material, historical, and psychological contexts (Bronfennbrenner, 1977; Buss, 1987).

Piaget's (1953) theory divides intellectual development into four major periods: sensorimotor (birth to 2 years); preoperational (2 years to 7 years); concrete operational (7 years to 11 years); and formal operational (11 years and beyond). From a Piagetian framework, problem solving begins in the sensorimotor stage. The young infant is learning to relate information from his or her sensory systems, including vestibular input, proprioception, vision, hearing, touch, taste, and smell. The child is organizing this information along with a growing understanding of objects and people, a foundation that gives the child better means to get needs met and goals accomplished. Needs and goals change as the child matures; therefore, the problems he or she needs to solve are different at various developmental levels. The following, based on the work of Piaget (1962) and Uzgiris and Hunt (1975), summarizes how problem solving evolves as the child develops:

From ages 6 to 9 months, the child's basic problem is how to acquire the objects he or she wants and how to make an interesting event recur with body movement. Infants first display intentional means–end behavior at about 7 or 8 months age when they begin to solve simple problems involving completion of one intermediate step prior to achievement of the goal. Examples involving manual retrieval of an object include removing a cover to search for a hidden object (Diamond, 1985; Piaget, 1953) and releasing one object to take hold of another (Bruner, 1970; Piaget, 1953).

From ages 9 to 12 months, the child is learning how to perform actions and how to use adults to achieve desired results.

From ages 12 to 18 months, the child is learning more about what makes things work. He or she knows objects, their parts, their mechanisms, their relationships to other objects, and how people can have an effect on objects.

From ages 18 to 24 months, the child is learning to think about his or her actions. Combined with increasing fine motor skills and emerging language skills, the child can explore with more precision and take instruction from adults.

From ages 2 to 4 years, the child's problem solving involves taking acquired knowledge and applying it to new situations. Problem solving involves reasoning from situation to situation.

Problem solving for a child age 5 and older depends on his or her ability to build an integrated understanding of the rules governing how things work.

OPERATIONAL DEFINITIONS

Problem-solving behavior follows problem situations that have been characterized in many different ways. Morgan (1941, as cited in Sternberg, 1982, p. 271) suggested, "that a problem exists when there are some elements or conditions that are unknown, and the solution depends upon a discovery of how to deal with the unknown factors of the situation." Vinacke (1952) claims that a problem situation exists when there is an "obstacle" to overcome. Woodworth and Schlosberg (1954) argue that a problem situation exists when an individual has a goal but no clear means of achieving the goal. Johnson (1955) has suggested that a problem situation exists when an individual's first goal-directed response has proven unsuccessful.

Sternberg (1982) subdivided problems into well-defined spaces and ill-defined spaces. A problem with a well-defined problem space is one for which the steps to a solution can be clearly identified by the problem solver, and an ill-defined space is one for which the steps are not so clear. An example of a well-defined problem space is the "missionaries and cannibals" problem. This problem is one of a number of "river-crossing problems" in which a group of travelers must get across the river from one bank to another. What makes the task difficult is that the boat can only hold a certain number of people and only particular combinations of travelers are allowed. For example, the number of cannibals cannot exceed the number of missionaries or the cannibals will eat the missionaries. The problem is to figure out how to transport three missionaries and three cannibals across a river. A boat is available for transportation but will hold only two people at a time; it is possible to use the boat to transport just a single person at a time. The number of cannibals on either side of the river can never be allowed to exceed the number of missionaries. Performance on this task is quantifiable. One overall measure of performance is to count the number of moves needed to solve the problem; another is to track the amount of time spent solving the problem (Sternberg, 1982).

An example of an ill-defined problem space is the "two-strings" problem. Subjects are brought into a large room containing many objects, such as poles, ring stands, clamps, pliers, extension cords, tables, and chairs. The experimenter hangs two strings from the ceiling. One hangs near the center of the room, the other near a wall. The strings are of sufficient length to reach the floor. Subjects are told that their task is to tie the ends of the two strings together. It soon becomes apparent to subjects that the cords are far enough apart so that it is not possible to hold both in one's hands at the same time. The subjects must use the materials in the room to attain a solution to the problem. Ill-defined problem spaces such as this problem seem to depend on a major "insight" for their solution as opposed to well-defined problem spaces that seem to require several steps and several "insights" (Sternberg, 1982).

Examining problem-solving strategies in a social context led Shure (1999) to define effective problem solving as "the ability to think of alternative solutions to a problem (alternative-solution thinking) and the ability to understand the consequences of behavior (consequential thinking)" (p. 589). Shure (1988) argued that the most important problem-solving skill a child learns is how to think. Shure (1999) found that, across the age span and regardless of IQ and language skills, the ability to think of multiple alternative solutions to problems relates to positive peer relationships. Since the early 1970s, Shure and Spivack have proposed a theory of children's interpersonal cognitive problem-solving (ICPS) skills and developed tools to measure these skills in developmentally appropriate ways (Shure, 1993, 1999; Shure & Spivack, 1979). The ability to think of alternative solutions to real-life problems can be measured by the Preschool Interpersonal Problem Solving (PIPS) test (Shure & Spivack, 1974). This test examines the number of different and relevant solutions 4-year-olds generate when presented with age-appropriate problems (e.g., wanting a toy with which another child is playing). ICPS researchers have repeatedly found that well-adjusted children generate more relevant solutions than more poorly adjusted youngsters (Shure, 1993; Shure & Spivack, 1979). Other frequently used measures are the What Happens Next Game and the Means–End Problem-Solving Test. For additional information about these measures, see Butler and Meichenbaum (1981).

ANTECEDENTS OF PROBLEM-SOLVING BEHAVIOR

Independent problem solving is a high level cognitive activity requiring relatively sophisticated verbal and abstract reasoning skills. According to Nezu and Perri (1989), to successfully engage in social problem solving, one must possess several prerequisite skills:

1. Ability to express one's thoughts and feelings.
2. Ability to recognize and predict cause and effect relationships.
3. Ability to perceive and have empathy for another's perspective.
4. Ability to engage in abstract, creative thinking.
5. Belief that one's actions can have a significant impact on the environment.

Butler and Meichenbaum (1981) have proposed that self-appraisal may successfully predict effective problem-solving behavior. Ellis (1962) and Beck (1976) emphasized that an individual's beliefs or perceptions of the environment may affect behavior more than the actual reality of that environment. Social learning theory resulted from an integration of cognitive and behavioral approaches that emphasized the reciprocal nature of internal and external determinants of behavior. Experience with the environment influences the way a person interprets situations; that interpretation then guides the person's behavior, which, in turn, affects their perception of the environment. Through that sequence of events, a person develops judgments about "self-efficacy," or the degree to which one believes that he or she can execute behaviors and conceptualize alternative solutions to problems that lead to desired outcomes. A person's self-efficacy beliefs are a surprisingly reliable predictor of actual behavior (Bandura, 1977). Self-efficacy is believed to strongly influence which behaviors are initiated and the persistence and effort that is expended on those behaviors in the face of difficulty and obstacles. It is this persistence, effort, and motivation that sustain one to complete a problem task that may seem extremely difficult. The desire to have an effect on one's environment appears be an innate motivational force, exhibited even in early infancy (White, 1959). Very young children invest a great deal of energy in play and exploration leading to accomplishing tasks that they appear to define for themselves. These self-initiated behaviors seem to promote a sense of control and competence. When the child's efforts to initiate and follow through with an activity result in encouragement or success, a healthy sense of control develops, supporting persistence, problem solving, and optimism about one's ability to have an effect on the world. Harter (1982) developed a "personal sense of competence" scale for use with third- to ninth-grade children. This instrument assesses students' sense of competence on cognitive, social, and physical tasks and also yields a measure of general self-worth. The Personal Problem-Solving Inventory developed by Heppner and Petersen (1982) can be used with adults and measures how confident adults feel in their ability to solve problems they are confronted with. It is possible that dimensions such as self-efficacy, sense of competence, and problem-solving confidence strongly influence the execution of problem-solving behaviors (Durlak, 1983).

Soviet psychologist Vygotsky (1962) discussed the role of verbal mediation in a developing child's behavior, particularly in the area of self-regulation and the ability to problem-solve. Verbal mediation is the process of using language to achieve self-direction and self-regulation of behavior. This behavior has also been termed *private* or *self-directed speech* and can be thought of as talking to oneself in an effort to guide problem-solving or coping efforts. According to Vygotsky, who devoted much of his writings to this phenomena, private speech originates in social experience, becomes increasingly more internalized with age, is dependent on the child's cognitive level, and increases in usage with challenging tasks (Berk, 1992). Whereas Vygotsky (1962) emphasized the importance of this internalized language in self-regulation, private speech is used for a variety of other functions as well (Berk and Spuhl, 1995; Furrow, 1992). As with social speech, the range of functions include describing, planning, questioning, problem solving, and expression, although there are differences in the distribution of these categories in social and private situations and as a function of age.

Developmental psychologist Luria (1961) suggested that children learn verbal mediation in stages, with their behavior initially controlled by adult verbalizations that they gradually internalize to covert self-instructions. First, adults control the child's behavior through verbal direction. During the first 2½ years of life, adults become more effective in directing children's behavior through verbal means. This period coincides with the age in which enormous gains are made in word comprehension, complex sentence structure use, and language abstraction. In the second stage, the child uses overt speech to direct and guide his or her own actions. During the preschool years, children's speech starts to be used to regulate their own behavior. This stage can be observed when watching three-year-olds put together puzzles. You can sometimes hear them talking to themselves, saying, "no, that piece doesn't go there, it goes here, that's right!" This latter transformation occurs over a several-year period beginning during the preschool years and is associated with the task difficulty as well as cognitive maturity. Finally, during the later school years, private speech declines as regulation becomes more internalized, and private speech is transformed to thought. Private speech serves to motivate and provide strategies for solving problems, reducing errors, and increasing efficiency.

PROMOTION OF PROBLEM SOLVING

One index of the quality of the parent–child relationship during the early years is the attachment, or bond, between the child and parent (Ainsworth & Bowlby, 1991). The importance of the attachment relationship extends beyond infancy. Research findings indicate that securely attached toddlers were more confident when solving easy problems and were more likely to enlist their mothers' support when faced with difficult problems (Matas, Arend, & Sroufe, 1978). These results suggested to Bretherton (1985) that attention span and persistence might be influenced as well by the attachment relationship. It is theorized that a secure attachment provides the child with a "safe base" from which to explore the environment, thus increasing opportunities for learning, problem solving, and a sense of control or mastery (Ainsworth & Bowlby, 1991).

Busch-Rossnagel, Kanuf-Jensen, and Desrosiers (1995) described caregiving influences at different phases in the development of a child's problem-solving ability and the development of mastery motivation. In the first phase, which occurs from birth to about 9 months of life, contingent play interactions, the provision of stimulating toys that can provide feedback, contingent responsiveness to distress and vocalizations, and the expression of positive affect are caregiver behaviors that are related to instrumental and social aspects of the child's development. During the second year of life, children are better able to initiate activities and to persist in goal attainment. When this increase in autonomy is accompanied by parental scaffolding as a strategy to introduce new material, caregivers are better able to facilitate problem-solving abilities. Beginning around their second birthday, children can identify tasks they can do; caregiving behaviors that interfere with this emerging self-direction have been found to negatively impact persistence and motivation (Jennings & Connors, 1989). For instance, Busch-Rossnagel and colleagues (1995) found that reduced task persistence was found in children whose caregivers modeled behavior rather than asked questions. Children at this level seem to benefit from interaction that is not overly directive but that is marked by positive, affective exchanges, provision of challenging learning materials, and emotional and motivational support during joint play.

The role of problem solving in parenting is relatively unexplored, but the few studies available suggest a connection between problem-solving ability and parenting outcomes. Walker and Johnson (1986) found mothers' problem-solving self-appraisal was correlated with their global rating of confidence in parenting ability, as well as with social competence and fewer behavioral problems in their 5-year-old children. Children who have parents who engage in active problem solving in response to the child's distress have been found to show a higher level of competence in preschool (Roberts & Strayer, 1987).

CONCLUSIONS

Problem solving is a construct that clearly crosses multiple domains and has cognitive, behavioral, and affective dimensions. Problem solving has always been viewed as a crucial aspect of academic, intellectual functioning but has also been instrumental in helping individuals solve the problems of everyday life. Problem-solving capabilities are a product of both individual and contextual factors and play a major role in personal well-being. Competence and the ability to problem-solve are produced through transactions of the individual with his or her social, material, historical, and psychological contexts.

REFERENCES

Ainsworth, M. D. S., & Bowlby, J. (1991). An ethological approach to personality development. *American Psychologist, 46*, 333–341.

Ames, C. (1992). Achievement goals and the classroom motivational climate. In D. H. Schunk & J. L. Meece (Eds.), *Student perceptions in the classroom* (pp. 327–348). Hillsdale, NJ: Lawrence Erlbaum Associates.

Baltes, M. M., & Baltes, P. B. (Eds.). (1985). *The psychology of control and aging.* Hillsdale, NJ: Lawrence Erlbaum Associates.

Bandura, A. (1977). Self-efficacy: Toward a unifying theory of behavioral change. *Psychological Review, 84*, 191–215.

Bandura, A. (1986). *Social foundation of thought and action: A social cognitive theory.* Englewood Cliffs, NJ: Prentice Hall.

Beck, A. T. (1976). *Cognitive therapy and the emotional disorders.* New York: International Universities Press.

Berg, C. A. (1989). Knowledge of strategies for dealing with everyday problems from childhood through adolescence. *Developmental Psychology, 25*, 607–618.

Berk, L. E. (1992). Children's private speech: An overview of theory and the status of research. In R. M. Diaz & L. E. Berk (Eds.), *Private speech: From social interaction to self-regulation* (pp. 17–53). Hillsdale, NJ: Lawrence Erlbaum Associates.

Berk, L. E., & Sphul, S. T. (1995). Maternal interaction, private speech, and task performance in pre-school children. *Early Childhood Research Quarterly, 10,* 145–169.

Block, J., & Kremen, A. M. (1996). IQ and ego-resiliency: conceptual and empirical connections and separateness. *Journal of Personality and Social Psychology, 70,* 349–361.

Bretherton, I. (1985). Attachment theory: Retrospect and prospect. *Monographs of the Society for Research in Child Development, 50*(1–2, Serial No. 209), 3–35.

Bronfenbrenner, U. (1977). Toward an experimental ecology of human development. *American Psychologist, 32,* 513–531.

Bruner, J. S. (1970). The growth and structure of skill. In K. Connolly (Ed.), *Mechanisms of motor skill development* (pp. 63–92). London: Academic Press.

Busch-Rossnagel, N., Kanut-Jensen, E., & Desroseirs, F. S. (1995) Mothers and others: The role of the socializing environment in the development of mastery motivation. In R. H. MacTurk & G. A. Morgan (Eds.), *Mastery motivation: Origins, conceptualizations, and applications. Advances in applied developmental psychology* (Vol. 12, pp. 117–145). Norwood, NJ: Ablex.

Buss, D. M. (1987). Selection, evocation, and manipulation. *Journal of Personality and Social Psychology, 53,* 1214–1221.

Butler. L., & Meichenbaum, D. (1981). The assessment of interpersonal problem-solving skills. In P. C. Kendall & S. D. Hollon (Eds.), *Assessment strategies for cognitive behavioral interventions* (pp. 127–142). New York: Academic Press.

Ceci, S. J., & Bronfenbrenner, U. (1985). "Don't forget to take the cookies out of the oven": Strategic time-monitoring, prospective memory, and context. *Child Development, 56,* 175–190.

Charness, N., & Bieman-Copland, S. (1992). The learning perspective: Adulthood. In R. J. Sternberg & C. A. Berg (Eds.), *Intellectual development* (pp. 301–327). Cambridge University Press, NY.

Chi, M., & Ceci, S. (1987). Content knowledge: Its role, representation, and restructuring in memory development. In H. W. Reese & L. P. Lipsitt (Eds.), *Advances in child development and behavior* (Vol. 20, pp. 91–142). San Diego, CA: Academic Press, Inc.

Deci, E. L., & Ryan, R. M. (1985). *Intrinsic motivation and self-determination in human behavior.* New York: Plenum Press.

Diamond, A. (1985). Development of the ability to use recall to guide action, as indicated by infants performance on AB. *Child Development, 55,* 68–883.

Durlak, J. A. (1983). Social problem-solving as a primary prevention strategy. In R. D. Felner, L. A. Jason, J. N. Mortisugu, & S. S. Farber (Eds.), *Preventive psychology: Theory, research and practice* (pp. 31–161). Elsevier Science, US.

Dweck, C. S., & Leggett, E. L. (1989). A social-cognitive approach to motivation and personality. *Psychological Review, 95,* 256–273.

D'Zurilla, T. J., & Nezu, A. (1982). Social problem solving in adults. In P. C. Kendall (Ed.), *Advances in cognitive-behavioral research and therapy* (Vol. 1). New York: Academic Press.

Ellis, A. (1962). *Reason and emotion in psychotherapy.* New York: Lyle Stuart.

Friedman, S. L., Scholnik, E. K., & Cocking, R. R. (Eds.). (1987). *Blueprints for thinking.* Cambridge University Press, N.Y.

Furrow, D. (1992). Developmental trends in the differentiation of social and private speech. In R. M. Diaz & L. E. Berk (Eds.) *Private speech: From social interaction to self-regulation* (pp. 143–158). Hillsdale, NJ: Lawrence Erlbaum Associates.

Goldfried, M. R., & D'Zurilla, T. J. (1969). A behavioral-analytic model for assessing competence. In C. D. Spielberger (Ed.), *Current topics in clinical and community psychology* (Vol. 1). New York: Academic Press.

Harackiewicz, J. M. (1989). Performance evaluation and intrinsic motivation processes: The effects of achievement orientation and rewards. In D. Buss & N. Cantor (Eds.), *Personality psychology: Recent trends and emerging directions* (pp. 128–137). New York: Springer.

Harter, S. (1982). A new self-report scale of intrinsic versus extrinsic orientation in the classroom: Motivation and informational components. *Developmental Psychology, 17,* 300–312.

Heppner, P. P., & Peterson, C. H. (1982). The development and implications of a personal problem solving inventory. *Journal of Counseling Psychology, 29,* 66–75.

Jennings, K. D., & Connors, R. E. (1989). Mothers' interactional style and children's competence at 3 years. *International Journal of Behavioral Development, 12,* 2.

Johnson, D. M. (1955). *The psychology of thought and judgement*. New York: Harper & Row.

Luria, A. R. (1961). *The role of speech in the regulation of normal and abnormal behavior*. New York: Liveright.

MacTurk, R. H.,& Morgan, G. A. (Eds). Mastery motivation: Origins, conceptualizations, and applications. *Advances in applied developmental psychology* (Vol. 12). Norwood, NJ: Ablex.

Matas, L., Arend, R. A., & Sroufe, L. A. (1978). Continuity of adaptation in the second year: The relationship between quality of attachment and later competence. *Child Development, 49*, 3.

Morgan, J. J. B. (1941). *Psychology*. New York: Farrar & Rinehart.

Nezu, A. M., & Perri, M. G. (1989). Social problem-solving therapy for unipolar depression: An initial dismantling investigation. *Journal of Consulting and Counseling Psychology, 57*, 408–413.

Piaget, J. (1953). *The origin of intelligence in the child*. London: Routledge & Kegan Paul.

Piaget, J. (1962). *Play, dreams and imitation in childhood*. New York: Norton.

Pintner, R. (1921). Contribution to Intelligence and its measurement: A symposium. *Journal of Educational Psychology, 12*, 139–143.

Roberts, W., & Strayer, J. (1987). Parents' responses to the emotional distress of their children: Relations with children's competence. *Developmental Psychology, 23*, 415–422.

Rutter, M. (1987). Psychological resilience and protective mechanism. *American Journal of Orthopsychiatry, 57*(3), pp. 316–331.

Rutter, M., & Quinton, D. (1984). Long-term follow-up of women institutionalized in childhood: Factors promoting good functioning in adult life. *British Journal of Developmental Psychology, 18*, 225–234.

Sattler, J. (1992). *Assessment of children*. San Diego, CA: Sattler.

Shure, M. B. (1981). Social competence as a problem-solving skill. In J. D. Wine & M. D. Smye (Eds.), *Social competence* (pp. 201–219). New York: Guilford.

Shure, M. B. (1988). How to think, not what to think: A cognitive approach to prevention. In L. A. Bond & B. M. Wagner (Eds.), *Families in transition: Primary prevention programs that work. Primary prevention of psychopathology* (Vol. 11, pp. 170–199). Newbury Park, CA: Sage.

Shure, M. B. (1993). I can problem solve (ICPS): Interpersonal cognitive problem solving for young children. Special issue: Enhancing young childrens' lives. *Early Child Development and Care, 96*, 49–64.

Shure, M. B. (1999, April). Preventing violence: The problem-solving way. *Juvenile Justice Bulletin*, 1–11.

Shure, M. B., & Spivack, G. (1974). *The problem-solving approach to adjustment*. San Francisco: Jossey-Bass.

Shure, M. B., & Spivack, G. (1979). Interpersonal cognitive problem solving and primary prevention: Programming for preschool and kindergarten children. *Journal of Clinical Child Psychology, 8*, 89–94.

Spivack, G., Platt, J. J., & Shure, M. B. (1976). *The problem-solving approach to adjustment*. San Francisco: Jossey-Bass.

Sternberg, R. (1982). *Handbook of human intelligence*. New York: Cambridge University Press.

Sternberg, R. J., & Kolligan, J., Jr. (1990). *Competence considered*. New Haven, CT: Yale University Press.

Terman, L. M., & Merrill, M. A. (1932). *Measuring intelligence*. Boston: Houghton Mifflin.

Uzgiris, I. C., & Hunt, J. M. (1975). *Assessment in infancy: Ordinal scales of psychological development*. Urbana, IL: University of Illinois Press.

Vinacke, W. E. (1952). *The psychology of thinking*. New York: McGraw-Hill.

Vygotsky. L. S. (1962). *Thought and language*. Boston: Cambridge University Press.

Vygotsky. L. S. (1978). *Mind in society: The development of higher psychological processes*, Cambridge, MA: Harvard University Press.

Walker, L. O., & Johnson, L. B. (1986). *Preschool children's socio-emotional development: Endogenous and environmental antecedents in early infancy*. Final report to the Hogg Foundation for Mental Health.

White, R. W. (1959). Motivation reconsidered: The concept of competence. *Psychological Review, 66*, 297–333.

Wolin, S. J., & Wolin, S. (1994). *The resilient self: How survivors of troubled families rise above adversity*. New York: Villard Books.

Woodworth, R. S., & Schlosberg, H. (1954). *Experimental psychology*. New York: Holt, Rinehart & Winston.

25

Language and Literacy

Brian MacWhinney
Carnegie Mellon University, Pittsburgh, PA

Marc H. Bornstein
*National Institute of Child Health
and Human Development, Bethesda, MD*

INTRODUCTION

Almost every human child learns to speak language (Lenneberg, 1967). As long as a basic social link is established between the child and his or her caregivers, language learning will occur. The seemingly easy task of learning language relies on other impressive accomplishments in the physical, perceptual, cognitive, and social spheres of development. Because of this, language development is fundamentally linked to the child's overall well-being.

Communication is the process of exchanging information, ideas, and feelings between individuals. Although language is not the only medium for communication (e.g., nonconventional gestures), it is the most typical form and the one that is used in school and work settings. In a literate society, proficient control of language provides keys for further success and well-being. In order to achieve access to economic and social power during the transition from childhood to the workplace, children must demonstrate a continually growing control of language. For children from working-class backgrounds, failing to attain higher forms of literacy can serve as barriers to entry into the middle class.

TECHNICAL ISSUES IN LANGUAGE STUDY

Human language involves both receptive and productive use. Receptive language use occurs during the comprehension or understanding of words and sentences. Productive language use involves idea generation and the articulation of words in speech. Typically, the child demonstrates new language abilities first in comprehension and then only later in production. For example, children comprehend their first words by 9 months or even earlier, but only produce their first word after 12 months. Children are able to comprehend 50 words by about 15 months, but do not produce 50 words in their own speech until about 20 months. More generally, children acquire words into their receptive vocabulary more than twice as fast as into their productive vocabulary.

The four basic structural components of language are phonology, semantics, grammar, and pragmatics. Phonology is the system of the sound segments that we use to build up words. Each language has a different set of these segments or phonemes, and children quickly come to recognize and then produce the speech segments that are characteristic of their native language. Semantics is the system of meanings that are expressed by words and phrases. In order to serve as a means of communication between people, words must have a shared or conventional meaning. Picking out the correct meaning for each new word is a major learning task for the child. Grammar is the system of rules by which words and phrases are arranged to make meaningful statements. Children need to learn how to use the ordering of words to mark grammatical functions such as subject or direct object. Pragmatics is the system of patterns that determine how we can use language in particular social settings for particular conversational purposes. Children need to learn that conversations customarily begin with a greeting, require turn-taking, and concern a shared topic. They need to adjust the content of their communications to match their listener's interests, knowledge, and language ability. Literate control of language involves the use of printed material and formal spoken dialog to express increasingly complex social, cognitive, and linguistic structures.

Language growth is marked by very notable individual differences in both developmental status and rates of change. Children at the same chronological age may be operating on very different levels in terms of language skill (Fenson et al., 1994). Moreover, young girls are often more verbal than young boys. For example, Huttenlocher, Haight, Bryk, Seltzer, and Lyons (1991) found that girls started to spurt in their vocabulary before boys, independent of the vocabulary to which they were exposed.

The approaches and instruments used to study language development are quite straightforward. Some involve simply recording and transcribing what children say (MacWhinney, 2000). Other studies use controlled experimentation that ask children to answer questions, repeat sentences, or make grammaticality judgments. We can also study children by asking their parents to report about them. Each of these methods has different goals, and each also has unique possibilities and pitfalls associated with it. Having obtained a set of data from children or their parents, we next need to group these data into measures of particular types of language skills, such as vocabulary, sentences, concepts, or conversational abilities.

Overall measures of the child's productions and parental input can sometimes obscure the fine-grained dynamics of the learning process. By themselves, frequency and diversity do not lead to successful language learning. It is also important for parents to adjust their linguistic input to the child's level of language ability or just slightly beyond it. If the child says, "Bobby no like it," the most effective response is one that reformulates or recasts the child's meaning, as in "Oh, Bobby doesn't like it?" A careful analysis of interactions between parents and their children shows that children soon come to follow their parent's lead when presented with gentle expansions in this form (Bohannon, MacWhinney, & Snow, 1990). More severe attempts at overt correction are usually less successful. For example, the parent could say, "No, don't say 'no like it', say 'doesn't like it'." Unfortunately, this type of overt didactic correction tends to confuse the child and interrupt the flow of the conversation.

Children learn more from accurate input than from correction. In this sense, it is best to help children with language learning by focusing on positive cases, rather than errors. Consider the case of a child who produces "goed" instead of "went". This is a typical case of the process of pattern overgeneralization in language learning. Rather than overtly correcting this child for the error, it is better to simply recast or rephrase the production using "went". The reinforcement of the correct target in the child's auditory lexicon will eventually lead to its dominance over the erroneous overgeneralization.

THEORETICAL AND EMPIRICAL REVIEW
OF THE LANGUAGE LITERATURE

Linguists tend to think of language as having a universal core from which individual languages select out a particular configuration of features, parameters, and settings (Chomsky, 1982). From this perspective, the shape of language development is determined by how formal universal constraints play out during the child's development. Although children in different countries learn very different languages, linguists tend to see all children as acquiring basically the same set of abstract structures and relations. By delineating the common characteristics involved in all cases of language learning, linguists are able to further clarify the basic structural aspects of human language.

An alternative approach to the dynamics of language development is to assume the perspective of the child. By taking this perspective, we can understand the challenges the child faces and the ways in which each are overcome. One scholar who attempted to assume this viewpoint was William James (1890), who described the world of the newborn as a "blooming, buzzing confusion." However, we now know that, on the auditory level at least, the newborn's world is remarkably well structured. The cochlea and auditory nerve provide extensive preprocessing of signals for pitch and intensity. In the 1970s and 1980s, researchers (Aslin, Pisoni, Hennessey, & Perey, 1981) discovered that human infants were specifically adapted at birth to perceive contrasts such as that between /p/ and /b/, as in *pit* and *bit*. Subsequent research showed that even chinchillas are capable of making this distinction. This suggests that much of the basic structure of the infant's auditory world can be attributed to fundamental processes in the mammalian ear. Moreover, there is evidence that some of these early perceptual abilities are lost as the infant begins to acquire the distinctions actually used by the native language (Werker, 1995). Beyond this basic level of auditory processing, it appears that infants have a remarkable capacity to record and store sequences of auditory events (Saffran, Newport, & Aslin, 1996). It is as if the infant has a tape recorder in the auditory cortex that records input sounds, replays them, and accustoms the ear to their patterns.

Children tend to produce their first words sometime between 9 and 12 months. One-year-olds have about 5 words in their vocabulary on average, although individual children may have none or as many as 30; by 2 years, average vocabulary size is more than 150 words, with a range among individual children from as few as 10 to as many as 450 words. Children possess a vocabulary of about 14,000 words by 6 years of age (Templin, 1957); adults have an estimated average of 40,000 words in their working vocabulary at age 40 (McCarthy, 1954).

Whereas vocabulary development is marked by spectacular individual variation, the development of grammatical and syntactic skills is highly stable across children. Children's early one-word utterances do not yet trigger the need for syntactic patterns because they are still only one word long. By the middle of the second year, when children's vocabularies grow to between 50 and 100 words, they begin to combine words in what has been termed "telegraphic speech." Utterances typical of this period include forms such as "where Mommy," "my shoe," "dolly chair," and "allgone banana."

At this same time, children are busy learning to adjust their language to suit their audience and the situation. Learning the pragmatic social skills related to language is an ongoing process. Parents go to great efforts to teach their children to say "please" and "thank you" when needed, to be deferential in speaking to adults, to remember to issue an appropriate greeting when they meet someone, and not to interrupt when others are speaking. Children fine tune their language skills to maintain conversations, tell stories, argue for favors, tattle on their classmates, or ask for favors. Early on, they also begin to acquire the metalinguistic skills involved in thinking and making judgments about language.

Beyond the basic skills of reading and spelling lie more advanced forms of literate expression. Children vary markedly in their ability to articulate explanations, narratives, arguments, and logical analyses. Gifted children often excel in the acquisition of specialized vocabulary, which further supports the child's entry into the worlds of literature, scientific discourse, and cultural analysis. Through literate activities such as reading and writing, language provides the means for self-learning and self-expression. The acquisition of reading and literacy poses a set of developmental challenges to the child (Bruner, 1987; Nelson, 1998). The human species has been using spoken language for at least 200,000 years. The ability to produce and comprehend rapid speech has been supported by nearly 10,000 generations of natural selection. However, writing and reading have arisen in the last 5,000 years, and adaptation to these tasks is supported by only 250 generations of natural selection. Thus, it is not surprising to find that so many children have trouble learning to read and are diagnosed as "dyslexic" (Booth, Perfetti, MacWhinney, & Hunt, 2000).

Communication skills are good indicator of the child's current developmental progress. They are also the primary vehicle of development in other domains. For instance, language facilitates growth in cognitive skills such as categorization, reasoning, and problem solving, particularly when such tasks involve abstractions. Beginning about 2 years of age, language is used as the major indicator of intellectual functioning. In using language, children are able to talk about the causes, consequences, and objects of their emotional experience (Bloom, 1995), thereby learning how to regulate their emotions.

DEVELOPMENTAL STABILITY OF LANGUAGE

During the first five years, the stages of language acquisition are marked by a series of fairly well defined milestones. In the 1st month, newborns respond to the human voice; by their 9th month, infants understand simple words; by their 18th month, toddlers comprehend simple questions; by their 48th month, children can correctly interpret complex commands. In the 2nd month, newborns begin to coo; around their 12th month, infants produce their first words; between 18 and 24 months, toddlers produce simple sentences; by 48 to 60 months, children have mastered the basics of grammar almost completely. They are able to invert auxiliaries when asking questions, compose complex sentences with embedded clauses, add particles for negatives and passives, and control selection of the correct complementizer (*for*, *to*, and *that*).

In adolescence, the focus of education is no longer on the mechanics of language and literacy, but rather on the use of literacy and oral language skills to gather, interpret, and convey information. In adulthood, success is also contingent on literate command of reading, writing, and formal oral expression. The link between literacy skills and economic success was examined in the recent National Adult Literacy Study (Kirsch, Jungeblut, Jenkins, & Kolstad, 1993). In this national survey, individuals with more limited literacy skills were less likely to be employed, earned less, and were more likely to be employed in non-professional occupations than were those who displayed more advanced skills. Not surprisingly, poverty was much more common among individuals with the lowest literacy skills. In addition, better literacy was also associated with one indication of good citizenship practices—voting in elections. It has also been found that literacy skills can act in a protective fashion for children at high risk because of poverty and familial problems (Werner & Smith, 1982).

Moreover, individual differences in language tend to be stable in the sense that children who have more words in their vocabularies at 2 years will be the children who are performing better in verbal tests of intelligence at 4 years (Bornstein & Haynes, 1998). Children who acquire language early are often regarded as "advanced," whereas the failure to use language productively is one of the most common markers of developmental delay. Early language development is one of the best predictors of long-term cognitive and communicative skills. Hart and Risley (1995) reported that in 29 of the 42 children they followed from preschool to school age both vocabulary growth and usage at age 3 were correlated with vocabulary comprehension, global language, and reading comprehension at 9–10 years of age.

FACTORS THAT AFFECT THE DEVELOPMENT OF LANGUAGE

Language is enormously complex. Fortunately, children can rely on a wide range of support mechanisms to move them continually through the language learning process. Support can come from parents, peers, schools, and other organizations. Each new experience in which the child engages is a new opportunity for language learning. Often these new experiences involve use of language in new social contexts with new groups, outside of the familiar family context. To the degree that teachers and parents can use these learning activities to promote literate practices, the child will become more and more competent in language use.

Children come to the language-learning task with a strong desire to communicate. Children's very early sensitivities to sound and their earliest vocal expressions give evidence of strong biological influences. Very soon, however, verbal perception and production become subject to the linguistic environments provided by parent, home, and culture. Language growth builds on a foundation of parent–child interaction, but it includes ever-expanding contexts outward from the family to community, social class, and cultural context.

Thus, language learning begins with the give-and-take of social interactions between child and parent. Parents often take advantage of periods of joint visual attention to label or comment on what the child is looking at. Mothers, fathers, caregivers, and even older children often use "baby talk" or "motherese" when addressing very young children. Motherese has several unique characteristics that distinguish it from speech directed to adults, including short sentences, greater repetition and questioning, and higher and more variable intonation. Specific parent-provided experiences or aspects of the environment have significant roles to play in the growth of specific verbal skills in children (Belsky, Rovine, & Taylor, 1984; Goldfield, 1987; Tamis-LeMonda, Bornstein, Baumwell, & Damast, 1996).

Children must speak to others and be spoken to in order to learn language; exposure to spoken language on television cannot substitute for actual interactive conversation. For example, Dutch children with extensive exposure to German television do not learn German (Snow et al., 1976). Learning of language and literacy depend on a wide array of social, situational, and linguistic supports. Children growing up in cultures with less access to parental input may show some delay in the acquisition of certain aspects of language (Scollon, 1976).

One of the best predictors of a child's vocabulary development is the amount and diversity of input the child receives (Huttenlocher et al., 1991). We also know that verbal input can be as great as three times more available in educated families (Hart & Risley, 1995) than in less educated families. These facts have led educators to suspect that basic and pervasive differences in the level of social support for language learning lie at the root of many learning problems in the later school years. Social interaction (quality of attachment, parent responsiveness, involvement, sensitivity, control style) and general intellectual climate (providing enriching toys, reading books, encouraging attention to surroundings) predict developing language competence in children as well (van IJzendoorn, Dijkstra, & Bus, 1995). Relatively uneducated and economically disadvantaged mothers talk less frequently to their children compared with more educated and affluent mothers, and correspondingly, children of less educated and less affluent mothers produce less speech. Socioeconomic status relates to both child vocabulary and to maternal vocabulary (Fenson et al., 1994). Middle-class mothers expose their children to a richer vocabulary, with longer sentences, and a greater number of word roots.

As children move on to higher stages of language development and the acquisition of literacy, they rely increasingly on broader social institutions. They may rely on Sunday School teachers as their source of knowledge about Biblical language, prophets, and the geography of the Holy Land. They will rely on science teachers to gain vocabulary and understandings about friction, molecular structures, the circulatory system, and DNA (Keil, 1989). They will rely on peers to introduce them to the language of the streets, verbal dueling, and the use of language for courtship. They will rely on the media for exposure to the verbal expressions of other ethnic groups and religions. When they enter the workplace, they will rely on their co-workers to develop a literate understanding of work procedures, union rules, and methods for furthering their status. By reading to their children, by telling stories, and by engaging in supportive dialogs, parents set the stage for their child's entry into the world of literature and schooling. Here, again, the parent and teacher must teach by displaying examples of the execution and generation of a wide variety of detailed literate practices, ranging from learning to write through outlines to taking notes in lectures (Connors & Epstein, 1995).

CONCLUSIONS

Children need to know language for many purposes, not the least of which include carrying on extended conversations, comprehending and composing narratives, providing reasoned answers, and just plain learning.

Language encompasses impressive accomplishments in the physical, perceptual, cognitive, and social spheres of development. It is a complex "system" with multiple components, multiple antecedents, and multiple implications. There is a bidirectional relation between successful language and literacy learning and children's well-being. In order to participate successfully in the family and the peer group, the child needs to develop adequate control of language and verbal expression.

Language is a unique marker of humanity. It distinguishes the human species from the rest of the creation, and it allows us to share our thoughts and feelings. Language is the most complex skill that any of us will ever master. Despite this sophistication, nearly every human child succeeds in learning language. This suggests that language is optimally shaped to mesh with our neurological, physical, cognitive, and social abilities. Although all children achieve the basic use of language, they differ markedly in the extent to which they acquire the more elaborated aspects of language and literate practices. Successful learning can facilitate well-being, but it must be provided within an appropriate sociological context. By better understanding the ways in which literate practices are treated within the various subcultures in American society, we can promote the child's learning and the growth of democratic society.

REFERENCES

Aslin, R. N., Pisoni, D. B., Hennessey, B. L., & Perey, A. J. (1981). Discrimination of voice onset time by human infants: New findings and implications for the effects of early experience. *Child Development*, *52*, 1135–1145.

Belsky, J., Rovine, M., & Taylor, P. (1984). The Pennsylvania Infant and Family Development Project: III. The origins of individual differences in infant–mother attachment: Maternal and infant contributions. *Child Development*, *55*, 718–728.

Bloom, L. (1995). *The transition from infancy to language: Acquiring the power of expression.* New York: Cambridge University Press.

Bohannon, N., MacWhinney, B., & Snow, C. (1990). No negative evidence revisited: Beyond learnability or who has to prove what to whom. *Developmental Psychology*, *26*, 221–226.

Booth, J. R., Perfetti, C. A., MacWhinney, B., & Hunt, S. B. (2000). The association of rapid temporal perception with orthographic and phonological processing in children and adults with readng impairment. *Scientific Studies of Reading*, *4*, 101–132.

Bornstein, M., & Haynes, O. M. (1998). Vocabulary competence in early childhood: Measurement, latent construct, and predictive validity. *Child Development*, *69*, 654–671.

Bruner, J. (1987). *Actual minds, possible worlds.* Cambridge, MA: Harvard University Press.

Chomsky, N. (1982) Some concepts and consequences of the theory of government and binding. Cambridge, MA: M. I. T. Press.

Connors, L. J., & Epstein, J. L. (1995). Parent and school partnerships. In M. H. Bornstein (Ed.), *Handbook of parenting* (Vol. 4, pp. 437–457). Mahwah, NJ: Lawrence Erlbaum Associates.

Fenson, L., Dale, P. S., Reznick, J. S., Bates, E., Thal, D. J., & Hartung, J. (1994). Variability in early communication development. *Monographs of the Society for Research in Child Development*, *59* (Serial No. 242).

Goldfield, B. (1987). The contributions of child and caregiver to referential and expressive language. *Applied Psycholinguistics*, *8*, 267–280.

Hart, B., & Risley, T. R. (1995). *Meaningful differences in the everyday experience of young American children.* Baltimore: Paul H. Brookes.

Huttenlocher, J., Haight, W., Bryk, A., Seltzer, M., & Lyons, T. (1991). Early vocabulary growth: Relation to language input and gender. *Developmental Psychology*, *27*, 236–248.

James, W. (1890). *The principles of psychology.* New York: Holt, Rinehart, & Winston.

Keil, F. C. (1989). *Concepts, kinds, and cognitive development.* Cambridge, MA: MIT Press.

Kirsch, I. S., Jungeblut, A., Jenkins, L., & Kolstad, A. (1993). *Adult literacy in America: A first look at the results of the National Adult Literacy Survey.* Princeton, NJ: Educational Testing Service.

Lenneberg, E. H. (1967). *Biological foundations of language.* New York: Wiley.

MacWhinney, B. (2000). *The CHILDES project: Tools for analyzing talk.* Mahwah, NJ: Lawrence Erlbaum Associates.

McCarthy, D. (1954). Manual of child psychology. In L. Carmichael (Ed.), *Language development in children.* New York: Wiley.

Nelson, K. (1998). *Language in cognitive development: The emergence of the mediated mind.* New York: Cambridge University Press.

Saffran, J. R., Newport, E. L., & Aslin, R. N. (1996). Word segmentation: The role of distributional cues. *Journal of Memory and Language, 35,* 606–621.

Scollon, R. (1976). *Conversations with a one year old: A case study of the developmental foundation of syntax.* Honolulu, HI: University Press of Hawaii.

Snow, C. E., Arlman-Rupp, A., Hassing, Y., Jobse, J., Joosten, J., & Vorster, J. (1976). Mothers' speech in three social classes. *Journal of Psycholinguistic Research, 31,* 424–444.

Tamis-LeMonda, C. S., Bornstein, M. H., Baumwell, L., & Damast, A. M. (1996). Responsive parenting in the second year: Specific influences on children's language and play. *Early Development and Parenting, 5,* 173–183.

Templin, M. (1957). *Certain language skills in children.* Minneapolis, MN: University of Minnesota Press.

van IJzendoorn, M. H., Dijkstra, J., & Bus, A. G. (1995). Attachment, intelligence, and language: A meta-analysis. *Social Development, 4,* 115–128.

Werker, J. F. (1995). Exploring developmental changes in cross-language speech perception. In L. Gleitman & M. Liberman (Eds.), *An invitation to cognitive science: Vol. 1. Language* (pp. 87–106). Cambridge, MA: MIT Press.

Werner, E. E., & Smith, R. S. (1982). *Vulnerable but not invincible: A study of resilient children.* New York: McGraw-Hill.

26

Educational Achievement

Stephen B. Plank
Douglas J. MacIver
Johns Hopkins University, Baltimore, MD

INTRODUCTION

Malcolm X called education a "passport for the future, for tomorrow belongs to the people who prepare for it today" (cited in Madhere et al., 1997, p. 1). Unfortunately, in most high-poverty schools, most students have diminished future prospects because they do not receive the high-quality learning opportunities, expert teaching, and supportive learning environments they need to reach the levels of educational achievement that are generally associated with better postsecondary educational opportunities and careers, higher economic returns, and developmental well-being. This chapter discusses how educational achievement has been most productively operationalized at different points throughout childhood, summarizes the evidence on the continuity and short- and long-term benefits of educational achievement, and discusses the factors that have been identified as promoting and impeding educational achievement. Special attention is paid to those factors that are alterable—those factors that, if changed, can increase the numbers of students from high-poverty schools who receive a passport for the future.

TECHNICAL ISSUES:
OPERATIONALIZING EDUCATIONAL ACHIEVEMENT

Ready to Learn

Measures of early educational achievement focus on whether children start school "ready to learn." The National Education Goals Panel (1999) has made school readiness its first goal. But what exactly is meant by the concept? Several trends can be identified in the ways readiness is conceptualized. First, readiness once seemed to refer to something that resided solely "within the child" that could be measured and used in reaching decisions about educational placement and instruction. In recent years, however, there has been a tendency to view readiness as an interactive property of the child and his or her parents and teachers (Graue, 1993; Meisels, Dorfman, & Steele, 1992). It can be defined as the state in which the capacities and competencies of the child match the expectations and requirements of the adults and school in his or her life (Karweit, 1999b). As such, the concept is relative: The same child might be deemed ready to enter kindergarten in one place, or in the eyes of one parent or teacher, but not ready in another setting. Much variation exists in parents' and educators' definitions of when a child is ready to learn. The aspects of readiness that are often articulated include not only abilities that would seem to be very proximate to future academic success (e.g., counting ability and recognition of letters) but also more distal building blocks (e.g., ability to sit still and pay attention, ability to follow classroom rules, having familiarity with books and having been read to by a parent).

Achievement Test Scores

By the time they reach first grade, most children begin experiencing one or more achievement tests every week that assess what they have learned following a unit or course of study. Of course, most of these tests are curriculum-embedded and teacher-made achievement tests rather than standardized achievement tests (Dorr-Bremme & Herman, 1986), but the administration by school districts of formal standardized achievement tests each year to students in grades 1 through 11 or 12 is not unusual (Linn, Graue, & Sanders, 1990). In most schools, in addition to district testing, some or all of the students may be required to take extra achievement tests (Linn, 1992). For example, students participating in certain specially funded programs are almost always given standardized achievement tests, often twice a year. This is the case, for instance, for students served by Title I, the federally administered program that provides extra money for academic programs in schools serving large numbers of poor students. Furthermore, almost all states administer standardized assessments to all students in selected grade levels in several content areas (National Research Council, 1999). In many states these include minimum competency tests that determine students' eligibility for graduation or promotion (Bond & King, 1995; National Research Council, 1999).

The most recent wave of reform has led to important changes to achievement tests and the accountability systems that rely on these tests (Linn, 2000). Because past uses of high stakes standardized tests frequently led to a narrowing of the curriculum and an overemphasis on basic skills (Resnick & Resnick, 1992), many new tests or subtests have been developed and widely administered that emphasize performance-based approaches to assessment that feature the use of more authentic and open-ended performance tasks. These tests are intended to be "tests worth teaching to" and to be aligned with specific content and performance standards that are demanding.

Report Card Grades

For upper elementary and secondary students and for many parents, the most salient indicators of students' short-term educational accomplishments are the marks they receive on their report cards. During the first few years of schooling, report cards frequently assess students' mastery of specific skills (e.g. "Knows letter sounds") usually with only three rating categories per skill (e.g., Succeeding, Progressing, or Needs Improvement). As students progress through school, the number of academic items marked becomes smaller—each item typically reflects a broad content area such as reading—but with a greater number of rating categories (typically, A, A–, B+, B, B–, C+, C, etc., or a percentage system). Report card marks typically reflect students' performance on teacher-made or curriculum-embedded tests, projects, presentations, reports, routine class and homework assignments, and participation during classroom discussions (Natriello, 1992).

Retention in Grade and Dropping Out

Two educational events that are frequently used as indicators of low achievement are grade retention and dropping out of school. In some cases, however, these events do not reflect achievement per se (what the affected students know and are able to do) but rather reflect attendance problems and/or relational problems (e.g., a student might display average achievement and still might not earn promotion or a diploma due to chronic absenteeism or a student may choose to leave school due to being estranged from teachers, administrators, or peers).

THEORETICAL AND EMPIRICAL REVIEW: WHY EDUCATIONAL ACHIEVEMENT MATTERS

It is generally accepted that educational achievement is a positive characteristic—something to be desired and encouraged in every child. It can be argued that greater educational achievement brings both individual and collective benefits. Here we focus on individual benefits.

Prior achievement has little impact on children's ability perceptions or other motivational outcomes during the early elementary grades. Instead, virtually all children have very high self-perceptions of competence during their first few years of school-ing (Benenson & Dweck, 1986; Eshel & Klein, 1981; Marsh, Barnes, Cairns, & Tidman, 1984; Nicholls, 1978, 1979; Pintrich & Blumenfeld, 1985; Stipek, 1981; Stipek & Tannatt, 1984) and their persistence on academic tasks does not decline as a consequence of failure until the fifth or sixth grade (Miller, 1985; Rholes, Blackwell, Jordan, & Walters, 1980). Nicholls (1978, 1979) found that children's self-ratings of ability were not significantly related to grades given by the teacher until the third or fourth grade. Because young children view ability as "incremental" (something that increases through practice and effort) rather than as a stable trait, they remain quite optimistic about their potential even in the face of low grades or other indications of low achievement (Stipek & MacIver, 1989; Newman & Spitzer, 1998).

In contrast, upper elementary students rely heavily on grades to evaluate their ability (Blumenfeld, Pintrich, & Hamilton, 1986; MacIver, 1987, 1988; Nicholls, 1978, 1979). As a result, once children reach the upper elementary grades, one of the most important short-term benefits of receiving high marks is that these marks help students maintain confidence in their ability. Such confidence has been shown to be critical in determining whether upper elementary and secondary students will persist and try harder, especially in the face of difficulty (Eccles & Wigfield, 1985; MacIver, Stipek, & Daniels, 1991; Andrews & Debus, 1978; Diener & Dweck, 1978; Licht, Kistner, Ozkaragoz, Shapiro, & Clausen, 1985; Weiner, 1979). For ex-ample, Helmke (1987) found that students' math-ability perceptions at the end of fifth grade had a positive impact on the quality of students' later efforts (e.g., on their perseverance and on their active engagement during instruction in sixth grade). Brown and Inouye's (1978) data indicated that the higher students' expec-tancies were concerning their ability to solve anagrams, the longer they persisted on anagrams for which they were unable to find solutions. Likewise, Hallerman and Meyer (1978, cited in Meyer, 1987) found that perceived ability was strongly pre-dictive of the persistence of teenage students on insoluble achievement tasks, re-gardless of whether the tasks were portrayed as normatively easy or normatively difficult. Students who perceived their ability for the achievement task as high ex-hibited high persistence at both "easy" and "difficult" tasks. Similarly, Licht et al. (1985) found that, for both learning-disabled and non-learning-disabled children, the tendency to attribute one's failures to insufficient ability was negatively related to persistence on a reading task. Increases in students' ability perceptions have been shown to lead to increases in student effort in junior and senior high school courses and to increases in students' valuing of the subject matter covered in those courses (MacIver et al., 1991).

Not only does educational achievement affect student motivation, it also affects students' access to certain opportunities and placements at times of transition from one year or level of schooling to the next—opportunities and placements from which low-achieving individuals may be restricted. Specifically, during primary and secondary schooling, low achievement may lead educators to require a student to repeat a grade rather than being promoted to the next one. While it is actively debated whether retention is the best decision for struggling students, most parents, educators, and researchers would agree that it is most desirable for a student not to exhibit the low achievement that makes retention a consideration in the first place (Alexander, Entwisle, & Dauber, 1994; Karweit, 1999a; Shepard & Smith, 1989).

A student's prior achievement is also often used to guide decisions about his or her placement within a structure of ability groups or tracks (e.g., vocational, general, or college preparatory; Oakes, Gamoran, & Page, 1992). Sadly, it has been documented that the quality and quantity of instruction and other resources are often markedly diminished in the lowest tracks within schools that utilize tracking. Experts disagree as to whether this diminished quality and quantity is a remediable unintended consequence of an otherwise sound educational practice or a reflection of a fundamentally inequitable system (Hallinan, 1994; Oakes, 1994).

In addition to placements and opportunities while one remains within the formal education system, achievement levels also affect one's likelihood of persisting within the system. Achievement (in terms of standardized tests and grades) is negatively related to the likelihood of dropping out of high school (Finn, 1989). A few studies have dramatically shown that the roots of dropping out of high school can be detected (probabilistically) in students' low achievement and other problematic experiences as early as first grade (Alexander, Entwisle, & Horsey, 1997; Ensminger & Slusarick, 1992). For those who complete high school, achievement during the K–12 years is positively related to the likelihood of pursuing postsecondary education (Hearn, 1991; Hossler, Schmidt, & Vesper, 1999; Plank & Jordan, 2001).

Finally, educational achievement and the development of cognitive skills affect placement and success in the adult world of work. It has been shown that one's level of formal schooling affects adult wages and job type (Arum & Hout, 1998; Blau & Duncan, 1967; Kerckhoff, 1995). Additionally, basic cognitive skills (e.g., mathematics skill as of 12th grade), as distinct from formal schooling, affect wages in adulthood. In fact, there is evidence that the association between cognitive skills and wages has gotten stronger in recent decades (Murnane, Willett, & Levy, 1995). At the same time, however, there is evidence that potential employers do not rely as directly as they might on new workers' educational achievements and acquired skills in making hiring decisions (Gamoran, 1994; Rosenbaum, DeLuca, Miller, & Roy, 1999). Regarding the sorts of jobs sought by youth who do not attend college, it has been claimed that the limited contact between U.S. employers and high schools means that employers who hire high school graduates have difficulty judging their ability at entry, meaning that student skills are not initially rewarded (Rosenbaum & Kariya, 1991). An ironic and distressing implication is that the very employers who decry youths' poor in-school preparation may be inadvertently contributing to the problem as they signal to students and schools that grades and test scores have only trivial influence on hiring decisions, thus weakening the incentive for students (especially those who plan to end their formal schooling with high school graduation) to strive for high grades and test scores (Rosenbaum, 1996).

DEVELOPMENTAL CONTINUITY OF ACHIEVEMENT
OVER THE LIFE SPAN

Across a sample of children, do those who were the highest achievers (in a school, city, state, or nation) at age 7 tend to be the highest achievers at ages 11 and 15 as well? Similarly, do early academic difficulties foretell later academic difficulties?

The Beginning School Study (BSS) provides one source for examining the continuity of achievement during the elementary and middle school years. BSS began with a sample of 825 children who attended first grade in Baltimore public schools in 1982. Alexander, Entwisle, and colleagues have followed the cohort longitudinally since then (Alexander & Entwisle, 1988; Alexander et al., 1994; Entwisle, Alexander, & Olson, 1997). We used these data to examine the correlation between students' earlier and later achievement test scores at four-year lags and at an eight-year lag. For BSS students, the correlation between reading comprehension on the California Achievement Test in Spring 1983 (when the students were in first grade and most were 6- or 7-year-olds) and reading comprehension in Spring 1987 is .58. The correlation after an eight-year lag (between 1983 and 1991) is almost as strong (.54). Once students have completed primary grades, achievement becomes even more predictable across four-year intervals. For example, the correlation between reading comprehension in Spring 1987 and Spring 1991 is .78. For mathematics achievement, the correlations are slightly higher, with a coefficient of .65 between 1983 and 1987 scores, a coefficient of .61 between 1983 and 1991, and a coefficient of .79 between 1987 and 1991 (all correlations taken from a correlation matrix provided by K. Alexander in a personal communication, April 28, 2000).

Achievement test scores in middle school remain highly predictive of future achievement test scores throughout high school. For example, the National Education Longitudinal Study of 1988 provides a representative sample of students who were 8th graders in the United States in 1988 (Ingels et al., 1994). For standardized measures of mathematics achievement, the correlation between 1988 scores and 1992 scores is .83 (based on 12,531 cases). In the subject areas of reading, science, and history/social studies, the associations are almost as great.

FACTORS AFFECTING THE DEVELOPMENT
AND ENHANCEMENT OF EDUCATIONAL ACHIEVEMENT

Parent–Child Interactions

Hart and Risley (1995) reveal strong associations between parent–child interactions during the first 3 years of a child's life and language development at age 3. Five aspects of parent–child communication—language diversity, feedback tone, symbolic emphasis, guidance style, and responsiveness—not only are strong predictors of the rate of vocabulary growth, vocabulary use, and IQ test score at age 3, but are equally predictive of vocabulary and language development at age 9. A striking finding is that, for this study's sample, 3-year-olds from professional families used more different words in their cumulative monthly vocabularies than did parents on welfare. The study does not lead one to conclude that poor, less educated parents are bad parents, but it does help one to understand why two different children,who may even have begun to use words at the same age, arrive at preschool or kindergarten with such different levels of academic readiness.

While the five parenting characteristics are significantly correlated with socioeconomic status (SES) across a sample of welfare, working class, and professional families, the strong associations between parent–child interaction and achievement measures lose none of their strength in analyses restricted to working class families, where the correlation between parenting styles and SES is near zero. This study shows the effects of early childhood experiences on later academic achievement, and serves as a strong corrective to anyone who believes that a child's intelligence and achievement are mostly genetically based.

Socioeconomic and Demographic Factors

Grissmer, Kirby, Berends, and Williamson (1994) used a sophisticated research design to estimate student achievement levels in the United States in 1970, 1975, and 1990. A first implication of their study is that average achievement probably improved in absolute terms in the United States over those years; this is a more encouraging picture than the one often portrayed in popular opinion and the media. Further, these researchers concluded that most of the improvement for non-Hispanic White students between 1970 and 1990 could be attributed to changes in family contexts—especially rising levels of parental education and shrinking family sizes, both of which are positively associated with student achievement. In contrast, for Hispanic and African American students, only about a third of the improvement in achievement between 1970 and 1990 could be accounted for by changing family and demographic conditions. The researchers inferred that much of the remaining improvement for Hispanics and African Americans could be explained by changes in the ways schools operate, public policies, and public investment in education.

The study by Grissmer and colleagues provides some encouraging news about educational achievement in the United States, showing, among other things, that achievement levels are not fixed or unalterable. Their study, like the one by Hart and Risley, also highlights aspects of family context that are predictive of student achievement. But the encouraging news about improvements in average achievement in the United States is accompanied by persistent achievement gaps linked to race, parental education, and family income. These gaps have been documented elsewhere as well (e.g., Duncan & Brooks-Gunn, 1997; Duncan, Yeung, Brooks-Gunn, & Smith, 1998; Hedges & Nowell, 1999; Jencks & Phillips, 1998). Further, there is strong evidence that when individual disadvantages, such as poverty, are concentrated within neighborhoods, detrimental effects on children's developmental outcomes are multiplied (Brooks-Gunn, Duncan, & Aber, 1997).

A study like that by Hart and Risley provides much insight into some family- and home-based reasons for lagging school achievement for disadvantaged students. So too do studies documenting the fact that poor and minority students lose the most academic ground to their wealthier and European American counterparts during summer months, when schools are not in session (Borman, 2000; Cooper, Nye, Charlton, Lindsay, & Greathouse, 1996; Entwisle & Alexander, 1992, 1996; Heyns, 1978). It is clear that opportunities and resources within the home and community that differ between families have strong effects on achievement. But it is equally clear that, beyond the home, children's schooling experiences differ systematically in association with SES, geographic location, and race in ways that affect the rates of students' educational progress.

Educators' Inattention to the Technical Core of Schooling

While it is true that economic, social, cultural, familial, and bureaucratic factors contribute to the low achievement of students, it is important to recognize that in high-poverty schools, low student achievement is actively manufactured (Balfanz & MacIver, 2000). This occurs when inattention to the technical core of schooling (e.g., curriculum, instructional materials, academic learning time, and professional development) results in students receiving impoverished learning opportunities of little substance or value (Balfanz, 1997, 2000; Wilson & Corbett, 1999). Achievement suffers when students are not provided a coherent, consistent, and increasingly complex standards-based curriculum that builds year after year in a systematic and strategic way (Balfanz, MacIver, & Ryan, 1999). Achievement suffers when struggling students are not provided with organized and sustained extra-help opportunities during the school day that help them succeed in a curriculum that challenges and engages them (MacIver, Balfanz, & Plank, 1998; Wilson & Corbett, 1999). Teachers' effectiveness and students' learning both suffer when teachers are not provided with ongoing subject- and grade-specific professional development that gives them the content knowledge, instructional strategies, classroom management advice, and hands-on experience they need to successfully implement new standards-based instructional programs or to teach a subject with which they have limited experience (Elmore, 1997; Killion, 1999; Killion & Hirsh, 1998; MacIver & Balfanz, 2000). Teachers' effectiveness and student learning also suffer when teachers do not know what their teaching assignment is going to be until the start of the school year and/or their teaching assignment is switched from a subject or grade level for which they have been recently trained to one for which they have not (Ruby, 1999). Teachers' ability to teach also suffers when they are not provided with the instructional materials they need until well into the school year. It also suffers when poor scheduling, inefficient human resource utilization, inattention to human relations, and ineffective discipline policies create a chaotic and unruly school climate (Balfanz, 2000). All of these problems commonly occur in high-poverty schools and work together to manufacture low levels of student achievement. In trying to address the myriad problems and larger social context that confront high-poverty schools, educators often overlook the fundamentals.

CONCLUSIONS

This chapter began by discussing some of the main ways educational achievement is defined and measured. For young children, readiness to learn and readiness to begin schooling involve the degree to which the capacities and competencies of a child match the expectations and requirements established by the adults and the school in his or her life. As children get older and progress through school, curriculum-embedded tests, standardized achievement tests, and report card grades become the primary indicators of achievement. In addition to these, grade retention and dropping out of school are often interpreted as indicators of low achievement when they occur.

We asserted that educational achievement matters and should be encouraged in every child because it sparks motivation and persistence, especially as children reach the upper elementary grades. Further, high achievement permits access to certain coveted opportunities and placements within the educational system while low achievement limits opportunity and access. Finally, achievement levels affect an individual's likelihood of persisting within the formal education system, and affect placement, success, and rewards in the adult world of work.

Achievement trajectories begin to be predictable or established as early as age 3—certainly as early as first grade. There tends to be a high degree of continuity regarding which children are high achievers and which are low achievers within a population over spans of 8 years or more.

Achievement levels are not fixed or unalterable, however. Among the environmental factors known to affect the development of educational achievement are the quality and quantity of parent-child communication during the first 3 years of a child's life, parental education levels (and the corresponding implications for childhood experiences), family size (and the corresponding implications for childhood experiences), and the specific character of curriculum, instruction, and structured learning time encountered during schooling.

A More Promising Future?

Toward the end of this chapter, we stressed some of the problems frequently encountered within schools serving disadvantaged populations. To counterbalance that distressing listing, however, we wish to conclude on a hopeful note. There is evidence that when schools provide students with high-quality learning opportunities, impressive gains in student achievement can follow. The achievement gap between disadvantaged and advantaged youth can narrow rather than increase over time. In order to provide these high-quality learning opportunities, teachers must have access to well-designed curricular materials, as well as ongoing professional development and support. There are currently some comprehensive school reform models that take seriously the idea of forming partnerships with schools to establish these crucial components for student success. Success for All/Roots & Wings (Slavin & Madden, 2000; Slavin, Madden, Dolan, & Wasik, 1996), Different Ways of Knowing (Catterall, 1995; Hovda & Kyle, 1997; Petrosko, 1997; Wang & Sogin, 1996), and the Talent Development Middle School (Balfanz & MacIver, 2000; MacIver, MacIver, Balfanz, Plank, & Ruby, 2000; MacIver et al., 2001) are three examples of reform models with solid research bases that have shown the ability to assist schools in improving the educational opportunities for students and, consequently, educational achievement. Whether schools attempt to establish excellent learning environments on their own or in collaboration with external partners, it is clear that the student potential with which they are entrusted is too precious and fragile to treat with anything less than our best efforts.

REFERENCES

Alexander, K. L., & Entwisle, D. R. (1988). Achievement in the first two years of school: Patterns and processes. *Monographs of the Society for Research in Child Development, 53*(2, Serial No. 218).

Alexander, K. L., Entwisle, D. R., & Dauber, S. L. (1994). *On the success of failure: A reassessment of the effects of retention in the primary grades.* New York: Cambridge University Press.

Alexander, K. L., Entwisle, D. R., & Horsey, C. S. (1997). From first grade forward: Early foundations of high school dropout. *Sociology of Education, 70,* 87–107.

Andrews, G. R., & Debus, R. L. (1978). Persistence and the causal perception of failure: Modifying cognitive attributions. *Journal of Educational Psychology, 70,* 154–166.

Arum, R., & Hout, M. (1998). The early returns: The transition from school to work in the United States. In Y. Shavit & W. Muller (Eds.), *From school to work: A comparative study of educational qualifications and occupational destinations* (pp. 471–510). New York: Oxford University Press.

Balfanz, R. (1997, March). *Mathematics for all in two urban schools: A view from the trenches.* Paper presented at the annual meeting of the American Educational Research Association, Chicago.

Balfanz, R. (2000). Why do so many urban public school students demonstrate so little academic achievement? The underappreciated importance of time and place. In M. G. Sanders (Ed.), *Schooling at risk: Research, policy, and practice in the education of poor and minority adolescents* (pp. 37–62). Mahwah, NJ: Lawrence Erlbaum Associates.

Balfanz, R., & MacIver, D. (2000). Transforming high-poverty urban middle schools into strong learning institutions: Lessons from the first five years of the Talent Development Middle School. *Journal of Education for Students Placed at Risk, 5,* 137–158.

Balfanz, R., MacIver, D. J., & Ryan, D. (1999, April). *Achieving algebra for all with a facilitated instructional program: First year results of the Talent Development Middle School Mathematics Program.* Paper presented at the annual meeting of the American Educational Research Association, Montreal, Canada.

Benenson, J., & Dweck, C. (1986). The development of trait explanations and self-evaluations in the academic and social domains. *Child Development, 57,* 1179–1187.

Blau, P. M., & Duncan, O. D. (1967). *The American occupational structure.* New York: Wiley.

Blumenfeld, P., Pintrich, P., & Hamilton, V. (1986). Children's concepts of ability, effort, and conduct. *American Educational Research Journal, 23,* 95–104.

Bond, L. A., & King, D. (1995). *State high school graduation testing: Status and recommendations.* Oak Brook, IL: North Central Regional Educational Laboratory.

Borman, G. D. (2000). The effects of summer school: Questions answered, questions raised. Commentary. *Monographs of the Society for Research in Child Development, 65*(1, Serial No. 260).

Brooks-Gunn, J., Duncan, G. J., & Aber, L. (Eds.). (1997). *Neighborhood poverty: Context and consequences for children.* New York: Russell Sage Foundation.

Brown, I., & Inouye, K. (1978). Learned helplessness through modeling: The role of perceived similarity in competence. *Journal of Personality and Social Psychology, 36,* 900–908.

Catterall, J. S. (1995). *Different Ways of Knowing: 1991–94 National Longitudinal Study, program effects on students and teachers (final report).* Los Angeles, CA: University of California at Los Angeles, Graduate School of Education and Information Studies.

Cooper, H., Nye, B., Charlton, K., Lindsay, J., & Greathouse, S. (1996). The effects of summer vacation on achievement test scores: A narrative and meta-analytic review. *Review of Educational Research, 66,* 227–268.

Diener, C. I., & Dweck, C. S. (1978). An analysis of learned helplessness: Continuous changes in performance, strategy, and achievement cognitions following failure. *Journal of Personality and Social Psychology, 36,* 451–462.

Dorr-Bremme, D. W., & Herman, J. L. (1986). *Assessing student achievement: A profile of classroom practices* (CSE Monograph 11). Los Angeles, CA: University of California, Center for the Study of Evaluation.

Duncan, G. J., & Brooks-Gunn, J. (Eds.). (1997). *Consequences of growing up poor.* New York: Russell Sage.

Duncan, G. J., Yeung, W. J., Brooks-Gunn, J., & Smith, J. R. (1998). How much does childhood poverty affect the life chances of children? *American Sociological Review, 63,* 406–423.

Eccles, J., & Wigfield, A. (1985). Teacher expectations and student motivation. In J. B. Dusek (Ed.), *Teacher expectations* (pp. 185–226). Hillsdale, NJ: Lawrence Erlbaum Associates.

Elmore, R. F. (1997). *Investing in teacher learning: Staff development and instructional improvement in Community School District #2, New York City.* New York: National Commission on Teaching and America's Future, Teachers College Columbia University.

Ensminger, M. A., & Slusarick, A. L. (1992). Paths to high school graduation or dropout: A longitudinal study of a first-grade cohort. *Sociology of Education, 65,* 95–113.

Entwisle, D. R., & Alexander, K. L. (1992). Summer setback: Race, poverty, school composition, and mathematics achievement in the first two years of school. *American Sociological Review, 57,* 72–84.

Entwisle, D. R., & Alexander, K. L. (1996). Further comments on seasonal learning. In A. Booth & J. F. Dunn (Eds.), *Family-school links: How do they affect educational outcomes?* (pp. 125–136). Mahwah, NJ: Lawrence Erlbaum Associates.

Entwisle, D. R., Alexander, K. L., & Olson, L. S. (1997). *Children, schools, and inequality.* Boulder, CO: Westview Press.

Eshel, Y., & Klein, Z. (1981). Development of academic self-concept of lower-class and middle-class primary school children. *Journal of Educational Psychology, 73,* 287–293.

Finn, J. D. (1989). Withdrawing from school. *Review of Educational Research, 59,* 117–142.

Gamoran, A. (1994). *The impact of academic course work on labor market outcomes for youth who do not attend college: A research review.* Unpublished manuscript prepared for the National Assessment of Vocational Education, U.S. Department of Education. Madison, WI.

Graue, M. E. (1993). *Ready for what? Constructing meanings of readiness for kindergarten.* Albany, NY: State University of New York Press.

Grissmer, D. W., Kirby, S. N., Berends, M., & Williamson, S. (1994). *Student achievement and the changing American family.* Santa Monica, CA: RAND Corp.

Hallinan, M. T. (1994). Tracking: From theory to practice. *Sociology of Education, 67,* 79–84.

Hart, B., & Risley, T. R. (1995). *Meaningful differences in the everyday experience of young American children.* Baltimore, MD: Brookes.

Hearn, J. C. (1991). Academic and nonacademic influences on the college destinations of 1980 high school graduates. *Sociology of Education, 64,* 158–171.

Hedges, L. V., & Nowell, A. (1999). Changes in the black-white gap in achievement test scores. *Sociology of Education, 72,* 111–135.

Helmke, A. (1987). *Mediating processes between children's self-concept of ability and mathematics achievement: A longitudinal study* (Paper No. 6). Munich, Germany: Max Planck Institute for Psychological Research.

Heyns, B. (1978). *Summer learning and the effects of schooling.* New York: Academic Press.

Hossler, D., Schmidt, J., & Vesper, N. (1999). *Going to college: How social, economic, and educational factors influence the decisions students make.* Baltimore: Johns Hopkins University Press.

Hovda, R. A., & Kyle, D. W. (1997). *Different Ways of Knowing Study B: Research and evaluation report.* Louisville, KY: Galef Institute-Kentucky, Collaborative for Teaching and Learning.

Ingels, S. J., Dowd, K. L. Baldridge, J. D., Stipe, J. L., Bartot, V. H., & Frankel, M. R. (1994). *NELS:88 second follow-up: Student component data file user's manual.* Washington, DC: National Center for Education Statistics.

Jencks, C., & Phillips, M. (Eds.). (1998). *The Black-White test score gap.* Washington, DC: Brookings Institution Press.

Karweit, N. L. (1999a). *Grade retention: Prevalence, timing, and effects.* Baltimore: Center for Research on the Education of Students Placed At Risk.

Karweit, N. L. (1999b). *Maryland kindergarten survey report.* Baltimore: Center for Research on the Education of Students Placed At Risk.

Kerckhoff, A. C. (1995). Institutional arrangements and stratification processes in industrialized societies. *Annual Review of Sociology, 15,* 323–347.

Killion, J. (1999). *What works in the middle: Results-based staff development.* Oxford, OH: National Staff Development Council.

Killion, J., & Hirsh, S. (1998, March 18). A crack in the middle. *Education Week on the Web.* Retrieved March 19, 1998 from the World Wide Web: http://www.edweek.org

Licht, B. G., Kistner, J. A., Ozkaragoz, T., Shapiro, S., & Clausen, L. (1985). Causal attributions of learning disabled children: Individual differences and their implications for persistence. *Journal of Educational Psychology, 77,* 208–216.

Linn, R. L. (1992). Achievement testing. In M. C. Alkin (Ed.), *Encyclopedia of educational research* (6th ed., pp. 1–12). New York: MacMillan.

Linn, R. L. (2000). Assessments and accountability. *Educational Researcher, 29*(2), 4–16.

Linn, R. L., Graue, M. E., & Sanders, N. M. (1990). Comparing state and district results to national norms: The validity of the claims that "everyone is above average." *Educational Measurement: Issues and Practice, 9*(3), 5–14.

MacIver, D. (1987). Classroom factors and student characteristics predicting students' use of achievement standards during ability self-assessment. *Child Development, 58,* 1258–1271.

MacIver, D. (1988). Classroom environments and the stratification of students' ability perceptions. *Journal of Educational Psychology, 80,* 495–505.

MacIver, D., & Balfanz, R. (2000). *The school district's role in helping high poverty schools become high performing.* Aurora, CO: Mid-continent Research for Education and Learning.

MacIver, D. J., Balfanz, R., & Plank, S. B. (1998). An elective replacement approach to providing extra help in math: The Talent Development Middle Schools' Computer- and Team-Assisted Mathematics Acceleration (CATAMA) program. *Research in Middle Level Education Quarterly, 22*(2), 1–23.

MacIver, D. J., MacIver, M. A., Balfanz, R., Plank, S. B., & Ruby, A. (2000). Talent Development Middle Schools: Blueprint and results for a comprehensive whole-school reform model. In M.G. Sanders (Ed.), *Schooling students placed at risk: Research, policy, and practice in the education of poor and minority adolescents* (pp. 261–288). Mahwah, NJ: Lawrence Erlbaum Associates.

MacIver, D. J., Stipek, D. J., & Daniels, D. H. (1991). Explaining within-semester changes in student effort in junior high school and senior high school courses. *Journal of Educational Psychology, 83,* 201–211.

MacIver, D. J., Young, E., Balfanz, R., Shaw, A., Garriott, M., & Cohen, A. (2001). High quality learning opportunities in high poverty middle schools: Moving from rhetoric to reality. In T. Dickinson (Ed.), *Reinventing the middle school* (pp. 155–175). New York: Routledge Falmer.

Madhere, S., Hogarth, A., Brown, J., Bynum, D., Cotton, L., Mgoqi, C., Salomon, G., & Spurlock, H. (1997). *Active affirmation.* Washington, DC: Howard University, Center for Research on Education of Students Placed at Risk.

Marsh, H., Barnes, J., Cairns, L., & Tidman, M. (1984). Self-description questionnaire: Age and sex effects in the structure and level of self-concept for preadolescent children. *Journal of Educational Psychology, 77,* 581–596.

Meisels, S. J., Dorfman, A., & Steele, D. M. (1992). *Contrasting approaches to assessing young children's school readiness and achievement.* Washington, DC: U.S. Department of Education, National Center for Education Statistics, Office of Educational Research and Improvement.

Meyer, W.-U. (1987). Perceived ability and achievement-related behavior. In F. Halisch & J. Kuhl (Eds.), *Motivation, intention, and volition* (pp. 73–86). Berlin, Germany: Springer-Verlag.

Miller, A. (1985). A developmental study of the cognitive basis of performance impairment after failure. *Journal of Personality and Social Psychology, 49*, 529–538.

Murnane, R. J., Willett, J. B., & Levy, F. (1995). The growing importance of cognitive skills in wage determination. *Review of Economics and Statistics, 77*, 251–266.

National Education Goals Panel. (1999). *The National Education Goals report: Building a nation of learners.* Washington, DC: U.S. Government Printing Office.

National Research Council. (1999). *High stakes: testing for tracking, promotion, and graduation.* Washington, DC: National Academy Press.

Natriello, G. (1992). Marking systems. In M. C. Alkin (Ed.), *Encyclopedia of educational research* (6th ed., pp. 772–776). New York: MacMillan.

Newman, R. S., & Spitzer, S. (1998). How children reason about ability from report card grades: A developmental study. *The Journal of Genetic Psychology, 159*, 133–146.

Nicholls, J. (1978). The development of the concepts of effort and ability, perceptions of academic attainment and the understanding that difficult tasks require more ability. *Child Development, 49*, 800–814.

Nicholls, J. (1979). Development of perception of own attainment and causal attributions for success and failure in reading. *Journal of Educational Psychology, 71*, 94–99.

Oakes, J. (1994). More than misapplied technology: A normative and political response to Hallinan on tracking. *Sociology of Education, 67*, 84–89.

Oakes, J., Gamoran, A., & Page, R. N. (1992). Curriculum differentiation: Opportunities, outcomes, and meanings. In P. W. Jackson (Ed.), *Handbook of research on curriculum* (pp. 570–608). Washington, DC: American Educational Research Association.

Petrosko, J. M. (1997). *Different Ways of Knowing Study A: Implementation of student-centered teaching and learning practices and student assessment results for Research Demonstration Site (RDS) Schools participating in Different Ways of Knowing.* Louisville, KY: Galef Institute-Kentucky, Collaborative for Teaching and Learning.

Pintrich, P., & Blumenfeld, P. (1985). Classroom experience and children's self-perceptions of ability, effort, and conduct. *Journal of Educational Psychology, 77*, 646–657.

Plank, S. B., & Jordan, W. J. (2001). Effects of information, guidance, and actions on postsecondary destinations: A study of talent loss. *American Educational Research Journal, 38*, 947–979.

Resnick, L. B., & Resnick, D. P. (1992). Assessing the thinking curriculum: New tools for educational reform. In B. G. Gifford & M. C. O'Conner (Eds.), *Changing assessments: Alternative views of aptitude, achievement, and instruction* (pp. 37–75). Boston: Kluwer Academic Publishers.

Rholes, W., Blackwell, J., Jordan, C., & Walters, C. (1980). A developmental study of learned helplessness. *Developmental Psychology, 16*, 616–624.

Rosenbaum, J. E. (1996). Policy uses of research on the high school-to-work transition. *Sociology of Education, Extra Issue*, 102–122.

Rosenbaum, J. E., DeLuca, S., Miller, S. R., & Roy, K. (1999). Pathways into work: Short- and long-term effects of personal and institutional ties. *Sociology of Education, 72*, 179–196.

Rosenbaum, J. E., & Kariya, T. (1991). Do school achievements affect the early jobs of high school graduates in the United States and Japan? *Sociology of Education, 64*, 78–95.

Ruby, A. (1999, April). *An implementable curriculum approach to improving science instruction in urban schools.* Paper presented at the annual meeting of the American Educational Research Association, Montreal, Canada.

Shepard, L. A., &. Smith, M. L. (Eds.). (1989). *Flunking grades: Research and policies on retention.* London: Falmer.

Slavin, R. E., & Madden, N. A. (2000). Roots & Wings: Effects of whole-school reform on student achievement. *Journal of Education for Students Placed At Risk, 5*, 109–136.

Slavin, R. E., Madden, N. A., Dolan, L. J., & Wasik, B. A. (1996). *Every child, every school: Success for All.* Thousand Oaks, CA: Corwin.

Stipek, D. (1981). Children's perceptions of their own and their classmates' ability. *Journal of Educational Psychology, 73,* 404–410.

Stipek, D., & MacIver, D. (1989). Developmental change in children's assessment of intellectual competence. *Child Development, 60,* 521–538.

Stipek, D., & Tannatt, L. (1984). Children's judgments of their own and their peers' academic competence. *Journal of Educational Psychology, 76,* 75–84.

Wang, M. C., &. Sogin, D. (1996). *Different Ways of Knowing Study C: Arts in education in Kentucky schools research report.* Louisville, KY: Galef Institute-Kentucky, Collaborative for Teaching and Learning.

Weiner, B. (1979). A theory of motivation for some classroom experiences. *Journal of Educational Psychology, 71,* 3–25.

Wilson, B. L., & Corbett, H. D. (1999). *No excuses: The eighth grade year in six Philadelphia middle schools.* Philadelphia: Philadelphia Education Fund.

27

Moral Development in Childhood

Daniel Hart

Debra Burock

Bonita London

Amanda Miraglia

Rutgers University, Camden, NJ

INTRODUCTION

Americans are fascinated with and frightened by children and adolescents who commit serious crimes. Television news, newsmagazines, and newspapers are dominated for weeks at a time with minute detail of youth homicides and elaborate speculation concerning the motivations of those involved. Indeed, the news stories for 1998 and 1999 most closely followed by the American public focused on adolescents who killed classmates. The news on the 1999 Littleton, Colorado, school shootings were followed closely by 68% of Americans, whereas only 31% reported following the impeachment trial of the President of the United States with the same level of interest (The Pew Research Center, 2000a). The media-supported image of a young conscience-less generation leads to a majority of the American adult population judging itself to be pessimistic about the future moral standards in the country.

No doubt, delinquent, criminal, and even sociopathic behavior in children is far too common and deserving of societal concern. However, the near exclusive focus on the maladaptive warps social policy and social science. Social policy suffers because the majority of youth who are on track to develop into moral adults are overlooked in the rush to punish the minority that has gone astray. This leads to greater spending on prisons than on higher education (Ambrosio & Schiraldi, 1997), laws to treat juvenile offenders as adult criminals, and so on. Although social science can learn a great deal from the study of pathology, an understanding of healthy development cannot be derived wholly from those who do not reflect it.

In this review, we focus on moral development in childhood. Indeed, the fascination with immoral behavior occludes from our recognition the fact that most children evolve in positive directions. While it would be rash to assert that as children grow older they become more "moral" in some absolute sense—there are few areas of psychological functioning that show simple linear improvement with time—there is ample evidence to indicate that they become more sophisticated in their moral thought and action.

Our overview of morality in children proceeds in five steps. First, the constituents of morality are mentioned and briefly described. Second, the development of each constituent is outlined. Third, the associations of the constituents to each other, to healthy psychological development, and to the contexts of children's lives are reviewed. We believe that it is at these intersections that society can most influence the paths that moral development will follow; because of the importance of these intersections for policy, we review sample studies in order to illustrate the field's current state of knowledge. Fourth, we examine the connections of the achievements of childhood to the moral lives of adolescents and adults. Finally, we reconsider the notion of moral development as a facet of healthy development.

THE CONSTITUENTS OF MORAL LIFE IN CHILDREN

To begin the discussion of moral development in childhood, it is necessary to sketch the outlines of moral life. What it means exactly for adults to be "moral" has yet to be settled. There are interesting and important debates about the essential nature of morality among philosophers (for a useful overview, see Williams, 1995) and psychologists (Turiel's 1998 discussion is especially thoughtful). There is a similar lack of consensus about the details of moral life in childhood. Nonetheless, most accounts include in the domain of the moral characteristics of human life that are reflective of the actor's consideration of prescriptive, other-centered values. For example, donating money to feed hungry children is widely perceived as genuinely moral. This is because there is a prescriptive quality to this action ("everyone ought to do the same") and because an other-centered value is relevant ("the welfare of others"). In contrast, the purchase of a new television for one's own use seemingly lacks the qualities that elicit the sense that morality adheres to the action. Consequently, whereas there is no widely accepted denotation that permits unambiguous identification of the elements of the moral domain, agreement about prototypical elements is substantial.

To provide an adequate account of the prototypical elements of morality in children and adults, three central features must be included: *moral judgment*, *moral emotions*, and *moral action*. These facets of moral life are connected to each other. Moral judgments precipitate actions and follow from them as well (often to justify a course of action to another). Similarly, sympathy serves to energize action on behalf of others and pride often follows from it. Moral judgment and moral emotions not only are psychologically related to moral action, they are necessary criteria for an action to be judged moral at all. As we have pointed out elsewhere (Hart, Burock, & London, in press), judgment and emotion are integral to our notion of moral life. For example, although a dialysis machine indisputably provides an important service to the individual dependent on it due to impaired kidneys, we do not ascribe moral value to the actions of the dialysis machine. This is because the machine's actions are not associated with the forms of thought and emotion that permeate most connotations of morality.

THE DEVELOPMENT OF THE CONSTITUENTS

Judgment

Moral judgment may be the most frequently considered component of moral development in childhood. Its prominence in developmental investigation can be traced directly to the work of Piaget (1932/1965) and Kohlberg (1984). Piaget was the first to elicit moral judgments from children of different ages in order to elucidate the age-related changes in moral understanding. Piaget categorized children's interpretations of intentional and accidental transgressions of rules into two types of moral judgment. Young children show little understanding of or concern for the intentions of others in making moral ascriptions about these others' behaviors. Instead, younger children seem most concerned with respecting the rules that were established by adults and judge harshly transgressions of these rules even if unintentional. Older children showed the second type of judgment and judge transgressions of rules in light of the intentions and mutual agreements of the individuals involved in the social conflict (for a thoughtful consideration of Piaget's theory, see Lapsley, 1996). Piaget believed that peer discussion, in which two or more individuals have relatively equal status and power, thus requiring negotiation rather than an assertion of power to resolve moral disputes, are fundamental to the transition from the first type of moral judgment to the second type.

Like Piaget, Kohlberg (1984) studied age-related change in moral judgment, considering the judgments of children but also those of adolescents and adults. Kohlberg elicited judgments by posing dilemmas and then asking individuals to respond to them. The best known of these is the *Heinz Dilemma*:

> In Europe, a woman was near death from a very bad disease, a special kind of cancer. There was one drug that the doctors thought might save her. It was a form of radium that a druggist in the same town had recently discovered. The drug was expensive to make, but the druggist was charging ten times what the drug cost him to make. He paid $200 for the radium and charged $2,000 for a small dose of the drug. The sick

woman's husband, Heinz, went to everyone he knew to borrow the money, but he could get together only about $1,000, which was half of what it cost. He told the druggist that his wife was dying and asked him to sell it cheaper or let him pay later. But the druggist said, "No, I discovered the drug and I'm going to make money from it." Heinz got desperate and broke into the man's store to steal the drug for his wife. (Kohlberg, 1984, p. 12)

The participant was asked to judge what Heinz should do in this situation, and the responses were then categorized into five stages of moral judgment development. Kohlberg confirmed Piaget's observation that young children judge actions in light of rules determined by powerful adult figures, and labeled this stage *Heteronomous Morality*. At the second stage, *Instrumental Morality*, the intentions of others are considered in moral judging, but only insofar as these intentions bear on one's own instrumental goals. The essence of the third stage, *Interpersonal Normative Morality*, is a concern for how others judge the self. An understanding of the diversity of perspectives and pursuits of self and others, and the necessity for the coordination of these pursuits within a codified framework in order to prevent anarchy marks the fourth stage, labeled *Social System Morality*. The final stage, *Human Rights and Social Welfare Morality*, is evident in responses to the dilemma characterized by a concern for fundamental human rights coordinated by ethical principles.

Responses characteristic of the first two stages are common in early and middle childhood, and are largely displaced by reasoning characteristic of stages 3 and 4 in adolescence. Stage 5 understanding of moral issues emerges in early adulthood, but only among a minority of adults.

The fascinating, often contentious, and generally productive debate about the developmental trends in moral reasoning proposed by Piaget and Kohlberg cannot be reviewed here, due to space limitations. However, three brief points are relevant for our goals in this review. First, hundreds of studies have replicated the general finding that moral judgment becomes increasingly sophisticated with age and follows in part the trajectory that Piaget and Kohlberg sketched. Second, there is considerable evidence to indicate that the methods used by Piaget and Kohlberg, which rely heavily on verbal production to demonstrate competence, underestimate the moral sophistication of young children. Third, researchers have provided compelling evidence to indicate that children's moral understanding is richly differentiated, reflecting moral engagement with a range of issues (the moral status of laws, obligations to friends, responsibility to act altruistically, etc.) that are not easily assimilated to the moral types and moral stages of Piaget and Kohlberg (see Killen & Hart, 1995, and Turiel, 1998, for a discussion of these).

Emotion

Moral emotion as a force in moral development has long had advocates (e.g., Hoffman, 1975). In recent years, new discoveries concerning the contribution of emotion to morality, a reaction against the cognitive, reflective theories of Piaget and

Kohlberg, and the emergence of an evolutionary perspective emphasizing morality's biological origins in social emotions (e.g., Kagan, 1984; Wilson, 1993) have together led to a paradigmatic shift toward emotion in research in moral development.

Central to the advances of emotivist approach is the demonstration that particular types of emotion, for example sympathy, predictably lead to action to benefit others. Eisenberg and her colleagues (see Eisenberg, this volume, and Eisenberg & Fabes, 1998, for a review) have shown in a series of studies that sympathy, an emotional reaction of concern arising from the perception of another's distress, but not empathy, the identification of another's distress, increases the likelihood of prosocial behavior in children and adolescents. Empathy may not be directly related to prosocial responding because it often leads to distress rather than concern in the observer. For example, a child may correctly infer that a friend is suffering from the taunts of a bully (empathy) but become upset and anxious (distress) rather than feel concern (sympathy). Distress and sympathy show distinct patterns of emotional reactivity, with the former associated with negative emotional tone and a lack of emotional modulation and the latter with positive mood and emotional regulation (for a detailed but concise description, see Eisenberg's chapter in this volume).

There have been few studies focusing directly on age-related change in sympathy over the course of childhood and adolescence. Nonetheless, the relations of sympathy to emotion-regulation and perspective-taking, two constructs that are known to develop in childhood and adolescence, make it almost certain that the capacity to sympathize grows with age. The increased capacity of older children for sympathy does not lead to dramatic increases in experienced sympathy, because emotional life is also regulated by appraisals of situations and social contexts that often inhibit or dampen sympathy. An important direction for future research is to identify the changes in patterns of construals and contexts common at different ages that lower and heighten sympathetic responding.

Action

Moral action is most often studied under the title of *prosocial behavior*.[1] Prosocial behavior includes a range of actions the results of which are intended to benefit others: sharing, helping, and so on. There is no set of actions that represent well the domain of prosocial behavior; without such a set, it is difficult to judge accurately how much prosocial behavior in general increases or decreases over the course of childhood. Nonetheless, based on their meta-analysis of studies that have examined the relation of age to one or more prosocial behaviors, Fabes and Eisenberg (1998) concluded that there is a slight but reliable tendency for older children to act more prosocially than younger children. There are likely multiple sources for age-related increase in prosocial behavior. Older children have a wider repertoire of actions that can be employed to benefit others and greater ability to discern when others are in need.

---

[1]For a review of prosocial behavior, empathy, and sympathy, see Eisenberg's chapter, pp. 253–266 of this volume.

Relations Among Constituents

Moral judgment, moral emotions, and moral action have been briefly described in the preceding sections, and each corresponds to a more or less distinct research tradition. One of the central tasks for the future is to understand how these constituents are interrelated. We know from decades of research that moral judgment is related to moral action. However, the same research has illustrated that judgment does not always lead to action; that actions are not always preceded by reflective appraisal of obligation; and that judgment and action can be seemingly incompatible. The same broad pattern holds true for the relation of emotion to the other moral constituents. There is ample evidence demonstrating a connection of emotion to moral action and moral judgment, but the paths of influence are not straightforward. The effective promotion of moral development will require a more thorough understanding of the interconnections among judgment, emotion, and action than the current research provides.

MORAL DEVELOPMENT IN THE CONTEXTS OF THE CHILD

To this point, the overview of moral development has focused on the nature of moral life and the development of its constituents in childhood. This focus on moral life serves to highlight the domain of interest in this chapter. In this section, we look at the relation of moral development to other components of psychological functioning and to the child's multiple social contexts. Moral development is one current in the river of development; focusing on it alone is useful for identifying its characteristic features but misleading to the extent that it suggests a component that can be separated from the whole.

Indeed, there is now considerable evidence to indicate that features of the child and his or her social world influence the course of moral development. Illustrative connections are cited in Table 27.1. The rows of Table 27.1 correspond to the features of moral life described previously. The columns of Table 27.1 are broad categories of the child and the social world. These categories have been selected because they (a) correspond to the most frequently studied influences on moral development, and (b) span intra-individual features (personality) to social structural variables (social class). The categories should not be interpreted as constituting a theoretical description of the only or even central influences on development and moral development—a task that remains for future development.

Academic Ability

Academic ability (or academic achievement or IQ) is one of the most frequently studied correlates of moral characteristics in childhood. The research evidence is particularly strong concerning the relation of ability to moral judgment development. Hart, Keller, Edelstein, and Hofmann (1998) found that ability measured at age 7 predicted

TABLE 27.1

Associations of Moral Components to Features of Children and Their Social Worlds

	Individual		Relationships		Social Contexts	
	Academic Ability	Personality	Peers	Familial	Social Class	Neighborhoods
Moral Judgment	Evidence for an association: Strong Sample study: Associated with more sophisticated reasoning (Hart, Keller, Edelstein, & Hoffman, 1998)	Evidence for an association: Strong Sample study: Resilient personality increases the rate of development (Hart, Keller, Edelstein, & Hoffman, 1998)	Evidence for an association: Moderately strong Sample study: reflective, supportive, discussion style predictive of a faster rate of development (Walker, Hennig, & Krettenauer, in press)	Evidence for an association: Moderately strong Sample study: Reflective, supportive family discussion associated with development (Walker & Taylor, 1991)	Evidence for an association:Strong Sample study: Higher social classes show advantage	Absent
Moral Emotion	Evidence for an association: Absent	Evidence for an association: Strong Sample study: Associated with emotion regulation Eisenberg, Fabes, Shepard, Murphy, Jones, and Guthrie (1998)	Evidence for an association: Absent	Evidence for an association: Weak Sample study: Parental sympathy associated with sympathy in boys (Eisenberg, Fabes, Schaller, Carlo, & Miller 1991)	Evidence for an association: Absent	Evidence for an association: Absent
Moral Action	Evidence for an association: Strong Sample study: Reading comprehension associated with adolescent community service (Hart, Atkins, & Hart, 1999)	Evidence for an association: Strong Sample study: Childhood emotion regulation associated adolescent community service (Hart, Atkins, & Hart, 1998)	Evidence for an association: Weak Sample study: Facilitated by peers engaged in community service (Youniss & Yates, 1997)	Evidence for an association: Strong Sample study: Community service by adults in family increase likelihood of children's adolescents' participation (Nolin, Chaney, & Chapman, 1997)	Evidence for an association: Weak Sample study: Volunteer community service is correlated with family income (Hart, Atkins, & Hart, 1998)	Evidence for an association: Weak Sample study: Participation in clubs, teams found to facilitate community service (Hart, Atkins, & Hart, 1998)

the developmental sophistication of moral judgment in late childhood and adolescence measured on the Kohlberg measure and on a related index even after controlling for social class and personality factors. One plausible explanation for this association is that there are broad similarities in the tasks used to measure the two domains: to perform well on measures of academic ability, one must focus attention and think analytically, and the same skills are important for moral reasoning on the Kohlberg task. Even though the association of academic ability to moral judgment sophistication has been replicated in many studies (for a review, see Rest, 1983), it is important to note that the magnitude of the relation is small to modest. This means that moral judgment sophistication and academic ability are largely independent of each other, and consequently that the development of moral reasoning cannot be explained by the same factors that yield academic ability.

The same conclusion probably holds for the association of academic ability to moral emotions and to moral action. The relation of moral emotions to cognitive and personality factors (see Eisenberg & Fabes, 1998, for a review) that are in turn associated with academic ability lead to the inference that moral emotion and academic ability are correlated with each other (we have been unable to find directly relevant research, however). Moral action is associated with academic ability (for an overview, see Eisenberg & Fabes, 1998). For example, Hart, Atkins, and Ford (1999) have found that reading comprehension measured on a standardized test was a predictor of voluntary community service in a nationally representative sample of older children and adolescents.

The positive connections of moral development to academic ability and academic achievement, while small, do suggest that contexts that foster growth of one domain are supportive of development in the other. In other words, there is no evidence to indicate that moral development must come at the expense of poor academic achievement, or that academic pursuits necessarily interfere with the growth of moral judgment, emotion, or action.

Personality

The evidence and theory linking personality to moral functioning are much stronger than for the association of ability to moral development. Moral life—judgment, emotion, action—often involves social interaction with others. This social interaction requires regulation of the self's emotions, reflective initiation of action, habitual responses to the behaviors of others, and so on. Many of these processes are at the heart of notions of personality.

Hart and his colleagues (Hart, Keller, Edelstein, & Hofmann, 1998) found that ego-resiliency, the ability to adapt to circumstances and to regulate emotions (Block & Kremen, 1996), was associated with moral judgment development in childhood and adolescence. Ego-resiliency was measured when children were 7 years old and moral judgment 5 and 8 years later. Children who were high in ego-resiliency at age 7, in comparison to those who were low at age 7, were higher in moral judgment at age 12 and developed at a faster rate between ages 12 and 15. Academic ability at age 7 predicted to moral judgment sophistication at age 12, but not to the rate of development between ages 12 and 15. Hart et al. interpreted this pattern to mean that children high in ego-resiliency were better able than children low in ego-resiliency to learn from daily experiences that were relevant to moral issues, and consequently developed at a faster rate.

Consistent with the findings just reported, Eisenberg et al., (1998) found that emotion regulation and the associated capacity to avoid intense negative emotions are predictive of sympathy. Parents rated emotion regulation and negative emotionality in children ages 4 to 6 years of age and again when the children were 2 years older. The tendency to respond sympathetically was rated by teachers when the children were 8 to 10 years of age. Negative emotionality at 4–6 and 6–8 was found to be negatively correlated with sympathetic responding. The results suggest that emotional regulation that decreases the likelihood of intense negative affect is associated with higher levels of sympathy.

Finally, resilience and emotion regulation are predictive of prosocial action. Hart, Atkins, and Ford (1998) used data from the National Longitudinal Survey of Youth, Child Data, to examine the relation of many factors to voluntary community service. In one analysis, they used temperament ratings made when children were 6 years old. These ratings, made by the mothers, focused on the child's ability to regulate emotions and to form healthy relationships with parents and were averaged into a single index. Hart, Atkins, and Ford found that children who were high on this measure of emotion regulation were more likely to be involved in voluntary community service at age 14 than children low on the measure. Once again, the results suggest the importance of adaptive personality on moral functioning.

Peer Relationships

A key assumption in the theoretical work of Piaget (1932) and Kohlberg (1984) is that moral judgment development is largely a consequence of the child's efforts to reconcile moral conflicts through collaborative social exchanges, rather than a process of passive internalization of adult rules. Consequently, Piaget and Kohlberg argued that peer interactions, which permit the joint exploration of moral issues, are powerful contexts for moral development. There is some evidence to support this claim. For example, Walker, Hennig, and Krettenauer (2000) examined the relation of discussions about moral issues in a laboratory in children and adolescents to moral judgment development in the four years following the observations. Walker and his colleagues found that peer interactions characterized by efforts to understand fully discussion partners' perspectives were predictive of subsequent moral judgment development. This finding suggests that children and adolescents who participate effectively in peer discussions of moral issues develop at a faster rate than do those whose peer interactions do not involve moral collaboration, a pattern consistent with the theories of Piaget and Kohlberg.

There is little research directly focusing on the influence of peers on moral emotions or on moral action in childhood (Eisenberg & Fabes, 1998). A range of theoretical perspectives would predict that peers do influence moral emotion and moral action; the cognitive-developmental tradition of Piaget and Kohlberg, as noted earlier, views peers as a constructive influence on development, and certainly social learning would predict that children will model themselves after peers whose moral actions are well received. There is also abundant evidence to indicate that peer influence is very instrumental in delinquent activity (Taylor, Iacono, & McGue, 2000) which is often inconsistent with moral action (though not necessarily the opposite of it; see Hart, Burock, & London, in press). While theory and findings from related areas are suggestive, it remains a task for future research to identify the nature and magnitude of connections of peers to moral emotion and action.

Relationships With Parents

Family life and parental behavior are generally regarded as very powerful influences on development. As just one example of this pervasive belief concerning the origins of human behavior, consider poll results that reveal that the American public regards "poor upbringing" to be more central than media depictions of violence or peer pressure to an explanation of school violence (The Pew Research Center, 2000b). The extent of parental behavior and family experiences on children's behavior is difficult to assess because in most families children also share genes with their parents. Consequently, it is difficult to determine if similarities between parents and their children are a consequence of shared experience or shared genes. Although there are research designs that escape this problem (adopted children and their adoptive parents, for example), these research designs have rarely been applied to the study of moral development. This means that the abundant research demonstrating an association between characteristics of parents and moral characteristics in their children that is reviewed below does not permit any conclusions about the relative contributions of behavior and genes.

There is substantial evidence to indicate that the quality of parent–child relationships and the quality of parent–child moral discussion are related to the rate of moral judgment development. Hart (1988) found that young adolescents who had good relationships with their parents developed at a faster rate than did adolescents with poor relationships. Walker and Taylor (1991) observed discussions between adolescents and their parents in the laboratory, and found that parents who used a Socratic, supportive discussion style fostered moral judgment development in their children. Parents using other discussion styles were less successful in supporting development in their children.

Moral emotions also are related to parental characteristics. Eisenberg, Fabes, Schaller, Carlo, and Miller (1991) measured sympathy and negative affectivity in children and sympathy in parents. The results suggested that parents who were themselves sympathetic had children who were sympathetic (particularly true for sons) and who were prepared to avoid negative emotion and distress when witnessing another in need.

There is also considerable evidence to indicate an association between parents and their children in prosocial behavior. In a recent national survey concerning community service, the results indicated adult participation in community service substantially increased the likelihood of participation among children and adolescents living in the same home (Nolin, Chaney, & Chapman, 1997). This finding is consistent with much of the research concerning the relation of parents and their children in regards to prosocial behavior (Hart, Yates, Fegley, & Wilson, 1995).

The pattern of associations between parents' and children's characteristics is consistent across judgment, emotion, and action. It is important to note that the magnitude of most of the associations is moderate, with most of the studies finding that parental characteristics account for less than 20% of the variation in children's moral constituents. Moreover, it is likely that some of the similarity between parents and children on some dimensions is attributable to shared genes. These two facts lead to the conclusion that parental behavior does affect moral development, but that its influence is probably more circumscribed than recognized by the general public.

Social Class

The relation of social class to psychological characteristics has long been studied. For much of the research on children, social class as a construct is intended to refer to a set of loosely correlated environmental characteristics including parents, peers, schools, neighborhood qualities, and cultural norms that is hypothesized to influence how children develop. Children from higher social classes, typically indexed by parental education and income, are usually thought to enjoy the developmental benefits of greater parental, peer, academic, and neighborhood resources than are available to children of lower social classes. A great deal of research suggests that social class is correlated with more favorable developmental outcomes, and we shall mention below a few representative studies reaching this conclusion that are relevant to moral development in childhood. However, the consistency of findings regarding the relation of social class to development is itself in need of further research, because relatively little is known about *why* social class and development are closely connected.

Moral judgment sophistication is associated with social class. Colby, Kohlberg, Gibbs, and Lieberman (1982) report that children and adolescents in higher social classes receive higher scores for moral judgment sophistication on the Kohlberg measure than do children and adolescents from families in lower social classes. Although little is known about the relation of social class on moral emotions, social class may be related to prosocial behavior (Eisenberg & Fabes, 1998). Children in higher social classes are more likely than children in the lower social classes to engage in prosocial behavior in the community. Research with large nationally representative samples consistently shows that community service participation is positively associated with social class (Hart et al., 1998; Nolin et al., 1997).

Neighborhood Effects

In recent years, considerably more attention has been paid to the effects of children's neighborhoods on development. The study of neighborhood effects on development addresses, in part, some of the limitations noted above inherent in the investigation of social class. In particular, most studies of neighborhood effects seek to identify the influence of living in particular neighborhoods while controlling for parental characteristics such as income and education. In a sense, then, the notion of social class is analytically split into features of the environment (the neighborhood) and qualities of parents (education, income). The premise is that the culture of a neighborhood exerts considerable influence on children's development.

The initial research on neighborhood effects has largely focused on the development of antisocial behavior (Elliott et al., 1996). To our knowledge, there is no research that assesses the effects of neighborhoods on moral judgment or on moral emotions. However, there is some research to indicate that neighborhood resources, such as youth organizations and teams, facilitate children's entry into voluntary community service (Hart et al., 1998). Certainly these topics deserve serious attention in future research.

Despite gaps in the knowledge base sketched in Table 27.1, the overall pattern is clear: Moral development is facilitated by an adaptive personality, supportive peer and parental relationships, and family and neighborhood environments favored with resources. The range of influences on moral development means that small changes in any one area are unlikely to have dramatic effects on moral development. For example, the influence of a single new friend is likely to be small, assuming that personality, other friends, parents, social class, and the neighborhood remain the same because these factors continue to exert their influence on the developmental course.

DEVELOPMENTAL CONTINUITY OF CHILDHOOD ACHIEVEMENTS

If moral life in childhood had few implications for later development, then it could be considered a transitory phase of interest but of little consequence. Crawling and walking in infancy are of this nature; there is substantial variability in the age at which infants begin to crawl and walk, but, except in instances of extreme delay, the age at which these behaviors emerge has no implications for later development. Consequently, there are no needs to consider how to foster the development of crawling and walking in infants.

There has been relatively little research that has examined the extent to which moral development in childhood lays the groundwork for moral development in adulthood. However, studies conducted for other purposes can offer some insight into this issue.

Moral Judgment

In Kohlberg's (Colby, Kohlberg, Gibbs, & Lieberman, 1983) longitudinal study of moral judgment development between ages 10 and 36, correlations from one testing point to the next one 3 to 4 years later are of moderate magnitude. However, it is important to note that the cross-age correlations in average stage scores presented by Colby et al. (1982) underestimate the true continuity because these correlations have not been corrected for attenuation due to measurement unreliability. To get a better sense of true continuity, we have calculated the reliability of measurement for each age group (necessary, because the reliability will vary according to the age of the subjects) by applying the Spearman-Brown formula to the three parts of Kohlberg's moral judgment test (Forms A, B, and C). These reliability estimates were then used to correct the correlations reported by Colby et al. The corrected correlations are reported in Table 27.2.

We offer two observations about the pattern in Table 27.2. First, it is clear that moral judgment, even at age 10, is predictive of moral judgment at later ages. This suggests that moral judgment in childhood is the foundation on which later development occurs. Second, the magnitude of the continuity from adolescence through adulthood is quite high, with a median correlation (corrected) of .82. This may mean that moral judgment development is more easily influenced in childhood than in adolescence or adulthood, age ranges in which individual differences are firmly established.

There are no comparable studies from which to estimate the continuity of moral emotions or of moral action from childhood into adulthood. However, ego-resilience, a personality trait associated with emotion regulation that in turn is important for moral emotions, shows some continuity between ages 7 and 19 (Hart, Keller, Edelstein, & Hofmann, 1997). The stability of judgment and ego-resilience over time suggests that there ought to be continuity in moral behavior over time. There are a few lines of research consistent with such an inference. For example, McAdams (1988) studied the lives of individuals who participated as young adults in the civil rights movement, participation presumably motivated in part by moral principles. Both researchers found that participation in young adulthood was predictive of a lifelong commitment to social activism. While these studies of social and political activism are suggestive, there is clearly a need for investigations focusing directly on the continuity of moral behavior from childhood to adulthood.

In summary, the available research evidence suggests that moral life in childhood is connected to moral development in adolescence and adulthood. Moreover, the pattern of correlations for moral judgment suggests (though certainly does not prove) that plasticity may be greater in childhood than in adolescence, and conse-

TABLE 27.2
Cross-Age Continuity Estimates for the Weighted Average Moral Judgment Score
(Corrected for Attenuation)

Age:	*Age*						
	10	*13–14*	*16–18*	*20–22*	*24–26*	*28–30*	*32–34*
13–14	.58	1.00					
16–18	.59	.91	1.00				
20–22	.47	.61	.80	1.00			
24–26	.25	.88	.82	.81	1.00		
28–30	–.32	.87	.80	.57	1.00	1.00	
32–33		.78	.54	.92	1.00	1.00	1.00
Mean Weighted Average Score	189	246	290	327	357	361	375

quently childhood may be a particularly useful age range in which to intervene to support healthy development.

CONCLUSIONS

The weight of evidence presented to this point suggests that moral development is fostered by influences that are consistent with healthy development in other areas. Supporting children so that they can succeed in school, form resilient personalities, acquire sound relationships, and live in supportive neighborhoods will contribute to successful development.

While moral development in childhood is largely consistent with the development of other domains, the opportunities of adolescence and adulthood may make more difficult the integration of all domains. For example, commitments to pursue lines of moral action over sustained periods of time that involve some cost can be observed in even young adolescents but are unknown in childhood. For adolescents, then, there is the possibility that the pursuit of moral goals can interfere with schoolwork, friendships, and so on (see Hart, Yates, Fegley, & Wilson, 1995, for a discussion). Our point is that although moral development is broadly consistent with the development of other talents and qualities in childhood, developmental trajectories in adolescence may be more varied.

REFERENCES

Ambrosio, T.-J., & Schiraldi, V. (1997). *From classrooms to cellblocks: A national perspective* [On-line]. Washington DC: The Justice Policy Institute. Available: http://www.cjcj.org/jpi/highernational.html

Block, J., & Kremen, A. M. (1996). IQ and ego-resiliency: Conceptual and empirical connections and separateness. *Journal of Personality and Social Psychology, 70,* 349–361.

Colby, A., Kohlberg, L., Gibbs, J., & Lieberman, M. (1983). A longitudinal study of moral judgment. *Monographs of the Society for Research in Child Development, 48*(1–2).

Eisenberg, N., & Fabes, R. A. (1998). Prosocial development. In W. Damon (Series Ed.) & N. Eisenberg (Vol. Ed). *Handbook of child psychology: Vol. 3, Social, emotional, and personality development* (5th Ed., pp. 701–778). New York: Wiley.

Eisenberg, N., Fabes, R. A., Schaller, M., Carlo, G., & Miller, P. A. (1991). The relations of parental characteristics and practices to children's vicarious emotional responding. *Child Development, 62,* 1393–1408.

Eisenberg, N., Fabes, R. A., Shepard, S., Murphy, B. C., Jones, S., & Guthrie, I. K. (1998). *Contemporaneous and longitudinal prediction of children's sympathy from dispositional regulation and emotionality. Developmental Psychology, 34,* 910–924.

Hart, D. (1988). A longitudinal study of adolescents' socialization and identification as predictors of adult moral judgment development. *Merrill-Palmer Quarterly, 34,* 245–260.

Hart, D., Atkins, R., & Ford, D. (1998). Urban America as a context for the development of moral identity in adolescence. *Journal of Social Issues, 54,* 513–530.

Hart, D., Atkins, R., & Ford, D. (1999). Family influences on the formation of moral identity in adolescence: Longitudinal analyses. *Journal of Moral Education, 28,* 375–386.

Hart, D., Burock, D., London, B., & Atkins, R. (in press). Prosocial development in childhood. In A. Slater & G. Bremner (Eds.) *Introduction to Developmental Psychology.* Oxford: Blackwell.

Hart, D., Keller, M., Edelstein, W., & Hofmann, V. (1998). Childhood personality influences on social–cognitive development: A longitudinal study. *Journal of Personality and Social Psychology, 74,* 5, 1278–1289.

Hart, D., Yates, M., Fegley, S., & Wilson, G. (1995). Moral commitment in Inner-City adolescents. M. Killen & D. Hart (Eds.), *Morality in everyday life: Developmental perspectives. Cambridge studies in social and emotional development.* New York, NY: Cambridge University Press.

Hoffman, M. L. (1975). Developmental synthesis of affect and cognition and its implications for altruistic motivation. *Developmental Psychology, 11,* 607–622.

Kagan, J. (1984). *The nature of the child.* New York: Basic Books.

Killen, M., & Hart, D. (Eds.). (1995). *Morality in everyday life: Developmental perspectives.* New York: Cambridge University Press.

Kohlberg, L. (1984). *The psychology of moral development : the nature and validity of moral stages.* San Francisco: Harper & Row.

Lapsley, D. (1996). *Moral psychology.* Boulder, Colorado: Westview Press.

McAdams, D. P. (1988). Personal needs and personal relationships. In S. Duck & D. F. Hay et al. (Eds.), *Handbook of personal relationships: Theory, research and interventions* (pp. 7–22). New York, NY: Wiley.

Nolin, M. J., Chaney, B., & Chapman, C. (1997). *Student participation in community service activity.* Washington, DC: U.S. Department of Education, National Center for Education Statistics.

Piaget, J. (1932). *The moral judgment of the child.* New York: Harcourt, Brace. (Original work published 1965)

Rest, J. (1983). Morality. In J. Flavell & E. Markman (Eds.), *Handbook of child psychology: Vol. 3* (4th ed., pp. 556–629). New York: Wiley.

Taylor, J., Iacono, W. G., & McGue, M. (2000). Evidence for a genetic etiology of early-onset delinquency. *Journal of Abnormal Psychology, 109,* 634–643.

The New York Times. (1999). *Complete results.* [On-line]. Available: http://www.nytimes.com/library/national/101799mag-poll-results.html

The Pew Research Center. (2000b). *A year after Columbine public looks to parents more than schools to prevent violence*. [On-line]. Available: http://www.people-press.org/april00rpt.htm

Turiel, E. (1998). The development of morality. In N. Eisenberg (Ed.), *Handbook of child psychology: Vol. 3. Social, emotional, and personality development* (5th ed., pp. 863–932).

Walker, L., Hennig, K., & Krettenauer, T. (2000). Parent and peer contexts for children's moral reasoning development. *Child Development, 71*, 1033–1048.

Walker, L., & Taylor, J. H. (1991). Family interactions and the development of moral reasoning. *Child Development, 62*, 264–283.

Williams, B. (1995). Ethics. In A. C. Grayling (Ed.), *Philosophy* (pp. 545–582). New York: Oxford University Press.

Wilson, J.Q. (1993). *The moral sense*. New York: The Free Press.

28

Creativity and Talent

Ellen Winner
Boston College

INTRODUCTION

Gifted children have always intrigued us, inspiring fascination and awe as well as intimidation and envy. They have been feared as oddballs, and rejected as nerds. Our schools often refuse to alter the curriculum for such children and insist that they can take care of themselves. As a result these children often suffer in our schools. Gifted children are our most important national resource, for from these children will emerge many of the adults who shape our thinking and our culture. Thus a better understanding of these children is in order so that they may be better served, and so that their gifts can be nurtured.

TECHNICAL ISSUES

Creativity and Talent: Description and Operational Definitions

In what follows, I use the term *gifted* to refer to talented children, and I argue that this term refers to children with talent in any area. Because I argue that a certain form of creativity is an inextricable part of giftedness, I do not speak separately about gifted versus creative children. When I refer to gifted children, then, I refer to talented children who, by definition, are creative in their area of high ability, as outlined next.

Whereas the term *gifted children* is most often used to refer to intellectually gifted (high IQ) children, giftedness can manifest itself in any domain. Systematic study of the gifted began in the 1920s with Lewis Terman's longitudinal study of

1,528 children with IQs averaging 151 (Terman, 1925). Since Terman's time, a consensus has developed that giftedness is often not captured by the unidimensional measure of IQ. Psychometric researchers have differentiated mathematical and verbal giftedness through the early administration of the math and verbal Scholastic Assessment Tests (Stanley, 1973). Other researchers have gone farther, arguing that giftedness should refer to high ability in any area, including music, spatial reasoning, interpersonal understanding, leadership, morality, and so on. (Gardner, 1983; Renzulli, 1978; Winner, 1996). Consistent with this broad view, the U.S. Office of Education has defined gifted children as those capable of high performance in general intellectual ability (as in Terman's approach), specific academic aptitude (as in Stanley's approach), creative or productive thinking, leadership, the visual and performing arts, and psychomotor ability (Marland, 1971).

Talented or gifted children, no matter what their domain of gift, are children with three characteristics. First, gifted children are precocious: they pass milestones in their domain of ability at an earlier age than do typical children, and make more rapid progress in this domain. Gifted children may begin to read fluently at the age of 3 or 4, without any extended instruction; They may play a musical instrument like a highly trained adult; they may turn everyday experiences into mathematical problems to play with, moving from arithmetic to algebra before their peers have learned their multiplication tables or division (Feldman, 1991; Radford, 1990; Winner, 1996).

Second, gifted children are intrinsically motivated and display a "rage to master." They exhibit intense (almost obsessive) interest and an ability to focus their attention sharply. The combination of such intense interest in a domain, along with an ability to learn easily in that domain, can lead to high achievement unless emotional factors interfere.

The third characteristic of the gifted is related to creativity. Gifted children are not just faster—they are different. They learn in qualitatively different ways from typical children. One way in which this is manifested is that they need a minimum of scaffolding, or support, from adults to master their domain. In fact, much of the time they simply teach themselves. They make discoveries about their domain that motivate them to continue. Often, such children invent rules in their domain and devise unusual ways of solving problems (Winner, 1996).

Because gifted children make discoveries in their domain of gift by themselves, and because they often invent unusual ways of solving problems, they can be considered creative. But gifted children are creative in a "little-c" sense of creativity; that is, they make discoveries on their own and they solve problems in new ways. They are not, however, creative in the big-C sense; that is, they do not revolutionize their domain and they do not invent new forms of mathematics or new forms of music. They do not ask new questions never asked before by the major figures in the domain. Big-C creativity means transforming a domain the way that Picasso and Braques transformed the domain of painting with the invention of cubism or the way that Einstein transformed Newtonian physics. Major changes in a domain are brought about by creative masters who have spent a minimum of 10 years first mastering the existing domain (Gardner, 1993; Simonton, 1994).

Creativity and Talent: Available Indicators

Indicators of giftedness are linked to definitions of giftedness. Traditionally, researchers have defined giftedness as high general intelligence. The most commonly used indicator of giftedness defined in this way is the IQ test, but a high IQ is an indicator only of intellectual giftedness. The Stanford-Binet IQ test, Terman's revision of Binet's original test, is made up of a variety of paper and pencil tasks that measure verbal, logical, and mathematical ability (and to a small extent, spatial ability). The test includes measures of the ability to define words, to show how two words are different, to explain how two objects are similar or different, to summarize an orally presented story, to solve verbal puzzles, to read stories and state their moral, to listen to a string of numbers and say them backwards, to solve math problems, to complete visual–spatial patterns, and so forth. A score of around 100 is average intelligence, and 50% of all people score close to 100. A score of 130, almost two standard deviations above the mean, is a common entrance requirement for gifted programs in schools. About 2%–3% of children are predicted to have IQs of 130 or higher; only about 1% have IQs of 140 and higher; only 1 in 10 to 30,000 have IQs of 160 or higher; and IQs of 180 or above are predicted to be as rare as 1 in a million. However, it has been reported that highly gifted children emerge with a higher incidence that would be statistically predicted, suggesting that IQ is not normally distributed (Silverman, 1989).

Other theories of intellectual giftedness call for other kinds of indicators. For example, according to one theory, tests of the ability to solve "insight problems" (in which one must see something in a new way) are the best indicators of intellectual giftedness (Davidson, 1986). Insight problems require one to think about a problem in a new, non-obvious way. For example, consider the following insight problem from Davidson (1986): "Suppose you and I have the same amount of money. How much money must I give you so that you have ten dollars more than I?" To solve this, one must resist the obvious but wrong answer of ten dollars and realize that the right answer is half that amount. According to another theory, indicators of giftedness must include a measure of task commitment (motivation) and creativity (Renzulli, 1978). Nonetheless, it is fair to say that the most widely used measure of intellectual (scholastic) giftedness is the IQ test.

The assumption underlying the use of a global IQ score as an indicator of intellectual giftedness is that academically gifted children are generally gifted across all intellectual areas. Some children are indeed globally gifted in this way—showing high ability in reading, verbal ability, logical analytic thinking, and mathematics. These children are "notationally" gifted, able to master readily the two kinds of notational symbol systems valued in school: language and number.

Whereas globally gifted children exist, many other academically gifted children present a less balanced picture, and unevenness between verbal and mathematical abilities is common. Many of Terman's participants had greater strengths and interests in reading than math, or the reverse. And when assessed by difficult tests without low ceilings, academically gifted children often reveal quite uneven profiles, showing that an extreme gift in one scholastic area does not imply a gift as extreme in another area. For example, the higher the IQ, the lower the correlation among subtests of the IQ test (Detterman & Daniel, 1989). In addition, children with IQs of 120 or higher show sharper discrepancies between verbal and performance IQ scores than do those with lower IQs (Wilkinson, 1993). Another study found that 42% of intellectually gifted adolescents, who scored in the top 0.5% on the SATs, had over one standard deviation of difference between their math and their verbal scores. And among those who scored in the top .01% in math, 72% displayed this kind of differentiated profile (Achter, Lubinski, & Benbow, 1996). We should not be surprised by such unevenness because the mathematics is so different a domain from that of language.

Uneven profiles of intellectually gifted children also occur because giftedness in one area may be accompanied by a learning disability in another area. We do not know how many children are both gifted and learning disabled, but in 1985 it was estimated that between 120,000 and 180,000 such children existed in American schools (Davis & Rimm, 1985). One of the most common combinations is that of an academic gift along with a language-based learning disability such as dyslexia (Reis, Neu, & McGuire, 1995).

Of course an IQ test cannot identify giftedness in areas not covered by the IQ test. Thus, an IQ test cannot be used as an indicator of artistic or musical giftedness. A gift in music or art can exist alongside an average IQ. Correlations between musical ability and IQ are positive but low: Above an average IQ level, IQ does not predict musical ability. Nor does high musical ability predict a high IQ (Shuter-Dyson & Gabriel, 1981). Indeed, a gift in music or art can exist alongside even a subnormal IQ. We know this from the existence of savants, individuals who are retarded and/or autistic but who have exceptional musical or artistic ability (Miller, 1999; Selfe, 1977; Treffert, 1989). We do not have standardized measures of giftedness in music or art, but it is abundantly obvious to teachers and parents when a child is gifted in such a domain. These children stand out in terms of the three characteristics mentioned at the outset of this chapter: They are precocious and learn rapidly, they are highly motivated, and they make discoveries on their own and solve problems in unusual ways.

If IQ and musical giftedness do not correlate, how can we explain the fact that musically gifted children tend to do well academically (Csikszentmihalyi, Rathunde, & Whalen, 1993)? One possible explanation is that all that we know about the relation between music, IQ, and academic performance comes from studies of children taking classical musical lessons. These children tend to come from middle and upper middle class families, and thus their musical ability is confounded with socioeconomic status (SES). In addition, these children are taught to read musical notation and are required to practice regularly. Both of these activities might transfer to school performance. We know nothing about the academic performance of musically gifted children who engage in rebellious anti-authority music (rock, rap), or who do not read music notation. It is likely that such children would not excel in school; hence, we could account for the strong academic performance of the musically gifted child as due to either SES or to the concomitants of musical training (notation and disciplined practice).

THEORETICAL AND EMPIRICAL REVIEW OF THE LITERATURE

Overview of Theory and Evidence Supporting Creativity and Talent as Positive Characteristics

Giftedness involves both an inborn biological capacity as well as the right kind of environment for the inborn capacity to develop. Some have tried to account for the high achievement of gifted and creative individuals only in terms of environmental factors, such as hard work and intensive training (e.g., Ericsson, Krampe, & Tesch-Romer, 1993). However, there is no evidence that allows us to rule out the necessity of an innate component. Evidence for a biological basis includes the fact that gifted children reveal high ability at a very early age, often before any regimens of intensive training have set in. Simonton (1999) proposed a model of innate talent that is multidimensional and dynamic. According to this model, achievement in any domain is based on multiple innate components. Some domains rest on more innate components than others. Each component develops independently, and the level of ability achieved is the result of a multiplicative composite of these components. Giftedness is likely to manifest itself only when all of the required components are inherited and thus present. This conceptual model predicts many of the things we know about giftedness, especially its rarity and the uneven profiles of gifted individuals.

It would be difficult to dispute the claim that creativity and talent are positive characteristics. Talented (gifted) children typically go on to become high achieving and successful adults, as discussed in more detail later. For example, the "greatest" classical composers tended to have been prodigies as children (Simonton, 1991), the Terman children grew up to be high achievers (Terman & Oden, 1959), and there is other evidence that the greater the childhood gift, the greater the adult eminence (Cox, 1926; Shuter-Dyson & Gabriel, 1981). However, only a small fraction of gifted children go on not only to be high achievers but also to make major creative breakthroughs in their domain of high ability. To be sure, as discussed later, giftedness and big-C creativity are not always accompanied by happiness. Nonetheless, giftedness and creativity are positive characteristics in the sense that individuals with these characteristics are those who make the most important advances in human culture.

Gifted children are our most important human capital. These are the individuals most likely to make scientific discoveries and artistic contributions, and to become our great social and political leaders. Of course, the particular kind of contribution that they go on to make (e.g., whether in science, the arts, politics, morality, etc.) depends on the domain in which they show a gift at an early age.

This is not to say that there are no late bloomers. Late bloomers are children not identified as gifted in any clearly defined domain but who, in young adulthood, discover a domain in which they can make a contribution and go on to become genuinely creative in that area. Examples of late bloomers include Charles Darwin and Igor Stravinsky. However, late bloomers were most likely not typical children. As a child, for example, Darwin showed unusual interests and high levels of curiosity, but no one could predict from the child what the adult would become. Often such children discover their domain in college where they first encounter it. As children, these individuals were most likely gifted even if they were not identified as such.

Despite the existence of late bloomers, it is fair to say that gifted children, those who are identified as gifted in childhood, are more likely to make major contributions to human society than are typical children. Therefore, it is of practical significance for societies to nurture and promote the development of these children's high abilities. In the final section of this chapter, I discuss what we know about the factors most likely to promote the development of giftedness. Of course, there is a moral imperative to promote the development of abilities in all children. However, there is no zero sum game: We can promote the development of abilities in gifted children without taking away from the nurturing of abilities in other kinds of children.

What is known about the relation between giftedness and well-being? Whereas moderately gifted children (in whatever domain) are socially and emotionally well adjusted, this is not true of gifted children with more extreme levels of ability. Children with profound intellectual gifts have a higher than average rate of social and emotional problems (Hollingworth, 1942; Janos & Robinson, 1985).

One obvious explanation for this is that children with exceptionally high ability in any area face social and emotional problems because they are out of step with their peers. They thus have difficulty making friends unless they are exposed to others like themselves. In addition, these children are almost always bored and under-challenged in school, leading to negative attitudes toward school, and sometimes to underachievement and school drop-out.

Gifted children are more introverted and lonely than the typical child both because they have so little in common with others and because they need and want to be alone to develop their talent (Gallagher, 1990; Janos & Robinson, 1985; Silverman, 1993). Introverts derive their energy from themselves, they prefer low levels of stimulation from the outside, and hence they often avoid social occasions. They do not make friends easily, they spend much time alone, and they are less in tune with the values of the dominant culture. These qualities describe not only the high IQ gifted child but also children gifted in music, art, and athletics: Adolescents talented academically or in art or athletics spend about 5 more hours a week alone than do typical adolescents (Csikszentmihalyi et al., 1993). Some gifted children turn inward because they are ostracized for being different. But gifted children of all types are also introverted because they know how to be alone, they derive plea-sure from solitude, and they need to be alone in order to develop their talent.

Research on giftedness has suffered from various kinds of methodological weaknesses. Researchers have studied gifted children and compared them to aver-age ones, but the gifted children studied are already identified as gifted. We thus do not know how many potentially gifted children never get recognized because they grow up in environments where their gifts are not nurtured. In addition, though there have been many retrospective studies of gifted children and eminent adults, prospective studies are lacking. Retrospective studies have revealed much about the concomitants of talent (e.g., that most gifted children have grown up in enriched en-vironments and have parents with high standards); however, retrospective studies do not allow us to determine whether any of these concomitants are either necessary or sufficient. Only with prospective longitudinal studies can we discover which concomitants are necessary, which (if any) are sufficient, and which are only char-acteristic. To cite one example of the problem, currently we have no way of know-ing how many children there are in enriched environments with parents with high standards who do *not* grow up gifted, nor do we know how many children there are in non-enriched environments who might have grown up gifted had they had an en-riched environment.

Developmental Stability of Creativity and Talent Over the Life Span

Not all gifted children go on to become high achieving and creative adults. Some gifted children drop out of their domain of high ability. This can occur if they do not encounter a stimulating and nurturing family environment. Similarly, a lack of challenge in school can lead intellectually gifted children to underachieve and to become disaffected with academic pursuits. However, longitudinal studies of gifted children suggest that most do go on to become high achievers. The children studied by Terman typically became experts in a well-established domain such as medicine, law, business, or the academy (Terman & Oden, 1959; for other longi-tudinal studies, see Subotnik & Arnold, 1994, and Subotnik, Kassan, Summers, & Wasser, 1993).

Although gifted children tend to become high-achieving adults, only a fraction eventually become big-C creators. Those who do so must make a painful transition from being a gifted child (one who can learn rapidly and effortlessly in an estab-lished domain) to an adult creator (someone who disrupts and ultimately remakes a domain; Gardner, 1993). A high IQ child who can solve complex math problems wins acclaim. But as a young adult, she must come up with some new way to solve some unsolved mathematical problem or discover a new problem. Otherwise, she will not alter the domain of mathematics. The same situation applies in the arts: Gifted children are applauded for the technical feats, but if they do not eventually go beyond technical skills to expression and innovation, they remain experts and do not become domain creators.

It is not surprising that most gifted children, even the most extreme, those we would call prodigies, do not become domain creators. Individuals who are domain creative have a different personality structure from the typical gifted child: They are rebellious, they have a desire to alter the status quo, and they have often suffered childhoods of stress and trauma (Goertzel, Goertzel, & Goertzel, 1978; Sulloway, 1996). In addition, there is a higher than average incidence of manic depression in domain creators. Though most creators do not have manic depression, people of this ilk are more likely to suffer from this disease than are ordinary people (Jamison, 1993; Ludwig, 1995).

FACTORS AFFECTING DEVELOPMENT AND PROMOTION OF CREATIVITY AND TALENT

Gifted children typically report that their families were far more important to their development than their schooling (Winner, 1996). The families of gifted children are child-centered (Freeman, 1979). Gifted children typically grow up in enriched family environments with a high level of intellectual and/or artistic stimulation. Parents of gifted children typically have high expectations and also model hard work and high achievement themselves (Bloom, 1985). And gifted children who grow up in "complex" families—those that combine both stimulation are nurturance—turn out to be happier, more alert, more engaged, and more goal directed than equally gifted children who grow up in families with one only or neither of these traits (Csikszentmihalyi et al., 1993). Gifted children from such complex families report more states of "flow" (states in which they are deeply engaged) and more often report experiencing high energy. They were also rated by teachers as original, independent, and working up to their potential. Those who lost interest in their domain of talent reported having parents who were either too directive or too uninvolved. However, we cannot conclude for sure that any of these family characteristics are causally implicated in promoting the development of giftedness because these findings are purely correlational. They are suggestive, however.

Training and hard work have also been shown to be associated with the development of talent (Bloom, 1985). No gifted child develops into a gifted adult without intensive training and years of work. But this finding does not mean that hard work is sufficient. It is most probably not. A typical child cannot and will not work as intensively as a gifted child. But hard work is surely necessary for giftedness to develop into expertise.

CONCLUSIONS

Parents and schools ought to model high expectations if children (including gifted ones) are to reach their potential. All too often, American schools underchallenge their students. International comparisons show that American children, no matter what their ability level, perform below most European and East Asian nations

(Mullis et al., 1998). The gap between American students and others is greatest for those at the highest levels of ability (Ross, 1993). We simply do not know how many more high potential children there are who never develop their talent because they are not challenged by parents or schools, and are instead captured by the potent messages from their peer culture that it is more cool to play video games and hang out at the mall than to read or play a musical instrument.

While this chapter has focused on giftedness and its relation to well-being, children of ordinary ability levels can develop enjoyment by focusing on one area and learning to develop real skill in that area, whether this be in an art form (playing a musical instrument, learning ceramics) or a more academic area (reading, math). All too often our children flit from one activity to another without ever sticking to something long enough to develop their ability in one particular area. Even children of typical ability levels can gain flow and well-being from mastering a skill.

REFERENCES

Achter, J., Lubinski, D., & Benbow, C. (1996). Multipotentiality among the intellectually gifted: "It was never there in the first place, and already it's vanishing." *Journal of Counseling Psychology, 43*(1), 65–76.

Bloom, B. (1985). *Developing talent in young people.* New York: Ballantine.

Cox, C. (1926). *Genetic studies of genius: Vol. 2. The early mental traits of three-hundred geniuses.* Stanford, CA: Stanford University Press.

Csikszentmihalyi, M., Rathunde, K., & Whalen, S. (1993). *Talented teenagers: The roots of success and failure.* New York: Cambridge University Press.

Davidson, J. E. (1986). The role of insight in giftedness. In R. J. Sternberg & J. E. Davidson (Eds.), *Conceptions of Giftedness* (pp. 201–222). New York: Cambridge University Press.

Davis, G. A., & Rimm, S. B. (1985). *Education of the gifted and talented.* Englewood Cliffs, NJ: Prentice-Hall.

Detterman, D., & Daniel, M. (1989). Correlations of mental tests with each other and with cognitive variables are highest for low IQ groups. *Intelligence, 15,* 349–359.

Ericsson, K. A., Krampe, R., & Tesch-Romer, C. (1993). The role of deliberate practice in the acquisition of expert performance. *Psychological Review, 100*(3), 363–406.

Feldman, D. H., with Goldsmith, L. T. (1991). *Nature's gambit: Child prodigies and the development of human potential.* New York: Teachers College Press.

Freeman, J. (1979). *Gifted children: Their identification and development in a social context.* Lancaster, England: MPT Press.

Gallagher, A. (1990). Personality patterns of the gifted. *Understanding Our Gifted, 3*(1), 11–13.

Gardner, H. (1983). *Frames of mind: The theory of multiple intelligences.* New York: BasicBooks.

Gardner, H. (1993). *Creating minds: An anatomy of creativity seen through the lives of Freud, Einstein, Picasso, Stravinsky, Eliot, Graham and Gandhi.* New York: BasicBooks.

Goertzel, M. G., Goertzel, V., & Goertzel, T. G. (1978). *Three hundred eminent personalities.* San Francisco: Jossey-Bass.

Hollingworth, L. (1942). *Children above 180 IQ, Stanford-Binet origin and development.* Yonkers, NY: World Book.

Jamison, K. (1993). *Touched with fire: Manic depressive illness and the artistic temperament.* New York: Free Press.

Janos, P., & Robinson, N. (1985). Psychosocial development in intellectually gifted children. In F. Horowitz & M. O'Brien (Eds.), *The gifted and talented: Developmental perspectives* (pp. 149–195). Washington, DC: American Psychological Association.

Ludwig, A. M. (1995). *The price of greatness: Resolving the creativity and madness controversy.* New York: Guilford.

Marland, S. P., Jr. (1971). *Education of the gifted and talented: Report to the Congress of the United States by the Commissioner of Education.* Washington, DC: U.S. Government Printing Office.

Miller, L. (1999). The savant syndrome: Intellectual impairment and exceptional skill. *Psychological Bulletin, 125*(1), 31–46.

Mullis, I. V. S., Martin, M. O., Beaton, A. E., Gonzales, E. J., Kelly, D. L., & Smith, T. A. (1998). *Mathematics and science achievement in the final year of secondary school: IEA's Third International Mathematics and Science Study.* Boston: Boston College; Center for the Study of Testing, Evaluation, and Educational Policy.

Radford, J. (1990). *Child prodigies and exceptional early experience.* London: Harvester.

Reis, S. M., Neu, T., & McGuire, J. (1995). *Talents in two places: Case studies of high ability students with learning disabilities who have achieved.* (Research Monograph No. 95113). National Research Center on the Gifted and Talented. Storrs, CT: University of Connecticut.

Renzulli, J. (1978). What makes giftedness? Re-examining a definition. *Phi Delta Kappa, 60*, 180–184.

Ross, P. O. (1993). *National excellence: A case for developing America's talent.* Washington, DC: U.S. Department of Education, Office of Educational Research and Improvement.

Selfe, J. (1977). *Nadia: A case of extraordinary drawing ability in an autistic child.* London: Academic Press.

Shuter-Dyson, R., & Gabriel, C. (1981). *The psychology of musical ability* (2nd ed.). London: Methuen.

Silverman, L. K. (1989, November). *Lost: One IQ point per year for the gifted.* Paper presented at the 36th annual National Association for the Gifted Convention, Cincinnati, OH.

Silverman, L. K. (1993). The gifted individual. In L. K. Silverman (Ed.), *Counseling the gifted and talented* (pp. 3–28). Denver, CO: Love.

Simonton, D. K. (1991). Emergence and realization of genius: The lives and works of 120 classical composers. *Journal of Personality and Social Psychology, 61*, 829–840.

Simonton, D. K. (1994). *Greatness: Who makes history and why.* New York: Guilford Press.

Simonton, D. K. (1999). Talent and its development: An emergenic and epigenetic model. *Psychological Review, 106*(3), 435–457.

Stanley, J. C. (1973). Accelerating the educational progress of intellectually gifted youths. *Educational Psychologist, 10*, 133–146.

Subotnik, R., & Arnold, A. (Eds.). (1994). *Beyond Terman: Contemporary longitudinal studies of giftedness and talent.* Norwood, NJ: Ablex.

Subotnik, R., Kassan, L., Summers, E., & Wasser, A. (1993). *Genius revisited: High IQ children grown up.* Norwood, NJ: Ablex.

Sulloway, F. (1996). *Born to rebel: Birth order, family dynamics, and creative lives.* New York: Pantheon.

Terman, L. M. (1925). *Genetic studies of genius: Vol. 1. Mental and physical traits of a thousand gifted children.* Stanford, CA: Stanford University Press.

Terman, L. M., & Oden, M. H. (1959). *Genetic studies of genius: Vol. 5. The gifted group at mid-life: Thirty-five years' follow-up of the superior child.* Stanford, CA: Stanford University Press.

Treffert, D. A. (1989). *Extraordinary people.* New York: Bantam Press.

von Karolyi, C. (1999). *Developmental dyslexia and visual-spatial strength: Is there a relationship?* Manuscript submitted for publication.

Wilkinson, S. C. (1993). WISC-R profiles of children with superior intellectual ability. *Gifted Child Quarterly, 37*(2), 84–91.

Winner, E. (1996). *Gifted children: Myths and realities.* New York: BasicBooks.

PART IV

ADULT DEVELOPMENT DOMAIN

Edited by

Corey L. M. Keyes
Emory University, Atlanta, GA

29

Adolescence and Emerging Adulthood: The Critical Passage Ways to Adulthood

Jacquelynne Eccles

Janice Templeton
University of Michigan, Ann Arbor

Bonnie Barber

Margaret Stone
University of Arizona, Tucson

INTRODUCTION

In the previous chapters, the authors laid out a diverse set of assets needed for successful development during childhood. Some of the authors have included adolescence; others have not. In the subsequent chapters, the authors discuss a diverse set of assets linked to successful lives during adulthood. In this chapter, we focus on adolescence and emerging adulthood (Arnett, 2000) as the pivotal periods between childhood and adulthood; we refer to the people in these two periods as youth. The learning and development that takes place from birth to adolescence, of course, continues during adolescence and emerging adulthood. But more importantly, the need to be prepared for the transition into adulthood becomes increasingly salient during these years. It is during these periods of life that individuals must acquire and consolidate the skills, attitudes, values, and social capitol needed to move from dependence on one's family to both self-reliance and the adult forms of interdependence coupled with the kinds of strong social connections needed for both one's own well-being and the parenting of the next generation.

In this chapter, we outline what these skills, values, attitudes, and social capitol might be. First, however, we summarize the critical developmental challenges facing youth in America. These challenges are numerous and quite complex. The psychological assets described in the previous chapters are essential for dealing with these challenges (Larson, 2000; Lerner, Fisher, & Weinberg, 2000; Scales & Leffert, 1999; Wheaton, 1990). It is important to have these issues in mind as one considers the assets needed both for well-being during adolescence and emerging adulthood and for a successful transition into and through adulthood.

It is also important to understand why this chapter focuses on the period from age 10 to age 25. There is general agreement that the adolescent years are critically important for the successful transition to adulthood. In the last 10 to15 years, developmentalists have also begun to focus on ages from 18 to 25 as equally important transitional years. In the past, these years (18–25) were considered part of adulthood. But rapid demographic, sociocultural and labor market changes have made these years more transitional. As recently as the 1960s, the transition into adulthood in most western industrialized countries (particularly in the United States and Canada) was well defined for most social class groups. Adolescents finished high school and either went to college or into the labor market or the military. People generally married and began families in their early 20s. Thus people were usually launched into adulthood by their early 20s and there were only a limited number of fairly well defined pathways from adolescence into adulthood.

This is no longer the case (see Arnett, 2000, for details). The median age for marriage and childbearing has moved up to the late 20s. Both the length of time and proportion of youth in some form of tertiary education have increased dramatically. Finally, the heterogeneity of passage through this period of life has exploded. There is no longer a small easily understood set of patterns for the transition to adulthood—making the years between 18 and 25 as challenging a period of life as adolescence. In the USA, the level of challenge is especially high for noncollege youth and for members of several ethnic minority groups, particularly Blacks and Hispanics for the following reasons: (a) unlike many European and Asian industrialized countries, there is very little institutional support for the transition from secondary school to work in the United States creating what the William T. Grant Foundation (WTGF, 1988) labeled a "floundering" period in their important report, *The Forgotten Half*; and (b) stereotypes about the competence of Blacks and Hispanics, coupled with lower levels of "soft skills" (Murnane & Levy, 1996) and the loss of employment options in many inner city communities (Wilson, 1997) have made employment of Black and Hispanic youth (particularly males) quite problematic. Given these changes and the increasing complexity and heterogeneity of acceptable lifestyles during the third decade of life, Arnett (2000) recently argued for the importance of looking at this period of life as a fundamental transitional period in its own right. He labeled this period *emerging adulthood*. We agree with his argument and have included this period as a central focus in this chapter.

CORNERSTONES OF DEVELOPMENT DURING ADOLESCENCE AND EMERGING ADULTHOOD

The years from age 10 to 25 are marked by major changes at all levels. Among the most dramatic are the biological changes associated with puberty. These include dramatic shifts in the shape of the body, major increases in gonadal hormones, and changes in brain architecture. These biological shifts are directly linked to increases in sexual interest and changes in both cognitive and physical capacities. But there are also major social changes associated with school and work and with the changing roles adolescents and young adults are expected to play by friends, parents, teachers, coaches, and so on. Finally, there are major psychological changes linked to increasing social and cognitive maturity. In fact, very few developmental periods are characterized by so many changes at so many different levels.

With rapid change comes a heightened potential for both positive and negative outcomes (Rutter & Garmezy, 1983; Wheaton, 1990). Although most individuals pass through these two developmental periods without excessively high levels of "storm and stress, " a substantial number of individuals experience difficulty that extends well into young adulthood (Eccles et al., 1993; Arnett, 1999). For example among adolescents, between 15% and 30% (depending on ethnic group) drop out of school before completing high school, 10% to 15% drink alcohol on a regular basis (weekly), and between 7% and 16% (depending on sex and ethnic group) have had suicidal thoughts or have tried to commit suicide in the last 12 months. In addition, the arrest rate is higher than any other age group (Office of Educational Research and Improvement, 1988). Similarly, there is great variation in the functioning of youth during emerging adulthood. Most White middle- and upper-class youth, for example, go to college right out of high school. Many of these graduate and then move into prestigious career-ladder jobs. The story is not so rosy for many other youth in the United States. In a report on non-college youth (*The Forgotten Half*), Sherrod and his colleagues outlined the problems faced by poor youth in this country. Recent studies suggest that these adolescents find it difficult to get jobs that take advantage of the vocational training they got in high school. Their occupational plans are often met with frustrated expectations as they encounter a floundering period of alternately low paid work and unemployment resulting from employers' reluctance to hire recent high school graduates for career-ladder positions

(WTGF, 1988). In turn, these repeated episodes of unemployment undermine general well-being during emerging adulthood.

Adolescence and emerging adulthood are particularly important for life course development because these are times when individuals make many choices and engage in a wide variety of behaviors that have the potential to influence the rest of their lives. For example, adolescents pick which high school courses to take, which after-school activities to participate in, and which peer groups to join. They begin to make future educational and occupational plans and to implement these plans through secondary school course work and out-of-school vocational and volunteer activity choices. Finally, some experiment with quite problematic behaviors linked to drug and alcohol consumption and unprotected sexual intercourse. Similarly, in the emerging adulthood years, individuals make choices related to education, vocational training, entry into the labor market, transitions within the labor market, moving out of one's natal family home, spouse selection, and parenthood. Given the power that these choices and behaviors can have over future options and opportunities, it is critical that we understand what influences whether youth stay on a healthy, productive pathway or move onto more problematic, and potentially destructive, pathways as they pass through this important developmental period.

In his theoretical model of life span development, Erik Erikson (1963, 1968) outlined a set of tasks that are particularly salient for individuals between the ages of 10 and 25; namely developing a sense of mastery, a sense of identity and a sense of intimacy. Others have expanded these tasks to include establishing autonomy, dealing with sexuality and intimacy, and finding a niche for oneself in the worlds of education and work (e.g., Havighurst, 1972; Levinson, 1978). In many cultural groups in Western industrialized countries, the challenges of adolescence translate into several more specific tasks: (a) the shift in one's relationship with one's parents from one of dependency and subordination to one that reflects the adolescents' increasing mature role in their community (in some cultures this shift involves greater independence from one's parents and greater decision-making power over one's own life; in other cultures this shift involves taking greater responsibility for supporting one's natal family and increased participation in community decision-making), (b) exploring new social and sexual roles, (c) the emergence of intimate partnerships, (d) social and personal identity formation, (e) planning one's future and taking the appropriate actions to further these plans, and (f) acquiring a range of skills and values necessary for the successfully transition into work, partnering, parenting, and citizenship (Eccles & Gootman, 2002).

Similarly, emerging adulthood is characterized by specific tasks and challenges. As individuals make the transition into adulthood in this society, they become more and more independent from their natal families. As a consequence, they need to play a much more active role in their own development. This involves (a) managing and coordinating multiple demanding life roles, (b) refining the skills necessary to succeed in these roles, (c) finding meaning and purpose in the roles one has selected, or has ended up in for any number of reasons, (d) developing a mature view of one's strengths and limitations, (e) coping with both foreseen and unforeseen events and life changes, (f) making changes in one's life course if necessary and (g) then coping with both the planning and implementation of these new choices.

As made clear by Erikson (1968), each of the tasks of adolescence and emerging adulthood is played out in a complex set of social contexts and in both cultural and historical settings (see also Bronfenbrenner, 1979; Eccles et al., 1993). For example, the array and severity of risks for adolescents has increased dramatically over the last 30 years as communities have become more transient and less homogeneous, drugs have become more widely available, and social norms have become less rigid and proscribed. Similarly, the passage from 18 to 25 has become increasingly complex during the last 40 years as the transition to adulthood has become more extended in time and less homogeneous in the array of transitional and end-state patterns (Arnett, 2000). These changes have created a situation in which the tasks of emerging adulthood must be carried out in a climate of extreme uncertainty about both one's current options and the implications of one's choices for future options and barriers.

Optimal progress on each of these tasks depends on the psychosocial, physical, and cognitive assets of the individual (Erikson, 1963; Wheaton, 1990). Because transition and change are primary characteristics of both of these life periods, personal and social assets that facilitate coping with change will be critical for successful functioning during these periods. Optimal progress also depends on the developmental appropriateness of the social contexts encountered by individuals as they pass through these periods of life. Repeated exposure to developmentally inappropriate and unsupportive social contexts during these years can undermine the coping skills of even the most resilient youth (Rutter & Garmezy 1983; Rutter, 1988; Werner & Smith, 1982, 1992). This complexity must be taken into account when one thinks about successful development during this period of life.

Equally important is the longer term consequences of well-being during these two periods for the successful transition into adulthood. Failure to deal with these tasks adequately will place restrictions on adult options that are very hard to overcome.

We now turn to a more detailed discussion of the specific changes and challenges of adolescence and emerging adulthood.

Puberty

During early adolescence, most individuals experience a growth spurt and increased sexual libido, develop primary and secondary sex characteristics, and become fertile as a result of the hormonal changes associated with puberty. These hormonal changes can also have a weak impact on such behaviors as aggression, sexuality, and mood swings although these relations are weak and are often moderated by social experiences (Buchanan, Eccles, & Becker, 1992). Learning how to manage these feelings and to develop mature sexual relations with other youth is one of the major developmental tasks throughout adolescence and emerging adulthood.

In general, pubertal changes begin earlier for girls than for boys. There are also major individual differences in the timing, sequencing, and magnitude of pubertal development within each sex. Some children begin their pubertal changes earlier than others and the timing of pubertal development can have major implications for many aspects of life depending on the cultural beliefs and norms associated with pubertal changes. Do these individual differences in timing matter? In a study of the consequences of early maturation for Swedish women, Stattin and Magnusson (1990) found that early maturing girls obtain less education and marry at a younger age than the later maturing girls. These researchers suggested that this difference is due the fact that early maturing females tend to join older peer groups and date older males which, in turn, leads the girls to drop out of school in order to marry the men they date. In addition, school achievement is valued less than early entry into the job market and marriage by their peer social network. Once again, however, having the types of psychological assets outlined in previous chapters and reviewed later in this chapter reduce the likelihood of the early maturing girls being pulled unto a early marriage/lower education life trajectory.

Cognitive Maturation

Over the adolescent years, youth learn to think abstractly, to reflect on themselves and events in their lives, to process information more efficiently, to consider multiple dimensions of problems simultaneously, and to manage their learning and problem solving better (Keating, 1990; Perry, 1970; Wigfield, Eccles, & Pintrich, 1996). Most theorists agree that these types of cognitive skills are critical for a successful transition into adulthood. These kinds of cognitive skills also facilitate both identity development and maturation in moral reasoning; both of which can influence future life planning and engagement in both positive and problematic behaviors. Finally, these kinds of cognitive skills also affect adolescents' view of other people. With increasing cognitive maturity, adolescents become more interested in understanding others' internal psychological characteristics, and friendships come to be based more on perceived similarity in these characteristics (Selman, 1980). When coupled with prosocial values and the opportunity to think about tolerance and human interaction, these skills can lay the groundwork for developing better inter-group relationships and commitments to civic involvement.

Changes in Social Relationships

Changes in Natal Family Relations.   Parent-child relations change in dramatic ways during both adolescence and young adulthood (Buchanan et al., 1992;

Collins, 1990; Eccles & Gootman, 2002; Grotevant, 1998; Youniss, 1980). As they mature, adolescents often want increasing independence and autonomy, particularly regarding family rules and roles. These desires can lead to family conflicts. Research suggests, however that these conflicts are more likely to focus on such issues as dress and appearance, chores, and dating than on more core issues such as education, politics, and spirituality (Collins, 1990). Nonetheless, maintaining strong ties to one's family is a very important asset for both the adolescent years and the transition into adulthood (Grotevant, 1998).

Relationships with one's natal family generally improve during late adolescence and emerging adulthood. Although most youth move out of their parents' home sometime during this period, many come back for periods of time and even more continue to rely on their parents for financial support (Goldscheider & DaVanzo, 1985. WTGF, 1988). The quality of these relationships is critical to well-being during emerging adulthood (Roberts & Bengton, 1996; Schultheiss & Blustein, 1994).

Changes in the Role of Non-Familial Adults. Equally important, however, is the creation of new relationships with non-familial adults. Increasing evidence suggests that adolescence is a time when youth seek out other adult relationships—often teachers, coaches, parents of one's friends, and/or spiritual leaders. Research on mentoring has repeatedly demonstrated the importance of these relationships in adolescents' lives in particular. Strong mentors can even overcome some of the negative effects of a poor relationship with one's parents as well as involvement in problematic peer groups (see Scales & Leffert, 1999).

Changes in the Role of Friendships and Peer Groups. The importance of peer groups and activities done with peers increases dramatically over the adolescent years. For some adolescents, peer acceptance and peer activities become more important than academic achievement, leading to declines in academic achievement that can compromise the successful transition to adulthood (Savin-Williams & Berndt, 1990; Youniss, 1980; Wigfield, Eccles, Mac Iver, Reuman, & Midgley, 1991). In addition, for some youth, confidence in one's physical appearance and social acceptance is a more important predictor of self-esteem than confidence in one's cognitive/academic competence (Harter, 1990).

In part because of the importance of social acceptance during adolescence, friendship networks during this period often are organized into relatively rigid cliques that differ in social status within school and community settings (see Brown, 1990). The existence of these cliques reflects, in part, adolescents' need to establish a sense of identity: Belonging to a group is one way to solve the problem of "who am I." The impact of these cliques on adolescent development depends on the nature of the peer culture within one's cliques. Participation in cliques involved in high levels of problem behaviors may expose adolescents to excessive peer pressure to engage in such behaviors—possibly compromising one's successful transition to adulthood (see Savin-Williams & Berndt, 1990). Having the social skills and personal confidence necessary to resist this pressure is a very important asset during this period of development.

The Emergence of Romantic Partnerships.   As adolescents mature, the role of peers expands: Peers become romantic partners and spouses as well as friends. We know very little about this shift in the roles of peers. Most of the work has focused on the role of marriage in helping youth recover from a problematic adolescence (e.g., Bachman, Wadsworth, O'Malley, Johnston, & Schulenberg, 1997; Jessor, Donovan, & Costa, 1991; Rutter, 1988; Werner & Smith, 1992). These studies suggest that one primary role of marriage is to decrease the amount of time individuals spend with friends who engage in problematic behaviors (Horney, Osgood, & Marshall, 1995; Osgood, Wilson, O'Malley, Bachman, & Johnston, 1996; Sampson & Laub, 1993). There are also lower rates of alcohol abuse in young adults in committed partnerships, including but not limited to marriage (Meschke, Barber, & Eccles, 1998; Miller-Tutzauer, Leonard, & Windle, 1991; Sadava & Pak, 1994). Finally, there is strong evidence that involvement with an intimate partner is related to greater mental and physical well-being for both men and women (Dimitrovsky, Schapira-Beck, & Itskowitz, 1994; Elliot, 1996; Sadava & Pak, 1994; Werner & Smith, 1992).

We know much less about the characteristics that lead to involvement with various kinds of romantic partners. As noted earlier, early maturation is associated with early marriage and cohabitation. Working-class life trajectories are also associated with earlier commitments to romantic partners. In contrast, enrollment in tertiary education and more middle-class life trajectories are associated with later commitments to romantic partners. It is also true that adolescents with fewer of the assets discussed in early chapters and later in this chapter are also more likely to form unstable romantic partnerships with people who also have fewer psychological assets (e.g., Furstenberg, Brooks-Gunn, & Morgan, 1987; Werner & Smith, 1992).

The transition to romantic partnerships is also linked to identity constructs. For example, young women with a strong commitment to work and higher education express less interest in dating and are less likely to marry during their 20s than their peers with lower commitments to education and careers; interestingly, the opposite is true for men. (Thornton, Axinn, & Teachman, 1995; Matula, Huston, Grotevant, & Zamutt, 1992). This work shows the need to look at the interface between the various adult roles adolescents and emerging adults are moving towards in understanding the impact of each on well-being.

There is also a burgeoning literature on what predicts successful romantic partnerships, but reviewing this work is beyond the scope of this chapter.

Becoming a Parent.   There is a large body of research focused on impact of the transition to parenthood on emotional well-being. Typically, the transition to parenthood is associated with a decrease in maternal depression, particularly in comparison with the time prior to becoming a parent (Anderson, Fleming, & Steiner, 1994; Hock, Schirtzinger, Lutz, & Widaman, 1995). However, in one study, the self-esteem of childless women was both higher and showed greater improvement over time that the self-esteem of mothers (Elliot, 1996).

As with research on all transitions, associations between the transition to parenthood and socioemotional well-being are moderated by other factors, such as spousal behavior and previous levels of marital satisfaction. Specifically, young women who report high levels of marital satisfaction are less depressed following the transition to parenthood than women who report lower levels of marital satisfaction (Hock et al., 1995). Likewise, young women whose husbands are less involved in child care report greater decreases in marital satisfaction than women whose husbands are more involved (Levy-Shiff, 1994). Finally, levels of maternal depression pre- and postpartum are associated with such factors as body image, pain tolerance, self-confidence, and maternal involvement with child (Anderson et al., 1994).

Finally, there is also a large literature on the negative consequences of becoming a parent too young (Furstenberg et al, 1987). Teenage parenting is linked to lower educational and occupational attainment, lower lifetime earnings, and more difficulties in all types of adult transitions including forming stable romantic partnerships and coping with life events of all kinds. As was the case for timing of marriage and cohabitation, early maturation in females, working-class life trajectories, limited educational and occupational involvements and family-focused personal identities predict early transition into parenthood (Furstenberg, et al., 1987; Stattin & Magnusson, 1990; Werner & Smith, 1992).

Educational Transitions

Secondary School Transitions.   For some individuals, the adolescent years are marked by a downward spiral in academic performance leading to academic failure and school dropout (Simmons & Blyth, 1987). Similar declines have been documented for interest in school, intrinsic motivation, self-concepts/ self-perceptions, and confidence in one's intellectual abilities (Eccles, Wigfield, & Schiefele, 1999; Wigfield et al., 1996). A variety of explanations have been offered to explain these "negative" school achievement-related changes: Some have suggested that declines such as these result from the intraspsychic upheaval assumed to be associated with adolescent development (see Arnett, 1999). Others have suggested that it is the coincidence of the timing of multiple life changes (e.g., Simmons & Blyth, 1987). Still others have suggested that it is the nature of junior and senior high school environments themselves, rather than the transition per se, that is important (see Eccles et al., 1993; Entwisle, 1990; Wigfield et al., 1996). According to Person-Environment Fit Theory, behavior, motivation, and mental health are influenced by the fit between the characteristics individuals bring to their social environments and the characteristics of these social environments. Individuals are not likely to do very well, or be very motivated, if they are in social environments that do not fit their psychological needs. If the social environments in the typical secondary schools do not fit very well with the psychological needs of adolescents, then Person-Environment Fit Theory predicts a decline in the adolescents' motivation, interest, performance, and behavior as they move into this environment. Evidence suggests that this is the case (Eccles, et al., 1993). Personal assets such as confidence in one's ability to succeed, good coping skills, high self-esteem, and good social skills help adolescents deal with these school-related stressors (Lord, Eccles, & McCarthy, 1994).

Transition to College.   At the completion of secondary school, about half of America's youth go to college; the other half move into a variety of work and non-work settings. In thinking about the differences in these two trajectories, one needs to consider the multiple roles college plays in young adult development. In addition to greatly increased occupational prospects, going to college provides youth with many opportunities and challenges. The college years afford a safe milieu in which to explore ideas, opportunities, and lifestyles, while delaying the assumption of adult responsibilities (Sherrod et al., 1993; Wigfield et al., 1996). Living in a college residence greatly increases opportunities for self-governance, but provides a protected environment in which to adjust to new-found independence. Individuation from parents and freedom to direct one's own lifestyle increases (Flanagan et al., 1993). These characteristics of college life should provide the young adult with the opportunity to explore their own identities in a somewhat protected context.

The demands and norms of college life, however, can also be challenging and stressful: Individuals often face unfamiliar academic expectations, changes in sources of social support, and social norms that encourage high levels of risk behaviors, particularly alcohol use (Compas, Wagner, Slavin, & Vannatta, 1986; Prentice & Miller, 1993; Schulenberg & Maggs, 2000). Binge drinking, for example, peaks during the college years particularly for those students (like non-athletes) who were not heavy drinkers in high school (Barber, Eccles & Stone, 2001). Similarly, many youth drop out of college. In fact, only 52% of those enrolling in college receive their initial degree objective within 5 years. The high attrition rates during college (near 50%) have stimulated social scientists and educators to consider the relation of a wide range of predictors and college success (e.g., Rice, Cole, & Lapsley, 1990). However, this work is still in its infancy. Certainly the kinds of personal assets discussed later are likely to be key.

Only half of American youth attend postsecondary education (WTGF, 1988). The other half not only misses out on the many educational benefits provided by college, they may also miss out on the developmental moratorium of exploration and experimentation enjoyed by those who attend college full-time (Sherrod et al., 1993). Except for individuals who join the military, non-college youth do not have the option of living semi-independently in a supervised group living situation such as a college dormitory. They also tend to marry and have children earlier, dramatically increasing their responsibilities and decreasing opportunities for exploration. Earlier entry into the adult roles of worker, spouse, and parent are associated with lower educational and occupational attainment (Marini, 1985, 1987), and, for less resilient youth, with more problematic social and psychological development as well (Hogan & Astone, 1986; Sherrod et al., 1993). In addition, non-college youth face difficult challenges in the world of work without adequate social supports. In an economy characterized by high unemployment and deflated academic credentials, even high school graduates experience great difficulty finding full-time, stable, adequately paid, and satisfying work.

College and non-college youth differ in another interesting way: The non-college roles of individuals in their 20s, particularly that of employee, are generally associated with greater responsibilities and fewer freedoms than the role of college student. Non-college young adults are likely to have designated daily start and end hours of employment, that, when not met, could result in job loss. Non-college youth are also likely to marry earlier, which potentially increases their responsibilities to others as well. Interestingly these are exactly the contextual characteristics linked to declines in problem behaviors and alcohol consumption (Bachman et al., 1997). Thus, while non-college bound youth are more likely to be involved in risky and problematic behavior than college-bound youth during adolescence, the desistence rates for these behaviors are higher in those non-college youth who take on these adult role responsibilities than for college youth.

Transition From School to Work in the Labor Market

In our society, individuals are expected to move from school into the labor market. However, at this point in our history the transition from school to the labor market is less clear cut than even 30 years ago. Youth leave school at such varying times as before completing high school, after high school, after some college, after completing a community college degree, after completing a 4-year college degree, or after a postgraduate degree. These different groups can move back and forth between unemployment, one or more part-time jobs, a series of "dead-end" jobs, or a stable long-term job. Some individuals initially drop out of high school and college, but then return (Weidman & Friedmann, 1984). Additionally, schooling and employment may take place concurrently; many youth take on part-time work while still attending high school (Greenberger & Steinberg, 1986) and college.

Controversy has arisen about the advisability of work during the high school years. The critical issue is how much and what kind of work. Some evidence suggests that taking on too much work (more than 20 hours per week), particularly in low-quality jobs, can have detrimental effects on school achievement, alcohol use, and involvement in problem behaviors (Mortimer, Finch, Shanahan, & Rye, 1992; Steinberg & Dornbusch, 1991).

Although this transition is not the same for all youth, many researchers have focused on what factors are associated with a successful transition. Compared to those adolescents who drop out of high school, those with a high school degree are better prepared for low-skill, low-wage jobs (Klerman & Karoly, 1994); the accumulation of both academic and vocational credits in high school increases the chances of employment, reduces the duration of unemployment, and increases earnings (Rumberger & Daymont, 1984). Many researchers have examined the value of vocational education courses taken during the high school on later employment and earnings (Arum & Shavit 1995; Hotchkiss & Dornsten, 1987). The results are mixed. For example, some have found that vocational courses during high school have little or no positive effects on subsequent employment (Hamilton & Hurrelmann, 1994; Hamilton & Powers, 1990; Kantor, 1994). Others have found that the positive effects of vocational courses depend on the gender of the adolescent or young adult. One research group found an increase in employment for both men and women, but an increase in wages only for men (Kang & Bishop, 1989); another group found consistently positively effects on the employment and wages of women, but less consistent effects for men (Lewis, Hearn, & Zilbert, 1993).

Data on the relation of a college degree to future employment outcomes are less ambiguous: Obtaining a college predicts higher income and job status (Fournier & Payne, 1994; Kandel, Mossell, & Kaestner, 1987; Krau, 1989). For example, according to the U.S. Bureau of the Census, in 1995 the average income of high school graduates was $21, 431; the average income for those with some college or an associate's degree was $23, 862; the average income jumped to $36, 980 for individuals with a college degree. In addition, longitudinal data from the National Longitudinal Study of Youth (NLSY) indicates that non-college youth face greater unemployment problems as adults than youth who go on to college, and that unemployment and unsatisfactory employment are related to lower self-esteem (Dooley, 1995).

The process of transitioning from school to employment is likely to be influenced by experiences in multiple life domains, including family relationships, leisure activities, peer relationships, identity, and mental health (Krau, 1989). For example, Way and Rossmann (1995) found that parenting practices influence the transition from school to work through their impact on adolescents' readiness for this transition. They defined readiness as a composite of vocational identity, work effectiveness skills, a career indecision scale, and post-high school plans. As predicted, they found a proactive parenting style (similar to authoritative parenting) was positively related to readiness while a dominating parenting style (similar to authoritarian parenting) was negatively related to readiness. Other researchers have found that the kinds of psychological assets discussed in this and earlier chapters also facilitate the transition to employment (e.g., Barling & Kelloway, 1999; Furstenberg et al. 1987; Sampson & Laub, 1993; Werner & Smith, 1992).

The complexity of the influences on this transition, however, is well illustrated by the work on the relation of adolescent drinking and drug use to young adult employment outcomes. One research group found that high school drug use (including alcohol, marijuana use, cigarettes, hard drugs) significantly predicted lower college involvement, more work force involvement, and drug use in young adulthood; additionally, low high school GPA predicted earlier entry into future full-time employment (Newcomb & Bentler, 1986). On the other hand, Kandel and colleagues (Kandel et al., 1987) found no significant effect of high school drug use on the individual's first job or income, after controlling for a variety of variables during high school (including parents' years of schooling, fathers' occupational prestige, number of siblings, race, delinquency index, frequency of attending religious services, peer activity index, GPA, frequent talks about education and occupation with fathers) and concurrently at the time of first job (including educational attainment and marital status). Clearly, this second study provides a much better picture of the potential processes through which alcohol use might be associated with adult occupational trajectories. For most youth, alcohol use takes place as part of a larger system of behaviors and social networks. Consequently, its association with adult outcomes likely depends on its larger significance. For example, in our work, we have identified two groups of heavy high school drinkers: a popular, well-adjusted group and a multiple-problem group. Because alcohol use means something very different in these two groups, it is likely to have very different long-term consequences for young adult and adult occupational outcomes (Barber et al., 2001; see also Bachman et al., 1997).

Work-related experiences also have implications for both mental health and adult social and psychology development. The impact of both unstable employment and unemployment more generally during the 20s has received considerable research attention. A number of studies have documented the impact of employment per se on socioemotional well-being, with unemployed individuals and young adults who have been laid off reporting much higher levels of distress and psychiatric problems than employed individuals (e.g., Feehan, McGee, Williams, & Nada-Raja, 1995; Timms, 1996; Winefield & Tiggemann, 1989). In addition, the financial strain associated with unemployment during the 20s was related to greater depression in both marital partners, which in turn was related to lower levels of support and increased undermining behavior in the marital relationship (Vinokur, Price, & Caplan, 1996). Other studies have documented the bi-directional relations between young adult work experiences and such psychological characteristics as personality and values (Van der Velde, Feij, & Taris, 1995).

Summary

In this section, we have outlined the major developmental challenges likely to affect well-being during adolescence and emerging adulthood. We have also pointed out how particular skills, attitudes, values, and social capitol might help adolescents and young adults cope with these challenges and prepare for the transition into adulthood. In the next section, we summarize the evidence for the protective role of these skills, attitudes, values, and social assets.

PERSONAL AND SOCIAL ASSETS

Having laid out the major developmental challenges associated with adolescence and emerging adulthood, we now turn to a discussion of the personal and social assets likely to facilitate both optimal passage through these periods of life and optimal transition into adulthood. In this section, we review what we know about the personal and social assets that predict both concurrent well-being and optimal future life transitions.

Developmental scientists have repeatedly debated whether there are core human needs and how their fulfillment might relate to positive development. For example, Freud argued that well-being depends on the "successful" fulfillment of one's needs for mastery and love. Erikson proposed the following set of characteristics as key to healthy psychological development: trust (which he linked to positive emotional relationships with caring adults), a strong sense of self-sufficiency, initiative, a strong sense of industry (confidence in one's ability to master the demands of one's world), identity, and intimacy. Many contemporary theorists have suggested a similar set of needs (e.g, Bandura, 1994; Connell & Wellborn, 1991; Deci & Ryan, 1985; Elder, 1998; Levinson, 1978; Rutter & Garmezy, 1983). These include a sense of personal efficacy, intrinsic motivation, a desire for mastery, social connectedness, good emotional coping skills, planfulness, a sense of optimism, and attachment to conventional prosocial institutions.

Over the last 10 or so years, many lists of assets have been proposed. Three recent reviews include one by Lerner and his colleagues (Lerner, Fisher, & Weinberg, 2000), one by the Search Institute (Scales & Leffert, 1999), and one by the National Research Council (Eccles & Gootman, 2002). Of these, the review by Scales and Leffert is the most comprehensive. They listed the following assets as critical for successful passage through adolescence and into adulthood:

Commitment to learning (achievement motivation, school engagement, doing school work, and other intellectual activities).
Positive values (caring, equality and social justice, integrity, honesty, responsibility, and restraint).
Social competencies (Planning and decision-making, interpersonal and cultural competence, resistance skills, and peaceful conflict resolution skills).

Positive identity (personal power, self-esteem, sense of purpose, optimism about one's future).

Positive use of time.

Autonomy and the opportunity to make a meaningful difference.

By and large, research supports these suggestions. Longitudinal studies have shown strong relations of these personal assets to a variety of indicators of a successful transition into adulthood. For example, in her pioneering longitudinal study of poor children and their families on Kauai, Emmy Werner and her colleagues concluded that high levels of the following personal characteristics predict successful passage through adolescence and adulthood: health, good cognitive skills, positive social skills, well-developed self-regulatory and coping/adaptation skills, an engaging personality, high levels of self-confidence, positive self-esteem, and either spirituality or a strong sense of meaningfulness in one's life. They concluded that the following social assets are also very important: strong and positive social connections to both one's family and other positive organizations and networks. Clausen (1993) and Elder (1974) reached similar conclusions based on their work with the Berkeley and Oakland Growth Studies and Clausen added planfulness to the list (see also work by Block, 1971; Cairns & Cairns, 1994; Compas et al., 1986; Elder & Conger, 2000; Furstenberg, Brooks-Gunn, & Morgan, 1987; Furstenberg et al., 1999; Jessor et al., 1991; Sampson & Laub, 1993).

In reviewing this work and related studies of resilience and adolescent development, Eccles and Gootman (2002) organized the key psychological and social assets around three general categories: intellectual, psychological, and social assets. Those assets with the strongest longitudinal evidence are summarized in Table 29.1 (adapted from Eccles and Gootman, 2002). Many of these assets overlap with the assets reviewed in earlier chapters. Consequently, the reader has already been exposed to massive amounts of empirical support for the importance of most of these assets. In this chapter, we focus on the predictive role of these assets for well-being during adolescence and for the successful transition into adulthood. But it is important to note that we know much less about the strength of these associations for the transition to adulthhood than we know about their strength for younger children. In particular, we know very little about the relative importance of each of these assets for the wide variety of positive adult outcomes that would signify a successful transition to adulthood. On the one hand, it is likely that having more assets and assets across all three categories is better than having only a few. On the other hand, it is also clear that some individuals do quite well on some aspects of adult development with only a limited number of assets in each category.

For this review, we focused on two types of empirical studies: studies that link various psychological and social characteristics to concurrent indicators of positive development during adolescence and young adulthood and studies that link these types of characteristics longitudinally to subsequent indicators of positive development during young adulthood and adulthood. Studies of the first type (those using concurrent indicators of well-being) have documented positive associations among such indicators of adolescent and young adult well-being as good mental health, average or better school performance, positive peer relations, good problem-solving skills, and little to no involvement in such problematic behaviors as gang membership, excessive drug and alcohol use, school failure, school dropout, delinquency, and early pregnancy. Longitudinal studies have linked these kinds of adolescent characteristics to such indicators of adult well-being as completing high school, completing tertiary education, successful transition into the labor market (i.e., obtaining and keeping a job that pays at least a living wage), staying out of prison, avoiding drug and alcohol abuse and addiction, turning around a problematic adolescent trajectory, entering a stable and supportive intimate relationship (usually assessed in terms of one's marital partner), and involvement in civic and community activities. Together these two broad types of studies provide a growing body of consistent evidence supporting the importance of the set of characteristics summarized in Table 29.1. In this chapter we focus on the findings from the longitudinal studies.

Intellectual Assets

The evidence is quite good regarding the positive link of life skills, school academic success, planfulness and good decision-making skills for positive outcomes during both adolescence and young adulthood on such indicators as mental health, school completion, adult levels of educational and occupational attainment, positive moral values and prosocial behaviors, good parent child relations, attachment to prosocial friends and romantic partners, participation in volunteer activities, and avoidance of problematic behavior patterns (see Cairns & Cairns, 1994; Clausen, 1993; Eccles & Gootman, 2002; Elder & Conger, 2000; Entwisle, 1990; Furstenberg et al., 1987; Jessor et al., 1991; Sampson & Laub, 1993; Scales & Leffert, 1999; Warner & Smith, 1992). However, although several studies have documented the importance of life skills training for positive development during adolescence, we know little about which particular life skills and competencies are most important for youth in different cultural, ethnic, gender, and social class contexts. More generally, we also know little about the extent to which these life skills actually facilitate the successful transition into adulthood. Logic suggests that they should but more empirical work is needed to substantiate these hypothesized relations.

Psychological Assets

Longitudinal evidence is also strong for the predictive importance of good mental health, self-regulation skills, mastery motivation, confidence in one's competence in those domains valued most by the individual, optimism, and planfulness

Table 29.1

Personal and Social Assets Linked to Adolescent and Adult Well-Being
(Adapted from Eccles and Gootman, 2002)

Intellectual Assets

Knowledge of essential life and vocational skills
Good decision-making and problem-solving skills
School success
Planfulness

Psychological Assets

Good mental health
Positive self-esteem
Emotional self-regulation skills
Coping and conflict resolution skills
Positive achievement motivation
Confidence in one's ability to accomplish one's goals
Optimism coupled with realism
Coherent and positive personal and social identity
Spirituality and/or a sense of purpose in life
Strong moral character
A sense that one is making a meaningful contribution to one's community

Social Assets

Good relationships with parents, peers, and other adults
Strong sense of being connected to, and valued by, larger social networks and social institutions
   such as schools, churchs, out of school youth development centers

for a wide variety of indicators of subsequent well-being during both adolescence and emerging adulthood (e.g., Aseltine & Gore, 1993; Bandura, 1994; Block, 1971; Clausen, 1993; Compas et al., 1986; Connell, Halpern-Felsher, Clifford, Crichlow, & Usinger, 1995; Connell & Wellborn, 1991; Deci & Ryan, 1985; Eccles et al., 1998; Elder & Conger, 1999; Jessor et al., 1991; Lord et al., 1994; Luthar & Zigler, 1992; Scales & Leffert, 1999; Werner & Smith, 1992).

Far fewer studies have investigated the relation of such moral and value-based characteristics as prosocial values, spirituality, moral character, personal responsibility, a sense that one is making a meaningful contribution to one's community, and personal identity with other indicators of adolescent and adult well being (Eccles & Gootman, 2002). Nonetheless, the few available studies support their importance (e.g., see Benson, Masters & Larson, 1997; DuRant, R. H., Getts. A., Cadenhead, C., Emans, S. J., & Woods, E., 1995; Eisenberg, Carlo, Murphy, & Van Court, 1995; Elder & Conger, 2000; Erikson, 1968; Marcia, 1980; Markus & Wurf, 1987; Scales & Leffert, 1999; Waterman, 1982; Wentzel, 1991; Werner & Smith, 1992). Recent work on the important relations of service learning with both well-being during adolescence and civic involvement in adulthood is providing some of the strongest evidence for these types of assets (Youniss, McLellan, & Yates, 1996).

Finally, some very recent work has focused on role of psychological assets linked to ethnic identity formation and culturally sensitive values. These studies are beginning to provide support for the importance of a coherent and positive ethnic identity for such indicators of adolescent well-being as high self-esteem, confidence in one's ability to accomplish one's goals, commitment to doing well in school, a sense of purpose in life, and academic success (e.g., Beauvis, 2000; Castro, Boyer, & Balcazar, 2000; Cross, 1991; Ford & Harris. 1997; Leong, Chao & Hardin, 2000; Phelan & Davidson, 1993; Phinney, 1990; Spencer, 1995). A few of these studies have now also shown that a strong and positive ethnic identity can help adolescents of color to resist the negative impact of experiences with racial and ethnic discrimination (see also Wong, Eccles, & Sameroff, 1998). Whether these psychological assets also facilitate a successful transition to adulthood remains to be determined. In addition, we know very little about how these types of assets are related to either the well-being of White Americans or to the nature of intergroup interactions and racial tolerance. Knowing such information is very important given our increasingly multicultural society.

Social Assets

Finally, there is strong longitudinal evidence of the predictive power of connectedness, integration, feelings of belonging, and institutional attachments for such objective indicators of well-being during adolescence and young adulthood as secondary school success, mastery of a wide variety of life skills, adult educational and occupational attainment (Eccles & Goodman, 2002; Scales & Leffert, 1999). These social assets also predict such subjective indicators of adult well-being as positive mental health, confidence in one's ability to accomplish one's goals, optimism, and good self-regulation skills. Finally, these social assets predict smoother transitions into such key adult roles as partner, spouse, parent, worker and active community member (e.g., Cairns & Cairns, 1994; Elder & Conger, 2000; Furstenberg et al., 1999; Goodenow, 1992; Rice et al., 1990; Wentzel, 1991; Werner & Smith, 1992).

CONCLUSIONS

We had two goals in this chapter: (a) to provide an overview of the tasks that face individuals as they pass through adolescence and the early years of adulthood, and (b) to summarize what we know from longitudinal studies about the assets that facilitate successful coping with and adaptation to these tasks and the demands inherent in passage into adulthood in the United States. We argued that adolescence and emerging adulthood are two of the most challenging periods of human development. Adolescence, in particular, is a time of massive changes in all dimensions of life, ranging from the dramatic physical changes associated with puberty to the social changes associated with increasing independence from one's natal family and the beginnings of intimate relationships that can lead to long term partnering and new family formation.

In the second half of the chapter, we outlined the evidence regarding the assets likely to help youth through these two periods of life. We organized these assets under three broad categories: intellectual, psychological, and social. Within each of these general areas, we summarized the evidence from longitudinal studies regarding the specific assets that predict successful transitions into adulthood. These assets are listed in Table 29.1. We also concluded that we know relatively little about how these assets combine to facilitate healthy development. Few studies have included more than a couple of these assets at one time. Consequently, we just do not know which assets are the most important for which aspects of a successful transition into adulthood. It is unlikely that one needs all of these assets. Instead, youth are likely to do quite well with several different profiles of assets. Evidence also suggests that having more assets is better than having only a few (i.e., the effects of the assets in studies that measure more than one asset are additive). Finally, it is important to note that exposure to repeated negative life events can undermine the healthy development and successful passage to adulthood of even those adolescents who have multiple assets (Cui & Vallant, 1996). Consequently, it is critical that supportive environments be made available for all young people (Eccles & Gootman, 2002).

REFERENCES

Anderson, V. N., Fleming, A. S., & Steiner, M. (1994). Mood and the transition to motherhood. *Journal of Reproductive and Infant Psychology, 12*, 69–77.

Arum, R., & Shavit, Y. (1995). Secondary vocational education and the transition from school to work. *Sociology of Education, 68*, 187–204.

Arnett, J. J. (1999). Adolescent storm and stress, reconsidered. *American Psychologist, 54,* 317–326.

Arnett, J. J. (2000). Emerging adulthood: A theory of development from the late teens through the twenties. *American Psychologist, 55,* 469–480.

Aseltine, R. H., & Gore, S. (1993). Mental health and social adaptation following the transition from high school. *Journal of Research on Adolescence, 3*, 247–270.

Bachman, J. G., Wadsworth, K. N., O'Malley, P. M., Johnston, L. D. & Schulenberg, J. E. (1997). *Smoking, drinking, and drug use in young adulthood: The impacts of new freedoms and responsibilities*. Mahwah, NJ, Lawrence Erlbaum Associates.

Baltes, P. B., Lindenberger, U., & Staudinger, U. M. (1998). Life-span theory in developmental psychology. In W. Damon & R. M. Lerner (Eds.), *Handbook of child psychology 5th edition: Vol. 1. Theoretical models of human development* (pp. 1029–1144). New York: Wiley.

Bandura, A. (1994). *Self-efficacy: The exercise of control*. New York: Freeman.

Barber, B. L., Eccles, J. S., & Stone, M. R. (2001). Whatever happened to the Jock, the Brain, and the Princess? Young adult pathways linked to adolescent activity involvement and social identity. *Journal of Adolescent Research, 16*, 429–455.

Barling, J., & Kelloway, E. K. (1999). *Young workers: Varieties of experience.* Washington, DC: American Psychological Association.

Beauvais. F. (2000). Indian adolescence: Opportunity and challenge. In R. Montemayor, G. R. Adams, & T. P. Gullotta (Eds.), *Adolescent diversity in ethnic, economic, and cultural contexts* (pp. 110–140). Thousand Oaks, CA: Sage.

Benson, P. L., Masters, K. S., & Larson, D. B. (1997). Religious influences on child and adolescent development. In J. D. Noshpitz & N. E. Alessi (Eds.), *Handbook of child and adolescent psychiatry: Vol 4 Varieties of development* (pp. 206–219). New York: Wiley.

Block, J. (1971). *Lives through time.* Berkeley, CA: Bancroft.

Bronfenbrenner, U. (1979). *The ecology of human development: Experiments by nature and design.* Cambridge, MA: Harvard University Press.

Brown, B. B. (1990). Peer groups and peer cultures. In S. S. Feldman & G. R. Elliott (Eds.), *At the threshold: The developing adolescent* (pp. 171–196). Cambridge, MA: Harvard University Press.

Buchanan, C. M., Eccles, J. S., & Becker, J. B. (1992). Are adolescents the victims of raging hormones: Evidence for activational effects of hormones on moods and behaviors at adolescence. *Psychological Bulletin, 111,* 62–107.

Cairns, R. B., & Cairns, B. D. (1994). *Lifelines and risks: Pathways of youth in our time.* Cambridge, UK: Cambridge University Press.

Castro, F. G., Boyer, G. R., & Balcazar, H. G. (2000). Healthy adjustment in Mexican American and other Hispanic adolescents. In R. Montemayor, G. R. Adams, & T. P. Gullotta (Eds.), *Adolescent diversity in ethnic, economic, and cultural contexts* (pp. 141–178). Thousand Oaks, CA: Sage.

Clausen, J. A. (1993). *American lives: Looking back at the children of the great depression.* New York: The Free Press.

Collins, W. A. (1990). Parent-child relationships in the transition to adolescence: Continuity and change in interaction, affect, and cognition. In R. Montemayor, G. R. Adams, & T. P. Gullotta (Eds.), *From childhood to adolescence: A transitional period?* (pp. 85–106). Beverly Hills, CA: Sage.

Compas, B. E., Wagner, B. M., Slavin, L. A., & Vannatta, K. (1986). A prospective study of life events, social support, and psychological symptomatology during the transition from high school to college. *American Journal of Community Psychology, 14,* 241–257.

Connell, J. P., Halpern-Felsher, B. L., Clifford, E., Crichlow, W., & Usinger, P. (1995). Hanging in there: Behavioral, psychological, and contextual factors affecting whether African-American adolescents stay in high school. *Journal of Adolescent Research, 10,* 41–63.

Connell, J. P., & Wellborn, J. G. (1991). Competence, automomy, and relatedness: A motivational analysis of self-system processes. In R. Gunnar & L. A. Sroufe (Eds.), *Minnesota symposia on child psychology* (Vol. 23, pp. 43–77). Hillsale, NJ: Lawrence Erlbaum Associates.

Cross, W. E. (1991). *Shades of black: Diversity in African-American identity.* Philadelphia: Temple University Press.

Cui, X., & Vaillant, G. E. (1996). Antecedents and consequences of negative life events in adulthood: A longitudinal study. *American Journal of Psychiatry, 153,* 21–26.

Deci, E. L., & Ryan, R. M. (1985). *Intrinsic motivation and self-determination in human behavior.* New York: Plenum Press.

Dimitrovsky, L., Schapira-Beck, E. & Itskowitz, R. (1994). Locus of control of Israeli women during the transition to marriage. *Journal of Psychology, 128,* 537–545.

Dooley, D. (1995). Effect of unemployment on school leavers' self-esteem. Journal of *Occupational & Organizational Psychology, 68,* 177–192.

DuRant, R. H., Getts, A., Cadenhead, C., Emans, S. J., & Woods, E. (1995). Exposure to violence and victimization and depression, hopelessness, and purpose of life among adolescents living in and around public housing. *Journal of Developmental and Behavioral Pediatrics, 16,* 233–237.

Eccles, J. S., & Barber, B. L. (1999). Student council, volunteering, basketball, or marching band: What kind of extracurricular involvement matters? *Journal of Adolescent Research, 14,* 10–43.

Eccles. J. S., & Gootman, J. (Eds.). (2002). *Community Programs to Promote Youth Development.* Washington DC: National Academy Press.

Eccles, J. S., Midgley, C., Buchanan, C. M., Wigfield, A., Reuman, D., & Mac Iver, D. (1993). Developmental during adolescence: The impact of stage/environment fit. *American Psychologist, 48,* 90–101.

Eccles, J. S., Wigfield, A., & Schiefele, U. (1998). Motivation to Succeed. In N. Eisenberg (Ed.), *Handbook of Child Psychology*, (Vol. 3, 5th ed., pp. 1017–1095). New York: Wiley.

Eisenberg, N., Carlo, G., Murphy, B., & Van Court, P. (1995). Prosocial development in late adolescence: A longitudinal study. *Child Development, 66,* 1179–1197.

Entwisle, D. R. (1990). Schooling and the adolescent. In S. S. Feldman & G. R. Elliott (Eds.), *At the threshold: The developing adolescent* (pp. 197–224). Cambridge, MA: Harvard University Press.

Elder, G.H. (1974). *Children of the Great Depression*. Chicago: University of Chicago Press.

Elder, G. H. (1998). The life course and human development. In W. Damon & R. M. Lerner (Eds.), *Handbook of child psychology: Theoretical model of human development* (Vol. 1, 5th ed., pp. 939–992). New York: Wiley.

Elder, G. H., & Conger, R. (2000). *Children of the land*. Chicago: University of Chicago Press.

Elliot, M. (1996). Impact of work, family and welfare receipt on woman's self-esteem in young adulthood. *Social Psychology Quarterly, 59*, 80–95.

Erikson, E. H. (1963). *Childhood and society*. New York: Norton.

Erikson, E. H. (1968). *Identity, youth and crisis*. New York: Norton.

Feehan, M., McGee, R., Williams, S. M., & Nada-Raja, S. (1995). Models of adolescent psychopathology: Childhood risk and the transition to adulthood. *Journal of the American Academy of Child and Adolescent Psychiatry, 34,* 670–679.

Flanagan, C., Schulenberg, J., & Fuligni, A. (1993). Living arrangements and parent-adolescent relationships during the college years. *Journal of Youth and Adolescence, 22,* 171–189.

Ford, D. Y., & Harris, J. J. (1996). Perceptions and attitudes of Black students toward school: School achievement and other educational variables. *Child Development, 67,* 1144–1152.

Fournier, V., & Payne, R. (1994). Change in self construction during the transition from university to employment: A personal construct psychology approach. *Journal of Occupational & Organizational Psychology, 67,* 297–314.

Fuligni, A. (in press). Family obligation and the academic motivation of adolescents from Asian, Latin American, and European backgrounds. *New directions in child development.*

Furstenberg, F., Jr., Brooks-Gunn, J., & Morgan, P. (1987). *Adolescent mothers in later life*. New York: Cambridge University Press.

Furstenberg, F., Cook, T., Eccles, J., Elder, G., & Sameroff, A. (1999). *Managing to make it*. Chicago: University of Chicago Press.

Goldscheider, F. K., & DaVanzo, J. (1985). Living arrangements and the transition to adulthood. *Demography, 22,* 545–563.

Goodenow, C. (1993). Classroom belonging among early adolescent students: Relationships to motivation and achievement. *Journal of Early Adolescence, 13,* 21–43.

Greenberger, E., & Steinberg, L. D. (1986). The workplace as a context for the socialization of youth. *Journal of Youth & Adolescence, 10*, 185–210.

Grotevant, H. D. (1998). Adolescent development in family contexts. In W. Damon & N. Eisenberg (Eds.), *Handbook of child psychology: Social, emotional, and personality development*, (Vol. 3, 5th ed., pp. 1097–1150). New York: Wiley.

Hamilton, S. F., & Hurrelmann, K. (1994). The school-to-career transition in Germany and the United States. *Teachers College Record, 96,* 329–344.

Hamilton, S. F., & Powers, J. L. (1990). Failed expectations: Working class girls' transition from school to work. *Youth & Society, 22,* 241–262.

Harter, S. (1990). Causes, correlates and the functional role of self-worth: A life-span perspective. In R. J. Sternberg & J. Kolligian (Eds.), *Competence considered* (pp. 67–97). New Haven, CT: Yale University Press.

Havighurst, R. J. (1972). *Developmental tasks and education* (3rd ed). New York: McKay.

Hock, E., Schirtzinger, M. B., Lutz, W. J., & Widaman, K. (1995). Maternal depressive symptomalogy over the transition to parenthood: Assessing the influence of marital satisfaction and marital sex role traditionalism. *Journal of Family Psychology, 9*, 79–88.

Hogan, D. P., & Astone, N. M. (1986). The transition to adulthood. *Annual Review of Sociology, 12,* 109–130.

Horney, J., Osgood, D. W., & Marshall, I. H. (1995). Criminal careers in the short-term: Intra-individual variability in crime and its relation to local life circumstances. *American Sociological Review, 60*, 655–673.

Hotchkiss, L., & Dorsten, L. (1987). Curriculum effects on early post-high school outcomes. *Research in the sociology of education and socialization, 7*, 191–219.

Jessor, R., Donovan, J. E., & Costa, F. M. (1991). *Beyond adolescence: Problem behavior and young adult development.* New York: Cambridge University Press.

Kandel, D. B., Mossell, P., & Kaestner, R. (1987). Drug use, the transition from school to work and occupational achievement in the United States. Special Issue: Juvenile substance use and human development: New perspectives in research and prevention. *European Journal of Psychology of Education, 2*, 337–363.

Kang, S., & Bishop, J. (1989). Vocational or academic coursework in high school: Complements or substitutes? *Economics of Education Review, 8*, 133–148.

Kantor, H. (1994). Managing the transition from school to work: The false promise of youth apprenticeship. *Teachers College Record, 95*, 442–461.

Keating, D. P. (1990). Adolescent thinking. In S. S. Feldman & G. R. Elliott (Eds.), *At the threshold: The developing adolescent* (pp. 54–89). Cambridge, MA: Harvard University Press.

Klerman, J. A., & Karoly, L. A. (1994). Young men and the transition to stable employment. *Monthly Labor Review*, 31–48.

Krau, E. (1989). The transition in life domain salience and the modification of work values between high school and adult employment. *Journal of Vocational Behavior, 34*, 100–116.

Larson, R. W. (2000). Toward a psychology of positive youth development. *American Psychologist, 55*, 170–183.

Leong, F. T. L., Chao, R. K., & Hardin, E. E. (2000). Asian American adolescents: A research review to dispel the model minority myth. In R. Montemayor, G. R. Adams, & T. P. Gullotta (Eds.), *Adolescent diversity in ethnic, economic, and cultural contexts* (pp. 179–209). Thousand Oaks, CA: Sage

Lerner, R. M., Fisher, C. B., & Weinberg, R. A. (2000). Toward a science for and of the people: Promoting civil society through the application of developmental science. *Child Development, 71*, 11–20.

Levy-Shiff, R. (1994). Individual and contextual correlates of marital change across the transition to parenthood. *Developmental Psychology, 30*, 591–601.

Levinson, D. J. (1978). *The seasons of a man's life.* New York: Ballantine.

Lewis, D., Hearn, J., & Zilbert, E. (1993). Efficiency and equity effects of vocationally focused postsecondary education. *Sociology of Education, 66*, 188–205.

Lord, S. E., Eccles, J. S., & McCarthy, K. A. (1994). Surviving the junior high school transition: Family processes and self-perceptions as protective and risk factors. *Journal of Early Adolescence, 14*, 162–199.

Luthar, S. S., & Zigler, E. (1992). Intelligence and social competence among high-risk adolescents. *Development and Psychopathology, 4*, 287–299.

Marcia, J. E. (1980). Identity in adolescence. In J. Adelson (Ed.), *Handbook of adolescent psychology* (pp. 149–173). New York: Wiley.

Marini, M. M. (1985). Determinants of the timing of adult role entry. *Social Science Research, 14*, 309–350.

Marini, M. M. (1987). Measuring the process of role change during the transition to adulthood. *Social Science Research, 16*, 1–38.

Markus, H., & Wurf, E. (1987). The dynamic of self-concept: A social psychological perspective. *Annual Review of Psychology, 38*, 299–337.

Matula, K. E., Huston, T. L., Grotevant, H. D., & Zamutt, A. (1992). Identity and dating commitment among women and men in college. *Journal of Youth and Adolescence, 21*, 339–356.

Meschke, L. L., Barber, B. L., & Eccles, J. S. (1998, February). *The power of love: Romantic relationships and change in risk-taking behavior.* Paper presented at the biennial meeting of the Society for Research on Adolescence, San Diego, CA.

Miller-Tutzauer, C., Leonard, K. E., & Windle, M. (1991). Marriage and alcohol use: A longitudinal study of "maturing out." *Journal of Studies on Alcohol, 52*, 434–440.

Mortimer, J. T., Finch, M., Shanahan, M., & Ryu, S. (1992). Work experience, mental health, and behavioral adjustment in adolescence. *Journal of Research on Adolescence, 2*, 25–57.

Murnane, Richard J., & Levy, F. (1996). *Teaching the new basic skills : principles for educating children to thrive in a changing economy.* New York: Free Press.

Newcomb, M. D., & Bentler, P. M. (1986). Drug use, educational aspirations, and work force involvement: The transition from adolescence to young adulthood. *American Journal of Community Psychology, 13,* 303–321.

Office of Educational Research and Improvement (1988). *Youth Indicators 1988.* Washington DC: U.S. Government Printing Office.

Osgood, D. W., Wilson, J. K., O'Malley, P. M., Bachman, J. G., & Johnston, L. D. (1996). Routine activities and individual deviant behavior. *American Sociological Review, 61,* 635–655.

Perry, W. G., Jr. (1970). *Forms of intellectual and ethical development in the college years: A scheme.* NY: Holt, Rinehart, & Winston.

Phelan, P., & Davidson, A. L. (Eds.). (1993). *Renegotiating cultural diversity in American schools.* New York: Teachers College Press.

Phinney, J. S. (1990). Ethnic identity in adolescents and adults: A review of research. *Psychological Bulletin, 108,* 499–514.

Prentice, D. A., & Miller, D. T. (1993). Pluralistic ignorance and alcohol use on campus: Some consequences of misperceiving the social norm. *Journal of Personality and Social Psychology, 64,* 243–256.

Rice, K., Cole, D., & Lapsley, D. (1990). Separation-individuation, family cohesion, and adjustment to college: Measurement validation and test of a theoretical model. *Journal of Counseling Psychology, 37,* 195–202.

Roberts, R. E. L., & Bengton, V. L. (1996). Affective ties to parents in early adulthood and self-esteem across 20 years. *Social Psychology Quarterly, 59,* 96–106.

Rumberger, R., & Daymont, D. (1984). The economic value of academic and vocational training acquired in high school. In M. E. Borus (Ed.), *Youth and the labor market: Analysis of the national longitudinal survey.* Kalamazoo, MI: W. E. Upjohn Institute for Employment Research.

Rutter, M. (Ed.). (1988). *Studies of psychosocial risk: The power of longitudinal data.* New York: Cambridge University Press.

Rutter, M., & Garmezy, N. (1983). Developmental psychopathology. In P. H. Mussen & E. M. Hetherington (Eds.), *Handbook of child psychology: Vol. 4. Socialization, personality, and social development* (pp. 775–911). New York: Wiley.

Sadava, S. W. & Pak, A.W. (1994). Problem drinking and close relationships during the third decade of life. *Psychology of Addictive Behaviors, 8,* 251–258.

Sampson, R. J., & Laub, J. H. (1993). *Crime in the making: Pathways and turning point through life.* Cambridge, MA: Harvard University Press.

Savin-Williams, R. C., & Berndt, T. (1990). Friendships and peer relations during adolescence. In S. S. Feldman & G. R. Elliot (Eds.), *At the threshold: The Developing Adolescent.* Palo Alto, CA: Stanford University Press.

Scales, P.C., & Leffert, N. (1999). *Developmental assets: A synthesis of the scientific research on adolescent development.* Minneapolis, MN: Search Institute.

Schulenberg, J., & Maggs, J. L. (2000). *A developmental perspective on alcohol use and heavy drinking during adolescence and the transition to young adulthood.* Report prepared for the National Institute of Alcohol Addiction and Abuse. Ann Arbor, MI.

Schultheiss, D. E. S., & Blustein, D. L. (1994). Role of adolescent-parent relationships and college student development and adjustment. *Journal of Counseling Psychology, 41,* 248–255.

Selman, R. L. (1980). *The growth of interpersonal understanding.* New York: Academic Press.

Sherrod, L. R., Haggerty, R. J., & Featherman, D. L. (1993). Introduction: Late adolescence and the transition to adulthood. *Journal of Research on Adolescence, 3,* 217–226.

Simmons, R. G., & Blyth, D. A. (1987). *Moving into adolescence: The impact of pubertal change and school context.* Hawthorn, NY: Aldine de Gruyter.

Spencer, M. B. (1995). Old issues and new theorizing about African-American youth: A phenomenological variant of the ecological systems theory. In R. L. Taylor (Ed.), *Black youth: Perspectives on their status in the United States* (pp. 37–70). New York: Praeger.

Stattin, H., & Magnusson, D. (1990). Pubertal maturation in female development. In D. Magnusson (Ed.), *Paths through life* (Vol. 1). Hillsdale, NJ: Lawrence Erlbaum Associates.

Steinberg, L. D., & Dornbusch, S. M. (1991). Negative correlates of part-time employment during adolescence: Replication and elaboration. *Developmental Psychology, 27*, 304–313.

Thornton, A., Axinn, W. G., & Teachman, J. (1995). The influence of school enrollment and accumulation on cohabitation and marriage in early adulthood. *American Sociological Review, 60*, 762–774.

Timms, D. W. G. (1996). Social mobility and mental health in a Swedish cohort. *Social Psychiatry and Psychiatric Epidemiology, 31*, 38–48.

Van der Velde, M. E. G., Feij, J. A., & Taris, T. W. (1995). Stability and change of person characteristics among young adults: The effect of the transition from school to work. *Personality & Individual Differences, 18*, 89–99.

Vinokur, A. D., Price, R. H., & Caplan, R. D. (1996). Hard times and hurtful partners: How financial strain affects depression and relationship satisfaction of unemployed persons and their spouses. *Journal of Personality & Social Psychology, 71*, 166–179.

Waterman, A. L. (1982) Identity development from adolescence to adulthood: An extension of theory and a review of research. *Developmental Psychology, 18,* 341–358.

Way, W. L., & Rossmann, M. M. (1996). Family contributions to adolescent readiness for school-to-work transition. *Journal of Vocational Education Research, 21*, 5–35.

Weidman, J. C., & Friedmann, R. R. (1984). The school-to-work transition for high school dropouts. *Urban Review, 16*, 25–42.

Wentzel, K. R. (1991). Social competence at school: Relation between social responsibility and academic achievement. *Review of Educational Research, 61*, 1–24.

Werner, E. E., & Smith, R. S. (1982). *Vulnerable but invincible: A study of resilient children*. New York: McGraw-Hill.

Werner, E. E., & Smith, R. S. (1992). *Overcoming the odds*. Ithaca, NY: Cornell University Press.

Wheaton, B. (1990). Life transitions, role histories, and mental health. *American Sociological Review, 55*, 209–223.

Wigfield, A., Eccles, J., Mac Iver, D., Reuman, D., & Midgley, C. (1991). Transitions at early adolescence: Changes in children's domain-specific self-perceptions and general self-esteem across the transition to junior high school. *Developmental Psychology, 27*, 552–565.

Wigfield, A., Eccles, J. S., & Pintrich, P. R. (1996). Development between the ages of eleven and twenty-five. In D. C. Berliner & R. C. Calfee (Eds.), *The handbook of educational psychology,* (pp. 148–185). New York: Macmillan.

William T. Grant Foundation (1988). *The forgotten half: Pathways to success for America's youth and young families*. Washington, DC: The William T. Grant Commission on Work, Family, and Citizenship.

Wilson, W. J. (1987). *The truly disadvantaged: The inner city, the underclass, and public policy*. Chicago: University of Chicago Press.

Winefield, A. H., & Tiggemann, M. (1989). Unemployment duration and affective well-being in the young. *Journal of Occupational Psychology, 62*, 327–336.

Wong, C., Eccles, J. S., & Sameroff, A. (1998). *Ethic identity as a buffer against racial discrimination*. Unpublished manuscript, under review. Ann Arbor, MI.

Youniss, J. (1980). *Parents and peers in social development*. Chicago: University of Chicago.

Youniss, J., McLellan, J. A., & Yates, M. (1997). What we know about engendering civic identity. *American Behavioral Scientist, 40,* 620–631.

30

Physical Health
and Adult Well-Being

Edward L. Schneider
University of Southern California, Los Angeles

Lucy Davidson
The Center for Child Well-being, Decatur, GA

INTRODUCTION

> Health is a state of complete physical, mental and social well-being, and not merely the absence of disease or infirmity.
>
> —World Health Organization (1948, p. 2)

In its constitution, the World Health Organization addressed the interdependence of physical health and social-emotional well-being along with the appreciation of health as more than freedom from impairment. Although components of health and well-being are mutually interrelated, what role does physical health play in this totality of well-being? The colloquial maxim is, "When you've got your health, you've got everything." But, do you? Most people would not say that positive physical health inevitably produces positive social and emotional well-being. But how essential is physical health as a foundation for other dimensions of well-being? And how dependent is subjective well-being on objective measures of physical health?

An extensive literature relates adult physical health to aspects of overall well-being. These studies are largely point in time snapshots examining quality of life in adult populations with specific physical illnesses or comparisons of general physical health with psychosocial function/satisfaction. Adult physical health is seen as a greater or lesser determinant of well-being according to outcome measures that are weighted more toward functional capacity or subjective satisfaction. Adult onset physical disability affects social and occupational roles in ways that can negatively impact well-being. Additionally, some adult physical conditions have direct brain effects that produce symptoms of depression and thereby diminish well-being. This chapter also provides guidance on health behaviors that affect physical well-being throughout adulthood and enhance quality of life.

LITERATURE REVIEW

Quality of Life and Subjective Well-Being

Recently, the Centers for Disease Control and Prevention (CDC) have developed a combined measure of adult physical health and subjective well-being called the health-related quality of life (HRQOL; CDC, 2000). HRQOL is defined as "an individual's or group's perceived physical and mental health over time" and reported as healthy/unhealthy days in a month. The four questions used to assess HRQOL are self-report items of perception and functional status: (a) self-rated general health, (b) number of days in the past 30 when physical health was not good, (c) number of days in the past 30 when mental health was not good, and (d) number of days in the past 30 with limitations of usual activity due to poor physical or mental health.

When these questions were part of the Behavioral Risk Factor Surveillance System, a continuous, state-based, random telephone survey of adults over 18 living in the community, respondents averaged 24.7 composite healthy days a month. However, younger and older adults showed different proportions of mental and physical health problems. While the average number of healthy days declined only modestly with increasing age, young adults reported worse mental health than the older adults and the older adults reported more physical health problems than younger adults. Perceived mental and physical health also showed little overlap in the total number of unhealthy days reported. Implications of HRQOL are that older, community-dwelling adults' sense of subjective well-being is not markedly influenced by their perceived physical health. This does not address the full spectrum of physical health and well-being, though. Older adults whose physical health is compromised such that they require skilled nursing care or most assisted living arrangements would not appear in the community-based sample. HRQOL surveys cannot completely inform the degree of adaptive functioning or minimum physical health conditions necessary to experience subjective well-being.

Another useful metric for quality of life is the quality-adjusted life-year (QALY). The QALY captures measurement of the quality of life along with length of life. QALYS can be used to compare the life impact of more severe physical impairment than HRQOL because they are not restricted to community-based measurement. As a hypothetical example, if an older adult survives a hip fracture for 4 years but with major decrements to quality of life (QOL) including nursing home placement, their QOL might be 0.5 and the 4 years of remaining life would be counted as 2 QALYS based on $0.5 \times 4 = 2$. If the hip fracture had been prevented and the older adult lived 6 more years in full health, those years would rate 6 QALYS. The net effect of some investment in physical well-being that prevented the hip fracture would be 4 QALYS, not just the 2 additional years of survival. (Gold, Siegel, Russell, & Weinstein, 1996)

Like many qualitative measures, the QOL portion of QALY calculation can vary widely from study to study. In one meta-analysis of health-related quality of life after stroke, QOL estimates ranged from –0.02 to 0.71 for major stroke, from 0.12 to 0.81 for moderate stroke, and from 0.45 to 0.92 for minor stroke (Tengs, Yu, & Luistro, 2001). Additionally, myriad QOL questionnaires and other instruments have been developed for specific disease states because in assessing the effects of treatment, researchers want to inquire about QOL components most likely to be affected by the disease or treatments being compared (Fletcher, 1988) and minimize the respondent time burden. For instance, body image and self-esteem may be QOL components important to measure among breast cancer patients and social isolation more important to track among patients with tuberculosis. Questionnaires may be self-administered or employ trained interviewers and new questionnaires may not go through rigorous determinations of reliability, construct validity, or respondent acceptability (Andresen, Rothenberg, & Kaplan, 1998). All these factors make it difficult to make comparisons across studies or compare the impact of various physical disorders on adult subjective well-being as measured by QOL ratings.

More generic QOL measurements are often combined with objective measures of physical health, such as an exercise tolerance test or tumor staging, to inform the impact assessment of physical health on overall well-being. Five commonly used QOL measurements that have been combined with objective measures across many physical disorders are the Medical Outcomes Trust's Short Form–36 (SF-36), the Physician's QOL Index, the Sickness Impact Profile (SIP), the Quality of Well Being (QWB), and the Patient's Self-Rating Scale (Meyers, Gage, & Hendricks, 2000; Tandon, 1990). Overall QOL shows lower correlation with dimensions of objective physical health than its psychological components. For example, the objective severity of neurological disorders, such as spinal cord injury or ALS (amyotrophic lateral sclerosis), is less associated with diminished patient-rated QOL unless the patient has a co-occurring depressive illness or other psychological disorder (Manns & Chad, 1999; Simmons et al., 2000). Differences between patient- and physician-rated QOL demonstrate physician relative over valuation of physical impairment among functions affecting QOL when QOL is defined similarly to well-being in this book: "Quality of life refers to the capacities to engage in and derive satisfaction from socially and psychologically meaningful thought and behavior" (Meyers et al., 2000).

Physical Domain Is Not Independent of Other Domains

Social and behavioral aspects of aging interact with every element in the physical domain. For example, one of the clearest risk factors for disability in later life is the strength of the social support system available to an older person (Mendes de Leon et al., 1999). Strong social networks not only lower the risk of physical disability but also increase the likelihood of recovery from acute disability. Whereas, depression in later life can separately restrict social networks and increase the risk for physical disability (Steffens, Hays, & Krishnan, 1999). Physical disability, in turn, can circumscribe networks of social support. Other dimensions of social and emotional well-being—self-esteem, optimism, and mastery—predict positive adjustment after adverse health events, such as heart disease with coronary angioplasty (Helgeson, 1999). Therefore, the relative contributions of the physical domain are difficult to separate from the social and psychological domains that influence the health and well-being of older persons.

The Lynds' classic sociological study of community, named Middletown, USA, was based in Muncie, Indiana (Lynd & Lynd, 1929). More recently, older "Middletown" adults were studied to identify factors most associated with their life satisfaction (Morris, 1990). Among community-dwelling adults over 60, subjective physical health status was one of the six variables accounting for most of the variance in overall life satisfaction. The six variables were subjective health status, satisfaction with current home, life satisfaction now compared with young adulthood, contact with someone they trust or confide in, loneliness, and serious consideration of moving to a retirement complex. When asked, "How would you describe general satisfaction with life at the present?" 75% of the older adults responded *excellent* or *good*. Results were interpreted in terms of life satisfaction being upheld by psychological, social, and environmental continuity. Through this lens, physical well-being assumes significance among older adults as a prerequisite to continuity.

The Role of Environmental Factors Increases with Aging

Environmental factors are important in extending physical well-being across the life course. In the Swedish Twin Study, older adult identical and non-identical twins raised together and raised apart were examined for their genetic and environmental contributions to chronic diseases and disorders (Rowe & Kahn, 1998). With aging, the relative impact of the environmental component increased decade by decade. The salience of environmental effects over the life course supports the importance of health behaviors (that determine environmental exposures and conditions) in influencing the quality of health in later life.

Positive Health Behaviors Need to Start in Childhood

Animal studies have supported the role of a nurturing environment in infancy on adult physical well-being. A recent study of mice with the gene for Huntington's chorea, a devastating disease of middle age, showed that animals placed in a nurturing environment during their development had a delay in the onset of their disease (van Dellen, Blakemore, Deacon, York, & Hannan, 2000). Among adults, educational attainment is a strong predictor of health and well-being, even after controlling for income, occupation, and race. Higher education has a compression effect on illness and disability like that shown in animal studies—deferring onset to later in the life course. In these studies, educational attainment may be a marker for multiple psychosocial resources that are developed within the same early environment that supports educational attainment (Barnfather & Ronis, 2000).

   Most of the factors described below that influence physical health and well-being in later life need to be established during childhood. For example, the extent of bone mass development by early adulthood will directly determine the risk of osteoporosis in late life. Thus, childhood consumption of adequate calcium coupled with sufficient physical activity will build up the adequate bone mass that may prevent hip fractures seven decades later. Many health behaviors need to be re-emphasized in early adulthood to sustain their contributions to health promotion and disease prevention. Milk consumption declines in early adulthood (Klesges et al., 1999). Drinking milk and eating dairy products to get enough calcium in the diet, then, is a health behavior that needs to be emphasized in adulthood, as well as childhood and adolescence, in order to prevent disability later in life.

CRITICAL HEALTH BEHAVIORS IN ADULTHOOD

The following health behaviors are most critical in maintaining physical well-being. They are factors that can be promoted by community actions, health care providers, and organizations for older adults. As Surgeon General David Satcher announced with the launch of major, national health goals and objectives called Healthy People 2010, "Building on two decades of success in Healthy People initiatives, Healthy People 2010 is poised to address the concerns of the 21st century … The first goal, which addresses the fact that we are growing older as a Nation, is to increase the quality and years of healthy life" (U.S. Department of Health and Human Services, 2000, Foreword [unnumbered]). The Surgeon General emphasized the quality of healthy life, not only extending longevity. The determinants of adult physical health identified below were selected to emphasize the value-added years that positive physical well-being can add to living.

Restorative Sleep

Sleep is the daily voluntary loss of consciousness that permits the refreshment of the body's resources. Getting sufficient sleep is critical across the life span because it can impact the behavior and health of children and adults (Ancoli-Israel, 1996). Sleep is also one of the critical determinants of successful aging. Those who get, on average, 7 to 8 hours of sleep a night, enjoy the greatest health and longevity. Lack of sleep can cause a variety of ailments, ranging from loss of energy to depression. Chronic sleep deprivation can lead to depression of the immune system and, thus, increase susceptibility to viruses and bacteria.

Getting a good night's sleep becomes increasingly difficult with age (Ancoli-Israel, 1996). It becomes harder to get to sleep, and people wake up more frequently in the middle of the night and have more difficulty falling back to sleep. As a result, they spend more time in bed and yet get less sleep. Older persons also have less slow wave and REM (rapid eye movement) sleep. Older adults also suffer from more sleep disorders, including disordered breathing (apnea) and periodic limb movements in sleep (PLMS; Ancoli-Israel, 1997).

Fortunately, there are several ways to improve sleep. A randomized control study of depressed older volunteers showed that exercise could improve the quality of sleep and reduce their depression (Singh, Clements, & Fiatarone, 1997a). A number of other studies have confirmed the effect of physical exercise on improving sleep (King, Oman, Brassington, Bliwise, & Haskell, 1997).

A proper sleeping environment is another crucial factor in insuring sleep quality. Ambient light and sound can deter sleep. Obvious remedies to reduce light include thick, opaque curtains over windows, skylights, and other routes for light to reach the sleeping environment. Reduction of noise is more difficult but can be accomplished by thick drapes over windows and other techniques to soundproof the sleeping environment. If noise is unavoidable (e.g., the person sleeps next to an interstate highway), then it may be necessary to introduce soothing noises into the environment to offset the disruptive sounds. There are many commercial sound machines that produce the sounds of surf or running water that are helpful. It is also critical to avoid stimulants prior to sleep. Many individuals inadvertently consume caffeine prior to attempting sleep in the form of chocolate or soft drinks. Lastly, alcohol and nicotine (in the form of tobacco smoke), both of which can be stimulants, are frequently consumed at night.

Getting enough sunlight appears to be another important factor in preparing the body for a restful night's sleep. While this may be difficult in northern latitudes during mid-winter, intense light seems to be critical in keeping circadian rhythms intact. It is a particularly difficult problem for institutionalized older persons who frequently wind up sleeping during the day and staying up all night. Interventions to increase light exposure appear to work. A group of older women treated with intense bright morning light had improved quality of sleep (Kobayashi et al., 1999).

As indicated earlier, sleep plays a critical role across the life course but grows increasingly important with age.

Resistance Training

Resistance training comprises those weight-training exercises that strengthen and provide tone to muscles. In practice, this means exercising with lower weights than employed to build muscle bulk but using more repetitions to improve muscle strength and tone. There are few scientists researching the relationship of resistance training to aging. While aerobic exercise has been accepted enthusiastically by baby boomers looking towards health and self-sufficiency in old age, resistance training has not been as widely embraced.

Resistance training has been linked to both decreased disability and increased longevity in older persons. In the landmark study in this area, Fiatarone et al. (1990) started a group of nonagenarian residents on a high intensity weight-training program. The control group received nutritional supplements. Subsequent disability and mortality were then measured in both groups. In the weight-training group, morbidity and mortality were significantly reduced. Since then, a number of studies have demonstrated the beneficial effects of weight training for older individuals (Ades, Ballor, Ashikaga, Utton, & Nair, 1996; McCartney, Hicks, Martin, & Webber, 1995; Snow-Harter, Bouxsein, Lewis, Carter, & Marcus, 1992).

Maintaining independence is the most important physical goal of older persons. This involves the ability to conduct the activities of daily living (ADLs) without assistance. These defined ADLs are the ability to walk, bathe, dress, eat, and toilet. Of these, walking is the most important ADL. Resistance training for the lower extremities is of particular importance because it may prevent disability through insuring the ability to walk and by preventing falls. In a study of outpatient volunteers, resistance training of the lower extremities resulted not only in increased lower body strength but also increased walking speeds (Ades et al., 1996).

Resistance training promotes independence by reducing the impact of several diseases that afflict older adults. These conditions include osteoporosis, depression, osteoarthritis, diabetes, and hypertension. One of the great threats to independence in older persons is a hip fracture, which is usually the result of a fall onto an osteoporotic hip. Weight training is as effective as aerobic exercise in increasing bone mineral density and thus reducing the risk of hip fracture. A study of college women assigned to aerobic exercise or weight training found that both groups had significant but similar improvements in bone mineral density (Snow-Harter et al., 1992).

Resistance training can also be effective in reducing minor depression. In a study comparing a cognitive intervention and weight training three times a week, the weight-training group had a significant reduction in their scores on measures of depression (Singh, Clements, & Fiatarone, 1997b). Many older disabled persons with osteoarthritis of the knee can have lessened disability, increased physical performance, and less pain by participating in either an aerobic exercise or a resistance training program (Ettinger et al., 1997). With aging, the risk for developing Type II diabetes escalates rapidly. Weight training can be effective in the treatment of this condition, reducing the need for glucose lowering mediations (Eriksson, 1999). A prospective study of weight training found that this intervention could lower blood pressure in a group of older persons (Martel et al., 1999).

In summary, weight training can promote independence and reduce the impact of many of the chronic diseases of aging, including osteoporosis, osteoarthritis, depression, hypertension, and diabetes. Resistance training is helpful at all ages but becomes a critical part of the weekly routine after age 40.

Aerobic Exercise

Aerobic exercise is defined as physical activity that increases the heart rate to 75% of maximum capacity. The knowledge base has grown over the last decade to the point where sufficient evidence supports the effect of aerobic exercise on health and longevity. Of all the interventions available to older persons, aerobic exercise has been demonstrated to have the most wide-ranging and consistent beneficial effects. Studies of older Americans have shown that aerobic exercise can increase longevity and improve cardiovascular fitness, cognitive function, mood, sleep, and endurance, as well as protect against many of the chronic diseases and disorders of aging.

Several studies have convincingly demonstrated that lifelong exercise increases longevity. For example, a prospective study of Harvard graduates indicated that longevity was directly related to the amount of physical activity in this group (Lee, Hsieh, & Paffenbarger, 1995; Paffenbarger, Hyde, Wing, & Hsieh, 1986). Vigorous activity produced the best results, followed by moderate activity (Lee & Paffenbarger, 2000). Low levels of physical activity did not have any beneficial effects on longevity. Further analysis of this group indicated that the amount of distance walked, stories climbed, and degree of vigorous activities among these graduates were the most significant predictors of increased longevity (Lee & Paffenbarger, 2000). Even modest walking has been demonstrated to increase longevity (Hakim et al., 1998). Of great importance to today's aging population, current levels of exercise appear to be even more significant than exercise during youth in extending life expectancy (Bijnen, Feskens, Caspersen, Nagelkerke, Mosterd, & Kromhout, 1999).

Aerobic exercise both improves health and prevents a variety of diseases. It improves health by improving mood, sleep, and cardiopulmonary fitness and by helping to maintain weight control. There is abundant anecdotal evidence of the beneficial effects of exercise on mood. However, there are few good published studies in this important area. One 10-week study compared a group of seniors engaged in a low-impact moderate exercise program with a control group and found that the exercising seniors had improved psychological vigor (Engels, Drouin, Zhu, & Kazmierski, 1998).

In the previous section on sleep, the beneficial effects of exercise on sleep were discussed. Aerobic exercise may also assist in weight loss programs, where its chief benefit is maintaining the weight loss (Votruba, Horvitz, & Schoeller, 2000). Aerobic exercise will also help prevent the following diseases and disorders: arteriosclerotic cardiovascular disease, hypertension, diabetes, and osteoporosis.

While aerobic exercise at any age will increase vital capacity, a measure of cardiopulmonary fitness, the increases at older ages are particularly impressive. In a recent study in Japan, 65 seniors were randomly assigned to exercise and control groups. After just 6 months, the exercise group had substantially increased their vital capacity to a level found in those 5 years younger (Tsuji et al., 2000). In addition to improving blood flow to the heart and brain, exercise training also improves peripheral vascular blood flow (Beere, Russell, Morey, Kitzman, & Higginbotham, 1999).

Risk of heart attack and stroke is inversely related to the degree of daily physical activity (Bijnen, Caspersen, Feskens, Saris, Mosterd, & Kromhout, 1998; Ellekjaer, Holmen, Ellekjaer, & Vatten, 2000; Gartside, Wang, & Glueck, 1998; Lee, Hennekens, Berger, Buring, & Manson, 1999). Among the ways that exercise may mediate its protective effect against heart disease is through its beneficial effects on body weight, blood pressure, serum cholesterol, and glucose tolerance (Lee et al., 1999). Hypertension is linked to the absence of vigorous activity (Paffenbarger & Lee, 1997). Furthermore, some hypertension can be successfully treated through a program of aerobic exercise coupled with resistance training (Dengel, Hagberg, Pratley, Rogus, & Goldberg, 1998).

There is a clear association between the risk of developing Type II adult-onset diabetes and the amount of aerobic exercise. The Harvard study of physicians revealed a dose–response association between exercise frequency and risk of Type II diabetes (Manson et al., 1992). The importance of starting an exercise program early in life is underscored by a Japanese study of glucose tolerance in men in their 50s, which showed that those who had the highest levels of physical fitness in their 30s had the best glucose tolerance in their 50s (Takemura, Kikuchi, Inaba, Yasuda, & Nakagawa, 1999).

One of the most important risk factors for a hip fracture is lack of exercise (Kanis et al., 1999). In a study of American women, higher levels of leisure time, sport activity, and household chores and fewer hours of sitting daily significantly reduced the risk for hip fracture (Gregg, Cauley, Seeley, Ensrud, & Bauer, 1998).

Continuance is a major problem for older persons starting an exercise program. Greater efforts need to be directed toward maintaining exercise programs with seniors, as participation declines with age (Sallis et al., 1986). Unfortunately, some of the factors that negatively affect participation are self-efficacy (Oman & King, 1998), being overweight, having physical complaints, and anxiety (Klonoff, Annechild, & Landrine, 1994); most of these are conditions that could be ameliorated by exercise.

The beneficial effects of exercise increase as a function of the time and effort expended in physical activities. Even gardening or housework will improve the chances of health and longevity over those who do not have any physical activities. However, exercising too vigorously may have adverse consequences. Marathoners have an increased frequency of joint problems related to the trauma of excessive running. There is also the additional risk of heart arrythmias for those with very high levels of physical activity (Jensen-Urstad, Bouvier, Saltin, & Jensen-Urstad, 1998).

Nutrition

Nutrition encompasses the nutrients, vitamins, and minerals in our diet that affect our health and well-being. Because nutrition is such an inclusive topic, discussion in this chapter is limited to three significant aspects of nutrition for aging: antioxidant, bone, and heart protection.

Antioxidant Protection.   Oxidative damage is constantly occurring in every body cell. It can be accelerated by smoking, pollution, and certain toxins, such as iron. One of the more dangerous molecules is the free radical of oxygen, the superoxide radical. It is highly reactive and can lead to damage to the cell membrane, proteins, and DNA. The accumulation of free radical oxidative damage has been postulated as being a critical component in the aging of cells, tissues, and organs (Ames & Shigenaga, 1992).

Oxidative damage has been proposed to play a critical role in the formation of several diseases associated with aging, including diabetes (Schleicher, Wagner, & Nerlich, 1997), cardiovascular disease (Bankson, Kestin, & Rifai, 1993), cancer (Loft & Poulsen, 1996), Alzheimer's disease (Christen, 2000), Parkinson's disease (Zhang et al., 1999), and ALS (Ferrante et al., 1997). Low levels of antioxidants have also been implicated in age-related disorders such as macular degeneration (Snodderly, 1995), which is the leading cause of blindness in older Americans.

The appreciation of the role of antioxidants in the diseases of aging has led to the development of clinical trials to assess the effect of antioxidants in the prevention and/or treatment of these conditions. Several large clinical trials are now taking place to assess whether taking supplemental vitamins E and C will reduce the risk of heart attacks and strokes. Studies have shown that antioxidants such as vitamin E may be able to prevent the oxidation of LDL cholesterol, which may play a critical role in stimulating the development of arterial wall damage (Bunout et al., 2000). A trial of very large doses of vitamin E was successful in slowing the progression of Alzheimer's disease, although the effect was not substantial (Grundman, 2000).

The most abundant sources of antioxidants are fruits and vegetables. They not only contain vitamin C, but also many other antioxidants such as lycopene, lutein, zeaxanthine, and beta-carotene. Unfortunately, only about 10% of Americans consume the five to nine portions of fruits and vegetables recommended to prevent diseases related to oxidative damage. Many individuals attempt to get their antioxidants via supplements. However, the average antioxidant supplement contains the amounts of vitamins E and C to meet the RDAs, but not to prevent oxidative damage. Experts in the field of aging research endorse higher levels of antioxidants and the best way to get them is through fruits and vegetables.

Building Strong Bones.   A hip fracture is a devastating event for an older man or woman. A consistent risk factor for a hip fracture is bone mineral density (BMD; Melton, Atkinson, O'Connor, O'Fallon, & Riggs, 1998; Mussolino, Looker, Madans, Langlois, & Orwoll, 1998; Tromp et al., 2000). BMD can be increased by resistance training and aerobic exercise. Smoking, which lowers BMD, increases the risk of hip fracture (Cornuz, Feskanich, Willett, & Colditz, 1999). This risk increases as the number of cigarettes smoked increases. Smoking cessation reduces the risk, which continues for 10 years after cessation (Cornuz et al., 1999). Getting enough calcium to build BMD is a challenge given the low levels of milk and dairy products consumed by Americans (Klesges et al., 1999). Vitamin D is critical for the efficient absorption of calcium. Low vitamin D levels were found in women who fractured their hips (LeBoff et al., 1999). A less clear relationship exists between the risk of hip fracture and protein intake; low protein intake appears to be related to increased risk (Munger, Cerhan, & Chiu, 1999).

The reason for the extremely high frequency of hip fractures in postmenopausal women is that estrogen helps to maintain BMD. Unfortunately, most postmeno-pausal women who have osteoporosis are unaware that they have this condition (MMWR, 1998). Prevention of hip fractures should focus on increasing bone density through exercise, adequate intake of calcium and vitamin D, as well as consid-eration of estrogen replacement therapy for post–menopausal women. Once osteoporosis is diagnosed, a number of treatments are available, including estrogen replacement, calcitonin, and biphosphonates (Deal, 1997).

The hesitancy regarding estrogen replacement therapy is related to the increased risk of breast cancer in women receiving this therapy. An alternative to estrogen re-placement therapy is the use of Specific Estrogen Receptor Modulators (SERMs; Bryant & Dere, 1998; Dhingra, 1999). SERMs have estrogen-like effects, such as building bone density, but do not increase the risk of breast cancer. In fact, one SERM, Tamoxifen, has been successfully used in the prevention of breast cancer (Osborne, 1999). Loss of testosterone with aging places men at greater risk of bone fractures (Seeman, 1999). This is the rationale for the hormone replacement ther-apy of older men who have low testosterone levels. However, this must be weighed with the potential increased risk of prostate cancer and heart disease that testoster-one might induce. Clinical trials are underway to assess the risks and benefits of tes-tosterone replacement therapy.

Preventing Heart Disease.   Heart disease is a leading cause of death among older Americans. Nutrition plays a critical role in the causation of cardiovascular disease. Increased consumption of cholesterol and saturated fats has been known for decades to increase the risk of heart attack and stroke. Furthermore, elevated LDL-cholesterol and a low LDL-cholesterol/HDL-cholesterol ratio were associ-ated with increased incidence of coronary artery disease. Although high blood LDL-cholesterol levels still place older Americans at risk for heart attacks (Benfante & Reed, 1990), this risk diminishes with age. For example, in the Hono-lulu Heart Study of older men, their previous cholesterol levels were a more impor-tant risk factor than their present cholesterol levels for determining risk of coronary artery disease (Hakim et al., 1999). A diet rich in fruits and vegetables will lower risk. As mentioned earlier, antioxidants may prevent the oxidation of LDL-cholesterol, which may be one of the earliest events in arterial wall disease.

Blood homocysteine levels are emerging as another nutrition-related risk factor. Homocysteine blood levels increase with aging (Moustapha & Robinson, 1999). Although there are epidemiological studies which show significant correlations between the risk of heart disease and blood homocysteine level, it is still not clear whether homocysteine is a causative agent or just a marker for another atherogenic process (Christen, Ajani, Glynn, & Hennekens, 2000). Blood homocysteine levels can be lowered effectively by increasing consumption of folic acid and vitamins B6 and B12 (Undas, Domagala, Jankowski, & Szczeklik, 1999; Vermeulen et al., 2000).

National studies of risk factors for heart disease have shown that fish consumption is significantly inversely related to the risk of heart disease (Gartside, Wang, & Glueck, 1998). A more recent analysis of the same data set (NHANES I) suggested that consumption of fish was not related to cardiovascular deaths but was significantly related to decreased overall mortality (Gillum, Mussolino, & Madans, 2000). The substances in fish that have been proposed to be protective are called the long-chain n-3 polyunsaturated fatty acids (PUFAs). As PUFAs are found in fish, they are also called 3-omega fish oils, (von Schacky, 2000). In animal studies and in some preliminary human studies, these PUFAs can prevent arrythmias, which are a common cause of cardiac death (Siscovick et al., 2000).

Consumption of whole grains may be another protective nutritional factor. The comprehensive Harvard Nurses Study has recently shown that consumption of whole grains can significantly lower the risk of heart disease independently of fiber, vitamin B6, vitamin E, and folate content (Liu et al., 1999).

Weight Maintenance

Weight maintenance comprises the maintenance of Body Mass Index (BMI) in the appropriate range. Across most of the life course, extra weight brings extra risk for a variety of diseases including cardiovascular disease, diabetes, certain cancers, and hypertension. There is little question that obesity at any age is dangerous. However, in the last decades of life, it is not clear whether following the National Heart Institute guidelines, which recommend a BMI of less than 25, will promote health and longevity. Recent studies have shown that being slightly overweight in older adulthood may actually extend life expectancy and diminish the risk of disability.

Can a few pounds be protective? One hypothesis is that extra padding around the hips reduces the risk of hip fracture. Total body weight is one of the chief risk factors for a hip fracture (greater weight = lower risk; Ensrud, Lipschutz et al., 1997). Recent loss of weight is another risk factor for hip fracture risk (Ensrud, Cauley, Lipschutz, & Cummings, 1997). Furthermore, a low BMI predicts increased risk of death related to hip fracture (Meyer, Tverdal, & Falch, 1995).

CONCLUSIONS

Physical health has a significant impact on adult well-being through its contribution to independent living, social continuity and connectedness, emotional health, and adaptive functioning. Measures of physical well-being have been developed to assess objective physical status and quality of life. Specific diseases are not necessarily associated with lowered subjective quality of life measures unless emotional disorders, such as depressive illness, are also present.

Positive health behaviors can extend years of life and enhance quality of life among older adults. Most of the positive health behaviors interact with each other. For example, aerobic exercise will promote better sleep, elevate depressive mood, and help with weight maintenance. These health behaviors need to be supported during child development and, once established, maintained across the life course. It is never too early to develop healthy habits that ensure proper nutrition, sleep, aerobic exercise, and weight training. It is also never too late to begin these health habits.

ACKNOWLEDGMENT

The authors would like to thank Rebecca Morris for her assistance in preparing this manuscript.

REFERENCES

Ades, P. A., Ballor, D. L., Ashikaga, T., Utton, J. L., & Nair, K. S. (1996). Weight training improves walking endurance in healthy elderly persons. *Annuals of Internal Medicine*, *124*(6), 568–572.

Ames, B. N., & Shigenaga, M. K. (1992). Oxidants are a major contributor to aging. *Annals of the New York Academy of Sciences*, *663*, 85–96.

Ancoli-Israel, S. (1996). *All I want is a good night's sleep*. St. Louis, MO: Mosby.

Ancoli-Israel, S. (1997). Sleep problems in older adults: Putting myths to bed. *Geriatrics*, *52*(1), 20–30.

Andresen, E. M., Rothenberg, M. P. A., & Kaplan, R. M. (1998). Performance of a self-administered mailed version of the quality of well-being (QWB-SA) questionnaire among older adults. *Medical Care*, *36*(9), 1349–1360.

Bankson, D. D., Kestin, M., & Rifai, N. (1993). Role of free radicals in cancer and atherosclerosis. *Clinics in Laboratory Medicine*, *13*(2), 463–480.

Barnfather, J. S., & Ronis, D. L. (2000). Test of a model of psychosocial resources, stress, and health among undereducated adults. *Research in Nursing & Health*, *23*, 55–66.

Beere, P. A., Russell, S. D., Morey, M. C., Kitzman, D. W., & Higginbotham, M. B. (1999). Aerobic exercise training can reverse age-related peripheral circulatory changes in healthy older men. *Circulation*, *100*(10), 1085–1094.

Benfante, R., & Reed, D. (1990). Is elevated serum cholesterol level a risk factor for coronary heart disease in the elderly? *JAMA*, *263*(3), 393–396.

Bijnen, F. C., Caspersen, C. J., Feskens, E. J., Saris, W. H., Mosterd, W. L., & Kromhout, D. (1998). Physical activity and 10-year mortality from cardiovascular diseases and all causes: The Zutphen Elderly Study. *Archives of Internal Medicine*, *158*(14), 1499–1505.

Bijnen, F. C., Feskens, E. J., Caspersen, C. J., Nagelkerke, N., Mosterd, W. L., & Kromhout, D. (1999). Baseline and previous physical activity in relation to mortality in elderly men: The Zutphen Elderly Study. *American Journal of Epidemiology*, *150*(12), 1289–1296.

Bryant, H. U., & Dere, W. H. (1998). Selective estrogen receptor modulators: an alternative to hormone replacement therapy. *Biologie Medicale*, *217*(1), 45–52.

Bunout, D., Garrido, A., Suazo, M., Kauffman, R., Venegas, P., de la Maza, P., Petermann, M., & Hirsch, S. (2000). Effects of supplementation with folic acid and antioxidant vitamins on homocysteine levels and LDL oxidation in coronary patients. *Nutrition*, *16*(2), 107–110.

Centers for Disease Control and Prevention. (2000, November). *Measuring healthy days*. Atlanta, GA: Author.

Christen, W. G., Ajani, U. A., Glynn, R. J., & Hennekens, C. H. (2000). Blood levels of homocysteine and increased risks of cardiovascular disease: Causal or casual? *Archives of Internal Medicine*, *160*(4), 422–434.

Christen, Y. (2000). Oxidative stress and Alzheimer disease. *American Journal of Clinical Nutrition*, *71*(2), 621S–629S.

Cornuz, J., Feskanich, D., Willett, W. C., & Colditz, G. A. (1999). Smoking, smoking cessation, and risk of hip fracture in women. *American Journal of Medicine*, *106*(3), 311–314.

Deal, C. L. (1997). Osteoporosis: Prevention, diagnosis, and management. *American Journal of Medicine*, *102*(1A), 35S–39S.

Dengel, D. R., Hagberg, J. M., Pratley, R. E., Rogus, E. M., & Goldberg, A. P. (1998). Improvements in blood pressure, glucose metabolism, and lipoprotein lipids after aerobic exercise plus weight loss in obese, hypertensive middle-aged men. *Metabolism*, *47*(9), 1075–1082.

Dhingra, K. (1999). Antiestrogens: Tamoxifen, SERMs and beyond. *Investigational New Drugs*, *17*(3), 285–311.

Ellekjaer, H., Holmen, J., Ellekjaer, E., & Vatten, L. (2000). Physical activity and stroke mortality in women. Ten-year follow-up of the Nord-Trondelag health survey, 1984–1986. *Stroke*, *31*(1), 14–18.

Engels, H. J., Drouin, J., Zhu, W., & Kazmierski, J. F. (1998). Effects of low-impact, moderate-intensity exercise training with and without wrist weights on functional capacities and mood states in older adults. *Gerontology*, *44*(4), 239–244.

Ensrud, K. E., Cauley, J., Lipschutz, R., & Cummings, S. R. (1997). Weight change and fractures in older women. Study of Osteoporotic Fractures Research Group. *Archives of Internal Medicine*, *157*(8), 857–863.

Ensrud, K. E., Lipschutz, R. C., Cauley, J. A., Seeley, D., Nevitt, M. C., Scott, J., Orwoll, E. S., Genant, H. K., & Cummings, S. R. (1997). Body size and hip fracture risk in older women: A prospective study. Study of Osteoporotic Fractures Research Group. *American Journal of Medicine*, *103*(4), 274–280.

Eriksson, J. G. (1999). Exercise and the treatment of type 2 diabetes mellitus. An update. *Sports Medicine*, *27*(6), 381–391.

Ettinger, W. H., Jr., Burns, R., Messier, S. P., Applegate, W., Rejeski, W. J., Morgan, T., Shumaker, S., Berry, M. J., O'Toole, M., Monu, J., & Craven, T. (1997). A randomized trial comparing aerobic exercise and resistance exercise with a health education program in older adults with knee osteoarthritis. The Fitness, Arthritis and Seniors Trial. *JAMA*, *277*(1), 25–31.

Ferrante, R. J., Browne, S. E., Shinobu, L. A., Bowling, A. C., Baik, M. J., MacGarvey, U., Kowall, N. W., Brown, R. H., Jr., & Beal, M. F. (1997). Evidence of increased oxidative damage in both sporadic and familial amyotrophic lateral sclerosis. *Journal of Neurochemistry*, *69*(5), 2064–2074.

Fiatarone, M. A., Marks, E. C., Ryan, N. D., Meredith, C. N., Lipsitz, L. A., & Evans, W. J. (1990). High-intensity strength training in nonagenarians. Effects on skeletal muscle. *JAMA*, *263*, 3029–3034.

Fletcher, A. E. (1988). Measurement of quality of life in clinical trials of therapy. *Recent Results in Cancer Research*, *111*, 216–230.

Gartside, P. S., Wang, P., & Glueck, C. J. (1998). Prospective assessment of coronary heart disease risk factors: The NHANES I epidemiologic follow-up study (NHEFS) 16-year follow-up. *Journal of the American College of Nutrition*, *17*(3), 263–269.

Gillum, R. F., Mussolino, M., & Madans, J. H. (2000). The relation between fish consumption, death from all causes, and incidence of coronary heart disease. The NHANES I Epidemiologic Follow-up Study. *Journal of Clinical Epidemiology*, *53*(3), 237–244.

Gold, M. R., Siegel, J. E., Russell, L. B., & Weinstein, M. C. (1996). *Cost-effectiveness in health and medicine.* New York: Oxford University Press.

Gregg, E. W., Cauley, J. A., Seeley, D. G., Ensrud, K. E., & Bauer, D. C. (1998). Physical activity and osteoporotic fracture risk in older women. Study of Osteoporotic Fractures Research Group. *Annals of Internal Medicine*, *129*(2), 81–88.

Grundman, M. (2000). Vitamin E and Alzheimer disease: The basis for additional clinical trials. *American Journal of Clinical Nutrition*, *71*(2), 630S–636S.

Hakim, A. A., Curb, J. D., Burchfiel, C. M., Rodriguez, B. L., Sharp, D. S., Yano, K., & Abbott, R. D. (1999). Screening for coronary heart disease in elderly men based on current and past cholesterol levels. *Journal of Clinical Epidemiology*, *52*(12), 1257–1265.

Hakim, A. A., Petrovitch, H., Burchfiel, C. M., Ross, G. W., Rodriguez, B. L., White, L. R., Yano, K., Curb, J. D., & Abbott, R. D. (1998). Effects of walking on mortality among nonsmoking retired men. *New England Journal of Medicine*, *338*(2), 94–99.

Helgeson, V. S. (1999). Applicability of cognitive adaption theory to predicting adjustment to heart disease after coronary angioplasty. *Health Psychology*, *18*(6), 561–569.

Jensen-Urstad, K., Bouvier, F., Saltin, B., & Jensen-Urstad, M. (1998). High prevalence of arrhythmias in elderly male athletes with a lifelong history of regular strenuous exercise. *Heart*, *79*(2), 161–164.

Kanis, J., Johnell, O., Gullberg, B., Allander, E., Elffors, L., Ranstam, J., Dequeker, J., Dilsen, G., Gennari, C., Vaz, A. L., Lyritis, G., Mazzuoli, G., Miravet, L., Passeri, M., Perez Cano, R., Rapado, A., & Ribot, C. (1999). Risk factors for hip fracture in men from southern Europe: The MEDOS study. Mediterranean Osteoporosis Study. *Osteoporosis International*, *9*(1), 45–54.

King, A. C., Oman, R. F., Brassington, G. S., Bliwise, D. L., & Haskell, W. L. (1997). Moderate-intensity exercise and self-rated quality of sleep in older adults. A randomized controlled trial. *JAMA*, *277*(1), 32–37.

Klesges, R. C., Harmon-Clayton, K., Ward, K. D., Kaufman, E. M., Haddock, C. K., Talcott, G. W., & Lando, H. A. (1999). Predictors of milk consumption in a population of 17- to 35-year-old military personnel. *Journal of the American Dietetic Association*, *99*(7), 821–826; quiz 827–828.

Klonoff, E. A., Annechild, A., & Landrine, H. (1994). Predicting exercise adherence in women: The role of psychological and physiological factors. *Preventive Medicine*, *23*(2), 257–262.

Kobayashi, R., Kohsaka, M., Fukuda, N., Sakakibara, S., Honma, H., & Koyama, T. (1999). Effects of morning bright light on sleep in healthy elderly women. *Psychiatry and Clinical Neurosciences*, *53*(2), 237–238.

LeBoff, M. S., Kohlmeier, L., Hurwitz, S., Franklin, J., Wright, J., & Glowacki, J. (1999). Occult vitamin D deficiency in postmenopausal U.S. women with acute hip fracture. *JAMA*, *281*(16), 1505–1511.

Lee, I. M., Hennekens, C. H., Berger, K., Buring, J. E., & Manson, J. E. (1999). Exercise and risk of stroke in male physicians. *Stroke*, *30*(1), 1–6.

Lee, I. M., Hsieh, C. C., & Paffenbarger, R. S., Jr. (1995). Exercise intensity and longevity in men. The Harvard Alumni Health Study. *JAA*, *273*(15), 1179–1184.

Lee, I. M., & Paffenbarger, R. S., Jr. (2000). Associations of light, moderate, and vigorous intensity physical activity with longevity. The Harvard Alumni Health Study. *American Journal of Epidemiology*, *151*(3), 293–299.

Liu, S., Stampfer, M. J., Hu, F. B., Giovannucci, E., Rimm, E., Manson, J. E., Hennekens, C. H., & Willett, W. C. (1999). Whole-grain consumption and risk of coronary heart disease: Results from the Nurses' Health Study. *American Journal of Clinical Nutrition*, *70*(3), 412–419.

Loft, S., & Poulsen, H. E. (1996). Cancer risk and oxidative DNA damage in man. *Journal of Molecular Medicine*, *74*(6), 297–312.

Lynd, R. S., & Lynd, H. M. (1929). *Middletown: A Study in American Culture.* New York: Harcourt, Brace, Jovanovich.

Manns, P. J., & Chad, K. E. (1999). Determining the relation between quality of life, handicap, fitness, and physical activity for persons with spinal cord injury. *Archives of Physical Medical Rehabilitation*, *80*, 1566–1571.

Manson, J. E., Nathan, D. M., Krolewski, A. S., Stampfer, M. J., Willett, W. C., & Hennekens, C. H. (1992). A prospective study of exercise and incidence of diabetes among U.S. male physicians. *JAMA*, *268*(1), 63–67.

Martel, G. F., Hurlbut, D. E., Lott, M. E., Lemmer, J. T., Ivey, F. M., Roth, S. M., Rogers, M. A., Fleg, J. L., & Hurley, B. F. (1999). Strength training normalizes resting blood pressure in 65- to 73-year-old men and women with high normal blood pressure. *Journal of the American Geriatrics Society*, *47*(10), 1215–1221

McCartney, N., Hicks, A. L., Martin, J., & Webber, C. E. (1995). Long-term resistance training in the elderly: Effects on dynamic strength, exercise capacity, muscle, and bone. *Journals of Gerontology. Series A, Biological Sciences and Medical Science*, *50*(2), B97–B104.

Melton, L. J., IV, Atkinson, E. J., O'Connor, M. K., O'Fallon, W. M., & Riggs, B. L. (1998). Bone density and fracture risk in men. *Journal of Bone and Mineral Research*, *13*(12), 1915–1923.

Mendes de Leon, C. F., Glass, T. A., Beckett, L. A., Seeman, T. E., Evans, D. A., & Berkman, L. F. (1999). Social networks and disability transitions across eight intervals of yearly data in the New Haven EPESE. *Journal of Gerontology Series B Psychological Sciences–Social Sciences*, *54*(3), S162–S172.

Meyer, H. E., Tverdal, A., & Falch, J. A. (1995). Body height, body mass index, and fatal hip fractures: 16 years' follow-up of 674,000 Norwegian women and men. *Epidemiology*, *6*(3), 299–305.

Meyers, A. R., Gage, H., & Hendricks, A. (2000). Health-related quality of life in neurology. *Archives of Neurology*, *57*(8), 1224–1227.

Morris, D. C. (1990). *Views regarding health, home, and other influences on life satisfaction in Middletown, USA*. (Report No. 316789). Washington, DC: U.S. Department of Education, Office of Educational Research and Improvement. (ERIC Document Reproduction Service No. CG 022 336)

Morbidity and Mortality Weekly Report (MMWR). (1998). Osteoporosis among estrogen-deficient women—United States, 1988–1994. *MMWR*, *47*(45), 969–973.

Moustapha, A., & Robinson, K. (1999). Homocysteine: An emerging age-related cardio-vascular risk factor. *Geriatrics*, *54*(4), 41, 44–46, 49–51.

Munger, R. G., Cerhan, J. R., & Chiu, B. C. (1999). Prospective study of dietary protein intake and risk of hip fracture in postmenopausal women. *American Journal of Clinical Nutrition*, *69*(1), 147–152.

Mussolino, M. E, Looker, A. C., Madans, J. H., Langlois, J. A., & Orwoll, E. S. (1998). Risk factors for hip fracture in white men: The NHANES I Epidemiologic Follow-up Study. *Journal of Bone and Mineral Research*, *13*(6), 918–24.

Oman, R. F., & King, A. C. (1998). Predicting the adoption and maintenance of exercise participation using self-efficacy and previous exercise participation rates. *American Journal of Health Promotion*, *12*(3), 154–161.

Osborne, M. P. (1999). Breast cancer prevention by antiestrogens. *Annals of the New York Academy of Sciences*, *889*, 146–151.

Paffenbarger, R. S., Jr., Hyde, R. T., Wing, A. L., & Hsieh, C. C. (1986). Physical activity, all-cause mortality, and longevity of college alumni. *New England Journal of Medicine*, *314*(10), 605–613.

Paffenbarger, R. S., Jr., & Lee, I. M. (1997). Intensity of physical activity related to incidence of hypertension and all-cause mortality: An epidemiological view. *Blood Pressure Monitoring*, *2*(3), 115–123.

Rowe, J. W., & Kahn, R. L. (1998). *Successful aging*. New York: Pantheon Books.

Sallis, J. F., Haskell, W. L., Fortmann, S. P., Vranizan, K. M., Taylor, C. B., & Solomon, D. S. (1986). Predictors of adoption and maintenance of physical activity in a community sample. *Preventive Medicine*, *15*(4), 331–341.

Schleicher, E. D., Wagner, E., & Nerlich, A. G. (1997). Increased accumulation of the glycoxidation product N(epsilon)-(carboxymethyl)lysine in human tissues in diabetes and aging. *Journal of Clinical Investigation*, *99*(3), 457–468.

Seeman, E. (1999). The structural basis of bone fragility in men. *Bone*, *25*(1), 143–147.

Simmons, Z., Bremer, B. A., Robins, R. A., Walsh, S. M., & Fischer, S. (2000). Quality of life in ALS depends on factors other than strength and physical function. *Neurology*, *55*(3), 388–392.

Singh, N. A., Clements, K. M., & Fiatarone, M. A. (1997a). A randomized controlled trial of the effect of exercise on sleep. *Sleep*, *20*(2), 95–101.

Singh, N. A., Clements, K. M., & Fiatarone, M. A. (1997b). A randomized controlled trial of progressive resistance training in depressed elders. *Journal of Gerontology Series A Biological Sciences–Medical Sciences*, *52*(1), M27–M35.

Siscovick, D. S., Raghunathan, T., King, I., Weinmann, S., Bovbjerg, V. E., Kushi, L., Cobb, L. A., Copass, M. K., Psaty, B. M., Lemaitre, R., Retzlaff, B., & Knopp, R. H. (2000). Dietary intake of long-chain n-3 polyunsaturated fatty acids and the risk of primary cardiac arrest. *American Journal of Clinical Nutrition*, *71*(1 Suppl.), 208S–212S.

Snodderly, D. M. (1995). Evidence for protection against age-related macular degeneration by carotenoids and antioxidant vitamins. *American Journal of Clinical Nutrition*, *62*(6 Suppl.), 1448S–1461S.

Snow-Harter, C., Bouxsein, M. L., Lewis, B. T., Carter, D. R., & Marcus, R. (1992). Effects of resistance and endurance exercise on bone mineral status of young women: A randomized exercise intervention trial. *Journal of Bone and Mineral Research*, *7*(7), 761–769.

Steffens, D. C., Hays, J. C., & Krishnan, K. R. (1999). Disability in geriatric depression. *American Journal of Geriatric Psychiatry*, *7*(1), 34–40.

Takemura, Y., Kikuchi, S., Inaba, Y., Yasuda, H., & Nakagawa, K. (1999). The protective effect of good physical fitness when young on the risk of impaired glucose tolerance when old. *Preventive Medicine*, *28*(1), 14–19.

Tandon, P. K. (1990). Applications of global statistics in analyzing quality of life data. *Statistics in Medicine*, *9*, 819–827.

Tengs, T. O., Yu, M., & Luistro, E. (2001). Health-related quality of life after stroke: a comprehensive review. *Stroke*, *32*(4), 964–971.

Tromp, A. M., Ooms, M. E., Popp-Snijders, C., Roos, J. C., & Lips, P. (2000). Predictors of fractures in elderly women. *Osteoporosis International*, *11*(2), 134–140.

Tsuji, I., Tamagawa, A., Nagatomi, R., Irie, N., Ohkubo, T., Saito, M., Fujita, K., Ogawa, K., Sauvaget, C., Anzai, Y., Hozawa, A., Watanabe, Y., Sato, A., Ohmori, H., & Hisamichi, S. (2000). Randomized controlled trial of exercise training for older people (Sendai Silver Center Trial; SSCT): Study design and primary outcome. *Journal of Epidemiology*, *10*(1), 55–64.

Undas, A., Domagala, T. B., Jankowski, M., & Szczeklik, A. (1999). Treatment of hyperhomocysteinemia with folic acid and vitamins B12 and B6 attenuates thrombin generation. *Thrombosis Research*, *95*(6), 281–288.

U.S. Department of Health and Human Services. (2000, November). *Healthy people 2010: Understanding and improving health* (2nd ed.). Washington, DC: U.S. Government Printing Office.

Van Dellen, A., Blakemore, C., Deacon, R., York, D., & Hannan, A. J. (2000). Delaying the onset of Huntington's in mice. *Nature*, *404*(67–79), 721–722.

Vermeulen, E. G., Stehouwer, C. D., Twisk, J. W., van den Berg, M., de Jong, S. C., Mackaay, A. J., van Campen, C. M., Visser, F. C., Jakobs, C. A., Bulterjis, E. J., & Rauwerda, J. A. (2000). Effect of homocysteine-lowering treatment with folic acid plus vitamin B6 on progression of subclinical atherosclerosis: A randomised, placebo-controlled trial. *Lancet*, *355*(9203), 517–522.

von Schacky, C. (2000). N-3 fatty acids and the prevention of coronary atherosclerosis. *American Journal of Clinical Nutrition*, *71*(1 Suppl), 224S–227S.

Votruba, S. B., Horvitz, M. A., & Schoeller, D. A. (2000). The role of exercise in the treatment of obesity. *Nutrition*, *16*(3), 179–188.

Wannamethee, S. G., Shaper, A. G., Whincup, P. H., & Walker, M. (2000). Characteristics of older men who lose weight intentionally or unintentionally. *American Journal of Epidemiology*, *151*(7), 667–675.

World Health Organization. (1948). *Constitution of the World Health Organization*. Available http://www.who.int/ratebooks/official-records/constitution.pdf

Zhang, J., Perry, G., Smith, M. A., Robertson, D., Olson, S. J., Graham, D. G., & Montine, T. J. (1999). Parkinson's disease is associated with oxidative damage to cytoplasmic DNA and RNA in substantia nigra neurons. *American Journal of Pathology*, *154*(5), 1423–1429.

31

Social and Emotional Engagement in Adulthood

Donald C. Reitzes

Department of Sociology
Georgia State University, Atlanta

INTRODUCTION

As part of the formidable task of conceptualizing adult development, Rowe and Kahn (1997, 1998) defined "successful aging" in terms of three main components. The first two are quite predictable. Successful aging entails: (1) a low probability of disease and disease-related disability; and (2) high cognitive and physical functional capacity. The third component, engagement with life, may have surprised some readers. Engagement with life, they argue, contains interpersonal relations and productive activities. The former includes contacts and transactions with others, exchanges of information, emotional support, and direct assistance; and the latter includes all activities, paid and unpaid that create goods and services of economic value (Rowe & Kahn, 1997). These authors noted it has long been recognized that isolation and lack of connectedness to others are predictors of morbidity and mortality. More recently, they cite a series of MacArthur Foundation supported studies that suggest that social support has positive consequences for both physical and emotional health.

Interpersonal relations and productive activities tend to occur within social roles. In this chapter, symbolic interactionism and identity theory (Burke, 1980; Stryker, 1980) are used to frame the review of social and emotional engagement in adulthood.

Past work has either focused on the broad theoretical processes and consequences of role engagement or on the investigation of specific roles. The challenge is to develop a solid theoretical framework for understanding and measuring engagement and then to review the empirical literature on the processes and consequences of engagement in specific roles. The first task will be to operationally define engagement as the process by which individuals become involved and invested in their roles. Attention will focus on five roles: volunteer, neighbor, friend, church/religious, and grandparent. The next step will be to review both theoretical understanding of the consequence of role engagement and the empirical studies that explore the consequences of role engagement. This will be followed by a consideration of the stability and continuity of social and emotional engagement over the life span, and finally a review of the factors that influence engagement in the five roles.

TECHNICAL ISSUES

Before one can meaningfully consider the measurement of social and emotional engagement, one has to begin with a working understanding or operational definition of what it means. Social engagement suggests the positive character of social interaction or social relations. Indeed, Rowe and Kahn (1997) turned to Durkheim's understanding of social integration to serve as a theoretical foundation for their formulation of engagement. Durkheim ([1897] 1951) argued that suicide was not completely a consequence of psychological processes but systematically related to the quantity and quality of social ties. In particular, he noted that individuals with greater and stronger social ties were less likely to commit suicide. Connections to family, especially marital ties, generate a sense of responsibility and obligation that inhibits acting out a self-destructive impulse. In addition, social ties provide the value and direction to one's life to avoid a sense of worthlessness and meaninglessness that may lead to suicide. Thus, social engagement incorporates both a connection to others and a sense of purpose that is a component of those ties. Rowe and Kahn (1997) proceeded to suggest that social engagement contains two dimensions: activities and social supports. Both have generated a research literature. After briefly reviewing social activity and social support studies, an operational definition of social engagement as a role and identity process will be proposed.

Activity theory (Havighurst & Albrecht, 1953; Tobin & Neugarten, 1961) began with the finding that more active middle-aged and older people tended to be happier and better adjusted. The thesis was that adults find social approval and ego involvement in social activities. Lemon, Bengtson, and Peterson (1972) organized activities into three sets: (1) informal activities, including interactions with relatives, friends, and neighbors; (2) formal activities, including social participation in voluntary organizations; and (3) solitary activities, including watching television, reading, and working on hobbies. The recent research suggests that activities, even Rowe and Kahn's "productive activities," is too general. For example, Lee and Shehan (1989) argued that activities need to be more directly linked to specific other people, such as work friends or adult children, if the positive consequences of activities are to be understood. An understanding of social and emotional engagements needs to be more textured and contextual than a summary measure of all activities. Instead, there must be recognition that activities with specific others or in relation to specific roles may be of differential importance to people and produce different positive consequences.

The last decade has witnessed an explosion of research on the topic social support. Social support refers to helpful activities that lead a person to feel loved and cared, esteemed and valued, and to feel a sense of belonging and connection to a social group or set of other people (Cobb, 1976). In a review of the literature, House, Landis, and Umberson (1988) noted that a broad variety of studies show that "more socially isolated or less socially integrated individuals are less healthy, psychologically and physically, and more likely to die" (p. 540). Recent studies have found that the impact of social support on physical and mental health varies among three factors: (1) the quantity of support (Lin & Ensel, 1984); (2) who is providing the support (Dean, Kolody, & Wood, 1990); and (3) subjective assessment of support (Thompson, et al., 1989).

Operational Definition

The review of the activity and social support literature suggests that social and emotional engagement needs to be understood as more than just a summary of social ties. Indeed, ties to a close friend refer to support of a different kind than ties to a formal organization member. An operational definition of engagement needs to consider the nature and character of social relations and social connections. In addition, the finding that solitary activities may have positive consequences for self-esteem implies that engagement does not necessarily require the physical presence of others to be supportive or beneficial. For example, writing a letter to a friend may provide an individual with the opportunity to feel "needed" or "sharing an experience" with a significant other. Similarly, reading a report may be an important part of being a volunteer. The social support literature also suggests that it is worthwhile to consider the quality of social ties as well as the quantity of support in assessing the contribution of social ties on physical and mental health.

Social and emotional engagement, therefore, must be understood in part as an investment by an individual into a relationship as well as an opportunity for social participation. Rather than proceeding with an operational definition based on either activities or social support, a more parsimonious strategy is to consider emotional and social engagement in terms of role participation and identity construction. Roles, from a symbolic interactionist perspective, are shared norms that apply to the occupants of social positions (Heiss, 1981; LaRossa & Reitzes, 1993). They are systems that enable role occupants, and others with whom they interact, to anticipate future behaviors and to maintain regularity in their social interactions. Roles specify not only knowledge, ability, and motivation but also expectations about the proper extent, direction, and duration of feelings and emotions (Hochschild, 1979). They also may vary in their relation to social positions. Formal roles, such as club member, bank teller, or father, refer to a position in a social organization, group, or institution, while informal roles, such as best friend or lover, identify an interactional or interpersonal position. The meanings for formal and informal roles are not totally fixed and prescribed but there may be more room for variations in the meaning of informal roles. Identities refer to self-meanings in a role (LaRossa & Reitzes, 1993). Thus, within the role of neighbor, individuals construct their identities as a particular or distinctive neighbor. One person may view him/herself as a sociable friend; another may view him/herself as a confident neighbor. Stryker (1980) argued that identities form the units that make up a person's self conception.

Social and emotional engagement could conceivably cover all roles and identities that a person develops in adulthood. However, for the purposes of this review, attention will focus on voluntary roles and exclude occupational and immediate family (spouse, sibling, and parent) roles and identities. Lee and Shehan (1989), reflecting on the finding that friendship interaction positively affects morale among the elderly whereas interaction with an adult child does not, proposed that kinship relations are bound by norms of obligations while friendship ties, in contrast, are based on mutual choice. A consequence is that interaction with friends, if they persist, is more likely to be productive and positive. Beyond the role of friend, this investigation will cover the voluntary roles of neighbor, voluntary member of a formal organization, and (church) religious role. The grandparent role will also be investigated in part because it has the character of a voluntary role. Thoits (1992) found that after family and occupation, the most commonly held roles were that of friend, neighbor, churchgoer, group member, and community volunteer among a representative sample of Indianapolis adults over the age of 18.

Theoretical and Empirical Review

One of the strengths of a symbolic interactionist perspective, as the theoretical framework for social and emotional engagement, is its recognition that role learning is a life-long process that is never complete or finished. Roles are not "scripts" or internalized sets of fully-formed norms; rather, roles entail the active involvement of the person with other people in working out shared meanings of a social position and provide the opportunity for the person to infuse roles with intrinsic and subjective meanings (Stryker, 1980; Turner, 1956). It is helpful to begin by considering role learning and role enactment as the outcome of two processes: (1) "identification of" roles; and (2) "identification with" roles (Reitzes and Mutran, 1994; Stone 1962).

"Identification of" focuses on the processes of learning role meanings. Part of that process includes learning the social meanings shared by occupants of the role (Turner, 1956). Role contents can be formal expectations, such as legal responsibilities and liabilities associated with being a neighbor, or rules and regulations of a voluntary organization. They also can be informally developed but nevertheless share expectations that are part of the culture of a community with respect to the role of neighbor. "Identification of" also contains the complementary process by which actual individuals in specific situations negotiate the more detailed aspects of the role expectations. What emerges from the interaction among actual neighbors is a working definition of what is right and proper in the particular situation and enables individuals to work out unique and idiosyncratic role definitions within the context of a generally shared role (Goffman, 1959). So, in terms of engagement, "identification of" highlights that role learning is an ongoing process that requires the active involvement and participation of a person throughout the duration of role occupancy.

"Identification of" roles focuses on learning the shared contents of roles. The most frequently used measure of role engagement is role occupancy. Does the person belong to a church or voluntary organization? Does he/she interact with others as a neighbor, friend, or grandparent? Variations on role occupancy include measures of breadth or scope of role involvement, including the number of voluntary organization affiliations or number of different types of organizations; and extent or depth of role involvement, such as the frequency of visits with grandchildren or the amount of time spent in role-related activities. By itself, role occupancy is a rather narrow indicator of role engagement and the ways that individuals identify roles.

Another "identification of" role engagement measure deals with the meanings of roles. Recently there has been interest in the meanings and scope of the religious and grandparent roles. Pollner (1989) explored perception of a person's relationship to God, which suggests one of the meanings of the religious role. Divine relationships were measured by three questions that probe perceptions of: (1) closeness to God; (2) frequency of prayer; and (3) frequency of feeling close to a spiritual force. Thomas (1990) used factor analysis and found three underlying dimensions of the grandparent role meanings: (1) symbolic meanings of being a grandparent, such as a valued elder or connecting oneself with the past; (2) nurturance, including perceiving the role to include caretaking responsibility; and (3) authority, interpreting grandparenting as including responsibility for advising and disciplining grandchildren. Similar measures could and should be developed for the other roles. The recognition that roles may have different meanings for people at different stages in the life cycle highlights that variations in role meanings may influence role outcomes.

"Identification with" refers to the processes by which an individual invests roles with intrinsic self meanings. Foote (1951) argued that roles, viewed merely as status and position, are "empty bottles of behaviors and formal relations" and would be poor predictors of behavior. It is the infusion of self into roles that accounts for interests, involvements, and motivated action in social situations. Five variables capture some of these dimensions of role engagement.

Probably the most common qualitative assessment is role satisfaction, which taps how happy or satisfied one is with membership in a voluntary organization, neighbor, religious or friend role, or being a grandparent. Wheaton (1990) argued that the consequences of role loss depend on whether a person is satisfied in the role. So, the loss of a satisfying role increased stress, while the loss of a dissatisfying role, such as a divorce from an unhappy marriage, may reduce depression and anxiety. Similarly, Keyes (1995) reported results that suggest that being positive about one's roles increases a person's well-being.

Commitment suggests an investment of self into a role. Stryker and Serpe (1994) identified two dimensions of commitment. Interactional commitment refers to the social networks and personal relationships that a person would lose and miss if he/she lost a role. It recognizes that as a result of role occupancy, a person develops valued social ties that enhance the personal stake in the role. Thus, Stryker and Serpe have probed respondents about their involvement in student organizations and whether they had met any friends through student activities to measure interactional commitment to the college student role. Affective commitment measures a sense of personal attachment to a role. Measures include items that tap subjective attachment or a sense of personal loss if one was no longer a role occupant. Johnson, Caughlin, Huston (1999) identified three types of commitment: (1) personal commitment, which is similar to affective commitment and refers to the positive attractions of staying in a role; (2) moral commitment, a sense of moral obligation to stay in a role and role relationships; and (3) structural commitment, similar to interactional commitment, and refers to irretrievable investments in a role.

Salience as defined by Stryker (1980) refers to the probability of invoking a role. Individuals choose to enact more salient roles more frequently and in more diverse settings. Stryker and Serpe (1994) measured student role salience by asking respondents, " How likely would it be upon meeting a person for the first time to identify yourself as a student?" For the grandparent role, measures of salience would be to ask respondents how likely it would be to announce that you are a grandparent upon meeting someone at a party or social event, showing friends pictures of grandchildren, or displaying pictures of grandchildren at work. Centrality measures the importance that a person attributes to a role. Measures could include asking respondents to rank order their role, to identify their three most important roles, or to assess the importance of one or more roles. Stryker and Serpe (1994) found that centrality and salience measures were correlated but not identical and that they independently influenced time in the student role.

Identity meanings are the meanings that individuals attribute to themselves in a role (Burke, 1980). Mortimer, Finch, and Kumka (1982) defined four meaning dimensions among late adolescents that remained stable over time and influenced their adaptation to adult roles. Reitzes and Mutran (1994) adapted three of these dimensions to measure identity meanings in roles in middle and old age: (1) competent is an evaluation dimension that captures a sense of self as active and successful in a role; (2) confident is an affective dimension with identity meanings of being relaxed, happy and confident in a role; and (3) sociable refers to being interested in others with meanings such as warm, open, and social; they found that competent identity meanings in the worker role, confident meanings in the parent role, and sociable meanings in the spouse role influence self-esteem among middle-aged working men and women.

Outcomes of Role Engagement

Social engagement as a component of "successful aging" (Rowe & Kahn, 1998) is proposed to have beneficial consequences for adults. Similarly, a theoretical understanding of social activities (Lemon et al., 1972), social support (House, et al., 1988), and roles and identities (Stryker & Serpe, 1994) suggests that engagement should encourage both physical and mental health. This section reviews research findings that investigate the consequences of role engagement.

Most research articles on engagement in the roles of volunteer, neighbor, friend, religious participant, or grandparent dealt either with characteristics of the role occupants or with identifying factors that influence role performance. There has been much less attention to the issue of role outcome or the consequences of role engagement. The studies that do explore the outcomes of role engagement on a person's health and well-being have typically focused on the role participation. However, role engagement is a much broader and more extensive process. Much less studied have been the consequences of "identification with" roles such as outcomes of increased commitment or importance of a role or the beneficial consequences of a positive identity in a role.

STABILITY AND CONTINUITY OF LIFE SPAN

Theoretical Concepts

Robert C. Atchley, in a professional career that spans over thirty years, has focused on the issue of continuity in human behavior and on the question of how to explain the findings that a large proportion of older adults show considerable consistency over time in their patterns of activity and social relationships (Atchley, 1999). He proposed that a powerful motivation for people is to actively and intentionally strive to maintain stability and continuity as they adapt to the present and plan for the future. His continuity theory contains four elements: internal continuity; external continuity, adaptative capacity, and developmental goals. Individuals are also motivated to maintain consistent self concepts. Atchley described internal continuity in terms of three self concepts that motivate behavior: (1) personal agency or self-confidence; (2) personal goals; and (3) emotional resilience.

Using a data set derived from a twenty-year longitudinal quantitative study (i.e., the Ohio Long-Term Care Research Project) of a small midwestern town beginning in 1975, Atchley investigated the impact of earlier self-confidence on later self-confidence. Regression analysis revealed that the strongest factor that explained self-confidence in 1977 was self-confidence in 1975. Similarly, self-confidence in 1977 had a strong positive effect on self-confidence in 1981, as did self-confidence

Table 31.1

Summary of Research on Outcomes of Role Engagement

Researchers	Roles	Population Studied	Constructs in Measures	Outcomes	Effects
Young & Glasgow (1998)	Volunteer	Men and women ≥ 60 in non-Metropolitan Middle Atlantic Region	Instrumental social participation	Perceived heath	(+) effect for men and women
			Expressive social participation	Perceived health	(+) for women
Musick, Herzog, & House (1999)	Volunteer	Men and women ≥ 65 (national sample)	Number of voluntary groups and time in role	Mortality	(↓) with strongest effect for those volunteering for only one organization
Lee & Shehan (1989)	Volunteer, Neighbor, Friend	Men and women ≥ 55 living in state of Washington	Frequency of interaction in role	Self-esteem	(+) effects of friends for both men and women
					(+) effect of volunteering for women
Goudy & Goudeau (1982)	Friend, Volunteer, Neighbor	Men and women ≥ 55 living in Iowa	Number of friends, number of voluntary association memberships, number of known local people, community attachment	Life satisfaction, Quality of life	(+) effects of friends and neighbors on both outcomes
					(+) effect of volunteer ties on quality of life
					(+) effects of community attachment (identification with neighbors) on both outcomes
Roberto & Scott (1984)	Friend, Neighbor	Urban, middle class women ≥ 65 in one locality	Equity in giving and receiving help	Morale	(↑) for equitably benefitted women vs. overbenefitted women

Study	Role	Sample	Role meanings	Outcome	Findings
					(↑) for underbenefitted vs. overbenefitted woman
					(0) difference between equitably and underbenefitted women
Pollner (1989)	Religious role	Adults ≥ 18 (national sample)	Role meanings ("divine relations")	General satisfaction, Happiness, Life excitement, Life satisfaction with place of residence, non-work activities, family life, friendship & health	(+) effect of divine relations on all 4 outcomes
Ellison, Gay, & Glass (1989)	Religious role	Adults ≥ 18 (national sample)	Denominational affiliation, frequency of attendance, devotional intensity	Life satisfaction	(+) effect of being Baptist, southern Baptist and "other" Baptist; (+) effect of attendance; (+) effect of devotional intensity
Ellison (1991)	Religious role	Adults ≥ 18 (national sample)	Religious identity meaning ("existential certainty"); Religious role meanings ("divine interactions")	Life satisfaction, Happiness	(+) effects of divine interactions and existential certainty on life satisfaction; (+) effect of existential certainty on happiness
Thomas (1990)	Grandparent	Men and women 43 to 86 years old in Wisconsin	Grandparent role meanings (nurturance, symbolic meaning)	Moral, Self-esteem	(+) effect of role meanings (nurturance) on morale; (−) effect of role meaning (symbolic importance) on self-esteem

433

in 1981 on self-confidence in 1991 and self-confidence in 1991 on 1995. Continuity in self-confidence completely overshadowed the effects of social background characteristics and health.

External continuity refers to social arrangements people create to meet their needs and included lifestyle factors such as living arrangements, household composition, marital status, and income adequacy, as well as activities such as employment activities, volunteer services, social activities, and family activities. Investigating the pattern of activities across data collected in 1975, 1977, 1979, 1981, 1991, and 1995, regression analysis revealed that earlier activity levels, measured as overall aggregate, consistently and powerfully influenced later activity levels. Similarly, activity levels in 1975 had the single strongest effect on activity levels in 1995. Other factors considered included age, education, gender and health in 1995. Two other patterns are noteworthy. First, looking at patterns of change, Atchley found that over 51% of his respondents had maintained continuity in their patterns of activity from 1975 to 1995; 3% increased and 38% decreased their activities, 4% experienced a decline but then returned to their previous level of activities, and 4% experienced intermediate increases but eventual declines in activities. Second, over the twenty years, a majority of respondents demonstrated continuity in levels of being with friends, being with children, attending church, gardening, and reading. Atchley (1999) concluded that continuity of activities was the norm.

The third element is adaptive capacity. It focuses on the process by which individuals adjust and respond to changes in physical and social circumstances. Adaptive capacity contains resources, such as adequate income, good health, physical functioning, and adequate social support; but it also includes the anticipation of problems and the creation of conditions that neutralize potential difficulties. Examples of these coping strategies include a positive outlook, sustained relationships, articulated personal goals. Atchley distilled his quantitative and qualitative data into four patterns or styles that reflect how people cope with functional limitations over time: (1) consolidation, the offsetting of losses in some activities due to functional limitations by increasing other activities; (2) decline with continuity, captures reduced activities level as a result of functional limitations but in a wide variety of customary activities; (3) decline with some offsetting increases, by which respondents were able to maintain a positive outlook by remaining at least partially involved in their customary activities; and (4) disengagement, which reflects people who stopped participating in customary activities with leads to declines in activities and declines in morale. The data reveal that more than 41% of respondents had adopted the consolidation approach, 17% following the decline with some offsets approach, and 21% in each of the remaining modes.

Why is there consistency in behavior throughout the life span? Atchley (1999) proposed that the desire to maintain internal consistency, adequate resources and support provided by the external social environment, and active individuals applying adaptive strategies, are three elements or partial answers. The fourth element is goals for personal development. Atchley suggested that consistent application of personal goals provides directions for action and yardsticks to evaluate individual decisions and aspirations. To test this proposition, he compared the importance attributed to 17 goals in 1975 with responses to the same list 20 years later. Consistency was defined as either having the same score over the six waves of data collection or having a score that fluctuated but was either still important or unimportant to the respondent. The findings revealed that there was 90% consistency in self goals, such as being self-reliant or doing things for others, over the 20 years; 80% consistency in goals relating to others or being a religious person; and at least 50% consistency in goals related to socioeconomic status, such as having a satisfying job or being prominent in the community.

While Atchley's continuity theory does not explicitly apply a symbolic interactionist perspective or role engagement, it is clear that his discussion of internal consistency reflects the theme that individual desire to maintain self concepts; and external consistency recognizes the importance of social support in role engagement. Further, goals for personal development can be understood as part of the process of learning and negotiating role meanings; while coping strategies emerge as individuals strive to maintain role commitments and support identity meanings.

Empirical Findings

One of the most interesting sets of findings that explore the longitudinal aspects of role engagement was reported by Moen et al. (1992). They were particularly curious about the implications of role engagement in early adulthood on health outcomes later in adulthood. The study drew on data from a two-wave sample of women living in upstate New York in 1956 and reinterviewed thirty years later in 1986. While the overall number of roles occupied in 1956 did not influence either duration of physical health or mental health, involvement in clubs and organizations in 1956 did have a statistically significant positive effect on health measures in 1986, as well as continued participation in voluntary roles. A role engagement perspective suggests that participation in voluntary organizations may have contributed to positive self conception and health in 1956 and continued to serve as a reference for good health and self conception later in life.

Taken as a whole, the longitudinal findings suggest that there are long-term effects of role engagement. Involvement in voluntary organization roles early in adulthood had positive consequences for women thirty years later (Moen et al., 1992); and adolescents who participated in volunteer activities were less likely to be engaged in criminal behavior four years later (Uggen & Janikula, 1999). In addition, patterns of role engagement persist over time. Participation in voluntary organizations when young adults were in their twenties increased the likelihood of their participating in the same kind of organizations in their thirties (Janoski, Musick, & Wilson, 1998; Janoski &Wilson, 1995). However, the long term effects of role engagements may be different for men and women due to a combination of gender socialization and work histories (Rotolo, 2000).

TABLE 31.2

Summary of Research on Longitudinal Effects of Role Engagement

Researchers	Roles	Population Studied	Time Interval or Dates	Constructs or Measures	Outcomes	Effects
Moen et.al (1992)	Volunteer	Women living in upstate NY	1965 & 1986	Membership in organizations or clubs	Health	(+) effect of voluntary role in 1956 on health in 1986
Uggen & Janikula (1999)	Volunteer	Adolescents in St. Paul, Minnesota	1988–1995	Volunteer work	Criminal arrests	(−) effect of volunteering on arrests 4 years later
Janoski & Wilson (1995)	Volunteer	High school students (national sample)	1965 1973 1982	Community-oriented volunteering	Number of organizational memberships	(+) effect of community involvement of subjects in their 20s on subjects in their 30s
Janoski & Wilson (1995)	Volunteer	High school students (national sample)	1965 1973 1982	Volunteer work (early)	Volunteer work (later)	(+) effect of early volunteering or later volunteering
Fischer & Oliker (1983)	Friend	Adults in Northern California	Cross-sectional data	Social participation	Number of friends	Young married women who worked had same number of friends as men
						(−) effect of leaving labor force on friends for young women but not men
						Between ages 34-64, women gained friends while men lost them
						By age 65, women had more friends then men

Study	Type	Sample	Time	Predictors	Outcome	Findings
Rotolo (2000)	Volunteer	Adults in 10 Nebraska communities	Cross-sectional	Marriage, children, employment	Joining voluntary organizations	(+) effects of marriage and having young children for men
						(+) effect of working full-time and school-aged children for women Leaving volunteering organizations
					Leaving voluntary organization	(+) effect of employment status on leaving voluntary organizations for men and women
						(+) effect of school-aged children on leaving rates for women but not men
Somary & Stricker (1998	Grandparent	Men & women before and after birth of first grandchild	1–2 years	Gender, satisfaction	Role satisfaction	Grandmothers more satisfied then grandfathers
King & Elder	Grandparent	Men and women in rural Iowa	1989	Knowing ones own grandparents	Involvement with grandchildren	(+) effect of knowing ones own grandparent on involvement with grandchildren

Table 31.3

Summary of Research on Factors that Affect Role Engagement

Researchers	Roles	Population Studied	Constructs or Measures	Antecedent Factors	Effects
Wilson & Musick (1997a)	Volunteer	Adults > 25 (national sample)	Volunteering	Human Capital	(+) effect of human capital on volunteering
				Social Capital	(+) effect of social capital on volunteering
				Cultural Capital	(+) effect of cultural capital on volunteering
Wislon & Musick (1997b)	Volunteer	Adults > 25 (national sample)	Volunteering	Self-directed occupations	(+) effect of self-directed occupations on volunteering
Wilson & Musick (1998)	Volunteer	Adults > 21 (national sample)	Volunteering	Formal social interaction, social capital, number of friends	(+) effects of formal social interaction, social capital, and number of friends on volunteering
Wilson & Musick (1999)	Volunteer	Adults > 25 (national sample)	Volunteering over time	Human Capital, Social Capital	(+) effects of human capital and social capital in volunteering over 3 periods
Lammers (1991)	Volunteer	Adult volunteers at a crisis information telephone service (one locality)	Continued volunteering	Identity meanings, interpersonal ties to other volunteers	(+) effects of identity meanings and interpersonal ties on continued volunteering
Okun (1994)	Volunteer	Adults 60 $\geq$	Frequency of volunteering	Identity Meanings	(+) effect of identity meanings on frequency of volunteering
Penner & Finkelstein (1998)	Volunteer	Adult volunteers for a HIV/AIDS organization	Extensiveness of participation	Satisfaction with organization	(+) effect of satisfaction with organization on extensiveness of participation
				Commitment to role	(+) effect of commitment to role on extensiveness of participation

Lee, Piliavin & Call (1999)	Volunteer (blood donor)	Adults ≥ 19 (national sample)	Intention to donate blood, money, or time	Past identity	(+) effects of past identity on intention to donate blood, money or time
Verbrugge (1983)	Friend	White males 21–64 years old in Detroit	Contact with friends	Social background factors	(+) effects of young and elderly adults, never-married, students, production workers and sales on contact with friends
					(+) effects of friends with similar marital status, political preference and residential proximity on contact with friends
Milardo (1982)	Friend	University students	Friendship ties	Intimate ties	(+) effect of network overlap
Waite & Harrison (1992)	Friend	Women between 44–56 years old (national sample)	Contact with friends	Social background	(+) effects of employment health and income
Logan & Spitze (1994)	Neighbor	Adults ≥ 40 living in Albany - Schenectady - Troy. NY	Family neighbors & local ties	Length of residence	(+) effects of length of residence and family neighbors on local lies
Campbell & Lee (1992)	Neighbor	Adults in selected Nashville, TN neighborhoods	Contact with neighbors	Gender	Women knew more of their neighbors by name and talked to them more than men
				Age	Young and old adults have less contact with neighbors than middle-aged adults
				Marriage	(+) effect of contact with neighbors
Ellison & London (1992)	Neighbor	African-American adults (national sample)	Neighborhood participation	Social background	(+) effects of income, gender, and age on neighborhood participation
				Self-esteem	(+) effect on neighborhood participation

continued on next page

TABLE 31.3 (continued)

Researchers	Roles	Population Studied	Constructs or Measures	Antecedent Factors	Effects
Ellison & Sherkat (1995)	Religious role	African-American adults (national sample)	Attend church services	Region social background	Blacks in rural south attend church services more then blacks in other regions
					(+) effects of age, female, married, and education
Ross (1990)	Religious role	Adults > 18 in Illinois	Role meanings (personal efficacy & trust in God)	Religious affiliation and social background	(−) effects of people with no affiliation and age
					(+) effects of men and education
Krause (1991)	Religious role	Adults ≥ 60 (national sample)	Role frequency and role subjectivity (centrality & salience)	Gender and race	(+) effects of women and blacks on attending church and higher subjective religiosity scores
Whitbeck, Hoyt, & Huck (1993)	Grandparent	Parents of 7th graders and their parents in a Midwest state	Role contract and quality	Proximity and parents	(+) effects of parents on contact and quality of ties between grandparents and grandchildren
Thomas (1990)	Grandparent	Grandparents in Wisconsin	Role satisfaction and role important	Gender	Grandmothers had greater role satisfaction Grandfathers place greater emphasis on role
King & Elders (1998)	Grandparent	Families in Iowa	Role meanings (self-efficiency)	Contact with parent and grandchildren	(+) effect of contact with parents
					(+) effects of role quality and role activity

Factors that Affect Role Engagement

As noted earlier, most of the current empirical work on role engagement is devoted to identifying factors that influence role performance. Wilson, in a series of articles, has developed an integrated theory of volunteer work based on three contributing forms of capital. The model may be applied to factors that influence all five roles. Human capital refers to resources, such as education, income, and health, that enable individuals to make productive activities possible. Social capital identifies the resources that may be associated with social connections such as information and trust that increase the likelihood of role engagement. Wilson and Musick (1997a) measure social capital with two indicators: informal social interaction and number of children in the household. Cultural capital reflects values and beliefs that encourage participation and was measured by religiosity as indicated by church attendance, practicing prayer, and extent to which the person values helping others. Findings revealed that: (1) among the human capital variables, socioeconomic status had a positive effect on volunteering; (2) both of the social capital variables, number of children in the household and number of informal interactions, have positive effects on volunteering; and (3) the values of helping and religiosity, the two cultural capital variables, exert positive effects on volunteer behavior. Thus, each kind of capital contributes to voluntary role participation and by extension may influence engagement in other roles. Although not as numerous, other studies explored the impact of "identification with" factors, such as identity meanings, commitment, and salience, on role engagement (e.g., Lammers, 1991; Lee, et al., 1999; Okun, 1994; Penner & Finkelstein, 1998). These studies suggest that the process of infusing roles with self meanings influence role performance and behavior.

CONCLUSIONS

Past empirical and theoretical works on adult development, including Rowe and Kahn's (1977) "successful aging," have described the positive outcomes of social and emotional engagement in terms of social activities and social support. A persistent problem with this approach is that not all activities and social ties are equally important or beneficial to a person. Not only are summary measures of all relationships difficult to interpret, but also specific ties need to be understood in their own social context. Ties to a close friend refer to support of a different kind than ties to a formal organization member. In addition, research needs to focus not only on the quantity but the quality of the social relationships to fully appreciate the beneficial consequences of social engagement. Therefore, social and emotional engagement must be understood as an individual's investment in relationships as well as an opportunity for social participation.

Symbolic interaction and identity theory (Stryker, 1980) provides a parsimonious perspective by considering engagement as the ongoing process of participating in roles and constructing identities. Engagement could conceivably cover all roles and identities. However, for the purpose of this review, attention focused on the five adult roles of voluntary organization member, neighbor, friend, church/religious organization member, and grandparent. "Identification of" the role, begins with the learning of shared social meanings and expectations that identify occupants of a social position. Role contents may be formal, such as legal responsibilities of being a member of a voluntary organization, or informal, such as the expectations for being a good neighbor or friend. Role measures include role occupancy and the number and frequency of role interactions, and the extent or depth of the role involvement; but also measures of the shared content and meanings of roles.

Role learning also entails establishing self-meanings, or an identity, in a role. It is the fusion of self and role, the "identification with" the role that accounts for motivated action in social situations. Five measures capture some of the ways that individuals add self meaning and affect to their roles. Role satisfaction taps how satisfied one is with his/her role. Commitment refers to an individual's social and personal "stake" or investment in a role. Salience, in turn, describes the willingness of a person to invoke a role and be acknowledged as a role occupant. Centrality reflects the importance that a person attributes to a role. Lastly, identity meanings indicate the ways that a person views her/himself in a role. One of the first conclusions to be drawn from the review of the literature is that most research still employs a very limited set of measures, often only role occupancy, to investigate role engagement. A negative consequence of this practice is to potentially seriously underestimate the impact of the personal meanings of social and emotional engagement.

What are the consequences of role engagement? Several theoretical orientations suggest that role engagement is expected to have a positive effect on psychological well-being and physical health. Beginning with the latter, a dramatic demonstration of the outcome of role engagement was provided by Moen et al. (1992). They found that involvement in clubs and organizations influenced the physical health of women thirty years later. The findings suggest that engagement in voluntary organization roles may have directly influenced physical health or indirectly influenced health through their contribution to positive self conceptions. Two other studies found that social participation and voluntary group membership have positive effects on health for men and women aged 60 and over (Musick, Herzog, & House, 1999; Young & Glasgow, 1998). These findings support the expectation that role participation influences physical health, sometimes 30 years later. However, the measures of role engagement were limited to role occupancy. Future research would benefit by including more "identification with" measures.

A more extensive set of role engagement variables have been used to explore the impact of roles on psychological well-being. Two studies reported that interactions with friends and neighbors have positive effects on self-esteem and life satisfaction for older adults (Goudy & Goudeau, 1982; Lee & Shehan, 1989); while a measure that resembles commitment to the community or neighbor role was the single strongest factor to influence life satisfaction (Goudy & Goudeau, 1982). Turning to the religious role, measures of religious role meanings and the religious identity influenced well-being and happiness (Ellison, Gay, & Glass, 1989; Pollner, 1989); and Thomas (1990) explored the implications of several grandparent role meanings and found that some role meanings increased but others decreased self-esteem. Taken as a whole, these findings suggest a promising possibility for future research. The inclusion of a broad range of role and identity variables may demonstrate the consistent and positive impact of role engagement on well-being.

By far, most work on role engagement has concentrated on identifying factors that influence role occupancy. Seven trends emerge when one looks at factors that influence role engagement across the five roles. Earlier levels of role involvement tend to influence later levels of involvement (#1). Atchley (1999) proposed that stability and continuity is powerful motivation for people and found that role activities in 1975 were the single strongest predictors of role activities twenty years later in 1995. Moen et al. (1992) found this to be true for the volunteer role over a 30 year period; while Janoski and Wilson (1995) found that volunteering in one's twenties predicts volunteering in one's thirties. Putman (2000) recognizes that there tends to be stability in patterns of involvement but noted that there are generational differences in social engagement. Older cohorts were very engaged in social activities and have been replaced by less-involved adults. Generational differences in values as well as levels of engagement may persist over time.

Three important themes were foreshadowed in Fischer and Oliker's (1983) study of the role of friend. First, they found that there were differences in role engagement by gender but subtle differences that seem to reflect combinations of gender socialization and labor force participation (#2). Thus, while men and women had the same total number of friends, young, childless women who worked had fewer friends than young men, while marriage and having children had a stronger effect on the friendship patterns of women than on men. Similarly, Somary and Stricker (1998) found that while women were more satisfied with the grandparent role than men, both men and women scored higher than they expected on role satisfaction and there were no differences by gender in interaction with grandchildren.

Second, work role characteristics, such as employment status and occupation, as well as family factors, such as being married and having children, powerfully influence engagement in other roles (#3). Rotolo (2000) found that for men, marriage increased rates of joining voluntary associations as did having young school-aged children; while for women, working full-time and having school-aged children increased rates of joining voluntary associations. Work and family role affect the time and opportunity for other roles. But the issue is also the relative salience of one's roles. Adults order roles in salience hierarchy with more salient roles occupying more time and being invoked in more varied situations. Waite and Harrison (1992) studied how middle-aged women balance their roles. They found that middle-aged women give priority in their allocation of their time first to children or other relatives who live with them, followed by children and parents who live outside the home, then siblings and in-laws, and finally friends. The findings suggest that it is critical to investigate role engagement in the context of a person's hierarchy of roles and identities.

Third, Fischer and Oliker's (1983) findings suggest that patterns of role engagement may vary by stage in the life cycle (#4). So, by age 65, women who earlier in their lives tended to have fewer friendship ties than men, report more friends than did men. Campbell and Lee (1992) found that age was curvilinearly related to neighborhood networks with young and old adults having less contact with neighbors than middle-aged adults, while marriage was associated with larger networks within the neighborhood. Roberto (1990) noted that timing of grandparenthood influences the quality of the role experience with "on-time" grandmothers feeling more comfortable in the role than "early" grandmothers.

Three other themes emerge across the study of the five roles. As one would expect, resources, what Wilson and Musick (1997a) call "human capital" including education, income, and health, facilitate role activities and engagement (#5). They found that socioeconomic status has a positive effect on volunteering; in addition, Wilson and Musick (1997b) reported that people employed in self-directed occupations and self-employment are more likely to volunteer; while Wilson and Musick (1999) concluded that education also increases the likelihood of continued volunteering over time. Similarly, Krause (1991) found that adults with health problems and financial difficulties attend church less than other adults.

Among the five adult roles under consideration, engagement in one role may encourage engagement in other roles (#6). So, for example, Wilson and Musick (1998) found that church attendance and interactions with friends and neighbors were among the factors that tend to increase volunteering. Logan and Spitze (1994) concluded that neighboring and neighborhood ties are increased when adult children or parents live in the same neighborhood. Ellison and London (1992) reported that participation in voluntary organizations had a positive effect on interactions with neighbors for a sample of African Americans. Returning for a moment to family ties, Whitbeck, Hoyt, and Huck (1993) conclude that parents (adult children) served as mediators of both the quality and the frequency of grandparent-grandchildren interactions.

Finally, there is evidence to support the expectation that the greater the "identification with" roles the greater the role participation (#7). Penner and Finkelstein (1998) followed volunteers for an organization that serves people with HIV/AIDS over a year. They found that satisfaction with the organization and volunteer activities was positively correlated with length of service and that commitment to the organization encouraged more extensive participation. Lammers (1991) investigated duration of service among volunteers at a crisis and information telephone service and found that identity meanings, such as perceiving the work as challenging, interesting, and requiring responsibility, and positive interpersonal ties to other volunteers were the two strongest factors that influenced pursuing volunteer service beyond training. Similarly, Okun (1994) noted that identity meanings of being productive as a volunteer, and seeing volunteering as fulfilling a moral obligation increased the frequency of volunteering; and King and Elder (1998) found that grandparents who feel most efficacious in the role tend to have more contact with grandchildren and higher quality relationships than other grandparents.

In conclusion, this review suggests that a symbolic interaction and identity theory provide a robust framework for understanding social and emotional engagement in adults. However, future studies should include a broader set of role engagement measures, especially measures of role satisfaction, commitment, salience, centrality, and identity meanings. In addition, future research plans would benefit by investigating several adults roles and their interplay, as well as considering possible gender differences in role engagement and differences by stages in the life cycle. Continued research on the dynamics of adult role engagement should be particularly helpful as researchers develop intervention strategies to maintain and enhance the well-being of adults and children.

REFERENCES

Atchley, R. C. (1999). *Continuity and adaptation in aging: Creating positive experiences*. Baltimore: The Johns Hopkins University Press.

Burke, P. J. (1980). The self: Measurement implications from a symbolic interactionist perspective. *Social Psychology Quarterly, 43*, 18–29.

Campbell, K. E., & Lee, B. A. (1992). Sources of personal neighbor networks: Social integration, need, or time? *Social Forces, 70*, 1077–1100.

Cobb, S. (1976). Social support as a moderator of life stress. *Psychosomatic Medicine, 38*, 300–314.

Dean, A., Kolody, B., & Wood, P. (1990). Effects of social support from various sources on depression in elderly persons. *Journal of Health and Social Behavior, 31*, 148–161.

Durkheim. E. [1897] (1951). *Suicide: A study in sociology*. Trans. by J. A. Spaulding & G. Simpson. Glencoe, IL: Free Press.

Ellison, C. (1991). Religious involvement and subjective well-being. *Journal of Health and Social Behavior, 32*, 80–99.

Ellison, C. G., Gay, D. A., Glass, T. A. (1989). Does religious commitment contribute to individual life satisfaction? *Social Forces, 68*, 100–123.

Ellison, C., & London, B. (1992). The social and political participation of black Americans: Compensatory and ethnic community perspectives revisited. *Social Forces, 70*, 681–701.

Ellison, C. G., & Sherkat, D. E. (1995). The "semi-involuntary institution" revisited: Regional variations in church participation among black Americans. *Social Forces, 73*, 1415–1437.

Fischer, C. S., & Oliker, S. J. (1983). A research note on friendship, gender, and the life cycle. *Social Forces, 62*, 124–133.

Foote, N. N. (1951). Identification as the basis for a theory of motivation. *American Sociological Review, 26*, 14–21.

Goffman. E. (1959). *The presentation of self in everyday life*. New York: Doubleday.

Goudy, W. J., & Goudeau, J. F. (1982). Social ties and life satisfaction of older persons: Another evaluation. *Journal of Gerontological Social Work, 4*, 35–50.

Havighurst, R. J., & Albrecht, R. (1953). *Older people*. New York: Longmans, Green.

Hayslip, B., Shore, R. J., Henderson, C. E., & Lambert, P. L. (1998). Custodial grandparenting and the impact of grandchildren with problems on role satisfaction and role meaning. *Journal of Gerontology: Social Sciences, 53B*, jS164–S173.

Heiss, J. (1981). Social roles. In M. Rosenberg & R. H. Turner (Eds.), *Social psychology: Sociological perspectives* (pp. 94–129). New York: Basic Books.

Hochschild, A. R. (1979). Emotion work, feeling rules, and social structure. *American Journal of Sociology, 85*, 551–575.

House, J. S., Landis, K. R., & Umberson, D. (1988). Social relationships and health. *Science, 241*, 540–545.

Janoski, T., Musick, M., & Wilson, J. (1998). Being volunteered? The Impact of social participation and pro-social attitudes on volunteering. *Sociological Forum, 13*, 495–519.

Janoski, T., & Wilson, J. (1995). Pathways to voluntarism: Family socialization and status transmission models. *Social Forces, 74*, 271–292.

Johnson, M. P., Caughlin, J. P., & Huston, T. L. (1999). The tripartite nature of marital commitment: Personal, moral, and structural reasons to stay married. *Journal of Marriage and the Family, 61*, 160–177.

Keyes, C. L. M. (1995). *Social functioning and social well-being: Studies of the social nature of personal well-ness.* Madison, WI: Unpublished PhD dissertation.

King, V., & Elder, G. H. (1997). The legacy of grandparenting: childhood experiences with grandparents and current involvement with grandchildren. *Journal of Marriage and the Family, 59*, 848–859.

King, V., & Elder, G. H. (1998). Perceived self-efficacy and grandparenting. *Journal of Gerontology: Social Sciences, 53B*, S249–S257.

Krause, N. (1991). Stress, religiosity, and abstinence from alcohol. *Psychology and Aging, 6*, 134–144.

Lammers, J. C. (1991). Attitudes, motives, and demographic predictors of volunteer commitment and service duration. *Journal of Social Service Research, 14*, 125–140.

LaRossa, R., & Reitzes, D. C. (1993). Symbolic interactionism and family studies. In P. G. Boss, W. J. Doherty, R. LaRossa, W. R. Schumm, & S. K. Steinmetz (Eds.), *Sourcebook of family theories and methods: A contextual approach* (pp. 135–163). New York: Plenum Press.

Lee, G. R., & Shehan, C. L. (1989). Social relations and the self-esteem of older persons. *Research on Aging, 11*, 427–442.

Lee, L., Piliavin, J. A., & Call, V. R. A. (1999). Giving time, money, and blood: Similarities and differences. *Social Psychology Quarterly, 62*, 276–290.

Lemon, B. W., Bengtson, V. L., & Peterson, J. A. (1972). An exploration of the activity theory of aging: Activity types and life satisfaction among in-movers to a retirement community. *Journal of Gerontology, 27*, 511–523.

Lin, N., & Ensel, W. M. (1984). Depression-mobility and its social etiology: The role of life events and social support. *Journal of Health and Social Behavior, 25*, 176–188.

Logan, J. R., & Spitze, G. D. (1994). Family neighbors. *American Journal of Sociology, 100*, 453–476.

Milardo, R. M. (1982). Friendship networks in developing relationships: Converging and diverging environments. *Social Psychology Quarterly, 3*, 162–172.

Moen, P., Dempster-McClain, D., & Williams, R. M. (1992). Successful aging: A life-course perspective on women's multiple roles and health. *American Journal of Sociology, 97*, 1612–1638.

Mortimer, J. T., Finch, M. D., & Kumka, D. (1982). Persistence and change in development: The multidimensional self-concept. *Life-Span Development and Behavior, 4*, 263–313.

Musick, M. A., Herzog, A. R., & House, J. S. (1999). Volunteering and mortality among older adults: Findings from a national sample. *Journal of Gerontology: Social Sciences, 54B*, S173–S180.

Okun, M. A. (1994). The relation between motives for organizational volunteering and frequency of volunteering by elders. *The Journal of Applied Gerontology, 13*, 115–126.

Penner. L. A., & Finkelstein, M. A. (1998). Dispositional and structural determinants of volunteerism. *Journal of Personality and Social Psychology, 74*, 525–537.

Peters-Golden, H. (1982). Breast cancer: Varied perceptions of social support in the illness experience. *Social Science and Medicine, 16*, 483–491.

Pollner, M. (1989). Divine relations, social relations, and well-being. *Journal of Health and Social Behavior, 30*, 92–104.

Putnam, R. D. (2000). *Bowling alone: The collapse and revival of American community.* New York, NY: Simon and Schuster.

Reitzes, D. C., & Mutran, E. J. (1994). Multiple roles and identities: Factors influencing self-esteem among middle-aged working men and women. *Social Psychology Quarterly, 57*, 313–325.

Roberto, K. A. (1990). Grandparent and grandchild relationships. In T. H. Brubaker (Ed.), *Family relationships in later life* (2nd ed., pp. 100–112). Newbury Park, CA: Sage Publications.

Roberto, K. A., & Scott, J. P. (1984). Friendship patterns among older women. *International Journal of Aging and Human Development, 19*, 1–10.

Ross, C. E. (1990). Religion and psychological distress. *Journal for the Scientific Study of Religion, 29*, 236–245.

Rotolo, T. (2000). A time to join, a time to quit: the influence of life cycle transitions on voluntary association membership. *Social Forces, 78*, 1133–1161.

Rowe, J. W., & Kahn, R. L. (1997). Successful aging. *The Gerontologist*, *37*, 433–440.

Rowe, J. W., & Kahn, R. L. (1998). *Successful aging*. New York: Pantheon Books.

Somary, K., & Stricker, G. (1998). Becoming a grandparent: A longitudinal study of expectations and early experiences as a function of sex and lineage. *The Gerontologist*, *38*, 53–61.

Stone, G. P. (1962). Appearance and the self. In A. Rose (Ed.), *Human behavior and social processes* (pp. 86–118). Boston: Houghton Mifflin.

Stryker, S. (1980). *Symbolic interaction: A social structural version*. Menlo Park, CA: Benjamin/ Cummings.

Stryker, S., & Serpe, R. T. (1994). Identity salience and psychological centrality: Equivalent, overlapping or complementary concepts? *Social Psychology Quarterly*, *57*, 16–35.

Thoits, P. A. (1992). Identity structures and psychological well-being: Gender and marital status comparisons. *Social Psychology Quarterly*, *55*, 236–256.

Thomas, J. L. (1989). Gender and perceptions of grandparenthood. *International Journal of Aging and Human Development*, *29*, 269–282.

Thomas, J. L. (1990). Grandparenthood and mental health: Implications for the practitioner. *Journal of Applied Gerontology*, *9*, 464–479.

Thompson, S. C., Sobolew-Shubin, A., Graham, M. A., & Janigian, A. S. (1989). Psychosocial adjustment following a stroke. *Social Science and Medicine*, *28*, 239–247.

Tobin, S. S., & Neugarten, B. L. (1961). Life satisfaction and social interaction in the aging. *Journal of Gerontology*, *16*, 344–346.

Turner, R. (1956). Role-taking, role standpoint, and reference-group behavior. *American Journal of Sociology*, *61*, 316–328.

Uggen, C., & Janikula, J. (1999). Volunteering and arrest in the transition to adulthood. *Social Forces*, *78*, 331–362.

Verbrugge, L. M. (1983). A research note on adult friendship contact: A dyadic perspective. *Social Forces*, *62*, 78–83.

Waite, L. J., & Harrison, S. C. (1992). Keeping in touch: How women in mid-life allocate social contacts among kith and kin. *Social Forces*, *70*, 637–655.

Wheaton, B. (1990). Life transitions, role histories, and mental health. *American Sociological Review*, *55*, 209–223.

Whitbeck, L. B., Hoyt, D. R., & Huck, S. M. (1993). Family relationship history, contemporary parent-grandparent relationship quality, and the grandparent-grandchild relationship. *Journal of Marriage and the Family*, *55*, 1025–1035.

Wilson, J., & Musick, M. (1997a). Who cares? Toward an integrated theory of volunteer work. *American Sociological Review*, *62*, 694–713.

Wilson, J., &, Musick, M. A. (1997b). Work and volunteering: The long arm of the job. *Social Forces*, *76*, 251–272.

Wilson, J., & Musick, M. (1998). The contribution of social resources to volunteering. *Social Science Quarterly*, *79*, 799–814.

Wilson, J., & Musick, M. A. (1999). Attachment to volunteering. *Sociological Forum*, *4*, 243–272

Young, F. W., & Glasgow, N. (1998). Voluntary social participation and health. *Research on Aging*, *20*, 339–362.

32

Cognitive Styles and Well-Being in Adulthood and Old Age

Derek M. Isaacowitz

Martin E. P. Seligman
University of Pennsylvania, Philadelphia

INTRODUCTION

Cognitive styles are the habitual ways that individuals attend to, remember, frame, and interpret information provided by their environment. The classification of a variable as cognitive indicates most generally that the construct involves the way a person tends to see the world; from their general outlook to their specific response to stimuli. We argue in this chapter that cognitive also includes processes as diverse as the ways individuals choose what areas of life are most salient to them, how people perceive time, and how they intentionally structure and perceive their social relations and social network. Thus, we take cognitive in its most general sense as we try to understand the role of cognitive variables in processes of successful aging.

Our goal in this chapter is to argue that this broad conception of cognitive styles allows for the most variance in successful aging to be explained. We use an emotion-centered definition of successful aging to match the dependent variables that tend to be used in studies of cognitive styles, which arose primarily in the study of depression. So, we consider a positive affective profile in which depressive symptoms and negative affect are absent or minimal and positive affect and life satisfaction are moderate or high as indicating successful individual aging. Maintaining the well-regulated emotional system implied by our definition of successful aging is no small accomplishment given the changes that may come with age; however, successful emotion regulation seems to be the rule rather than exception for many middle-age and older people (Carstensen & Charles, 1998; Carstensen, Isaacowitz, & Charles, 1999), though this may be less true in very old age (Isaacowitz & Smith, 2000; Mroczek & Kolarz, 1998; Suzman, Manton, & Willis, 1992). We aim in this chapter to review evidence that links individual differences in cognitive style variables to individual differences in these affective indicators of successful development in adulthood and old age, with attention whenever possible to how these processes may unfold developmentally.

The idea that cognitive processes and styles may be causes, rather than merely symptoms, of affective experience originated with Aaron Beck's cognitive formulation of depression. According to Beck's (1967) theory, distortions in cognitive processes are not simply a result of being depressed, but instead may be a cause of the depression itself. Thus, interventions based on correcting these distortions appear to be a successful therapeutic intervention for depression in adults (DeRubeis, Gelfand, Tang, & Simons, 1999). Typical cognitive distortions common in depressed people include overgeneralization and catastrophic thinking; in general, these styles involve a "lens" through which negative information from the environment is highlighted in cognitive processing, while potentially neutral or positive information is ignored. Interestingly, according to theory, it is not the case that nondepressed individuals process information without cognitive distortions. Instead, they distort positive information to promote their good moods—so, for instance, a nondepressed person would overgeneralize from a positive piece of information rather than a negative one. Empirically, one aspect of the theory that has received the most support is the notion that depressed people have more negative cognitions about the self than do nondepressed individuals (Haaga, Dyck, & Ernst, 1991).

What the cognitive model of depression has contributed to the understanding of psychological well-being in adults is the idea that the lenses through which people see the world not only correlate with how they feel at any moment, but may also affect how they feel later. A similar idea arose from work on stress appraisal, based on the observation that people may react very differently to stressful events depending on how they interpret those events (Lazarus & Folkman, 1984). The notion that individual differences in ways of processing information from the world can be a key mechanism in the etiology of later well-being forms the basis for much of this chapter. We consider several types of cognitive style variables that have been either theorized or shown to impact affective experience and psychological well-being in adult populations. These styles include explanatory style, dispositional optimism and pessimism, being selective about goals and social relationships, hardiness, perceived control over the environment, and wisdom.

EXPLANATORY STYLE

In the late 1970s, psychologists who had been studying learned helplessness revised the original theory to account for apparent individual differences in the tendency to become helpless when faced with uncontrollable stressful situations (see Seligman & Isaacowitz, 2000, for a further review of these historical developments). This reformulation focused on differences in people's explanations for the causes of events in their environment (Abramson, Seligman, & Teasdale, 1978). When events occur, people attempt to explain why they happened; these explanations appear to fall along three dimensions. First, an individual will decide if the event was due to their own actions or to some other force, also known as the internal–external dimension. The second dimension, stable–temporary, involves discerning whether the cause of the event is one that will persist over time or is limited only to that one instance. The final dimension, global–specific, concerns whether the cause of the event is one that will affect many areas of a person's life or will instead be isolated to just one life domain.

Importantly, individuals tend to have a stylistic way of explaining events. This explanatory style can be measured in two primary ways: through self-report questionnaire or with a coding system. The Attributional Style Questionnaire (ASQ; Peterson et al., 1982) asks individuals to give perceived causes for 12 vignettes in the affiliation and achievement domains; half are positive and half are negative. Then, the individual rates their perceived cause on the three explanatory style dimensions. Versions of the questionnaire have also been developed specifically for use with children (CASQ; Seligman et al., 1984), adults (Dykema, Bergebower, Doctora, & Peterson, 1996), and older adults (Isaacowitz & Seligman, in press). For those individuals who are not able to complete a self-report questionnaire, a coding system was devised that can take verbatim transcripts and yield explanatory style scores (Content Analysis of Verbatim Explanations [CAVE]; Schulman, Castellon, & Seligman, 1989).

A style of explaining negative events with causes that are internal, stable, and global became known as a "pessimistic explanatory style." In contrast, an optimistic explanatory style involves making external, temporary, and specific causal explanations for negative events (Peterson & Seligman, 1984). Using the CAVE coding system, Burns and Seligman (1989) investigated the stability of these habitual explanatory styles throughout adulthood. The researchers had 30 older adults answer questions about their lives at the moment and provide either diaries or letters they had written during their teens or 20s. Then, the CAVE system was used to derive explanatory style scores for each individual as a young adult and as an old adult. Very high stability of explanatory style for negative events was found across a 50-year period. However, explanatory style for positive events did not emerge as stable over that time period.

The correlation between this cognitive variable and emotion arises from the multitude of findings linking a pessimistic explanatory style with depressive symptoms, at least in some populations. Peterson and Seligman (1984) reviewed a variety of evidence, including critical longitudinal data, showing that a pessimistic explanatory style predicts increases in depressive symptoms over time. This occurs in a diathesis-stress context, in which a pessimistic explanatory style serves as a vulnerability for depression when paired with a stressful negative event. For example, college students with a pessimistic explanatory style who did badly on a midterm exam have been shown in several studies to experience the most enduring depressive symptoms after receiving their disappointing score (Metalsky, Abramson, Seligman, Semmel, & Peterson, 1982; Metalsky, Halberstadt, & Abramson, 1987).

The Origins of Explanatory Style

Explanatory style appears to arise fairly early in childhood and may have a genetic component. Schulman, Keith, and Seligman (1993) gave the Attributional Style Questionnaire to monozygotic and dizygotic twin pairs. For monozygotic twins, who share identical genetic material, optimism as measured by composite score on the ASQ demonstrated a highly significant intraclass correlation of .48. In contrast, the intraclass correlation between dizygotic twins, who share only half of their genetic material, was zero. Although this suggests a genetic component to explanatory style, the researchers speculate that it is not optimism per se that may be directly heritable; instead, what may be heritable is a propensity to have success or failure experiences, which in turn influences the development of explanatory style. Indeed, there is evidence among older adults that some types of life events are heritable (though uncontrollable events were not found to have a genetic component; Saudino, Pedersen, Lichtenstein, McClearn, & Plomin, 1997).

What, then, is the evidence for developmental trajectories of explanatory style among children? A large study of children aged 9 to 11 found not only that a pessimistic explanatory style was correlated with depressive symptoms, but also that children with a pessimistic explanatory style were more likely to become depressed over the course of the year. Additionally, depression seemed to lead to a more pessimistic enduring style in children over the course of a year (Nolen-Hoeksema, Girgus, & Seligman, 1986). In a 5-year longitudinal study of third graders, negative events appeared to best predict depression among the children when they were younger, but as they got older, a pessimistic explanatory style emerged as a predictor of depression (Nolen-Hoeksema, Girgus, & Seligman, 1992). Explanatory style predicted depression both as a "main effect" over time and also in diathesis-stress interaction with negative events in the older children. In other words, pessimistic children were more likely to get depressed over time, but pessimistic children who experienced negative life events had an even greater chance of becoming depressed. Importantly, experiencing depression appeared to predict an enduring decline in children's explanatory style, making them more pessimistic. The finding that this maladaptive explanatory style is present even in schoolchildren and can both be a risk factor for depression as well as responsive to events in the environment led researchers to attempt interventions aimed at changing the explanatory style of very pessimistic children and thereby to prevent depression.

The prevention program, known as the Penn Resiliency Program, uses a variety of techniques to try to improve the explanatory style of children at-risk for depression as well to improve their social and problem-solving skills. For example, children in the program learn ways to dispute their automatic negative thoughts about the causes of events, to search for evidence, and to evaluate situations more realistically. The program involves 12 two-hour sessions during or after school. Compared to students in a no-intervention control, 5th- and 6th-grade students in the prevention program showed fewer depressive symptoms at the end of the program (Jaycox, Reivich, Gillham, & Seligman, 1994) and showed a 50% lower rate of moderate to severe depressive symptoms at 2-year follow-up (Gillham, Reivich, Jaycox, & Seligman, 1995). Current research is comparing the program to a similar one without the cognitive components, to determine whether change in explanatory style is indeed motivating these encouraging prevention findings. Recently, a similar program with college students was shown to prospectively reduce rates of depression in young adults (Seligman, Schulman, DeRubeis, & Hollon, 1999).

Explanatory Style Across the Life Span

A number of studies have explored the links between explanatory style and mental and physical health outcomes in older populations. One study used the CAVE technique to evaluate the relationship between explanatory style and immune function in a population of relatively healthy older adults (Kamen-Siegel, Rodin, Seligman, & Dwyer, 1991). Those participants who displayed a more pessimistic explanatory style also had worse immune function, as indicated by T-helper cell/T-suppressor cell ratio and T-lymphocyte response to mitogen challenge. These analyses controlled for a number of possible intervening variables, such as general health and depression. Interestingly, more pessimistic older participants in this sample also reported higher levels of depressive symptoms, though it is important to note that these measures were taken simultaneously and thus did not involve any prospective prediction.

The Grant Study of Harvard graduates has been used to link explanatory style early in life with health outcomes later in adulthood (Peterson, Seligman, & Vaillant, 1988). At age 25, participants in the study described wartime experiences; these descriptions were then analyzed with the CAVE technique so that an explanatory style score could be assigned to each participant. The researchers then determined whether explanatory style at age 25 predicted physical health, as rated by physicians, of each participant from ages 30 to 60. These physician exams were conducted every 5 years during the study period. To make these analyses more conservative, the researchers controlled for physical and mental health at age 25 when evaluating the predictive relationship of early explanatory style to later physical health. A more pessimistic explanatory style at 25 significantly predicted worse physical health at age 45, 55, and 60, using partial correlations in which initial mental and physical health were controlled. At least through early and middle adulthood in this elite sample, a pessimistic explanatory style appears to predict declining health.

Until recently, no study had directly assessed whether a pessimistic explanatory prospectively predicted increased depression in older adults, in the presence of life stressors or otherwise. The body of research showing this particular prospective relationship simply had not been extended through the adult life span. Several years ago, we conducted the first study to determine the role of explanatory style in predicting affect change among community-dwelling older adults (Isaacowitz & Seligman, 2001). To measure explanatory style, we modified the ASQ to make the items more appropriate for older people (e.g., changing "you do a project which is highly praised" to "your performance as a volunteer is highly praised"). We then followed our sample of 71 community-dwelling adults age 64 to 94 for a full year, tracking changes in depressive symptoms (as measured by the Beck Depression Inventory) as well as life stressors experienced. We found the opposite effect than had been hypothesized based on previous work in younger populations. Specifically, at 6-month and 1-year follow-up, the older adults who scored as most optimistic in the affiliation domain showed the highest levels of depressive symptoms when they experienced several life stressors during the follow-up period. Optimists with no life events had very low levels of depressive symptoms, whereas the more pessimistic participants were in the middle, regardless of presence or absence of life stressors.

We have recently completed a new study in which we followed a second cohort of community-dwelling older adults and traced the relationship of explanatory style to effect change over time (Isaacowitz & Seligman, in press). We eliminated the achievement items from our measure of explanatory style, because they seemed particularly irrelevant to our elderly subjects, and replaced them with items concerning the more relevant health and cognitive domains (e.g., "your doctor says you are in good shape" and "you fall and break your hip"). This new measure of explanatory style in older adults (the OAASQ) had slightly improved psychometric properties as compared with the measure in the first study. The diathesis-stress relationship found in the previous study did not replicate in this sample; however, the only predictor of depressive symptom change over a six-month period in this study was composite score of explanatory style for health/cognitive items. Controlling for baseline depressive symptoms and life stressors over the 6-months, explanatory style for health/cognitive items was positively correlated with increases in depressive symptoms as measured by the CES-D. That is, those participants whose scores reflected more optimism on the health/cognitive items also tended to get more depressed over time. Though this is not a replication of the original effect, the notion that extremely optimistic explanatory styles may be maladaptive for community-dwelling older adults did receive further support from the results.

The key to the shift in adaptiveness of different explanatory styles that appears to take place throughout adulthood may involve the nature of the life events and life stressors faced by adults of different ages. Explanatory style was developed primarily in college student populations; in these groups, the negative life events include failing exams, breaking up with boy/girlfriends and the like. In these cases, a more optimistic explanatory style aligns with an accurate explanation, as these events are usually caused by fairly transient changeable circumstances. This is not the case when the life events of older adults are considered. Most common life events among older adults involve serious illnesses and close friends dying (Murrell, Norris, & Hutchins, 1984); these events are rather different than failing an exam and may be seen as involving more stable (and perhaps global) causes. Interestingly, this partially matches age differences in ASQ scores found by Lachman (1990). Compared to younger adults, her sample of older adults tended to explain negative events with more stable yet specific attributions, suggesting that they may be able to "compartmentalize" negative events, even when these stressors seem to arise from causes that are not transient in nature.

Thus, accuracy may shift away from extreme optimism to more balanced perspectives as people get older and the life events they face may shift. Coping may be the way in which these changes link to affective outcomes. According to Seligman (1990), those with an optimistic explanatory style tend towards active, problem-focused coping strategies; in other words, they try to produce change in the world and solve problems externally. This is an adaptive strategy, but only in certain contexts. Specifically, active problem-focused coping is a useful strategy when the problem in question is amenable to change, and when the actor possesses the necessary resources to enact these changes. However, if either the problem is not amenable to change, or the actor does not have the necessary resources to enact the changes, then active problem-focused coping will be a time-consuming strategy that is likely to fail. For someone who has been an optimist during their entire adult life and has successfully taken charge of problems they face, encountering problems that they cannot fix may be an assault to their life view, and therefore may be rather demoralizing.

In contrast, those adults with a more pessimistic explanatory style may prefer emotion-focused coping strategies rather than trying first for external control attempts. They may be at an advantage when facing certain events characteristic of late life, such as a close friend dying, because they will cut quickly to emotion regulation strategies rather than spending valuable time and energy on active coping attempts that are doomed to failure. Emotion-focused coping may be the only realistic way of responding to certain types of stressors, such as a losing a best friend, and pessimists may be at an advantage in their avoidance of problem-focused coping and preference for emotional coping in those situations where problem-focus turns out to be impossible.

This role of explanatory style in successful development across adulthood depends on the context in which the cognitions are enacted. What is most adaptive, it appears, is an explanatory style that is accurate concerning the events being faced by the person at their developmental point. During childhood and young adulthood, it appears that a more optimistic explanatory style matches up best with the reality of stressors faced. The emerging evidence we described above suggests that extreme optimism is inaccurate for older adults, and that a less optimistic style may be more realistic. We suspect that the changing contexts that would make extreme optimism maladaptive are true only for old age, and we are currently investigating the predictive value of explanatory style in a middle-aged population to determine whether this is indeed the case.

DISPOSITIONAL OPTIMISM

Scheier and Carver (1985, 1993) proposed an alternative conception of optimism than the one used in the explanatory style framework. They consider dispositional optimism to be a generalized positive expectancy about the future, whereas dispositional pessimism involves generalized negative expectations. This future-oriented definition of optimism is more closely related to lay conceptions of the meaning of the term. The Life Orientation Test (LOT; Scheier & Carver, 1985) measures dispositional optimism and pessimism. The scale consists of four optimism items ("I'm always optimistic about my future"), 4 pessimism items ("If something can go wrong for me it will"), and four filler items ("I enjoy my friends a lot"). Originally, the pessimism items were reverse-coded and added to the optimism items, yielding one total dispositional optimism–pessimism score, with higher scores indicating more dispositional optimism. However, it now appears that the optimism and pessimism scales may be somewhat independent, with different correlates and predictive relationships, at least among older adults (Mroczek et al., 1993; Robinson-Whelen, Kim, MacCallum, & Kiecolt-Glaser, 1997). Thus, many researchers who use the LOT now evaluate the two scales separately.

Several studies have compared scores on the LOT with scores on the ASQ to determine the relationship between an individual's explanatory style and dispositional optimism. Hjelle, Belongia, and Nesser (1996) found the two scores to be only moderately correlated in a sample of college students. In a sample of community-dwelling adults, scores on the LOT and the OAASQ were uncorrelated (Isaacowitz & Seligman, in press). Later, we discuss evidence suggesting that the measures also diverge in their predictive power over time, at least among older adults.

In the early years of research on dispositional optimism, a controversy emerged concerning the unique character of the construct. Some argued that the LOT measured general tendencies toward negative affectivity, rather than any unique aspect of a person's cognitive style. In one set of studies, relationships between the LOT and outcome measures were reduced to zero when they controlled for neuroticism, though the neuroticism-symptom relationship survived controlling for dispositional optimism (Smith, Pope, Rhodewalt, & Poulton, 1989). Scheier, Carver, and Bridges (1994) responded with evidence suggesting that the relationship between dispositional optimism and the outcomes of depression and coping styles did survive controlling for neuroticism, trait anxiety, self-mastery and self-esteem.

Despite these controversies concerning the uniqueness of the LOT, it has been used in many studies to predict important outcomes among adults of various ages. For instance, one study followed a group of middle-aged men through coronary bypass surgery and their recovery from it (Scheier et al., 1989). Those men who displayed more dispositional optimism prior to their surgery showed evidence of more problem-focused coping; more importantly, they also recovered and returned to normal life faster, and showed a higher quality of life six months postoperatively, as compared to subjects who scored as less optimistic on the LOT before surgery.

Bromberger and Matthews (1996) followed a large sample of middle-aged women over a 3-year period. They found that more pessimistic women who experienced ongoing stress during the follow-up period tended to have high levels of depressive symptoms at the end of the follow-up period. This suggests a diathesis-stress relationship, with dispositional pessimism (in this study, meaning lower scores on one continuous dispositional optimism–pessimism scale) as a vulnerability factor for depression for middle-aged women when combined with stress.

Another large study tested whether the LOT predicted changes in psychological well-being in middle-aged and older women over a 1-year period (Robinson-Whelen et al., 1997). In this study, some of the participants were caregiving for sick relatives; this constituted the "stressed" sample; a noncaregiving, nonstressed sample was also followed.

The researchers looked separately at dispositional optimism and pessimism in this study, and evaluated whether either could predict changes in measures of depression, anxiety, perceived stress, and self-rated health. Using multisample structural equation modeling, the researchers found that only pessimism predicted change over the year: increased anxiety, increased perceived stress and worsening perceived health. Neither predicted change in depressive symptoms over the year. The path coefficients for optimism and pessimism were not significantly different from each other, though this may have been a function of the relatively small samples.

What differences did the researchers find between the stressed and nonstressed samples? There were no differences between the stressed and nonstressed samples in the predictive relationships described above, suggesting "main effect" rather than diathesis-stress effects of the cognitive style variable on psychological well-being. Despite this similarity, however, there were some other important differences between the stressed and nonstressed samples (Robinson-Whelen et al., 1997). There was no difference in the factor structure of the LOT; however, the correlation between the optimism and pessimism scales differed between the two samples. In the nonstressed sample, the two scales were uncorrelated, whereas they were negatively correlated in the stressed sample. Furthermore, the scales were more strongly correlated with concurrent levels of depression and anxiety in the stressed sample. Finally, those individuals who were caregiving showed lower levels of dispositional optimism and a trend towards higher pessimism than the nonstressed controls. This suggests that this particular cognitive style may be sensitive to individual life experiences and circumstances, and perhaps is a particularly malleable "lens" through which adults may process information.

Research also suggests that dispositional optimism and pessimism's predictive value may shift across the adult life span, at least in the domain of health outcomes

(Schulz, Bookwala, Knapp, Scheier, & Williamson, 1996). These researchers followed a large sample of adults undergoing radiation treatment for cancer over an 8-month period. They investigated the relationship between dispositional optimism, pessimism, and depressive symptoms and mortality in this sample. They found that pessimism predicted mortality in the sample, but only among those participants aged 59 or younger. This relationship did not replicate among older participants. Neither optimism nor depression related to mortality in this sample. The authors therefore concluded that there is some unique quality to expecting bad things to happen in the future that may be particularly maladaptive, but only for younger adults. This is because older adults may be using pessimism as a coping strategy to deal with anticipated or actual losses while maintaining some sense of control.

Interestingly, we have found results consistent with this argument in our recent cohort of 93 community-dwelling older adults, aged 60 to 99 (Isaacowitz & Seligman, in press). At baseline, dispositional optimism and pessimism were uncorrelated, so we evaluated the two scales as potentially separable predictors of affective changes over time. Neither dispositional optimism nor pessimism predicted changes in depressive symptoms over a 6-month period, either as main effects or interacting with life stressors. However, these generalized expectancy variables both did predict increases in positive affect over the six-month period, suggesting that pessimism may cease to be quite so maladaptive in terms of depressive symptomatology for older adults, but that expecting positive things in the future may still confer some affective benefits in this population.

The Origins of Dispositional Optimism

Given the evidence that dispositional optimism may be a cognitive style that predicts psychological well-being in adults, the obvious next question concerns the origins of these styles. One study of identical and fraternal middle-aged twins reared together or apart examined the degree to which dispositional optimism and pessimism may be heritable (Plomin et al., 1992). Both dispositional optimism and pessimism produced heritability estimates of approximately 25% using twin and adoption analyses. Unlike many psychological variables, there was a shared environment effect for dispositional optimism, but not for dispositional pessimism. All twin pairs evaluated in this study also completed measures of depression and life satisfaction; both dispositional optimism and pessimism emerged as independent predictors of these mental health measures. This suggests several tentative conclusions about the origins of dispositional optimism. First, the two scales may function independently, but both may have a significant genetic component. Second, shared aspects of the home environment may contribute to dispositional optimism but not pessimism. Importantly, both appear to have a substantial amount of variance likely attributable to unique aspects of individual experience. This is consistent with the findings discussed above demonstrating that the individual experience of being a caregiver may serve to lower levels of dispositional optimism (Robinson-Whelen et al., 1997).

Adding to a preliminary understanding of the roots of dispositional optimism before adulthood, one large study of adolescents in sixth and seventh grade investigated whether dispositional optimism predicted resilience in the face of stressful events (Herman-Stahl & Petersen, 1996). In this research, a single dispositional optimism scale was formed by combining the optimism and pessimism items of the LOT such that higher scores indicated higher optimism. Participants were interviewed twice over a 1-year period, and were divided based on prior experiences and symptomatology at baseline into one of four groups: positively adjusted (low stress, few depressive symptoms), resilient (high stress, few depressive symptoms), negatively adjusted (low stress, high depressive symptoms), and vulnerable (high stress, high depressive symptoms). At both baseline and follow-up, youth without symptoms reported higher levels of dispositional optimism than those with symptoms. Interestingly, resilient youth appeared to display more dispositional optimism than vulnerable youth, leading the authors to speculate that optimism may play a role in stress resilience, in a diathesis-stress framework. However, while this study was longitudinal, the researchers did not use the prospective component to test whether those adolescents who were stressed over the study year did not become depressed if they were optimistic, which would be a more stringent test of the stress resilience hypothesis. While this study illuminates the potential benefits of optimism early in life, it does not contribute much to the attempt to understand the roots of the style.

Indeed, there is not much research relevant to the nongenetic origins of dispositional optimism and pessimism. Scheier and Carver (1993) speculate that children may learn to expect future success from past success, and future failure from past failure. Parents may influence the future expectancies of their children both by modeling behaviors and cognitive approaches for them, and by instructing them in problem-solving. To the extent that children feel like they have the skills to face problems, they will likely feel optimistic about their future.

Personal Optimism

Reker and Wong (1985) developed a future-oriented notion of optimism, known as personal optimism, which is highly similar to dispositional optimism. Personal optimism is measured by asking participants to list positive events they expect in the future and how confident they are that these events will happen. Recently, Reker (1997) looked at the cross-sectional relationship between personal optimism and depressive symptoms in both community-dwelling and insitutionalized older adults. Interestingly, personal optimism uniquely related to lower levels of depressive symptoms among institutionalized elderly; there was no unique relationship between the two constructs among community-dwelling participants. These findings are consistent with work finding no predictive effect of dispositional optimism or pessimism on depression in older people (Isaacowitz & Seligman, in press; Robinson-Whelen et al., 1997). These results also suggest that gloomy expectations for the future may lose their affective maladaptiveness for community-dwelling older people, while positive expectancies may lose some of their buffering ability in this population.

BEING SELECTIVE ABOUT GOALS

While we are emphasizing affective and emotional experiences as indicators of successful aging in the present chapter, another school of thought has used process rather than outcome to indicate aging successfully (Baltes & Carstensen, 1996; Freund, Li, & Baltes, 1999). In this section, we try to combine these two perspectives and consider how the processes considered in these theories of successful development may lead to positive affective outcome.

Selective Optimization with Compensation

The two primary theories that have considered processes in defining successful aging are selective optimization with compensation (SOC model; Baltes & Baltes, 1990; Marsiske, Lang, Baltes, & Baltes, 1995), and the optimization in primary and secondary control model (OPS model; Heckhausen & Schulz, 2000; Schulz & Heckhausen, 1996). According to the former model, successful human development at any age involves the orchestration of the three processes of selection, optimization and compensation in an action-theoretical sense. Although SOC is often referred to as a meta-theory, it can most be easily be defined using an action-theoretical framework in which success involves the accomplishment of goals. Selection then refers to choosing which goals are most salient, either proactively (elective selection) or in response to real or anticipated losses (loss-based selection). Optimization means mobilizing resources to maximize performance in goal-related domains, whereas compensation involves the investment of resources to maintain functioning in important domains despite losses in previously available resources. These processes take on special importance in the context of aging, when resources become more constrained and goals therefore become more difficult to achieve.

The SOC model has been tested in various ways. For instance, one published study explicitly looked at the connection between general endorsement of SOC-relevant principles (e.g., "I always focus on the one most important goal at a given time" to measure elective selection, and "I make every effort to achieve a given goal" to assess optimization) and indices of psychological well-being (Freund & Baltes, 1998). Using data from participants in the Berlin Aging Study (aged 70–100), the researchers found that those participants who used more SOC-related strategies also scored higher on measures of successful aging: higher subjective well-being, more positive emotions, and less loneliness. These relationships remained even after controlling for a host of other possible personality-type predictor variables, such as neuroticism.

We believe that the SOC model approximates a cognitive-type predictor of successful aging, especially the model's assertion that selecting goals and domains in the face of limited time and resources and trying to maximize functioning in those domains is important for adaptive development. Some individuals are selective about the goals that they pursue, and others are not. There are likely both age effects and individual differences in these processes. If the cognitive strategy of being selective about which goals to pursue and which domains to keep salient is indeed related to positive affective outcomes in adulthood and old age, then these processes may function analogously to explanatory style and optimism in linking person-level differences in information processing with successful emotion regulation in old age.

Optimization in Primary and Secondary Control

According to the OPS model, humans are primarily motivated by a desire for control over their environment. There are two major types of control: primary control involves behavior aimed at the external environment, whereas secondary control involves intrapsychic processes. While opportunities for primary and secondary control change over the adult life span (Schulz & Heckhausen, 1996), primary control is always considered preferable. Each type of control strategy can be divided into two subprocesses: selective and compensatory. Selective primary control involves behaviors aimed at accomplishing a selected goal, whereas selective secondary control consists of mental commitment to a chosen goal. Compensatory processes are called on whenever progress toward a goal appears blocked in some way. Compensatory primary control involve external aids to facilitate goal accomplishment; compensatory secondary control, in contrast, primarily consists of disengagement from goals that are no longer feasible, though it can also involve social comparisons and attribution processes that allow the person the feel better about their own performance. For example, an individual who had a goal of running a marathon may start training every day (selective primary control) and will also decide that marathon-running is a key to good health and is thus very important (selective secondary control). However, if the marathon is only a week away and the individual is not able to run 20, much less 26, miles, she or he may take several courses of action: hire a trainer or change his or her diet to improve their performance in time for the marathon (compensatory primary control), or decide that running marathons is overrated and silly and plan to start swimming instead (compensatory secondary control).

Although primary control is preferable, when a goal is actually unattainable, compensatory secondary control processes of disengagement from the goal are critical so that energy can be saved for maintaining primary control in other domains. In other words, continuing to try to reach a goal that is unattainable is a waste of resources and will detract from an individual's ability to maintain primary control with respect to other goals. According to the model, then, disengagement from unattainable goals should be important for maintaining psychological well-being. One study has looked at partnership goals in a sample of individuals of different ages who had recently separated from romantic relationships (Wrosch & Heckhausen, 1999). The researchers believed that relationship goals would be more attainable for newly separated young adults than for those who were in later middle age following the break-up; thus, younger adults would focus more on achieving these goals. For the older adults, the goal of finding a new romantic partner would be considerably less attainable; in this case, disengagement from the goal would be more appropriate and adaptive according to the OPS model. Consistent with these predictions, the younger people in the sample endorsed more goals related to relationships, whereas the late midlife members of the sample appeared to be more disengaged from the goal of finding a partner. Importantly, they also appeared to endorse more social goals that did not have to do with romantic partnership, suggesting that they were using the resources saved by disengaging from romantic partnership goals to invest more in other social relationships.

Most relevant to this chapter on cognitive style aspects of well-being in adulthood, concerns predictors of improvement in the emotional lives over time of the separated individuals. In general, over the 15-month period from the first interview until the longitudinal follow-up, separated individuals tended to report increased positive affect and decreased negative affect. Most interesting from a developmental perspective was the following finding: when predicting change in emotional well-being over time, an interaction between age and compensatory secondary control strategies emerged. For young adults, use of compensatory secondary control strategies involving disengagement from partnership goals was related to declines in emotional well-being over time, whereas for older adults the endorsement of these same strategies predicted improvements in well-being over the 15 months (Wrosch & Heckhausen, 1999).

Goal Selectivity: A Summary

Perhaps the take-home message of theory and empirical work on the relationship between goal selectivity and well-being is that Kenny Rogers was right in "The Gambler," and that individuals need to know when to "hold 'em," and "when to walk away." Engagement in some number of attainable goals and disengagement from unattainable goals seem likely to be important cognitive strategies for well-being in adulthood. There is some theoretical rationale for the assertion that a pruning down of salient life domains may also be adaptive as adults get older and both have fewer resources available for optimizing performance across many domains, and also face an increasingly negative gain/loss ratio (Heckhausen, Dixon, & Baltes, 1989). With an increasing number of loss events, investing commitment in many life domains sets an individual up with a high probability of experiencing a salient loss in one or more of those selected life areas. Being selective about what constitutes a salient life domain may be a way of regulating emotional responses to life events when resources are limited and losses are fairly common.

SOCIAL SELECTIVITY

Selectivity may not be specific to goals and life domains but may also be a component of well-being in social relations as people get older. While it has long been observed that adults seem to have fewer social contacts as they get older, only recently have these changes begun to be understood as potentially proactive processes desirable to the aging adult. Socioemotional selectivity theory (Carstensen et al., 1999) argues that, as adults get older, they intentionally narrow down their social networks to focus primarily on their closest social partners. This happens not because of age per se, but rather because increasing age is a strong proxy for the future being limited, and for impending endings. According to socioemotional selectivity theory, when people sense that their future is limited, they focus on emotions and on emotion regulation over other possible goals (e.g., acquiring new information), and they make decisions based on this focus. If emotion regulation is the goal, then it does not make good sense to make many new acquaintances and friends, as novel social partners can be quite unpredictable in their effects on emotion. Familiar social partners, in contrast, are more reliable in their impact on emotions and are a safer bet for social contact when emotion regulation is the goal. In support of this finding, it appears that age reductions in social contacts and social networks are more common among less central as opposed to more central members of social networks (Lang & Carstensen, 1994).

What is cognitive, however, about the theory of social selectivity? Several aspects of the theory at least suggest "cognitive styles" that might relate to well-being as adults get older, though for the most part these aspects of the theory have not yet been evaluated empirically. The first place in the theory that cognitive processes may play a role is that individuals are constantly assumed to be keeping track of time, and monitoring whether their future seems open-ended or limited. If the future is assessed as being limited, then the theory asserts that emotion will become more salient in all domains and decisions (Carstensen et al., 1999). Evidence from cognitive aging research supports the assertion that emotions may indeed become more central to cognitive processes as people age (Isaacowitz, Charles, & Carstensen, 2000). One hypothesized outcome of this emotion focus is an increased focus on close social partners and an elimination of less close social partners, which may result in a perception of an individual's social network as being more "emotionally dense" or packed with closer social partners.

This theory may then lead to three potential "cognitive style" individual difference variables. The first would be time orientation, the degree to which an individual views her future as extended or limited. According to the theory, viewing the future as limited rather than expansive would lead to a focus on emotions. This would then lead into the second possible individual difference variable, namely, the degree to which an individual focuses cognitive processing on the domain of emotion. Finally, emotion-focus is hypothesized to lead to a pruning down of social network members to only the closest, and thus to a perception of an individual's social network as "emotionally dense" or filled primarily with close social partners. Each of these should be correlated with each other; and, more importantly, if being socially selective is an adaptive response to situations in which the future is limited, then they should be related simultaneously and prospectively to measures of psychological well-being, at least among those whose future genuinely is limited.

Socioemotional selectivity theory researchers have only recently become interested in the individual difference aspect and adaptiveness of being a socially selective person. In a study on age pattern in the social networks of African Americans and Caucasian Americans of different ages, Fung, Carstensen, and Lang (2001) looked at the correlation between emotional density (the final individual difference variable described earlier) and a measure of happiness in participants of different ages. The two constructs were correlated only among young adults, and for them the correlation was negative. That is, a higher level of emotional density was related to less happiness in younger people, consistent with the assertion that focus on close social partners is adaptive only for those actually facing an ending and thus a limited future. The significant negative correlation in younger adults was partially attenuated when perceived health, education, and SES were controlled in the analyses.

Can any of the other social selectivity-relevant variables be linked to psychological well-being? Now that there is good evidence that older people may focus more on emotional material in their cognitive processing of information (Isaacowitz et al., 2000), the individual difference question arises: Do individuals differ in the extent to which they focus on emotions in their cognitive processing, and is an increased emotion-focus adaptive? This is a question which no research to date has addressed (though there is a body of research suggesting that focusing on emotions in cognitive processing leads to less efficient performance; Johnson, Nolde, & De Leonardis, 1996). Similarly, surprisingly little research has looked at individual differences in time perspective and the functional value of different time perspectives at different ages (see Zimbardo & Boyd, 1999, for one attempt to study time perspective as an individual difference variable and connect the construct to adaptive outcomes). However, Keyes and Ryff (1999) suggest that time perspective shifts across adulthood, with middle age holding the temporal orientation most balanced between past and future.

HARDINESS

Kobasa and colleagues (Kobasa, 1979; Kobasa, Maddi, & Kahn, 1982; Kobasa & Puccetti, 1983) have proposed the construct of "hardiness" to account for individual differences in resilience in the face of stress. Hardiness has been defined as the presence of three personality dispositions in an individual: commitment, control, and challenge. Commitment is whether a person feels connected to what they are doing, whether they feel there is a purpose to their activities, and whether they have an active, approach-centered orientation to their lives. Control revolves around whether an individual feels that they can influence what happens in their environment. This includes decisional control, or choosing a plan to deal with stress; cognitive control, or dealing with stressors through framing and interpretation; and coping skill, which involves the desire to be successful in dealing with all stressors. Finally, challenge refers to an individual's perception of change as being normal and desirable, rather than disruptive.

Hardiness is a cognitive individual difference variable because it involves the way a person processes information from the environment. Certainly, the cognitive control component is most explicitly about information processing. However, commitment is also highly cognitive: whether a person feels a sense of purpose and meaning in their activities is very much tied in to their interpretation of events and their framing of information. Even challenge involves a lens through which people view stimuli in their environment, as they can view events either as being part of a desirable change trajectory, or as merely being roadblocks to their happiness.

In the original study on hardiness, Kobasa (1979) hypothesized that the presence of the three previously mentioned personality dispositions would make stressful experiences less likely to lead to negative health outcomes, thus predicting resilience to stress. She compared two groups of middle and upper level executives. Members of both groups had experienced roughly equivalent amounts of stress in the 3 years before the study; what distinguished the groups was whether they reported becoming ill following their stressful experiences. The dimensions of hardiness were measured with a variety of questionnaires. For instance, one measure of decisional control was the Internal-External Locus of Control Scale. When a discriminant function analysis was used to compare the two groups of executives, those who had high stress but did not experience illness endorsed a more internal locus of control, more commitment to the self, a more active stance toward their environment, and a greater sense of meaning from their activities.

Kobasa et al., (1982) followed a sample of executives over a period of 5 years to determine the impact of hardiness on later illness. These researchers found main effects of stressful life events and hardiness on later physical illness, with less stress and more hardiness predicting lower levels of subsequent illness. However, they also found an interaction effect of stress and hardiness, in which hardiness was most beneficial for those with the most stress in their lives. Thus, this research supports the assertion that the configuration of trait-like factors collectively termed *hardiness* may have important physical health benefits. What remains unclear from even this prospective work is whether this style has benefits for psychological well-being as well, though this would seem likely from the physical health findings. Additionally, the degree to which cognitive aspects of hardiness are the "active ingredients" in these effects is not clear, though it seems that each of the three components of hardiness involve a substantial cognitive component.

A final study investigated the relationship between hardiness and other contextual factors in individuals' environments (Kobasa & Puccetti, 1983). In this study, hardiness was measured in a group of businessmen. In addition, they reported on stressful events and physical health symptoms over the previous three years, as well as their level of support from work superiors and family, and levels of social assets such occupational level and church attendance. The researchers found several interesting main effects and interactions among hardiness, stressors, and social resources. More stressful events predicted more physical illness, whereas higher levels of hardiness predicted lower levels of physical illness. For those with high levels of stress, having a supportive boss protected against physical illness, but having a supportive family did not. Interestingly, having family support predicted declining health only among those participants who rated low in hardiness. Social assets did not predict physical health.

These findings suggest that applying a hardiness-type strategy, such as seeing life as meaningful and challenging, may be protective against physical illness and thus an important part of well-being in adulthood, but that it is only one component among many potential influences on health and well-being. In particular, other aspects of the context of stress, such as the support available, may also impact whether stress leads to physical illness. Nonetheless, the evidence still points to the adaptive value in adulthood of hardiness.

Similar to many of the other cognitive styles discussed in this review, there is some theory but little empirical evidence concerning the origins of hardiness. Kobasa and colleagues (1982) speculate that hardiness might arise from certain features of the early childhood environment: the experience of a wide range of events, an environment that stimulates and supports cognitive skills like imagination, positive response for taking initiative, and parents who model and teach the aspects of hardiness. However, without any evidence to back up these claims, they remain sheer speculations.

PERCEPTIONS OF CONTROL

Both hardiness and the OPS model, described earlier, include control as a critical component of cognitive styles related to well-being in adulthood and old age. Both approaches include a consideration of both behavioral and cognitive means of being in control over the environment, though the OPS model explicitly argues for the universal primacy of external, behavioral control (Heckhausen & Schulz, 1999). Other research has focused not on the degree to which individuals exercise control over their environment as the key to successful development and psychological well-being, but rather on perceptions of control as the critical predictor of well-being. Feeling in control may certainly be considered a cognitive style that affects information processing. The landmark study in this field, conducted in the 1970s, demonstrated that changing nursing home residents' perceptions of how much control they could exert over their day-to-day life appeared to have a dramatic impact on their daily activity and risk for mortality (Langer & Rodin, 1976; Rodin & Langer, 1977). In many ways, this study started a field of inquiry into the importance of feeling in control of life. Other areas of research that have supported the general notion that feeling in control of situations is adaptive regardless of the actual objective level of environmental control include depressive realism (Alloy & Abramson, 1979) and positive illusions (Taylor, 1983).

What, then, is the evidence on how perceived control changes over the life-span, and how these perceptions actually relate to measures of psychological well-being? Although there is accumulating evidence for age differences on measures of control in specific life domains, this research has not adequately connected these changes in control to measures of psychological well-being in individuals. For example, Mirowsky (1995) found declines in overall sense of control with advancing age among adults over age 50. Using data from the MacArthur Studies of Successful Midlife Development, Lachman and Weaver (1998b) looked at self-perceived control across seven domains of functioning in this large sample of adults aged 25 to 75. Using these cross-sectional data, the researchers found age patterns that differed by domain. Older adults rated themselves as having more control in the domains of work, finances, and marriage; younger adults scored higher on control over sex life and relationship with children. These age patterns replicated across demographic groups. These findings suggest that any studies of general control (which have produced inconsistent findings, with some suggesting increased internality and others pointing toward increased externality with age; see Fung, Abeles, Carstensen, 1999, for a review) may be missing many of the interesting age differences in perceived control.

What effect, then, does feeling in control have on feeling good? One study has used an Experience Sampling Method (ESM) to determine whether perceptions of control actually predict psychological well-being in individuals' lives (Larson, 1989). In this study, several samples of different ages (adolescents, adults, and a sample of retired older adults) were beeped at random times during the day to report how much they felt in control at that moment as well as their level of happiness. The control questions asked how much the individual felt in control of the situation they were in and how much they felt they would be in control of the outcome of the situation. Two types of analyses were conducted. First, Larson evaluated the relationship between moment-to-moment control and happiness within individuals to determine whether variations in how much control individuals felt in the moment related to how happy they felt. In contrast to theories and laboratory experiments asserting that losses of control are demoralizing, variations in perceived control were only minimally correlated with changes in affect within individuals. This seems to be true for nondistressed individuals only, as adults with psychopathology studied in earlier research showed a much stronger correlation between control and affect in the moment.

Second, average daily levels of perceived control more strongly correlated with affect in these nondisturbed adult samples, suggesting that people who in general feel more control over their environment also tend to be happier in general. This average daily rating is akin to a cognitive style or lens through which individuals process environmental stimuli, demonstrating individual variability in the extent to which they see their environment as one which they can generally control (Larson,

1989). The stronger correlation between average daily control and happiness than between moment-to-moment measures suggests that this stylistic measure may be a component of psychological well-being in nondisturbed individuals of different ages. These individuals can experience small losses of control without experiencing much distress, and they can benefit over time from their generalized feeling of being in control over most things.

Historically many psychologists have argued that an internal locus of control, or feeling in control of a situation, is always preferable in terms of psychological well-being (see Skinner, 1996; Schulz & Heckhausen, 1996). However, there has been a growing realization that perceiving more control over situations is not always advantageous in terms of psychological well-being (see Clark-Plaskie & Lachman, 1999, for an example from the adult development literature). This debate has been particularly heated in the health psychology literature. The traditional approach relates strongly to Bandura's (1977) self-efficacy theory: It is adaptive for an individual to believe that certain actions will lead to certain outcomes (outcome expectancy) and that they can produce those actions (efficacy expectations).

Recently, Carver and colleagues (2000) have argued that the literature showing psychological benefits of perceived control has confounded control beliefs with the more general expectancy that positive outcomes will take place in the future. In other words, the apparent benefits of control beliefs may derive not from these beliefs per se but rather from the general belief that the outcome will be positive regardless of perceived control over it. To test this potential confound, they conducted two studies of patients in the early stages of breast cancer. They attempted to disentangle the potential confounds by asking separate questions about participants' expectations for whether they will remain cancer-free in the future and whether they thought their cancer outcome would be primarily under their own control or primarily outside their control. Across both studies, cross-sectional data suggested that only expectancies predicted measures of emotional distress. Neither perceived control nor the interaction of expectancies and control predicted distress in these samples. The authors argue that perceived control may only be useful in situations in which personal agency is necessary for the accomplishment of a particular outcome. In many other cases, confidence that good things will happen may be a better predictor of psychological well-being than control.

Recent work in life span developmental psychology supports the idea that there are boundaries on the adaptive value of perceived control. While the OPS model discussed earlier argues for the universal primacy of actual control, it also posits that attempting to maintain control over a goal that is unlikely to be reached (e.g., because a developmental deadline has passed making accomplishment of the goal impossible or much less likely; e,g., the effect of menopause on a woman's goal of having a child) is not an adaptive strategy (Wrosch & Heckhausen, 1999). Interestingly, evidence points to the adaptive function of secondary control strategies (as opposed to trying to control or alter the situation) for children facing painful, uncontrollable medical procedures (Weisz, McCabe, & Denning, 1994). In some situations, feeling in control (an internal locus) would lead people to feel responsible for situations which may in fact not be amenable to change, thus potentially leading to demoralization and declines in psychological well-being.

WISDOM

In addition to the SOC-model, Paul Baltes and his research group in Berlin have worked on another construct that may be thought of as a cognitive style related to successful aging. According to Baltes and Staudinger (2000), wisdom is "an expertise in the conduct and meaning of life" (p. 124). They consider the content of the expert system to be "fundamental pragmatics of life" such as understanding what a good human life is and what the ways are of achieving it. The emphasis is on skill in dealing with problems that lack clear-cut optimal solutions. From the beginning, this definition of the structure and content of wisdom locates it as a cognitive process with potential individual differences.

Baltes and colleagues specify five criteria for wisdom. The first two criteria emerge from the fact that wisdom is considered a type of expertise. Expertise in any domain requires extensive factual and procedural knowledge about the domain; that is, knowing what the domain is and how it works. In the case of wisdom, this involves basic knowledge of what life is like (how aging works, etc.) and how to deal with life, such as advice-giving and problem-solving.

The other criteria are specific to wisdom and are considered metacriteria superimposed on the two general expertise-related criteria. The first of these three is life span contextualism, or understanding that human behavior takes place in a complex context involving factors, such as point in the life span and the particular historical and cultural moment. The second metacriteria is relativism of values, meaning that wisdom involves an appreciation that only some priority systems are universal and that many are culturally based. The final metacriteria is concern with and understanding of uncertainty, especially concerning the constrained nature of human's ability to understand the world and know the future (Baltes & Standinger, 2000).

To measure wisdom-related performance, the Berlin group devised a procedure in which individuals respond to life problems, such as a teenage girl who wishes to get married. Individual responses to the problems are reported aloud, recorded, transcribed, and finally coded by judges on scales representing the five criteria. A wise response is rated high on all five criteria. Perhaps the most interesting result to emerge using this research paradigm involves the relationship of age to wisdom. In cross-sectional research with adults of different ages, there appear to be no age differences in wisdom-related performance from age 25 to 75. The acquisition of wisdom appears to be focused in the 15–25 age range, during which time wisdom appears to increase. At the other end of the life span, wisdom-related performance declines after 75, probably because of decline in other cognitive processes at that point (Baltes & Staudinger, 2000). Age, however, is not a sufficient condition for becoming wise.

Recently, Baltes and Freund (in press) have made a link between the SOC-model and the Berlin group's work on wisdom. They have argued that, although SOC provides a model for the structure of successful goal pursuit, it is wisdom that specifies the appropriate content for such goal strivings. In other words, wisdom is the cognitive style that allows individuals to know the right goals to pursue, while following the strategies of selection, optimization, and compensation gives the individual the best possible chance of actually accomplishing those goals. While the authors offer several case examples of the link between wise goals and SOC processes, the further delineation of this relationship is a matter for future research.

A final issue in the wisdom paradigm concerns the interactive nature of the phenomenon. While we consider wisdom a potential individual difference cognitive style for the purpose of the present review, Staudinger and Baltes (1996) have proposed that individuals are not perfect carriers of wisdom; instead, wisdom results from individuals interacting with each other. To demonstrate this, they conducted an experiment in which people completed wisdom tasks in one of four conditions: alone, after discussing the problem with a significant other, after having an internal dialogue about the problem with a person of their choice, or as part of a group in which each member had time to think about it themselves individually. Interactive conditions facilitated wisdom-related performance in this study, regardless of whether they were public or private (internal dialogue). Thus, while wisdom may be most easily conceptualized in individual difference terms, it may be the case that it can only be fully understood in interpersonal context. Nonetheless, it may still be used, perhaps best in combination with the SOC-model, to identify different cognitive strategies adults may possess and use, and to try to map these styles onto variation in the success of affective outcomes.

CONCLUSIONS

One problem raised by the research reviewed in this paper is the frequent disconnect between research done with children and research done with adults. Though there has been some research on explanatory style, dispositional optimism, and perceived control in children as well as research on adolescent wisdom (see Weisz, Sweney, Proffitt, & Carr, 1993, for an example of work on control beliefs in childhood depression, and Weisz et al., 1994, for work relevant to the OPS model in children), many of the potential cognitive predictors of well-being in adulthood and old age have not been sufficiently extended downward to childhood. Thus, we have little understanding of where these cognitive styles come from; instead, we just know the levels of them that seem to typify young adults (in some cases).

Similarly, we have little understanding of how malleable these cognitive styles may be, both in adults and in children. Preliminary evidence from prevention work targeting explanatory style suggests that this cognitive style can indeed be changed through didactic training. Indirect evidence from studies comparing older individuals in different life contexts suggests that context can affect levels of dispositional optimism and pessimism. However, we know very little about the contexts and plasticity of these constructs. Furthermore, we know just about nothing about the broader context in which these styles may develop and go on to influence psychological well-being. For example, how do these styles interact with socioeconomic differences? It may be the case that certain cognitive styles are only adaptive in certain circumstances (see, e.g., Lachman & Weaver, 1998a).

From our own research, for example, we have found that the emotional density of an older person's social network is negatively correlated with depressive symptoms among Caucasian participants, suggesting that being socially selective is related to more psychological well-being for them. However, these two measures were uncorrelated in an African American sample of the same age (Isaacowitz & Seligman, in press). It may be the case that social selectivity is only adaptive for older adults in those contexts more likely to be experienced by Caucasians. One possibility is that African American older adults may use church as an important source of psychological strength more so than do Caucasians; this would lead some African American older people to have very large social networks (many members of the church community) and also high levels of well-being. Other research has suggested that being socially selective may be very adaptive for Japanese American older adults who survived internment camps during World War II, but is correlated with maladaptive outcomes (e.g., higher depressive symptoms) among Holocaust survivors of the same age, suggesting that the different contexts of these two groups of older adults make selectivity have differential effects (Isaacowitz, Smith, & Carstensen, 2001). Future research will need to determine what contextual factors might lead to differences in the adaptiveness of different cognitive styles.

Assuming that research in the near future will be able to more clearly delineate the contexts (i.e., at what age, in what groups) in which each of these possible elements actually does contribute to well-being, the next step will be to determine how these elements might be promoted in relevant populations. Findings from prevention programs targeting explanatory style in children and young adults at risk for depression (Gillham et al., 1995; Jaycox et al., 1995; Seligman et al., 1999) suggest that at least explanatory style may be promoted through didactic-type training. However, this is only a very first step towards understanding how to promote explanatory style, and reminds us how far we have to go in understanding how these cognitive style elements develop and may be promoted.

Nonetheless, even with this observation, we may still make a preliminary conclusion on the basis of the evidence presented in this review that the following cognitive style elements may very well contribute to well-being in adulthood and old age: a realistic explanatory style, sensitive to the changes in the nature of life events with age; the absence of dispositional pessimism; selectivity in goal pursuit and social relations when resources become limited; perceptions of control when control is good to have and confidence when control is irrelevant; a fair amount of hardiness; and expertise in the pragmatics of life, or wisdom. Empirical evidence is strongest for the first two elements. The challenge for the future will be to specify the conditions in which these cognitive styles are in fact elements of well-being in adulthood and old age and how they can then be promoted in those with suboptimal levels.

REFERENCES

Abramson, L. Y., Seligman, M. E., & Teasdale, J. D. (1978). Learned helplessness in humans: Critique and reformulation. *Journal of Abnormal Psychology, 87*, 49–74.

Alloy, L. B., & Abramson, L. Y. (1979). Judgment of contingency in depressed and nondepressed students: Sadder but wiser? *Journal of Experimental Psychology: General, 108*, 441–485.

Baltes, P. B., & Baltes, M. M. (1990). Psychological perspectives on successful aging: The model of selective optimization with compensation. In P. B. Baltes & M. M. Baltes (Eds.), *Successful aging: Perspectives from the behavioral sciences* (pp. 1–34). New York: Cambridge University Press.

Baltes, M. M., & Carstensen, L. L. (1996). The process of successful ageing. *Ageing and Society, 16*, 397–422.

Baltes, P. B., & Freund, A. M. (in press). The intermarriage of wisdom and selective optimization with compensation (SOC): Two meta-heuristics guiding the conduct of life. To appear in C. L. M. Keyes & J. Haidt (Eds.), *Flourishing: The positive person and the good life.* Washington, DC: American Psychological Association.

Baltes, P. B., & Staudinger, U. M. (2000). Wisdom: A metaheuristic (pragmatic) to orchestrate mind and virtue toward excellence. *American Psychologist, 55*, 1222–1236.

Bandura, A. (1977). *Social learning theory.* Englewood Cliffs, NJ: Prentice Hall.

Beck, A. T. (1967). *Depression: Clinical, experimental, and theoretical aspects.* New York: Harper & Row.

Bromberger, J. T., & Matthews, K. A. (1996). A longitudinal study of the effects of pessimism, trait anxiety, and life stress on depressive symptoms in middle-aged women. *Psychology & Aging, 11*, 207–213.

Burns, M. O., & Seligman, M. E. (1989). Explanatory style across the life span: Evidence for stability over 52 years. *Journal of Personality & Social Psychology, 56*, 471–477.

Carstensen, L. L., & Charles, S. T. (1998). Emotions in the second half of life. *Current Directions in Psychological Science, 7*, 144–149.

Carstensen, L. L., Isaacowitz, D. M., & Charles, S. T. (1999). Taking time seriously. A theory of socioemotional selectivity. *American Psychologist, 54*, 165–181.

Carver, C. S., Harris, S. D., Lehman, J. M., Durel, L. A., Antoni, M. H., Spencer, S. M., & Pozo-Kaderman, C. (2000). How important is the perception of personal control? Studies of early stage breast cancer patients. *Personality and Social Psychology Bulletin, 26*, 139–149.

Clark-Plaskie, M., & Lachman, M. E. (1999). The sense of control at midlife. In S. L. Willis & J. D. Reid (Eds.), *Life in the middle* (pp. 181–208). San Diego, CA: Academic Press.

DeRubeis, R. J., Gelfand, L. A., Tang, T. Z., & Simons, A. D. (1999). Medications versus cognitive behavior therapy for severely depressed outpatients: Mega-analysis of four randomized comparisons. *American Journal of Psychiatry, 156*, 1007–1013.

Dykema, J., Bergbower, K., Doctora, J. D., & Peterson, C. (1996) An Attributional Style Questionnaire for general use. *Journal of Psychoeducational Assessment, 14*, 100–108.

Freund, A. M., & Baltes, P. B. (1998). Selection, optimization, and compensation as strategies of life management: Correlations with subjective indicators of successful aging. *Psychology & Aging, 13*, 531–543.

Freund, A. M., Li, K. Z. H., & Baltes, P. B. (1999). Successful development and aging: The role of selection, optimization, and compensation. In J. Brandtstädter & R. M. Lerner (Eds.), *Action and self-development* (pp. 401–434). Thousand Oaks, CA: Sage.

Fung, H. H., Abeles, R. P., & Carstensen, L. L. (1999). Psychological control in later life: Implications for life-span development. In J. Brandtstädter & R. M. Lerner (Eds.), *Action and self-development* (pp. 345–372). Thousand Oaks, CA: Sage.

Fung, H. H., Carstensen, L. L., & Lang, F. R. (2001). Age-related patterns of social relationships among African-Americans and Caucasian-Americans: Implications for socioemotional selectivity across the life span. *International Journal of Aging and Human Development, 52*, 185–206.

Gillham, J., Reivich, K., Jaycox, L., & Seligman, M. E. P. (1995). Prevention of depressive symptoms in school children: Two year follow up. *Psychological Science, 6*, 343–351.

Haaga, D. A., Dyck, M. J., & Ernst, D. (1991). Empirical status of cognitive theory of depression. *Psychological Bulletin, 110*, 215–236.

Heckhausen, J., Dixon, R. A., & Baltes, P. B. (1989). Gains and losses in development throughout adulthood as perceived by different adult age groups. *Developmental Psychology, 25*, 109–121.

Heckhausen, J., & Schulz, R. (1995). A life-span theory of control. *Psychological Review, 102*, 284–304.

Heckhausen, J., & Schulz, R. (1999). The primacy of primary control is a human universal: A reply to Gould's (1999) critique of the life-span theory of control. *Psychological Review, 106*, 605–609.

Heckhausen, J., & Schulz, R. (2000). Selectivity in life-span development: Biological and societal canalizations and individuals' developmental goals. In J. Brandtstädter & R. M. Lerner (Eds.), *Action and self-development* (pp. 67–103). Thousand Oaks, CA: Sage.

Herman-Stahl, M., & Petersen, A. C. (1996). The protective role of coping and social resources for depressive symptoms among young adolescents. *Journal of Youth and Adolescence, 25*, 733–753.

Hjelle, L., Belongia, C., & Nesser, J. (1996). Psychometric properties of the Life Orientation Test and the Attributional Style Questionnaire. *Psychological Reports, 78*, 507–515.

Isaacowitz, D. M., Charles, S. T., & Carstensen, L. L. (2000). Emotion and cognition. F. I. M. Craik & T. A. Salthouse (Eds.), *The Handbook of Aging and Cognition* (2nd ed., pp. 593–631). Mahwah, NJ: Lawrence Erlbaum Associates.

Isaacowitz, D. M., & Seligman, M. E. P. (2001). Is pessimistic explanatory style a risk factor for depressive mood among community-dwelling older adults? *Behaviour Research and Therapy, 39*, 255–273.

Isaacowitz, D. M., & Seligman, M. E. P. (in press). A cognitive styles approach to emotion and aging. *International Journal of Aging and Human Development.*

Isaacowitz, D. M., & Smith, J. (2000). *Positive and Negative Affect in Very Old Age: Extending Mroczek & Kolarz (1998) into Late Life.* Manuscript submitted for publication.

Isaacowitz, D. M., Smith, T. B., & Carstensen, L. L. (2002). *Socioemotional selectivity and mental health among trauma survivors in old age.* Manuscript submitted for publication.

Jaycox, L. H., Reivich, K. J., Gillham, J., & Seligman, M. E. (1994). Prevention of depressive symptoms in school children. *Behaviour Research & Therapy, 32*, 801–816.

Johnson, M. K., Nolde, S. F., & De Leonardis, D. M. (1996). Emotional focus and source monitoring. *Journal of Memory and Language, 35*, 135–156.

Kamen-Siegel, L., Rodin, J., Seligman, M. E., & Dwyer, J. (1991). Explanatory style and cell-mediated immunity in elderly men and women. *Health Psychology, 10*, 229–235.

Keyes, C. L. M., & Ryff, C. D. (1999). Psychological well-being in midlife. In S. L. Willis & J. D. Reid (Eds.), *Life in the middle* (pp. 161–180). San Diego, CA: Academic Press.

Kobasa, S. C. (1979). Stressful life events, personality, and health: An inquiry into hardiness. *Journal of Personality & Social Psychology, 37*, 1–11.

Kobasa, S. C., Maddi, S. R., & Kahn, S. (1982). Hardiness and health: A prospective study. *Journal of Personality & Social Psychology, 42*, 168–177.

Kobasa, S. C., & Puccetti, M. C. (1983). Personality and social resources in stress resistance. *Journal of Personality & Social Psychology, 45*, 839–850.

Lachman, M. E. (1990). When bad things happen to older people: Age differences in attributional style. *Psychology and Aging, 5*, 607–609.

Lachman, M. E., & Weaver, S. L. (1998a). The sense of control as a moderator of social class differences in health and well-being. *Journal of Personality and Social Psychology, 74*, 763–773.

Lachman, M. E., & Weaver, S. L. (1998b). Sociodemographic variations in the sense of control by domain: Findings from the MacArthur studies of midlife. *Psychology & Aging, 13*, 553–562.

Lang, F. R., & Carstensen, L. L. (1994). Close emotional relationships in late life: Further support for proactive aging in the social domain. *Psychology & Aging, 9*, 315–324.

Langer, E. J., & Rodin, J. (1976). The effects of choice and enhanced personal responsibility for the aged: a field experiment in an institutional setting. *Journal of Personality & Social Psychology, 34*, 191–198.

Larson, R. (1989). Is feeling "in control" related to happiness in daily life? *Psychological Reports, 64*, 775–784.

Lazarus, R. S., & Folkman, S. (1984). *Stress, appraisal, and coping.* New York: Springer.

Marsiske, M., Lang, F. R., Baltes, P. B., & Baltes, M. M. (1995). Selective optimization with compensation: Life-span perspectives on successful human development. In R. A. Dixon & L. Backman

(Eds.), *Compensating for Psychological Deficits and Declines* (pp. 35–79). Mahwah, NJ: Lawrence Erlbaum Associates.

Metalsky, G. I., Abramson, L. Y., Seligman, M. E., Semmel, A., & Peterson, C. (1982). Attributional styles and life events in the classroom: vulnerability and invulnerability to depressive mood reactions. *Journal of Personality & Social Psychology, 43*, 612–617.

Metalsky, G. I., Halberstadt, L. J., & Abramson, L. Y. (1987). Vulnerability to depressive mood reactions: Toward a more powerful test of the diathesis-stress and causal mediation components of the reformulated theory of depression. *Journal of Personality & Social Psychology, 52*, 386–393.

Mirowsky, J. (1995). Age and the sense of control. *Social Psychology Quarterly, 58*, 31–43.

Mroczek, D. K., & Kolarz, C. M. (1998). The effect of age on positive and negative affect: A developmental perspective on happiness. *Journal of Personality and Social Psychology, 75*, 1333–1349.

Mroczek, D. K., Spiro, A., Aldwin, C. M., Ozer, D. J., & Bossé, R. (1993). Construct validation of optimism and pessimism in older men: Findings from the normative aging study. *Health Psychology, 12*, 406–409.

Murrell, S. A., Norris, F. H., & Hutchins, G. L. (1984). Distribution and desirability of life events in older adults: Population and policy implications. *Journal of Community Psychology, 12*, 301–311.

Nolen-Hoeksema, S., Girgus, J. S., & Seligman, M. E. (1986). Learned helplessness in children: A longitudinal study of depression, achievement, and explanatory style. *Journal of Personality & Social Psychology, 51*, 435–442.

Nolen-Hoeksema, S., Girgus, J. S., & Seligman, M. E. (1992). Predictors and consequences of childhood depressive symptoms: A 5-year longitudinal study. *Journal of Abnormal Psychology, 101*, 405–422.

Peterson, C., & Seligman, M. E. (1984). Causal explanations as a risk factor for depression: Theory and evidence. *Psychological Review, 91*, 347–374.

Peterson, C., Seligman, M. E., & Vaillant, G. E. (1988). Pessimistic explanatory style is a risk factor for physical illness: A thirty-five-year longitudinal study. *Journal of Personality & Social Psychology, 55*, 23–27.

Peterson, C., Semmel, A., von Baeyer, C., Abramson, L. T., Metalsky, G. I., & Seligman, M. E. P. (1982). The Attributional Style Questionnaire. *Cognitive Therapy and Research, 6*, 287–300.

Plomin, R., Scheier, M. F., Bergeman, C. S., Pedersen, N. L., Nesserroade, J. R., & McClearn, G. E. (1992). Optimism, pessimism and mental health: A twin/adoption analysis. *Personality & Individual Differences, 13*, 921–930.

Reker, G. T. (1997). Personal meaning, optimism, and choice: Existential predictors of depression in community and institutional elderly. *The Gerontologist, 37*, 709–716.

Reker, G. T., & Wong, P. T. P. (1985). Personal optimism, physical and mental health. In J. E. Birren & J. Livingston (Eds.), *Cognition, stress and aging* (pp. 134–173). Englewood Cliffs, NJ: Prentice-Hall.

Robinson-Whelen, S., Kim, C., MacCallum, R. C., & Kiecolt-Glaser, J. K. (1997). Distinguishing optimism from pessimism in older adults: Is it more important to be optimistic or not to be pessimistic? *Journal of Personality & Social Psychology, 73*, 1345–1353.

Rodin, J., & Langer, E. J. (1977). Long-term effects of a control-relevant intervention with the institutionalized aged. *Journal of Personality & Social Psychology, 35*, 897–902.

Saudino, K. J., Pedersen, N. L., Lichtenstein, P., McClearn, G. E., & Plomin, R. (1997). Can personality explain genetic influences on life events? *Journal of Personality & Social Psychology, 72*, 196–206.

Scheier, M. F., & Carver, C. S. (1985). Optimism, coping, and health: Assessment and implications of generalized outcome expectancies. *Health Psychology, 4*, 219–247.

Scheier, M. F., & Carver, C. S. (1993). On the power of positive thinking: The benefits of being optimistic. *Current Directions in Psychological Science, 2*, 26–30.

Scheier, M. F., Carver, C. S., & Bridges, M. W. (1994). Distinguishing optimism from neuroticism (and trait anxiety, self-mastery, and self-esteem): A reevaluation of the Life Orientation Test. *Journal of Personality & Social Psychology, 67*(6), 1063–1078.

Scheier, M. F., Matthews, K. A., Owens, J. F., Magovern, G. J., Sr., Lefebvre, R. C., Abbott, R. A., & Carver, C. S. (1989). Dispositional optimism and recovery from coronary artery bypass surgery: The beneficial effects on physical and psychological well-being. *Journal of Personality & Social Psychology, 57*(6), 1024–1040.

Schulman, P., Castellon, C., & Seligman, M. E. (1989). Assessing explanatory style: The content analysis of verbatim explanations and the Attributional Style Questionnaire. *Behaviour Research & Therapy, 27*, 505–512.

Schulman, P., Keith, D., & Seligman, M. E. (1993). Is optimism heritable? A study of twins. *Behaviour Research & Therapy, 31*, 569–574.

Schulz, R., Bookwala, J., Knapp, J. E., Scheier, M., & Williamson, G. M. (1996). Pessimism, age, and cancer mortality. *Psychology & Aging, 11*, 304–309.

Schulz, R., & Heckhausen, J. (1996). A life span model of successful aging. *American Psychologist, 51*, 702–714.

Seligman, M. E. P. (1990). *Learned Optimism*. New York: Knopf.

Seligman, M. E. P., & Isaacowitz, D. M. (2000). Learned helplessness. In *The Encyclopedia of Stress* (Vol. 2, pp. 599–603). San Diego, CA: Academic Press.

Seligman, M. E., Peterson, C., Kaslow, N. J., Tanenbaum, R. L., Alloy, L. B., & Abramson, L. Y. (1984). Attributional style and depressive symptoms among children. *Journal of Abnormal Psychology, 93*, 235–238.

Seligman, M. E. P., Schulman, P., DeRubeis, R. J., & Hollon, S. D. (1999). The prevention of depression and anxiety. *Prevention and Treatment*. [electronic journal].

Skinner, E. A. (1996). *Perceived control, motivation, and coping*. Thousand Oaks, CA: Sage.

Smith, T. W., Pope, M. K., Rhodewalt, F., & Poulton, J. L. (1989). Optimism, neuroticism, coping, and symptom reports: An alternative interpretation of the Life Orientation Test. *Journal of Personality & Social Psychology, 56*, 640–648.

Staudinger, U. M., & Baltes, P. B. (1996). Interactive minds: A facilitative setting for wisdom-related performance? *Journal of Personality and Social Psychology, 71*, 746–762.

Suzman, R. M., Manton, K. G., & Willis, D. P. (1992). Introducing the oldest old. In R. M. Suzman, D. P. Willis, & K. G. Manton (Eds.), *The oldest old* (pp. 3–14). New York: Oxford University Press.

Taylor, S. E. (1983). Adjustment to threatening events: A theory of cognitive adaptation. *American Psychologist, 38*, 1161–1173.

Weisz, J. R., McCabe, M. A., & Denning, M. D. (1994). Primary and secondary control among children undergoing medical procedures: Adjustment as a function of coping style. *Journal of Consulting and Clinical Psychology, 62*, 324–332.

Weisz, J. R., Sweeney, L., Proffitt, V., Carr, T. (1993). Control-related beliefs and self-reported depressive symptoms in late childhood. *Journal of Abnormal Psychology, 102*, 411–418.

Wrosch, C., & Heckhausen, J. (1999). Control processes before and after passing a developmental deadline: Activation and deactivation of intimate relationship goals. *Journal of Personality & Social Psychology, 77*, 415–427.

Zimbardo, P. G., & Boyd, J. N. (1999). Putting time in perspective: A valid, reliable individual-differences metric. *Journal of Personality and Social Psychology, 77*, 1271–1288.

33

Dimensions of Well-Being and Mental Health in Adulthood

Corey L. M. Keyes
Mary Beth Waterman
Emory University, Atlanta, GA

INTRODUCTION

Studies of the occurrence and distribution of mental illnesses in the United States (Kessler & Zhao, 1999; Keyes & Lopez, 2002) suggest that as many as 50% of adults will remain free of serious mental illness over their lifetimes with 90% of the adult population remaining free of major depression in a given year. Are adults who remain free of mental illnesses annually and over a lifetime mentally healthy and productive? This is a pivotal question for everyone interested in the well-being of adults. Proponents of mental *health* distinguish this state from the mere absence of mental *illnesses* (Keyes & Shapiro, in press). This chapter examines three aspects of subjective well-being—psychological, social, and emotional—that impact mental health. Emotional well-being is characterized as a positive feeling state, and social and psychological well-being are characterized as positive functional states. Focusing on individuals 18 years old or older, we then review evidence indicating the beneficial social and economic outcomes that are associated with higher levels of subjective well-being, and identify multiple determinants of subjective well-being for adults.

Mental health, according to the Surgeon General's Report (U.S. Department of Health and Human Services, 1999) is "… a state of successful performance of mental function, resulting in productive activities, fulfilling relationships with people, and the ability to adapt to change and to cope with adversity" (p. 4). For about 50 years, social scientists have called for a definition of mental health that is more than the absence of mental illnesses (Jahoda, 1958; Smith, 1958). In 1958, M. Brewster Smith lamented that "positive" mental health is a "slogan" rather than an empirical concept or variable.

Although the Surgeon General's Mental Health Report was years in the making, much remains to be done to make mental health truly a positive construct and not just a de-stigmatizing synonym for mental illness. For about 40 years, social scientists have attempted to conceptualize and measure the many dimensions of subjective well-being. Subjective well-being reflects individuals' perceptions and evaluations of their own lives in terms of their affective states and their psychological and social functioning, all being critical dimensions of mental health.

How can mental health be operationalized? In health or illness, symptoms are subjective evidence of the person's condition. Symptoms indicate a bodily or mental state as perceived by the individual. Signs are objective findings identified by an examiner. Operationalizing mental health involves connecting subjective indications of well-being (symptoms of mental health) and objective indicators of cognitive, emotional, and social functioning (signs of mental health). We have found that certain constellations of symptoms cluster in mental health (Keyes, 2001; Mechanic, 1999) and that their level of intensity and duration are important in the same ways as symptoms of illness.

SUBJECTIVE WELL-BEING AND MENTAL HEALTH

Positive Feelings: Emotional Well-Being

The emotional well-being cluster of symptoms reflects the presence and absence of positive feelings about life operationalized as evaluations of happiness and satisfaction with life, and the balance of positive to negative affect experiences over a time period. Thus, emotional well-being can be conceptualized as the balance of feelings (positive and negative) experienced in life (Bradburn, 1969) and the perceived feelings (happiness and satisfaction) (Andrews & Withey, 1976).

Most single-item measures of life satisfaction are adaptations of Cantril's (1965) Self-Anchoring Scale, which asks respondents to "rate their life overall these days" on a scale from 0 to 10, where 0 means the "worst possible life overall" and 10 means "the best possible life overall." Variants of Cantril's (1965) measure have been used extensively in numerous studies worldwide and have been applied to the measurement of avowed happiness with life (Andrews & Robinson, 1991; Andrews & Withey, 1976). Single-item indicators and multi-item scales of life satisfaction and happiness have also been developed and employed extensively (see Diener, 1984, p. 546, for a list of measures of emotional well-being).

Most measures of positive and negative affect investigate the frequency or the duration of time that a respondent reports the experience of symptoms of positive and negative affect. For example, individuals are often asked to indicate how much of the time during the past 30 days they have felt six types of negative and six types of positive indicators of affect. Response choices for time are "all," "most," "some," "a little," or "none of the time." Symptoms of negative affect typically include so sad nothing could cheer you up, nervous, restless or fidgety, hopeless, that everything was an effort, and worthless. Symptoms of positive affect typically involve feeling cheerful, in good spirits, extremely happy, calm and peaceful, satisfied, and full of life. Estimates of internal reliability of the multi-item scales of satisfaction and happiness (see, e.g., Diener, 1993) and positive and negative affect (see, e.g., Mroczek & Kolarz, 1998) usually exceed .80.

Studies clearly support a proposed factor structure of emotional well-being with a more cognitive domain of life satisfaction (i.e., quality of life) and a more affective domain (i.e., happiness; Bryant & Veroff, 1982). However, the debate over the structure of positive and negative affect continues to this day. Are positive and negative affect opposite ends of a single continuum (i.e., highly correlated), or are positive and negative feelings relatively independent (i.e., modestly correlated) dimensions of well-being? Evidence supports the unidimensional and the bidimensional model (Diener & Emmons, 1984; Keyes, 2000; Russell & Carroll, 1999; Watson & Tellegen, 1985; Zautra, Reich, Davis, Potter, & Nicolson, 2000).

However, some scholars maintain that the inconclusiveness of the evidence can be assigned to artifacts of measurement. Prior to the demonstrated validity of frequency as a response choice (see Diener, Sandvik, & Pavot, 1991), measures of emotional well-being tended to confound the frequency and intensity of emotional experience. Measures of the intensity of positive affect and of negative affect are strongly and positively correlated. Measures of the frequency of the experience of symptoms of positive and negative affect are negatively and modestly correlated. (Diener, Larson, Levine, & Emmons, 1985). Nonrandom measurement errors between indicators of positive and negative affect may also suppress the negative correlation between the latent constructs of positive and negative affect (Green, Goldman, & Salovey, 1993).

Positive Functioning: Psychological Well-Being

Mental health is more than the presence and absence of affective states. Subjective well-being includes measures of the perceived presence and absence of positive functioning in life (Jahoda, 1958; Ryff, 1989). Positive functioning encompasses six dimensions of psychological well-being: self-acceptance, positive relations with others, personal growth, purpose in life, environmental mastery, and autonomy (see Keyes & Ryff's 1999 review). Each dimension of psychological well-being contributes to mental health.

Self-acceptance requires the maintenance of esteem for one's self while facing complex and sometimes unpleasant personal aspects of the self. In addition, individuals accumulate a past and have the capacity to recall and remember themselves through time. Healthy individuals perceive themselves positively across the life course and accept all parts of themselves. *Positive relations with others* consist of the ability to cultivate warm, intimate relationships with others. It also includes the presence of satisfying social contacts and relations. *Autonomy* measures the degree to which people seek self-determination and personal authority, in a society that at times requires obedience and compliance. However, healthy individuals seek to understand their own values and ideals. In addition, healthy individuals see themselves guiding their own behavior and conduct from internalized standards and values.

Environmental mastery is the active engagement of the environment to mold it to meet one's needs and wants. Healthy individuals recognize personal needs and desires and also feel capable of, and permitted to, take an active role in getting what they need from their environments. *Purpose in life* captures the adult's perception of having direction in life, even when the world offers none or provides unsatisfactory alternatives. Healthy individuals see their daily lives as fulfilling a direction and purpose, and therefore, they view their personal lives as meaningful. Last, *personal growth* is the ability and desire to enhance existing skills and talents, and to seek opportunities for further personal development. In addition, healthy individuals are open to experience and have the capacity to identify challenges in a variety of circumstances.

Positive Functioning: Social Well-Being

Still, there is more to mental health than emotional and psychological well-being. Keyes (1998) has asscrtcd that positive functioning includes social challenges and tasks, and proposed five dimensions of social well-being. Thus, the triad comprising mental health includes the subjective feeling and functional states of emotional, psychological, and social well-being.

Whereas psychological well-being (and its component, positive relations with others) represents more private and personal criteria for evaluation of one's functioning, social well-being epitomizes the more public and societal criteria whereby people evaluate their functioning in life. These societal dimensions consist of social coherence, social actualization, social integration, social acceptance, and social contribution.

Social integration is the evaluation of the quality of one's relationship to society and community. Integration is therefore the extent to which people feel they have something in common with others who constitute their social reality (e.g., their neighborhood), as well as the degree to which they feel that they belong to their communities and society. *Social contribution* is the evaluation of one's value to society. It includes the belief that one is a vital member of society, with something of value to give to the world. *Social coherence* is the perception of the quality, organization, and operation of the social world, and it includes a concern for knowing about the world. Social coherence is analogous to meaningfulness in life (Mirowsky & Ross 1989; Seeman, 1959) and involves appraisals that society is discernable, sensible, and predictable.

Social actualization is the evaluation of the potential and the trajectory of society. This is the belief in the positive evolution of society and the sense that society has potential that is being realized through its institutions and citizens. *Social acceptance* is the construal of society through the character and qualities of other people in general. Individuals must function in a public arena that consists primarily of strangers. Individuals who illustrate social acceptance trust others, think that others are capable of kindness, and believe that people can be industrious. Socially accepting people hold favorable views of human nature and feel comfortable with others.

THE STRUCTURE OF WELL-BEING: FACTOR MODELS

Several studies using community and nationally representative samples have supported the theory that social and psychological well-being are structured as discrete factors. Confirmatory factor models have revealed that the proposed five-factor theory of social well-being provides the best fit (Keyes, 1998), and the proposed six-factor theory of psychological well-being is the best-fitting model (Ryff & Keyes, 1995). Moreover, the factors of social and psychological well-being are mutually distinct. The scales of social and psychological well-being correlated as high as .44, and exploratory factor analysis revealed two correlated ($r = .34$) factors with the scales of social well-being loading on a separate factor from the items measuring happiness, satisfaction, and the overall scale of psychological well-being (Keyes, 1996).

Measures of social well-being also are factorially distinct from traditional measures (happiness and satisfaction) of emotional well-being (Keyes, 1996). Measures of emotional well-being (positive and negative affect, life satisfaction) are factorially distinct from the measures of psychological well-being (Keyes, Shmotkin, & Ryff, 2002).

While the three major dimensions—emotional, psychological, and social well-being—are factorially distinct, underlying components for emotional and for psychological well-being may link attributes within each of those dimensions. McGregor and Little's (1998) factor analysis yielded two distinct factors that share an underlying emotional factor (including depression, positive affect, and life satisfaction) and an underlying psychological functioning factor (including four of the psychological well-being scales: personal growth, purpose in life, positive relations with others, and autonomy).

Conceptualizing Mental Health

Table 33.1 summarizes the psychological, social, and emotional dimensions of subjective well-being as they were measured (italicized statements) in the MacArthur Foundation's Successful Midlife in the U.S. (MIDUS) Study.

Empirically, mental health and mental illness are not opposite ends of a single health continuum. Measures of psychological well-being (in two studies summarized in Ryff & Keyes, 1995) correlated on average –.51 with the Zung depression inventory and –.55 with the Center for Epidemiological Studies depression (CESD)

TABLE 33.1

Subjective Well-Being: Dimensions and Operational Definitions

Psychological Well-Being	Social Well-Being	Emotional Well-Being
Self-Acceptance: possess positive attitude toward the self; acknowledge and accept multiple aspects of self; feel positive about past life.	**Social Acceptance**: have positive attitudes toward people; acknowledge others and generally accept people, despite others' sometimes complex and perplexing behavior.	**Positive Affect**: experience symptoms that suggest enthusiasm, joy, and happiness for life
• I like most parts of my personality • When I look at the story of my life, I am pleased with how things have turned out so far • In many ways, I feel disappointed about my achievements in life (−)	• People who do a favor expect nothing in return • People do not care about other people's problems (−) • I believe that people are kind	• During the last 30 days, how much of the time did you feel cheerful; in good spirits; extremely happy; calm and peaceful; satisfied; and full of life?**
Personal Growth: have feeling of continued development and potential and are open to new experience; feel increasingly knowledgeable and effective.	**Social Actualization**: care about and believe society is evolving positively; think society has potential to grow positively; thing self-society is realizing potential.	**Negative Affect**: absence of symptoms that suggest that life is undesirable and unpleasant.
• For me, life has been a continuous process of learning, changing, and growth • I think it is important to have new experiences that challenge how I think about myself and the world • I gave up trying to make big improvements changes in my life a long time ago (−)	• The world is becoming a better place for everyone • Society has stopped making progress (−) • Society isn't improved for people like me (−)	• During the last 30 days, how much of the time did you feel so sad nothing could cheer you up; nervous; restless or fidgety; hopeless; that everything was an effort; worthless?**
Purpose in Life: have goals and a sense of direction in life; past life is meaningful; hold beliefs that give purpose to life.	**Social Contribution**: feel they have something valuable to give present and to society; think their daily activities are valued by their community.	**Life Satisfaction**: is a sense contentment, peace, and satisfaction from small discrepancies between wants and needs with accomplishments and attainments.
• Some people wander aimlessly through life, but I am not one of them	• I have something valuable to give to the world	

- I live life one data at a time and don't really think about the future (–)
- I sometimes feel as if I've done all there is to do in life (–)

- My daily activities do not create anything worthwhile for my community
- I have nothing important to contribute to society (–)

- During the past 30 days, how much of the time did you feel satisfied: full of life?**
- Overall these days, how satisfied are you with your life? (0–10, where 0 = terrible and 10 = delighted)
- Satisfaction may be measured in life domains such as work, home, neighborhood, health, intimacy, finances, parenting, etc.

Happiness: having a general feeling and experience of pleasure, contentment, and joy.

- Over all these days how happy are you with your life***
- How frequently have you felt (joy, pleasure, happiness) in the past week, month, or year?

Environmental Mastery: feel competent and able to manage a complex environment; choose or create personally suitable community.

- The demands of everyday life often get me down (–)
- In general, I feel I am in charge of the situation in which I live
- I am good at managing the responsibilities of daily life

Social Coherence: see a social world that is intelligible, logical, and predictable; care about and are interested in society and contexts.

- The world is too complex for me (–)
- I cannot make sense of what's going on in the world (–)
- I find it easy to predict what will happen next in society

Autonomy: are self–determining, independent, and regulate internally: resist social pressures to think and act in certain ways; evaluate self by personal standards.

- I tend to be influenced by people with strong opinions (–)
- I have confidence in my own opinions, even if they are different from the way most other people think
- I judge myself by what I think is important, not by the values of what others think is important

Social Integration: feel part of community; think they belong, feel supported, and share commonalities with community.

- I don't feel I belong to anything I'd call a community (–)
- I feel close to other people in my community
- My community is a source of comfort

483

continued on next page

TABLE 33.1   (continued)

Psychological Well–Being	Social Well–Being	Emotional Well–Being
Positive Relations With Others: have warm, satisfying, trusting relationships; are concerned about others' welfare; capable of strong empathy, affection, and intimacy; understand give–and–take of human relationships.		
• *Maintaining close relationships has been difficult and frustrating for me* (–)		
• *People would describe me as a giving person, willing to share my time with others*		
• *I have not experienced many warm and trusting relationships with others* (–)		

Note: A negative sign in parenthesis indicates that the item is reverse scored. Response options range from strongly disagree (1), moderately disagree (2), or slightly disagree (3) to neither agree nor disagree (4), slightly agree (5), moderately agree (6), to strongly agree (7).
** Indicates response range from all the time (1), most the time (2), some of the time (3), a little of the time (4), none of the time (5).
*** Indicates response range from worse possible situation (0) to best possible situation (10).

scale. Indicators and scales of life satisfaction and happiness (i.e., emotional well-being) also tend to correlate around −.40 to −.50 with scales of depression symptoms (see Frisch, Cornell, Villanueva, & Retzlaff, 1992).

Confirmatory factor analyses of the subscales of the CESD and the scales of psychological well-being scales in a sample of U.S. adults supported the two-factor theory (Keyes, Ryff, & Lee, 2001). That is, the best-fitting model was one where the CESD subscales were indicators of the latent factor that represented the presence and absence of mental illness (see also Headey, Kelley, & Wearing, 1993). The psychological well-being scales were indicators of a second latent factor that represented the presence and absence of mental health. In short, mental health is not merely the absence of mental illnesses; it is not simply the presence of high levels of subjective well-being. Mental health is best viewed as a complete state consisting of the relative presence or absence of mental illness (depression) and mental health symptoms.

Toward Application of Subjective Well-Being and Mental Health

Well-being may be regarded as the goal of a good life or the means to living a good life. Aristotle deemed happiness, one aspect of well-being, the summum bonum of life. Happiness was an end rather than a means, because its consummation was so intoxicating that happiness muted all subsequent desire and motivation. As Socrates put it, happiness would render individuals "contented pigs." The alternative perspective shows the utility of happiness as the proverbial carrot at the end of life's stick, maintaining the individual's motivation to be a productive and ethical citizen.

Happiness or well-being, then, is the reward for a life well-lived (Becker, 1992; Veenhoven, 1988). Alternatively, happiness or well-being may be a means to an end. Here, the objective of life is to live in a satisfying, productive, and healthy manner. Rather than rendering individuals content with their lot in life, well-being may propel individuals to constructively create, produce, and participate in their communities. Facets of adult mental health and well-being have been studied under many different names, like happiness, that do not necessarily map completely onto subjective well-being as identified in the MacArthur Foundation's MIDUS Study. Nonetheless, examining these applications can illustrate many benefits of supporting mental health and well-being during adulthood.

A growing body of research suggests that facets of well-being are associated with a host of positive outcomes in the business sector (Harter, Schmidt, & Keyes, in press; Spector, 1997). Employees who are more satisfied with life and their work tend to be more cooperative, and more helpful to their colleagues, are more punctual and time efficient, show up for more days of work, and stay with a company longer than dissatisfied employees. Investigation of the happy-productive worker clearly links emotional well-being with positive management evaluations of work performance. Employees who report experiencing a greater balance of positive emotional symptoms over negative emotional symptoms received higher performance ratings from supervisors than employees who report feeling more negative than positive symptoms of emotion (Wright & Bonnett, 1997; Wright & Cropanzano, 2000; Wright & Staw, 1999).

Meta-analyses of the association between employee workplace satisfaction and perceptions of personal growth and relationships at work are reliably correlated with positive outcomes for the business. That is, businesses with more employees who have high levels of employee well-being also tend to report greater customer satisfaction and loyalty, greater profitability, more productivity, and lower rates of turnover (Harter & Schmidt, 2000; Harter et al., in press). Analyses conservatively estimate that companies with the most employees in the highest quartile of well-being report dramatically higher monetary returns than companies with most employees in the lowest quartile of well-being (Harter & Schmidt, 2000; Harter et al., in press).

Emotional well-being may prevent the onset of disability among older adults. In a sample of older (65 to 99 years old) Hispanic adults without limitations of daily life at baseline, Ostir and colleagues (Ostir, Markides, Black, & Goodwin, 2000) found that those with high positive affect were half as likely as the adults with low positive affect to have died or to have acquired limitations of activities of daily life 2 years later. These findings controlled for sociodemographic variables, functional physical status, lifestyle (i.e., smoking and drinking), and negative affect scores at baseline. Emotional well-being may buffer older adults from declines in physical health.

Lewinsohn, Redner, and Seeley (1991) investigated the association of perceived quality of life with current depression and future depression as measured by the CESD scale. Operationalized as perceived happiness and satisfaction with domains of life, quality of life correlated in the range of −.48 to −.60 with the CESD scale. Low levels of life satisfaction and happiness at time 1 among nondepressed subjects were associated with an increased risk for depression at the time 2 follow-up. This study suggests that lower levels of well-being may increase the risk for the onset of some mental illnesses. Conversely, the promotion of adult well-being may protect against some mental illnesses.

The risk of suicide may be increased among persons with lower levels of subjective well-being. Weerasinghe and Tepperman (1994) stated that they could not locate a single study directly investigating the relationship between perceived happiness and suicide. However, the same authors identified several factors (viz. marriage, religion, and employment) that studies have shown to promote happiness as well as correlate with lower risk of suicide. This association is separate from the linkage of low well-being, mood disorders, and suicide risk.

Low levels of social well-being as evidenced by low social integration and low social contribution may also increase the risk of suicide (see Rebellon, Brown, & Keyes, 2001). Recently, analyses of 20 years' data from the Finnish twin cohort study related lower life satisfaction and suicide (Koivumaa-Honkanen et al., 2001). Life satisfaction was operationalized as a composite of the following items: perceived interest in life, happiness with life, ease of living, and feelings of loneliness. After controlling for sociodemographic variables, health status, health habits, and physical activity, the authors found that low levels of life satisfaction placed men at very high risk of suicide, relative to men who had higher levels of life satisfaction.

Maintenance therapy that promotes well-being may prevent or delay recurrence of depression (Keyes & Lopez, 2002). As many as 70% of depressed patients relapse within 6 months of their original symptom remission (Ramana et al., 1995). Maintenance therapy, a continuation phase of therapy following the initial remission of symptoms, has reduced the relapse rate for major depressive disorder (U.S. Department of Health and Human Services, 1999). Booster sessions of cognitive behavioral therapy or continuation of therapy supporting psychological well-being has prevented recurrence of depression (Fava, 1999; Fava, Rafanelli, Grandi, Conti, & Belluardo, 1999).

Individuals with higher levels of subjective well-being tend to experience positive mood states that facilitate mental and physical functioning (Diener, Suh, Lucas, & Smith, 1999). Positive emotions have been shown to facilitate and improve cognition and immune system function. On a daily level, individuals who feel more positively tend to engage in more creative and efficient thought processes (Csikszentmihalyi, 1990; Fredrickson, 1998; Isen, 1987), are more attentive to self-relevant health risk information (Reed & Aspinwall, 1998), and have enhanced immune system functioning (Salovey, Rothman, Detweiler, & Steward, 2000).

DETERMINANTS OF WELL-BEING AND MENTAL HEALTH

Studies show that overall measures of emotional and psychological well-being are relatively stable over time. However, specific aspects of well-being may vary in response to external events and changes in the environment. Much remains to be learned about determinants of well-being and mental health. Some factors may be truly causal, such as genetic predisposition, without being sole or proximal determinants of any condition. Other factors, such as personality traits, may mediate the effects of causal factors. Demographic variables, such as age, gender, or socioeconomic status, may be proxies for other, as yet unspecified, causal factors.

Brief descriptions of some determinants of well-being and mental health follow. Many of these determinants have been studied in their relationship to the outcomes of happiness and life satisfaction, rather than overall well-being or mental health. Additionally, happiness and life satisfaction have not carried uniform operational definitions or been measured uniformly across these studies. This methodological inconsistency limits comparisons across studies and may account for some divergence in outcomes.

Age

Some studies have shown that overall happiness or mood decreases in older adults, whereas other studies have found that life satisfaction either increases or plateaus with age. Even though studies have shown that positive and negative affect are experienced differently by the young and the old (Diener, 1984), older adults appear to experience more positive affect with age (Mroczek & Kolarz, 1998). Interestingly, studies suggest that women may become less happy with age, whereas men become happier (Argyle, 1999).

In several studies employing community and national samples, Ryff (1989; Ryff & Keyes, 1995) found that environmental mastery and autonomy increased with age. At the same time, purpose in life and personal growth showed dramatic declines with age. Measures of self-acceptance and positive relations did not reliably shown age differences.

The limitations of studies on this topic have lead researchers to believe that getting older may not be the cause of lower emotional well-being (Diener et al., 1999). Although happiness cannot change age, can the effect of age on happiness be causal? Cohort differences for older people, such as education and expectancy levels, could explain the relationship. Despite the fact that the effects of age on happiness are small, there are several reasons for the relationship. Numerous studies have found that older people are in worse health, have lower incomes after retirement, are less likely to be married, and have lower aspirations. Yet, older people are more satisfied, perhaps because the gap between their goals and achievement is narrower (Campbell, Converse, & Rogers, 1976) or because they have had time to adapt to their situation (Argyle, 1999).

Sex and Race

Though women are more prone to depression and men to antisocial behaviors, overall, men and women report equivalent degrees of happiness and life satisfaction (Myers, 2000). Several studies have found that Caucasians report greater happiness than African Americans. The disparity in levels of happiness between ethnic groups may be attributable in part to differences in income levels, education, and job status. Although the greatest effect of ethnicity on happiness is seen among those with higher occupational status, education, or income, when controlling for these factors, the effect of ethnicity on happiness is reduced or negligible (Veenhoven, 1994). Perceived self-esteem is also lower among black Americans than whites, which can also affect measures of happiness and well-being (Campbell et al., 1976).

Education

Many studies have correlated educational levels and measures of happiness. When looking at positive and negative affect separately, the relationship between education and positive affect was clearly shown, whereas there was no relationship found between negative affect and education (Bradburn, 1969). The primary impact that education has on emotional well-being is from its influence on both occupation and income. However, when controlling for income, the effect of education on emotional well-being is reduced (Diener, Sandvik, Seidlitz, & Diener, 1993). If occupation is held constant, the effect of education on emotional well-being becomes quite small or disappears (Glenn & Weaver, 1979).

Income

Although most people would claim that wealth cannot buy happiness, there is, at least in part, a relationship between money and well-being (Myers, 2000). A strong ecological correlation has been found between national economic growth and well-being. However, the individual correlation between personal income and measures of happiness has been found to be quite small (Haring, Stock, & Okun, 1984). Further, the relationship between income and well-being is stronger at the lower end of the income scale (Diener et al., 1993). The relationship that exists may be due to the benefits financial resources have on meeting basic needs such as health care, shelter, and nutrition (Diener et al., 1999).

Employment

Positive affect, satisfaction, self-esteem, and apathy are all influenced by employment status. Studies have found that more people who are employed describe themselves as more "happy" than do people who are unemployed (Argyle, 1999). Additionally, retired people, though not working, are happier than those who do work (Campbell et al., 1976). When controlling for the effect of income, education, family support, and other variables, the effects of employment on happiness are reduced, but still remain (Argyle, 1999).

Social Ties and Relationships

Humans have a need to belong to social groups. Most people will say that having satisfying close relationships with family, friends, or significant others are very important to happiness and meaningfulness in life (Myers, 2000). There are benefits to having close relationships; relationships are a source of health and happiness. Numerous studies reviewed by Ornish (1998) have shown that being loved and emotionally supported has substantial health effects. Perceptions of social relationships have also shown to influence well-being (Ornish, 1998). There are several possible reasons for the effect of social support on health. Social ties provide opportunities for confiding problems and painful feelings and those who have strong social ties have better health behaviors (Myers, 1999).

Marriage

Many studies support the relationship between intimate attachments and happiness with marriage being one of the strongest correlates (Argyle, 1999). Married people express greater life satisfaction than those who are single, widowed, divorced, or separated (Myers, 1999). Even after controlling for age, gender, income, and other variables, the positive effects of marriage are still found, although greater for women than for men. Although marriage can be a source of conflict, overall, marriage is associated with happiness and general life satisfaction (Argyle, 1999).

Friends and Leisure

The correlation between social support and emotional well-being has been found in several studies. People who are in relationships cope better with adverse life events; the more friends and confidants people have, the more likely they are to feel happy (Myers, 1999). A correlation of 0.40 has been found between happiness and leisure satisfaction and leisure activities. However, after controlling for employment, social class, and other variables, the correlation between happiness and leisure activities was reduced by half (Veenhoven, 1994). There are many reasons why leisure activities affect happiness. Leisure activities such as sports and exercise can induce positive mood, decrease depression and anxiety, and help one cope better with stressful tasks. Some activities may be "mood-inducing" directly, like dancing and music (Argyle, 1999).

Volunteering

Social participation can provide a means for people to fulfill various "self-focused needs." Volunteer activity is one such way to meet these needs (Cantor & Sanderson, 1999). The benefits of volunteering are immense (Argyle, 1999); not only will society benefit from the volunteer work, but the individual can receive personal rewards as well (Cantor & Sanderson, 1999). Several functions are served by voluntary activity, which may elucidate how voluntary behavior affects well-being. Clary and Snyder (1999) have identified at least six functions of volunteering. First, individuals volunteer in order to express or act on important values like humanitarianism. In this way, volunteering can affirm one's worldview and create feeling of authenticity and positive affect. Second, individuals may volunteer to learn more about the world or exercise skills that are often unused. In this way, volunteering can lead to personal growth and social contribution. Third, individuals may volunteer to develop psychologically, and this may lead to both personal growth and a sense of acceptance of oneself. Continuing the theme of growth, volunteering can function as a source for gaining career-related experience. Last, volunteering often permits individuals to develop new and strengthen old social relationships. In this way, volunteering can generate positive relations with others and enhance social integration (Keyes & Ryff, 1998).

Social Roles

Studies consistently show that individuals who occupy more, rather than fewer, social roles report higher levels of well-being and lower levels of distress and depression (e.g., Thoits, 1983). However, Keyes' (1996) research strongly suggests that the benefits of multiple roles is due in large part to the fact that adults add social involvement roles that may serve to promote their well-being and buffer them from the stressors of other roles. Rietschlin (1998) found that volunteers were buffered from stressors. Even after adjusting for perceived mastery, self-esteem, and perceived social support, volunteers who experienced significant stress burden reported lower levels of depression than nonvolunteers who also experienced significant stress burden.

Religion

Studies that measure religion as attendance tend to find correlations between religion and subjective well-being. Individuals who are more religious are happier, perhaps because religion gives people a sense of meaning and purpose. The effect of religion on happiness was found to be positive and of moderate strength. However, when controlling for attendance at religious services, demographic variables, and social contacts, the effect size is reduced. The primary means by which religion promotes happiness is the social support that church members receive (Argyle, 1999).

Genetic Predisposition

Although temporary factors like mood can influence well-being, emotional well-being is actually somewhat stable across situations and across the life course. A study of twins by Tellegen and colleagues (1988) supported the idea that people have a genetic predisposition to be either happy or unhappy. Although the twin study showed a substantial effect of heritability on affective well-being, other studies have shown the effects to be much smaller (Deiner et al., 1999).

Personality Traits

The most consistent relationship between personality and emotional well-being has been found when examining extraversion and neuroticism. Multiple studies have shown that extraversion and neuroticism are closely linked to emotion and affect (Diener, Sandvik, Pavot, & Fujita, 1992; Diener et al., 1999). Extraversion is the main personality dimension that correlates with happiness, perhaps because extraverts participate more in social activities that induce good moods, they exchange smiles more, and they possess certain social skills that are conducive to social relationships (Argyle, 1997).

Self-Esteem

Other traits also correlate with affective well-being. Many studies have found high self-esteem to be a strong predictor of emotional well-being (Diener, 1984). However, a growing body of research suggests that the relationship of self-esteem to mental health outcomes, such as well-being, depends on the daily fluctuations of self-esteem. The stability of self-esteem is operationalized by the magnitude of fluctuations in self-esteem measured over a short period of time (e.g., 1 week; see Kernis, Grannemann, & Mathis, 1991). No or small fluctuations reveal stable levels of esteem. Only stable levels of low self-esteem are linked with measures of mental illness. In particular, individuals who have stable and low self-esteem report significantly lower profiles of mental health than individuals with unstable and low esteem and individuals with high self-esteem.

Control and Optimism

Personal control and self-efficacy have been associated with adults' well-being. Personal control is the belief that individual action will increase good outcomes and decrease bad outcomes. Believing in one's ability to affect outcomes has consistently been correlated with well-being (Peterson, 1999). Similarly, internality, which is attributing outcomes to one's self, as opposed to external factors, has consistently been shown to be related to happiness, although the direction of causality is unknown. Optimism, on the other hand, is the belief that only good things will happen in one's life. A number of studies have suggested that those who are optimistic have higher levels of emotional well-being at times of stress than people who are less optimistic. Studies have shown that optimists adapt better to certain situations like going away to college or recovering from heart surgery, but this may be due in part to coping skills (Pervin, 1996).

Goals and Aspirations

Personality also influences the goals that people try to achieve. Goals can be an important concept for understanding emotional well-being. The types of goals, the structure of the goals, the success in attaining goals, and the rate of progress towards goals can all affect a person's emotions and life satisfaction. Additionally, one's commitment to set goals can lead to a sense of structure and meaning in life, and may help in coping with problems (Deiner et al., 1999). Although there may also be conflict between one's goals and one's desires, and having unattainable goals may be detrimental, personal goals are still important to well-being (Ryan & Deci, 2000). The influence of aspirations on happiness and emotional well-being has been the topic of many studies. Some believe that happiness is threatened by aspirations that are too high. People may become discouraged, anxious, or bored due to inappropriate levels of aspiration. However, it may not be the attainment of the goal that affects well-being, but rather the process of moving toward the goal. Although aspirations do not directly predict emotional well-being, they do help in the understanding of well-being (Deiner et al., 1999).

CONCLUSIONS

Social scientists have examined subjective well-being in adults across the dimensions of positive emotional feelings, positive psychological functioning, and positive social functioning. The identified factors in emotional well-being are positive affect, negative affect, life satisfaction, and happiness. Psychological well-being factors are self-acceptance, personal growth, purpose in life, environmental mastery, autonomy, and positive relations with others. Social well-being factors are social acceptance, social actualization, social contribution, social coherence, and social integration. In this model, mental health represents both the absence of mental illnesses and the presence of high levels of subjective well-being (symptoms) that represent emotional vitality and strong, positive functioning. Flourishing adults represent the epitome of mental health (Keyes & Lopez, 2002).

Many benefits have been shown to accrue from high levels of adult subjective well-being. They include business productivity, workplace satisfaction, and protection against some mental illnesses and physical disabilities. The utility of adult well-being also stems from its association with the predisposition to experience positive feeling states (e.g., Yardley & Rice, 1990). A bounty of research has shown that the experience of daily positive mood and emotion promotes creativity, problem solving, and immune functioning. Research also suggests that well-being is associated with behaviors and feeling that constitute social capital, i.e., feelings of trust, a sense of social responsibility, and reciprocal social ties. Data now indicate that adults with high levels of well-being are more active and engaged in their communities through volunteering, voting, community involvement to solve local problems. Moreover, adults with high levels of social and psychological well-being also tend to feel high levels of civic responsibility, engage in the provision of more emotional supports to more people, and see themselves as sources of the intergenerational transmission of important social skills.

Multiple influences determine well-being and mental health. They include education, employment, social relationships, leisure and volunteer activities, religion, and personality traits. Because emotional well-being tends to be associated with emotional states that are viewed as unstable and fluctuating, the temporal stability of elements of emotional well-being has been extensively studied. Studies revealed that measures of emotional well-being and psychological well-being were relatively stable over time with some tendency to increase with age. When the measurement of well-being reflected the quality of relationships with other people and communities, women reported higher levels of well-being than men. All elements of well-being increased with income and education, and were usually higher among employed rather than unemployed adults.

Social ties and social relationships that provide social integration and supportive relationships are consistently correlated with elevated emotional, psychological, and social well-being. In particular, married adults and adults who regularly participate in religious activities, civic organizations, and volunteer service report higher levels of well-being than unmarried adults and adults who are uninvolved in the institutions of their communities. Last, intrapersonal perceptions that convey a sense of hope and optimism, a sense of control over outcomes and efficacy over behavioral performance, consistently predict elevated levels of well-being. There is mounting evidence that the pursuit and accomplishment of intrinsically rewarding goals are associated with higher levels of well-being. Well-being in adulthood should be viewed as a means rather than solely as an end in life because it supports productivity, life satisfaction, socially desirable behaviors, and positive mental and physical health.

REFERENCES

American Psychiatric Association. (1987). *Diagnostic and statistical manual of mental disorders* (3rd ed.). Washington, DC: Author.

Andrews, F. M., & Robinson, J. P. (1991). Measures of subjective well-being. In J. P. Robinson, P. R. Shaver, & L. S. Wrightsman (Eds.), *Measures of personality and social psychological attitudes* (Vol. 1, pp. 61–114). San Diego, CA: Academic Press.

Andrews, F. M., & Withey, S. B. (1976). *Social indicators of well-being: Americans' perceptions of life quality.* New York: Plenum.

Argyle, M. (1997). Is happiness a cause of health? *Psychology and Health, 12,* 769–781.

Argyle, M. (1999). Causes and correlates of happiness. In D. Kahneman & E. Deiner (Eds.), *Well-being: The foundations of hedonic psychology* (pp. 353–373). New York: Russell Sage Foundation.

Becker, L. C. (1992). Good lives: Prolegomena. *Social Philosophy and Policy, 9,* 15–37.

Bradburn, N. M. (1969). *The structure of psychological well-being.* Chicago: Aldine.

Bryant, F. B., & Veroff, J. (1982). The structure of psychological well-being: A sociohistorical analysis. *Journal of Personality and Social Psychology, 43,* 653–673.

Campbell, A., Converse, P. E., & Rodgers, W. L. (1976). *The quality of American life: Perceptions, evaluations, and satisfactions.* New York: Russell Sage Foundation.

Cantor, N., & Sanderson, C. A. (1999). Life task participation and well-being: The importance of taking part in daily life. In D. Kahneman & E. Deiner (Eds.), *Well-being: The foundations of hedonic psychology* (pp. 230–243). New York: Russell Sage Foundation.

Cantril, H. (1965). *The pattern of human concerns.* New Brunswick, NJ: Rutgers University Press.

Clary, E. G., & Snyder, M. (1999). The motivations to volunteer: Theoretical and practical consideration. *Current Directions in Psychological Science, 8,* 156–159.

Csikszentmihalyi, M. (1990). *Flow: The psychology of optimal experience.* New York: Basic Books.

Diener, E. (1984). Subjective well-being. *Psychological Bulletin, 95,* 542–575.

Diener, E. (1993). Assessing subjective well-being: Progress and opportunities. *Social Indicators Research, 31,* 103–157.

Diener, E., & Emmons, R. A. (1984). The independence of positive and negative affect. *Journal of Personality and Social Psychology, 47,* 1105–1117.

Diener, E., Larsen, R. J., Levine, S., & Emmons, R. A. (1985). Intensity and frequency: Dimensions underlying positive and negative affect. *Journal of Personality and Social Psychology, 48,* 1253–1265.

Diener, E., Sandvik, E., Pavot, E., & Fujita, F. (1992). Extraversion and subjective well-being in a U.S. national probability sample. *Journal of Research in Personality, 26,* 205–215.

Diener, E., Suh, E. M., Lucas, R. E., & Smith, H. L. (1999). Subjective well-being: Three decades of progress. *Psychological Bulletin, 125,* 276–302.

Diener, E., Sandvik, E., Seidlitz, L., & Diener, M. (1993). The relationship between income and subjective well-being: Relative or absolute? *Social Indicators Research, 28,* 195–223.

Fava, G. A. (1999). Well-being therapy: Conceptual and technical issues. *Psychotherapy and Psychosomatics, 68,* 171–179.

Fava, G. A., Rafanelli, C., Grandi, S., Conti, S., & Belluardo, P. (1999). Prevention of recurrent depression with cognitive behavioral therapy. *Archives of General Psychiatry, 56*, 479–480.

Fredrickson, B. L. (1998). What good are positive emotions? *Review of General Psychology, 2*, 300–319.

Frisch, M. B., Cornell, J., Villanueva, M., & Retzlaff, P. J. (1992). Clinical validation of the Quality of Life Inventory: A measure of life satisfaction for use in treatment planning and outcome assessment. *Psychological Assessment, 4*, 92–101.

Glenn, N. D., & Weaver, C. N. (1979). A note on family situation and global happiness. *Social Forces, 57*, 960–967.

Green, D. P., Goldman, S. L., & Salovey, P. (1993). Measurement error masks bipolarity in affect ratings. *Journal of Personality and Social Psychology, 64*, 1029–1041.

Haring, M. J., Stock, W. A., & Okun, M. A. (1984). A research synthesis of gender and social class as correlates of subjective well-being. *Human Relations, 37*, 645–57.

Harter, J. K., & Schmidt, F. L. (2000). *Validation of a performance-related and actionable management tool: A meta-analysis and utility analysis.* Gallup Technical Report, Lincoln, NE: The Gallup Organization.

Harter, J. K., Schmidt, F. L., & Keyes, C. L. M. (in press). Well-being in the workplace and its relationship to business outcomes: A review of the Gallup studies. In C. L. M. Keyes & J. Haidt (Eds.), *Flourishing: Positive psychology and the life well-lived.* Washington, DC: American Psychological Association.

Headey, B., Kelley, J., & Wearing, A. J. (1993). Dimensions of mental health: Life satisfaction, positive affect, anxiety and depression. *Social Indicators Research, 29*, 63–82.

Headey, B., & Wearing, A. J. (1989). Personality, life events, and subjective well-being: Toward a dynamic equilibrium model. *Journal of Personality and Social Psychology, 57*, 731–739.

Isen, A. M. (1987). Positive affect, cognitive processes, and social behavior. In L. Berkowitz (Ed.), *Advances in experimental social psychology* (Vol. 20, pp. 203–253). San Diego, CA: Academic Press.

Jahoda, M. (1958). *Current concepts of positive mental health.* New York: Basic Books.

Kernis, M. H., Grannemann, B. D., & Mathis, L. C. (1991). Stability of self-esteem as a moderator of the relation between level of self-esteem and depression. *Journal of Personality and Social Psychology, 61*, 80–84.

Kessler, R. C., & Zhao, S. (1999). The prevalence of mental illness. In A. V. Horwitz & T. L. Scheid (Eds.), *A handbook for the study of mental health: Social contexts, theories, and systems* (pp. 58–78). New York: Cambridge University Press.

Keyes, C. L. M. (1996). Social functioning and social well-being: Studies of the social nature of personal wellness (Doctoral dissertation, University of Wisconsin, 1995) *Dissertation Abstracts International: Section B: Sciences & Engineering, 56*(12-B).

Keyes, C. L. M. (1998). Social well-being. *Social Psychology Quarterly, 61*, 121–140.

Keyes, C. L. M. (2000). Subjective change and its consequences for emotional well-being. *Motivation and Emotion, 24*, 67–84.

Keyes, C. L. M. (2001). Definition of mental disorders. In C. E. Faupel & P. M. Roman (Eds.), *The encyclopedia of criminology and deviant behavior, volume four: Self destructive behavior and disvalued identity* (pp. 373–376). London: Taylor and Francis.

Keyes, C. L. M. (in press). Complete mental health: An agenda for the 21st century. In C. L. M. Keyes & J. Haidt (Eds.), *Flourishing: Positive psychology and the life well-lived.* Washington, DC: American Psychological Association.

Keyes, C. L. M., & Lopez, S. J. (2002). Toward a science of mental health: Positive directions in diagnosis and interventions. In C. R. Snyder & S. J. Lopez (Eds.), *Handbook of positive psychology* (pp. 45–59). New York: Oxford University Press.

Keyes, C. L. M., & Ryff, C. D. (1998). Generativity in adult lives: Social structural contours and quality of life consequences. In D. McAdams & E. de St. Aubin (Eds.), *Generativity and adult development: Perspectives on caring for and contributing to the next generation* (pp. 227–263). Washington, DC: American Psychological Association.

Keyes, C. L. M., & Ryff, C. D. (1999). Psychological well-being in midlife. In S. L. Willis & J. D. Reid (Eds.), *Middle aging: Development in the third quarter of life* (pp. 161–180). Orlando, FL: Academic Press.

Keyes, C. L. M., Ryff, C. D., & Lee, S.-J. (2001). *Somatization and mental health: A comparative study of the idiom of distress hypothesis.* Manuscript submitted for publication.

Keyes, C. L. M., & Shapiro, A. (in press). Social well-being in the United States: A descriptive epidemiology. In C. D. Ryff, R. C. Kessler, & O. G. Brim, Jr. (Eds.), *A portrait of midlife in the United States.* Chicago: University of Chicago Press.

Keyes, C. L. M., Shmotkin, D., & Ryff, C. D. (2001). Optimizing well-being: The empirical encounter of two traditions. *Journal of Personality and Social Psychology, 82,* 1007–1022.

Koivumaa-Honkanen, H., Honkanen, R., Viinamäki, H., Heikkilä, K., Kaprio, J., & Koskenvuo, M. (2001). Life satisfaction and suicide: A 20-year follow-up study. *American Journal of Psychiatry, 158,* 433–439.

Lewinsohn, P. M., Redner, J. E., & Seeley, J. R. (1991). The relationship between life satisfaction and psychosocial variables: New perspectives. In F. Strack, M. Argyle, & N. Schwarz (Eds.), *Subjective well-being: An interdisciplinary perspective* (pp. 141–169). Oxford, England: Pergamon.

McGregor, I., & Little, B. R. (1998). Personal projects, happiness, and meaning: On doing well and being yourself. *Journal of Personality and Social Psychology, 74,* 494–512.

Mechanic, D. (1999). Mental health and mental illness: Definitions and perspectives. In A. V. Horwitz & T. L. Scheid (Eds.), *A handbook for the study of mental health: Social contexts, theories, and systems* (pp. 12–28). New York: Cambridge University Press.

Mirowsky, J., & Ross, C. E. (1989). *Social causes of psychological distress.* New York: Aldine.

Mroczek, D. K., & Kolarz, C. M. (1998). The effect of age on positive and negative affect: A developmental perspective on happiness. *Journal of Personality and Social Psychology, 75,* 1333–1349.

Myers, D. (2000). The funds, friends, and faith of happy people. *American Psychologist, 55,* 56–67.

Myers, D. G. (1999). Close relationships and quality of life. In D. Kahneman & E. Diener (Eds.), *Well-being: The foundations of hedonic psychology* (pp. 374–391). New York: Russell Sage Foundation.

Myers, D. G., & Diener, E. (1995). Who is happy? *Psychological Science, 6,* 10–19.

Ornish, D. (1998). *Love and survival.* New York: HarperCollins.

Ostir, G. V., Markides, K. S., Black, S. A., & Goodwin, J. S. (2000). Emotional well-being predicts subsequent functional independence and survival. *Journal of the American Geriatrics Society, 48,* 473–478.

Pervin, L. A. (1996). *The science of personality.* New York: Wiley.

Peterson, C. (1999). Personal control and well-being. In D. Kahneman & E. Diener (Eds.), *Well-being: The foundations of hedonic psychology* (pp. 288–301). New York: Russell Sage Foundation.

Ramana, R., Paykel, E. S., Cooper, Z., Hayhurst, H., Saxty, M., & Surtees, P. G. (1995). Remission and relapse in major depression: A two-year prospective follow-up study. *Psychological Medicine, 25,* 1161–1170.

Rebellon, C., Brown, J., & Keyes, C. L. M. (2001). Mental illness and suicide. In C. E. Faupel & P. M. Roman (Eds.), *The encyclopedia of criminology and deviant behavior: Vol. 4, Self destructive behavior and disvalued identity* (pp. 426–429). London: Taylor and Francis.

Reed, M. B., & Aspinwall, L. G. (1998). Self-affirmation reduces biased processing of health-risk information. *Motivation and Emotion, 22,* 99–132.

Rietschlin, J. (1998). Voluntary association membership and psychological distress. *Journal of Health and Social Behavior, 39,* 348–355.

Russell, J., & Carroll, J. M. (1999). On the bipolarity of positive and negative affect. *Psychological Bulletin, 125,* 3–30.

Ryan, R. M., & Deci, E. L. (2000). Self-determination theory and the facilitation of intrinsic motivation, social development, and well-being. *American Psychologist, 55,* 68–78.

Ryff, C. D. (1989). Happiness is everything, or is it? Explorations on the meaning of psychological well-being. *Journal of Personality and Social Psychology, 57,* 1069–1081.

Ryff, C. D., & Keyes, C. L. M. (1995). The structure of psychological well-being revisited. *Journal of Personality and Social Psychology, 69,* 719–727.

Salovey, P., Rothman, A. J., Detweiler, J. B., & Steward, W. T. (2000). Emotional states and physical health. *American Psychologist, 55,* 110–121.

Seeman, M. (1959). On the meaning of alienation. *American Sociological Review, 24,* 783–791.

Smith, M. B. (1959). Research strategies toward a conception of positive mental health. *American Psychologist, 14,* 673–681.

Spector, P. E. (1997). *Job satisfaction: Application, assessment, cause, and consequences.* Thousand Oaks, CA: Sage.

Suh, E., Diener, E., & Fujita, F. (1996). Events and subjective well-being: Only recent events matter. *Journal of Personality and Social Psychology, 70*, 1091–1102.

Tellegen, A., Lykken, D. T., Bouchard, T. J., Wilcox, K. J., Rich, S., & Segal, N. L. (1988). Personality similarity in twins reared apart and together. *Journal of Personality & Social Psychology, 54*, 1031–1039.

Thoits, P. A. (1983). Multiple identities and psychological well-being: A reformulation and test of the social isolation hypothesis. *American Sociological Review, 48*, 174–187.

U.S. Department of Health and Human Services. (1999). *Mental health: A report of the Surgeon General*. Rockville, MD: Author.

Veenhoven, R. (1988). The utility of happiness. *Social Indicators Research, 20*, 333–354.

Veenhoven, R. (1994). *World database of happiness: Correlates of happiness: 7837 findings from 603 studies in 69 nations 1911–1994, Vols. 1–3*. Rotterdam, Netherlands: Erasmus University.

Watson, D., & Tellegen, A. (1985). Toward a consensual structure of mood. *Psychological Bulletin, 98*, 219–235.

Weerasinnghe, J., & Tepperman, L. (1994). Suicide and happiness: Seven tests of the connection. *Social Indicators Research, 32*, 199–233.

Wright, T. A., & Bonett, D. G. (1997). The role of pleasantness and activation-based well-being in performance prediction. *Journal of Occupational Health Psychology, 2*, 212–219.

Wright, T. A., & Cropanzano, R. (2000). Psychological well-being and job satisfaction as predictors of job performance. *Journal of Occupational Health Psychology, 5*, 84–94.

Wright, T. A., & Staw, B. M. (1999). Affect and favorable work outcomes: Two longitudinal tests of the happy-productive worker thesis. *Journal of Organizational Behavior, 20*, 1–23.

Yardley, J. K., & Rice, R. W. (1990). The relationship between mood and subjective well-being. *Social Indicators Research, 24*, 101–111.

Zautra, A. J., Reich, J. W., Davis, M. C., Potter, P. T., & Nicolson, N. A. (2000). The role of stressful events in the relationship between positive and negative affects: Evidence from field and experimental studies. *Journal of Personality, 68*, 927–951.

PART V

OVERARCHING ISSUES AND THEMES

Edited by

Marc H. Bornstein
National Institute of Child Health and Human Development, Bethesda, MD

Lucy Davidson
The Center for Child Well-being, Decatur, GA

34

Child Well-Being:
From Elements to Integrations

Richard M. Lerner
Tufts University, Boston, MA

Marc H. Bornstein
*National Institute of Child Health
and Human Development, Bethesda, BD*

D. Camille Smith
Centers for Disease Control and Prevention, Atlanta, GA

INTRODUCTION

Well-being is an integrative concept in at least two senses. First, well-being connotes that all levels of organization involved in the ecology of human development combine to support feelings of, self-reflections about, and actual physical and behavioral attributes pertinent to health and positive physiological and behavioral functioning. Well-being connotes then that all these levels act in concert as an integrated or "fused" developmental system (Ford & Lerner, 1992; Lerner, 1998a; Thelen & Smith, 1998). Accordingly, well-being is a holistic notion of the individual or, better, of the "individual-context relational system," and thus involves person-oriented, as compared to variable-oriented, scholarship (Magnusson, 1999a, 1999b; Magnusson & Stattin, 1998). Second, well-being connotes that healthy and positive physiological and behavioral functioning at one point in time are associated with such functioning at other points in time. To have well-being, the integrated developmental system must be maintained over time.

To appreciate why well-being involves positive, healthy integrations across levels of organization over time, we note that well-being would be absent if one level within the fused, dynamic developmental system is poorly functioning or if there is an absence of temporal continuity in the positive functioning of this system. For instance, an individual could not be construed to be in a state of well-being if her or his physiological functioning were dysfunctional, if problems of affect or cognitive deficits existed, or if social relationships were disordered (e.g., if she or he experienced abusive or neglectful parenting). Similarly, well-being would be absent if the child were a target of racial or ethnic prejudice or discrimination, lived under conditions of persistent and pervasive poverty, or had to grow up under conditions of community violence or national war. Moreover, if well-being at one point in time was not related to well-being at subsequent times in life, then the concept of well-being could not be used to understand development. The well-being concept would be irrelevant for understanding the life span.

Accordingly, all elements (variables, processes) at the multiple levels of organization within the developmental system must be functioning in a positive manner for well-being to exist. In addition, the quality of the within- and across-time relations among elements is key to specifying the conditions under which well-being emerges, exists, and develops. The integrative, relational character of well-being imposes special problems for research aimed at describing and explaining these conditions and for applications that attempt to use such knowledge for policy engagement and program design.

RESEARCH ISSUES IN WELL-BEING

Problems of both description and explanation exist in regard to conducting research about the character of, and conditions promoting, well-being. The manner in which these problems are resolved shapes the research agendum associated with the study of well-being.

Descriptive Issues

To study well-being we must use measures that describe the relations among elements in the developmental system. As a consequence, any measure of a single element within the developmental system (e.g., of emotion, cognition, or personality), no matter how psychometrically well-developed in regard to classic test theory (Baltes, Reese, & Nesselroade, 1977), will need to be extended in at least two respects. At the least, the link between that measure and at least one other measure (typically at a different level of organization) within the developmental system must be developed in order to capture at least some feature of the relational character of well-being. In other words, interlevel units of analysis must be developed.

For example, measures have been developed of the "goodness of fit" between attributes of behavioral individuality (e.g., regarding temperament or academic abilities; Chess & Thomas, 1999; Eccles & Midgley, 1989; Eccles, Wigfield, & Blumenfeld, 1993; Lerner & Lerner, 1983) and the demands for behavior present in the home or school. In turn, several multivariate statistical innovations in relational and/or systems analyses have been introduced to provide indices of the relations involved in well-being. These methods range from the categorical procedures involved in configural frequency analysis (von Eye, 1990a, 1990b; von Eye & Schuster, 2000) to procedures for assessing dynamic behaviors, cognitions, or skills (Fischer & Bidell, 1998; Molenaar, 1986; Thelen & Smith, 1998).

To illustrate, in configural frequency analysis (von Eye, 1990b) one is able to identify patterns of multiple category membership that occur at frequencies greater than expected (these patterns are called *types*) and less than expected (*antitypes*). Since either types or antitypes may include categories that include both individual-level behaviors (e.g., the presence or absence of delinquent or violent behaviors, passing grades in school, or safe sexual practices) as well as contextual variables (e.g., the presence or absence in a child's life of authoritative or authoritarian parents, a safe neighborhood, or a well-funded school), configural frequency analysis can be used to identify patterns of person–context covariation (e.g., Taylor et al., in press).

In addition, qualitative research (e.g., Burton, 1990; Jarrett, 1998; Taylor, 1990, 1993), including ethnographic and cultural anthropological methods (Mistry & Saraswathi, in press; Rogoff, 1998), has been employed to assess the person–context system. For instance, structured, open-ended interviews with youth and older family members may be coded for the presence of themes that portray individuals' relations with features of their context (e.g., the role of neighborhood social support in facilitating healthy development among poor children and parents; Jarrett, 1998).

However, it is important to note that, at this writing, no measurement procedure or statistical analysis technique has elicited a consensus among scholars in regard to constituting the preferred means through which to assess the developmental system. One reason for this lack of agreement about methods to-be-used is that there has been no specification of the design criteria for devising such methods and no comparison between extant measures and these criteria.

The research challenges that exist in regard to indexing the relations involved in well-being are complicated by another measurement issue that arises in regard to assessing the developmental system. This issue is one of developmental measurement (of developmental test theory, if you will; Baltes et al., 1977). Measures of well-being must be useful across both levels of organization *and* ontogenetic and historical time. Simply, to develop useful measures of well-being, one needs to establish measurement equivalence between a relational index within one period of ontogeny (and/or history; Elder, 1998) and a relational index at another time in life (or history).

In turn, several questions arise in regard to developing relational measures that are valid across time. For instance, "What constitutes a significant change in the relational process?" and "What constitutes a significant change in the parameters (person and context)?" Simply, "How much time does matter?" The empirical answers to these questions are dependent on the degree to which the index of a target relation is reliably sensitive to change in both the relation and its components. Since all of these measures are assumed to constantly change, the issues of measurement equivalence that may be raised involve not just time but, as well, settings and individual differences among people and within a person over time (i.e., there exist interindividual differences in intraindividual change trajectories).

Measuring change simultaneously at multiple levels of analysis, with the hope of showing how the timing of these changes constitutes a source of well-being, raises also the issue of what has been termed the "nonequivalent temporal metric" (Lerner, Chaudhuri, & Dowling, in press; Lerner, Skinner, & Sorell, 1980). This concept denotes that rates of change within and across levels of analysis are not necessarily the same. On the individual/psychological level, for instance, cognitive, personality, and emotional changes do not necessarily proceed at comparable rates, either intra- or interindividually (cf. Riegel, 1977). Despite such within-level differences, it may be the case that months or years represent a useful (i.e., sensitive) developmental division ("along the x axis") to measure changes in individual/psychological processes. However, to appraise the effects of changes in people arising as a consequence of new social policies it may be most reasonable to use decades as the smallest sensible temporal division. For example, Sarason (1973) raised this point in regard to why intellectual interventions aimed at the individual/ psychological level of analysis can be evaluated for their effectiveness along temporal divisions of "months-" or "years-to-change," whereas biocultural interventions (e.g., Project Head Start) may need to be evaluated with divisions of decades or even centuries.

Even if we knew the best way to divide time in order to detect changes in well-being, there would still be other information we lacked about the character of developmental changes in well-being. For instance, it is still uncertain if there are particular trajectories that well-being takes across the life course. Whereas we believe that, for well-being to exist, there must exist positive and healthy integrations across levels and time in the developmental system, it is unknown, once a given point of integration is reached, whether well-being emerges "full-blown" as a digital (all or none) phenomenon (see Figure 34.1a). Alternatively, is it the case that, although well-being emerges after a given point of integration is reached, there are intraindividual differences in how much well-being exists in particular areas of functioning (Figure 34.1b)? In turn one can speak of "more of less" well-being (after the minimal system requirement is met), and as such describe well-being as growing and developing in an analog (graded and linear) way (see Figure 34.1c). Perhaps well-being is best described as following a curvilinear growth function (Figure 34.1d)?

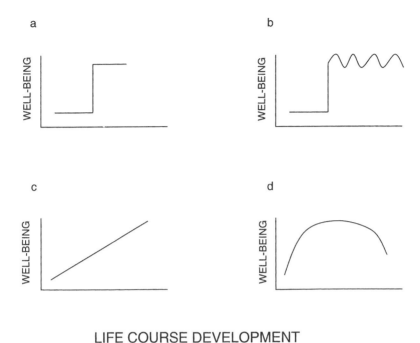

LIFE COURSE DEVELOPMENT

FIG. 34.1.   Possible growth trajectories for the development of well-being across the life course: (a) Achieving well-being is a digital (all or none) phenomenon; (b) after a particular level of well-being is reached, there are intraindividual differences in how much well-being exists in particular domains; (c) the growth of well-being is an analog (graded and linear) function; (d) well-being as a curvilinear function.

Of course, interindividual differences in trajectories may exist, and for each person the answers to these questions may be different. A key question here is whether well-being is stable or instable and, if there is instability, is it associated with some features of well-being more than others. As a consequence of these issues, a key descriptive task in regard to understanding well-being across the life span is to ascertain whether well-being is (a) an individually unique (i.e., idiosyncratic or idiographic) process, (b) a group or subgroup (i.e., general or nomothetic) phenomenon, or as is more likely (c) a phenomenon having both individual/idiographic and group/nomothetic components (Lerner, in press-a).

As emphasized by Werner (1957), answering questions about the continuity-discontinuity and stability-instability of a phenomenon may not be entirely, or even primarily, an empirical issue. Rather, answers to such questions are embedded in theories of development, and the explanatory models associated with them (Lerner, 2002a).

Explanatory Issues

Different theoretical models of the structure of well-being may be posited. For instance, independent of whether or not one views the components of well-being as idiographic or nomothetic in character, one may forward models of the organization of well-being as varying in either manifest or latent structures (see Figure 34.2). Are the elements of well-being specific or general, and do they exist on the surface only or share a latent structure (Figure 34.2a shows such specificity of individual elements of well-being, Figure 34.2b shows elements of well-being sharing a latent structure)? Is well-being one wholistic entity (Figure 34.3a) *or* is well-being multiple related elements that have achieved the same level of development or different levels of development (Figure 34.3b) *or* is well-being multiple unre-

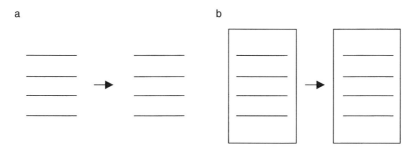

FIG. 34.2.   The organization of well-being may vary in regard to (a) individual manifest elements or (b) latent structures that embrace different elements.

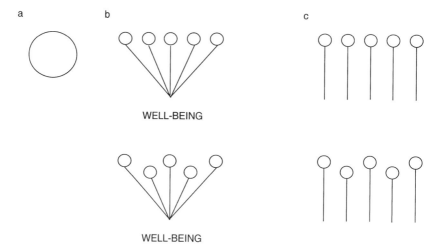

FIG. 34.3.   (a) Well-being may be a holistic entity. Well-being may be differently structured (b) within or (c) across levels of organization.

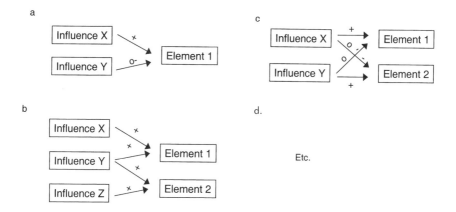

FIG. 34.4.   Well-being may be promoted by different mechanisms at different levels of organization. (a) It could be that X influences some aspect of well-being positively, but Y has a zero or negative influence on well-being. (b) It could be that X or Y influences one element of well-being, whereas Y or Z influences another. (c) It could be that X influences one element of well-being positively, but another element negatively or not at all, whereas Y does the reverse. (d) And so on.

lated elements that have achieved the same or different levels of development (see Figure 34.3c)? Independent of these varying ideas about the structure of well-being is the possibility that models of the promotion of well-being include general mechanisms that promote well-being across levels and domains. Alternatively, models may specify that well-being is promoted by different mechanisms at different levels (see Figure 34.4).

Unfortunately, extant research in developmental science has not provided sufficient knowledge to afford an empirical basis for discriminating the relative validity or utility of these various structural models. As such, we cannot yet specify the character of the structure of well-being within or across ontogenetic periods. We do not know if well-being in one instantiation at one age translates (evolves into) well-being in another instantiation at another age. Nevertheless, despite this state-of-the-art, the holistic and integrative character of well-being enables us to judge some theoretical models as of more potential use than others.

For instance, Sameroff (1983), Overton and Reese (1973; see also Overton, 1998 and Reese & Overton, 1970), and Lerner (2002a) have discussed main effects, or nature-nurture-split, models of developmental structure and change. In contrast, these scholars have also discussed various forms of interactional models of developmental structure and change (i.e., weak, moderate, and strong models). The former (main effect) type of model stresses, through ontological reductionism, the sole role of either environmental or genetic sources of behavioral structure and developmental change (e.g., see Bijou & Baer, 1961, and Rowe, 1994, respectively); such approaches are unable to accommodate the integrative and fused relations in the developmental system that are at the core of the holistic and person-centered concept of well-being and that reflect the relationism that defines the actual ecology of human development (Bronfenbrenner & Morris, 1998; Overton, 1998). Simply, main effects models are fictions in the sense that the environment cannot influence development independent of the genotype, just as genetic make-up is not wholly determinative of phenotype outside of experience and environment.

Similarly, weak and moderate forms of interaction theory would not be useful as explanatory frames for the study of well-being. In the weak types of interaction model, nature and nurture add their influences to behavior and development (in a genetically predetermined sequence; e.g., Erikson, 1959; Freud, 1954). In the moderate interaction model, the influences of nature and nurture are combined in a manor analogous to the interaction term in an analysis of variance (e.g., Piaget, 1960) to affect well-being. Thus, the former type of theory orders the two sources of behavior and development (nature and nurture) in terms of their primacy. The latter theory sees both sources as equal in influence in shaping behavior and development but treats the two sources as existing separately. Thus, both of these two instances of interaction theories reflect as well the counterfactual split conceptions of the world and do not lend themselves to the study of the integrations involved in well-being. They are as fictitious as are split theoretical conceptions.

Models that stress the strong, transactional, fused, or dynamic interactional association between nature and nurture processes do constitute frames useful for the study of such integrations (e.g., see Lerner, 1998b, 2002, for discussions of these types of theories). More sophisticated and faithful to the reality of the developmental system, these dynamic, relational theories see, for instance, child characteristics (e.g., temperament) influencing parent-provided experience and, reciprocally, experience influencing child well-being through time. As the fused relations between parent and child continue across the life span, each partner in the relation continues to change as a consequence of the influence of the other person on them (e.g., Lewis & Lee-Painter, 1974; Lewis & Rosenblum, 1974). Moreover, the fusion of the parent–child relationship within the multiple proximal and distal levels of the ecology of human development is both an influence on and is influenced by the changing parent–child relationship (Lerner, Rothbaum, Boulos, & Castellino, in press).

Thus, from the perspective of these dynamic, relational models of the developmental system, well-being is not situated in the individual. Rather, it is, as we stressed at the beginning of this chapter, a state that depends on the quality of the integrations within a person *and* between her or him and the multiple levels of her or his context. Accordingly, research pertinent to such an integrative understanding of well-being will index (e.g., through the sorts of interlevel units of analysis discussed earlier) dynamic aspects of development and multiple contexts of development. Clearly, taking into consideration multiple developmental contexts is critical to explicating the origins, development, and status of well-being across the life span. As such, the integrative, relational approach to well-being brought to the fore by a strong interactional model of nature and nurture has important implications for research about the development of well-being.

Features of a Research Agendum for the Study of Well-Being

Conceptualizing well-being as a transactional, systemic, embedded state does not preclude the empirical assessment of different components of well-being at different levels. What a dynamic developmental systems approach does regard as less useful sui generis, however, is emphasis on molecular studies to the exclusion of consideration of a larger systems analysis. From the integrative perspective involved in strong interactional theories, multiple factors should be considered together synergistically; such scholarship will have more predictive power than research that assesses and analyzes alone parts of the integrated system.

In regard to such prediction, then, it may be valuable both to look at proportions of variance accounted for inside the traditional general linear model and to analyze odds ratios (the ratio of the odds that someone with well-being in some specific or general fashion was exposed to a specific experience to the odds that someone without that element of well-being was exposed to the same developmental experience). Similarly, examining effect sizes, beyond proportion of variance accounted for, will begin to tell us more about what affects well-being systematically; effects sizes are standard indexes that allow the interpretation of phenomena comparably across procedures and studies.

Typically, well-being has been measured retrospectively; however, retrospective studies suffer from several shortcomings including (a) the difficulty of unconfounding causes and consequences; (b) the biases that are in evidence when individuals with good or poor developmental outcomes are directly compared (there is sometimes no way for researchers to remain ignorant of the obvious and associated histories); (c) retrospective reports are notoriously poor in quality; and (d) in retrospective studies appropriate controls are often lacking. Therefore, it is only prospective studies of children, looking at the unfolding of multiple aspects of well-being and documenting the multiple systems of child development, that will lead to a deep understanding of factors that influence well-being.

The study of well-being must be multivariate and multilevel, and data from all levels should be triangulated both for reasons of psychometric adequacy per se and because such a procedure will enable relations within and across levels to be more richly described. For instance, standardized tests, assessments, parent reports, self-reports, and behavioral observations are all useful. Contextually sensitive profiles may provide kinds of information about well-being that is not available from standardized instruments or even aggregated multivariate approaches at a given time point.

As we see from the foregoing chapters in this volume, well-being has been studied in laboratory settings as well as in naturalistic situations. The new frontiers of well-being will collect data at biological as well as behavioral levels and attempt to map these two spheres onto one another.

Conclusions about Research Issues

The integrative, relational character of well-being requires description to be multi-variate and multilevel and to use change-sensitive measures of person–context relations. In turn, explanations of the structure and development of well-being must be able to account for the fused relations in the developmental system. Thus, theoretical models associated with strong, dynamic, or transactional approaches to nature and nurture hold the greatest promise for furthering understanding of the conditions under which well-being occurs and develops.

The integrative, relational character of well-being, and the dynamic, developmental systems model within which well-being seems most usefully embedded, have important implications as well for applications aimed at promoting well-being. These applications pertain to both policy engagement and program design.

ISSUES FOR APPLICATION: TOWARD THE PROMOTION OF WELL-BEING

Issues of explanation raised by developmental systems models of human development lead directly to the approach taken to application by users of this theoretical perspective. Explanatory research involves the introduction (through manipulation or statistical modeling) of variation into such person-context relations. These planned variations in the course of human life are predicated on (a) theoretical ideas about the source of particular developmental phenomena (for specific combinations of people and contexts); or on (b) theoretically guided interests about the extent to which a particular developmental phenomenon (e.g., cognitive development in early childhood) shows systematic change in structure and/or function (i.e., *plasticity* across the life span; Baltes, 1987; Lerner, 1984). In the case of either (a) or (b), such researcher introduced variation is an attempt to simulate the "natural" variation of life; if theoretical expectations are confirmed, the outcomes of such investigations provide an explanation of how developmental change occurs within a person or group.

Given the developmental systems focus on studying person–context relations within the actual ecology of human development, explanatory investigations of well-being by their very nature constitute intervention research. In other words, the goal of developmental contextual explanatory research is to understand the ways in which variations in ecologically "valid" person-context relations account for the character of actual or potential trajectories of human development, that is life paths enacted in the "natural laboratory" of the "real world."

Therefore, to gain understanding of how theoretically relevant variations in such person-context relations may influence actual or to-be-actualized developmental trajectories of well-being, the researcher may introduce policies and/or programs as "experimental manipulations" of the proximal and/or distal natural ecology. Evaluations of the outcomes of such interventions become, then, a means to bring data to bear on theoretical issues pertinent to changing person–context relations and, more specifically, to the plasticity in human development that may exist, or that may be capitalized on, to enhance well-being across the life span (Lerner, 2002a). In other words, a key theoretical issue for explanatory research in the development of well-being is the extent to which changes—in the multiple, fused levels of organization comprising human life—can alter the structure and/or function of the development of well-being.

Of course, independent of any researcher-imposed attempts to intervene in the course of the development of well-being, the naturally occurring events experienced by people constantly shape, texture, and help direct the course of their lives. That is, the accumulation of the specific roles and events a person experiences across life—involving normative age-graded events, normative history-graded events, and non-normative events (Baltes, 1987; Baltes, Reese, & Lipsitt, 1980)—alters each person's developmental trajectory in a manner that would not have occurred had another set of roles and events been experienced. The between-person differences in within-person change that exist as a consequence of these naturally occurring experiences attest to the magnitude of the systematic changes in structure and function—the plasticity—that characterizes human life (Lerner, 1984).

Explanatory research is necessary, however, to understand what variables, from what levels of organization, are involved in particular instances of plasticity that have been seen to exist. In addition, such research is necessary to determine what instances of plasticity may be created by science or society in order to promote well-being. In other words, explanatory research is needed to ascertain the extent of human plasticity or, in turn, the limits of plasticity (Lerner, 1984). From a developmental systems perspective, the conduct of such research requires the scientist to alter the natural ecology of the person or group he or she is studying. Such research may involve proximal and/or distal variations in the context of human development (Lerner & Ryff, 1978); however, in any case, these manipulations constitute theoretically guided alterations of the roles and events a person or group experiences at, or over, a portion of the life span.

These alterations are indeed, then, interventions: They are planned attempts to alter the system of person–context relations constituting the basic process of change; they are conducted in order to ascertain in the service of the promotion of well-being the specific bases of, or to test the limits of, particular instances of human plasticity (Baltes, Dittmann-Kohli, & Dixon, 1984; Baltes, Smith, & Staudinger, 1992). These interventions are a researcher's attempt to substitute designed person–context relations for naturally occurring ones, a substitution effected in an attempt to understand the process of changing person–context relations that provide the basis of the development of well-being. In short, then, from the perspective of developmental systems theory, basic research in human development is intervention research.

Accordingly, the cutting-edge of theory and research in applications pertinent to the promotion of well-being lies in the use of the conceptual and methodological expertise of developmental science in the "natural ontogenetic laboratory" of the real world. Multilevel, and hence, qualitatively and quantitatively multivariate, and longitudinal research methods must be used by scholars from multiple disciplines to derive, from theoretical models of person–context relations, programs of research that involve the design, delivery, and evaluation of interventions aimed at enhancing—through scientist-introduced variation—the course of well-being.

In short, in the developmental systems model of well-being there is a stress on ontological (and on epistemological, we would add) relationism and contextualization. These emphases have brought to the fore of scientific, intervention, and policy concerns issues pertinent to the functional importance of diverse person–context interactions.

The Substantive Importance of Diversity

As greater study has been made of the actual contexts within which children and families live (e.g., Bronfenbrenner & Morris, 1998; Burton, 1990; Jarrett, 1998; Sampson, Raudenbush, & Earls, 1997), behavioral and social scientists have shown increasing appreciation of the interrelated patterns of diversity of individual and family development that comprise the range of human structural and functional characteristics. Bornstein (1995), in discussing infancy, captured the importance of this focus on diversity in the specificity principle, which "states that specific experiences at specific times exert specific effects over specific aspects of infant growth in specific ways" (p. 21). The diversity that requires such specificity involves, for instance, racial, ethnic, gender, physical ability, cohort, family, community, national, and cultural variation. Unfortunately, to the detriment of the knowledge base in human development, such diversity has not been a prime concern of empirical analysis (but see Fisher & Brennan, 1992; Fisher, Jackson, & Villarruel, 1998; Graham, 1992; Hagen, Paul, Gibb, & Wolters, 1990; McAdoo, 1995; McLoyd, 1998; Spencer, 1990).

Yet, there are several reasons why this diversity must become a key focus of concern in the study of well-being among children and adolescents (Lerner, 1991). Diversity of people and their settings means that one cannot assume that general rules of development either exist for, or apply in the same way to, all children and families. Accordingly, a research agendum that emphasizes the person and his or her diversity is necessary. This agendum should focus on diversity and context while at the same time attending to commonalities of individual development, contextual changes, and mutual influences between the two. In other words, diversity should be placed at the fore of the research agendum about well-being. Then, with a knowledge of individuality, it is possible to determine empirically parameters of commonality, of interindividual generalizability. Thus, we should no longer make a priori assumptions about the existence of generic developmental laws pertinent to well-being or of the primacy of such laws, even if they are found to exist, in providing key information about the trajectory of well-being of a given person or group. Again, the specificity principle (Bornstein, 1995) is the key concept organizing applied theory and research about the development of well-being.

In short, then, integrated multidisciplinary and developmental research devoted to the study of diversity and context must be moved to the fore of scholarly concern about well-being. In addition, however, scholars involved in such research must have at least two other concerns, ones deriving from the view that basic, explanatory research in human development is, in its essence, intervention research.

Implications for Policies and Programs

Research about the development of well-being that is concerned with one or even a few instances of individual and contextual diversity cannot be assumed to be useful for understanding the life course of all people. Similarly, policies and programs derived from such research, or associated with it in the context of a researcher's tests of ideas pertinent to human plasticity, cannot hope to be applicable, or equally appropriate and useful, in all contexts or for all individuals. Accordingly, developmental and individual differences-oriented policy development and program (intervention) design and delivery may be integrated fully with the approach to research for which we are calling.

As emphasized in developmental systems thinking, the variation in settings within which people live means that studying development in a standard (e.g., a "controlled") environment does not provide information pertinent to the actual (ecologically valid) developing relations between individually distinct people and their specific contexts (for example, their particular families, schools, or communities). This point underscores the need to conduct research in real-world settings and highlights the ideas that (a) Policies and programs constitute natural experiments (i.e., planned interventions for people and institutions), and (b) the evaluation of such activities becomes a central focus in the developmental contextual research agendum we have described (Lerner & Miller, 1993).

In this view, then, policy and program endeavors do *not* constitute secondary work, or derivative applications, conducted after research evidence has been compiled. Quite to the contrary, policy development and implementation, and program design and delivery, become integral components of the present vision for well-being research; the evaluation component of such policy and intervention work provides critical feedback about the adequacy of the conceptual frame from which this research agenda should derive. In short, a synthetic approach to research, policy, and programs, predicated on a developmental systems perspective, will facilitate substantial progress toward understanding and promoting of child well-being. The integrative, applied developmental science agendum we envision should engender better efforts to be made in promoting positive and healthy youth development.

Enhancing Well-Being: The Promotion of Positive Youth Development

Researchers and policy makers have the laudable and well-intentioned goal to develop interventions, remediations, or preventions that are geared to address children's disorders, deficits, and disabilities. However, from the perspective we have presented about the way the developmental system may be engaged to promote well-being, the challenge of innovations in applied research and policy and program applications is on the development and promotion of positive behaviors in youth. New successes might arise from building on individual competencies that enhance contextual support for such development (Benson, 1997; Benson, Leffert, Scales, & Blyth, 1998; Leffert et al., 1998; Scales, Benson, Leffert, & Blyth, 2000).

Developmental science points to three general origins of characteristics and values pertinent to positive youth development: Children, child effects, and parenting (broadly conceived). Clearly, children contribute directly to their own development through their attributes of individuality and by the influence they exert on others, notably their caregivers (Lerner & Busch-Rossnagel, 1981; Lerner & Walls, 1999). Despite the plasticity of such endogenous processes in the child, without attending to promoting variation in the key contexts of child development—for instance, the family (e.g., in regard to the behavior of parents)—we will be constraining our opportunity to engage the relational and integrative developmental system to promote positive youth development (e.g., the "Five Cs" of such development, i.e., competence, confidence, connection, character, and caring/compassion; Lerner, 2002b).

Parent-provided environments and experiences can contribute directly and indirectly to children's well-being. It is the principal and continuing task of parents in each generation to prepare children of the next generation for the physical, economic, and psychosocial situations in which those children must survive and hopefully thrive (Bornstein, 1995; LeVine, 1977; Scales et al., 2000). Many factors influence the development of children, but parents are the "final common pathway" to childhood oversight and caregiving, adjustment, and success.

Mothers and fathers (as well as siblings, other family members, and even children's nonfamilial daycare providers) guide the development of children via many means. All prominent theories of human development put experience in the world as either the principal source of individual growth or as a major contributing component. It falls to parents (and other caregivers) to shape most, if not all, of young children's direct experiences, and we think that parents influence their children's well-being both by the beliefs they hold and by the behaviors they exhibit. These, then, are the most logical targets of policies and programs.

Parenting beliefs include perceptions about, attitudes toward, and knowledge of all aspects of parenting and childhood, and each can play a telling part in the promotion of well-being in children. (More than one quarter of new parents in America today believes that she or he cannot influence the development of their newborn infant's mental abilities, for example; Zero-to-Three, 1997). Perhaps more salient in the phenomenology of childhood, however, are parents' and caregivers' direct behaviors, the tangible experiences they provide children. Furthermore, parents influence their children's well-being in indirect ways. One example is by virtue of their influence on one another (e.g., marital support and communication). Parents also influence their children's well-being because they are decision-makers and citizens: From the perspective of an ecological model of child development, parents influence the social health or toxicity of the environments their children inhabit through their politics. Ultimately, citizens shape the quality of daycare, the adequacy of schools, and availability of children's opportunities in their community.

Sorrowfully, it is not the case that overall level of, say, stimulation a child experiences directly affects the child's overall level of functioning and compensates for selective deficiencies: Simply providing an adequate financial base, a big house, or the like does not guarantee, or even speak to, a child's development of an empathic personality, verbal competence, or other valued capacities and strengths. As noted earlier, the specificity principle asserts that specific experiences parents provide children at specific times exert specific effects over specific aspects of child well-being in specific ways. Moreover, no one factor in life is determinative and trumps all others but, from a developmental systems perspective, many factors—environment, experience, genetics, and biology and their transaction—influence the development of well-being.

To fathom the nature of effective child policies and programs (of which the parent–child relationship is one useful focus) requires therefore a multivariate and dynamic stance. It is only by taking multiple factors into consideration that we can appreciate individual, dyadic, family, and society level contributions to child well-being. For instance, we may want to pay particular attention to assessing biological contributions to shyness and intelligence, or peer influences on risk taking, or the role of the family in the formation of values and life aspirations (Lerner, 2002b). As all parents know, childrearing is akin to trying to "hit a moving target," the toddler emerging out of the infant, the youth emerging out of the toddler. In order to exert appropriate influence and guide their children toward well-being, parents must constantly and effectively adjust their interactions, cognitions, emotions, affections, and strategies to the age-graded activities, abilities, and experiences of their children.

Imagine, then, a program whose goal is to promote infant, child, and adolescent well-being in the physical, cognitive, and social spheres of development through the active participation of parents. Parents are, after all, the corps available in the greatest numbers to lobby and labor for children.

Legacy for Children is One Such Program

Legacy for Children is a set of randomized, controlled, longitudinal research projects. The intent is to examine the potential for improvement in child developmental outcomes through programs designed to influence parenting behavior. The Legacy sites have developed a group-based parenting intervention that focuses on a variety of parenting topics and specific parenting practices that are correlated with optimal child development. In other words, parental behaviors facilitate the elements of well-being. Although some of the correlation may be due to genetic factors, parental characteristics and behaviors are the most predictive factors influencing a child's outcome. Legacy for Children organizes these specific parent behaviors into parental commitment and responsibility, nurturing and supportive relationships, verbal and cognitive stimulation, and social/behavioral guidance.

The multiple pathways and dynamics of parenting and child development make for really a quite challenging and frankly messy situation. Nonetheless, the good news is that we can foster virtually all elements of child well-being. To do so, we can identify some common sources of influence to target. For example, responsive and empathic parenting, parental interest in children's learning, emphasis on success, use of rational disciplinary procedures, and providing an enriched environment are all associated with increases in children's intelligence.

If we are fatalists, we accept the environment we live in. If we are not, we take the personal, social, and political steps to construct environments with appropriate stimulation for our children, to organize our children's daycare, to promote their associations with positive peers, to make sure our community affords adequate schooling, and to enroll our children in growth promoting extracurricular activities (church or temple, boy or girl scouts, little league or soccer).

As our children go off on their own, parenthood and citizenship ultimately mean having facilitated a child's self-confidence, capacity for intimacy, achievement motivation, pleasure in play and work, friendships with peers, and continuing academic success and fulfillment—the elements of well-being. It is only through comprehensive and integrated programs, however, that parent, family, and community contexts may usefully affect children's attaining well-being. That reaching these goals challenges us does not mean we should shrink from them.

In fact, there is a growing research literature that may motivate our efforts in this regard. Using conceptual models and methods that are predicated on a developmental systems orientation (Lerner, Chaudhuri, & Dowling, in press), this research demonstrates that, when the strengths—or assets—of young people are integrated with those of their families and community, well-being exists and positive youth development, thriving, and healthier communities are promoted.

Engaging the Developmental System to Promote Well-Being

What programs may engage the developmental system in a manner that serves well-being and that promotes the positive development of young people? One answer is provided by Damon (1997), who has envisioned the creation of a "youth charter" in each community in our nation and the world. The charter consists of a set of rules, guidelines, and plans of action that each community can adopt to provide their youth with a framework for development in a healthy manner. Damon describes how youth and significant adults in their community (e.g., parents, teachers, clergy, coaches, police, business leaders, and government) can create partnerships to pursue a common ideal of positive moral development and intellectual achievement.

Embedding youth in a caring and developmentally facilitative community can promote their ability to develop morally and to contribute to civil society. In a study of about 130 African American parochial high school juniors, working at a soup kitchen for the homeless as part of a school-based community service program was associated with identity development and with the ability to reflect on society's political organization and moral order (Yates & Youniss, 1996).

In a study of over 3,100 high school seniors (Youniss, Yates, & Su, 1997), the activities engaged in by youth were categorized into school-based, adult-endorsed norms or engagement in peer fun activities that excluded adults. Youth were then placed into groups that reflected orientations to (a) school–adult norms, but not peer fun (the *School* group); (b) peer fun but not school–adult norms (the *Party* group); or (c) both (a) and (b) (the *All-around* group). The School and the All-around seniors were both high in community service, religious orientation, and political awareness. In turn, the Parry group seniors were more likely to use marijuana than were the School group (but not the All-around group) seniors (Youniss et al., 1997).

Furthermore, African American and Latino adolescents who were nominated by community leaders for having shown unusual commitments to caring for others or for contributions to the community were labeled *care exemplars* and compared to a matched group of youth not committed to the community (Hart & Fegley, 1995). The care exemplars were more likely than the comparison youth to describe themselves in terms reflective of moral characteristics, to show commitment to both their heritage and to the future of their community, to see themselves as reflecting the ideals of both themselves and their parents, and to stress the importance of personal philosophies and beliefs for their self-definitions (Hart & Fegley, 1995).

Damon (1997) envisioned that, by embedding youth in a community where service and responsible leadership are possible, the creation of community-specific youth charters could enable adolescents and adults to, together, systematically promote the positive development of youth. Youth charters can create opportunities to actualize both individual and community goals to eliminate risk behaviors among adolescents and promote in them the ability to contribute to high quality individual and community life. Through community youth charters, youth and adults may work together to create a system wherein individual well-being and, simultaneously, civil society are maintained and perpetuated (Damon, 1997).

What, precisely, must be brought together by such charters to ensure the promotion of such positive youth development? Benson and his colleagues at Search Institute in Minneapolis, Minnesota, believe that what is needed is the application of assets (Benson, 1997; Benson et al., 1998; Leffert et al., 1998; Scales et al., 2000). They stress that positive youth development is furthered when actions are taken to enhance the strengths of a person (e.g., a commitment to learning, a healthy sense of identity), a family (e.g., caring attitudes toward children, rearing styles that both empower youth and set boundaries and provide expectations for positive growth), and a community (e.g., social support, programs that provide access to the resources for education, safety, and mentorship available in a community; Benson, 1997). Across these categories of strengths or developmental assets, Benson et al. (1998) specify that there are 20 internal and 20 external attributes that comprise the resources needed by youth for positive development.

Benson and his colleagues have found that the more developmental assets possessed by an adolescent the greater is his or her likelihood of positive, healthy development. For instance, in a study of 99,462 youth in Grades 6 through 12 in
public and/or alternative schools from 213 U.S. cities and town who were assessed during the 1996/1997 academic year for their possession of the 40 assets
noted earlier, Leffert et al. (1998) found that the more assets present among youth
the lower the likelihood of alcohol use, depression/suicide risk, and violence. For
instance, the level of alcohol use risk for youth in Grades 6 to 8 combined and for
youth in Grades 9 to 12 combined decreases with the possession of more assets.
Youth with zero to 10 assets have the highest risk, followed by youth with 11 to 20
assets, youth with 21 to 30 assets, and youth with 31 to 40 assets. Thus, consistent
with Benson's (1997) view of the salience of developmental assets for promoting
healthy behavior among young people, the fact that the last group has the lowest
level of risk shows the importance of the asset approach in work aimed at promoting
positive development in our nation's children and adolescents. Moreover, similar
trends were found for males and females in regard to depression/suicide risk, and
for combinations of males and females in different grade groupings in regard to violence risk. This congruence strengthens the argument for the critical significance of
a focus on developmental assets in the promotion of positive youth development
and, as such, in the enhancement of the capacity and commitment of young people
to contribute to civil society.

Other data from Benson and his colleagues provide direct support for this argument. Scales et al., (2000) measured a concept termed thriving among 6,000 youth
in Grades 6 to 12, evenly divided across six ethnic groups (American Indian, African American, Asian American, Latino, European American, and Multiracial).
Thriving was defined as involving seven attributes: school success, leadership, valuing diversity, physical health, helping others, delay of gratification, and overcoming adversity. Most, if not all, of these attributes are linked to the presence of
prosocial behavior (e.g., helping others, delay of gratification) and to the behaviors
requisite for competently contributing to civil society (e.g., valuing diversity, leadership, overcoming adversity). The greater the number of developmental assets
possessed by youth, the more likely they were to possess the attributes of thriving,
for example, in regard to helping others, valuing diversity, and leadership.

There are other data that support the importance of focusing on developmental assets in both understanding the bases of positive youth development and in using that
knowledge to further civil society. Luster and McAdoo (1994) sought to identify the
factors that contribute to individual differences in the cognitive competence of African American children in early elementary grades. Consistent with an assets-based
approach to promoting the positive development of youth (Benson, 1997; Scales &
Leffert, 1998), they found that favorable outcomes in cognitive and socioemotional
development were associated with high scores on an advantage index. This index was
formed by scoring children on the basis of the absence of risk factors (e.g., pertaining
to poverty or problems in the quality of the home environment) and the presence of

more favorable circumstances in their lives. Luster and McAdoo (1994) reported that, whereas only 4% of the children in their sample who scored low on the advantage index had high scores on a measure of vocabulary, 44% of the children who had high scores on the advantage index had high vocabulary scores. Similar contrasts between low and high scorers on the advantage index were found in regard to measures of math achievement (14% vs. 37%, respectively), word recognition (0% vs. 35%, respectively), and word meaning (7% and 46%, respectively).

Luster and McAdoo (1996) later extended the findings of their 1994 research. Seeking to identify the factors that contribute to individual differences in the educational attainment of African American young adults from low socioeconomic status, Luster and McAdoo found that assets linked with the individual (cognitive competence, academic motivation, and personal adjustment in kindergarten) and the context (parental involvement in schools) were associated longitudinally with academic achievement and educational attainment.

CONCLUSIONS

Well-Being and the Positive Development of America's Young People

Consistent with the perspective forwarded by Benson (1997), and the data provided by Leffert et al. (1998) and by Luster and McAdoo (1994, 1996), we can see the individual and contextual assets of youth are linked to their positive development. These data legitimize the idea that the enhancement of such assets will be associated with the promotion of positive youth development.

These data also underscore the importance of integrating the strengths of young people, their families, and their communities in the service of well-being. As suggested by the developmental systems perspective that frames our approach to well-being, such a synthetic approach to well-being seems to have both substantial empirical validity and, as a consequence, may be an optimally productive frame for policy and program innovations aimed at increasing the probability of well-being across the life span of current and future generations. We believe that the benefit of such applications of developmental science will accrue not only for our nation's young people but, because today's youth are the future stewards of our democracy, for civil society in our nation.

When we provide our nation's youth with the resources for their well-being; when we insure that families have the capacity to provide children with boundaries and expectations, fulfillment of physiological and safety needs, a climate of love and caring, the inculcation of self esteem, the encouragement for growth, positive values, and positive links to the community; and when we instill the commitment and capacity in communities to give all children a healthy start, a safe environment, caring and reliable adults, an education resulting in marketable skills, and opportunities to "give back" to their communities by volunteering and serving, we will ensure that current and future generations of young people develop the Five Cs of positive youth development. When these five sets of outcomes are developed in youth, civil society is enhanced. Through the intergenerational effect these youth may initiate in rearing of their own children, these youth can positively affect the rearing of subsequent generations (Bornstein, 1995).

REFERENCES

Baltes, P. B. (1987). Theoretical propositions of life-span developmental psychology: On the dynamics between growth and decline. *Developmental Psychology, 23*, 611–626.

Baltes, P. B., Dittmann-Kohli, F., & Dixon, R. A. (1984). New perspectives on the development of intelligence in adulthood: Toward a dual-process conception and a model of selective optimization with compensation. In P. B. Baltes & O. G. Brim, Jr., (Eds.), *Life-span development and behavior* (Vol. 6). New York: Academic Press.

Baltes, P. B., Lindenberger, U., & Staudinger, U. M. (1998). Life-span theory in developmental psychology. In W. Damon (Series Ed.) & R. M. Lerner (Vol. Ed.), *Handbook of child psychology: Vol. 1. Theoretical models of human development* (5th ed., pp. 1029–1144). New York: Wiley.

Baltes, P. B., Reese, H. W., & Lipsitt, L. P. (1980). Life-span developmental psychology. *Annual Review of Psychology, 31*, 65–110.

Baltes, P. B., Reese, H. W., & Nesselroade, J. R. (1977). *Life-span developmental psychology: Introduction to research methods.* Monterey, CA: Brooks/Cole.

Baltes, P. B., Smith, J., & Staudinger, U. M. (1992). Wisdom and successful aging. In T. B. Sonderegger (Ed.), *Nebraska Symposium on Motivation, 39*, 123–167. Lincoln, NE: University of Nebraska.

Baltes, P. B., Staudinger, U. M., & Lindenberger, U. (1999). Life span psychology: Theory and application to intellectual functioning. In J. T. Spence, J. M. Darley, & D. J. Foss (Eds.), *Annual Review of Psychology* (Vol. 50, pp. 471–507). Palo Alto, CA: Annual Reviews.

Benson, P. (1997). *All kids are our kids: What communities must do to raise caring and responsible children and adolescents.* San Francisco: Jossey-Bass.

Benson, P. L., Leffert, N., Scales, P. C., & Blyth, D. A. (1998). Beyond the "village" rhetoric: Creating healthy communities for children and adolescents. *Applied Developmental Science, 2*(3), 138–159.

Bijou, S. W., & Baer, D. M. (Eds.). (1961). *Child development: A systematic and empirical theory.* New York: Appleton-Century-Crofts.

Bornstein, M. H. (1995). Parenting infants. In M. H. Bornstein (Ed.), *Handbook of Parenting* (Vol. 1, pp. 3–39). Mahwah, NJ: Lawrence Erlbaum Associates.

Bronfenbrenner, U., & Morris, P. A. (1998). The ecology of developmental process. In W. Damon (Series Ed.) & R. M. Lerner (Vol. Ed.), *Handbook of child psychology: Vol. 1. Theoretical models of human development* (5th ed., pp. 993–1028). New York: Wiley.

Burton, L. M. (1990). Teenage childbearing as an alternative life-course strategy in multigeneration black families. *Human Nature, 1*(2), 123–143.

Cairns, R. B. (1998). The making of developmental psychology. In W. Damon (Series Ed.) & R. M. Lerner (Vol. Ed.), *Handbook of child psychology: Vol. 1. Theoretical models of human development* (5th ed., 419–448). New York: Wiley.

Chess, S., & Thomas, A. (1999). *Goodness of fit: Clinical applications from infancy through adult life.* New York: Brunner/Mazel.

Damon, W. (1997). *The youth charter: How communities can work together to raise standards for all our children.* New York: Free Press.

Eccles, J. S., & Midgley, C. (1989). Stage-environment fit: Developmentally appropriate classrooms for young adolescents. In C. Ames & R. Ames (Eds.), *Research on motivation in education. Goals and cognitions* (Vol. 3, pp. 139–186). New York: Academic Press.

Eccles, J. S., Wigfield, A., Harold, R., & Blumenfeld, P. B. (1993). Age and gender differences in children's self- and task perceptions during elementary school. *Child Development, 64*, 83–847.

Elder, G. H., Jr. (1998). The life course and human development. In W. Damon (Series Ed.) & R. M.
    Lerner (Vol. Ed.), *Handbook of child psychology: Vol. 1. Theoretical models of human development*
    (5th ed., pp. 939–991). New York: Wiley.
Erikson, E. H. (1959). Identity and the life cycle. *Psychological Issues, 1*, (pp. 50–100).
Fischer, K. W., & Bidell, T. (1998). Dynamic development of psychological structures in action and
    thought. In W. Damon (Series Ed.) & R. M. Lerner (Vol. Ed.), *Handbook of child psychology: Vol. 1.
    Theoretical models of human development* (5th ed., pp. 467–561). New York: Wiley.
Fisher, C. B., & Brennan, M. (1992). Application and ethics in developmental psychology. In D. L.
    Featherman, R. M. Lerner, & M. Perlmutter (Eds.), *Life-span development and behavior* (Vol. 11,
    pp. 189–219). Hillsdale, NJ: Lawrence Erlbaum Associates.
Fisher, C. B., Jackson, J. F., & Villarruel, F. A. (1998). The study of African American and Latin Ameri-
    can children and youth. In R. M. Lerner (Ed.), *Handbook of child psychology: Vol. 1 Theoretical
    models of human development* (5th ed., pp. 1145–1207). New York: Wiley.
Ford, D. L., & Lerner, R. M. (1992). *Developmental systems theory: An integrative approach.* Newbury
    Park, CA: Sage.
Freud, S. (1954). *Collected works, standard edition.* London: Hogarth.
Garbarino, J., Kostelny, K., & Dubrow, N. (1998). *No place to be a child: Growing up in a war zone.* San
    Francisco: Jossey-Bass.
Graham, S. (1992). "Most of the subjects were white and middle class": Trends in published research on
    African Americans in selected APA journals, 1970–1989. *American Psychologist, 47*, 629–639.
Hagen, J. W., Paul, B., Gibb, S., & Wolters, C. (1990). *Trends in research as reflected by publications in
    Child Development: 1930–1989.* Paper presented at the Biennial meeting of the Society for Re-
    search on Adolescence, Atlanta, GA.
Hart, D., & Fegley, S. (1995). Prosocial behavior and caring in adolescence: Relations to self-under-
    standing and social judgment. *Child Development, 66*, 1346–1359.
Jarrett, R. L. (1998). African American children, families, and neighborhoods: Qualitative contributions
    to understanding developmental pathways. *Applied Developmental Science, 2*, 2–16.
Leffert, N., Benson, P., Scales, P., Sharma, A., Drake, D., & Blyth, D. (1998). Developmental assets:
    Measurement and prediction of risk behaviors among adolescents. *Applied Developmental Science,
    2*(4), 209–230.
Lerner, J. V., & Lerner, R. M. (1983). Temperament and adaptation across life: Theoretical and empirical
    issues. In P. B. Baltes & O. G. Brim, Jr. (Eds.), *Life-span development and behavior* (Vol. 5, pp.
    197–231). New York: Academic Press.
Lerner, R. M. (1984). *On the nature of human plasticity.* New York: Cambridge University Press.
Lerner, R. M. (1991). Changing organism-context relations as the basic process of development: A de-
    velopmental-contextual perspective. *Developmental Psychology, 27*, 27–32.
Lerner, R. M. (1998a). Theories of human development: Contemporary perspectives. In W. Damon (Se-
    ries Ed.) & R. M. Lerner (Vol. Ed.), *Handbook of child psychology: Vol. 1. Theoretical models of hu-
    man development* (pp. 1–24). New York: Wiley.
Lerner, R. M. (Ed.). (1998b). *Handbook of Child Psychology: Vol. 1. Theoretical models of human de-
    velopment.* (5th ed.). New York: Wiley.
Lerner, R. M. (2002a). *Concepts and theories of human development* (3rd ed.). Mahwah, NJ: Lawrence
    Erlbaum Associates.
Lerner, R. M. (2002b). *Adolescence: Development, diversity, context, and application.* Upper Saddle
    River, NJ: Prentice-Hall.
Lerner R. M., & Busch-Rossnagel, N. A. (Eds.). (1981). *Individuals as producers of their development:
    A life-span perspective.* New York: Academic Press.
Lerner, R. M., Chaudhuri, J., & Dowling, E. (in press). Methods of contextual assessment and assessing
    contextual methods: A developmental contextual perspective. In D. M. Teti (Ed.), *Handbook of re-
    search methods in developmental psychology.* Cambridge, MA: Blackwell.
Lerner, R. M., & Miller, J. R. (1993). Integrating human development research and intervention for
    America's children: The Michigan State University model. *Journal of Applied Developmental Psy-
    chology, 14*, 347–364.

Lerner, R. M., Rothbaum, F., Boulos, S., & Castellino, D. R. (2002). A developmental systems perspective on parenting. In M. R. Bornstein (Ed.), *Handbook of parenting: Vol. 2. Biology and ecology of parenting* (pp. 315–344). Mahwah, NJ: Lawrence Erlbaum Associates.

Lerner, R. M., & Ryff, C. (1978). Implementation of the life-span view of human development: The sample case of attachment. In P. B. Baltes (Ed.), *Life-span development and behavior* (Vol. 1, pp. 1–44). New York: Academic Press.

Lerner, R. M., Skinner, E. A., & Sorell, G. T. (1980). Methodological implications of contextual/dialectic theories of development. *Human Development, 23*, 225–235.

Lerner, R. M., & Walls, T. (1999). Revisiting individuals as producers of their development: From dynamic interactionism to developmental systems. In J. Brandtsdädter & R. M. Lerner (Eds.), *Action and development: Origins and functions of intentional self-development* (pp. 3–36). Thousand Oaks, CA: Sage.

Levine, R. A. (1977). Child rearing as cultural adaptation. In P. H. Liederman, S. R. Tulkin, & A. Rosenfeld, (Eds.), *Culture and infancy: Variations in the human experience* (pp. 15–27). New York: Academic Press.

Lewis, M., & Lee-Painter, S. (1974). An interactional approach to the mother-infant dyad. In M. Lewis & L. A. Rosenblum (Eds.), *The effect of the infant on its caregivers* (pp. 21–48). New York: Wiley.

Lewis, M., & Rosenblum, L. A. (Eds.). (1974). *The effect of the infant on its caregivers.* New York: Wiley.

Luster, T., & McAdoo, H. (1996). Family and child influences on educational attainment: A secondary analysis of the High/Scope Perry Preschool data. *Developmental Psychology, 32*(1), 26–39.

Luster, T., & McAdoo, H. P. (1994). Factors related to the achievement and adjustment of young African American children. *Child Development, 65*, 1080–1094.

Magnusson, D. (1999a). Holistic interactionism: A perspective for research on personality development. In L. A. Pervin & O. P. John, (Eds.), *Handbook of personality: Theory and research* (2nd ed., pp. 219–247). New York: Guilford Press.

Magnusson, D. (1999b). On the individual: A person-oriented approach to developmental research. *European Psychologist, 4*, 205–218.

Magnusson, D., & Stattin, H. (1998). Person-context interaction theories. In W. Damon (Series Ed.) & R. M. Lerner (Vol. Ed.), *Handbook of child psychology: Vol. 1. Theoretical models of human development* (5th ed., pp. 685–759). New York: Wiley.

McAdoo, H. P. (1995). Stress levels, family help patterns, and religiosity in middle- and working-class African American single mothers. *Journal of Black Psychology, 21*, 424–449.

McLoyd, V. C. (1998). Children in poverty: Development, public policy, and practice. In W. Damon (Series Ed.) , and I. E. Sigel & K. A. Renninger (Vol. Eds.), *Handbook of psychology: Vol. 4. Child psychology in practice* (pp. 135–208). New York: Wiley.

Mischel, W., & Shoda, Y. (1995). A cognitive-affective system theory of personality: Reconceptualizing situations, dispositions, dynamics, and invariance in personality structure. *Psychological Review, 102*, 246–268.

Mistry, J., & Saraswathi, T. S. (in press). Cultural context of child development. In R. M. Lerner, M. A. Easterbrooks, & J. Mistry (Eds.), *Comprehensive Handbook of Psychology: Vol. 6. Developmental Psychology.* New York: Wiley.

Molenaar, P. C. M. (1986). On the impossibility of acquiring more powerful structures: A neglected alternative. *Human Development, 29*, 245–251.

Overton, W. (1998). Developmental psychology: Philosophy, concepts, and methodology. In W. Damon (Series Ed.) & R. M. Lerner (Ed.), *Handbook of child psychology: Vol. 1. Theoretical models of human development* (5th ed., pp. 107–187). New York: Wiley.

Overton, W. F., & Reese, H. W. (1973). Models of development: Methodological implications. In J. R. Nesselroade & H. W. Reese (Eds.), *Life-Span Developmental Psychology: Methodological Issues.* New York: Academic Press.

Piaget, J. (1960). *The child's conception of the world.* Paterson, NJ: Littlefield, Adams.

Reese, H. W., & Overton, W. F. (1970). Models of development and theories of development. In L. R. Goulet & P. B. Baltes (Eds.), *Life-span developmental psychology: Research and theory.* New York: Academic Press.

Riegel, K. F. (1977). The dialectics of time. In N. Datan & H. W. Reese (Eds.), *Life-Span Developmental Psychology: Dialectical Perspectives on Experimental Research.* New York: Academic Press.

Rogoff, B. (1998). Cognition as a collaborative process. In D. Kuhn & R. S. Siegler (Eds.), *Handbook of Child Psychology: Vol. 2. Theoretical models of human development* (5th ed. pp. 679–744) New York: Wiley.

Rowe, D. C. (1994). *The limits of family influence: Genes, experience, and behavior.* New York: Guilford Press.

Sameroff, A. J. (1983). Developmental systems: Contexts and evolution. In P. H. Mussen (Series Ed.) & W. Kessen (Vol. Ed.), *Handbook of child psychology: Vol. 1. History, theory, and methods* (pp. 237–294). New York: Wiley.

Sampson, R., Raudenbush, S. W., & Earls, F. (1997). Neighborhoods and violent crime. A multilevel study of collective efficacy. *Science, 277*, 918–924

Sarason, S. B. (1973). Jewishness, Blackish-ness and the nature-nurture controversy. *American Psychologist, 28*, 962–971.

Scales, P., Benson, P., Leffert, N., & Blyth, D. A. (2000). The contribution of developmental assets to the prediction of thriving among adolescents. *Applied Developmental Science, 4*(2).

Scales, P., & Leffert, N. (1999). *Developmental assets: A synthesis of the scientific research on adolescent development.* Minneapolis, MN: Search Institute.

Spencer, M. B. (1990). Development of minority children: An introduction. *Child Development, 61*, 267–269.

Taylor, C. S., Lerner, R., von Eye, A., Balsano, A. B., Dowling, E. M., Anderson, P. M., Bobek, D. L., & Bjelobrk, D. (in press). Individual and ecological assets and positive developmental trajectories among gang and community-based organization youth. In Lerner, R. M., Taylor, C. S., & von Eye, A. (Eds.). (in press), *Pathways to positive development among diverse youth. New directions for youth development: Theory, practice, and research.* San Francisco: Jossey-Bass.

Taylor, C. S. (1990). *Dangerous society.* East Lansing, MI: Michigan State University Press.

Taylor, C. S. (1993). *Girls, gangs, women, and drugs.* East Lansing, MI: Michigan State University Press.

Thelen, E., & Smith, L. B. (1998). Dynamic systems theories. In W. Damon (Series Editor) & R. M. Lerner (Vol. Ed.), *Handbook of child psychology: Vol. I. Theoretical models of human development* (5th ed., pp. 563–633). New York: Wiley.

von Eye, A. (1990a). *Introduction to Configural Frequency Analysis: The search for types and antitypes in cross-classifications.* Cambridge: Cambridge University Press.

von Eye, A. (1990b). *Statistical methods in longitudinal research: Principles and structuring change.* New York: Academic Press.

von Eye, A., & Schuster, C. (2000). The road to freedom: Quantitative developmental methodology in the third millennium. *International Journal of Behavioral Development, 24*, 35–43.

Werner, H. (1957). The concept of development from a comparative and organismic point of view. In D. B. Harris (Ed.), *The concept of development* (pp. 125–148). Minneapolis, MN: University of Minnesota Press.

Yates, M., & Youniss, J. (1996). Community service and political-moral identity in adolescents. *Journal of Research on Adolescence, 6*, 271–284.

Youniss, J., Yates, M., & Su, Y. (1997). Social integration: Community service and Marijuana use in high school seniors. *Journal of Adolescent Research, 12*, 245–262.

Zero-to-Three. (1997). *Key findings for a nationwide survey among parents of zero-to-three-year-olds.* Washington, DC: Peter D. Hart Research Associates, Inc.

35

Well-Being and the Future: Using Science Based Knowledge to Inform Practice and Policy[1]

Lucy Davidson
Mark L. Rosenberg
The Center for Child Well-being, Decatur, GA

Kristin A. Moore
Child Trends, Washington, DC

INTRODUCTION

Science works to improve well-being across the life course by contributing to decision making in public policy and practice. Yet, the capacity of science to inform policy and practice is affected by many challenges that face child well-being as a new field of study and interest. Some of these challenges are easily identifiable as "scientific" because they are matters of theory, research methodology, or information technology. Other challenges affect our ability to apply what can be learned through science. These applications are limited by (a) the social will and resources that the public is willing to invest in children's well-being, (b) cultural assumptions

[1]This chapter is dedicated to our parents: Ruth Hortense Kindgren Anderson, Donald Frank Anderson, Margaret Shearer Davidson, William E. Davidson, Jr., Lillian Rosenberg, and Ruben Rosenberg, "Parents are like shuttles on a loom. They join the threads of the past with threads of the future and leave their own bright patterns as they go."—*Fred Rogers.*

about determinants of well-being and whether they can be changed, and (c) social disparities that limit access to resources for those whose physical, cognitive, and social-emotional capacities are less developed and reinforce access and availability for those whose capacities are already strong. Additional challenges and alternate approaches are that:

- Few sources bring together information about the different dimensions of child development and even fewer attempt to integrate this information across developmental stages. A more holistic approach would help link scientific information and those interested in children.
- Children are often viewed as a collection of problems or at risk conditions. Focus on a more strengths-based approach including foundational strengths of well-being can under gird success and happiness across the life course.
- Some dimensions of child well-being are underappreciated areas (social and emotional development) that have a huge impact on more visible areas of interest (cognitive performance in school). Social and emotional development needs to be built into existing interventions.
- Not all sectors of the community are attentive to child health and development. Developing a strong social will to support child well-being depends on engaging a broad group of stakeholders.
- Decision makers need an accessible evidence base of what works that communities can adapt to local circumstances. Clear and accessible information about practices and policies that work could help communities build on success instead of starting from scratch, program by program.
- Appropriate measures and indicators are unavailable for tracking some of the most important outcomes for child well-being. A larger set of usable indicators would help decision makers understand the value of their investment in child well-being.
- Strategic action to eliminate disparities in child health and development is hampered by inequitable resource allocation. Scientific information about the relative costs and benefits of various choices can impact decisions about resources.

THE SCIENTIFIC IMPLICATIONS

Almost all scholarly research carries practical and political implications. Better that we should spell these out ourselves than leave that task to people with a vested interest in stressing only some of the implications and falsifying others. (Coontz, 1992, p. B2)

As a social historian and scholar of the American family, Stephanie Coontz was particularly mindful of the duty that scientists and academicians have to include among their scholarly responsibilities, reflection and communication about the implications of their research. This concern for the practical and political implications of scientific inquiry is never more critical than when one's focus is the well-being of children. Thoughtful program-, policy-, and systems-level actions require evaluation of multiple simultaneous and complex inputs. Good science that explores the well-being of children has much to say about public policy and practice on behalf of children. Even the gaps in current science and measurement have implications for investment in child well-being because practice doesn't wait for science to catch up. Scientific knowledge is only one component in the applied decision making of policy and practice, but without the active engagement of scientists, ideology can steal that role.

This chapter highlights the nexus of science, public policy, and practice in child well-being. We consider next steps in applied science and scientific theory that help connect the knowledge presented in preceding chapters to the work of communities, practitioners, and public systems. The primary focus of other sections of the book has been the foundational elements of well-being across physical, cognitive, and social and emotional development. These elements have been described for individuals, although they are co-determined and supported by the wider environment and culture. We now consider how knowledge of the foundational elements of well-being, child development, and parenting can contribute to decision making and be integrated with wider social and political co-determinants of well-being.

In some ways, the U.S. social/cultural/ political framework may give science a potentially larger role in decisions affecting child well-being than countries where well-being is framed in terms of rights. The United States may think of child well-being as a natural unfolding of developmental potential where action outside the family is generally not warranted until problems arise. For instance, government action may be viewed as justified when there are problems whose scale requires a collective or a public solution and the public response will actually save future public expenditure. In this framework, science may be called on to identify causal relationships and the possible impacts of alternative actions taken. The rights perspective does not ask science why something should be done but shares an interest in what science may be able to demonstrate as empirically effective to do.

The European Union (EU) and Scandinavian countries have taken a more rights-based approach to child well-being that does not look to science to demonstrate that action is indicated (Commission of the European Communities, 2000). For instance, quality child care, children's health services, and early education are basic rights, not interventions for problems where science has demonstrated a positive cost–benefit analysis for public investment. The foundational capabilities examined in this book are individual dimensions, and they are never developed exclusively by or through individual actions. Within the U.S. context, science is needed to expand ways to study and understand the social and systemic determinants of well-being. Learning more about the roles of organizations, systems, and the wider environment in shaping child well-being can contribute to progress along side the sphere determined by families' autonomous choices.

The word *element* was a deliberate and strategic selection to anchor the examination of child well-being throughout this book. The expression *foundational element of well-being* suggests a factor that is a fundamental precursor to other aspects of well-being across the life course and a characteristic that stands on its own, something which is not a product or a differently named subordinate of some other factor. Attention to the actions and conditions that support a foundational element can be expected to benefit children in the here and now as well as transfer a beneficial effect for well-being more broadly across the life course.

Obviously, identifying these foundational elements of well-being represents a challenging task. Yet, it seems reasonable to use the notion of elements to anchor a vision and a goal. If the real world application is much more complex, we can at least seek to outline a theory and identify the crucial antecedent factors that will enhance application. If the research base is not commensurate with the task, we can work to improve available research. If the measurements for concepts and indicators data are not ready, then we need to expand the stock.

Although identifying foundational elements of well-being, their functions, and mutual interactions is an extraordinarily complex and incomplete task, foundational elements can serve to anchor a vision and goal for children. The Center for Child Well-being, Child Trends, and many other organizations and people interested in the well-being of children share a vision of all children having the supports, strengths, and opportunities they need to grow and experience fulfilling lives. In this vision, science, policy, and practice that promote well-being would help children develop satisfying relationships, optimal health, lifelong learning abilities, social responsibility, and purposefulness. Review of the available research suggests a number of clear directions for future work to maximize scientific contributions to policy and practice. These include:

- The development and application of more coherent theory.
- Improvements in measurement to produce better indicators for child well-being.
- Integration of findings from trans-disciplinary research and contributed across different cultures and regions.
- Execution of more sophisticated research studies to guide interventions beyond single-factor programs.
- Use of scientific analysis and information technology to provide accessible registries of effective interventions.
- Development of science-based tools, such as national indices of child well-being, that can help shape public will.

IMPLICATIONS FOR THEORY

The *helping professions* are defined by the Penguin Dictionary of Psychology (Reber, 1995) as:

> Collectively, all those professions whose theories, research and practice focus on the assistance of others, the identification and resolution of their problems and the extension of knowledge of the human condition to further those aims. (p. 332)

This chapter considers the theoretician, per se, a member of the helping professions because theory, research, and practice are integrated to support child well-being. The study of human development and well-being is dispersed across many disciplines. Too often professionals in each discipline keep to themselves or work jointly with colleagues only in the same discipline. They develop their own theories, constructs, and methods and remain insulated from other social and biological sciences. Yet, public health researchers, developmentalists, economists, sociologists, philosophers, statisticians, and other researchers all have theoretical contributions to make in child well-being. Often, interaction across disciplines creates a synergy, such that the study of large questions moves forward more rapidly when theorists and researchers from different disciplines collaborate.

This project examining foundational elements has been organized around a broad paradigm that identifies three domains of well-being: physical health and safety, cognitive development, and social and emotional development. In addition, researchers on the project generally have accepted and employed an ecological model to examine influences on development within these domains (Bronfenbrenner, 1979, 1982). Moreover, developmental distinctions across the stages of childhood have been incorporated both implicitly and explicitly. The choice of these three rather general conceptual frameworks has enabled researchers from very different fields to work together comfortably. However, greater theoretical precision would enable more rapid advances.

One of the most vexing theoretical issues is the definition of *well-being*. The scholars contributing to this book have proposed and used the following definition:

> Well-being is a state of successful performance throughout the life course integrating physical, cognitive, and social-emotional functions that results in productive activities deemed significant by one's cultural community, fulfilling social relationships, and the ability to transcend moderate psychosocial and environmental problems. Well-being also has a subjective dimension in the sense of satisfaction associated with fulfilling one's potential.

Operationalizing any definition becomes problematic. The specific studies of well-being that are cited in this book reflect many disparate and implicit definitions of well-being that have informed, but not yet articulated a coherent theory.

Consensus on some operational outcomes, for instance, that well-being implies being free of incapacitating health problems or being literate in mathematics as well as the written word, is straightforward. Other, less obvious, outcome considerations point to the interdependence of theory and operational definition. Does something represent well-being because it is enjoyable or fulfilling in the present, or is it necessary that it contribute to positive characteristics later in life, such as adult social connectedness? Some emphasize the "being" aspect of well-being while others posit that "becoming" must always be considered. If positive outcomes exclusive to childhood were sufficient, the door might be open to calling virtually any child capacity an element of well-being that someone, somewhere considered a positive outcome.

Theory also must address the role of genetic influences. Although the importance of genetic factors is widely acknowledged (Collins et al., 2000), the mechanisms through which genetic endowment affects development, the relative impacts of genetic and extrinsic factors on development, and the mutual interactions among genetic and environmental influences are all incompletely understood. More precise theories of genetic expression in human development and the impact of development upon the instantiations of well-being across the life course await further research.

In addition, theories need to articulate how family and community influences interact. Beyond genetic factors, a complex array of family and community factors influence development. Are some of these family and community influences candidates to be elements of well-being? Chapters in this volume focus on parent–child, sibling and peer relationships. Beyond these social relationships, where do influences, such as family income, health insurance, family structure, housing, and community social capital fit into a theory? They are not child outcomes, but they are important inputs that need to be incorporated into a functional theory of well-being.

Clearly, many of these theoretical issues ask questions of philosophy as well as science. Integrating philosophical perspectives of "the good life" into a theory of positive development and well-being is a task that has only begun. All of these refinements in theory and research must serve as a bridge to service providers, rather than widening a gulf. *From Neurons to Neighborhoods: The Science of Early Childhood Development* cautions:

> As the rapidly evolving science of early childhood development continues to grow, its complexity will increase and the distance between the working knowledge of service providers and the cutting edge of the science will be staggering. The professional challenges that this raises for the early childhood field are formidable. (National Research Council and Institute of Medicine, 2000, p. 12)

THE MEASUREMENT OF WELL-BEING

> Nothing tends so much to the advancement of knowledge as the application of a new instrument.   —Sir Humphrey Davy (Hager, 1995)

Even given theoretical guidance, numerous issues of measurement remain to be addressed. Ideally, a single set of measures would exist for each well-being construct that could be used in basic research, evaluation studies, and in social indicator or monitoring efforts. Measures for some constructs, such as educational attainment, already exist. Other constructs are extremely difficult to measure, even in a laboratory setting, for example, sympathy and empathy. Developing measures appropriate for large-scale survey interviews represents an even greater challenge, particularly in a culturally diverse nation. In addition, it is necessary to identify the ranges of quantitative values or "scores," that are considered to define positive outcomes.

The selection of cut-offs gives significant decision-making power to the researchers who develop the measure and the cut-off. Of course, the distribution of the sample, natural break points, and the substantive interpretation of the items in the scale or index provide input into this decision. Infinitely more of some characteristics of well-being does not mean infinitely greater well-being. For example, measures of positive self-esteem need a cut-off point that differentiates good self-esteem from grandiosity. In defining cut-offs and categorical variables, it would be helpful to incorporate evidence about how the range of scores relates to concurrent life satisfaction and to positive outcomes in the future. For instance, subjective satisfaction and quality of life are more global areas that have been measured and could provide some referent for establishing desirable ranges of well-being elements.

Some relevant outcomes, especially problem behaviors such as substance abuse or teen pregnancy, are already well measured. However, other outcomes, especially positive outcomes, await stronger conceptual and theoretical development, for example, character. More in the middle, and urgently awaiting new research, are outcomes where there is some conceptual clarity but where reliable and valid measures do not exist. An example of such an outcome would be leadership.

One purpose of this book has been to advance the conceptual clarity of foundational elements of well-being so that better outcome measures can be developed. It is important that individuals from diverse populations contribute as surveys are developed and normed. For example, the attributes of leadership may vary across cultural groups such as Asian Americans and African Americans, and it is crucial to include items that tap leadership as viewed from within these groups. Similarly, responses may differ by age and gender, and it is essential to obtain input from boys and girls and from men and women in designing questions. Accordingly, as scales and indices are developed, tested, and revised, it is important that this work be conducted with individuals of different economic, age, gender, and cultural backgrounds (Sugland et al., 1995).

A related question is the source of data. Adolescents are more accurate respondents to questions about risk taking, such as sexual behavior or substance abuse, than parents or teachers, who lack information regarding the degree to which adolescents engage in these behaviors. If adolescent respondents are already the best information source for some topics, could we assume that adolescent self-report will be the best data source for information about positive behaviors and attributes? More particularly, would adolescents provide the most valid and reliable information about many or most of the elements of well-being? Triangulation to cross-check responses across multiple respondents may help, if we have theory or validity information to inform our use of the data obtained.

For younger children, data collection difficulties are different but still substantial. Children as young as 10 years old have been interviewed by telephone (National Commission on Children, 1991), and children as young as 7 have been interviewed in person about their families, their feelings, and their activities (Zill & Peterson, 1981). For other constructs, parents need to be the primary sources of information. In general, mothers have turned out to be better informants about their children's lives than fathers (Federal Interagency Forum on Child and Family Statistics, 1998). However, on a case-by-case basis, the most knowledgeable parent is increasingly being selected as the respondent, reflecting the fact that mothers are not inevitably the best informed about the child (Moore & Ehrle, 2000). Beyond parents, teachers represent a useful and independent point of view and one that reflects a different context (Bos et al., 1999; Hongling, Mahoney, & Cairns, 1999).

Even though most respondents enjoy participating in surveys about child and family topics (Moore & Peterson, 1989), extremely long surveys are expensive and some respondents may not be willing to participate if the burden on their time is too great. Therefore, it is necessary to develop scales that are reliable and valid, but also brief (Moore, Halle, & Mariner, 2000).

Assessing the test–retest reliability and validity of measures is recommended but done too seldom (e.g., Tout, Zaslow, Mariner, & Halle, 1998). In addition, the use of cognitive interviewing techniques to examine whether questions are working in the ways that question designers intended is not done as often as would be advisable (DeMaio, Rothgeb, & Hess, 1998). If items are to be used as indicators of child well-being, as outcome measures in research studies, and as goals for programs, researchers must increase attentiveness to measurement quality.

INDICATORS OF WELL-BEING

The adequacy of child well-being indicators is contingent on the underlying measurement science. Indicators are measures of desired outcomes for which data are available. Indicators do not measure every dimension of an outcome but stand for important markers of the outcome (Melaville, 1997). For example, ensuring that babies are "born healthy" may be an important community outcome to quantify. A quantifiable indicator for the general well-being goal of having babies "born healthy" could be the proportion of infants that weigh at least 2,500 grams at delivery. Birth weight represents only one aspect of the "born healthy" outcome, but an indicator may identify one measurable aspect for which data can be obtained to represent the broader outcome of interest.

This is an era of public devolution in funding and decision making on behalf of children. It is an era that endorses data-driven decision making and results-based accountability. When sound, nonpartisan, quantitative evidence is not accessible to decision makers, children get shortchanged. Useful indicators can serve as a lever to advance positive action for well-being, support results-based programming, and stimulate investment in child development. Things that cannot be measured or tracked over time through indicators do not garner public support, scientific understanding, sustainable investment, or comparable outcome information to stimulate best practices.

Creating categorical variables can make indicators user-friendly and understandable. For example, knowing that the mean leadership score in 1990 was 3.652, while in 2000 the mean score was 3.855 is not very useful because policy makers, service providers, the media, and parents will not know how to interpret this information. On the other hand, if we report as a categorical variable that in 1990, 24% of teens were leaders in their communities compared with 32% in 2000, the information will be more understandable and useful. In this way, the proportion of the population in poverty has become an important indicator (Federal Interagency Forum on Child and Family Statistics, 2000), even though few Americans know precisely how poverty is defined or know what the mean or median family income levels are for the current year.

Selection of indicators also requires careful consideration of causation. To illustrate, having straight teeth could reflect having greater family disposable income and nothing more. If so, and higher disposable family income does not create current life satisfaction and positive outcomes in adulthood, we would not want to include straight teeth as an indicator of well-being. If having straight teeth, either through genetic endowment or expensive orthodontia, actually serves as a valid indicator of overall physical attractiveness, and *if* physical attractiveness is a determinant of well-being (causal), then having straight teeth might be a serviceable indicator of well-being.

In this hypothetical example, straight teeth would be a particularly valuable indicator because it also points to an intervention that would support well-being. Interventions to straighten children's teeth would enhance their well-being, if the assumptions just mentioned applied. Positive indicators reflect strengths or assets to support well-being rather than markers of risk factors for poor well-being. As such, positive indicators (time reading to young children) are more likely to direct attention to interventions that can improve well-being than negative indicators (proportion of local third graders in the lowest quartile of national reading scores).

A series of related activities in partnership with agencies, organizations, and outside experts could expand the accessibility and utility of indicators for child well-being. Indicators relevant to well-being are scattered among many different state and national datasets provided by agencies in different sectors, for instance, commerce, health and human services, education, and juvenile justice. More negative, problem-focused (percentage of children in poverty) than positive, strengths-based (percentage of students who volunteer) indicators relating to child well-being have been measured. However, indicator information for child well-being would be more available and accessible if organized by developmental stages and presented in a searchable CD-ROM format and on the Web. This information would comprise an Indicators Directory for Child Well-Being.

A searchable directory to house this information could be created if national level data sets across relevant domains were disaggregated for specific indicators of child and family well-being. Such a directory would support interdisciplinary work in child and family well-being and provide information to myriad constituencies that need reliable information for their work on behalf of children. This directory should be searchable by key words in categories such as developmental stages (toddler, adolescent), type of indicator (behavior, health outcome, economic security, family characteristics), and demographics of the sample (urban/rural, ethnicity).

Relevant data sets would be accessed from a broad spectrum of reliable monitoring systems that are under government direction: commerce, juvenile justice, health and human services, education, and so on. Multiple characteristics would be recorded for each indicator, for example, description of the indicator, data source, years of available data, sponsor of the data source, and mode of administration, survey sample design, level of analysis, and so forth. Assembling these existing indicators will also serve to identify gaps in the current pool of child well-being indicators and stimulate expansion of the pool of relevant indicators and their more regular monitoring.

A directory of indicators would support the applied work of many kinds of people interested in child health and development: community planners, practitioners, policy makers, child serving organizations, scientists, journalists, and advocates. The primary value for some users would be in the directory's easy access to valid and reliable, current, quantitative information on a wide range of measures that impact children. The existing quantitative information may be invisible to potential users because it is scattered across so many specialty surveys and not publicly accessible, although in the public domain. These indicators can be used to direct attention and resources to underserved aspects of child health and development. They provide nonpartisan information to address misperceptions about the well-being of children in the United States and to influence social will for progress.

What can be measured can be supported and improved. The directory could capture positive indicators that provide more direct measures of broad goals that many communities share, such as having children healthy and ready to learn when they enter school. For others, the directory could identify existing instruments with modules of questions that could be used in surveys of the local population to gather community-specific information for needs assessment or tracking progress.

RESEARCH TO INFORM INTERVENTIONS, POLICY AND PRACTICE

One of the goals of research is to identify strategies to make life better. However, only a modest portion of the research on children is at a point where it can conclusively inform policy and practice. For example, a carefully conducted experimental intervention, such as the nurse home visiting program (Olds, Henderson, Kitzman, Eckenrode, Cole, & Tatelbaum, 1999), which shows significant and substantial evidence of impacts on children's development in the short run and over the longer term can be seen as ready for widespread replication. As Moore and Sugland (1996) term it, such programs are "next step" programs, in the sense that they are ready for immediate expenditure of public and/or private dollars to implement widely. Unfortunately, this robust an evidence base is rare, so that information for programmatic decisions must be augmented with other kinds of evidence.

Much of the research that is currently available is based on cross-sectional evidence, making it extremely difficult to ascertain causality. In addition, many databases include only local samples or samples that are highly selective or circumscribed. For example, some samples include only white children from affluent university towns, whereas other samples include only minority children from impoverished urban areas. To draw conclusions about the elements of well-being and actions that support their development, analyses need to be conducted on samples that are more diverse and ideally, that are broadly representative of the population.

Recently, though, important new sources of longitudinal data, such as the Early Childhood Longitudinal Study, Kindergarten Cohort, have become available, enabling researchers to establish the temporal ordering of developmental processes. This temporal ordering can contribute to the effective sequencing of actions supporting child well-being. Multivariate studies based on longitudinal data provide a second tier of evidence, termed "best bets" by Moore and Sugland. These studies do not provide the kind of explicit causal evidence produced by a well-conducted prospective study with random assignment to experimental conditions. They can suggest direction for policy and program intervention.

As national databases have expanded their content to include a variety of factors, researchers can examine whether a potential element of child well-being is truly a critical determinant of current life satisfaction and future well-being, or simply a correlate of other advantages. For example, the National Longitudinal Survey of Youth, both the 1979 and the 1997 cohorts, include information about family, school, employment, siblings, substance use, behavior problems, fertility, marriage, income, and other issues. This rich array of information makes it possible to control for numerous confounding factors and provide more compelling evidence regarding causality.

Without controlling for confounding variables, it is not possible to know whether the factor being studied is a determinant of child well-being or simply a reflection of some other factor. For instance, if children in single-parent families exercise less than children in two-parent families, is this finding due to something intrinsic in family structure, or is it determined by the lower family incomes and more dangerous, resource-poor neighborhoods common among many single parents? Thus, a concern for better research is not simply an academic nicety, but a crucial issue with important policy ramifications.

Research design characteristics and methods of analysis can be used to control for background factors such as parental education, poverty and family structure that might confound study outcomes. Sample selection that is diverse and representative of the populations of interest is helpful and also harder to construct than using a sample of convenience, such as a classroom. Researchers can use methods of analysis, such as fixed effects methods, that control for unmeasured influences that may be driving the results. For example, researchers might include State fixed effects in analysis models to control for economic or policy differences across States that might be affecting well-being. Family fixed effects could be included in models to control for unmeasured family variables that might be influencing well-being.

Researchers also need to develop new data resources to support longitudinal, multivariate analyses. This means including information on a variety of factors within the same database. The Panel Study of Income Dynamics, for example, has a long record of family economic, employment, family structure, attitudinal, and other information and has recently added modules on child well-being and family processes. The availability of these and other rich longitudinal databases is essential to moving forward research on foundational elements of child well-being.

Another critical research question is malleability. Can programs or policies affect an element of well-being? If a behavior such as shyness were determined entirely by genetic factors expressed as temperament, then it would not be programmatically sensible to focus on changing shyness, even if a large body of research indicated that it undermines well-being. However, scientists agree that nature and nurture are intertwined and coacting forces in development: "It is impossible to think of gene expression apart from the multiple environments in which it occurs. It is impossible to think of the manifestation of hereditary potential independently of the hierarchy of environments that shape its appearance" (National Research Council and Institute of Medicine, 2000, p. 40).

The role of environment in development may be more complex and person-specific than previously imagined. The task of researchers and of program developers is considerably more nuanced than had been envisioned by programs relying on simple behavior modification as a one-size-fits-all intervention or operated as if nature and nurture were separable.

Despite this complexity, random assignment experiments offer important opportunities to examine malleability and the magnitude of any effects that might be produced. How large an impact is it reasonable to anticipate? For outcomes that assess behavioral or cognitive elements, a change on the order of half a standard deviation or greater would be considered quite large (e.g., an 8-point change on a cognitive test with a standard deviation of 15 would be an important impact; Cohen, 1988). Multiple or very sustained inputs might be necessary to produce a large enough effect to be practically worthwhile as well as statistically significant. For instance, inputs from an intervention program, a benefit, and another support service combined might produce an effect of this magnitude. However, few studies have systematically varied inputs and examined the differential impacts achieved by input "doses" that vary in duration or magnitude. One implication is that potentially useful interventions may not demonstrate effectiveness when studied alone or over short periods of time. When practice and applied research combine several kinds of interventions, both outcomes and measurement of outcomes may be enhanced.

Given the cost and effort involved in implementing large-scale, high-quality interventions, policy makers and tax payers need to know how large an impact might be anticipated from a given "dose" of an input. For example, how much might a child's cognitive test scores rise as a result of spending one year in a high-quality preschool, compared with two years? Or how much might scores rise in a full-time program compared with a part-time program? In a full-year program compared with a part-year program?

Which program components produce the desired impacts and should be replicated with great fidelity wherever the program is implemented? Which program components should be adapted to fit cultural sub-groups and local conditions? Are impacts stronger or more positive for some sub-groups of children than others? What are those sub-groups? Most research cannot currently answer these very policy-relevant questions. A research agenda that identifies the most important programmatic questions and implements experimental studies designed to provide this information represents a critical next task for the scientific community. These kinds of research help move well-being interventions that have been efficacious under very controlled settings into real-world effective interventions that can be widely used.

A REGISTRY FOR INTERVENTIONS

In order to advance child well-being, communities, practitioners, policy makers, and advocates need to identify existing interventions that have had empirical support and can also fit their local needs and population. People entrusted to make funding and programming decisions for child health and development want to choose successful activities for their communities and want to know what works. Policy makers and practitioners want to go with the best available evidence, but may lack nonpartisan ways of finding out what that best evidence is or how separate pieces of information fit together. Scientists are asked for overall recommendations about what works, without a practical mechanism for assessing information from many separate studies. A registry of interventions would draw on the synthesis functions of science and research analysis, to create an applied product for policy and practice.

Practice and intervention information assembled into a registry could categorize the evidence for efficacy or effectiveness. Communities, practitioners, and policy makers could access and use information from successful programs that have been scientifically evaluated in order to extend programs into new settings and reach other groups of children. The registry could also house quantitative information formatted for scientists who would like to do meta-analyses, for instance a meta-analysis to determine the effect size of an intervention.

A registry to contain the evidence base of effective activities would enable those serving children and youth to make more informed decisions, as well as access information to support social will for child health and development. Activities in a registry would range in scope from multicomponent systems, to programs, to discrete interventions. Such a broad range of activities included could be useful in planning and evidence-based decision making if a registry were readily accessible over the web or via CD-ROM to a variety of consumers making decisions at the systems, agency, or program levels.

Consumers would need to be able to search by categories of interest as well as population characteristics for which activities supporting well-being work, sub-groups for whom they work best, under what circumstances, and to what degree. For example, an organization providing after school activities could search for implementation information about mentoring programs that have demonstrated effectiveness for teenage boys. They could compare the characteristics of successful mentoring programs to the program specifications they have under consideration.

Information in this registry could be searched by categories that would be practical for users, for example:

- Outcomes of interest according to specific well-being indicators.
- Risk or protective factors affected by the activity, such as problem solving or communication skills.
- Environment for the activity, such as school, pediatric clinic, or faith-based community organization.
- Structural level of activity, such as system, program, or individual intervention.
- Type of activity, such as home visitation or mentoring.
- Demographic information, such as developmental stage of the participants served or gender.
- Implementation information, such as cost or training required.

Additional studies and updates could be entered in the same system to keep the registry current.

To be useful and feasible, a registry must focus on a manageable number of outcomes that are valued by large numbers of communities, organizations, and providers. It must reflect a transdisciplinary perspective, because children are not sorted into academic fields of inquiry. It must reflect logical, defensible, replicable, and explicit criteria for inclusion and exclusion of studies and effectiveness categories. Effectiveness categories are generally grouped as proven, potential, and promising where the lowest category of effectiveness may be broad enough to include activities that (a) are logically consistent with a mainstream theory, (b) reflect expert opinion, and (c) have been implemented and are not known to cause harm. Transparency in describing categories of effectiveness while being able to share the best available practices helps programming decision makers draw from an evolving evidence base. If inclusion and exclusion criteria are unduly restrictive in an emerging field, practice has to draw more heavily on intuition than evidence.

Development of a registry melds science and information technology in the service of policy and practice to improve child well-being. Construction processes rely on software integration. Bibliographic management software is one type of software used to organize the data that will be abstracted and coded for a registry. The second type of software is used for meta-analysis. Planning for possible meta-analytic uses of the registry involves creating database fields that are compatible with meta-analysis software programs in the content and formatting of quantitative information. A database that is set up with meta-analysis as a possibility makes it easier for scientists to determine which kinds of interventions make what degree of difference. Meta-analyses contribute to the scientific knowledge base by combining outcomes across multiple studies. Thirdly, relational database software would need to be set up a registry to interface with the Web. This step allows wide consumer access and functional capacity to search for interventions that might benefit a particular community or developmental stage of children without wading through the totality of information.

A Web-based or CD-ROM registry would connect advances in research, measurement, and indicators to policy and practice. As a registry uses available research and existing information technology, it is feasible now. Barriers to development, however, include the academic disincentives to doing research synthesis instead of "original" research and the possible mismatch with donor-initiated funding priorities.

MODELING A NATIONAL INDEX OF WELL-BEING

Recently, a number of researchers have independently explored development of a national index of child well-being. They include Kenneth Land, presenting "Child Well-Being in the United States, 1975-1998: Some Findings from a New Index" (Land, Lamb, & Mustillo, 2001). In the same way that the United States uses composite measures in indices to track inflation, unemployment, and poverty, it is important to monitor the well-being of the population, particularly children (Hauser, Brown, & Prosser, 1997). Well-being can be tracked over time and across sub-groups (Moore, 1997) and could be the subject of a national index functionally analogous to the consumer price index.

Such a broad national index is primarily a tool for tracking social policy and its outcomes and for shaping social will. A composite index of well-being would weight the contribution of multiple domains of well-being, such as health, economic security, and social and emotional function to well-being. Similarly, a quantitative value for each domain would be determined by a weighted formula incorporating selected indicators that can be tracked over time. The technical aspects of index construction offer many viable solutions, but the critical issue is fitting logistical decisions such as the selection of relevant domains, indicator selection, and a weighting formula to an agreed on purpose for the index. The selections that are made in index composition and calculation methods shape what picture of child well-being is offered by the index. For instance, formulae that differentially weight data representing indicators of children's health can change whether the same index shows the well-being of children to be improving or declining over time (Johnson, 2001).

More stakeholders may support tracking a set of well-being indices for important domains, such as child health, educational development and others, than reporting by a single well-being index. Then, too, options for indicators to construct a single national index are more limited the further back in time one wishes to trace changes in well-being. The current selection of well-being indicators is wider than available in the past. Beginning a national index may be less politically charged if present-time indicators and a current calculus serve as the original benchmark rather than choosing historical indicators and a retrospective starting point for trends. However, some domain specific indices may be easier to construct retrospectively and more readily supported than a single overall index when tracking forward from some earlier point of social change is indicated.

An unresolved and technically challenging problem is the adjustment of available indicators within an index to proportionally represent the demographic distribution of children in the national population instead of a population group overrepresented by the particular indicator. For example, youth suicide rates might be an important indicator for the domain of emotional well-being. However, youth suicides in the United States occur predominantly among white males and their suicide rates increase markedly with age from 14 through 18. Using unadjusted youth suicide rates would overrepresent older white males as determinants of emotional well-being in a national index. Similar considerations of how to address the relative significance of different developmental stages during childhood in some overall calculus of child well-being have not been resolved.

CONCLUSIONS

In sum, while the evidence assembled in this book represents a critical and helpful compilation of the current knowledge base, one of the functions of this effort has been to highlight scientific gaps and limitations. Some of these gaps are theoretical, others are methodological, some reflect a paucity of data, and still others are analytic. It is clear that addressing these gaps would require a good decade of work. However, efforts to improve the well-being of today's children cannot be deferred until the next generation of scientific knowledge becomes available.

We have proposed steps to bridge science, policy, and practice in closing these gaps. Transdisciplinary collaboration among researchers to identify, measure, and monitor the elements of well-being and projects that meld research and information technology will provide an increasingly valuable foundation for improving the daily lives of children and enhancing their well-being across the life course. The scholars, researchers, and practitioners contributing to *Well-Being: Positive Elements Across the Life Course* have brought us closer to this goal. We hope that this book can accelerate progress by helping to mobilize the collective actions and resources needed to improve well-being for all children.

REFERENCES

Bos, H., Huston, A., Granger, R., Duncan, G., Brock, T., & McLoyd, V. (1999). *New hope for people with low incomes: Two-year results of a program to reduce poverty and reform welfare.* New York: Manpower Demonstration Research Corporation.

Bronfenbrenner, U. (1979). *The ecology of human development.* Cambridge, MA: Harvard University Press.

Bronfenbrenner, U. (1982). The context of development and the development of context. In R. M. Lerner (Ed.), *Developmental psychology: Historical and philosophical perspectives.* Hillsdale, NJ: Lawrence Erlbaum Associates.

Cohen, J. (1988). *Statistical power analysis for the behavioral sciences* (2nd ed.). Hillsdale, NJ: Lawrence Erlbaum Associates.

Collins, W. A., Maccoby, E. E., Steinberg, L., Hetherington, E. M., & Bornstein, M. H. (2000). Contemporary research on parenting: The case for nature and nurture. *American Psychologist, 55*(2), 218–232.

Commission of the European Communities. (2000). *Communication from the Commission, Building an Inclusive Europe,* Bruxelles, Belgium

Coontz, S. (1992). *Chronicle of Higher Education,* October 21, 1992, B2.

DeMaio, T., Rothgeb, J., & Hess, J. (1998). Improving survey quality through pretesting. *Proceedings of the Section on Survey Research Methods, American Statistical Association,* 50–58.

Federal Interagency Forum on Child and Family Statistics. (1998). *Nurturing fatherhood: Improving data and research on male fertility, family formation and fatherhood.* Washington, DC: Author.

Federal Interagency Forum on Child and Family Statistics. (2000). *America's children: Key national indicators of well-being, 2000.* Washington, DC: U.S. Government Printing Office.

Hager, T. (1995). *Force of Nature.* New York: Simon & Schuster.

Hauser, R., Brown, B. V., & Prosser, W. (Eds.). (1997). *Indicators of children's well-being.* New York: Russell Sage.

Hongling, X., Mahoney, J. L., & Cairns, R. B. (1999). Through a looking glass or a hall of mirrors? Self-ratings and teach-ratings of academic competence over development. *International Journal of Behavioral Development, 23*(1), 163–183.

Johnson, D. (2001, June). *Key Indicators of Child and Youth Well-being: Completing the Picture.* Panel discussion given at the Child Trends conference. Bethesda, MD.

Land, K. C., Lamb, V. L., & Mustillo, S. K. (2001, June). *Child well-being in the United States, 1975–1998: Some findings from a new index.* Presented at the Child Trends conference. Bethesda, MD.

Melaville, A. I. (1997) *A guide to selecting results and indicators: Implementing results-based budgeting.* The Finance Project. http://www.welfareinfo.org/results.htm

Moore, K. A. (1997). Criteria for indicators of child well-being. In R. M. Hauser, B. V. Brown, & W. R. Prosser (Eds.), *Indicators of children's well-being.* New York: Russell Sage Foundation.

Moore, K. A., & Ehrle, J. (2000). *Measuring child well-being at the state level: The reliability and utility of the National Survey of America's Families.* Washington, DC: Child Trends.

Moore, K. A., Halle, T. G., & Mariner, C. L. (2000). *Scaling back survey scales: How short is too short?* Washington, DC: Child Trends.

Moore, K. A., & Peterson, J. L. (1989). *The consequences of teenage pregnancy.* Washington, DC: Child Trends.

Moore, K. A., & Sugland, B. W. (1996). *Next steps and best bets: Approaches to preventing adolescent childbearing.* Washington, DC: Child Trends.

National Commission on Children. (1991). *Speaking of kids: A national survey of children and parents.* Washington, DC: Author.

National Research Council and Institute of Medicine. (2000). *From neurons to neighborhoods: The science of early childhood development.* J. P. Shonkoff & D. A. Phillips (Eds.). Washington, DC: National Academy Press.

Olds, D. L., Henderson, C. R., Jr., Kitzman, H. J., Eckenrode, J. J., Cole, R. E., & Tatelbaum, R. C. (1999). Prenatal and infant home visitation by nurses: Recent findings. *The Future of Children, 9*(1), 44–65.

Reber, A. S. (Ed.). (1995). *The Penguin dictionary of psychology.* London: Penguin Books.

Sugland, B. W., Zaslow, M., Smith, J. R., Brooks-Gunn, J., Coates, D., Blumenthal, C., Moore, K. A., Griffin, T., & Bradley, R. H. (1995). The early childhood HOME inventory and HOME-short form in differing racial/ethnic groups. Are there differences in underlying structure, internal consistency of subscales, and patterns of prediction? *Journal of Family Issues, 16*(5), 632–663.

Tout, K., Zaslow, M. J., Mariner, C. L., & Halle, T. (1998). Interviewer ratings of mother-child interaction and the home environment in the context of survey research: Contributions and concerns. *Methods Working Paper Series on Strengthening Survey Measures of the Mother-Child Relationship, #98.5.* Washington DC: Child Trends.

Zill, N., & Peterson, J. L. (1981). *Learning to do things without help.* Washington, DC: Child Trends.

About the Authors

BONNIE L. BARBER is an Associate Professor of Family Studies and Human Development at the University of Arizona. She completed her PhD in Developmental Psychology at the University of Michigan in 1990. In 2000, she was the Society for Research on Adolescence biennial meeting program co-chair. Her research interests include adolescent and young adult social relationships across life transitions and positive development in divorced families. She has also studied the effectiveness of empirically-based curricula for divorced mothers with adolescents and collaborated on a national outcome evaluation of programs for youth and families at risk. The Spencer Foundation and the William T. Grant Foundation have both funded her current longitudinal research on adolescence and the transition to young adulthood.

MARC H. BORNSTEIN is Senior Investigator and Head of Child and Family Research at the National Institute of Child Health and Human Development. He holds a BA from Columbia College and a PhD from Yale University. Bornstein was a Guggenheim Foundation Fellow and received a RCDA from the NICHD, the Ford Cross-Cultural Research Award from the HRAF, the McCandless Young Scientist Award from the APA, the US PHS Superior Service Award from the NIH, an Award for Excellence from American Mensa, and the Arnold Gesell Prize from the Theodor Hellbrügge Foundation. He has held faculty positions at Princeton University and New York University as well as visiting academic appointments in Munich, London, Paris, New York, and Tokyo. Bornstein is coauthor of *Development in Infancy* (4 editions) and general editor of *The Crosscurrents in Contemporary Psychology Series* (10 volumes). He also edited the *Handbook of Parenting* (Vols. I–V, 2 editions) and co-edited *Developmental Psychology: An Advanced Textbook* (4 editions) as well as multiple other volumes. He is author of several children's books and puzzles in *The Child's World* series. Bornstein is Editor Emeritus of *Child Development* and Editor of *Parenting: Science and Practice.* He has contributed scientific papers in the areas of human experimental, methodological, comparative, developmental, cross-cultural, neuroscientific, pediatric, and aesthetic psychology.

LISA J. BRIDGES is a Senior Research Scientist at The George Washington University and an independent consultant specializing in early childhood development, education, and research design and measurement. She is currently working on projects with the Institute for Research and Reform in Education and with Child Trends. Bridges received her PhD in Psychology from the University of Rochester and was previously affiliated with the University of California at Riverside. She is a past SRCD Executive Branch Public Policy Fellow at The National Institute of Child Health and Human Development, Demographic and Behavioral Sciences Branch.

WILLIAM M. BUKOWSKI is Professor of Psychology and University Research Chair at Concordia University in Montréal, Québec, Canada. He is also a member of Concordia's Centre for Research in Human Development. He was educated at Canisius College in Buffalo, New York, and at Michigan State University in East Lansing. Previously he was on the faculty of the University of Maine. His research program is focused on the features and effects of experiences with peers during the school-age and early adolescent periods. He is the editor of the *International Journal of Behavioral Development* and has been on the editorial boards of *Child Development, Journal of Abnormal Child Psychology,* and *Social Development.* Together with Andy Newcomb and Bill Hartup, he edited *The Company They Keep: Friendship in Childhood and Adolescence.*

DEBRA A. BUROCK is a doctoral student in the Clinical Developmental and School Psychology Program at Bryn Mawr College. Burock received her BA at Rutgers University-Camden College of Arts and Sciences. She is affiliated with the Bryn Mawr Cognition Laboratory where she is involved in research examining the effects of aging on memory, attention and perception. Her other research interests include the biological basis of anxiety and the effect of anxiolytic agents on neurological structures.

ANITA CHAWLA is currently a consultant with The National Academies of Science, Institute of Medicine. She is a graduate of Emory University, the University of Michigan Medical School, and the University of Michigan School of Public Health. Chawla completed her residency in internal medicine at Georgetown University. She previously worked for former President Carter at The Carter Center in Atlanta where she contributed to the Center's health projects, conflict resolution initiatives, and national policy issues. She has also designed and led research studies in the prevention of infectious diseases for the Centers for Disease Control and Prevention and the United States Public Health Service. In addition, Chawla has conducted research and published in the area of collaborative problem solving. She continues to practice medicine and sees patients in the community.

JEANETTE M. CONNER is Administrator of Clinical Trials and Follow-Up Projects for the Vermont Oxford Network, Burlington, Vermont. Conner was educated at the Universities of California, Los Angeles; Washington, Seattle; and Dartmouth Medical School, Center for the Evaluative Clinical Sciences, Hanover, New Hampshire. She previously was affiliated with Dartmouth Hitchcock Medical Center as an Instructor in Pediatrics. Currently, Conner is affiliated with the University of Vermont, College of Medicine Department of Pediatrics as an Associate Clinical Professor. Part of her doctoral studies included training at the Health Assessment Laboratory, Boston, where she worked on the Child Health Questionnaire. Conner has co-instructed survey research for the Evaluative Clinical Sciences Program at Dartmouth.

MARTHA J. COX is Professor of Psychology and Director of the Center for Developmental Science at the University of North Carolina at Chapel Hill. Cox was educated at the University of Illinois and the University of Virginia and was previously affiliated with the University of Evansville, Evansville, Indiana; the University of Texas Health Science Center at Dallas; the Timberlawn Psychiatric Research Foundation, Dallas, Texas; and the Western Carolina Center, Morganton, North Carolina. She also was a Fellow of the Bush Institute for Child and Family Policy at the University of North Carolina at Chapel Hill, North Carolina. Cox was the Co-Chair of the NIMH Research Consortium on Family Risk and Resilience and President of the Southwest Society for Research on Child Development. Cox has been an associate editor of the *Journal of Social and Personal Relationships* and on the editorial board of *Developmental Psychology, Journal of Family Psychology, Journal of Clinical Child Psychology, Journal of Family Issues,* and *Psychiatry.* She is the Series Co-Editor of *The Advances in Family Research Series*. She has recently co-edited *Conflict and Cohesion in Families* and *The Transition to Kindergarten.*

LUCY DAVIDSON is Clinical Associate Professor of Psychiatry at the Emory School of Medicine and Associate Director of Science at the Center for Child Well-being. She serves as expert consultant to the Office of the Surgeon General. She received her undergraduate and medical degrees from Emory University and Masters and specialists' degrees in education from Georgia State University. Her previous research and programmatic interests have concentrated on suicide and suicide prevention with special attention to epidemiology, policy, medical assessment, prevention planning, and public education. She is most recently co-editor of a special issue of *Suicide and Life Threatening Behavior* on bringing research to practice in suicide prevention and co-author of the *Surgeon General's Call to Action to Pre-*

vent Suicide. Davidson is a Fellow of the American Psychiatric Association and recipient of the U.S. Public Health Service Citation, American Foundation for Suicide Prevention Public Service Award, and SPAN Architect Award for the National Strategy for Suicide Prevention.

JAMES E. DEWEY is Executive Vice President Special Projects at Quality- Metric, Inc., Lincoln, Rhode Island. Dewey received his PhD from Purdue University in Health Education and teaches graduate courses in research methods at the University of Rhode Island. He is Past President of the Society of Prospective Medicine and has worked for the past sixteen years founding and building two technology-based health assessment companies. He currently works with Dr. John E. Ware, Jr., developer of the world's most widely used health outcomes tool, the SF-36(r).

LAURA J. DIETZ is a graduate student in the clinical psychology program at the University of Pittsburgh. She has completed requirements for a Masters degree and is currently working on the dissertation requirement for a PhD She received her undergraduate degree from Holy Cross College and has presented papers at several national and international meetings. Her primary research interests include the influence of parental psychopathology and family systems on young children's social/emotional development and adaptation.

JACQUELYNNE S. ECCLES (McKeachie Collegiate Professor of Psychology) received her PhD from UCLA. She has served on the faculty at Smith College, the University of Colorado, and the University of Michigan; in 1998-99, she was the Interim Chair of Psychology at Michigan. She was a member of the MacArthur Research Network on Successful Pathways through Adolescence, the SRA (Society for Research on Adolescence) Program Chair in 1996, served on the SRA Council, and is now President. She was also Program Chair and President for Division 35 of APA. She was on the CBASSE Committee of the National Academy of Science and chaired the NAS Committee on After School Programs for Youth. She is Chair of the MacArthur Foundation Network on Successful Pathways through Middle Childhood. Her awards include the Spencer Foundation Fellowship for Outstanding Young Scholar in Educational Research, the Sarah Goddard Power Award for Outstanding Service from the University of Michigan, the APS Cattell Fellows Award for Outstanding Applied Work in Psychology, SPSSI's Kurt Lewin Award for outstanding research, and the University of Michigan Faculty Recognition Award for Outstanding Scholarship. She has conducted research on topics ranging from gender-role socialization, teacher expectancies, and classroom influences on student motivation to social development in the family and school context. Her most recent work focuses on ethnicity and on the transition from mid to late adolescence and into adulthood.

NANCY EISENBERG is Regents' Professor of Psychology at Arizona State University. She has published over 250 books and papers on social, emotional, and moral development. She has been a recipient of Research Scientist Development Awards and a Research Scientist Award from the National Institute of Health (NIH and NIMH). She was President of the Western Psychological Association, has been associate editor of *Merrill-Palmer Quarterly* and *Personality and Social Psychology Bulletin,* and is editor of *Psychological Bulletin.* She has been on the governing council of the American Psychological Association and the Society of Research in Child Development and is a member of the U.S. National Committee for the International Union of Psychological Science (at the National Academy of Science). Her books include *The Roots of Prosocial Behavior in Children* and *The Caring Child,* as well as the editorship of Volume 3 *(Social, Emotional, and Personality Development)* of the *Handbook of Child Psychology.*

WILLIAM H. FOEGE is an epidemiologist who worked in the successful campaign to eradicate smallpox in the 1970s. He became Chief of the CDC Smallpox Eradication Program and was appointed director of the U.S. Centers for Disease Control in 1977. He attended Pacific Lutheran University, received his MD from the University of Washington, and MPH from Harvard University. In 1984, Foege and several colleagues formed the Task Force for Child Survival, a working group for the World Health Organization, UNICEF, The World Bank, the United Nations Development Program, and the Rockefeller Foundation. Its success in accelerating childhood immunization led to an expansion of its mandate in 1991 to include other issues that diminish the quality of life for children. Foege joined The Carter Center in 1986 as its Executive Director, Fellow for Health Policy, and Executive Director of Global 2000. In 1992, he resigned as Executive Director of The Carter Center, but continued in his role as a Fellow. He remained Executive Director of the Task Force for Child Survival and Development until October 1999. In January 1997, he joined the faculty of Emory University, where he was Presidential Distinguished Professor of International Health at the Rollins School of Public Health. In September 1999, Foege became a Senior Medical Advisor for the Bill and Melinda Gates Foundation. He retired from both Emory and the Gates Foundation in December 2001. Foege has championed many issues, but child survival and development, injury prevention, population, preventive medicine, and public health leadership are of special interest, particularly in the developing world. He is a strong proponent of disease eradication and control, and has taken an active role in the eradication of Guinea worm, polio and measles, and the elimination of River Blindness. He is the recipient of many awards, holds honorary degrees from numerous institutions, and was named a Fellow of the London School of Tropical Medicine and Hygiene in 1997. He is the author of more than 125 professional publications.

WILLIAM G. GRAZIANO is a Professor of Psychology at Texas A&M University. Graziano was educated at the University of Minnesota and was previously affiliated with the University of Georgia. He is a Fellow of Division 7, the

Developmental Psychology Division of the American Psychological Association. He has been associate editor of the *Journal of Personality*

ELIZABETH C. HAIR is a Research Associate at Child Trends, a non-profit, non-partisan research organization based in Washington, DC. She received her PhD from Texas A&M University. Hair's training is in social/developmental psychology and methodology, which allows for an inter-disciplinary perspective on issues related to children and families. Her research focuses on how family processes and individual differences in children can affect children's social emotional and cognitive development.

TAMARA HALLE is a Senior Research Associate and Content Area Manager for the Early Childhood Development area at Child Trends, a non-profit, non-partisan research organization based in Washington, DC. She received her PhD in developmental psychology from the University of Michigan. Prior to joining the Child Trends staff, she held an NICHD post-doctoral research fellowship at the Center for Developmental Science, an NICHD-funded, interdisciplinary research center located at the University of North Carolina at Chapel Hill. Halle's research interests focus on the interplay among family processes, children's social and cognitive development, and children's school readiness and achievement. She was an invited speaker and participant in the 14th Annual Rosalynn Carter Symposium on Mental Health Policy and an invited participant in the National Institute of Mental Health 5th Annual National Conference on Prevention Research. She has served as a reviewer of manuscripts for *Behavioral and Brain Sciences*, *First Language*, *Journal of Educational Psychology*, and *Psychology of Addictive Behaviors*.

DANIEL A. HART is Professor of Psychology and Associate Dean of Arts and Sciences at Rutgers University. Hart's research examines the development of identity, personality, and morality across the life span. In his most recent work, Hart is focusing on the influences of poverty and neighborhoods on the healthy development of youth. This work features both research and application. His new work makes use of national data sets to understand the problems confronting poor youth and the formation of new youth development and health promotion programs to address the problems identified in research.

KRISTINA S. M. HARTER is an advanced doctoral candidate in clinical psychology at the University of North Carolina at Chapel Hill. Her research focuses on family relationships and their role in individual psychological functioning and development. She has co-authored several book chapters in this area.

DENISE L. HAYNIE is a Staff Scientist in the Prevention Research Branch, Division of Statistics, Epidemiology, and Prevention Research at the National Institutes of Child Health and Human Development, National Institutes of

Health. She completed her MPH at Johns Hopkins School of Hygiene and Public Health and received her PHD in Developmental Psychology from The Catholic University of America. Prior to coming to NICHD, she was a Research Associate at the Laboratory for Children's Health Promotion at Georgetown University School of Medicine. Her research interests focus on adolescents' relationships with their parents and peers, particularly how these relationships impact health-related behaviors.

DEREK M. ISAACOWITZ is an Assistant Professor of Psychology at Brandeis University. He completed his undergraduate work at Stanford University and received a PhD in psychology from the University of Pennsylvania. He also has spent time as a visiting student at the Max Planck Institute for Human Development in Berlin, Germany. His primary research interests involve successful aging, optimism in old age, and emotion regulation throughout adulthood.

KAY DONAHUE JENNINGS is Associate Professor of Psychiatry and Psychology at the University of Pittsburgh. She is also the director of the Infancy and Early Childhood Program at the University of Pittsburgh Medical Center. Jennings was educated at the University of Michigan and the University of California at Berkley. She was previously affiliated with the National Institute of Child Health and Human Development in Washington, DC. She is a member of the American Psychological Association and the Society for Research in Child Development. She is the author of numerous articles published in peer-reviewed journals on children's development. Mastery motivation has been a primary focus of her research.

ROBERT V. KAIL is Professor of Psychological Sciences at Purdue University. He received his BA from Ohio Wesleyan University and his PhD in developmental psychology from the University of Michigan. He was previously affiliated with the Universities of Pittsburgh and Maryland. He was previously the associate editor for *Child Development* and is currently the editor of the *Journal of Experimental Child Psychology* and the editor of *Advances in Child Development and Behavior*. His research focuses on the causes and consequences of developmental change in speed of information processing. Kail is author of *The Development of Memory in Children* and *Children and Their Development* as well as co-author of *Human Development: A Life Span View*.

COREY L. M. KEYES is an Assistant Professor, jointly appointed in the Department of Sociology of Emory University and the Department of Behavioral Sciences and Health Education of the Rollins School of Public Health. Keyes received his PhD in Sociology from the University of Wisconsin, Madison. He is a member of the steering committee of the Society for the Study of Human Development, an associate of the John D. and Catherine T. MacArthur Foundation's Research Network on Successful Midlife Development, as well as a member of the Positive Psychology Network. He is co-editor of *Flourishing: Scientists Examine the Life Well-Lived* (forthcoming, American Psychological Association Press).

CAROLINE H. LEAVITT is a doctoral student in Counseling Psychology Program at Georgia State University and is specializing in the area of children and families. Prior to entering the doctoral program, she was a Research Associate at the Center for Child Well-being. Leavitt received a JD from Columbia University Law School and an MA from the Clinical and Counseling Psychology Department of Teachers College, Columbia University. She is a member of the American Psychological Association and has been the editor-in-chief of the *Columbia Journal of Environmental Law*.

RICHARD M. LERNER is the Bergstrom Chair in Applied Developmental Science at Tufts University. A developmental psychologist, Lerner received a PhD in 1971 from the City University of New York. He has been a fellow at the Center for Advanced Study in the Behavioral Sciences and is a fellow of the American Association for the Advancement of Science, the American Psychological Association, and the American Psychological Society. Prior to joining Tufts University, he was on the faculty and held administrative posts at Michigan State University, Pennsylvania State University, and Boston College, where he was the Anita L. Brennan Professor of Education and the Director of the Center for Child, Family, and Community Partnerships. During the 1994-95 academic year Lerner held the Tyner Eminent Scholar Chair in the Human Sciences at Florida State University. Lerner is the author or editor of 45 books and more than 300 scholarly articles and chapters. He edited Volume 1, on "Theoretical models of human development," for the fifth edition of the *Handbook of Child Psychology.* He is the founding editor of the *Journal of Research on Adolescence* and of *Applied Developmental Science.* He is known for his theory of, and research about, relations between life-span human development and contextual or ecological change. He has done foundational studies of adolescents' relations with their peer, family, school, and community contexts, and is a leader in the study of public policies and community-based programs aimed at the promotion of positive youth development.

BONITA E. LONDON is a doctoral student in social/personality psychology at Columbia University. London is a graduate of Rutgers University, where she majored in psychology and minored in women's studies. She was selected by the American Psychological Association to participate in the Summer Science Institute, conducting research at Johns Hopkins University. She has conducted research at several academic and applied institutions, focusing on phonological awareness in adolescents, salivary cortisol and adolescent personality types, and stereotype threat and academic performance. Currently, she is conducting research on interpersonal and race-based rejection sensitivity, implicit theories of intelligence and stereotype threat, and academic goal orientation of minority students. She is a co-author of a chapter reviewing the development of prosocial behavior in the forthcoming book *Introduction to Developmental Psychology.*

DOUGLAS J. MACIVER is a Principal Research Scientist and Director of the Talent Development Middle School Program at the Johns Hopkins University. Mac Iver received his PhD from the Developmental Psychology Program at the University of Michigan. His research focuses on middle level education, motivation and achievement in early adolescence, and the social structuring of schools. MacIver is co-author of *Education in the Middle Grades: National Practices and Trends.*

BRIAN MACWHINNEY is Professor of Psychology and Modern Languages at Carnegie Mellon University. He received a PhD in psycholinguistics from the University of California at Berkeley. He has developed a computational model of the acquisition of grammar and a functionalist account of the development of sentence processing. In 1984, he and Catherine Snow co-founded the CHILDES (Child Language Data Exchange System) Project for the computational study of child language transcript data. The CHILDES programs and database have now become an important component of the basic methodology of research in language acquisition. MacWhinney's work recently has focused on aspects of second language learning and the neural bases of language as revealed by the development of children with focal brain lesions. He has also begun to explore a new form of linguistic functionalism which views linguistic and discourse structure as emergent properties of cognitive and social grounding.

JAMES A. MERCY is the Associate Director for Science of the Division of Violence Prevention in the National Center for Injury Prevention and Control of the Centers for Disease Control and Prevention (CDC). He received his PhD in sociology from Emory University in Atlanta. After his graduation, Mercy began working at CDC as an Epidemic Intelligence Service Officer in a newly formed activity to examine violence as a public health problem. Over the two decades since he joined CDC, Mercy has conducted and overseen numerous studies of the epidemiology of youth suicide, family violence, homicide, and firearm injuries.

AMANDA M. MIRAGLIA is an undergraduate at Rutgers University, majoring in Psychology and Educational Development. She is a member of Kappa Delta Pi, national honor society in education. Miraglia has contributed to a study examining the relation of personality type to salivary cortisol. She has worked for a number of years with children with disabilities, particularly in classroom settings.

KRISTIN A. MOORE is a social psychologist and President and Senior Scholar of Child Trends, a non-profit, non-partisan research organization based in Washington, DC. She has been with Child Trends since 1982, studying trends in child and family well-being, the effects of family structure and social change on children, the determinants and consequences of adolescent parenthood, and the effects of welfare and welfare reform on children. Moore is a member of the Family and Child Well-Being Research Network established by the National Institute of Child Health and Human Development and serves on the Advisory Council for NICHD and as an advisor on teenage pregnancy and family issues for several national surveys. Moore helped establish the Task Force on Effective Programs and Research of The National Campaign to Prevent Teen Pregnancy and served as chair. She received the Presidential Award from the National Organization on Adolescent Pregnancy and Parenting in 1991, the Foundation for Child Development Centennial Award in 1999 for linking research on children's development to policies that serve the public interest, and two Hammer Awards, one for work on a public-private initiative to improve data on fathers and one for work on child and family statistics. In 2002 she was selected the Society for Adolescent Medicine's Visiting Professor in Adolescent Research.

STEPHEN B. PLANK is an assistant professor in the Department of Sociology and a research scientist at the Center for Social Organization of Schools, both at Johns Hopkins University. He received his BA from Northwestern University and his MA and PhD in sociology from the University of Chicago. He authored *Finding One's Place: Teaching Styles and Peer Relations in Diverse Classrooms* (Teachers College Press, 2000). He has also published articles and book chapters on middle school reform, peer influences on adolescents' career expectations, the transition to postsecondary education or work, and school choice.

ELIZABETH L. POLLARD is a Child Development Specialist at the Task Force for Child Survival and Development's Center for Child Well-Being. She has been with the Center for Child Well-being since 1999, studying child and family well-being, focusing her work on parenting and measurement issues. Currently, she directs the Center's Parenting Network. Pollard holds a BA in Psychology from the University of California, Santa Barbara, a MA in Marriage and Family Therapy from the University of San Diego, and a PhD in Child and Family Development from the University of Georgia. She has taught child development at the University of Georgia and has taught medical ethics to medical students, residents, and physicians for Tenet Healthcare and Emory University. She has presented scientific papers on parenting and child well-being at regional and national meetings, and developed the COSI: The Circle of Stress Index: A Measure of Parental Stress.

DONALD C. REITZES is Professor and Chair of the Sociology Department at Georgia State University in Atlanta. He received his doctoral training in sociology at Indiana University, Bloomington. Reitzes has served on the Editorial Boards of *Social Forces* and *Social Psychological Quarterly*. He has been an officer of Social Psychology Section of the American Sociological Association and is a fellow of the Gerontological Society of America. His research interests focus on symbolic interaction theory and the implications and applications of identity and self-concept on well-being and behavior. Recent published research studies include investigations of reciprocity between family generations, self-esteem and subjective responses to work among mature workers, the moderating effects of stress on depressive symptoms, friendship and social support for adult role identity, and the importance of racial-ethnic identity for blacks, whites, and multiracials. He is currently concluding a National Institute on Aging-funded, longitudinal investigation of self processes that influence middle-aged adults and their transition to retirement.

MARTHA F. ROGERS is a board certified pediatrician and an internationally known expert in the field of HIV/AIDS in women and children. She joined the Centers for Disease Control and Prevention (CDC) in 1981 and spent most of her 20 years at the CDC working in the effort to control the Acquired Immunodeficiency Syndrome (AIDS) worldwide pandemic. She was responsible for development of many of CDC's policies on HIV in children. One of the most important documents was published in 1995, recommending universal HIV testing of pregnant women in the United States. Rogers has published over 75 articles and has received several U.S. Public Health Service (USPHS) awards, including the Outstanding Service Medal and the Meritorious Service Medal. She is now the Director of Programs at the Center for Child Well-being, a project of the Task Force for Child Survival and Development.

MARK L. ROSENBERG is Executive Director of the Task Force for Child Survival and Development and is also the Executive Director of the Center for Child Well-being, a project of the Task Force. Rosenberg is board certified in both psychiatry and internal medicine, with training in public policy and public health. He was educated at Harvard University where he received his undergraduate degree as well as degrees in public policy and medicine. He completed a residency in internal medicine and a fellowship in infectious diseases at Massachusetts General Hospital, a residency in psychiatry at the Boston Beth Israel Hospital, and a residency in preventive medicine at the CDC. He is on the faculty at Morehouse Medical School, Emory Medical School, and the Rollins (Emory) School of Public Health. He served the Public Health Service for 20 years in enteric diseases, HIV/AIDS, and injury control. He was the founding director of the National Center for Injury Prevention and Control and attained the rank of Assistant Surgeon General.

EDWARD L. SCHNEIDER has been Executive Director of the University of Southern California's Ethel Percy Andrus Gerontology Center and Dean of the Leonard Davis School of Gerontology since December 1986. He is also the William and Sylvia Kugel Professor of Gerontology and a Professor of Medicine at the U.S.C. Keck School of Medicine. Dr. Schneider has 14 years of past experience at the National Institute on Aging as the head of the laboratory studying genetic aspects of aging, Associate Director for Biomedical Research, and Deputy Director.

He has served on faculties of Johns Hopkins University, Georgetown University, and the University of Colorado, and has written or co-written 12 books and published more than 160 articles in scientific publications and journals.

MARTIN E. P. SELIGMAN, works on learned helplessness, depression, and on optimism and pessimism. He is currently Fox Leadership Professor of Psychology and the Director of the Positive Psychology Network at the University of Pennsylvania. His bibliography includes over fifteen books and 150 articles on motivation and personality. Among his better-known works are Learned Optimism, What You Can Change & What You Can't, The Optimistic Child, Helplessness, and Abnormal Psychology (with David Rosenhan). He is the recipient of numerous awards including two Distinguished Scientific Contribution awards from the American Psychological Association. Dr. Seligman's research has been supported by a number of institutions including the National Institute of Mental Health (continuously since 1969), The National Institute of Aging, the National Science Foundation, and the Guggenheim Foundation. For 14 years, he was the Director of the Clinical Training Program at the University of Pennsylvania. His work has been featured in publications such as the New York Times, Time, Newsweek, U.S. News and World Report, and on television and radio shows. In 1996 Dr. Seligman was elected APA President, by the largest vote in modern history. His major initiatives concerned the prevention of ethnopolitical warfare and the study of Positive Psychology.

ROBERT S. SIEGLER is Teresa Heinz Professor of Cognitive Psychology at Carnegie Mellon University. He has been at Carnegie Mellon since receiving his PhD from SUNY at Stony Brook. In the ensuing years, he has published 5 books and 150 articles and book chapters. The books and articles have focused on children's reasoning and problem solving, particularly in scientific and mathematical domains. Among the books he has written are *How Children Discover New Strategies* (1989, with Eric Jenkins) and *Children's Thinking* (Third Edition, 1998). His book, *Emerging Minds*, was chosen one of the "Best Psychology Books of 1996" by the Association of American Publishers. Siegler also has served as associate editor of the journal *Developmental Psychology* and co-edited (with Deanna Kuhn) the 1998 *Handbook of Child Psychology: Cognition, Perception, and Language.*

BRUCE SIMONS-MORTON is Chief of the Prevention Research Branch in the Division of Epidemiology, Statistics, and Prevention Research at the National Institute of Child Health and Human Development, NIH, where he directs a program of research on child and adolescent health behavior. Simons-Morton was educated at the University of California at Santa Barbara, San Diego State University, The University of Northern Colorado, and The Johns Hopkins University School of Public Health. Previously he held academic positions at Temple University, The University of Texas Medical Branch, and the University of Texas School of Public Health. His current research focuses on adolescent problem behavior and injury prevention. He is the author of the textbook, *Introduction to Health Education and Promotion, Second Edition*. He is a past Vice President of the Society for Public Health Education and past Chairman of the Public Health Education Section of the American Public Health Association.

DAVID A. SLEET, is Associate Director for Science, Division of Unintentional Injury Prevention at the Centers for Disease Control and Prevention (CDC) in Atlanta. Sleet was educated at the University of Toledo (Health) and San Diego State University (Psychology), where he also taught and conducted research as a Professor in the School of Public Health and the Department of Exercise and Nutrition Sciences. He is a Fellow of the American Academy of Health Behavior and serves on the editorial board of the journal *Injury Control and Safety Promotion*. Sleet is former White House and Washington correspondent to Shape Magazine, served as a research psychologist at the US Department of Transportation, and was Acting Director of the Road Accident Prevention Research Unit in Perth, Western Australia. He is founder of the International Working Group on Behavioral Science and Unintentional Injury Prevention at CDC. He also developed "The Wellness Race," an educational board game for children and their families, and M-HAAPI, a Mental Health Appraisal and Promotion Instrument. He is on the teaching faculty in behavioral science at the Emory University Rollins School of Public Health.

D. CAMILLE SMITH is a Behavioral Scientist at the Centers for Disease Control and Prevention (CDC) in Atlanta. Smith was educated at Florida State University, George Washington University, and the University of Washington. Her research interests include the study of improving child developmental outcomes through programs designed to influence parenting behavior. Her professional experience includes statewide program planning and administration for young children with disabilities, university-based teaching in infant and child psychology, and direct service delivery with children and families. Smith has served as a member of the CDC Children's Health Initiative, CDC Child Care Working Group, the Pennsylvania Governor's Commission for Children and Families, as well as numerous planning projects designed to improve the well-being of children and families.

MARGARET R. STONE is a Research Associate in the Division of Family Studies and Human Development at the University of Arizona. Stone completed her graduate studies at the University of Wisconsin-Madison after completing undergraduate studies at the University of Kentucky, where she graduated Phi Beta Kappa. At the University of Wisconsin, she was awarded the Michael and Harriet O'Shea Fellowship for the study of adolescent development and education. Her primary scholarly interest has been in prototypic identities or "crowds" in secondary schools as emergent social cognitive categories through which adolescents interpret their social world and their own identities. Currently, she is particularly interested in employing longitudinal data to explore the ways that pre-adolescent personal characteristics and interests predict to adolescent social identities and the ways in which these identities, in combination with high school extra-curricular activities, structure adolescent and young adult development.

JANICE L. TEMPLETON received her BA and MA degrees in psychology from Wake Forest University. She is currently a doctoral student in the Combined Program in Education and Psychology at the University of Michigan. Her research interests focus on health and well-being throughout the life span with a specific interest in adolescence and the transition to adulthood.

RENÉE M. TOBIN is an assistant professor of school psychology at Illinois State University. She completed her doctoral degree at Texas A&M University.

THOMAS F TONNIGES is a Clinical Professor of Pediatrics at the University of Nebraska Medical Center. He completed his medical education at the University of Nebraska and Bridgeport Hospital, Bridgeport, CT. He is currently the Director of the Department of Community Pediatrics at the American Academy of Pediatrics (AAP). He has served on the Board of Directors of the AAP. His interests have included children with special health care needs, child abuse, and access to care. He has served on many state and national advisory boards. He is currently serving on an elected school board.

BRENDA L. VOLLING is Associate Professor of Psychology at the University of Michigan. She received her BS at the University of Illinois at Urbana-Champaign and completed her graduate studies at Penn State University with a PhD in Human Development and Family Studies. She was a NICHD post-doctoral fellow at the Carolina Consortium on Human Development before coming to the University of Michigan. Her research focuses on family relationships in infancy and early childhood and young children's social and emotional development.

MARY B. WATERMAN is a study manager in the Health Studies Sector of Westat, a statistical survey research corporation in Rockville, Maryland. She has also worked with such agencies as Emory University, the Arthritis Foundation, and the Centers for Disease Control and Prevention on various projects related to mental health and chronic disease prevention. Ms. Waterman received her MPH in behavioral sciences from the Rollins School of Public Health of Emory University.

NAOMI WENTWORTH is Associate Professor of Psychology and Director of Institutional Research at Lake Forest College in Lake Forest, Illinois and a Visiting Scientist in the Psychology Department at the University of Denver, Colorado. She was educated at the Universities of Massachusetts and Connecticut and previously was affiliated with the University of Illinois at Chicago.

ELLEN WINNER is Professor of Psychology at Boston College and Senior Research Associate at Project Zero, Harvard Graduate School of Education. Winner was educated at Radcliffe College and Harvard University. She is the author of *Invented Worlds: The Psychology of the Arts* (Harvard University Press, 1982), *The Point of Words: Children's Understanding of Metaphor and Irony* (Harvard University Press, 1986), and *Gifted Children: Myths and Realities* (Basic Books, 1996), which was awarded the Alpha Sigma Nu National Jesuit Book Award in Science. She is the co-editor of a double issue of the *Journal of Aesthetic Education* entitled "The arts and academic achievement: What the evidence shows." She is a past president of Division 10, the Psychology and the Arts Division of the American Psychological Association, and was awarded the Rudolf Arnheim Award for Outstanding Research by a Senior Scholar by this division in 2000. Her research focuses on the psychology of the arts, creativity, and giftedness.

SAM L. WITRYOL is Professor Emeritus in his 51st year at the University of Connecticut, where he participated in the initiation of the PhD program in Clinical Psychology, 1949–1959, and founded the PhD program in Child and Developmental Psychology in 1959, serving as Director for three and a half decades. Formally retired in 1992, he continues to teach Theories of Child Psychology and Tests and Measurements. The chronology of his research publications includes children's values, sociometry, paired comparison scaling, social intelligence, differential incentive effects on discrimination learning and memory, and curiosity. He is grateful for the collaboration of about 50 graduate students, who sometimes profited from his tutorial instruction and very often offered him ideas, research designs, stimulation, and, most important, friendship.

JONATHAN F. ZAFF is a research associate at Child Trends, a non-profit, non-partisan research organization dedicated to studying children, youth, and families. Zaff, a developmental psychologist, received his doctorate from University of Georgia. His research focuses on the positive social and emotional development of children and adolescents, with a specific emphasis on oppressed ethnic minority groups.

Author Index

Note: Page numbers in *italic* indicate bibliography references, page numbers followed by an *n* indicate a footnote.

A

Aagaard, P., 68, *79*
Aann, D. M., *203*
Aarnio, M., 73, *75*
Abbott, R., 90, *95*
Abbott, R. A., 457, *474*
Abbott, R. D., 414, 417, *420*
Abedin, M., 141, 144, *154*
Abeles, R. P., 467, *472*
Aber, J. L., 4, *9,* 172, *174,* 186, *187*
Aber, L., 347, *351*
Abramson, L. T., 241, 451, *474*
Abramson, L. Y., 451, 452, 467, *472, 474, 475*
Acevedo, M., 196, *201*
Acharya, U., 74, *77*
Achter, J., 374, *379*
Ackermann, C., 145, *154*
Acuna, J., 42, 43, *47*
Adams, 239, 241
Adams, G., 103, *106*
Adams-Taylor, S., 103, *106*
Adelson, E., 179, *187*
Ades, P. A., 413, *419*
Adler, N. E., 111, *119*
Ageton, S. S., 117, *120*
Ahadi, S. A., 141, *151*
Ahmed, K., 215, 217, *220*
Ainsworth, M. D. S., 144, *151,* 177, 178, 179, 185, *186,* 193, *200,* 327, *328*

Ajani, U. A., 418, *420*
Ajzen, I., 115, *120*
Alain, M., 228, *231*
Alan Guttmacher Institute, 103, *106,* 113, *118*
Albersheim, L., 184, *189*
Alberti, E. T., 287, 288, 289, *291*
Albrecht, R., 426, *445*
Albright, K., 57, *63*
Aldwin, C. M., 7, *9,* 456, *474*
Aleksandrovich, N., 68, *77*
Alemi, B., 150, *152*
Alessandri, S. M., 298, 299, *305*
Alexander, K. L., 345, 346, 348, *350, 351*
Alexander, R. A., 287, *293*
Alfred, E., 111, 114, *119*
Allander, E., 415, *421*
Allen, G. L., 275, *277*
Allen, L., 314, *319*
Allexander, J. M., 146, *151*
Allison, K. R., 68, 72, *75, 77*
Allman, A., 130, *136*
Alloy, L. B., 451, 467, *472, 475*
Allport, G. W., 6, *9,* 238, *246*
Almeida, D. M., *137*
Alnwick, D., 36, 38, *47*
Altkorn, D., 101, *107*
Altshuler, J. L., 162, *165*
AMA, 54
Amato, P. R., 210, *217*
Ambrosio, T.-J., 356, *369*

559

H

S

Subject Index

Note: Page numbers in *italic* refer to figures; those in **boldface** refer to tables.

A

Abcedarian Project, 318
Academic achievement
    autonomy and, 172
    benefits of, 343–345
    development stability of, 346
    factors affecting, 346–349
    measurement of, 342–343
    moral development and, 360–362
    novelty-seeking and, 287–288
    occupational success and, 345, 394
    peer relationships and, 229
    sibling relationships and, 211
Academic domain, coping in, 160
Acceptance, in peer group, 228, *see also* Self-acceptance; Social acceptance
Achievement tests, 342–343, 346
Action, moral, 359–360
Active moral regulation, 148
Activity theory, 426–427
Adaptive capacity, 434–435
Adolescence, *see also* Emerging adulthood; Puberty; Substance abuse
    assets needed in, 396–400, **399,** 517–519
    attachment and, 183
    cognitive development in, 388

educational transitions in, 391–393
emotions in, 129
moral development in, 368
overview of challenges in, 385–387
parent-child relationships and, 195, 388–389
processing speed in, 270–271
relationship changes in, 388–390
reproductive health in, 102–103
reproductive health services for, 103–105
safety in, 90–91, **93–94**
school-to-work transition during, 393–395
sibling relationships in, 210–211
working memory in, 270–271
Aerobic exercise, 414–415
Affective discomfort, 148
Age differences
    in mental health, 487–488
    in prosocial behavior, 261
Aging, *see* Cognitive styles; Mental health; Physical health, in adults; Role engagement; Successful aging
AIDS, *see* HIV
Alcohol use, *see also* Substance abuse
    in adolescence and emerging adulthood, 385, 392, 395
    as drug abuse, 111–113, **112**
    during pregnancy, 43, 288